T0180403

Lecture Notes in Artificial Intelligence   12164

Subseries of Lecture Notes in Computer Science

Series Editors

Randy Goebel
  University of Alberta, Edmonton, Canada
Yuzuru Tanaka
  Hokkaido University, Sapporo, Japan
Wolfgang Wahlster
  DFKI and Saarland University, Saarbrücken, Germany

Founding Editor

Jörg Siekmann
  DFKI and Saarland University, Saarbrücken, Germany

More information about this series at http://www.springer.com/series/1244

Ig Ibert Bittencourt · Mutlu Cukurova ·
Kasia Muldner · Rose Luckin ·
Eva Millán (Eds.)

Artificial Intelligence in Education

21st International Conference, AIED 2020
Ifrane, Morocco, July 6–10, 2020
Proceedings, Part II

 Springer

Editors
Ig Ibert Bittencourt 🆔
Federal University of Alagoas
Maceió, Brazil

Mutlu Cukurova 🆔
University College London
London, UK

Kasia Muldner 🆔
Carleton University
Ottawa, ON, Canada

Rose Luckin 🆔
University College London
London, UK

Eva Millán 🆔
University of Malaga
Málaga, Spain

ISSN 0302-9743   ISSN 1611-3349 (electronic)
Lecture Notes in Artificial Intelligence
ISBN 978-3-030-52239-1   ISBN 978-3-030-52240-7 (eBook)
https://doi.org/10.1007/978-3-030-52240-7

LNCS Sublibrary: SL7 – Artificial Intelligence

This Springer imprint is published by the registered company Springer Nature Switzerland AG
The registered company address is: Gewerbestrasse 11, 6330 Cham, Switzerland

Preface

The 21st International Conference on Artificial Intelligence in Education (AIED 2020) was held virtually during July 6–10, 2020. AIED 2020 was the latest in a longstanding series of a yearly international conference for high-quality research on ways to enhance student learning through applications of artificial intelligence, human computer interaction, and the learning sciences.

The theme for the AIED 2020 conference was "Augmented Intelligence to Empower Education." As AI in education systems becomes more mature and implemented at scale in real-world contexts, the value of supplementing human intelligence and decision making (e.g., teacher, tutor, peer-tutor) is more apparent than ever. While the paradigm of augmented intelligence is not new to the field, solid theoretical and/or empirical work in the area is limited. Thus, further work is needed to understand the balance of human and AI partnerships in systems that support student learning. The AIED community was convened in 2020 to present solutions for the key questions related to this theme, including the identification of the augmentation opportunities that would empower the stakeholders of education.

AIED 2020 was originally scheduled to visit the African continent for the first time and be co-located with Educational Data Mining (EDM 2020). However, the unprecedented COVID-19 pandemic made international traveling and in-person meetings impossible and AIED joined other conferences in becoming a virtual event. While this certainly brought new challenges, we were humbled by the response of our community during this difficult time. We are extremely grateful to the authors, the keynote speakers, the reviewers, and the other track chairs for making AIED possible. The virtual event included keynotes from Prof. Neil Heffernan on ways that tutoring systems can improve online learning, Prof. Yvonne Rogers on designing interactive technologies that augment humans, and Andreas Schleicher, director for the directorate of education and skills at OECD, with Lord Jim Knight, former school minister from the UK on how AI impacts upon the policymaking landscape in education. We want to extend a special thank you to the AIED Program Committee (PC) members and reviewers – your hard work and commitment was truly appreciated.

There were 184 submissions as full papers to AIED 2020, of which 49 were accepted as full papers (ten pages) with virtual oral presentation at the conference (for an acceptance rate of 26.6%), and 52 were accepted as short papers (four pages). Of the 30 papers directly submitted as short papers, 14 were accepted. Each submission was reviewed by three PC members. In addition, submissions underwent a discussion period (led by a leading reviewer) to ensure that all reviewers' opinions would be considered and leveraged to generate a group recommendation to the program chairs. The program chairs checked the reviews and meta-reviews for quality and, where necessary, requested for reviewers to elaborate their review. Final decisions were made by carefully considering both meta-reviews (weighed more heavily) scores and the discussions. Our goal was to conduct a fair process and encourage substantive and constructive reviews without interfering with the reviewers' judgment. We also took the constraints of the program into account, seeking to keep the acceptance rate within the typical range for this conference.

Beyond paper presentations and keynotes, the conference also included:

- An Industry and Innovation Track, intended to support connections between industry (both for-profit and non-profit) and the research community
- A series of four workshops across a range of topics, such as: empowering education with AI technology, intelligent textbooks, challenges related to education in AI (K-12), and optimizing human learning
- A Doctoral Consortium Track, designed to provide doctoral students with the opportunity to obtain feedback on their doctoral research from the research community

Special thanks goes to Springer for sponsoring the AIED 2020 Best Paper Award. As already mentioned above, we also want to acknowledge the wonderful work of the AIED 2020 Organizing Committee, the PC members, and the reviewers who made this conference possible.

May 2020

Ig Ibert Bittencourt
Mutlu Cukurova
Kasia Muldner
Rose Luckin
Eva Millán

Organization

General Conference Chair

Rose Luckin   University College London, UK

Senior Program Chair

Eva Millán   University of Malaga, Spain

Program Chairs

Ig Ibert Bittencourt   Universidade Federal de Alagoas, Brazil
Mutlu Cukurova   University College London, UK
Kasia Muldner   Carleton University, Canada

Advisory Board

Danielle McNamara   Arizona State University, USA
Ido Roll   Technion - Israel Institute of Technology, Israel

Workshop and Tutorial Chairs

Alexandra Cristea   Durham University, UK
Mingyu Feng   WestEd, USA
Richard Tong   Squirrel AI, China

Industry and Innovation Track Chairs

Elle Yuan Wang   ASU EdPlus, USA
Wei Cui   Squirrel AI, China

Doctoral Consortium Chairs

Janice Gobert   Rutgers University, USA
Kaska Porayska-Pomsta   University College London, UK

Program Committee

Adeniran Adetunji   University of Aberdeen, UK
Patricia Albacete   University of Pittsburgh, USA
Vincent Aleven   Carnegie Melon University, USA
Giora Alexandron   Weizmann Institute of Science, Switzerland

Michail Giannakos	Norwegian University of Science and Technology, Norway
Niki Gitinabard	North Carolina State University, USA
Janice Gobert	Rutgers University, USA
Alex Sandro Gomes	Universidade Federal de Pernambuco, Brazil
Monique Grandbastien	Université de Lorraine, France
Nathalie Guin	LIRIS, Université de Lyon, France
Gahgene Gweon	Seoul National University, South Korea
Rawad Hammad	University of East London, UK
Jason Harley	McGill University, Canada
Peter Hastings	DePaul University, USA
Neil Heffernan	Worcester Polytechnic Institute, USA
Martin Hlosta	The Open University, UK
Wayne Holmes	NESTA, UK
Ulrich Hoppe	University of Duisburg-Essen, Germany
Tomoya Horiguchi	Kobe University, Japan
Sharon Hsiao	Arizona State University, USA
Stephen Hutt	University of Colorado Boulder, USA
Paul S. Inventado	California State University Fullerton, USA
Seiji Isotani	University of São Paulo, Brazil
Sridhar Iyer	IIT Bombay, India
Patricia Jaques	UNISINOS, Brazil
Srecko Joksimovic	University of South Australia, Australia
Judy Kay	The University of Sydney, Australia
Carmel Kent	University College London, UK
Simon Knight	University of Technology Sydney, Australia
Kazuaki Kojima	Teikyo University, Japan
Emmanuel Kolog	University of Ghana, Ghana
Amruth Kumar	Ramapo College of New Jersey, USA
Rohit Kumar	Consultant (independent), USA
Jean-Marc Labat	UPMC Paris 6, France
Sébastien Lallé	The University of British Columbia, Canada
Andrew Lan	University of Massachusetts Amherst, USA
Nguyen-Thinh Le	Humboldt-Universität zu Berlin, Germany
Blair Lehman	Educational Testing Service, USA
James Lester	North Carolina State University, USA
Fuhua Lin	Athabasca University, Canada
Zitao Liu	TAL AI Lab, China
Yu Lu	Beijing Normal University, China
Vanda Luengo	Sorbonne Université, LIP6, France
Collin Lynch	North Carolina State University, USA
Michael Madaio	Carnegie Mellon University, USA
Laura Malkiewich	Columbia University, USA
Mavrikis Manolis	UCL Knowledge Lab, UK
Ye Mao	North Carolina State University, USA
Leonardo Marques	University of São Paulo, Brazil

Mirko Marras	University of Cagliari, Italy
Roberto M.-Maldonado	Monash University, Australia
Smit Marvaniya	IBM, India
Jeff Matayoshi	McGraw-Hill Education/ALEKS Corporation, USA
Noboru Matsuda	North Carolina State University, USA
Manolis Mavrikis	UCL Knowledge Lab, UK
Gordon McCalla	University of Saskatchewan, Canada
Kathryn Soo McCarthy	Georgia State University, USA
Bruce McLaren	Carnegie Mellon University, USA
Danielle McNamara	Arizona State University, USA
Muhammad Memon	Beijing University of Technology, China
Agathe Merceron	Beuth University of Applied Sciences Berlin, Germany
Sein Minn	Polytechnique Montreal, Canada
Tanja Mitrovic	University of Canterbury, New Zealand
Kazuhisa Miwa	Nagoya University, Japan
Riichiro Mizoguchi	Japan Advanced Institute of Science and Technology, Japan
Inge Molenaar	Radboud University, The Netherlands
Camila Canellas	Sorbonne University, France
Bradford Mott	North Carolina State University, USA
Kasia Muldner	Carleton University, Canada
Anabil Munshi	Vanderbilt University, USA
Iryna Nikolayeva	Sorbonne University, France
Roger Nkambou	Université du Québec à Montréal, Canada
Ange Tato	Université du Québec à Montréal, Canada
Amy Ogan	Carnegie Mellon University, USA
Ruth Okoilu	North Carolina State University, USA
Andrew Olney	University of Memphis, USA
Jennifer Olsen	École Polytechnique Fédérale de Lausanne, Switzerland
Solomon Oyelere	University of Eastern Finland, Finland
Ranilson Paiva	Universidade Federal de Alagoas, Brazil
Luc Paquette	University of Illinois at Urbana-Champaign, USA
Abelardo Pardo	University of South Australia, Australia
Zach Pardos	University of California, Berkeley, USA
Radek Pelánek	Masaryk University Brno, Czech Republic
Niels Pinkwart	Humboldt-Universität zu Berlin, Germany
Elvira Popescu	University of Craiova, Romania
Kaska Porayska-Pomsta	University College London, UK
Thomas Price	North Carolina State University, USA
Ramkumar Rajendran	IIT Bombay, India
Martina Rau	University of Wisconsin-Madison, USA
Genaro Méndez	Tecnologico de Monterrey, Mexico
M. Mercedes Rodrigo	Ateneo de Manila University, Philippines
Ido Roll	Technion - Israel Institute of Technology, Israel
Jonathan Rowe	North Carolina State University, USA

José A. Valiente	University of Murcia, Spain
Vasile Rus	The University of Memphis, USA
Demetrios Sampson	Curtin University, Australia
Olga C. Santos	aDeNu Research Group (UNED), Spain
Mohammed Saqr	University of Eastern Finland, Finland
Flippo Sciarrone	Roma Tre University, Italy
Shitian Shen	North Carolina State University, USA
Yu Shengquan	Beijing Normal University, China
Lei Shi	Durham University, UK
Sean Siqueira	Federal University of the State of Rio de Janeiro, Brazil
Caitlin Snyder	Vanderbilt University, USA
Sergey Sosnovsky	Utrecht University, The Netherlands
Angela Stewart	University of Colorado Boulder, USA
Pierre Tchounikine	University of Grenoble, France
Craig Thompson	The University of British Columbia, Canada
Armando Toda	University of São Paulo, Brazil
Richard Tong	Squirrel AI, China
Maomi Ueno	The University of Electro-Communications, Japan
Felisa Verdejo	Universidad Nacional de Educacin a Distancia, Spain
Rosa Vicari	Universidade Federal do Rio Grande do Sul, Brazil
Erin Walker	Arizona State University, USA
April Wang	University of Michigan, USA
Elle Yuan Wang	ASU EdPlus, USA
Chris Wong	University of Technology Sydney, Australia
Beverly Park Woolf	University of Massachusetts, USA
Sho Yamamoto	Kindai University, Japan
Xi Yang	North Carolina State University, USA
Bernard Yett	Vanderbilt University, USA
Diego Zapata-Rivera	Educational Testing Service, USA
Ningyu Zhang	Vanderbilt University, USA
Guojing Zhou	North Carolina State University, USA
Gustavo Zurita	Universidad de Chile, Chile

Additional Reviewers

Alvarez, Claudio	Herder, Tiffany
Alwahaby, Haifa	Ismail, Daneih
Anaya, Antonio R.	Jensen, Emily
Celepkolu, Mehmet	José, Jario
Corrigan, Seth	Ju, Song
Fraca, Estibaliz	Karp Gershon, Saar
Gao, Ge	Khan, Madiha
Ghosh, Aritra	Krumm
Harrison, Avery	Lee, William
He, Liqun	Li, Warren

Limbu, Bibeg
Mao, Ye
Marwan, Samiha
Medeiros Machado, Guilherme
Mohammadhassan, Negar
Morita, Jun'Ya
Ostrow, Korinn
Pathan, Rumana
Patikorn, Thanaporn
Praharaj, Sambit
Prasad, Prajish
Prihar, Ethan
Rajendran, Ramkumar
Rodriguez, Fernando
Serrano Mamolar, Ana
Shahriar, Tasmia
Shi, Yang

Shimmei, Machi
Singh, Daevesh
T. Lakshmi
Tenório, Thyago
Tobarra, Llanos
Tomoto, Takahito
Tong, Richard
Tsan, Jennifer
Varatharaj, Ashvini
Wang, Emma
Wang, Shuai
Wang, Zichao
Wiggins, Joseph
Yang, Xi
Zhang, Zheng
Zhou, Qi
Zhou, Xiaofei

International Artificial Intelligence in Education Society

Contents – Part II

Short Papers

Modelling Learners in Crowdsourcing Educational Systems 3
    Solmaz Abdi, Hassan Khosravi, and Shazia Sadiq

Interactive Pedagogical Agents for Learning Sequence Diagrams 10
    Sohail Alhazmi, Charles Thevathayan, and Margaret Hamilton

A Socratic Tutor for Source Code Comprehension 15
    Zeyad Alshaikh, Lasagn Tamang, and Vasile Rus

Scientific Modeling Using Large Scale Knowledge 20
    Sungeun An, Robert Bates, Jen Hammock, Spencer Rugaber,
    Emily Weigel, and Ashok Goel

Examining Students' Intrinsic Cognitive Load During Program
Comprehension – An Eye Tracking Approach 25
    Magdalena Andrzejewska and Agnieszka Skawińska

Sequence-to-Sequence Models for Automated Text Simplification 31
    Robert-Mihai Botarleanu, Mihai Dascalu, Scott Andrew Crossley,
    and Danielle S. McNamara

The Potential for the Use of Deep Neural Networks in e-Learning Student
Evaluation with New Data Augmentation Method 37
    Andrzej Cader

Investigating Transformers for Automatic Short Answer Grading 43
    Leon Camus and Anna Filighera

Predicting Learners Need for Recommendation Using Dynamic
Graph-Based Knowledge Tracing 49
    Abdessamad Chanaa and Nour-Eddine El Faddouli

BERT and Prerequisite Based Ontology for Predicting Learner's Confusion
in MOOCs Discussion Forums 54
    Abdessamad Chanaa and Nour-Eddine El Faddouli

Identification of Students' Need Deficiency Through a Dialogue System 59
    Penghe Chen, Yu Lu, Yan Peng, Jiefei Liu, and Qi Xu

The Double-Edged Sword of Automating Personalized Interventions in
Makerspaces: An Exploratory Study of Potential Benefits and Drawbacks . . .   64
  Edwin Chng, Sofya Zeylikman, and Bertrand Schneider

EdNet: A Large-Scale Hierarchical Dataset in Education   69
  Youngduck Choi, Youngnam Lee, Dongmin Shin, Junghyun Cho,
  Seoyon Park, Seewoo Lee, Jineon Baek, Chan Bae, Byungsoo Kim,
  and Jaewe Heo

Exploring Automatic Short Answer Grading as a Tool to Assist
in Human Rating   74
  Aubrey Condor

Multi-document Cohesion Network Analysis: Visualizing Intratextual
and Intertextual Links   80
  Maria-Dorinela Dascalu, Stefan Ruseti, Mihai Dascalu,
  Danielle S. McNamara, and Stefan Trausan-Matu

Mastery Learning Heuristics and Their Hidden Models   86
  Shayan Doroudi

Towards Practical Detection of Unproductive Struggle   92
  Stephen E. Fancsali, Kenneth Holstein, Michael Sandbothe,
  Steven Ritter, Bruce M. McLaren, and Vincent Aleven

What Happens When Gamification Ends?   98
  Miguel García Iruela, Manuel J. Fonseca, Raquel Hijón-Neira,
  and Teresa Chambel

Using Eye-Tracking and Click-Stream Data to Design Adaptive Training
of Children's Inhibitory Control in a Maths and Science Game   103
  Andrea Gauthier, Kaśka Porayska-Pomsta, Denis Mareschal,
  and The UnLocke Project Team

Prediction of Group Learning Results from an Aggregation of Individual
Understanding with Kit-Build Concept Map   109
  Yusuke Hayashi, Toshihiro Nomura, and Tsukasa Hirashima

Automatic Classification for Cognitive Engagement in Online Discussion
Forums: Text Mining and Machine Learning Approach   114
  Hind Hayati

Explaining Errors in Predictions of At-Risk Students in Distance
Learning Education   119
  Martin Hlosta, Tina Papathoma, and Christothea Herodotou

A General Multi-method Approach to Design-Loop Adaptivity
in Intelligent Tutoring Systems.................................. 124
   Yun Huang, Vincent Aleven, Elizabeth McLaughlin,
   and Kenneth Koedinger

Towards Improving Sample Representativeness of Teachers on Online
Social Media: A Case Study on Pinterest......................... 130
   Hamid Karimi, Tyler Derr, Kaitlin T. Torphy, Kenneth A. Frank,
   and Jiliang Tang

A Framework for Exploring the Impact of Tutor Practices on Learner
Self-regulation in Online Environments 135
   Madiha Khan-Galaria, Mutlu Cukurova, and Rose Luckin

Automated Personalized Feedback Improves Learning Gains
in An Intelligent Tutoring System............................... 140
   Ekaterina Kochmar, Dung Do Vu, Robert Belfer, Varun Gupta,
   Iulian Vlad Serban, and Joelle Pineau

Allowing Revisions While Providing Error-Flagging Support:
Is More Better?.. 147
   Amruth N. Kumar

Learner-Context Modelling: A Bayesian Approach 152
   Charles Lang

Distinguishing Anxiety Subtypes of English Language Learners Towards
Augmented Emotional Clarity.................................. 157
   Heera Lee, Varun Mandalapu, Andrea Kleinsmith, and Jiaqi Gong

Siamese Neural Networks for Class Activity Detection 162
   Hang Li, Zhiwei Wang, Jiliang Tang, Wenbiao Ding, and Zitao Liu

Deep-Cross-Attention Recommendation Model for Knowledge Sharing
Micro Learning Service....................................... 168
   Jiayin Lin, Geng Sun, Jun Shen, David Pritchard, Tingru Cui,
   Dongming Xu, Li Li, Ghassan Beydoun, and Shiping Chen

Investigating the Role of Politeness in Human-Human Online Tutoring 174
   Jionghao Lin, David Lang, Haoran Xie, Dragan Gašević,
   and Guanliang Chen

Raising Academic Performance in Socio-cognitive Conflict Learning
Through Gamification 180
   Zhou Long, Dehong Luo, Kai Kiu, Hongli Gao, Jing Qu,
   and Xiangen Hu

Towards Interpretable Deep Learning Models for Knowledge Tracing   185
    Yu Lu, Deliang Wang, Qinggang Meng, and Penghe Chen

Early Prediction of Success in MOOC from Video Interaction Features   191
    Boniface Mbouzao, Michel C. Desmarais, and Ian Shrier

Predicting Reading Comprehension from Constructed Responses:
Explanatory Retrievals as Stealth Assessment   197
    Kathryn S. McCarthy, Laura K. Allen, and Scott R. Hinze

An Approach to Model Children's Inhibition During Early Literacy
and Numeracy Acquisition   203
    Guilherme Medeiros Machado, Geoffray Bonnin, Sylvain Castagnos,
    Lara Hoareau, Aude Thomas, and Youssef Tazouti

Confrustion and Gaming While Learning with Erroneous Examples
in a Decimals Game   208
    Michael Mogessie, J. Elizabeth Richey, Bruce M. McLaren,
    Juan Miguel L. Andres-Bray, and Ryan S. Baker

Learning Outcomes and Their Relatedness Under Curriculum Drift   214
    Sneha Mondal, Tejas I. Dhamecha, Smriti Pathak, Red Mendoza,
    Gayathri K. Wijayarathna, Paul Gagnon, and Jan Carlstedt-Duke

Promoting Learning and Satisfaction of Children When Interacting
with an Emotional Companion to Program   220
    Elizabeth K. Morales-Urrutia, José Miguel Ocaña Ch.,
    Diana Pérez-Marín, and Celeste Pizarro-Romero

Automatic Grading System Using Sentence-BERT Network   224
    Ifeanyi G. Ndukwe, Chukwudi E. Amadi, Larian M. Nkomo,
    and Ben K. Daniel

Extended Multi-document Cohesion Network Analysis Centered
on Comprehension Prediction   228
    Bogdan Nicula, Cecile A. Perret, Mihai Dascalu,
    and Danielle S. McNamara

Supporting Empathy Training Through Virtual Patients   234
    Jennifer K. Olsen and Catharine Oertel

Generating Game Levels to Develop Computer Science Competencies
in Game-Based Learning Environments   240
    Kyungjin Park, Bradford Mott, Wookhee Min, Eric Wiebe,
    Kristy Elizabeth Boyer, and James Lester

An Evaluation of Data-Driven Programming Hints in a Classroom Setting . . .   246
Thomas W. Price, Samiha Marwan, Michael Winters,
and Joseph Jay Williams

Deep Knowledge Tracing with Transformers   252
Shi Pu, Michael Yudelson, Lu Ou, and Yuchi Huang

Relationships Between Body Postures and Collaborative Learning States
in an Augmented Reality Study   257
Iulian Radu, Ethan Tu, and Bertrand Schneider

Effect of Immediate Feedback on Math Achievement at the High
School Level   263
Renah Razzaq, Korinn S. Ostrow, and Neil T. Heffernan

Automated Prediction of Novice Programmer Performance Using
Programming Trajectories.   268
Miguel A. Rubio

Agent-in-the-Loop: Conversational Agent Support in Service of Reflection
for Learning During Collaborative Programming.   273
Sreecharan Sankaranarayanan, Siddharth Reddy Kandimalla,
Sahil Hasan, Haokang An, Christopher Bogart, R. Charles Murray,
Michael Hilton, Majd Sakr, and Carolyn Rosé

Toward an Automatic Speech Classifier for the Teacher.   279
Bahar Shahrokhian Ghahfarokhi, Avinash Sivaraman,
and Kurt VanLehn

Constructing Automated Revision Graphs: A Novel Visualization
Technique to Study Student Writing   285
Antonette Shibani

When Lying, Hiding and Deceiving Promotes Learning - A Case
for Augmented Intelligence with Augmented Ethics.   291
Björn Sjödén

Understanding Collaborative Question Posing During Computational
Modeling in Science   296
Caitlin Snyder, Nicole M. Hutchins, Gautam Biswas, Mona Emara,
Bernard Yett, and Shitanshu Mishra

Machine Learning and Student Performance in Teams   301
Rohan Ahuja, Daniyal Khan, Sara Tahir, Magdalene Wang,
Danilo Symonette, Shimei Pan, Simon Stacey, and Don Engel

Scanpath Analysis of Student Attention During Problem Solving
with Worked Examples   306
  Samantha Stranc and Kasia Muldner

Helping Teachers Assist Their Students in Gamified Adaptive Educational
Systems: Towards a Gamification Analytics Tool   312
  Kamilla Tenório, Geiser Chalco Challco, Diego Dermeval,
  Bruno Lemos, Pedro Nascimento, Rodrigo Santos,
  and Alan Pedro da Silva

Understanding Rapport over Multiple Sessions with a Social,
Teachable Robot.   318
  Xiaoyi Tian, Nichola Lubold, Leah Friedman, and Erin Walker

Exercise Hierarchical Feature Enhanced Knowledge Tracing.   324
  Hanshuang Tong, Yun Zhou, and Zhen Wang

Relationships Between Math Performance and Human Judgments
of Motivational Constructs in an Online Math Tutoring System   329
  Rurik Tywoniw, Scott A. Crossley, Jaclyn Ocumpaugh,
  Shamya Karumbaiah, and Ryan Baker

Automated Short-Answer Grading Using Deep Neural Networks
and Item Response Theory.   334
  Masaki Uto and Yuto Uchida

Automatic Dialogic Instruction Detection for K-12 Online
One-on-One Classes   340
  Shiting Xu, Wenbiao Ding, and Zitao Liu

Exploring the Role of Perspective Taking in Educational
Child-Robot Interaction   346
  Elmira Yadollahi, Marta Couto, Wafa Johal, Pierre Dillenbourg,
  and Ana Paiva

Evaluating Student Learning in a Synchronous, Collaborative Programming
Environment Through Log-Based Analysis of Projects.   352
  Bernard Yett, Nicole Hutchins, Caitlin Snyder, Ningyu Zhang,
  Shitanshu Mishra, and Gautam Biswas

Adaptive Forgetting Curves for Spaced Repetition Language Learning.   358
  Ahmed Zaidi, Andrew Caines, Russell Moore, Paula Buttery,
  and Andrew Rice

Learning from Interpretable Analysis: Attention-Based
Knowledge Tracing.   364
  Jia Zhu, Weihao Yu, Zetao Zheng, Changqin Huang, Yong Tang,
  and Gabriel Pui Cheong Fung

Industry and Innovation Papers

Identifying Beneficial Learning Behaviors from Large-Scale
Interaction Data   371
    Miruna Cristus, Oscar Täckström, Lingyi Tan, and Valentino Pacifici

A Gamified Solution to the Cold-Start Problem of Intelligent
Tutoring System   376
    Yang Pian, Yu Lu, Yuqi Huang, and Ig Ibert Bittencourt

Bridging Over from Learning Videos to Learning Resources Through
Automatic Keyword Extraction   382
    Cleo Schulten, Sven Manske, Angela Langner-Thiele,
    and H. Ulrich Hoppe

A Large-Scale, Open-Domain, Mixed-Interface Dialogue-Based ITS
for STEM   387
    Iulian Vlad Serban, Varun Gupta, Ekaterina Kochmar, Dung D. Vu,
    Robert Belfer, Joelle Pineau, Aaron Courville, Laurent Charlin,
    and Yoshua Bengio

Doctoral Consortium Papers

Contingent Scaffolding for System Safety Analysis   395
    Paul S. Brown, Anthony G. Cohn, Glen Hart, and Vania Dimitrova

The Exploration of Feeling of Difficulty Using Eye-Tracking
and Skin Conductance Response   400
    Chou Ching-En and Kaska Porayska-Pomsta

Sense of Agency in Times of Automation: A Teachers' Professional
Development Proposal on the Ethical Challenges of AI Applied
to Education   405
    Ana Mouta, Eva Torrecilla Sánchez, and Ana María Pinto Llorente

Improving Students' Problem-Solving Flexibility
in Non-routine Mathematics   409
    Huy A. Nguyen, Yuqing Guo, John Stamper, and Bruce M. McLaren

Workshop Papers

Optimizing Human Learning: Third International Workshop Eliciting
Adaptive Sequences for Learning (WASL 2020)   417
    Jill-Jênn Vie, Fabrice Popineau, Hisashi Kashima, and Benoît Choffin

Empowering Education with AI Technology – IEEE LTSC   420
    Robby Robson, Xiangen Hu, Jim Goodell, Michael Jay, and Brandt Redd

Second Workshop on Intelligent Textbooks   424
   Sergey Sosnovsky, Peter Brusilovsky, Richard G. Baraniuk,
   and Andrew S. Lan

2nd International Workshop on Education in Artificial Intelligence
K-12 (EduAI)   427
   Gerald Steinbauer, Sven Koenig, Fredrik Heintz, Julie Henry,
   Tara Chklovski, and Martin Kandlhofer

Author Index   431

Contents – Part I

Full Papers

Making Sense of Student Success and Risk Through Unsupervised
Machine Learning and Interactive Storytelling   3
    Ahmad Al-Doulat, Nasheen Nur, Alireza Karduni, Aileen Benedict,
    Erfan Al-Hossami, Mary Lou Maher, Wenwen Dou, Mohsen Dorodchi,
    and Xi Niu

Strategies for Deploying Unreliable AI Graders in High-Transparency
High-Stakes Exams   16
    Sushmita Azad, Binglin Chen, Maxwell Fowler, Matthew West,
    and Craig Zilles

AI Enabled Tutor for Accessible Training   29
    Ayan Banerjee, Imane Lamrani, Sameena Hossain, Prajwal Paudyal,
    and Sandeep K. S. Gupta

Introducing a Framework to Assess Newly Created Questions
with Natural Language Processing.   43
    Luca Benedetto, Andrea Cappelli, Roberto Turrin, and Paolo Cremonesi

Detecting Off-Task Behavior from Student Dialogue in Game-Based
Collaborative Learning.   55
    Dan Carpenter, Andrew Emerson, Bradford W. Mott, Asmalina Saleh,
    Krista D. Glazewski, Cindy E. Hmelo-Silver, and James C. Lester

Automated Analysis of Middle School Students' Written Reflections
During Game-Based Learning.   67
    Dan Carpenter, Michael Geden, Jonathan Rowe, Roger Azevedo,
    and James Lester

Can Ontologies Support the Gamification of Scripted Collaborative
Learning Sessions?   79
    Geiser Chalco Challco, Ig Ibert Bittencourt, and Seiji Isotani

Predicting Gaps in Usage in a Phone-Based Literacy Intervention System . . .   92
    Rishabh Chatterjee, Michael Madaio, and Amy Ogan

MACER: A Modular Framework for Accelerated Compilation
Error Repair.   106
    Darshak Chhatbar, Umair Z. Ahmed, and Purushottam Kar

Using Motion Sensors to Understand Collaborative Interactions
in Digital Fabrication Labs.   118
   Edwin Chng, Mohamed Raouf Seyam, William Yao,
   and Bertrand Schneider

Student Dropout Prediction   129
   Francesca Del Bonifro , Maurizio Gabbrielli, Giuseppe Lisanti,
   and Stefano Pio Zingaro

Real-Time Multimodal Feedback with the CPR Tutor   141
   Daniele Di Mitri, Jan Schneider, Kevin Trebing, Sasa Sopka,
   Marcus Specht, and Hendrik Drachsler

Impact of Methodological Choices on the Evaluation of Student Models   153
   Tomáš Effenberger and Radek Pelánek

Investigating Visitor Engagement in Interactive Science Museum Exhibits
with Multimodal Bayesian Hierarchical Models   165
   Andrew Emerson, Nathan Henderson, Jonathan Rowe, Wookhee Min,
   Seung Lee, James Minogue, and James Lester

Fooling Automatic Short Answer Grading Systems   177
   Anna Filighera, Tim Steuer, and Christoph Rensing

Using Neural Tensor Networks for Open Ended Short
Answer Assessment.   191
   Dipesh Gautam and Vasile Rus

The Sound of Inattention: Predicting Mind Wandering with Automatically
Derived Features of Instructor Speech   204
   Ian Gliser, Caitlin Mills, Nigel Bosch, Shelby Smith, Daniel Smilek,
   and Jeffrey D. Wammes

To Tailor or Not to Tailor Gamification? An Analysis of the Impact
of Tailored Game Elements on Learners' Behaviours and Motivation   216
   Stuart Hallifax, Elise Lavoué, and Audrey Serna

Improving Affect Detection in Game-Based Learning with Multimodal
Data Fusion   228
   Nathan Henderson, Jonathan Rowe, Luc Paquette, Ryan S. Baker,
   and James Lester

A Conceptual Framework for Human–AI Hybrid Adaptivity in Education . . .   240
   Kenneth Holstein, Vincent Aleven, and Nikol Rummel

Exploring How Gender and Enjoyment Impact Learning
in a Digital Learning Game 255
*Xinying Hou, Huy A. Nguyen, J. Elizabeth Richey,
and Bruce M. McLaren*

Neural Multi-task Learning for Teacher Question Detection
in Online Classrooms 269
*Gale Yan Huang, Jiahao Chen, Haochen Liu, Weiping Fu,
Wenbiao Ding, Jiliang Tang, Songfan Yang, Guoliang Li, and Zitao Liu*

A Data-Driven Student Model to Provide Adaptive Support During Video
Watching Across MOOCs 282
Sébastien Lallé and Cristina Conati

Transfer of Automated Performance Feedback Models to Different
Specimens in Virtual Reality Temporal Bone Surgery 296
*Jesslyn Lamtara, Nathan Hanegbi, Benjamin Talks,
Sudanthi Wijewickrema, Xingjun Ma, Patorn Piromchai, James Bailey,
and Stephen O'Leary*

Use of Adaptive Feedback in an App for English Language
Spontaneous Speech 309
*Blair Lehman, Lin Gu, Jing Zhao, Eugene Tsuprun,
Christopher Kurzum, Michael Schiano, Yulin Liu,
and G. Tanner Jackson*

Impact of Conversational Formality on the Quality and Formality
of Written Summaries 321
Haiying Li and Art C. Graesser

LIWCs the Same, Not the Same: Gendered Linguistic Signals
of Performance and Experience in Online STEM Courses 333
Yiwen Lin, Renzhe Yu, and Nia Dowell

SoundHunters: Increasing Learner Phonological Awareness in Plains Cree ... 346
*Delaney Lothian, Gokce Akcayir, Anaka Sparrow, Owen Mcleod,
and Carrie Demmans Epp*

Moodoo: Indoor Positioning Analytics for Characterising
Classroom Teaching 360
*Roberto Martinez-Maldonado, Vanessa Echeverria, Jurgen Schulte,
Antonette Shibani, Katerina Mangaroska, and Simon Buckingham Shum*

DETECT: A Hierarchical Clustering Algorithm for Behavioural Trends
in Temporal Educational Data.................................. 374
Jessica McBroom, Kalina Yacef, and Irena Koprinska

Effect of Non-mandatory Use of an Intelligent Tutoring System
on Students' Learning   386
  Antonija Mitrović and Jay Holland

Evaluating Crowdsourcing and Topic Modeling in Generating Knowledge
Components from Explanations.   398
  Steven Moore, Huy A. Nguyen, and John Stamper

Modeling the Relationships Between Basic and Achievement Emotions
in Computer-Based Learning Environments   411
  Anabil Munshi, Shitanshu Mishra, Ningyu Zhang, Luc Paquette,
  Jaclyn Ocumpaugh, Ryan Baker, and Gautam Biswas

Analysis of Task Difficulty Sequences in a Simulation-Based
POE Environment   423
  Sadia Nawaz, Namrata Srivastava, Ji Hyun Yu, Ryan S. Baker,
  Gregor Kennedy, and James Bailey

Affective Sequences and Student Actions Within Reasoning Mind   437
  Jaclyn Ocumpaugh, Ryan S. Baker, Shamya Karumbaiah,
  Scott A. Crossley, and Matthew Labrum

Helping Teachers Help Their Students: A Human-AI Hybrid Approach   448
  Ranilson Paiva and Ig Ibert Bittencourt

Comprehensive Views of Math Learners: A Case for Modeling
and Supporting Non-math Factors in Adaptive Math Software   460
  J. Elizabeth Richey, Nikki G. Lobczowski, Paulo F. Carvalho,
  and Kenneth Koedinger

Exploring the Impact of Simple Explanations and Agency on Batch Deep
Reinforcement Learning Induced Pedagogical Policies   472
  Markel Sanz Ausin, Mehak Maniktala, Tiffany Barnes, and Min Chi

Recommending Insightful Drill-Downs Based on Learning Processes
for Learning Analytics Dashboards   486
  Shiva Shabaninejad, Hassan Khosravi, Sander J. J. Leemans,
  Shazia Sadiq, and Marta Indulska

Using Thinkalouds to Understand Rule Learning and Cognitive Control
Mechanisms Within an Intelligent Tutoring System   500
  Deniz Sonmez Unal, Catherine M. Arrington, Erin Solovey,
  and Erin Walker

Remember the Facts? Investigating Answer-Aware Neural Question
Generation for Text Comprehension   512
  Tim Steuer, Anna Filighera, and Christoph Rensing

Raising Teachers Empowerment in Gamification Design of Adaptive
Learning Systems: A Qualitative Research   524
 Kamilla Tenório, Diego Dermeval, Mateus Monteiro,
 Aristoteles Peixoto, and Alan Pedro

Far from Success – Far from Feedback Acceptance? The Influence
of Game Performance on Young Students' Willingness to Accept Critical
Constructive Feedback During Play   537
 Eva-Maria Ternblad and Betty Tärning

Robust Neural Automated Essay Scoring Using Item Response Theory   549
 Masaki Uto and Masashi Okano

Supporting Teacher Assessment in Chinese Language Learning Using
Textual and Tonal Features   562
 Ashvini Varatharaj, Anthony F. Botelho, Xiwen Lu,
 and Neil T. Heffernan

Early Detection of Wheel-Spinning in ASSISTments   574
 Yeyu Wang, Shimin Kai, and Ryan Shaun Baker

Investigating Differential Error Types Between Human
and Simulated Learners   586
 Daniel Weitekamp, Zihuiwen Ye, Napol Rachatasumrit, Erik Harpstead,
 and Kenneth Koedinger

Studying the Interactions Between Science, Engineering,
and Computational Thinking in a Learning-by-Modeling Environment   598
 Ningyu Zhang, Gautam Biswas, Kevin W. McElhaney, Satabdi Basu,
 Elizabeth McBride, and Jennifer L. Chiu

Exploring Automated Question Answering Methods
for Teaching Assistance   610
 Brian Zylich, Adam Viola, Brokk Toggerson, Lara Al-Hariri,
 and Andrew Lan

Author Index   623

Short Papers

Short Papers

Modelling Learners in Crowdsourcing Educational Systems

Solmaz Abdi$^{(\boxtimes)}$, Hassan Khosravi, and Shazia Sadiq

The University of Queensland, Brisbane, Australia
`solmaz.abdi@uq.edu.au`

Abstract. Traditionally, learner models estimate a student's knowledge state solely based on their performance on attempting assessment items. This can be attributed to the fact that in many traditional educational systems, students are primarily involved in just answering assessment items. In recent years, the use of crowdsourcing to support learning at scale has received significant attention. In crowdsourcing educational systems, in addition to attempting assessment items, students are engaged with other various tasks such as creating resources, creating solutions, rating the quality of resources, and giving feedback. Past studies have demonstrated that engaging students in meaningful crowdsourcing tasks, also referred to as learningsourcing, has pedagogical benefits that can enhance student learning. In this paper, we present a learner model that leverages data from students' learnersourcing contributions alongside attempting assessment items towards modelling of students' knowledge state. Results from an empirical study suggest that indeed crowdsourced contributions from students can effectively be used in modelling learners.

Keywords: Learner modelling · Crowdsourcing · Educational systems · Learnersourcing

1 Introduction

Learner models capture an abstract representation of a student's knowledge state. By and large, learner models approximate a student's knowledge state solely based on their performance on assessment items. As a point of reference, many popular learner models such as Bayesian Knowledge Tracing (BKT) [9], Item Response Theory (IRT) [24], Adaptive Factor Models (AFM) [7], Performance Factor Analysis (PFA) [25], deep knowledge tracing (DKT) [27], collaborative filtering based models [1,28], Elo-based modes [3,26], and knowledge tracing machines (KTM) [29] only use responses of students to assessment items and information about them in their modelling. This can probably be attributed to the fact that in many educational learning systems, students are prominently involved in just answering assessment items (e.g., [22]).

In recent years, the use of crowdsourcing in education, often referred to as learnersourcing [21], to support learning at scale has received significant attention. Examples of tasks that have been learnersourced include creating resources

© Springer Nature Switzerland AG 2020
I. I. Bittencourt et al. (Eds.): AIED 2020, LNAI 12164, pp. 3–9, 2020.
https://doi.org/10.1007/978-3-030-52240-7_1

[12, 20], creating solutions and explanations [14, 32], rating quality [12, 20], giving feedback [23] and annotating videos [10, 31]. The adoption of learnersourcing approaches is often motivated by learning theories that promote higher-order learning [4] and have been demonstrated to enhance student learning [12, 18].

Building on the growing evidence that learnersourcing practices enhance learning, this paper explores whether information about the learnersourcing contributions of students can be leveraged towards modelling of learners. For this exploration, we make use of the knowledge tracing machines (KTMs) framework [29] for modelling student learning. Commonly, KTMs have been used as a framework for modelling learners based on a single task (attempting assessment items). We present an encoding extension on KTMs so that the framework can capture students' interactions across multiple types of tasks (multi-tasks). To evaluate our approach, we use two data sets collected from a crowdsourcing adaptive educational system called RiPPLE in which students are engaged with multiple types of tasks within the system. Results suggest that leveraging data associated with learnersourcing contributions of the students on some types of tasks such as content creation and content moderation can be used to improve the predictive performance of the learner model compared to traditional learner models. In addition, in recent years, OLMs have been extensively integrated into various educational tools to help students in monitoring, reflecting, planning, and regulating their learning [2, 5, 6, 8, 15, 16]. In the context of open learner models [6], updating models of the learners based on their crowdsourced contributions can further highlight the link between learnersourcing and learning as well as acknowledging their contribution. This may act as a method of incentivising student engagement with learnersourcing.

2   Approach

To infer learner models that incorporate data from learnersourced contributions alongside student assessment data, we present an encoding extension over the knowledge tracing machine (KTM) framework [29] so that interactions across multiple types of tasks (multi-tasks) can be captured. We denote students by $u_n \in \{u_1 \ldots u_N\}$, learning resources (items) by $q_m \in \{q_1 \ldots q_M\}$, and knowledge components (concepts) by $\delta_c \in \{\delta_1 \ldots \delta_C\}$. Each item can be tagged with one or more concepts. We denote the relationship between items and concepts by $\omega_{mc} \in \Omega_{M \times C}$, where ω_{mc} is 1 if item q_m is tagged with δ_c, and 0 otherwise. We further denote o_{nc} to keep track of the number of opportunities a student u_n has had on a concept δ_c at a given time.

Commonly, KTMs have been used as a generic framework for traditional computer-based educational systems where students are only involved in attempting assessment items available in the repository of the system. Therefore, the set of tasks, T, represented in these systems is only limited to one task. We present a simple extension that enables KTMs to capture and encode data on students interacting with more than one task. We denote different types of tasks that students are allowed to perform in relation to items by $t_k \in \{t_1 \ldots t_k\}$. Furthermore,

Students	Tasks	Resources	Concepts	Outcome
u_1	t_1	q_3	δ_1	0
u_1	t_1	q_1	$\delta_1 \sim \delta_2$	1
u_1	t_2	q_2	δ_2	1
u_1	t_3	q_1	$\delta_1 \sim \delta_2$	1
u_2	t_1	q_1	$\delta_1 \sim \delta_2$	0
u_2	t_1	q_3	δ_1	0
u_2	t_3	q_3	δ_1	1

(a)

Students		Tasks			Resources			Concepts		t_1		t_2		t_3		Outcome
u_1	u_2	t_1	t_2	t_3	q_1	q_2	q_3	δ_1	δ_2	$o_1^{t_1}$	$o_2^{t_1}$	$o_1^{t_2}$	$o_2^{t_2}$	$o_1^{t_3}$	$o_2^{t_3}$	
1	0	1	0	0	0	0	1	1	0	0	0	0	0	0	0	0
1	0	1	0	0	1	0	0	1	1	1	0	0	0	0	0	1
1	0	0	1	0	0	1	0	0	1	0	1	0	0	0	0	1
1	0	0	0	1	1	0	0	1	1	2	1	0	1	0	0	1
0	1	1	0	0	1	0	0	1	1	0	0	0	0	0	0	0
0	1	1	0	0	0	0	1	1	0	1	0	0	0	0	0	0
0	1	0	0	1	0	0	1	1	0	2	0	0	0	0	0	1

(b)

Fig. 1. (a) An example of a log file with 7 interactions from a crowdsourcing educational system with three types of tasks (b) On-hot encoded of the log for training KTM

we extend o_{nc} to o_{nc}^k to represent the number of opportunities a user u_n has had on a task t_k on a concept δ_c at a given time. Our proposed approach encodes and uses data from student, items, concepts, and opportunities on each of the tasks to infer a learner model $\Lambda_{N \times M}$ that estimate each student u_n's knowledge state for correctly attempting learning item q_m.

Figure 1 presents an example of the input file (part (a)) and its one-hot encoding (part (b)) for an educational system with multi-tasks using a chronologically ordered log file with seven observed interactions from an educational system based on two students, three tasks, three items and two concepts into a sparse vector for training KTM (for details, please see [29]).

3   Evaluation

Data Sets. We used two data sets obtained from an adaptive educational system called RiPPLE that recommends learning activities to students based on their knowledge state from a pool of learnersourced learning items [18]. RiPPLE enables students to create, attempt, moderate, rate, and leave comments on a range of items, including worked examples and multiple-choice questions. For this study, we consider three main types of tasks that students are allowed to perform in RiPPLE: (1) attempting items (Attempt), (2) creating new items (Create), and (3) moderating items (Moderate). The data sets are obtained from two courses, namely, 'Preparation for US Medical Licensing Examination (USMLE) (Medi) and 'Biological Fate of Drugs' (Pharm). For each of these two courses, the RiPPLE platform was used for 13 weeks of the semester. Each item in the repository is associated with one or more concepts (KC) covered in the course. Overall information about these data sets are provided in Table 1.

Table 1. overall statistics for data sets (# stands for number of).

Data Set	Students	Concepts	Resources	Records	#Attempt	#Create	#Moderate
Medi	179	4	619	16,052	13,249	615	2,188
Pharm	131	13	678	29,982	28,019	678	1,285

Table 2. Performance of different feature encoding for modeling learners

ID	Model	Medi			Pharm		
		ACC	AUC	NLL	ACC	AUC	NLL
m_1	IRT: Student, Item	0.698	0.711	0.567	0.785	0.771	0.451
m_2	AFM: Student, Concept, o^A	0.678	0.599	0.614	0.772	0.672	0.504
m_3	PFA: Student, Concepts, w^A, f^A	0.676	0.551	0.625	0.770	0.625	0.521
m_4	Baseline: Student, Item, Concepts, o^A	0.700	0.713	0.565	0.784	0.773	0.453
m_5	**Student, Item, Concepts, o^A, o^C, o^M**	**0.707**	**0.723**	**0.563**	**0.788**	**0.778**	**0.499**

Models for Comparison. We implemented the proposed model based on the encoding of students, items, concepts, opportunities on attempting (o^A), opportunities on creating (o^C), and opportunities on moderating items (o^M) as tasks in KTM. We compare the predictive performance of this model with traditional learner models, including IRT, AFM, and PFA. To provide a fair comparison between all models, we also made two considerations: (1) We implemented a baseline model within KTM based on the encoding of student, items, concepts, and opportunities on attempting items (o^A); (2) The pairwise interaction between features in KTM is set to zero (d = 0). For all models, we used 80% of data as the train set and predicted the outcomes on the remaining 20% as the test set. For both of the data sets, 400 epochs are used for training KTM.

Results. Table 2 compares the accuracy (ACC), area under the curve (AUC), and negative log-likelihood (NLL) of the model fit statistics related to each model. Our experimental results suggest that the learner model that leverages data related to content creation and content moderation activities (m_5) can more accurately estimate students' knowledge state compared to its baseline and the traditional learner models that only rely on students performance on attempting learning items. This outcome is aligned with past studies on learnersourcing [11–13,18,19,30] that suggest engaging students in higher-order learning impacts learning.

4   Discussion and Conclusion

In this paper, we presented a learner model that leveraged data from students' learnersourced contributions alongside traditional item-assessment data towards modeling the knowledge state of students in crowdsourcing educational systems. The results of our empirical studies suggest that incorporating data from students' contributions on some types of tasks associated with higher-order learning such as content creation and content moderation can be used to improve the predictive performance of the learner model. This, in turn, can improve the provided personalised feedback by the system and its adaptivity functionalities. Our findings can also have implications for learnersourcing systems that incorporate an open learner model (OLMs). Incorporating OLMs in crowdsourcing educational systems can have two benefits:

1. *Highlighting the link between learnersourcing and learning.* Updating a student's competency in a concept by creating or moderating resources on that concept can help the student better associate learnersourcing with learning.
2. *Acknowledging students' learningsourcing contributions.* Developing models that recognise students' learningsourcing contributions and associate it with their learning may incentivise students' engagement with learnersourcing tasks, which has been identified as a challenge in learnersourcing [17,31].

A major limitation of the presented evaluation is that the study was conducted on small data sets. Future directions include replicating this study across different disciplines with a larger number of students to evaluate the generalisability of our current findings.

References

1. Abdi, S., Khosravi, H., Sadiq, S.: Predicting student performance: the case of combining knowledge tracing and collaborative filtering. In: Proceedings of the International Conference on Educational Data Mining, pp. 545–548 (2018)
2. Abdi, S., Khosravi, H., Sadiq, S., Gasevic, D.: Complementing educational recommender systems with open learner models. In: Proceedings of the Tenth International Conference on Learning Analytics & Knowledge, pp. 360–365. Association for Computing Machinery, New York (2020)
3. Abdi, S., Khosravi, H., Sadiq, S., Gasevic, D.: A multivariate Elo-based learner model for adaptive educational systems. In: Proceedings of the Educational Data Mining Conference, pp. 462–467 (2019)
4. Bloom, B.S., et al.: Taxonomy of Educational Objectives. vol. 1: Cognitive Domain, pp. 20–24. McKay, New York (1956)
5. Bull, S., Ginon, B., Boscolo, C., Johnson, M.: Introduction of learning visualisations and metacognitive support in a persuadable open learner model. In: Proceedings of the Sixth International Conference on Learning Analytics & Knowledge, pp. 30–39. ACM (2016)
6. Bull, S., Kay, J.: Open learner models. In: Nkambou, R., Bourdeau, J., Mizoguchi, R. (eds.) Advances in Intelligent Tutoring Systems. SCI, vol. 308, pp. 301–322. Springer, Heidelberg (2010). https://doi.org/10.1007/978-3-642-14363-2_15
7. Cen, H., Koedinger, K., Junker, B.: Learning factors analysis – a general method for cognitive model evaluation and improvement. In: Ikeda, M., Ashley, K.D., Chan, T.-W. (eds.) ITS 2006. LNCS, vol. 4053, pp. 164–175. Springer, Heidelberg (2006). https://doi.org/10.1007/11774303_17
8. Cooper, K., Khosravi, H.: Graph-based visual topic dependency models: supporting assessment design and delivery at scale. In: Proceedings of the 8th International Conference on Learning Analytics and Knowledge, pp. 11–15. ACM (2018)
9. Corbett, A.T., Anderson, J.R.: Knowledge tracing: modeling the acquisition of procedural knowledge. User Model. User-Adapt. Interact. 4(4), 253–278 (1994)
10. Cross, A., Bayyapunedi, M., Ravindran, D., Cutrell, E., Thies, W.: Vidwiki: enabling the crowd to improve the legibility of online educational videos. In: Proceedings of the 17th ACM Conference on Computer Supported Cooperative Work & Social Computing, pp. 1167–1175 (2014)

11. Denny, P., Hamer, J., Luxton-Reilly, A., Purchase, H.: Peerwise: students sharing their multiple choice questions. In: Proceedings of the Fourth International Workshop on Computing Education Research, pp. 51–58. ACM (2008)
12. Denny, P., Luxton-Reilly, A., Hamer, J.: The peerwise system of student contributed assessment questions. In: Proceedings of the Tenth Conference on Australasian Computing Education, vol. 78, pp. 69–74. Citeseer (2008)
13. Dunlosky, J., Rawson, K.A., Marsh, E.J., Nathan, M.J., Willingham, D.T.: Improving students' learning with effective learning techniques: promising directions from cognitive and educational psychology. Psychol. Sci. Public Interest **14**(1), 4–58 (2013)
14. Heffernan, N.T., et al.: The future of adaptive learning: does the crowd hold the key? Int. J. Artif. Intell. Educ. **26**(2), 615–644 (2016)
15. Jivet, I., Scheffel, M., Specht, M., Drachsler, H.: License to evaluate: preparing learning analytics dashboards for educational practice. In: Proceedings of the 8th International Conference on Learning Analytics and Knowledge, pp. 31–40. ACM (2018)
16. Khosravi, H., Cooper, K.: Topic dependency models: graph-based visual analytics for communicating assessment data. J. Learn. Anal. **5**(3), 136–153 (2018)
17. Khosravi, H., Gyamfi, G., Hanna, B., Lodge, J.: Fostering and supporting empirical research on evaluative judgement via a crowdsourced adaptive learning system. In: Proceedings of the 10nth International Conference on Learning Analytics and Knowledge, LAK 2020. ACM, New York (2020)
18. Khosravi, H., Kitto, K., Joseph, W.: Ripple: a crowdsourced adaptive platform for recommendation of learning activities. J. Learn. Anal. **6**(3), 91–105 (2019)
19. Khosravi, H., Kitto, K., Williams, J.J.: Ripple: a crowdsourced adaptive platform for recommendation of learning activities. arXiv preprint arXiv:1910.05522 (2019)
20. Khosravi, H., Sadiq, S., Gasevic, D.: Development and adoption of an adaptive learning system: reflections and lessons learned. In: Proceedings of the 51st ACM Technical Symposium on Computer Science Education, pp. 58–64. Association for Computing Machinery, New York (2020). https://doi.org/10.1145/3328778.3366900
21. Kim, J., et al.: Learnersourcing: improving learning with collective learner activity. Ph.D. thesis, Massachusetts Institute of Technology (2015)
22. Koedinger, K.R., Anderson, J.R., Hadley, W.H., Mark, M.A.: Intelligent tutoring goes to school in the big city (1997)
23. Kulkarni, C., et al.: Peer and self assessment in massive online classes. ACM Trans. Comput.-Hum. Interact. (TOCHI) **20**(6), 1–31 (2013)
24. Lord, F.M.: Applications of Item Response Theory to Practical Testing Problems. Routledge (2012)
25. Pavlik Jr., P.I., Cen, H., Koedinger, K.R.: Performance factors analysis-a new alternative to knowledge tracing. Online Submission (2009)
26. Pelánek, R., Papoušek, J., Řihák, J., Stanislav, V., Nižnan, J.: Elo-based learner modeling for the adaptive practice of facts. User Model. User-Adapt. Interact. **27**(1), 89–118 (2017)
27. Piech, C., et al.: Deep knowledge tracing. In: Advances in Neural Information Processing Systems, pp. 505–513 (2015)
28. Thai-Nghe, N., Drumond, L., Horváth, T., Krohn-Grimberghe, A., Nanopoulos, A., Schmidt-Thieme, L.: Factorization techniques for predicting student performance. In: Educational Recommender Systems and Technologies: Practices and Challenges, pp. 129–153 (2011)

29. Vie, J.J., Kashima, H.: Knowledge tracing machines: factorization machines for knowledge tracing. In: Proceedings of the AAAI Conference on Artificial Intelligence, vol. 33, pp. 750–757 (2019)
30. Walsh, J.L., Harris, B.H., Denny, P., Smith, P.: Formative student-authored question bank: perceptions, question quality and association with summative performance. Postgrad. Med. J. **94**(1108), 97–103 (2018)
31. Weir, S., Kim, J., Gajos, K.Z., Miller, R.C.: Learnersourcing subgoal labels for how-to videos. In: Proceedings of the 18th ACM Conference on Computer Supported Cooperative Work & Social Computing, pp. 405–416 (2015)
32. Williams, J.J., et al.: Axis: generating explanations at scale with learnersourcing and machine learning. In: Proceedings of the Third ACM Conference on Learning@ Scale, pp. 379–388. ACM (2016)

Interactive Pedagogical Agents for Learning Sequence Diagrams

Sohail Alhazmi[✉], Charles Thevathayan, and Margaret Hamilton

RMIT University, Melbourne, Australia
{sohail.alhazmi,charles.thevathayan,
margaret.hamilton}@rmit.edu.au

Abstract. Students struggle to learn sequence diagrams (SDs), as the designs must meet the requirements without violating the constraints imposed by other UML diagrams. Providing manual timely feedback, though effective, cannot scale for large classes. Our pedagogical agent combining data dependencies and quality metrics with rule-based techniques capturing consistency constraints allowed generation of immediate and holistic feedback. The scaffolding approach helped to lower the cognitive overload. The pre- and post-tests and survey results revealed substantially improved learning outcomes and student satisfaction.

Keywords: Pedagogical agent · Constructivism · Interaction diagrams

1 Introduction

A multi-institutional study with 314 participants found that over 80% of graduating students were unable to create a software design or even a partial design [3]. The design and modelling skills are cognitively demanding skills needing formative feedback [10]. Formative feedback should be non-evaluative, supportive, timely and context specific [12]. Effective tutors use a scaffolding approach after diagnosing student difficulties [7]. Such an approach though highly effective cannot be used in large cohorts with fixed budgets. We posit, pedagogical agents can help fill this gap by augmenting domain knowledge with scaffolding skills of effective tutors.

Design patterns used for modeling complex interaction behaviors in the industry, rely on a good understanding of sequence diagrams (SDs) [5]. However, SDs posed the most difficulties among novices learning modeling [13]. Similarly when we analyze our own modeling tasks in the final exam, we found many students had no idea how SDs were constrained by other models. Many exhibited difficulties in identifying valid interacting-objects and constructing messages with appropriate arguments. Though students understood the role of objects, messages and arguments individually, they were daunted when considering all constraints imposed by other models, concurrently.

The cognitive load theory postulates that the cognitive load resulting from a task may potentially hamper learning [15]. Any strategy that involves more cognitive load than available working memory can deteriorate performance by overwhelming the learner [14]. Modelling SD overwhelms many learners as it involves a high number of interacting items that must be handled concurrently [14]. The direct correlation that

© Springer Nature Switzerland AG 2020
I. I. Bittencourt et al. (Eds.): AIED 2020, LNAI 12164, pp. 10–14, 2020.
https://doi.org/10.1007/978-3-030-52240-7_2

exists between cognitive load and self-efficacy [17], helps to explain why students exhibit poor self-efficacy in modelling SDs. We report the results of our ongoing studies where we have gradually raised types of constraints and goals the agent can handle with commensurate levels of support. The main contribution in this paper is to demonstrate how pedagogical agents augmenting domain knowledge with scaffolding techniques can assist novices learning modelling tasks by reducing the cognitive load. Our main research question is:

- Can pedagogical agents augmenting domain knowledge with scaffolding improve the learning outcomes of stragglers modeling sequence diagrams?

2 Related Work

Pedagogical agents are defined to be autonomous agents that support human learning, by interacting with students in the context of an interactive learning environment as a guide, critic, coach or wizard [4]. Pedagogical agents using scaffolding have been shown to enable significant improvement in students' learning outcomes [6]. Scaffolding is timely support given to students to foster problem-solving and design skills [2]. The key features of scaffolding are ongoing diagnosis, adaptivity and fading, but these features are neglected by some developing pedagogical agents for complex environments, often equating scaffolding to additional support [9]. Good tutors are usually able to adjust to the learning style of the student and use a scaffolded approach by giving just enough support to help students solve their problem. However, with increasing class sizes and diversity, tutors cannot provide the levels of support needed [8]. Intelligent agents can be made to give the right amount of hints by tracking the current and goal states and capturing the proficiency level of the learner [7].

3 Overview and Elements of the Pedagogy Agent

Our pedagogy agent permits a scaffolding approach providing gradual feedback on consistency, message validity, completeness and quality. Inputs to the pedagogy agent includes the description of class diagram, methods that must be called specifying particular order if needed, and the quality related metrics. The class diagram supplied together with AI rule-based techniques capturing domain constraints help enforce consistency. For example, the agent forbids a message to be dispatched to a target object if the class it belongs to does not have a corresponding method. The data and methods explicitly capturing data dependencies allow knowledge state in entities to be maintained, preventing data to be dispatched prematurely. In the second stage when student submits the sequence diagram, student will be asked to re-attempt if the specified methods based on use cases are not called or if they are called in incorrect order. In the final stage when a student has submitted a valid sequence diagram, design will be graded based on the qualitative metrics supplied. For example, if distributed design is specified as a quality-criteria, a poor grade will be awarded if most of the messages are originated by the same entity. Figure 1 shows a sample sequence diagram for a class diagram with 4 classes Doctor, Hospital, Patient and Appointment.

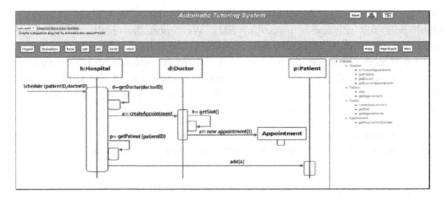

Fig. 1. A sample of a completed Sequence Diagram using our agent which must discharge its responsibilities by calling the Appointment constructor and the *add* method of *p:Patient*.

4   Results

All 243 students taking the first software engineering course were invited to the trial the agent, and out of the 94 students who volunteered only 68 proceeded to complete both tests and the survey. The average marks for pre- and post-tests were 46.25 and 61.25 respectively showing a 32% improvement. To study how the agent affects students with different grades, we analyzed the distribution of pre- and post- test marks in cycle 1, which had a substantial number of students as shown in Fig. 2. The distribution of test marks before and after using the agent suggests weaker students (especially those scoring only 0–49 in the pretests) had the greatest gains. Note the number of students scoring in the range 0–49 declined by nearly 60% from 32 students to 13 students, suggesting a pedagogical agent can significantly improve the performance of stragglers in design activities.

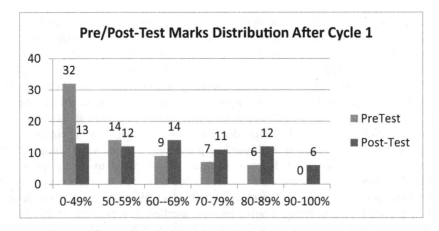

Fig. 2. Marks distribution in pre/posttests after cycle 1

We designed a survey to study the effectiveness of the pedagogical agent from students' perspectives. The survey included Likert-scale and open-ended questions. Students were asked to complete the survey at the end of the modelling activity and tests. The survey was completed by 68 students. Questions were primarily about the agent, student's difficulties and whether the agent can help them get over misconceptions. The results showed around 61.4% of students found learning UML diagrams difficult while over 79% of the students found the modelling agent with instant feedback beneficial for learning UML design. Most of the students found the agent allowed them to grasp the interdependencies between class diagrams and SDs. The overwhelmingly positive response (over 80% agree and over 45% strongly agree) to the three questions related to student confidence, understanding and awareness suggests pedagogical agents can play a key role in improving the self-efficacy of students.

5 Discussion

Success in modeling is generally recognized as requiring a certain level of cognitive development [3]. The cognitive load theory postulates the cognitive load resulting from a task may potentially hamper learning [15]. Decomposing an inherently difficult subject matter can help reduce the cognitive load by allowing subtasks to be first learnt individually [11]. Scaffolding has proven to be effective with diverse student cohorts as it helps to decompose complex problems into incremental constructivist steps [1, 16]. Our solution using a pedagogy agent approach allows cognitive load for modeling SDs to be gradually increased using scaffolding. In the initial stage consistency rules and data dependencies were enforced, before introducing valid completion criteria and grade for quality. Figure 2 depicts most of the weaker students had better learning improvement and displayed greater satisfaction in the second stage where greater scaffolding and multiple tasks were provided accompanied with context specific feedback.

6 Conclusion

Modelling sequence diagrams poses heavy cognitive load on students as constraints and rules imposed by other models must be analyzed concurrently, making it the most poorly performing UML artifact. Effective tutors use scaffolding techniques to teach cognitively demanding tasks. Augmenting a goal and constraint driven agent with such scaffolding techniques appears to substantially improve the learning outcomes in modelling sequence diagrams. The scaffolding techniques allow creation of student specific pathways with varying levels of cognitive challenges and support. The varying levels of support are provided through prompting, feedback, guidance and problem decomposition. Problem decomposition allows cognitive load to be reduced when necessary by enabling students to focus solely on one aspect at a time. This longitudinal study allowed data collected from experienced tutors, lecturers and participants to evolve a more personalized approach to teaching to our increasingly diverse student cohorts.

References

1. Alhazmi, S., Hamilton, M., Thevathayan, C.: CS for all: catering to diversity of master's students through assignment choices. In: Proceedings of the 49th ACM Technical Symposium on Computer Science Education, pp. 38–43, February 2018. https://doi.org/10.1145/3159450.3159464
2. Belland, B.R.: Scaffolding: Definition, Current Debates, and Future Directions. Springer, New York (2014). https://doi.org/10.1007/978-1-4614-3185-5_39
3. Eckerdal, A., Ratcliffe, M., Mccartney, R., Zander, C.: Can graduating students design software systems? ACM SIGCSE Bull. **38**(1), 403–407 (2006). https://doi.org/10.1145/1124706.1121468
4. Jondahl, S., Morch, A.: Simulating pedagogical agents in a virtual learning environment. In: CSCL 2002, Boulder (2002). https://doi.org/10.3115/1658616.1658705
5. Lu, L., Kim, D.: Required behavior of sequence diagrams: semantics and conformance. ACM Trans. Softw. Eng. Methodol. **23**(2), 15:1–15:28 (2014). https://doi.org/10.1145/2523108
6. Martha, A.S.D., Santoso, H.B., Junus, K., Suhartanto, H.: A scaffolding design for pedagogical agents within the higher-education context. In: International Conference on Education Technology and Computers. ACM, Amsterdam (2019). https://doi.org/10.1145/3369255.3369267
7. Merrill, D.C., Reiser, B.J., Ranney, M., Trafton, J.G.: Effective tutoring techniques: a comparison of human tutors and intelligent tutoring systems. J. Learn. Sci. **2**(3), 277–305 (1992). https://doi.org/10.1207/s15327809jls0203_2
8. Parvez, S.M., Blank, G.: Individualizing Tutoring with Learning Style Based Feedback. Intelligent Tutoring Systems, Montreal (2008)
9. Puntambekar, S., Hubscher, R.: Tools for scaffolding students in a complex learning environment: what have we gained and what have we missed? Educ. Psychol. **40**(1), 1–12 (2005). https://doi.org/10.1207/s15326985ep4001_1
10. Schaffer, H.E., Young, K.R., Ligon, E.W., Chapman, D.D.: Automating individualized formative feedback in large classes based on a direct concept graph. Front. Psychol. **8**, 260 (2017). https://doi.org/10.3389/fpsyg.2017.00260
11. Shibli, D., West, R.: Cognitive load theory and its application in the classroom. J. Chart. Coll. Teach. **8** (2019)
12. Shute, V.J.: Focus on formative feedback. Rev. Educ. Res. **78**(1), 153–189 (2008). https://doi.org/10.3102/0034654307313795
13. Sien, V.Y.: An investigation of difficulties experienced by students developing unified modelling language class and sequence diagrams. Comput. Sci. Educ. **21**(4), 317–342 (2011). https://doi.org/10.1080/08993408.2011.630127
14. Sin, T.: Improving Novice Analyst Performance in Modelling the Sequence Diagram in Systems Analysis: A Cognitive Complexity Approach. Florida International University, Miami (2009)
15. Sweller, J.: Cognitive load during problem solving: effects on learning. Cogn. Sci. **12**(2), 257–285 (1988). https://doi.org/10.1207/s15516709cog1202_4
16. Thevathayan, C., Hamilton, M.: Supporting diverse novice programming cohorts through flexible and incremental visual constructivist pathways. In: ACM Conference on Innovation and Technology in Computer Science Education, pp. 296–301. ACM, Lithuania (2015). https://doi.org/10.1145/2729094.2742609
17. Vasile, C., MariaMarhan, A., Singer, F.M., Stoicescu, D.: Academic self-efficacy and cognitive load in students. Soc. Behav. Sci. **12**, 478–482 (2011). https://doi.org/10.1016/j.sbspro.2011.02.059

A Socratic Tutor for Source Code Comprehension

Zeyad Alshaikh[(✉)], Lasagn Tamang[(✉)], and Vasile Rus[(✉)]

The University of Memphis, Memphis, TN 38152, USA
{zlshaikh,ljtamang,vrus}@memphis.edu

Abstract. Reported here are the findings of a comparative study on the effects of using a Socratic Intelligent Tutoring System for source code comprehension and learning computer programming. The result shows there are significant differences between the two groups where students who used Socratic Tutor ITS improved their knowledge by 45% in term of learning gain, developed a better understanding of concepts such as nested if-else and for loop, and improved their confidence level by 13%. Furthermore, the result of the Pearson product-moment correlation coefficient shows a positive correlation (r = 0.68) between feedback from the ITS and learning gain.

Keywords: Socratic method · Computer science education · Computer programming · Intelligent Tutoring System

1 Introduction

Introductory programming courses are difficult [10], frustrating [8], and often considered a major stumbling block for many students [15]. There is much evidence that drop-out and failure rates in introductory Computer Science courses such as CS1 and CS2 are high (30–40%) [3,12,16].

Intelligent Tutoring Systems have been proven to be beneficial solutions that can provide individualized, one-on-one instruction for all students [1], and improve the quality and effectiveness of computer programming instruction [14]. As a result, many ITS systems were developed as early as 1974 [7] to aid students on different programming phases [6,9,10,17,18].

In our case, we developed a dialogue-based intelligent tutoring system called Socratic Tutor to help novice programmers acquire deep and robust programming knowledge by engaging in source code understanding learning activities. The Socratic Tutor is inspired by the Socratic instructional strategy [4] in the form of a set of guiding questions meant to provide students a form of scaffolding by targeting key aspects of the instructional task. Furthermore, the developed system relies on self-explanation theories of learning [5] by implementing instructional strategies such as eliciting self-explanations through Socratic questioning.

Socratic Tutor ITS uses a natural language understanding (NLU) engine [2] to evaluate students' responses with respect by computing a semantic similarity score to model/benchmark correct answers and well-known misconceptions

© Springer Nature Switzerland AG 2020
I. I. Bittencourt et al. (Eds.): AIED 2020, LNAI 12164, pp. 15–19, 2020.
https://doi.org/10.1007/978-3-030-52240-7_3

created prior by experts. Therefore, the NLU engine enables the Socratic Tutor to immediately detect misconceptions and provide tailored feedback which was proven to have a positive benefit on learning [13]. The developed system provides help to students using a three-level feedback strategy where at level one the tutor explains briefly the target concept and gives the student a second chance to retry answering the original question. At levels two and three, the tutor asks questions in the form of multiple-choice and fill-in-the-blank questions.

This paper analyzes a comparative study of using the Socratic Tutor ITS for learning JAVA programming in Introductory to Computer Science courses (CS1 and CS2) focusing on arithmetic operations, nested $if - else$, $while$ loops, for loops, arrays, and class.

2   Research Questions

To understand Socratic Tutor's impact on students programming knowledge and other characteristics such as confidence, we have conducted a study focusing on the following research questions: (1) how much do students learn when using Socratic Tutor?, (2) how much do students learn on each targeted programming concept?, (3) how much does the Socratic Tutor have an impact on students' self-confidence?, and (4) what is the relationship between feedback and learning gains?

3   Method

Subjects who participated in the study were undergraduates ($n = 70$) enrolled in the Introductory to Computer Science course at a major 4-year Asian university. Half of the students were randomly assigned to a control group who used a scaled-down version of the Socratic Tutor system that only presents JAVA code examples and asks the participant to predict the output without providing any feedback or Socratic tutoring. The other half of the participants were assigned to a condition in which they used the Socratic Tutor. The Socratic Tutor asks to explain the code while trying to understand it and then predicts the output. After that, the tutor asks questions about the programming concepts used in the code. If a participant's answer is not correct or incomplete, the tutor initiates the three-level feedback mechanism.

3.1   Materials

Materials for this experiment included a self-confidence survey and a pre- and post-test. The self-confidence survey contained six questions with a 1–7 Likert scale where each question related to one programming concept. The pre- and post-test have similar levels of difficulty and contained 6 JAVA programs where each question assessed the student's understanding of a particular programming concept. For each question in the pre- and post-test, the participants were asked to predict the output of the code example.

3.2 Procedure

The experiment was conducted in a computer lab under supervision. First, participants were debriefed about the purpose of the experiment and were given a consent form. Those who consented took a self-confidence survey and the pre-test. Once they had finished the pre-test, an approximately 60-min tutoring session started. Finally, participants took the post-test and a post self-confidence survey.

3.3 Assessment

The pre and post-test questions were scored 1 when the student answer was correct and 0 otherwise. The learning gain score (LG) was calculated for each participant as follows [11].

$$LG = \begin{cases} \frac{post\text{-}test - pre\text{-}test}{6 - pre\text{-}test} & post\text{-}test > pre\text{-}test \\ \frac{post\text{-}test - pre\text{-}test}{pre\text{-}test} & post\text{-}test < pre\text{-}test \\ drop & pre\text{-}test = post\text{-}test = 6 \ or \ 0 \\ 0 & post\text{-}test = pretest \end{cases} \tag{1}$$

4 Results

4.1 Quantitative Analysis

Out of 70 participants, we dropped three participants from the treatment group and two from the control group because they had a perfect score in both tests and four students from the control group were dropped for not completing the experiment.

Table 1. Mean and Stander Deviation of Pre-test, post-test and Learning gain for control and treatment group

Section	n	Pre-test		Post-test		Learning gain (1)	
		Mean	SD	Mean	SD	Mean	SD
Control group	29	3.46	2.1	3.68	2	12%	9.1
Treatment group	32	3.47	1.8	4.8	1.3	57%	41

To understand how much do students learn when using Socratic Tutor, we analyzed the results from both groups in terms of average for pre-test, post-test, and learning gains as shown in Table 1. The results indicate that the learning gain of the treatment group was 45% higher and the results from a two-tailed t-test showed that there is a statistically significant difference between the two groups in learning gain scores (t = 3.6, df = 51, p < 0.05).

We analyzed the pre-post test improvement for each programming concept to understand how much do students learn on each programming concept when using Socratic Tutor. The results show between 10% and 33% higher improvement in treatment group, and there are a statistically significant differences in nested if-else ($t = -2.04$, $df = 56$, $p < 0.5$) and for loops ($t = -1.97$, $df = 54$, $p < 0.5$) concepts.

To understand how much does the Socratic Tutor affect students' self-confidence, we evaluated the pre-confidence and post-confidence scores. The results show that the treatment group participants improved their confidence level on average by 13% compared with -1.6% negative improvement in the control group. The result from an independent-sample t-test shows that the difference is statistically significant ($t = -3.1$, $df = 58$, $p < 0.05$).

To understand the relationship between the feedback and learning gains, we analyzed the relationship between the number of feedback each student received and his/her learning gains. The result shows that students received on average 15.4 feedback per tutoring session with a standard deviation of $SD = 7.1$. The relationship was investigated using the Pearson product-moment correlation coefficient. We found a strong, positive correlation between the number of feedback and learning gains ($r = 0.68$, $n = 32$, $p < 0.05$).

5   Conclusion

To understand the effectiveness of the Socratic Tutor ITS, we conducted a comparative study on seventy students who enrolled in Introductory to Computer Science course.

The seventy students were divided into two groups (1) control group where students have to read code and predict the output without any feedback from the system, and (2) treatment group where students interact with the Socratic Tutor.

The result shows that students who used Socratic-ITS improved their knowledge by 45% in term of learning gain, developed better understanding on concepts such as nested if-else and for loop, and improved their confidence level by 13%. Furthermore, the result of the Pearson product-moment correlation coefficient shows a positive correlation ($r = 0.68$) between feedback and learning gain.

Acknowledgments. This work as partially funded by the National Science Foundation under the award #1822816 (Collaborative Research: CSEdPad: Investigating and Scaffolding Students' Mental Models during Computer Programming Tasks to Improve Learning, Engagement, and Retention) to Dr. Vasile Rus. All opinions stated or implied are solely the authors' and do not reflect the opinions of the funding agency.

References

1. Anderson, J.R., Skwarecki, E.: The automated tutoring of introductory computer programming. Commun. ACM **29**(9), 842–849 (1986)
2. Banjade, R., et al.: Nerosim: a system for measuring and interpreting semantic textual similarity. In: Proceedings of the 9th International Workshop on Semantic Evaluation (SemEval 2015), pp. 164–171 (2015)
3. Beaubouef, T., Mason, J.: Why the high attrition rate for computer science students: some thoughts and observations. ACM SIGCSE Bull. **37**(2), 103–106 (2005)
4. Chang, K.E., Sung, Y.T., Wang, K.Y., Dai, C.Y.: Web/spl I.bar/soc: a socratic-dialectic-based collaborative tutoring system on the world wide web. IEEE Trans. Educ. **46**(1), 69–78 (2003)
5. Chi, M.T., De Leeuw, N., Chiu, M.H., LaVancher, C.: Eliciting self-explanations improves understanding. Cogn. Sci. **18**(3), 439–477 (1994)
6. Dadic, T., Stankov, S., Rosic, M.: Prototype model of tutoring system for programming. In: 28th International Conference on Information Technology Interfaces, pp. 41–46. IEEE (2006)
7. Danielson, R.L., Nievergelt, J.: An automatic tutor for introductory programming students (1974)
8. Johnson, W.L.: Understanding and debugging novice programs. Artif. Intell. **42**(1), 51–97 (1990)
9. Johnson, W.L., Soloway, E.: Proust: knowledge-based program understanding. IEEE Trans. Softw. Eng. **3**, 267–275 (1985)
10. Lane, H.C., VanLehn, K.: A dialogue-based tutoring system for beginning programming. In: FLAIRS Conference, pp. 449–454 (2004)
11. Marx, J.D., Cummings, K.: Normalized change. Am. J. Phys. **75**(1), 87–91 (2007)
12. Mcgettrick, A., Boyle, R., Ibbett, R., Lloyd, J., Lovegrove, G., Mander, K.: Grand challenges in computing: education-a summary. Comput. J. **48**(1), 42–48 (2005)
13. Mory, E.H.: Feedback research revisited. Handbook Res. Educ. Commun. Technol. **2**, 745–783 (2004)
14. Pillay, N.: Developing intelligent programming tutors for novice programmers. ACM SIGCSE Bull. **35**(2), 78–82 (2003)
15. Proulx, V.K.: Programming patterns and design patterns in the introductory computer science course. ACM SIGCSE Bull. **32**(1), 80–84 (2000)
16. Robins, A., Rountree, J., Rountree, N.: Learning and teaching programming: a review and discussion. Comput. Sci. Educ. **13**(2), 137–172 (2003)
17. Soloway, E.M., Woolf, B., Rubin, E., Barth, P.: Meno-II: An intelligent tutoring system for novice programmers. In: Proceedings of the 7th International Joint Conference on Artificial Intelligence, vol. 2, pp. 975–977. Morgan Kaufmann Publishers Inc. (1981)
18. Woods, P.J., Warren, J.R.: Rapid prototyping of an intelligent tutorial system. In: Proceedings of 12th Australian Society for Computers in Learning in Tertiary Education, pp. 557–563 (1995)

Scientific Modeling Using Large Scale Knowledge

Sungeun An[1]([✉]), Robert Bates[1], Jen Hammock[2], Spencer Rugaber[1], Emily Weigel[3], and Ashok Goel[1]

[1] School of Interactive Computing, Georgia Institute of Technology,
Atlanta, GA 30308, USA
sungeun.an@gatech.edu
[2] National Museum of Natural History, Smithsonian Institution,
Washington, DC 20002, USA
[3] School of Biological Sciences, Georgia Institute of Technology,
Atlanta, GA 30332, USA

Abstract. The intelligent research assistant, VERA, supports inquiry-based modeling by supplying contextualized large-scale domain knowledge in the Encyclopedia of Life. Learners can use VERA to construct conceptual models of ecological phenomena, run them as simulations, and review their predictions. A study on the use of VERA by college-level students indicates that providing access to large scale but contextualized knowledge helped students build more complex models and generate more hypotheses in problem-solving.

Keywords: Agent-based modeling · Inquiry-based modeling · Ecology · College-level education · Science education

1 Introduction

Research on learning about scientific modeling has revealed the need for cognitive assistance of several kinds [2,4,9,10]. In particular, scientific modeling requires domain knowledge, e.g., relationships between variables describing the system being modeled, as well as mathematical skills [9]. Thus, the question our research addresses is how can we scaffold the acquisition of domain knowledge involved in scientific modeling?

Of course, large amounts of knowledge about many domains are now readily accessible on the internet. However, much of this general-purpose knowledge is not particular to any specific task and thus difficult to comprehend by many learners. Our research hypothesis is that contextualized acquisition of this knowledge may help students achieve deeper understanding about the domain and generate richer models. The Virtual Ecological Research Assistant (VERA) supports scientific modeling in the domain of ecology using large scale domain knowledge through Smithsonian's Encyclopedia of Life (EOL; [7]). Preliminary results from the experiment indicate that contextualized access to ecological knowledge from EOL helped the students build more richer models in problem-solving.

I. I. Bittencourt et al. (Eds.): AIED 2020, LNAI 12164, pp. 20–24, 2020.
https://doi.org/10.1007/978-3-030-52240-7_4

2   VERA: A Research Assistant for Ecological Modeling

VERA is a web-based system intended for large-scale use and supports scientific modeling in three ways [1]. First, it provides a visual language with a well-defined semantics to represent conceptual models clearly. Second, it automatically translates a conceptual model into an agent-based simulation suitable for the ecological domain without requiring any programming skills or mathematical expertise. Third, it provides access to large scale biological knowledge through EOL to help the students construct the conceptual models and set the simulation parameters.

While other recent modeling systems (Co-Lab and PROMETHEUS) use equation-based modeling that consists of a set of equations and executions to evaluate them [3,5], VERA uses a visual language to specify conceptual models that automatically generate agent-based simulations and leverages contextualized domain knowledge to assist the process of construction of the models of ecological phenomena.

VERA is built on our previous work [6] that integrated Component-Mechanism-Phenomenon (CMP) models and their agent-based simulations. VERA contains three types of components: *biotic abiotic, and habitat*. VERA's taxonomy of interactions among biotic components is based on the ontology of the interactions used by EOL, in particular, Global Biotic Interactions (GloBI) [8]. The specific interactions it uses are *produces, consumes, becomes on death, and affects*. It uses an off-the-shelf agent-based simulation system called NetLogo [11] because agent-based simulations are especially well suited for ecological modeling. Running the simulation enables the user to observe how system variables change over time and to refine their models through a generate-evaluate-revise loop.

3   Contextualization of Domain Knowledge

EOL is the world's largest aggregated and curated database of species data with almost two million species and eleven million attribute records in the biological domain. VERA enables a learner to access EOL to find species of interest and automatically populate simulation parameters. VERA currently uses the following parameters specific to ecology from EOL: *lifespan, body mass, carbon biomass, respiratory rate, photosynthesis rate, assimilation efficiency, reproductive maturity, reproductive interval, and offspring count.*

3.1   Illustrative Example of Inquiry-Based Modeling Using VERA

In the following scenario, a learner wants to create a model of an observed food web to explore the predator-prey relationship between sheep and wolves. The learner begins by placing a biotic component into the conceptual model canvas, naming it "sheep," and clicking on "Lookup species on EOL." The system queries EOL for all matches to the scientific or common name "sheep" and checks for the existence of attribute records for each found species. The learner selects "domestic sheep," and VERA extracts the species attributes from EOL that are relevant to the agent-based simulation (see Fig. 1). This provides the learner with valuable data that a student would be hard-pressed to locate and make sense of, reducing the cognitive load in model creation.

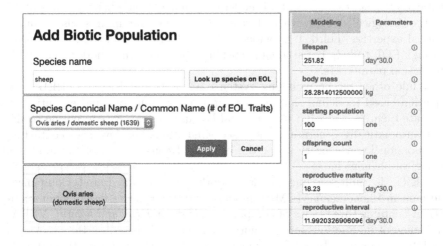

Fig. 1. Automatic filling of simulation parameters retrieved from EOL.

The learner carries on with the model construction to add a predator (wolf) and food source (grass) along with adding consumption interactions between the populations, leveraging EOL lookups with each component and interaction. In this way, our intrepid novice scientist has constructed a partial food web model revolving around the species of interest. VERA automatically spawns the simulation and displays the results as a set of graphs, for example, a graph indicating the changes in populations of various species over time (see Fig. 2).

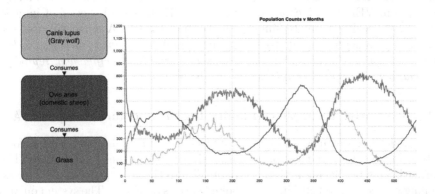

Fig. 2. A conceptual model of the relationships between species (left) and the simulation results generated from the conceptual model creating predator-prey cycle (right).

The learner may now experiment with different simulation parameters, revise the conceptual model, or generate an alternative hypothesis.

4   Lab Experiment

The goal of the study was to see if providing access to domain knowledge helps learners build richer models in problem solving. Fifteen self-selected students ($N = 15$) were recruited from a college-level general biology introductory course taught in Fall 2018. During the study, the students were asked to use VERA to explore multiple hypotheses to explain the decline in the sheep population. The students were also encouraged to actively use EOL when they needed information about a given species and later asked how often they used EOL while modeling.

4.1   Results

The students in our study developed models in VERA to evaluate their hypotheses and used EOL to get information about the species being modeled. The complexity of a model was calculated by adding the number of components in the conceptual model and the total number of relationships among the components. We found that access to ecological data from EOL helped students build more complex models and generate more hypotheses. The students who answered that they used the EOL frequently were found to come up with multiple hypotheses and build more complex models (Pearson product-moment correlation coefficients; $r = 0.38$; $r = 0.26$). We conjecture that information about the relationships between predator, prey, and competitors in the EOL knowledge-base may have led to the construction of more complex models. Interestingly, building complex models was associated with generating more hypotheses ($r = 0.66$). This means that the students who build more complex models are likely to have generated more hypotheses.

5   Conclusion

The research question in this work is how might we scaffold the acquisition of domain knowledge for students engaged in scientific modeling? The research hypothesis is that the contextualized acquisition of domain knowledge will help students build richer models. VERA contextualizes EOL's large scale domain knowledge to support modeling of ecological systems. The study with college-level students using VERA confirmed that contextualized acquisition of domain knowledge helped them construct more complex models and more explanatory hypotheses.

Acknowledgements. This research is supported by an US NSF grant #1636848 (Big Data Spokes: Collaborative: Using Big Data for Environmental Sustainability: Big Data + AI Technology = Accessible, Usable, Useful Knowledge!) and Georgia Tech seed grants through the Brooke Byers Institute for Sustainable Systems.

References

1. An, S., Bates, R., Hammock, J., Rugaber, S., Goel, A.: VERA: popularizing science through AI. In: Penstein Rosé, C., et al. (eds.) AIED 2018. LNCS (LNAI), vol. 10948, pp. 31–35. Springer, Cham (2018). https://doi.org/10.1007/978-3-319-93846-2_6

2. Bransford, J.D., Brown, A.L., Cocking, R.R., et al.: How People Learn, vol. 11. National Academy Press, Washington, DC (2000)

3. Bridewell, W., Sánchez, J.N., Langley, P., Billman, D.: An interactive environment for the modeling and discovery of scientific knowledge. Int. J. Hum Comput Stud. **64**(11), 1099–1114 (2006)

4. Hogan, K., Thomas, D.: Cognitive comparisons of students' systems modeling in ecology. J. Sci. Educ. Technol. **10**(4), 319–345 (2001)

5. van Joolingen, W.R., de Jong, T., Lazonder, A.W., Savelsbergh, E.R., Manlove, S.: Co-lab: research and development of an online learning environment for collaborative scientific discovery learning. Comput. Hum. Behav. **21**(4), 671–688 (2005)

6. Joyner, D.A., Goel, A.K., Papin, N.M.: MILA-S: generation of agent-based simulations from conceptual models of complex systems. In: Proceedings of the 19th International Conference on Intelligent User Interfaces, pp. 289–298 (2014)

7. Parr, C.S., et al.: The encyclopedia of life v2: providing global access to knowledge about life on earth. Biodiv. Data J. (2), e1079 (2014)

8. Poelen, J.H., Simons, J.D., Mungall, C.J.: Global biotic interactions: an open infrastructure to share and analyze species-interaction datasets. Ecol. Inform. **24**, 148–159 (2014)

9. Sins, P.H., Savelsbergh, E.R., van Joolingen, W.R.: The difficult process of scientific modelling: an analysis of novices' reasoning during computer-based modelling. Int. J. Sci. Educ. **27**(14), 1695–1721 (2005)

10. VanLehn, K.: Model construction as a learning activity: a design space and review. Interact. Learn. Environ. **21**(4), 371–413 (2013)

11. Wilensky, U., Resnick, M.: Thinking in levels: a dynamic systems approach to making sense of the world. J. Sci. Educ. Technol. **8**(1), 3–19 (1999)

Examining Students' Intrinsic Cognitive Load During Program Comprehension – An Eye Tracking Approach

Magdalena Andrzejewska$^{(\boxtimes)}$ⓘ and Agnieszka Skawińskaⓘ

Pedagogical University, Cracow, Poland
magdalena.andrzejewska@up.krakow.pl

Abstract. Programming as a cognitive activity requires the utilization of various kinds of mental models that involve different cognitive loads while students learn to program. The article discusses the results of an experiment aimed at answering the following question: are eye tracking based measures related to the intrinsic cognitive load (ICL) connected with program comprehension? Thirty one students of computer science took part in the experiment. They analyzed two program codes written in the C++ language to search for (1) logical errors (LER) and (2) syntax errors (SER). ICL was measured by subjective rating of the difficulty of each task. There were significant differences found for the subjective measures of intrinsic load, the effectiveness and the time of tasks performance, and the values of eye tracking parameters: fixation duration average (FDA) and saccade amplitude average (SAA) in two experiment conditions. Longer fixation and shorter saccades were associated with higher ICL. The results obtained suggest that FDA and SAA are eye tracking measures sensitive of intrinsic cognitive load.

Keywords: Cognitive load · Program comprehension · Eye tracking

1 Introduction

Studies conducted for many years consistently show that acquiring the skill of programming at its early stage poses difficulty to students [incl. 9]. Programming is a complex skill that, on the one hand, encompasses mechanisms of problem-solving and algorithm construction, and, on the other, demands knowledge of the syntax and semantics of the programming language [14]. It is, therefore, assumed that the experienced difficulties result to a significant extent from the excessive cognitive load (CL) occurring in the process of learning [15].

This paper approaches cognitive load as a triarchic concept, such as the one defined within the framework of the Cognitive Load Theory (CLT) which distinguish three types of cognitive load: intrinsic load (ICL) (related to the difficulty of a task, its structure or complexity, referring to an individual's effort load needed to learn a concept), extraneous load (ECL) (related to information presentation and instructional format), and germane load (GCL) (referring to the mental resources involved in

© Springer Nature Switzerland AG 2020
I. I. Bittencourt et al. (Eds.): AIED 2020, LNAI 12164, pp. 25–30, 2020.
https://doi.org/10.1007/978-3-030-52240-7_5

acquiring and automating schemata in the long-term memory [16]. Designing education-related materials following the principles of CLT and measuring cognitive load values has seen a growing interest in the field of research in recent years. A few of these studies have attempted to examine the application of the cognitive load theory in computer science education – especially in teaching programming [1, 11, 12, 17]. But despite many conducted studies, the problem of how to measure the cognitive load occurring during learning is still widely discussed [13]. Researchers are looking for measures designed to distinguish between the different types of load (ICL, ECL, GCL) [incl. 7, 10].

There are four dominant types of methods to address the measurement of cognitive load: subjective rating, performance-based measures, physiological measures, and behavioral measures [3]. Among the physiological measurements of CL, eye-based measures appear to be the most popular. The most common eye tracking measures of CL there are: changes in pupil size, blink rate and duration, saccade speed, and fixation duration [incl. 4, 8]. But it should be also mentioned that there are no threshold values of these indices that would allow for making inferences regarding the actual level of CL. Eye tracking methods have been shown to distinguish between tasks involving low cognitive loads and tasks involving high cognitive loads [5]. It has also been examined how cognitive load factors can be independently measured with eye tracking methods as well as how they are related to the subjective rating scale [6, 18]. But there seems to be an underrepresentation of eye tracking research that would apply to programming tasks, and – in particular – research investigating which eye movement parameters are sensitive to different types of cognitive load in the process of learning to program.

2   Current Study

The studies conducted so far have not yet analyzed the cognitive load involved in programming activities such as code debugging, in conditions where (1) the study subjects analyze a code without using an Integrated Development Environment (IDE) (where they can trace and run the program, which leads to the occurrence of additional factors disturbing the comprehension of the program) and (2) they analyze the exact same code but perform two different cognitive tasks – such as (a) searching for logical errors (LER) and (b) searching for syntax errors (SER). Given the above and with respect to the CLT principles, an assumption can be made that extraneous load (ECL)—which is related to the instructional format—should not differ between the two task versions. Therefore, this experiment design will be mainly related to ICL which is affected by the level of difficulty of the concept related to its complexity. It is con-sidered that the subject's prior knowledge determine the ICL [10]. These assumptions are similar to those adopted by [2].

In the light of the above, our research question is: what eye movement parameters are sensitive to intrinsic cognitive load that program comprehension imposes on a student? To address the research question, we examined several fixation and saccade parameters, excluding those that were correlated with each other. Finally, we focused on fixation duration and saccade length that were assumed to be the measures of the total cognitive load [8], i.e.: fixation duration average (ms) (FDA: the sum of the duration of all fixations divided by the number of fixations) and saccade amplitude average (°) (SAA: the sum of all saccade amplitudes divided by the number of saccades in the trial). Our analysis also included: time (ms), which refers to the number of milliseconds spent answering each task, and accuracy (%), meaning the percentage of errors reported by the subjects. These variables are also included in the research as performance-based measures of ICL [incl. 2].

3 Method

Experimental apparatus. Our study was conducted using the iViewX Hi-Speed eye tracker manufactured by SensoMotoric Instrument (SMI). The following SMI software was used to prepare the experiment and compile its results: Experiment Center and BeGazeTM 2.4.

Participants. Thirty four students of computer science participated in the study. The results of 3 subjects were removed from our analyses due to eye tracking measurement errors. The final sample resulted in 31 participants and consisted of 23 men and 8 women, aged between 21 and 29 (M = 23.90, SD = 1.66). All students completed a C++ programming course and had previously learned the concepts that were employed in the tasks they were asked to perform.

Procedure and material. After the subjects were familiarized with the experimental procedure, the eye tracking system was calibrated and validated. Next, each participant received two codes of short but complete programs written in C++. Each program offered a solution to the same problem, which was the implementation of an algorithm of sorting a ten-element table based on the *selection sort* method in a non-decreasing order. There were two separate programs that were presented in the same sequence to each participant. The first program contained four only logical errors (LER), the second code contained five only syntax errors (SER). Students were asked to find errors in both coding tasks and provide an answer orally. The codes were neither compiled nor run. The subjects had unlimited time to find the errors. In a short post-survey, study participants rated the difficulty level related to each task and their programming skills level (on a Likert scale from 1 (very easy/low) to 5 (very difficult/high)).

4 Results

Most of the students considered their programming skills to be on a medium level (M = 2.80, SD = 0.7, Me = 3, Q1 = 2, Q3 = 3); the sample seems to be quite homogeneous with respect to this feature. In the case of subjective measurement, the LER task imposed a higher intrinsic load as compared to the SER task (see: Table 1). Students rated searching for logical errors as more difficult than searching for syntax errors.

We studied the distribution of the gaze data: FDA, SAA, the performance data: Time, Accuracy, and Difficulty rating using the Shapiro-Wilk test, and found that only the FDA parameter followed the theoretical normal distribution (LER: $W = 0.943$, $p = 0.102$; SER: $W = 0.942$, $p = 0.097$). Thus, we decided to use a paired t-test for FDA and the Wilcoxon signed-rank test as a non-parametric test for the remaining variables.

Table 1. Wilcoxon test and paired t-test for the dependent variables

Variable	M			
	LER (high ICL)	SER (low ICL)	Z	p
Difficulty rating	3.6	2.8	3.587	0.000
Accuracy (%)	23.4	37.4	3.250	0.001
Time (ms)	238091.6	146887.5	3.155	0.002
SAA (°)	4.5	4.7	2.027	0.043
			t	p
FDA (ms)	251.5	233.6	4.602	0.000

If we refer to Table 1, we can see that there are significant differences both in the time and the task performance during searching for syntax versus logical errors. In the case of LER (high ICL), the subjects spent more time and found fewer errors compared to SER (low ICL). Furthermore, we found that students had a significantly higher FDA and a significantly lower SAA in the LER task (high ICL) compared to the SER task (low ICL), which suggests that these eye-based parameters are sensitive to ICL.

5   Conclusions

The outcomes of our study show that (1) FDA and SAA differed significantly in two task conditions, and that (2) longer fixation and shorter saccades were associated with a higher intrinsic cognitive load. The obtained findings suggest that these eye tracking measures are sensitive to ICL and therefore are a promising indicator of ICL related to the specific mental process of program analysis aimed at identifying logical and syntax errors. However, it was a preliminary study and therefore has some limitation that should be taken into consideration and addressed in future works. The aspects that need to be taken into account include: (1) increasing the number of subjects and comparing novice and expert results; (2) extending the scale of the subjective load assessment; (3) entering code difficulty levels; (4) introducing redundancy to measure ECL; (5) examining how ICL and ECL change in time intervals.

References

1. Asai, S., Phuong, D.T.D., Harada, F., Shimakawa, H.: Predicting cognitive load in acquisition of programming abilities. Int. J. Electr. Comput. Eng. 9(4), 3262–3271 (2019)
2. Ayres, P.: Using subjective measures to detect variations of intrinsic cognitive load within problems. Learn. Instr. 16(5), 389–400 (2006)
3. Chen, F., Zhou, J., Wang, Y., Yu, K., Arshad, S.Z., Khawaji, A., Conway, D.: Robust Multimodal Cognitive Load Measurement. Springer, Cham (2016). https://doi.org/10.1007/978-3-319-31700-7
4. Chen, S., Epps J., Ruiz, N., Chen, F.: Eye activity as a measure of human mental effort in HCI. In: Proceedings of the 16th International Conference on Intelligent User Interfaces, pp. 315–318. Association for Computing Machinery, Palo Alto (2011)
5. Chen, S., Epps, J.: Using task-induced pupil diameter and blink rate to infer cognitive load. Hum.-Comput. Interact. 29(4), 390–413 (2014)
6. Debue, N., Leemput, C.: What does germane load mean? An empirical contribution to the cognitive load theory. Front. Psychol. 5, 1099 (2014)
7. DeLeeuw, K.E., Mayer, R.E.: A comparison of three measures of cognitive load: evidence for separable measures of intrinsic, extraneous, and germane load. J. Educ. Psychol. 100(1), 223–234 (2008)
8. Holmqvist, K., Nyström, N., Andersson, R., Dewhurst, R., Jarodzka, H., Van de Weijer, J.: Eye tracking: a comprehensive guide to methods and measures. Oxford University Press, Oxford (2011)
9. Konecki, M.: Problems in programming education and means of their improvement. In: Katalinic, B. (ed.) DAAAM International Scientific Book 2014, pp. 459–470. DAAAM International, Vienna (2014)
10. Leppink, J., Paas, F., Van der Vleuten, C.P.M., Van Gog, T., Van Merrienboer, J.J.G: Development of an instrument for measuring different types of cognitive load. Behav. Res. Methods 45(4), 1058–1072 (2013)
11. Morrison, B.B., Dorn, B., Guzdial, M.: Measuring cognitive load in introductory CS: adaptation of an instrument. In: Proceedings of the ICER 2014: International Computing Education Research Conference, Glasgow, Scotland, UK, pp. 131–138 (2014)
12. Nolan, K., Mooney, A., Bergin, S.: Examining the role of cognitive load when learning to program. In: 3rd International Workshop on Eye-Movements in Programming, Joensuu, Finland, pp. 23–24 (2015)
13. Orru, G., Longo, L.: The evolution of cognitive load theory and the measurement of its intrinsic, extraneous and germane loads: a review. In: Longo, L., Leva, M.C. (eds.) H-WORKLOAD 2018. CCIS, vol. 1012, pp. 23–48. Springer, Cham (2019). https://doi.org/10.1007/978-3-030-14273-5_3
14. Robins, A., Rountree, J., Rountree, N.: Learning and teaching programming: a review and discussion. Comput. Sci. Educ. 13, 137–172 (2003)
15. Shaffer, D., Doube, W., Tuovinen, J.: Applying cognitive load theory to computer science education. In: Petre, M., Budgen, D., (eds.) 15th Annual Workshop of the Psychology of Programming Interest Group, pp. 333–346 (2003)
16. Sweller, J., Van Merrienboer, J.J.G., Paas, F.G.W.C.: Cognitive architecture and instructional design. Educ. Psychol. Rev. 10(3), 251–296 (1998)

17. Yousoof, M., Sapiyan, M.: Cognitive load measurement in learning programming using NASA TLX rating scale (Non Physiological Measures). In: Proceedings of the 13th International Conference on Applied Computer and Applied Computational Science, Kuala Lumpur, Malaysia, pp. 235–245 (2014)
18. Zu, T., Hutson, J., Loschky, L.C., Rebello, N.S.: Use of eye-tracking technology to investigate cognitive load theory. In: Proceedings of 2017 Physics Education Research Conference, pp. 472–475. American Association of Physics Teachers, Cincinnati, OH (2018)

Sequence-to-Sequence Models for Automated Text Simplification

Robert-Mihai Botarleanu[1], Mihai Dascalu[1,2($\boxtimes$)],
Scott Andrew Crossley[3], and Danielle S. McNamara[4]

[1] University Politehnica of Bucharest, 313 Splaiul Independentei,
060042 Bucharest, Romania
robert.botarleanu@stud.acs.pub.ro,
mihai.dascalu@cs.pub.ro
[2] Academy of Romanian Scientists, Str. Ilfov, Nr. 3,
050044 Bucharest, Romania
[3] Department of Applied Linguistics/ESL, Georgia State University,
Atlanta, GA 30303, USA
scrossley@gsu.edu
[4] Department of Psychology, Arizona State University, PO Box 871104, Tempe,
AZ 85287, USA
dsmcnama@asu.edu

Abstract. A key writing skill is the capability to clearly convey desired meaning using available linguistic knowledge. Consequently, writers must select from a large array of idioms, vocabulary terms that are semantically equivalent, and discourse features that simultaneously reflect content and allow readers to grasp meaning. In many cases, a simplified version of a text is needed to ensure comprehension on the part of a targeted audience (e.g., second language learners). To address this need, we propose an automated method to simplify texts based on paraphrasing. Specifically, we explore the potential for a deep learning model, previously used for machine translation, to learn a simplified version of the English language within the context of short phrases. The best model, based on an Universal Transformer architecture, achieved a BLEU score of 66.01. We also evaluated this model's capability to perform similar transformation to texts that were simplified by human experts at different levels.

Keywords: Natural language processing · Text simplification · Paraphrasing · Sequence-to-sequence model

1 Introduction

The process of simplifying texts affords better comprehension on the part of struggling readers. Text simplification generally involves manipulation at the syntactic, lexical, and discourse level. All simplified texts share the same goal: reducing a reader's cognitive load and increasing text comprehensibility on the part of the L2 reader [1, 2]. The basis for text simplification is the notion that if written content is accessible, then beginning level readers, such as second language (L2) readers, can use the input to better test and confirm language hypotheses [3]. In general, much of the language to

© Springer Nature Switzerland AG 2020
I. I. Bittencourt et al. (Eds.): AIED 2020, LNAI 12164, pp. 31–36, 2020.
https://doi.org/10.1007/978-3-030-52240-7_6

which beginning level readers are exposed has been simplified to make it easier to comprehend. For instance, most readings provided to L2 students contain less sophisticated words, fewer rare words, greater syntactic complexity, and more explicit cohesive devices such as connectives or lexical overlap between text segments [1, 2]. However, in almost all cases, a human has to manually simplify the text at the grammatical, syntactic, morphological, or lexical levels [4].

The aim of this paper is to propose a novel method of automatically simplifying texts using sequence-to-sequence Machine Learning models in order to paraphrase certain expressions into easier to understand, equivalent forms. Such an approach has strong potential to aid practitioners, teachers, and textbook writers to better meet the needs of students with lower reading skills.

2   Method

2.1   Corpora

Three datasets were used in the simplification algorithm. First, phrases and paraphrases were collected from the ParaPhrase DataBase (PPDB) [5], which consists of English pairs of phrases and paraphrases, with their associated alignment and entailment properties, with three types of paraphrases: lexical, phrasal and syntactic. For the purpose of this project, the PPDB XXXL English pack was filtered such that only those pairs of source-target phrases that correspond to equivalence entailments remained, with the target text being chosen as the one to maximize the Dale-Chall readability formula [6].

The second source of simplified data came from WordNet synonym sets. The WordNet lexical database [7] contains synsets (i.e., sets of synonyms) which can be used to generate synonym pairs by intersecting the synsets of various dictionary terms. Using these, we supplemented our paraphrasing data with additional pairs of synonyms to expand the number and range of potential rephrases. Age of acquisition (AoA) scores were used for establishing a simplification criterion (i.e., we selected which words in the synonym set were easier to understand based on AoA scores).

Another dataset integrated into the corpus consists of sentence aligned pairs between the Simple English Wikipedia entries and their corresponding English Wikipedia entries [8]. This corpus has been previously used for textual simplification and presents a good diversity of simplified sentence pairs.

The three simplified paraphrase sources in our corpus have significant differences when it comes to the scope and nature of the simplifications they provide, allowing for more robust model development. Synonyms from Wordnet tend to be only one word long, while PPDB typically has phrases of 6 to 8 words in length and the Simple Wikipedia aligned dataset uses entire phrases.

2.2   Model Architectures

The Transformer we used [9] followed an encoder-decoder architecture. The inputs consisted of sequences of word embeddings, which were then modified by adding a positional encoding that uniquely identifies each position in the text. The resulting embeddings were processed by a multi-head attention layer that consists of a self-attention distributed across a number of heads. Attention computes the compatibility function of a query Q given a set of corresponding key-value pairs (K-V). These relationships modeled by self-attention do not necessarily correspond to those typically understood in natural language (e.g., syntactic structure, coreferences etc.), but are rather some latent dependencies that arise from the text.

A variation of the Transformer is the Universal Transformer [10], an extension of the original architecture that is Turing complete. The Universal Transformer uses for recurrence either a separable convolutional or a neural network with a rectified linear unit activation and two affine transformations [10].

3   Results

BLEU scores [11], one of the frequently employed metrics for machine translation, were used to evaluate the models. BLEU scores range from 0 to 100, where 100 indicates that the translation is identical to the reference translation. The BLEU score is usually formed as a geometric mean of the individual n-gram precision scores combined with a brevity penalty, assigned so as to discourage shorter translations. In addition to the deep learning models described previously, the BLEU scores for a "Repeater" provide an estimate of the similarity between the normal and simplified phrases. Both the evaluation and the model training were conducted using the tensor2tensor library [12] (Table 1).

Table 1. BLEU scores for the tested models.

Model name	Train set	Development set	Test set
Repeater	59.72 (baseline)	60.24 (baseline)	60.24 (baseline)
Transformer	**78.76 (+19.04)**	64.92 (+4.68)	64.71 (+4.47)
Universal Transformer	69.99 (+10.27)	**66.00 (+5.76)**	**66.01 (+5.77)**

Transformer-based models attain BLEU scores that indicate good generalization, with the Universal Transformer model presenting less overfitting. Simplification is only performed on phrases instead of paragraphs or the whole text because the data present in the corpus is, at most, limited to sentences. Table 2 presents examples of paraphrase suggestions generated by the Transformer model.

Table 2. Sample paraphrases generated for an input essay in ascending order of BLEU scores.

Phrase	Reference simplification	Paraphrase choices	BLEU score
In problems	To the issues	In trouble, Because of problems	30.32
Represents the only	Was the sole	Is the only, Are the only	38.00
Errors that	The mistakes that	Mistake that, Mistakes that	42.88
And a violation of	A breach of the	And a breach of, And the breach of	59.46
Still underway	Still in progress	In progress, Still running	60.65
Provision of access	Give access	For access, Terms of access	70.71
Relevant provisions of the charter of	The provisions of the charter of	Provisions of the charter of, of provisions of the charter of	81.7

As a post-hoc analysis, we used a corpus of 100 texts [4] which were each simplified to three levels (advanced, intermediate, and elementary) to better assess the performance of the model on real world texts. We measure the uncased BLEU score for the Transformer model paraphrases generated on the advanced texts and compare them to their intermediate and elementary forms. We also try various probability thresholds which indicate the minimum joint probability of a candidate simplification. All evaluations are performed using the Transformer model. The results from Table 3 indicate that the more alterations the model is allowed to make (lower thresholds), the worse it performs. One reason for this may be the manner in which the human experts perform alterations in these texts, such as the use of sentence fusion, phrase splitting, phrase reordering. and the elimination of certain sequences of text wholesale. These alterations are beyond the capabilities of what our model has been trained to perform, although they provide insight into future directions for analysis.

Table 3. BLEU scores for the Transformer model's translations on the real-life testing corpus.

Threshold	Intermediate	Elementary
0.0	59.17	39.01
0.05	65.96	42.09
0.15	67.80	42.64
0.70	69.76	43.88

4 Conclusions

In this paper, we analyzed the capabilities of modern Neural Machine Translation models in the context of text simplification, via paraphrasing. By expanding on previous work done by Kauchak [8], we generate a text simplification dataset that includes samples of varying scopes: synonyms, few word idioms, and entire phrases. We set up our learning problem such that the models are trained to transform an English sequence into another, equivalent, sequence with higher readability. We then train Machine

Translation architectures consisting of encoder-decoder Neural Networks in order to evaluate how well they can transduce text written in English into a simpler form.

Our results suggest that human modifications to the text diverge from those found in the textual simplification corpora we used. The reference simplifications tended to include stylistic and structural alterations, such as fusing or breaking up phrases, eliminating portions of the text, and changing the structure of the document.

Our constructed dataset expands on those commonly used in text simplification and we show that the neural models examined in this study are indeed capable of generalizing on these data. A future avenue of research for this topic is the construction of a dataset that is better aligned with the kind of alterations humans make during essay simplification. This might require the addition of syntactic parsers, part of speech taggers, and tools that can measure elements of text cohesion including vectors of connectives and semantic representations across texts. This work and future endeavors of this kind have strong potential to make crucial contributions to students' capacity to understand and learn from text - a concern of a broad range of practitioners and researchers.

Acknowledgments. This work was supported by a grant of the Romanian National Authority for Scientific Research and Innovation, CNCS – UEFISCDI, project number PN-III 54PCCDI / 2018, INTELLIT – "Prezervarea și valorificarea patrimoniului literar românesc folosind soluții digitale inteligente pentru extragerea și sistematizarea de cunoștințe". This research was also supported in part by the Institute of Education Sciences (R305A190063) and the Office of Naval Research (N00014-17-1-2300 and N00014-19-1-2424). The opinions expressed are those of the authors and do not represent views of the IES or ONR.

References

1. Crossley, S.A., McNamara, D.S.: Assessing L2 reading texts at the intermediate level: an approximate replication of Crossley, Louwerse, McCarthy & McNamara (2007). Lang. Teach. **41**(3), 409–429 (2008)
2. Crossley, S.A., Louwerse, M.M., McCarthy, P.M., McNamara, D.S.: A linguistic analysis of simplified and authentic texts. Modern Lang. J. **91**(1), 15–30 (2007)
3. Hatch, E.M.: Second Language Acquisition: A Book of Readings. Newbury House Pub, Rowley (1978)
4. Allen, D.: A study of the role of relative clauses in the simplification of news texts for learners of English. System **37**(4), 585–599 (2009)
5. Ganitkevitch, J., Van Durme, B., Callison-Burch, C.: PPDB: the paraphrase database. In: Proceedings of the 2013 Conference of the North American Chapter of the Association for Computational Linguistics: Human Language Technologies, pp. 758–764 (2013)
6. Chall, J.S., Dale, E.: Readability Revisited: The New Dale-Chall Readability Formula. Brookline Books, Northampton (1995)
7. Miller, G.A.: WordNet: A lexical database for English. Commun. ACM **38**(11), 39–41 (1995)
8. Kauchak, D.: Improving text simplification language modeling using unsimplified text data. In: 51st Annual Meeting of the Association for Computational Linguistics, Vol. 1: Long papers, pp. 1537–1546. ACl, Sofia, Bulgaria (2013)

9. Vaswani, A., Shazeer, N., Parmar, N., Uszkoreit, J., Jones, L., Gomez, A.N., Kaiser, Ł., Polosukhin, I.: Attention is all you need. 31st Conference on Neural Information Processing Systems (NIPS 2017), Long Beach, CA, USA, pp. 5998–6008 (2017)
10. Dehghani, M., Gouws, S., Vinyals, O., Uszkoreit, J., Kaiser, Ł.: Universal Transformers. arXiv preprint, arXiv:1807.03819 (2018)
11. Papineni, K., Roukos, S., Ward, T., Zhu, W.-J.: BLEU: a method for automatic evaluation of machine translation. In: 40th Annual Meeting on Association for Computational Linguistics, pp. 311–318. ACL, Philadelphia, PA, USA (2002)
12. Vaswani, A., Bengio, S., Brevdo, E., Chollet, F., Gomez, A.N., Gouws, S., Jones, L., Kaiser, Ł., Kalchbrenner, N., Parmar, N.: Tensor2tensor for neural machine translation. arXiv preprint, arXiv:1803.07416 (2018)

The Potential for the Use of Deep Neural Networks in e-Learning Student Evaluation with New Data Augmentation Method

Andrzej Cader[✉]

Information Technology Institute, University of Social Sciences, Lodz, Poland
`acader@san.edu.pl`

Abstract. This study attempts to use a deep neural network to assess the acquisition of knowledge and skills by students. This module is intended to shape a personalized learning path through the e-learning system. Assessing student progress at each stage of learning in an individualized process is extremely tedious and arduous. The only solution is to automate assessment using Deep Learning methods. The obstacle is the relatively small amount of data, in the form of available assessments, which is needed to train the neural network. The specifity of each subject/course taught requires the preparation of a separate neural network. The paper proposes a new method of data augmentation, Asynchronous Data Augmentation through Pre-Categorization (ADAPC), which solves this problem. It has been shown that it is possible to train a very effective deep neural network with the proposed method even for a small amount of data.

Keywords: Deep Learning · e-learning · Deep neural networks · New data augmentation method

1 Introduction

Deep Learning (DL) methods in teaching began to spread after 2010 [1–3]. In recent years, a significant increase in the use of neural networks in teaching has been seen [4–6], and also in the field of student evaluation automation [7–9]. Two areas that automation applies to can be distinguished. The first relates to automated essay scoring and the second to automatic short answer grading, automatically classifying student responses as correct or not, based on a set of previous correct answers [10, 11]. Particularly interesting are attempts to use DL capabilities in the field of text analysis [12, 13]. Methods based on the use of recurrent neural networks [14–16], including bidirectional LTSM networks [5], dominate here.

The priority of modern education is to adapt the methods and pace of knowledge and skills transfer to the individual predispositions of each individual student. Such a strategy requires both the division of the entire learning process into small multi-variant stages, and also the assessment of the level of mastery of knowledge and skills at the end of each stage. It is possible to shape the course of the entire teaching process for

© Springer Nature Switzerland AG 2020
I. I. Bittencourt et al. (Eds.): AIED 2020, LNAI 12164, pp. 37–42, 2020.
https://doi.org/10.1007/978-3-030-52240-7_7

each student separately by using assessment that is carried out in stages. Such multi-variability of choice of further educational path is important – the choice of the type of next stage from among several options available, based on the result of the previous stage's evaluation. The assessment of a particular stage should be derived from many assessments that occur during various activities. These grades should be grouped under specific validation areas, e.g. test grades, practical tasks, own work, project grades, etc. The source of grades can be teachers or other students as part of group work, or it can be a self-assessment. Assessments can also come from automatic validation systems – automatic test evaluation, automatic text, image, speech, etc. The validation process in this system concept is very tedious and extremely burdensome for the tutor leading a given group of students – many rated persons, a very large number of stages, often very limited contact with the assessed student, many grades from various sources. In such a situation it is difficult to decide what final grade to make. It seems that in such a situation it is optimal to use an automatic system based on a properly trained neural network.

2   Comprehension and Data Preparation

This work presents the research stage of a broader program related to the development of a platform for personalized education of students at the University. Its purpose is to explore the possibility of creating a system for automatic validation of the teaching stages of a selected subject using DL methods. It is assumed that a deep neural network will be trained based on a small set of training data - student assessments.

The designed neural network should take into account the context defined by the environment in which the evaluation will take place. The specificity of assessment depends primarily on the structure and content transmitted in the educational process and the type of competences acquired by the student. In other words it depends on the subject being taught. Moreover, this condition will be determined by the specific curriculum, the assumed teaching objectives and even by different ways of organizing classes and the profile of the teaching staff. This means that in each specific case, training the neural network should be adapted to the conditions presented above. This leads to a significant reduction in the amount of training data available. In this case, it is difficult to use existing methods of data augmentation [17–19]. One of the possibilities is to use the properties of the student grade set, which was referred as data asynchronism.

Def. Asynchronous data - a set of data whose ranking (order) does not affect the information contained in this set. In particular, asynchronous data does not form a time series or sequence ordered in a different way in time or space.

From this definition, it follows that the set of feature values (grades) that determine the state of the student's knowledge and skills is a set of asynchronous data. The grades determine level of students mastery, to a large extent, regardless of the order in which they occur. Of course, this is some simplification resulting from the assumed model.

Lemma. Let B be a discrete set of N features describing the state of a given object: $B = \{c_1, c_2 \ldots \ldots c_N\}$ and which can take a finite number of v_{ij} values (i - feature number, j - number value). If all v_i sets are asynchronous data sets, then each combination of individual elements selected from each v_i set reflects a certain state of the object.

It follows from the above that for asynchronous data relating to object feature values, each combination of individual feature values can be an input vector of the neural network classifying the object's state. It should be clarified that individual combinations correspond to the detailed states, while the sequences of values of the attributes v_i represent the generalized state. Thus, by presenting many detailed vectors of the neural network, we are building a representation of the generalized state. The number of input vectors for each dataset is the product of the number of elements in each feature v_i.

A group of 80 students was selected for the experiment, whose grades generated training data for the neural network and a separate group of 40 students for the test set. Assessments were collected as part of the subject of physics in computer science at the University of Social Sciences in Lodz. Scores on a scale of 1 to 10 (0 means no rating) were issued in 12 categories: 1. Ability to create written studies; 2. Ability to prepare projects; 3. Level of solving theoretical sentences; 4. Ability to solve practical problems; 5. Ability to solve tests; 6. Substantive formulation of the oral answer; 7. Participation in the discussion and substantive activity; 8. Participation in consultations; 9. Own work; 10. Creativity; 11. Cooperation as part of group tasks; 12. Timeliness of tasks. The output of the trained network (labels) were the final grades issued by the tutor at the end of the semester (Table 1).

Table 1. Example of student assessments used to train the network.

Id	Labels	Cat_1	Cat_2	Cat_3	Cat_4	Cat_5	Cat_6	Cat_7	Cat_8	Cat_9	Cat_10	Cat_11	Cat_12
1	9	9, 8, 8	10, 8, 9	9, 9, 9	8, 8, 10	9, 8	9	7	5, 7	6, 8	9	9, 8	9, 9, 8
2	8	8, 9, 9	9, 6, 10, 7	8, 5, 10	7, 8, 8	9, 10	9	3	5, 8, 9	8, 7	0	6, 7	9, 10, 9
3	3	1, 2, 2, 4	3, 4, 2	2, 3	5, 4, 6	1, 9	2	1	1, 2	2, 1	2	1	5, 4, 3
4	4	7, 5, 5	5, 3	5, 4, 3, 6	7, 6	4, 6	4	4, 2	2, 4	3, 4	4	5	7, 8

Preparation of training data (80 students) included the following stages:

1. Assembling of all combinations of grades from Cat_1 to Cat_12 (one grade from each field) with the assignment of each combination of the same label, separately for each student (Id)
2. Random shuffle of all combinations
3. Separation of the set into train_data and train_labels and standard preparation of input data with normalization train_data.

560 688 training data were obtained using the procedure presented. At the stage of selecting the network model and tuning, a set of 160,000 validation data was temporarily separated from the training data. Test data were prepared on the basis of assessments of a separate group of 40 students. Test vectors were built from an average of individual categories rounded to the total value.

3 Experimental Results

Various models of neural networks and hyperparameter sets were considered in the validation process. The optimal turned out to be the use of a fully connected neural network with five dense layers. In layers 1 to 5, the *ReLU* activation function was used, and *Softmax* used in the output layer. The output layer neurons correspond to trained categories, which are final grades, expressed on a point scale from 0 to 10. The total number of parameters (weights and biases) was 84,043, all trained. The errors were computed based on *categorical cross-entropy* loss function and the *Adam* optimizer. Optimal mini-batch size = 100 selected. During NN training, it was determined that there was no need for regularization techniques. It is true that after 14 epochs, the effect of overfitting appeared, but up to this point the model obtained a surprisingly high training accuracy of 0.9982 (Fig. 1).

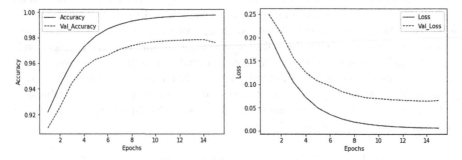

Fig. 1. Accuracy and loss function values calculated on the training (Accuracy, Loss) and validation (Val_Accurancy, Val_Loss) sets.

During testing, the results of prediction of the trained NN model were compared with the assessments proposed by the tutors. Because the *Softmax* output layer creates a probability distribution for individual categories (grades), the winning category is the one with the highest probability value. Out of 40 evaluated in 33 cases, the predictors were fully compatible with tutors' assessments. In four cases, the value of the prediction differed by one point from the tutor's assessment, in two by 2 points and in one by 4 points.

4 Conclusion

It has been shown that it is possible to use a deep neural network for extremely small amounts of data if they meet the asynchronous condition, i.e. independence of the way they are ordered. In this case, you can use a new method of data augmentation, which is technically called Asynchronous Data Augmentation through Pre-Categorization (ADAPC). Based on this method, you can train a medium-sized neural network that effectively classifies student achievement in the relatively narrow area of one subject (course) or module. This creates the possibility of quick and easy generation of artificial structures for automatic validation of educational processes. It should be emphasized that the ADAPC method can be used in many other areas in both classification and regression issues, provided that the processed data has the asynchronous feature. The model has been developed to meet the needs of a larger e-learning system as a link in profiling the individual education path of university students.

References

1. Romero, C., Ventura, S.: Educational data mining: a review of the state of the art. IEEE Trans. Syst. Man Cybern. Part C Appl. Rev. **40**(6), 601–618 (2010)
2. Romero, C., Ventura, S.: Data mining in education. Wiley Interdiscipl. Rev. Data Mining Knowl. Discov. **3**(1), 12–27 (2013)
3. Pena-Ayala, A.: Educational data mining: a survey and a data mining-based analysis of recent works. Expert Syst. Appl. **41**(4), 1432–1462 (2014)
4. Hu, B.: Teaching quality evaluation research based on neural network for university physical education. In: 2017 International Conference on Smart Grid and Electrical Automation (ICSGEA), pp 290–293. IEEE (2017). https://doi.org/10.1109/ICSGEA.2017.155
5. Kose, U., Arslan, A.: Optimization of self-learning in computer science engineering course: an intelligent software system supported by artificial neural network and vortez optimization algorithm. Comput. Appl. Eng. Educ. **25**, 142–156 (2017)
6. Lau, E.T., Sun, L., Yang, Q.: Modelling, prediction and classification of student academic performance using artificial neural networks. SN Appl. Sci. **1**, 982 (2019). https://doi.org/10. 1007/s42452-019-0884-
7. Zhao, S., Zhang, Y., Xiong, X., Botelho, A., Heffernan, N.: A memory-augmented neural model for automated grading. In: Proceedings of the Fourth ACM Conference on Learning @ Scale, pp. 189–192. ACM, Cambridge (2017)
8. Alvarado, J.G., Ghavidel, H.A., Zouaq, A., Jovanovic, J., McDonald, J.: A comparison of features for the automatic labeling of student answers to open-ended questions. In: Proceedings of the 11th International Conference on Educational Data Mining (2018)
9. Sales A., Botelho A., Patikorn T., Heffernan N.T.: Using big data to sharpen design-based inference in A/B tests. In: Proceedings of the 11th International Conference on Educational Data Mining (2018)
10. Taghipour, K., Ng, H.T.: A neural approach to automated essay scoring. In: Proceedings of the 2016 Conference on Empirical Methods in Natural Language Processing, pp. 1882–1891. Association for Computational Linguistics, Austin (2016)
11. Zhang, Y., Shah, R., Chi, M.: Deep learning + student modeling + clustering: a recipe for effective automatic short answer grading. In: Proceedings of the 9th International Conference on Educational Data Mining, pp. 562–567 (2016)
12. Choi, H., Wang, Z., Brooks, C., Collins-Thompson, K., Reed, B.G., Fitch, D.: Social work in the classroom? A tool to evaluate topical relevance in student writing. In: Proceedings of the 10th International Conference on Educational Data Mining (2017)
13. Neethu, G., Sijimol, P.J., Surekha, M.V.: Grading descriptive answer scripts using deep learning. Int. J. Innov. Technol. Explor. Eng. **8**(5), 991–996 (2019)
14. Tang, S., Peterson, J.C., Pardos, Z.A.: Deep neural networks and how they apply to sequential education data. In: Proceedings of the Third ACM Conference on Learning @ Scale (L@S 2016), pp. 321–324. ACM, New York (2016)

15. Okubo, F., Yamashita, T., Shimada, A., Ogata, H.: A neural network approach for students' performance prediction. In: Proceedings of the Seventh International Learning Analytics & Knowledge Conference (LAK 2017), pp. 598–599. ACM, New York (2017)
16. Wang, L., Sy, A., Liu, L., Piech, C.: Learning to represent student knowledge on programming exercises using deep learning. In: Proceedings of the 10th International Conference on Educational Data Mining, Cambridge, MA, USA, pp. 201–204 (2017)
17. Aggarwal, C.C.: Recommender Systems. Springer, Cham (2016)
18. Shorten, C., Khoshgoftaar, T.M.: A survey on image data augmentation for deep learning. J. Big Data **6**, 60 (2019). https://doi.org/10.1186/s40537-019-0197-0
19. Tan, Y.K., Xu, X., Liu, Y.: Improved recurrent neural networks for session-based recommendations. In: Proceedings of the 1st Workshop on Deep Learning for Recommender Systems, pp. 17–22 (2016)

Investigating Transformers for Automatic Short Answer Grading

Leon Camus[✉] and Anna Filighera[iD]

TU Darmstadt, Darmstadt, Germany
camus@algo.informatik.tu-darmstadt.de, anna.filighera@kom.tu-darmstadt.de

Abstract. Recent advancements in the field of deep learning for natural language processing made it possible to use novel deep learning architectures, such as the Transformer, for increasingly complex natural language processing tasks. Combined with novel unsupervised pre-training tasks such as masked language modeling, sentence ordering or next sentence prediction, those natural language processing models became even more accurate. In this work, we experiment with fine-tuning different pre-trained Transformer based architectures. We train the newest and most powerful, according to the glue benchmark, transformers on the SemEval-2013 dataset. We also explore the impact of transfer learning a model fine-tuned on the MNLI dataset to the SemEval-2013 dataset on generalization and performance. We report up to 13% absolute improvement in macro-average-F1 over state-of-the-art results. We show that models trained with knowledge distillation are feasible for use in short answer grading. Furthermore, we compare multilingual models on a machine-translated version of the SemEval-2013 dataset.

Keywords: Self-attention · Transfer learning · Short answer grading

1 Introduction

Online tutoring platforms enable students to learn individually and independently. To provide the users with individual feedback on their answers, the answers have to be graded. In large tutoring platforms, there are an abundant number of domains and questions. This makes building a general system for short answer grading challenging, since domain-related knowledge is frequently needed to evaluate an answer. Additionally, the increasing accuracy of short answer grading systems makes it feasible to employ them in examinations. In this scenario it is desirable to achieve the maximum possible accuracy, with a relatively high computational budget, while in case of tutoring a less computational intensive model is desirable to keep costs down and increase responsiveness. In this work, we experiment with fine-tuning the most common transformer models and explore the following questions:

© Springer Nature Switzerland AG 2020
I. I. Bittencourt et al. (Eds.): AIED 2020, LNAI 12164, pp. 43–48, 2020.
https://doi.org/10.1007/978-3-030-52240-7_8

Does the size of the Transformer matter for short answer grading? How well do multilingual Transformers perform? How well do multilingual Transformers generalize to another language? Are there better pre-training tasks for short answer grading? Does knowledge distillation work for short answer grading?

The field of short answer grading can mainly be categorized into two classes of approaches. The first ones represent the traditional approaches, based on hand-crafted features [14,15] and the second ones are deep learning based approaches [1,8,13,16,18,21]. One of the core constraints of short answer grading remained the limited availability of labeled domain-relevant training data. This issue was mitigated by transfer learning from models pre-trained using unsupervised pre-training tasks, as shown by Sung et al. [21] outperforming previous approaches by about twelve percent. In this study, we aim to extend upon the insights provided by Sung et al. [21].

2   Experiments

We evaluate our proposed approach on the SemEval-2013 [5] dataset. The dataset consists of questions, reference answers, student answers and three-way labels, represenenting the CORRECT, INCORRECT and CONTRADICTORY class. We translate it with the winning method from Wmt19 [2]. For further information see Sung et al. [21]. We also perform transfer learning from a model previously fine-tuned on the MNLI [22] dataset.[1]

For training and later comparison we utilize a variety of models, including BERT [4], RoBERTa [11], AlBERT [10], XLM [9] and XLMRoBERTa [3]. We also include distilled models of BERT and RoBERTa in the study [19]. Furthermore we include a RoBERTa based model previously fine-tuned on the MNLI dataset.

For fine tuning we add a classification layer on top of every model. We use the AdamW [12] optimizer, with a learning rate of 2e−5 and a linear learning rate schedule with warm up. For large transformers we extend the number of epochs to 24, but we also observe notable results with 12 epochs or less. We train using a single NVIDIA 2080ti GPU (11 GB) with a batch size of 16, utilizing gradient accumulation. Larger batches did not seem to improve the results. To fit large transformers into the GPU memory we use a combination of gradient accumulation and mixed precision with 16 bit floating point numbers, provided by NVIDIAs apex library[2]. We implement our experiments using huggingfaces transformer library [23]. We will release our training code on GitHub[3]. To ensure comparability, all of the presented models where trained with the same code, setup and hyper parameters (Table 1).

3   Results and Analysis

Does the size of the Transformer matter for short answer grading?
Large models demonstrate a significant improvement compared to Base models.

---

[1] https://www.nyu.edu/projects/bowman/multinli/.

[2] https://github.com/NVIDIA/apex.

[3] https://github.com/28Smiles/SAS-AIED2020.

improvement arises most likely due to the increased capacity of the model, as parameters allow the model to retain more information of the pre-training a.

w well do multilingual Transformers perform? The *XLM* [9] based dels do not perform well in this study. The *RoBERTa* based models (*XLM-BERTa*) seem to generalize better than their predecessors. *XLMRoBERTa* forms similarly to the base *RoBERTa* model, falling behind in the unseen stions and unseen domains category. Subsequent investigations could include -tuning the large variant on MNLI and SciEntsBank. Due to GPU memory straints, we were not capable to train the large variant of this model.

w well do multilingual Transformers generalize to another language? The models with multilingual pre-training show stronger generalization oss languages than their English counterparts. We are able to observe that the re of the multilingual model increases across languages it was never fine-tuned , while the monolingual model does not generalize.

e there better pre-training tasks for short answer grading? Transfer rning a model from MNLI yields a significant improvement over the same sion of the model not fine-tuned on MNLI. It improves the models ability to neralise to a separate domain. The models capabilities on the german version the dataset are also increased, despite the usage of a monolingual model. The son for this behavior should be further investigated.

oes knowledge distillation work for short answer grading? The usage models pre-trained with knowledge distillation yields a slightly lower score. wever, since the model is 40% smaller, a maximum decrease in performance about 2% to the previous state of the art may be acceptable for scenarios here computational resources are limited.

Conclusion and Future Work

this paper we demonstrate that large Transformer-based pre-trained models hieve state of the art results in short answer grading. We were able to show that odels trained on the MNLI dataset are capable of transferring knowledge to the sk of short answer grading. Moreover, we were able to increase a models overall ore, by training it on multiple languages. We show that the skills developed a model trained on MNLI improve generalization across languages. It is also own, that cross lingual training improves scores on SemEval2013. We show that nowledge distillation allows for good performance, while keeping computational sts low. This is crucial in evaluating answers from many users, like in online toring platforms.

Future research should investigate the impact of context on the classification. ncluding the question or its source may help the model grade answers, which ere not considered during the reference answer creation.

Table 1. Results on the SciEntsBank Dataset of SemEval 2013. Accuracy (Acc), macro-average-F1 (M-F1), and weighted-average-F1 (W-F1) are reported in percentage.

		English									German								
		Unseen answer			Unseen question			Unseen domain			Unseen answer			Unseen question			Unseen domain		
	Languages Trained	Acc	M-F1	W-F1	Acc	M-F1	W-F1	Acc	M-F1	W-F1	Acc	M-F1	W-F1	Acc	M-F1	W-F1	Acc	M-F1	W-F1
Baseline [5]	en	55.6	40.5	52.3	54.0	39.0	52.0	57.7	41.6	55.4	-	-	-	-	-	-	-	-	-
ETS [6]	en	72.0	64.7	70.8	58.3	39.3	53.7	54.3	33.3	46.1	-	-	-	-	-	-	-	-	-
SOFTCAR [7]	en	65.9	55.5	64.7	65.2	46.9	63.4	63.7	48.6	62.0	-	-	-	-	-	-	-	-	-
MEAD [17]	en	-	42.9	55.4	-	-	-	-	-	-	-	-	-	-	-	-	-	-	-
Graph [17]	en	-	43.8	56.7	-	-	-	-	-	-	-	-	-	-	-	-	-	-	-
Sultan et al. [20]	en	60.4	44.4	57.0	64.3	45.5	61.5	62.7	45.2	60.3	-	-	-	-	-	-	-	-	-
Saha et al. [18]	en	71.8	66.6	71.4	61.4	49.1	62.8	63.2	47.9	61.2	-	-	-	-	-	-	-	-	-
Marvaniya et al. [13]	en	-	63.6	71.9	-	-	-	-	-	-	-	-	-	-	-	-	-	-	-
Sung et al. [21]	en	75.9	72.0	75.8	65.3	57.5	64.8	63.8	57.9	63.4	-	-	-	-	-	-	-	-	-
BERT$_{\text{DISTILL}}$	en	69.2	67.2	69.2	56.6	54.7	56.6	61.4	49.7	61.4	38.8	26.2	38.8	33.7	21.5	33.7	51.7	29.5	51.7
BERT$_{\text{BASE}}$	en	72.8	70.6	72.8	57.3	56.0	57.3	63.4	54.6	63.4	45.0	37.0	45.0	40.5	32.9	40.5	59.0	41.7	59.0
BERT$_{\text{LARGE}}$	en	75.8	75.0	75.8	63.4	62.4	63.4	67.7	62.8	67.7	50.2	40.5	50.2	43.7	35.5	43.7	57.7	42.2	57.7
RoBERTa$_{\text{DISTILL}}$	en	74.8	73.2	74.8	56.9	55.2	56.9	65.1	55.6	65.1	48.0	40.4	48.0	44.1	36.7	44.1	58.2	40.2	58.2
RoBERTa$_{\text{BASE}}$	en	74.5	73.2	74.5	63.2	61.7	63.2	65.3	62.5	65.3	47.8	38.1	47.8	43.5	35.1	43.5	60.6	43.2	60.6
RoBERTa$_{\text{LARGE}}$	en	76.7	75.5	76.7	64.1	62.7	64.1	66.8	65.6	66.8	48.8	40.4	48.8	42.7	34.7	42.7	61.5	48.2	61.5
RoBERTa$_{\text{LARGE}}$	de	41.2	19.4	41.2	47.7	21.5	47.7	42.0	19.7	42.0	41.2	19.4	41.2	47.7	21.5	47.7	42.0	19.7	42.0
RoBERTa$_{\text{LARGE}}$	en, de	76.1	74.9	76.1	63.0	61.9	63.0	65.6	63.3	65.6	73.9	72.3	73.9	58.9	57.3	58.9	61.9	56.3	61.9
RoBERTa$_{\text{LARGE,MNLI}}$	en	78.8	78.3	78.8	**66.4**	**65.7**	**66.4**	**71.8**	**70.8**	**71.8**	52.6	49.3	52.6	46.1	42.5	46.1	60.1	51.9	60.1
RoBERTa$_{\text{LARGE,MNLI}}$	de	62.6	59.1	62.6	55.1	51.5	55.1	66.5	66.8	66.5	74.9	74.0	74.9	60.8	**59.0**	**60.8**	62.5	57.2	62.5
RoBERTa$_{\text{LARGE,MNLI}}$	en, de	**79.7**	**79.1**	**79.7**	66.3	65.3	66.3	69.4	69.1	69.4	**76.0**	**75.0**	**76.0**	**59.6**	58.4	**59.6**	**64.9**	**59.2**	**64.9**
AlBERT$_{\text{BASE}}$	en	72.6	71.4	72.6	57.6	55.2	57.6	60.1	52.3	60.1	37.0	31.5	37.0	30.0	24.9	30.0	40.6	31.8	40.6
AlBERT$_{\text{LARGE}}$	en	71.3	70.1	71.3	58.1	56.8	58.1	65.3	60.7	65.3	45.0	42.1	45.0	38.7	34.9	38.7	58.1	46.0	58.1
XLM$_{\text{MLM-TLM-XNLI}}$	en	72.6	71.2	72.6	57.6	55.5	57.6	56.3	44.8	56.3	48.0	47.4	48.0						
XLM$_{\text{MLM-TLM-XNLI}}$	de																		

Acknowledgements. We would like to thank Prof. Dr. rer. nat. Karsten Weihe, M.Sc. Julian Prommer, the department of didactics and Nena Marie Helfert, for supporting and reviewing this work.

References

1. Alikaniotis, D., Yannakoudakis, H., Rei, M.: Automatic text scoring using neural networks. arXiv preprint arXiv:1606.04289 (2016)
2. Barrault, L., et al.: Findings of the 2019 conference on machine translation (wmt19). In: Proceedings of the Fourth Conference on Machine Translation (Volume 2: Shared Task Papers, Day 1), pp. 1–61. Association for Computational Linguistics, Florence, August 2019. http://www.aclweb.org/anthology/W19-5301
3. Conneau, A., et al.: Unsupervised cross-lingual representation learning at scale. arXiv preprint arXiv:1911.02116 (2019)
4. Devlin, J., Chang, M.W., Lee, K., Toutanova, K.: Bert: Pre-training of deep bidirectional transformers for language understanding. arXiv preprint arXiv:1810.04805 (2018)
5. Dzikovska, M.O., et al.: Semeval-2013 task 7: The joint student response analysis and 8th recognizing textual entailment challenge. NORTH TEXAS STATE UNIV DENTON, Tech. rep. (2013)
6. Heilman, M., Madnani, N.: Ets: Domain adaptation and stacking for short answer scoring. In: Second Joint Conference on Lexical and Computational Semantics (* SEM), Volume 2: Proceedings of the Seventh International Workshop on Semantic Evaluation (SemEval 2013). pp. 275–279 (2013)
7. Jimenez, S., Becerra, C., Gelbukh, A.: Softcardinality: Hierarchical text overlap for student response analysis. In: Second Joint Conference on Lexical and Computational Semantics (* SEM), Volume 2: Proceedings of the Seventh International Workshop on Semantic Evaluation (SemEval 2013), pp. 280–284 (2013)
8. Kumar, S., Chakrabarti, S., Roy, S.: Earth mover's distance pooling over siamese lstms for automatic short answer grading. In: IJCAI, pp. 2046–2052 (2017)
9. Lample, G., Conneau, A.: Cross-lingual language model pretraining. arXiv preprint arXiv:1901.07291 (2019)
10. Lan, Z., Chen, M., Goodman, S., Gimpel, K., Sharma, P., Soricut, R.: Albert: A lite bert for self-supervised learning of language representations. arXiv preprint arXiv:1909.11942 (2019)
11. Liu, Y., et al.: Roberta: A robustly optimized bert pretraining approach. arXiv preprint arXiv:1907.11692 (2019)
12. Loshchilov, I., Hutter, F.: Fixing weight decay regularization in adam. arXiv preprint arXiv:1711.05101 (2017)
13. Marvaniya, S., Saha, S., Dhamecha, T.I., Foltz, P., Sindhgatta, R., Sengupta, B.: Creating scoring rubric from representative student answers for improved short answer grading. In: Proceedings of the 27th ACM International Conference on Information and Knowledge Management, pp. 993–1002 (2018)
14. Mohler, M., Bunescu, R., Mihalcea, R.: Learning to grade short answer questions using semantic similarity measures and dependency graph alignments. In: Proceedings of the 49th Annual Meeting of the Association for Computational Linguistics: Human Language Technologies-Volume 1, pp. 752–762. Association for Computational Linguistics (2011)

15. Mohler, M., Mihalcea, R.: Text-to-text semantic similarity for automatic short answer grading. In: Proceedings of the 12th Conference of the European Chapter of the ACL (EACL 2009), pp. 567–575 (2009)
16. Mueller, J., Thyagarajan, A.: Siamese recurrent architectures for learning sentence similarity. In: Thirtieth AAAI Conference on Artificial Intelligence (2016)
17. Ramachandran, L., Foltz, P.: Generating reference texts for short answer scoring using graph-based summarization. In: Proceedings of the Tenth Workshop on Innovative Use of NLP for Building Educational Applications, pp. 207–212 (2015)
18. Saha, S., Dhamecha, T.I., Marvaniya, S., Sindhgatta, R., Sengupta, B.: Sentence level or token level features for automatic short answer grading?: use both. In: Penstein Rosé, C., et al. (eds.) AIED 2018. LNCS (LNAI), vol. 10947, pp. 503–517. Springer, Cham (2018). https://doi.org/10.1007/978-3-319-93843-1_37
19. Sanh, V., Debut, L., Chaumond, J., Wolf, T.: Distilbert, a distilled version of bert: smaller, faster, cheaper and lighter. In: NeurIPS EMC2 Workshop (2019)
20. Sultan, M.A., Salazar, C., Sumner, T.: Fast and easy short answer grading with high accuracy. In: Proceedings of the 2016 Conference of the North American Chapter of the Association for Computational Linguistics: Human Language Technologies, pp. 1070–1075 (2016)
21. Sung, C., Dhamecha, T.I., Mukhi, N.: Improving short answer grading using transformer-based pre-training. In: Isotani, S., Millán, E., Ogan, A., Hastings, P., McLaren, B., Luckin, R. (eds.) AIED 2019. LNCS (LNAI), vol. 11625, pp. 469–481. Springer, Cham (2019). https://doi.org/10.1007/978-3-030-23204-7_39
22. Williams, A., Nangia, N., Bowman, S.: A broad-coverage challenge corpus for sentence understanding through inference. In: Proceedings of the 2018 Conference of the North American Chapter of the Association for Computational Linguistics: Human Language Technologies, Volume 1 (Long Papers), pp. 1112–1122. Association for Computational Linguistics (2018). http://aclweb.org/anthology/N18-1101
23. Wolf, T., et al.: Huggingface's transformers: State-of-the-art natural language processing. ArXiv arXiv:1910.03771 (2019)

Predicting Learners Need
for Recommendation Using Dynamic
Graph-Based Knowledge Tracing

Abdessamad Chanaa$^{(\boxtimes)}$ and Nour-Eddine El Faddouli

RIME Team, MASI Laboratory, E3S Research Center,
Mohammadia School of Engineers (EMI), Mohammed V University (UM5),
Rabat, Morocco
abdessamad.chanaa@gmail.com, nfaddouli@gmail.com

Abstract. Personalized recommendation as a practical approach to overcoming information overloading has been widely used in e-learning. Based on learners individual knowledge level, we propose a new model that can predict learners needs for recommendation using dynamic graph-based knowledge tracing. By applying the Gated Recurrent Unit (GRU) and the Attention model, this approach designs a dynamic graph over different time steps. Through learning feature information and topology representation of nodes/learners, this model can predict with high accuracy of 80,63% learners with low knowledge acquisition and prepare them for further recommendation.

Keywords: Node classification · Dynamic graph · Knowledge tracing · Recommendation · Gated Recurrent Unit (GRU)

1 Introduction

The personalized recommendation has been widely used in e-learning systems; It has been a practical approach to overcome information overloading by helping learners for better course selection [3,8]. However, the development of recommendation system must not only consider the capability of delivering the suitable learning material to the learner anytime, but also how to actively distinguish learners who need a recommendation at that time based on their past performance.

Knowledge tracing, on the other hand, is the process of modelling student knowledge over time to predict how learners will perform on future interactions accurately [5]. Knowledge tracing can identify suitable learners for a potential recommendation based on their knowledge level, thus providing more effective learning. It can be helpful for both learners and tutors, as predicting recommendation need in the right time can highly decrease drop out rate and increase learners engagement.

© Springer Nature Switzerland AG 2020
I. I. Bittencourt et al. (Eds.): AIED 2020, LNAI 12164, pp. 49–53, 2020.
https://doi.org/10.1007/978-3-030-52240-7_9

Recently, deep learning [2] and graph theory [11] are becoming two actives areas in e-learning. Previous work tries to predict student proficiency by modelling knowledge concepts into nodes using a deep graph neural network [9]. Although the efficiency of this approach, it focuses on knowledge concepts more than the learner. Also, this approach is not entirely taking into consideration the dynamic structure of the graph, which reflects the knowledge acquisition change over time steps.

In our paper, Based on [12], we propose a time-series node classification in a dynamic graph-based knowledge tracing approach. By modelling learners into nodes, we group learners in graphs based on a particular knowledge concept introduced by the tutor. Both nodes and graph topology are transforming over time, matching the knowledge tracing of learners. Through Gated Recurrent Unit (GRU) network [4] and the Attention Neural Network (ANN) [7], we propose to learn feature representation by aggregating the learner (presented by node) and its neighbours, then extract the network topology information at each different time step. The generated dependent temporal information will provide adequate information about the actual need for a future recommendation in the chosen knowledge concept for every individual learner presented in the graph.

2   Proposed Approach

Problem Definition: The problem we consider in this paper is supervised node classification. We suppose that the coursework is structured as $G = (\zeta^1, \zeta^2, ..., \zeta^T)$ where T is the number of time steps. $\zeta^t = (V, A^t, X^t, C)$ is the graph at time step t, where ζ^t denote a graph with nodes set V. Let $N = |V|$ denote the number of learners/nodes in our graph. Those nodes share a knowledge concept C as a dependency relationship, where $C = \{C_1, C_2, ..., C_m\}$ presents a knowledge concept where m is the number of existing knowledge concepts. Let $A^t \in R^{N \times N}$ be the adjacency matrix describing nodes connections where $A_{ij} = 1$ shows a shared knowledge concept C at time t between nodes i and j. A missing connection is signified by $A_{ij} = 0$. $X^t \in R^{N \times f}$ is the node attribute matrix where f is the dimension of the attribute features (the number of features/information presenting each learner). Both A^t and X^t change at different time steps, while V and C are fixed for all time steps.

Dynamic Graph Based Knowledge Tracing: As shown in the Fig. 1, first, the tutor chose an available knowledge concept. The knowledge tracing dataset is transformed into a dynamic graph that changes over time steps, where each node represents a learner with attribute features extracted and aggregated from his previous knowledge. All learners in the generated graphs share the same knowledge concept already chosen by the tutor. The idea behind node classification in a dynamic graph is to integrate both network structure information and node attribute information, using two connected GRU [12], an attribute GRU (A-GRU) and a topology GRU (T-GRU). First, attention neural network capture relevant node information and then aggregate important neighbours of

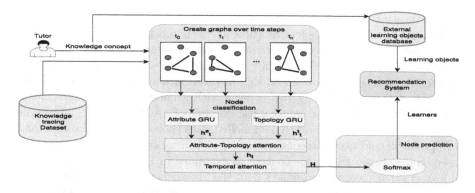

Fig. 1. The global architecture and workflow of the approach

a node. We use this neighbour representation along with node features vector of the previous state at each time step resulting in the new GRU state vector $h_t^A \in R^{d_h}$ that represents the A-GRU, where d_h is the state vector size. As for the T-GRU, it considers the topology context vectors of a node/learner at different time steps, resulting in the GRU state vector $h_t^T \in R^{d_h}$. Both T-GRU and A-GRU share the same calculation process of a standard GRU [1]. The attribute-topology attention determines the importance of attribute and topology at each time step; It receives the state vectors h_t^T and h_t^A and resolves respectively the attention values β_t^A and β_t^T. Therefore, the final state vector at time step t is: $h_t = [(\beta_t^T \times h_t^T)^\top \oplus (\beta_t^A \times h_t^A)^\top]^\top \in R^{2d_h}$. Moreover, temporal attention is added to detect the temporal influence in graph structure over multiple time step. The main objective of the temporal self-attentional layer is to capture the temporal variations in graph structure over multiple time steps. The attention model receives the state h_t and outputs the attention value α_t for each state. Using multiple-head self-attention [10], The final vector representation for the node is $\alpha \times H \in R^{2d_h}$, where $H = [h_1...h_t]$ represents the concatenation of all h_t and $\alpha \in R^T$ is the attention value of all different time steps. Finally, we used the cross-entropy loss and the Softmax function to estimate the node labels. Only the nodes that represent learners with low knowledge acquisition over time steps on the chosen knowledge concepts will be input to the recommendation system, alongside with learning objects matching that knowledge concept.

3   Experiment

3.1   Dataset

In order to evaluate our proposed approach, we adopt the dataset drawn from the ASSISTments learning platform[1] [6]. We reorganized the dataset by extracting

---

[1] https://sites.google.com/site/assistmentsdata/home/2012-13-school-data-with-affect.

and aggregating relevant features and then labelling it. We chose eight different features to represent the learner (time spent, number of correct answers, the hints count, the attempts count, frustration score, boredom score, confusion score and concentration score). Each learner is labelled with a binary value indicating whether the learner has low knowledge acquisition and needs a recommendation. The data was coded by two experts with a good inter-rater agreement. With the new labelled data, we took the example of «Addition and Subtraction Integers» as knowledge concept (the labelled data shows a 42% of learners that have problems and need a recommendation); Then we created a dynamic graph based on the chosen knowledge concept as explained in Table 1. This graph links all learners that pass an assignment with the knowledge concept «Addition and Subtraction Integers» over different time steps. The dataset alongside the generated graph is publicly available[2]. It is important to note that this experiment was conducted in Google Colab[3] with P100-PCIE-16 GB GPU and 25 GB RAM support settings.

Table 1. Reports on the graph data for the considered concept.

Knowledge concept	Assignments	Nodes	Features	Time steps	Labels
Addition and subtraction integers	151061	10732	8	10	2

3.2 Results and Discussion

The results are presented in Table 2. After several experiences, we notice that our model achieves the best performance under those parameters: batch size $= 2048$, learning rate $= 0.001$, number of epochs $= 30$, the state vector size $d_h = 12$. Our model combines the importance of chosen features that represent each learner of the graph, alongside with graph topology that represents the link between learners with the same knowledge concept. Using a dynamic representation of the graph over time steps, this approach will model better the learning acquisition of learners comparing to any static method that relies only on a static snapshot of the graph. The high accuracy also proves the effectiveness of the user attention model. In other words, this model can predict with high accuracy the need for a recommendation for each learner, which will highly decrease the dropout rate.

Table 2. Experiment results.

Knowledge concept	Accuracy	F1 score	AUC
Addition and subtraction integers	0,8063	0,8063	0,8342

---

[2] https://github.com/Abdessamad139/Predict-recommendation-need/.
[3] https://colab.research.google.com.

Additionally, this approach will also facilitate building an adaptive system for learners with a low acquisition.

4 Conclusion and Future Work

In this work, we exploit the use of node classification in a dynamic graph-based knowledge tracing approach to predict the needs for a recommendation for learners, using mainly the GRU and the Attention models. The experimental results have demonstrated the efficiency of the proposed approach. Future works will focus on building a framework matching the chosen learners for recommendation with suitable learning objects.

References

1. Bahdanau, D., Cho, K., Bengio, Y.: Neural machine translation by jointly learning to align and translate, pp. 1–15 (2014). http://arxiv.org/abs/1409.0473
2. Chanaa, A., El Faddouli, N.E.: Deep learning for a smart e-learning system. In: ACM International Conference Proceeding Series (2018). https://doi.org/10.1145/3289100.3289132
3. Chanaa, A., El Faddouli, N.E.: Context-aware factorization machine for recommendation in Massive Open Online Courses (MOOCs). In: 2019 International Conference on Wireless Technologies, Embedded and Intelligent Systems, WITS 2019, pp. 1–6 (2019). https://doi.org/10.1109/WITS.2019.8723670
4. Cho, K., van Merrienboer, B., Bahdanau, D., Bengio, Y.: On the properties of neural machine translation: encoder-decoder approaches, pp. 103–111 (2015). https://doi.org/10.3115/v1/w14-4012
5. Corbett, A.T., Anderson, J.R.: Knowledge tracing: modeling the acquisition of procedural knowledge. User Model. User Adap. Interact. 4(4), 253–278 (1994)
6. Feng, M., Heffernan, N., Koedinger, K.: Addressing the assessment challenge with an online system that tutors as it assesses. User Model. User Adap. Interact. 19(3), 243–266 (2009). https://doi.org/10.1007/s11257-009-9063-7
7. Kim, Y., Denton, C., Hoang, L., Rush, A.M.: Structured attention networks, pp. 1–21 (2017). http://arxiv.org/abs/1702.00887
8. Klašnja-Milićević, A., Ivanović, M., Nanopoulos, A.: Recommender systems in e-learning environments: a survey of the state-of-the-art and possible extensions. Artif. Intell. Rev. 44(4), 571–604 (2015). https://doi.org/10.1007/s10462-015-9440-z
9. Nakagawa, H., Iwasawa, Y., Matsuo, Y.: Graph-based knowledge tracing: modeling student proficiency using graph neural network. In: Proceedings of 2019 IEEE/WIC/ACM International Conference on Web Intelligence, WI 2019, pp. 156–163 (2019). https://doi.org/10.1145/3350546.3352513
10. Vaswani, A., et al.: Attention is all you need. In: Advances in Neural Information Processing Systems, pp. 5998–6008 (2017)
11. Vidal, J.C., Lama, M., Otero-García, E., Bugarín, A.: Graph-based semantic annotation for enriching educational content with linked data. Knowl. Based Syst. 55, 29–42 (2014). https://doi.org/10.1016/j.knosys.2013.10.007
12. Xu, D., et al.: Adaptive neural network for node classification in dynamic networks. In: ICDM. IEEE (2019)

BERT and Prerequisite Based Ontology for Predicting Learner's Confusion in MOOCs Discussion Forums

Abdessamad Chanaa$^{(\boxtimes)}$ ⓘ and Nour-Eddine El Faddouli ⓘ

RIME Team, MASI Laboratory, E3S Research Center, Mohammadia School
of Engineers (EMI), Mohammed V University (UM5), Rabat, Morocco
abdessamad.chanaa@gmail.com, nfaddouli@gmail.com

Abstract. The use of Massive Open Online Courses (MOOCs) is rapidly
increasing due to the convenience and ease that provide to learners. However, MOOCs suffer from high drop out rate owing mostly to the confusion and frustration going with the learning process. Based on MOOCs
discussion forums, this paper aims to explore different levels of confusion
in specific concept using prerequisite based ontology for extracting relevant posts, and Bidirectional Encoder Representations from Transformers (BERT) classification algorithm to describe the degree of confusion
for each post. The analysis of discussion posts from Stanford University
dataset affirms the effectiveness of our model. BERT achieve good classification accuracy; this will help in early drop out detection and also facilitate future support for learners in confusion state.

Keywords: Massive Open Online Courses (MOOCs) · Confusion ·
Text classification · Prerequisite based ontology · BERT classification
algorithm

1 Introduction

Over the few past years, Massive Open Online Courses (MOOCs) have witnessed
a significant evolution in the academic and industrial community. MOOCs give
more flexibility and convenience in taking the course through many helpful learning experiences to students, such as video lectures, assignments, exams. It also
provides the opportunity to connect and collaborate with others through discussion forums. Despite this great success, MOOCs still suffer from a high drop out
rate [7]. Although many causes exist for this problem, students' confusion and
frustration are one of the main reason behind it. Confusion can be defined as
a blockage or dilemmas where the learner is uncertain how to proceed with the
learning process. In MOOCs, there are several ways for learners to express confusion through retaking assessment or rewatching/slowing down videos. However,
in most cases, learners tend more to reveal their confusion via online discussion
forums through questions and posts, where each learner can express clearly his
struggles in more details [2,11].

© Springer Nature Switzerland AG 2020
I. I. Bittencourt et al. (Eds.): AIED 2020, LNAI 12164, pp. 54–58, 2020.
https://doi.org/10.1007/978-3-030-52240-7_10

Due to the absence of physical access to tutors, it is harder to early detect learners confusion about a particular concept or learning materials. On the other hand, Deep learning [5] and natural language processing (NLP) [9] are two artificial intelligence subfields used widely in e-learning. They aim to analyse learners posted messages and predict their different behaviours. Bidirectional Encoder Representations from Transformers (BERT) algorithm, is a new technique that reveals a very high performance over previous NLP techniques [1]. Published by Jacob Devlin in 2018 [6], BERT is based on attention mechanism that learns contextual relations between words in the text [10].

Our work aims to explore different levels of confusion in MOOCs discussion forums based on predetermined knowledge concept. We used ontologies to extract related terms to the chosen concept, then classify the selected messages using BERT classification algorithm. This method will help to identify the overall confusion level at each step of the learning process. It can also help distinguish learners with learning difficulties, then prepare them for a future process to increase their learning engagement and prevent drop out.

2   Proposed Approach

The overview of our proposed model is displayed in Fig. 1. Our approach is mainly composed of two principal subsystems: a prerequisite based ontology and a text classification using the BERT algorithm. First, at every end of the coursework, an intelligent tutor introduces the knowledge concept that should be acquired at this level of the learning process. The concepts generally do not exist alone; some concepts are the prerequisites of other concepts; Thus, for a student to master a chosen concept, he should usually master its prerequisites. Therefore, Based on OWL prerequisites ontology [3], we extract all the prerequisites of the introduced concept. The use of ontologies provides a useful tool for the representation of concepts, performance and relationships more adequately. After extracting all related prerequisites concepts, we filter by those concepts/terms all the messages posted in the discussion forums of MOOCs in this period. In this way, we only get posts related to the concept in question, alongside posts with the prerequisite concepts. This method will help to classify the confusion level based on only the chosen concept.

Before performing text classification, text pre-processing is a crucial step. Pre-processing transforms text into a more straightforward form for better performance for classification algorithms. We first perform noise removal and text cleaning (removing special characters, digits, lowercasing, . . .) then we proceed with normalization which includes transforming the text into a consistent form through two main techniques stemming and lemmatization [4].

The final step consists of BERT classification algorithm; BERT is a deep learning algorithm given state-of-the-art results on multiple natural language processing tasks. BERT is based on multi-layer bidirectional Transformer encoder, and multi-head attention network. It is published by Google, and it is trained based on the corpus of 3.3 billion texts. The model is able to learn the context of a word based on all its neighbourhood.

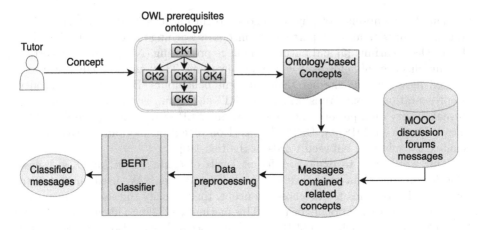

Fig. 1. Proposed approach workflow

BERT's attention model between encoder and decoder is crucial, and it is a function that maps the input (a query q and a key-value pairs k and v) to output as presented in Eq. 1:

$$Atten(q, K, V) = \sum_i \frac{e^{q.k_i}}{\sum_j e^{q.k_j}} v_i \qquad (1)$$

Based on contextual features within sentences and sequential features within the surrounding ones, we use the BERT classification algorithm to classify the selected messages into three different levels: confused, unconfused and neutral.

3   Experiment Settings

In our experiment, we used the Stanford MOOCPosts dataset that contains 29 604 learner forum posts from eleven Stanford university public online classes [2]. Those courses were chosen equally from three different domains: medicine, humanities/sciences and education. Each post was coded by three different independent coders. Each post in the MOOC Posts dataset was scored across six different dimensions, including the confusion. In the confusion dimension, coders ranked the confusion of the post on a scale of 1 to 7. A score of 1 means the post writer is not confused, while 7 means he is perplexed. We re-score the posts to limit confusion in three degrees, in the manner that posts with label inferior to 3.5 have the new label of 0 (unconfused). Posts with a label of 4 get the new label 1 (neutral), and the messages with score superior to 4.5 will be assigned the label 2 (confused).

As for the prerequisite based Ontology, we opt for the OWL (Ontology Web Language) which is a layer used below RDF (Resource Description Framework) to express logical constraints governing RDF triplets. We use this language to build our ontology, which is mainly used to build our vocabulary. By vocabulary, we mean the set of prerequisites concepts, their relationships that are formally expressed. As for the querying of data, it is done through a specific query language called SPARQL. We Use Python programming language for filtering posts by the resulting prerequisite concepts and Natural Language Toolkit (NLTK) library for messages pre-processing. Therefore, the final resulting corpus is input to Bert algorithm.

We use the BERT-Base pre-trained model, which has 12 layers, 768 hidden states, 12 heads and 110M parameters. The batch size is set to 30. We use Adam optimizer [8] as a learning rate optimization algorithm with hyper-parameters set to $\beta 1 = \beta 2 = 0, 9$.

4   Results and Evaluation

In our experiment, we took the example of «Statistic in medicine» as a chosen concept. The OWL ontology generates **14** different prerequisites concepts/terms: «probability», «median», «frequency», «mean», «function», «standard deviation».... From the 29 604 posts, only **7203** contain the chosen concept and its prerequisites. After pre-processing, then BERT classification algorithm, we achieve **68,16%** accuracy score, which is very high for this small corpus. The obtained result show significant performance, the combination of OWL prerequisite based ontology with text classification help the system to build a model that can predict the overall confusion score around a given concept on each course session. Also, this model helps us distinguish individual learners with high confusion rates. This will aid taking precaution to early preventing losing learners motivation and engagement; Since learners with much higher confusion are more likely to drop out the learning process.

5   Conclusion

In this paper, we explore the combination of OWL ontology with BERT classification algorithm on Mooc forum posts to analyse learners' confusion level through posted messages. This method shows high efficiency. It will provide practical guidance for improving student engagement and early preventing their drop out.

In future work, we will build a vector presenting different confused behaviour of learners during his learning process. This vector will be based mainly on the number of confused, unconfused and neutral messages produced by each learner. Also, in order to better evaluate our approach, We aim to process answers from directed questions such as interviews and questionnaires. Those methods of data collection might also be applicable to classify confusion.

References

1. Adhikari, A., Ram, A., Tang, R., Lin, J.: DocBERT: BERT for document classification. arXiv preprint arXiv:1904.08398 (2019)

2. Agrawal, A., Venkatraman, J., Leonard, S., Paepcke, A.: YouEDU: addressing confusion in MOOC discussion forums by recommending instructional video clips (2015)
3. Antoniou, G., Van Harmelen, F.: Web ontology language: OWL. In: Staab, S., Studer, R. (eds.) Handbook on Ontologies, pp. 67–92. Springer, Heidelberg (2004). https://doi.org/10.1007/978-3-540-24750-0_4
4. Balakrishnan, V., Lloyd-Yemoh, E.: Stemming and lemmatization: a comparison of retrieval performances (2014)
5. Chanaa, A., El Faddouli, N.E.: Deep learning for a smart e-learning system. In: Proceedings of the 2nd International Conference on Smart Digital Environment, pp. 197–202 (2018)
6. Devlin, J., Chang, M.W., Lee, K., Toutanova, K.: BERT: pre-training of deep bidirectional transformers for language understanding. arXiv preprint arXiv:1810.04805 (2018)
7. Jordan, K.: MOOC completion rates: the data (2015). http://www.katyjordan.com/MOOCproject.html. Accessed 05 May 2020
8. Kingma, D.P., Ba, J.: Adam: a method for stochastic optimization. arXiv preprint arXiv:1412.6980 (2014)
9. Robinson, C., Yeomans, M., Reich, J., Hulleman, C., Gehlbach, H.: Forecasting student achievement in MOOCs with natural language processing. In: Proceedings of the Sixth International Conference on Learning Analytics and Knowledge, pp. 383–387 (2016)
10. Vaswani, A., et al.: Attention is all you need. In: Advances in Neural Information Processing Systems, pp. 5998–6008 (2017)
11. Yang, D., Wen, M., Howley, I., Kraut, R., Rose, C.: Exploring the effect of confusion in discussion forums of Massive Open Online Courses. In: Proceedings of the Second (2015) ACM Conference on Learning @ Scale, pp. 121–130 (2015)

Identification of Students' Need Deficiency Through a Dialogue System

Penghe Chen, Yu Lu$^{(\boxtimes)}$, Yan Peng, Jiefei Liu, and Qi Xu

Advanced Innovation Center for Future Education, Faculty of Education,
Beijing Normal University, Beijing 100875, China
{chenpenghe,luyu,pengyan,liujiefe,xuqi}@bnu.edu.cn

Abstract. In the domain of moral education, students' need deficiency refers to the unsatisfied need that would result in problem behaviors. Timely and accurate identification of students' need deficiency is crucial to moral education and the students themselves. Previous psychology research focusing on distinct factors only provides scattered guidelines to identify such need deficiencies and meanwhile few teachers and parents have the related expertise, which makes the identification task difficult to accomplish. To address these issues, we develop a task-oriented dialogue system to help teachers and parents identify students' need deficiency through multi-turn dialogues. Specifically, relevant factors of need deficiency are summarized based on psychology theories, which provides a theoretical foundation for the newly proposed system. In addition, reinforcement learning methodology is adopted to learn dialogue policy to serve the designed dialogue system. Experimental results demonstrate that the developed dialogue system achieves its design objectives.

Keywords: Need deficiency · Problem behavior · Dialogue system

1 Introduction

In the moral education domain, students' need deficiency referring to the unsatisfied need is what drives students' problem behavior like playing truant and fighting in school [3,8]. In this work, based on Maslow's Hierarchy of Need [8], need deficiency is divided into five specific types: *physiological needs, safety needs, belongingness and love needs, esteem needs,* and *cognition needs.* Timely and accurate identification of students' need deficiency is crucial for reducing and modifying students' problem behavior. Past literature has demonstrated that effective moral education can promote behavioral advancement [5]. Targeting on this problem, extensive research has been conducted to analyze different factors of problem behavior and need deficiency. For instance, researchers found that uninvolved parenting style would lead to a higher probability of externalizing problems [11], and boys are more likely to perform aggressive behaviors [6]. These findings are informative for need deficiency identification, but too scattered to be employed systematically by teachers and parents without the expertise. Therefore, the education domain needs a system that not only encompasses relevant

© Springer Nature Switzerland AG 2020
I. I. Bittencourt et al. (Eds.): AIED 2020, LNAI 12164, pp. 59–63, 2020.
https://doi.org/10.1007/978-3-030-52240-7_11

psychology theories, but is also easy to use without the requirement of mastery on those theories.

With advancement in artificial intelligence, task-oriented dialogue system, aiming to complete a specific task through natural language interaction, has been applied to different fields, such as ticket booking [7], restaurant searching [13], disease diagnosis [12], moral education [10]. Adoption of dialogue system can significantly improve the service efficiency and accessibility in these domains. Hence, we are inspired to develop a task-oriented dialogue system for need deficiency identification, which presents three main advantages. Firstly, the dialogue system is designed according to psychology research findings, which guarantees the identification consistent with relevant theories. Secondly, unlike supervised classification model that requires information of each student's all aspects to make inference, the dialogue system depends on necessary information only and acquires them adaptively, which significantly reduces service cost but improves service applicability. Thirdly, the natural language based interaction makes dialogue system easy to use without mastering psychology theories necessarily. Note that the dialogue system is mainly designed as an assistant tool for giving professional suggestions on students' need deficiency behind problem behavior rather than directly providing the complete solution. We next explain the proposed dialogue system in detail.

2   Task-Oriented Dialogue System

As shown in Fig. 1, the proposed dialogue system consists of four main modules: Natural Language Understanding (NLU), Dialogue State Tracking (DST), Policy Learning (PL) and Natural Language Generation (NLG) [2]. The NLU module interprets user's input to identify the intention and the semantic slots. For example, user input "The student is boy." is interpreted as "inform(gender=boy)". With the output of NLU, the DST module updates the dialogue state which represents students' information. Based on dialogue state, the PL module decides next system action. Action can be like "inform(deficiency=belongingness and love needs)" to inform the need deficiency or "request(parenting style)" to inquiry more information. Subsequently, NLG composes a response based on system action using natural language. For instance, "request(parenting style)" generates output as "Do you know which kind of parenting style his family perform?". Through multi-turn dialogue, this system can acquire necessary information of a student and automatically infer need deficiency behind his problem behavior.

There are two main challenges in developing this dialogue system. One is how to properly define the semantic slots of need deficiency identification because they are the basis for dialogue state and system action design. The other is how to properly design the dialogue policy because it controls how to collect necessary information and infer the need deficiency. To solve these problems, we first summarize the main factors related to need deficiency identification based on previous psychology research findings. Specifically, based on Teacher's Report

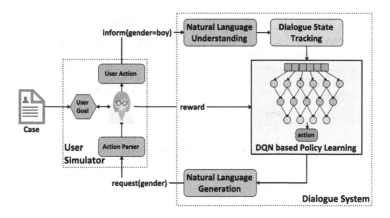

Fig. 1. Architecture of proposed dialogue system.

Form [1] and Problem Behavior Theory [4], we classify the relevant factors into three categories: problem behavior, internal individual characteristic and external environmental characteristic, which provides a foundation to define semantic slots and build the dialogue system. Secondly, we adopt reinforcement learning methodology, specifically deep Q-learning network (DQN) model [9], to learn dialogue policy so that the dialogue system can automatically request essential information from user to identify students' need deficiency. Meanwhile, to learn the dialogue policy, a user simulator is developed to emulate user based on real-life cases collected from an online platform. We next explain the DQN in detail.

By defining the **state** s_t as specific factors of problem behavior, internal individual characteristic and external environmental characteristic, the **action** a_t as *request* and *inform*, the **reward** r_t as system's immediate reward obtained at state s_t after taking the action a_t, the DQN model aims to find optimal Q-value $Q^*(s_t, a_t; \theta)$:

$$Q^*(s_t, a_t; \theta) = E_{s_{t+1}}[r_t + \gamma \max_{a_{t+1}}[Q^*(s_{t+1}, a_{t+1}; \theta)]|s_t, a_t], \tag{1}$$

where t and $t+1$ denote current step and next step respectively, $\gamma \in [0, 1]$ denotes the discount factor and θ denotes model parameters. The optimal policy $\pi^*(s_t)$ is defined as the actions generating the optimal Q-values at different states.

To learn model parameter θ, the ϵ-greedy learning strategy is employed to balance the trade-off between exploration and exploitation in reinforcement learning. In addition, the two techniques of experience replay and periodic parameter updating are also employed to train the model [9] through optimizing the loss function:

$$L(\theta) = E_{s_t, a_t}[(y - Q(s_t, a_t; \theta))^2], \tag{2}$$

where $y = r_t + \gamma \max_{a_{t+1}} Q(s_{t+1}, a_{t+1}; \theta^-)$ denotes the target optimal Q-value, and is computed by summing the current reward r_t and the optimal Q-value of subsequent step based on the target network θ^-.

Data Model		Training Data Size				
		50%	60%	70%	80%	90%
DQN Policy	Success	0.41	0.43	0.43	0.44	0.44
	Reward	-17.90	-15.33	-15.53	-15.70	-14.66
	Turns	5.26	6.09	7.44	9.61	11.11

Fig. 2. System performance of different sized training data.

3 Evaluation

Dataset. We obtain the data used to identify need deficiency from the real-life cases posted on an online moral education platform. In total, 689 cases are collected and converted into structured format in accordance with the defined moral education framework. Specifically, each case is manually annotated by two experts, and the Kappa value between these two annotations is 0.83. To ensure the data quality, cases with less information are excluded, thus create a dataset consisting of 628 cases to build the dialogue system.

Evaluation Result. In order to check the system performance of different sized training data, the experiments are conducted with 50%, 60%, 70%, 80%, 90% of data for training and the rest for testing. The results are presented at Fig. 2, where *success* denotes the success rate, *reward* denotes the average reward, and *turns* denotes the average turns. We have several significant findings from observing the result: Firstly, the dialogue system can achieve success rate between 0.4 and 0.44 for different-sized training data, showing the effectiveness of our system on identifying need deficiency. Secondly, the dialogue system returns result within just 11 turns on average, which means it has successfully recognized the essential factors to request and infer the need deficiency.

4 Conclusion

In this work, we designed and implemented a task-oriented dialogue system for identification of need deficiency in moral education. Based on factors summarized based on psychology theories, the DQN model of reinforcement learning was adopted to learn optimal dialogue policy. Experimental results demonstrated that the dialogue system can achieve success rate around 0.44 with only 11 dialogue turns on average.

Acknowledgment. This research is partially supported by the National Natural Science Foundation of China (No. 61807003), the Fundamental Research Funds for the Central Universities, and sponsored by CCF-Tencent Open Fund.

References

1. Achenbach, T.M., Rescorla, L.A., Maruish, M.: The Achenbach system of empirically based assessment (ASEBA) for ages 1.5 to 18 years. In: The Use of Psychological Testing for Treatment Planning and Outcomes Assessment, vol. 2, pp. 179–213 (2004)
2. Chen, H., Liu, X., Yin, D., Tang, J.: A survey on dialogue systems: recent advances and new frontiers. ACM SIGKDD Explor. Newsl. 19(2), 25–35 (2017)
3. Harper, F.D., Harper, J.A., Stills, A.B.: Counseling children in crisis based on Maslow's hierarchy of basic needs. Int. J. Adv. Couns. 25(1), 11–25 (2003)
4. Jessor, R., Jessor, S.L.: Problem Behavior and Psychosocial Development: A Longitudinal Study of Youth. Academic Press, New York (1977)
5. Jeynes, W.H.: A meta-analysis on the relationship between character education and student achievement and behavioral outcomes. Educ. Urban Soc. 51(1), 33–71 (2019)
6. Johnson, R.J., Kaplan, H.B.: Gender aggression and mental health intervention during early adolescence. J. Health Soc. Behav. 29(1), 53–64 (1988)
7. Li, X., Chen, Y.N., Li, L., Gao, J., Celikyilmaz, A.: End-to-end task-completion neural dialogue systems. arXiv preprint arXiv:1703.01008 (2017)
8. Maslow, A.H.: A theory of human motivation. Psychol. Rev. 50(4), 370 (1943)
9. Mnih, V., et al.: Human-level control through deep reinforcement learning. Nature 518(7540), 529 (2015)
10. Peng, Y., Chen, P., Lu, Y., Meng, Q., Xu, Q., Yu, S.: A task-oriented dialogue system for moral education. In: Isotani, S., Millán, E., Ogan, A., Hastings, P., McLaren, B., Luckin, R. (eds.) AIED 2019. LNCS (LNAI), vol. 11626, pp. 392–397. Springer, Cham (2019). https://doi.org/10.1007/978-3-030-23207-8_72
11. Pinquart, M.: Associations of parenting dimensions and styles with externalizing problems of children and adolescents: an updated meta-analysis. Dev. Psychol. 53(5), 873 (2017)
12. Tang, K.F., Kao, H.C., Chou, C.N., Chang, E.Y.: Inquire and diagnose: neural symptom checking ensemble using deep reinforcement learning. In: NIPS Workshop on Deep Reinforcement Learning (2016)
13. Wen, T.H., et al.: A network-based end-to-end trainable task-oriented dialogue system. arXiv preprint arXiv:1604.04562 (2016)

The Double-Edged Sword of Automating Personalized Interventions in Makerspaces: An Exploratory Study of Potential Benefits and Drawbacks

Edwin Chng[✉], Sofya Zeylikman, and Bertrand Schneider

Harvard University, Cambridge, MA 02138, USA
chng_weimingedwin@g.harvard.edu,
szeylikman@gmail.com,
bertrand_schneider@gse.harvard.edu

Abstract. While the affordance of a project-based and instructor-facilitated curriculum is a strength of makerspaces, they can be challenging learning environments for many students. This paper recognizes the need for instructors to personalize their approach in supporting students' needs. While there are opportunities to create automated systems to help instructors personalize their interventions, much care must be taken to prevent the introduction of unintended outcomes. In this study, we designed a weekly personalized intervention cycle based on students' self-reports. The effect of such personalized intervention was then evaluated using a repeated measure ANOVA. Findings suggest that students receiving personalized interventions were more time efficient in makerspaces and on assignments. Additionally, they reported a lower level of frustration. Students with personalized intervention, however, expressed a lower sense of community. This suggests that while additional data provided to instructors can support personalized assistance, a more nuanced approach may be needed to avoid unintended consequences.

Keywords: Personalized intervention · Makerspaces · Instructional support

1 Introduction

The dynamic nature of makerspaces can present challenges for instructors. In particular, students enter makerspaces from diverse backgrounds. This includes different levels of prior expertise, learning attitudes and working styles. Catering to students' learning needs is an almost impossible task without a good understanding of their individual backgrounds. The use of technology can support instructors in this area by aggregating relevant student information for the instructors to act on. However, cautionary tales from recent debates on algorithmic bias suggest that much consideration ought to be undertaken before committing to the design of a fully automated system for personalization. Therefore, the goal of this work is to conduct preliminary investigations into the design of a personalized intervention cycle to derive a more nuanced understanding of the effects of automated personalization.

© Springer Nature Switzerland AG 2020
I. I. Bittencourt et al. (Eds.): AIED 2020, LNAI 12164, pp. 64–68, 2020.
https://doi.org/10.1007/978-3-030-52240-7_12

2   Literature Review

A close examination of the benefits of makerspaces by Clapp et al. [1] indicates that the benefits of makerspaces lie in the development of students' "maker's mindset", which includes the development of a sense of agency and community spirit. The authors argue that, beyond the immediate transfer of technical skills, makerspaces imbue students with social-emotional skills and the ability to work in cross-disciplinary teams.

However, there are barriers to student learning in makerspaces [2]. For instance, students with little technical background might find entering the space to be daunting or encounter much difficulty when troubleshooting their projects. To complicate matters even further, diverse populations enter makerspaces with different levels of prior experience and expertise, abilities to seek help, and attitudes towards learning [3, 4]. This leads to an impossibility of a one-size-fits-all approach in teaching instruction. When facilitators provide personalized support, students not only overcome their difficulties more easily, but they also feel a greater sense of empowerment, which is critical for students who find makerspaces intimidating [5].

Despite the purported benefits of personalized instruction and maker-centered learning on a diverse population of students, we lack research-based guidelines for implementing this kind of instruction [2]. Thus, this research aims to derive a more nuanced understanding of personalization before the implementation of an automated personalization system.

3   Overview

3.1   Course Overview

Students in the digital fabrication course learn about digital fabrication tools like the use of basic electronics, microcontrollers, and laser cutters. In total, 24 graduate level students participated in this research study. The course is conducted at a makerspace located on the campus of a university in the northeastern United States.

3.2   Research Questions

Through conducting this study, we sought to understand the effect of personalized interventions on a student's learning experience as well as their maker's mindset. A student's learning experience encompasses a self-reflection of the student's mood, technical ability, and connection to others in the space. The maker's mindset includes a sense of agency and community [1]. Thus, our research questions are as follows:

1. What is the effect of personalized interventions on student learning experience?
2. What is the effect of personalized interventions on students' maker mindset?

4   Methods

We conducted a study in which a teaching team consisting of two co-instructors, two teaching assistants, and a lab manager were provided with information about 24 different students' individualized learning profiles. The effect of personalized interventions was studied by differentiating the information provided in these learning profiles. For students not receiving personalized interventions, their learning profiles included minimal information and simply stated the learning challenges encountered by each student. On the other hand, for students receiving personalized interventions, their profiles included specific interventions related to their learning challenges, as well as an overview of the students' individual learning progress. The suggested interventions were manually selected from an "intervention database" that contains suggestions from 32 makerspace facilitators and the overview of students' learning progress was automatically created using data collected from weekly and monthly student surveys. This formed the basis of our semi-automated approach. To determine the effect of personalization on students, we conducted a one-way ANOVA with repeated measures on the standardized survey scores.

5   Results

5.1   RQ 1 - Personalization Leads to Student Time Efficiency and Less Frustration in Learning

Table 1 shows the results for the dimensions of the student learning experience captured from weekly surveys that has statistically significant results between groups of students with and without personalized intervention. Based on the statistical analysis, we find that with personalized intervention, students spent significantly less time within the makerspace and on assignments. Students who received personalized intervention were also, on average, less frustrated than their peers.

Table 1. Effect of personalized intervention on student learning experience

Dimension of learning experience	One-way ANOVA with repeated measures (n = 24)	Personalized intervention (n = 12)	General feedback (n = 12)
Assignment time	$F(2, 41) = 8.01, p < 0.01$	−0.16 s.d.	0.06 s.d.
Makerspace time	$F(2, 41) = 5.44, p < 0.05$	−0.16 s.d.	0.05 s.d.
Frustration	$F(2, 41) = 6.34, p < 0.05$	−0.10 s.d.	0.15 s.d.

5.2   RQ 2 - Personalization Leads to Unexpected Lowering of Community Spirit

The last research question looks at the effect of personalized interventions on students' maker mindset. The results of the statistical analysis indicate that personalized interventions had no statistically significant impact on students' sense of agency, but they affected students' sense of community spirit. The negative score for students receiving personalized intervention shows that, on average, students with personalized interventions had a lower sense of community spirit (Table 2).

Table 2. Effect of personalized intervention on maker's mindset

Maker's mindset	One-way ANOVA with repeated measures (n = 24)	Personalized intervention (n = 12)	General feedback (n = 12)
Agency	$F(2, 41) = 0.60$, p = 0.4438	–	–
Community spirit	$F(2, 41) = 6.87$, p < 0.05	−0.07 s.d.	0.09 s.d.

6 Discussion

We found that students spent less time in the makerspace and on their assignments after receiving personalized intervention. One possible explanation is that their learning challenges were addressed adequately by the instructors. As a result, they became more time efficient in completing their coursework. Becoming more time efficient may also explain why students with personalized intervention felt less frustrated as compared to their peers. This result suggests that the benefits of personalization goes beyond the cognitive aspects of helping students and might provide emotional relief as well.

The result that students with personalized intervention felt a lower sense of community spirit was unexpected. One interpretation is that when students become more time efficient as a result of personalization, they spend less time in the makerspace socializing with peers to troubleshoot their problems. While this result is unexpected, it gives warning that a more nuanced approach in personalization may be needed to avoid unintended consequences. This is an important concern, since communities building and sharing with peers is integral to developing a student's maker's mindset.

7 Conclusion

Our research showed that personalization is a feasible endeavor in makerspaces. The use of surveys, an intervention database, and a student profile allowed us to create a semi-automated system of personalization to augment instructor decision making. While we considered aspects of learning beyond just students' technical skills, our efforts to personalize concluded in students that were more time efficient and less frustrated, but less connected to their communities. This prompts additional questions on how personalization and automation can be further nuanced to achieve different learning objectives, and our research serves as the beginning foundation for heading in this direction.

References

1. Clapp, E.P., Ross, J., Ryan, J.O., Tishman, S.: Maker-centered Learning: Empowering Young People to Shape their Worlds. Jossey-Bass, San Francisco (2016)
2. Litts, B.K.: Resources, facilitation, and partnerships: three design considerations for youth makerspaces. In: Proceedings of the 14th International Conference on Interaction Design and Children, pp. 347–350 (2015)
3. Sheridan, K., Halverson, E.R., Litts, B., Brahms, L., Jacobs-Priebe, L., Owens, T.: Learning in the making: a comparative case study of three makerspaces. Harv. Educ. Rev. **84**(4), 505–531 (2014)
4. Martinez, S.L., Stager, G.S.: The maker movement: a learning revolution. Learn. Lead. Technol. **41**(7), 12–17 (2014)
5. Keefe, J.W., Jenkins, J.M.: Personalized instruction. Phi Delta Kappa Fastbacks **532**(1–2), 7–49 (2005)

EdNet: A Large-Scale Hierarchical Dataset in Education

Youngduck Choi[1,2], Youngnam Lee[1], Dongmin Shin[1], Junghyun Cho[1],
Seoyon Park[1], Seewoo Lee[1,3], Jineon Baek[1,4], Chan Bae[1,3], Byungsoo Kim[1(✉)],
and Jaewe Heo[1]

[1] Riiid! AI Research, Seoul, Republic of Korea
{youngduck.choi,yn.lee,dm.shin,jh.cho,seoyon.park,seewoo.lee,jineon.baek,
chan.bae,byungsoo.kim,jwheo}@riiid.co
[2] Yale University, New Haven, USA
[3] UC Berkeley, Berkeley, USA
[4] University of Michigan, Ann Arbor, USA

Abstract. Advances in Artificial Intelligence in Education (AIEd) and
the ever-growing scale of Interactive Educational Systems (IESs) have led
to the rise of data-driven approaches for knowledge tracing and learning path recommendation. Unfortunately, collecting student interaction
data is challenging and costly. As a result, there is no public large-
scale benchmark dataset reflecting the wide variety of student behaviors
observed in modern IESs. Although several datasets, such as ASSIST-
ments, Junyi Academy, Synthetic and STATICS are publicly available
and widely used, they are not large enough to leverage the full potential of state-of-the-art data-driven models. Furthermore, the recorded
behavior is limited to question-solving activities. To this end, we introduce *EdNet*, a large-scale hierarchical dataset of diverse student activities
collected by *Santa*, a multi-platform self-study solution equipped with an
artificial intelligence tutoring system. *EdNet* contains 131,417,236 interactions from 784,309 students collected over more than 2 years, making it
the largest public IES dataset released to date. Unlike existing datasets,
EdNet records a wide variety of student actions ranging from question-
solving to lecture consumption to item purchasing. Also, *EdNet* has a
hierarchical structure which divides the student actions into 4 different levels of abstractions. The features of *EdNet* are domain-agnostic,
allowing EdNet to be easily extended to different domains. The dataset
is publicly released for research purposes. We plan to host challenges in
multiple AIEd tasks with *EdNet* to provide a common ground for the fair
comparison between different state-of-the-art models and to encourage
the development of practical and effective methods.

Keywords: Dataset · Education · Artificial intelligence · AIEd ·
Knowledge tracing

© Springer Nature Switzerland AG 2020
I. I. Bittencourt et al. (Eds.): AIED 2020, LNAI 12164, pp. 69–73, 2020.
https://doi.org/10.1007/978-3-030-52240-7_13

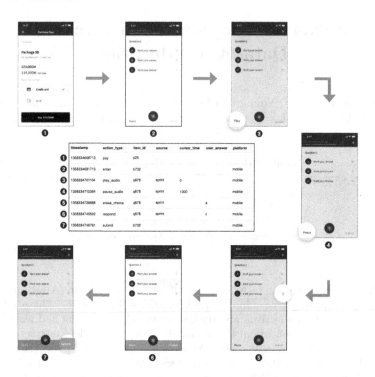

Fig. 1. A possible scenario of a student using *Santa* and example student data in *EdNet*. After the student purchases a 50-day pass (p25), they solve an LC question (q878). The timestamps at which they played and paused audio were recorded. They also eliminated 'a' and chose 'c' as an answer.

1   Introduction

In this paper, we introduce *EdNet*[1], a large-scale hierarchical dataset consisting of student interaction logs collected over more than 2 years from *Santa*[2], a multi-platform, self-study solution equipped with artificial intelligence tutoring system that aids students in preparing for the TOEIC® (Test of English for International Communication®) test. To the best of our knowledge, *EdNet* is the largest dataset open to the public, containing 131,441,538 interactions from 784,309 students. Aside from question-solving logs, *EdNet* also contains diverse student behaviors including but not limited to self-study activities, choice elimination, and course payment. *EdNet* has a hierarchical structure where the possible student actions in *Santa* are divided into 4 different levels of abstraction. This allows the researcher to select the level appropriate for the AIEd task at hand, for example, knowledge tracing or learning path recommendation.

---

[1] https://github.com/riiid/ednet.
[2] https://santatoeic.com.

Table 1. Comparison of Datasets in Education (ASSISTments [2,4], Synthetic-5 [5], Junyi Academy [1], STATICS-2011 [3] and EdNet). Here *logs* stands for interactions, and Synthetic-5, Junyi Academy, and Statics-2011 are renamed as Syn-5, Junyi, and Stat-2011.

	ASSISTments			Syn-5	Junyi	Stat-2011	EdNet			
	2009	2012	2015				KT1	KT2	KT3	KT4
# of students	4,217	46,674	19,917	4,000	247,606	335	784,309	297,444	297,915	297,915
# of questions	26,688	179,999	100	50	722	1,362	13,169	13,169	13,169	13,169
# of tags	123	265	–	5	41	27	188	188	293	293
# of lectures	0	0	0	0	0	0	0	0	1,021	1,021
# of logs	346,860	6,123,270	708,631	200,000	25,925,922	361,092	95,293,926	56,360,602	89,270,654	131,441,538
# of types of logs	3	3	1	1	1	5	1	3	4	13
Public available	Yes	Yes	Yes	Yes	Yes	No	Yes	Yes	Yes	Yes
Contents available	No	No	No	No	Yes	Yes	No	No	No	No
From real-world	Yes	Yes	Yes	No	Yes	Yes	Yes	Yes	Yes	Yes
Collecting period	1y	1y	1y	–	2y 2m	4m	2y 7m	1y 3m	1y 3m	1y 3m

2 EdNet

EdNet is a dataset consisting of all student-system interactions collected over a period spanning two years by *Santa*, a multi-platform AI tutoring service with approximately 780,000 students in South Korea. *Santa* is available through Android, iOS and the Web. It aims to prepare students for the TOEIC (Test of English for International Communication®) Listening and Reading Test. Each student communicates their needs and actions through *Santa*, to which the system responds by providing video lectures, assessing their response or giving expert commentary. *Santa*'s UI and data-gathering process is described in Fig. 1. As shown in the figure, the *EdNet* dataset contains various features of student actions such as the identity of the learning material consumed or the time spent by the student in solving a given problem. The following subsections describe properties of *EdNet*[3].

2.1 Large-Scale

EdNet is composed of a total of 131,441,538 interactions collected from 784,309 students of *Santa* since 2017. Each student has generated an average of 441.20 interactions while using *Santa*. Based on those interactions, *EdNet* makes it possible for researchers to access large-scale real-world IES data. Moreover, *Santa* provides a total 13,169 problems and 1,021 lectures tagged with 293 types of

---

[3] More detailed description of *EdNet* can be found in https://arxiv.org/abs/1912.03072.

skills, and each of them has been consumed 95,294,926 times and 601,805 times, respectively. To the best of our knowledge, this is the largest dataset in education available to the public in terms of the total number of students, interactions, and interaction types (Table 1).

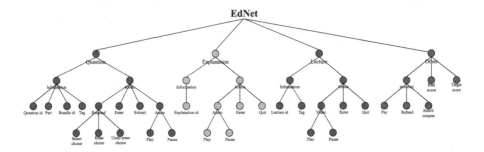

Fig. 2. Hierarchical structure of EdNet.

2.2 Diversity

EdNet offers the most diverse set of interactions among all existing public IES datasets (Table 1). The set of behaviors directly related to learning is also richer in *EdNet* than in other datasets, as *EdNet* includes learning activities such as reading explanations and watching lectures which aren't provided in other datasets. The richness of the data enables researchers to analyze students from various perspectives. For example, purchasing logs may help analyze student's engagement with the learning process.

2.3 Hierarchy

EdNet is organized into a hierarchical structure where each level contains different types of data points as shown in Fig. 2. To provide the various types of data in a consistent and organized manner, *EdNet* offers the data in four different datasets named KT1, KT2, KT3, KT4. As the postfix index of the datasets increases, the number of actions and types of actions involved also increase as shown in Table 1.

2.4 Multi-platform

In an age dominated by various devices spanning from personal computers to smartphones and AI speakers, IESs must offer access from multiple platforms in order to stay competitive. Accordingly, *Santa* is a multi-platform system available on iOS, Android and Web and *EdNet* contains data points gathered from both mobile and desktop users. *EdNet*'s platform-agnostic design allows the study of AIEd models suited for future multi-platform IESs, utilizing the data collected from different platforms in a consistent manner.

Acknowledgement. The authors would like to thank all the members of *Riiid!* for leading the *Santa* service successfully. *EdNet* could not have been compiled without their efforts.

References

1. Chang, H.S., Hsu, H.J., Chen, K.T.: Modeling exercise relationships in e-learning: a unified approach. In: EDM, pp. 532–535 (2015)
2. Feng, M., Heffernan, N., Koedinger, K.: Addressing the assessment challenge with an online system that tutors as it assesses. User Model. User-Adap. Interact. **19**(3), 243–266 (2009)
3. Koedinger, K.R., Baker, R.S., Cunningham, K., Skogsholm, A., Leber, B., Stamper, J.: A data repository for the EDM community: the PSLC DataShop. In: Handbook of Educational Data Mining, vol. 43, pp. 43–56 (2010)
4. Pardos, Z.A., Baker, R.S., San Pedro, M.O., Gowda, S.M., Gowda, S.M.: Affective states and state tests: Investigating how affect and engagement during the school year predict end-of-year learning outcomes. J. Learn. Anal. **1**(1), 107–128 (2014)
5. Piech, C., Bassen, J., Huang, J., Ganguli, S., Sahami, M., Guibas, L.J., Sohl-Dickstein, J.: Deep knowledge tracing. In: Advances in Neural Information Processing Systems, pp. 505–513 (2015)

Exploring Automatic Short Answer Grading as a Tool to Assist in Human Rating

Aubrey Condor[(✉)] [iD]

University of California, Berkeley, Berkeley, USA
aubrey_condor@berkeley.edu

Abstract. This project proposes using BERT (Bidirectional Encoder Representations from Transformers) as a tool to *assist* educators with automated short answer grading (ASAG) as opposed to replacing human judgement in high-stakes scenarios. Many educators are hesitant to give authority to an automated system, especially in assessment tasks such as grading constructed response items. However, evaluating free-response text can be time and labor costly for one rater, let alone multiple raters. In addition, some degree of inconsistency exists within and between raters for assessing a given task. Recent advances in Natural Language Processing have resulted in subsequent improvements for technologies that rely on artificial intelligence and human language. New, state-of-the-art models such as BERT, an open source, pre-trained language model, have decreased the amount of training data needed for specific tasks and in turn, have reduced the amount of human annotation necessary for producing a high-quality classification model. After training BERT on expert ratings of constructed responses, we use subsequent automated grading to calculate Cohen's Kappa as a measure of inter-rater reliability between the automated system and the human rater. For practical application, when the inter-rater reliability metric is unsatisfactory, we suggest that the human rater(s) use the automated model to call attention to ratings where a second opinion might be needed to confirm the rater's correctness and consistency of judgement.

Keywords: Assessment · Automated short answer grading · BERT · Natural Language Processing · Inter-rater reliability

1 Introduction

Although it has been shown that incorporating constructed response items in educational assessments is beneficial for student learning [2], the burden of time spent grading constructed response activities, as opposed to that of multiple choice questions, can deter educators from their use. In addition, the quality of human ratings of student responses can vary in consistency and reliability [15]. Using an automated system for grading free-text could help to alleviate this time

© Springer Nature Switzerland AG 2020
I. I. Bittencourt et al. (Eds.): AIED 2020, LNAI 12164, pp. 74–79, 2020.
https://doi.org/10.1007/978-3-030-52240-7_14

burden as well as produce more consistent ratings. However, from the educator's perspective, completely removing human judgement from assessment tasks is neither responsible nor realistic. Natural Language Understanding (NLU) models are not yet able to discern all the nuances of language as well as a human. In high-stakes grading situations, incorrect ratings can have dire consequences for students.

Recent Automated Short Answer Grading (ASAG) Research using the most state-of-the-art language models, trained on large quantities of data, is only able to predict human ratings correctly less than 85% of the time. Notable recent work includes Crossley et al. who used Latent Semantic Analysis (LSA) to assess student summarizations [3]. Mieskes et al. combined several different automated graders to create a superior ensemble grader [8]. Qi et al. created a hierarchical word-sentence model using a CNN and BLSTM model [9]. Sung et al. examined the effectiveness of pre-training BERT as a function of the size of training data, number of epochs and generalizability across domains [12]. In a separate study, Sung et al. pre-trained BERT on relevant domain texts to enhance the existing model for ASAG [11]. Dhamecha et al. introduced an iterative data collection and grading approach for analyzing student answers [5]. Finally, Hu et al. incorporated a technique called Recognizing Textual Entailment to investigate whether a given passage and question support the predicted answer [14].

We propose using a compressed version of the BERT model called bert-base to simplify the training process and show that with a relatively small amount of training data (less than 70 student answers per question), we can achieve high enough inter-rater reliability to assist a human grader in constructed response rating tasks.

2   Methods

2.1   Dataset

A data set called DT-Grade was used, consisting of short constructed answers from tutorial dialogues between students and an Intelligent Tutoring System called Deep Tutor, created at the University of Memphis Institute for Intelligent Systems [10]. About 1100 student responses, in 100 words or less, to conceptual questions relating to Newtonian Physics were randomly selected from 40, junior-level college students. Included in the data are 34 distinct questions with relative question context information. Initial ratings were completed by experts and each answer was annotated for correctness by categorizing it as one of four categories: correct, correct-but-incomplete, contradictory, and incorrect [1] (Fig. 1).

Question Context	Question	Student Answer	Rating
A car windshield collides with a mosquito ...	How does Newton's third law ...	the wildshield will apply a force ...	Incorrect
A rocket pushes a meteor with constant ...	Can you articulate Newton's ...	if there is zero net force on ...	Correct
...	...	...	...
...	...	...	...

Fig. 1. A snippet of the DT-Grade dataset

2.2 Data Pre-processing

We removed all records from the dataset where the number of answers per question was less than 20. Remaining were 28 distinct conceptual physics questions, and the number of student responses per question ranged from 20 to 69. The filtered dataset then contained 994 records. We collapsed the four rating categories into two so that we will have a binary response variable in order to start with the simplest version of the model. Correct responses were considered correct, and all others (correct-but-incomplete, contradictory and incorrect) were considered incorrect. The question context text was concatenated with the question text as well as the student's answer text before creating the input vector embeddings. The concatenated input texts were tokenized using the bert-base-uncased tokenizer [16] (Fig. 2).

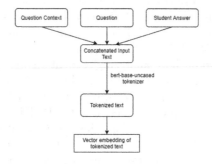

Fig. 2. Flow chart of data pre-processing

Training, validating, and testing data sets were created such that 70% of responses were randomly allocated to the training set, 15% to the validation set and 15% to the test set.

2.3 BERT Model

The language model we used, BERT, which stands for Bidirectional Encoder Representations from Transformers, was introduced in [4] as a revolutionary language representation model. It was the first to successfully learn by pre-training unlabeled text bidirectionally. Consequently, the model can be fine-tuned for many different tasks, such as ASAG, by adding only one additional layer to the existing deep neural network. We use a compressed version of the original BERT model, called bert-base, through a python package called fast-bert [13]. Fast-bert enables quick and simplified fine-tuning of the bert-base model for the assessment task at hand.

A simple grid search was used to tune the parameters and hyper-parameters of the model such that we achieve a high validation accuracy. The best results were observed with using a batch size of 8 (on a single GPU), a maximum sequence length of 512, 8 training epochs and a learning rate of 6e−5. In addition, the LAMB optimizer was used for training. Our particular ASAG task is essentially one of binary text classification - each response is classified as either Correct or Incorrect. Our model returns the predicted classification of response rating per input vector.

2.4 Cohen's Kappa

We used Cohen's Kappa as our metric for inter-rater reliability. It calculates the extent to which raters agree on rating assignments beyond what is expected by chance [7]. Cohen's Kappa is calculated as follows:

$$k = \frac{p_0 - p_e}{1 - p_e} \tag{1}$$

where p_0 = the relative observed agreement among raters and p_e = the hypothetical probability of chance agreement. A k value of 0 represents agreement equivalent to random chance, and a value of 1 represents perfect agreement between raters.

3 Results

The best model achieved a testing accuracy of 0.760 and a Cohen's Kappa statistic of 0.684. This represents the probability that the BERT model agrees with the human rater beyond random chance. With such a small amount of training data per question, we believe that these results provide evidence that transfer learning models such as BERT can remove a significant amount of human rating work, as well help achieve more consistent human ratings.

We must consider the question of whether an instructor would find the described system practical, and correspondingly whether the resulting Kappa statistic is good enough for real world use. One perspective is that, the human rater can incorporate context specific judgement about the extent to which they would like to examine the highlighted cases of disagreement. For example, if the assessment is used for low-stakes, formative purposes, it might not be practical for an educator to investigate rating mismatches in depth. However, if the questions will be used repeatedly in future assessments or the scoring is involved in a pass-fail discernment for a student, a detailed look into discrepancies may be appropriate.

4 Conclusion

In order for the field of education to adopt a willingness to embrace applicable research in Artificial Intelligence, researchers must consider the practicality and usefulness of new technologies from the educator's perspective. Such technologies should act as a support for teachers; not as independent, decision-making entities. This project represents a work-in-progress to continually investigate how we can leverage artificial intelligence to be in service of human decision making.

References

1. Banjade, R., Maharjan, N., Niraula, N., Gautam, D., Samei, B., Rus, V.: Evaluation dataset (DT-Grade) and word weighting approach towards constructed short answers assessment in tutorial dialogue context. In: Proceedings of the 11th Workshop on the Innovative Use of NLP for Building Educational Applications, San Diego, CA, pp. 182–187. Association for Computational Linguistics (2016). https://doi.org/10.18653/v1/W16-0520
2. Chi, M.T., De Leeuw, N., Chiu, M.H., LaVancher, C.: Eliciting self-explanations improves understanding. Cogn. Sci. **18**(3), 439–477 (1994)
3. Crossley, S.A., Kim, M., Allen, L., McNamara, D.: Automated Summarization Evaluation (ASE) using natural language processing tools. In: Isotani, S., Millán, E., Ogan, A., Hastings, P., McLaren, B., Luckin, R. (eds.) AIED 2019. LNCS (LNAI), vol. 11625, pp. 84–95. Springer, Cham (2019). https://doi.org/10.1007/978-3-030-23204-7_8
4. Devlin, J., Chang, M., Le, K., Toutanova, K.: BERT: pre-training of deep bidirectional transformers for language understanding (2018). arXiv:hep-th/9910001
5. Dhamecha, T.I., Marvaniya, S., Saha, S., Sindhgatta, R., Sengupta, B.: Balancing Human efforts and performance of student response analyzer in dialog-based tutors. In: Penstein Rosé, C., et al. (eds.) AIED 2018. LNCS (LNAI), vol. 10947, pp. 70–85. Springer, Cham (2018). https://doi.org/10.1007/978-3-319-93843-1_6
6. Holmes, W., Bialik, M., Fadel, C.: Artificial intelligence in education: promises and implications for teaching and learning. Center for Curriculum Redesign, Boston, MA (2019)
7. Louis, M., Field, R.: Interrater agreement measures: comments on $Kappa_n$, Cohen's Kappa, Scott's π, and Aickin's α. Underst. Stat. **2**(3), 205–219 (2003). https://doi.org/10.1207/S15328031US0203
8. Mieskes, M., Padó, U.: Work smart-reducing effort in short-answer grading. In: Proceedings of the 7th Workshop on NLP for Computer Assisted Language Learning, pp. 4294–4295. Linköping University Electronic Press, SLTC, Stockholm (2018)
9. Qi, H., Wang, Y., Dai, J., Li, J., Di, X.: Attention-based hybrid model for automatic short answer scoring. In: Song, H., Jiang, D. (eds.) SIMUtools 2019. LNICST, vol. 295, pp. 385–394. Springer, Cham (2019). https://doi.org/10.1007/978-3-030-32216-8_37
10. Rus, V., Niraula, N., Banjade, R.: DeepTutor: an effective, online intelligent tutoring system that promotes deep learning. In: Proceedings of the Twenty-Ninth AAAI Conference on Artificial Intelligence, Austin, TX, pp. 4294–4295. AAAI Press (2015). https://doi.org/10.5555/2888116.2888373
11. Sung, C., Dhamecha, T., Saha, S., Tengfei, M., Reddy, V., Rishi, A.: Pre-training BERT on domain resources for short answer grading. In: Proceedings of the 2019 Conference on Empirical Methods in Natural Language Processing and the 9th International Joint Conference on Natural Language Processing, Hong, Kong, CH, pp. 6071–6075. Association for Computational Linguistics (2019). https://doi.org/10.18653/v1/D19-1628
12. Sung, C., Dhamecha, T.I., Mukhi, N.: Improving short answer grading using transformer-based pre-training. In: Isotani, S., Millán, E., Ogan, A., Hastings, P., McLaren, B., Luckin, R. (eds.) AIED 2019. LNCS (LNAI), vol. 11625, pp. 469–481. Springer, Cham (2019). https://doi.org/10.1007/978-3-030-23204-7_39
13. Trivedi, K.: Fast-BERT. https://github.com/kaushaltrivedi/fast-bert. Accessed 25 Feb 2020

14. Hu, M., Wei, F., Peng, Y., Huang, Z., Yang, N., Li, D.: Read+ verify: machine reading comprehension with unanswerable questions. In Proceedings of the AAAI Conference on Artificial Intelligence, vol. 33, pp. 6529–6537, July 2019
15. Wind, S., Peterson, M.: A systematic review of methods for evaluating rating quality in language assessment. Lang. Test. **35**(2), 161–192 (2018). https://doi.org/10.1177/0265532216686999
16. Wolf, T., et al.: HuggingFace's transformers: state-of-the-art natural language processing. arXiv (2019) arXiv:1910.03771

Multi-document Cohesion Network Analysis: Visualizing Intratextual and Intertextual Links

Maria-Dorinela Dascalu[1], Stefan Ruseti[1], Mihai Dascalu[1,2(✉)],
Danielle S. McNamara[3], and Stefan Trausan-Matu[1,2]

[1] University Politehnica of Bucharest, 313 Splaiul Independentei,
060042 Bucharest, Romania
{dorinela.dascalu,stefan.ruseti,mihai.dascalu,
stefan.trausan}@upb.ro
[2] Academy of Romanian Scientists, Str. Ilfov, Nr. 3,
050044 Bucharest, Romania
[3] Department of Psychology, Arizona State University, PO Box 871104,
Tempe, AZ 85287, USA
dsmcnama@asu.edu

Abstract. Reading comprehension requires readers to connect ideas within and across texts to produce a coherent mental representation. One important factor in that complex process regards the cohesion of the document(s). Here, we tackle the challenge of providing researchers and practitioners with a tool to visualize text cohesion both within (intra) and between (inter) texts. This tool, Multi-document Cohesion Network Analysis (MD-CNA), expands the structure of a CNA graph with lexical overlap links of multiple types, together with coreference links to highlight dependencies between text fragments of different granularities. We introduce two visualizations of the CNA graph that support the visual exploration of intratextual and intertextual links. First, a *hierarchical view* displays a tree-structure of discourse as a visual illustration of CNA links within a document. Second, a *grid view* available at paragraph or sentence levels displays links both within and between documents, thus ensuring ease of visualization for links spanning across multiple documents. Two use cases are provided to evaluate key functionalities and insights for each type of visualization.

Keywords: Cohesion Network Analysis · Semantic links · Lexical overlap links · Coreference links · Graph visualizations

1 Introduction

Comprehension is a difficult and challenging process, for which learners need to understand words and sentences, connect ideas and link them to prior knowledge, while creating a coherent mental representation of the read text. One important factor in the comprehension process regards the cohesion of text [1], which considers the degree to which there are semantic links between ideas within a text. Cohesion is higher when there are multiple ideas and words that overlap and when the connections between ideas are explicit. Low cohesion text is more challenging to understand, particularly for

I. I. Bittencourt et al. (Eds.): AIED 2020, LNAI 12164, pp. 80–85, 2020.
https://doi.org/10.1007/978-3-030-52240-7_15

low knowledge and less skilled readers [2]. The process of overcoming cohesion gaps is even more challenging when learners are faced with multiple documents that require establishing connections both within and between disparate text fragments. Making connections across multiple texts is considerably more difficult than doing so within a single text. Some text fragments may be semantically linked, while other may be isolated, distal, and thus more difficult to recognize or infer.

While text cohesion is recognized as an important factor in comprehension and learning from text, there is currently no technique or tool available to visualize cohesive links between documents. We address this gap here, introducing Multi-document Cohesion Network Analysis (MD-CNA). CNA [3] relies on advanced natural language processing techniques, together with Social Network Analysis [4] measurements applied on the cohesion graph, to model discourse structure in terms of semantic links. The MD-CNA graph is a multi-layered graph that establishes semantic links between text elements of different granularities (i.e., the entire text, paragraphs, or sentences), including hierarchical inclusion links and links among elements of the same level. MD-CNA can be used to model both local and global cohesion, as it reflects the underlying semantic content of discourse within a document or between multiple texts [5].

In this study, we extend the CNA graph with lexical overlap links of two types (i.e., topic and content), together with coreference links, to better highlight dependencies between text fragments at different levels. We also introduce visualizations that highlight filtered links from the extended CNA graph, both within and between documents.

2   Method

The CNA graph [3] is centered mainly on semantic links computed using various models (e.g., Latent Semantic Analysis [6], Latent Dirichlet Allocation [7], word2vec [8], FastText [9], or Glove [10]), that can be established either between text elements of the same level (e.g., among sentences), or between different layers of the hierarchy (e.g., sentences relating to the constituent paragraphs). The CNA graph was extended for this study with two new types of links. First, *lexical overlap* is computed as a Jaccard distance over a bag of word representation of the text elements. Two types of measurements are performed after preprocessing the text using in spaCy[1]. *Content overlap* considers the usage of content words which include useful information from the text (i.e., lemmatized forms of words having as part-of-speech one of the following: nouns, verbs, adjectives, or adverbs). *Topic overlap* considers a more constrained view which takes into account only lemmas responsible for text contextualization and inducing actions (i.e., only nouns and verbs).

Second, *coreference links* are identified using NeuralCoref[2], which includes a mentions-detection module based on rules built on top of spaCy, together with a feed-forward neural-network to identify relevant pairs of mentions. The resulting clusters of

---

[1] https://spacy.io.

[2] https://github.com/huggingface/neuralcoref.

co-referring mentions are used to enrich the CNA graph structure. All follow-up visualizations rely on this extended CNA graph that is rendered both using only one reference text, as well as sequences of documents.

3   Visualization Use Cases and Discussion

Two types of visualizations are introduced here, together with preliminary use cases to illustrate their extensive applicability. First, a *hierarchical view* groups nodes by granularity level (i.e., document, paragraph, and sentence), followed by the rendering of different types of links from the MD-CNA graph using a tree-structure of discourse (see Fig. 1). The corresponding use case explores differences between high-low cohesion documents from the study performed by McNamara, Louwerse, McCarthy and Graesser [11]. All types of links are filtered within the rendered visualizations by minimum similarity thresholds available for each type of link. These values can be easily adjusted within the user interface. For this use case, topic overlap was set at 0.4, content overlap was established at 0.3, and high level of semantic similarity (0.7) was imposed.

Sentences from the same paragraph share its color. The size of each node is proportional to its semantic degree – i.e., the sum of all in-bound and out-bound semantic links above a statically imposed threshold, which ensures a sufficiently high semantic relatedness based on the context and readers (for Fig. 1, we considered the average plus standard deviation of all links, at each analysis level). On mouse-over, the link is colored in red, and a tooltip is displayed containing relevant details, including: link type, inter-connected text elements, similarity value (for content and semantic links) or pairs within the coreference cluster identified between the two nodes. The text from Fig. 1.a has low cohesion – only 2 semantic links are above the imposed threshold (i.e., links between sentences 1.1–1.4, and 1.6–1.9 respectively). The text was modified to increase its cohesion and, as expected, there are considerably more links (2 versus 4 topic overlap links, 6 versus 6 content overlap links, 6 versus 14 semantic links, and 3 versus 8 coreference links; 17 versus 32 total links), covering more text elements which are distributed throughout the entire document. Moreover, the semantic degree of most nodes is higher, mainly in the first 2 paragraphs.

The hierarchical view depicts only within document links, as the input consists of one text. The views are useful for analyzing text structure and cohesion, both locally at sentence level, as well as globally, between paragraphs. We can also observe cohesive sections of text and potential cohesion gaps, further providing improvement recommendations in terms of structure. Importantly, MD-CNA affords a *visual illustration* of cohesive links within a document, affording greater ease for researchers and educators in recognizing text cohesion and potentially increasing it for students.

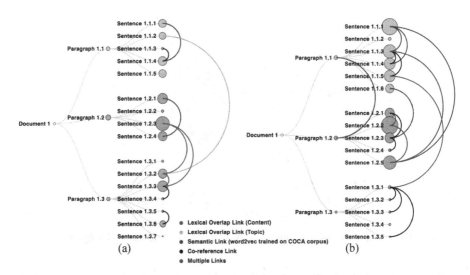

Fig. 1. CNA graph for a) low cohesion text; b) revised text having a high cohesion. (Color figure online)

Second, the *grid view* ensures ease of visualization for links spanning across multiple documents (see Fig. 2). The corresponding use case explores the task of multi-document comprehension on the collection of four documents used in the experiments performed by Nicula, Perret, Dascalu and McNamara [5]. Topic overlap was set at 0.1 due to a more diverse vocabulary, content overlap was kept at 0.2, while semantic similarity was increased to 0.75 to reduce the clutter generated by a dense semantic network.

This visualization shows connections both within (curved lines) and between documents (straight lines). The view can be rendered at two granularity levels (i.e., paragraph and sentence); for the second option, sentences have the same color as their corresponding paragraph. Documents are rendered as different columns in the grid, with constituent text elements displayed sequentially. As it can be observed, all documents are tightly related, with the 1st and 4th document containing many intratextual and intertextual semantic links. This second view enables researchers and educators to easily identify and trace semantically similar text segments between multiple documents, as well as to provide support to better target representative information (e.g., encourage bridging across multiple texts). This view can also be used to guide tutors to adequately order texts for presentation to learners, as well as to formulate comprehension questions that address a cohesive context spanning across multiple texts.

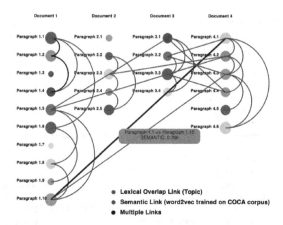

Fig. 2. CNA graph for multi-document analysis at paragraph level. (Color figure online)

In summary, the views provided in this study represent visual aids for researchers and educators to adequately evaluate and select texts to maximize cohesion flow and ease presentation of reading material. Our visualizations are designed to also scaffold readers to establish connections between texts and integrated concepts across documents, facilitating a more coherent understanding from separate sources of information.

Acknowledgments. This research was been funded by the "Semantic Media Analytics – SEMANTIC", subsidiary contract no. 20176/30.10.2019, from the NETIO project ID: P 40 270, MySMIS Code: 105976, the Operational Programme Human Capital of the Ministry of European Funds through the Financial Agreement 51675/09.07.2019, SMIS code 125125, the Institute of Education Sciences (R305A180144, R305A180261, and R305A190063), and the Office of Naval Research (N00014-17-1-2300 and N00014-19-1-2424). The opinions expressed are those of the authors and do not represent views of the IES or ONR.

References

1. McNamara, D.S.: SERT: self-explanation reading training. Discourse Process. **38**, 1–30 (2004)
2. O'Reilly, T., McNamara, D.S.: Reversing the reverse cohesion effect: good texts can be better for strategic, high-knowledge readers. Discourse Process. **43**(2), 121–152 (2007)
3. Dascalu, M., McNamara, D.S., Trausan-Matu, S., Allen, L.K.: Cohesion network analysis of CSCL participation. Behav. Res. Methods **50**(2), 604–619 (2018)
4. Scott, J.: Social Network Analysis. Sage, London (2017)
5. Nicula, B., Perret, C.A., Dascalu, M., McNamara, D.S.: Predicting multi-document comprehension: cohesion network analysis. In: Isotani, S., Millán, E., Ogan, A., Hastings, P., McLaren, B., Luckin, R. (eds.) AIED 2019. LNCS (LNAI), vol. 11625, pp. 358–369. Springer, Cham (2019). https://doi.org/10.1007/978-3-030-23204-7_30
6. Landauer, T.K., Dumais, S.T.: A solution to Plato's problem: the Latent Semantic Analysis theory of acquisition, induction and representation of knowledge. Psychol. Rev. **104**(2), 211–240 (1997)

7. Blei, D.M., Ng, A.Y., Jordan, M.I.: Latent Dirichlet allocation. J. Mach. Learn. Res. **3**(4–5), 993–1022 (2003)
8. Mikolov, T., Chen, K., Corrado, G., Dean, J.: Efficient estimation of word representation in vector space. In: Workshop at ICLR, Scottsdale, AZ (2013)
9. Bojanowski, P., Grave, E., Joulin, A., Mikolov, T.: Enriching word vectors with subword information. Trans. Assoc. Comput. Linguist. **5**, 135–146 (2017)
10. Pennington, J., Socher, R., Manning, C.D.: Glove: global vectors for word representation. In: The 2014 Conference on Empirical Methods on Natural Language Processing (EMNLP 2014), vol. 14. ACL, Doha (2014)
11. McNamara, D.S., Louwerse, M.M., McCarthy, P.M., Graesser, A.C.: Coh-Metrix: capturing linguistic features of cohesion. Discourse Process. **47**(4), 292–330 (2010)

Mastery Learning Heuristics and Their Hidden Models

Shayan Doroudi[✉]

University of California, Irvine, Irvine, CA 92697, USA
doroudis@uci.edu

Abstract. Mastery learning algorithms are used in many adaptive learning technologies to assess when a student has learned a particular concept or skill. To assess mastery, some technologies utilize data-driven models while others use simple heuristics. Prior work has suggested that heuristics may often perform comparably to model-based algorithms. But is there any reason we should expect these heuristics to be reasonable? In this paper, we show that two prominent mastery learning heuristics can be reinterpreted as model-based algorithms. In particular, we show that the N-Consecutive Correct in a Row heuristic and a simplified version of ALEKS' mastery learning heuristic are both optimal policies for variants of the Bayesian knowledge tracing model. By putting mastery learning heuristics on the same playing field as model-based algorithms, we can gain insights on their hidden assumptions about learning and why they might perform well in practice.

Keywords: Mastery learning · Heuristics · Learner models · N-CCR · Bayesian knowledge tracing · Change-point detection · CUSUM

1 Introduction

Mastery learning is an instructional technique popularized by Benjamin Bloom [7], but which at least dates back to progressive educational movements in the early twentieth century [17,24]. The idea is to give students just the right amount of instruction or practice that they need in order to mastery a particular topic before moving them on to the next topic. Today, mastery learning underlies many adaptive learning technologies, including Khan Academy, Duolingo, ASSISTments, ALEKS, and cognitive tutors like MATHia. Each of these platforms are being used by thousands to millions of students yearly, and as such, the way they assess mastery can have real consequences for students. A lot of work has been invested in developing statistical techniques to infer models of student learning that make predictions about whether a student has learned a skill, which could in turn be used in mastery learning [5,9,12,20,25]. However, in practice, many state-of-the-art adaptive learning systems assess mastery in simple ways, which are seemingly not very "intelligent" [4]. For example, some platforms use simple heuristics to assess whether students have reached mastery, such as having students receive practice on a skill until they answer questions correctly three times

© Springer Nature Switzerland AG 2020
I. I. Bittencourt et al. (Eds.): AIED 2020, LNAI 12164, pp. 86–91, 2020.
https://doi.org/10.1007/978-3-030-52240-7_16

in a row. Even platforms that use models of student learning often have the model parameters manually set by system designers or domain experts [10,22], rather than leveraging data-driven techniques.

One advantage of using simple heuristics is that they are interpretable and easy-to-convey to teachers, students, and other stakeholders. Moreover, they may seem intuitively reasonable. However, it is not clear whether these intuitions *in principle* align with (a) our understanding of how students learn or (b) inferences we can make about student mastery from the data.

In this paper, we present a means for better understanding mastery learning heuristics, by re-interpreting them as model-based algorithms. In particular, we show that the N-Consecutive Correct in a Row (N-CCR) heuristic used by ASSISTments and a simplified version of the mastery learning heuristic used by ALEKS are both optimal mastery learning policies for variants of the Bayesian knowledge tracing (BKT) model. By placing mastery learning heuristics in the same playing field as model-based mastery learning algorithms, we hope to better understand the theoretical assumptions about learning that mastery learning heuristics are making, and as such, help guide designers of adaptive learning systems to make more intentional decisions about what heuristics to use.

2   Background

In what follows, a *mastery learning policy* is any instructional policy that considers topics–skills, concepts, or knowledge components (KCs)–one at a time, and decides how many practice opportunities to give for the current topic before moving on to the next. In all of the mastery learning policies we consider, the decision will be made purely based on whether previous answers were correct or incorrect on the students' first attempt on each question for the same KC. An *optimal* mastery learning policy under a model is one that gives the optimal amount of practice subject to some accuracy threshold (e.g., 95% confidence that the student has mastered the skill).

A popular approach to mastery learning that underlies cognitive tutors, such as MATHia, is to use the Bayesian knowledge tracing (BKT) model. The standard BKT model for a single KC is a two-state hidden Markov model that assumes that after receiving a practice opportunity t, the student is in one of two knowledge states: the learned state, where they know the KC ($K_t = 1$), or the unlearned state, where they do not know the KC ($K_t = 0$) [12]. When the student begins using the adaptive learning system, BKT assumes they start in the unlearned state with probability $P(L_0) = P(K_1 = 1)$. If a student is in the unlearned state, every time they attempt a practice opportunity and receive feedback, they have some fixed probability of learning the KC, $P(T) = P(K_{t+1} = 1 | K_t = 0)$. When the student is in the learned state, they are assumed to stay there forever (i.e., no forgetting). Every time the student is given a practice opportunity, we can see whether they answered the question correctly ($C_t = 1$) or incorrectly ($C_t = 0$). If the student is in the unlearned state, they will answer correctly with some probability of guessing $P(G)$ and otherwise answer incorrectly. If the student is in the learned state, they will answer correctly unless they slip with probability $P(S)$. The BKT model for a single skill is thus fully described by four parameters: $P(L_0)$, $P(T)$, $P(G)$, and $P(S)$. When using the BKT model, one can continuously update the probability that the student has learned the KC so far $(P(K_t|C_1, C_2, \ldots, C_{t-1})$. The optimal mastery learning policy for the BKT model continues to give practice opportunities to the student until this probability exceeds some threshold, typically 0.95 [11,12].

3 N-CCR as a Model-Based Algorithm

The N-Consecutive Correct in a Row (N-CCR) heuristic keeps giving students practice problems on a given topic or skill until the student answers the problems correctly N times in a row. This heuristic is used in ASSISTments' Skill Builders exercises [6,15] and was previously used by Khan Academy [13]. Recently, Khan Academy has switched to a more gamified way of implementing mastery learning, where students can go through a series of Mastery Levels, but to reach the Proficient Level students still have to get a certain number of problems correct in a row [16].

We now show that N-CCR can be viewed as the optimal mastery learning policy for certain BKT models. Note that when using the N-CCR heuristic, if a student gives any number of consecutive correct answers less than N followed by an incorrect answer, then they are back in the same "state" as though they had not given any correct answers. Now suppose that the true model of learning is a BKT model. Then, this must mean once we see $C_{t-1} = 0$, the student is identified as having been in state $K_{t-1} = 0$, or $P(K_{t-1} = 0|C_{t-1} = 0) = 1$. Using Bayes' rule, it can be shown that this implies that the probability of slipping $P(S)$ must be zero. By setting the values of $P(G)$, $P(T)$, and $P(L_0)$ appropriately, it can be easily seen that N-CCR is the optimal mastery learning policy for some BKT model where $P(S) = 0$ and for a given accuracy (e.g., 95%). We demonstrate this precisely in the online supplementary material[1]. It is worth noting that the BKT model with $P(S) = 1$ was actually a well-studied model in the 1960s mathematical psychology community, known as the one-element model [8,14].

This re-formulation of N-CCR can help explain why it may seem to perform well in practice. For example, Pelánek and Řihák [19] showed in simulation that, even if students learn according to BKT models, the N-CCR heuristic (with the optimal value of N) often performs almost as good as the optimal BKT mastery learning policy. This may seem surprising, but our findings indicate that if $P(S)$ is small, then the best N-CCR heuristic will correspond to the mastery learning policy for a BKT model that might be close to optimal.

4   TOW as a Model-Based Algorithm

The Tug-of-War (TOW) Heuristic is what we are calling a mastery learning heuristic that gives points to students for answering questions correctly, removes

---

[1] https://bit.ly/aied2020-heuristics.

points for answering questions incorrectly (while keeping the minimum number of points at zero), and keeps giving practice until the student achieves a certain number of points. We will use $TOW_{+i,-j,N}$ to designate the specific TOW heuristic where the student gets i points for a correct answer, loses j points for an incorrect answer and needs N points for mastery. ALEKS, a prominent adaptive learning system, implements mastery learning using the $TOW_{+1,-1,5}$ heuristic (or $TOW_{+1,-1,3}$ in some cases) with a few differences[2] [2]. Previously, ALEKS used the $TOW_{+2,-1,5}$ and $TOW_{+2,-1,3}$ heuristics [23].

To see how some TOW heuristics can be interpreted as model-based algorithms, consider a variant of the BKT model where we make no assumptions as to how or when the student learns a KC. That is, $P(T)$ need not be a fixed probability (e.g., it can increase over time), it need not be the same for all students, and it need not even be probabilistic. Since we do not make assumptions about how students are learning, to implement mastery learning here, we simply want to detect when there appears to have been a sudden increase in the probability of answering correctly (from $P(G)$ to $1 - P(S)$). This is known as change-point detection, which is a well studied problem in statistics and fields like quality control [1,3,18]. Specifically, we can use the Bernoulli CUSUM chart algorithm [21]. We describe this method and how it can be applied to mastery learning in the online supplementary material[3]. Given that we do not make assumptions about the probability of learning, we cannot make any statement about how confident we are that the student has learned the skill. Instead, we can set the parameters such that 95% of students who have not learned the skill would have had at least a certain number of practice opportunities (which we can choose) before we would mistakenly declare mastery. It can be shown that a variety of TOW heuristics, including all of the ones mentioned above can be implemented using the CUSUM algorithm with an appropriate choice of parameters.

5 Conclusion

Given that these heuristics may be more principled than they might appear at first sight, perhaps their use in adaptive learning systems is warranted, especially given that they are much easier to communicate to students than complex model-based policies. However, other considerations need to also be taken into account. For example, the N-CCR heuristic might be demotivating for students given that a single "slip" punishes the student. On the other hand, if we believe students can slip, then perhaps the N-CCR heuristic should not be used altogether! All in all, a more comprehensive understanding of mastery learning heuristics and their hidden models can hopefully help us ensure that adaptive learning systems perform mastery learning in productive ways.

---

[2] In the ALEKS Learning Sequence, if the student gets two consecutive answers correct in a row, the student gets an extra point. Also, if the student revises an incorrect answer on their second attempt, they subsequently gain a point, netting zero points.

[3] https://bit.ly/aied2020-heuristics.

References

1. Adams, R.P., MacKay, D.J.: Bayesian online changepoint detection. arXiv preprint arXiv:0710.3742 (2007)
2. ALEKS: New ALEKS student module: reference guide (2016). https://www.aleks.com/resources/New_Student_Module_Ref_Guide.pdf
3. Aroian, L.A., Levene, H.: The effectiveness of quality control charts. J. Am. Stat. Assoc. **45**(252), 520–529 (1950)
4. Baker, R.S.: Stupid tutoring systems, intelligent humans. Int. J. Artif. Intell. Educ. **26**(2), 600–614 (2016)
5. Baker, R.S.J.D., et al.: Contextual Slip and prediction of student performance after use of an intelligent tutor. In: De Bra, P., Kobsa, A., Chin, D. (eds.) UMAP 2010. LNCS, vol. 6075, pp. 52–63. Springer, Heidelberg (2010). https://doi.org/10.1007/978-3-642-13470-8_7
6. Beck, J.E., Gong, Y.: Wheel-spinning: students who fail to master a skill. In: Lane, H.C., Yacef, K., Mostow, J., Pavlik, P. (eds.) AIED 2013. LNCS (LNAI), vol. 7926, pp. 431–440. Springer, Heidelberg (2013). https://doi.org/10.1007/978-3-642-39112-5_44
7. Bloom, B.S.: Learning for mastery. Eval. Comment **1**(2), 1–5 (1968)
8. Bower, G.H.: Application of a model to paired-associate learning. Psychometrika **26**(3), 255–280 (1961)
9. Cen, H.: Generalized learning factors analysis: improving cognitive models with machine learning. Ph.D. thesis (2009)
10. Cen, H., Koedinger, K.R., Junker, B.: Is over practice necessary?-Improving learning efficiency with the cognitive tutor through educational data mining. Front. Artif. Intell. Appl. **158**, 511 (2007)
11. Corbett, A.: Cognitive mastery learning in the act programming tutor. In: AAAI Tech. rep. SS-00-01 (2000)
12. Corbett, A.T., Anderson, J.R.: Knowledge tracing: modeling the acquisition of procedural knowledge. User Model. User-Adapt. Interac. **4**(4), 253–278 (1995)
13. Hu, D.: How Khan Academy is using machine learning to assess student mastery (2011). http://david-hu.com/2011/11/02/how-khan-academy-is-using-machine-learning-to-assess-student-mastery.html
14. Karush, W., Dear, R.: Optimal strategy for item presentation in a learning process. Manag. Sci. **13**(11), 773–785 (1967)
15. Kelly, K.M., Wang, Y., Thompson, T., Heffernan, N.T.: Defining mastery: knowledge tracing versus n-consecutive correct responses. In: Proceedings of the 8th International Conference on Educational Data Mining (2015)
16. Khan Academy: what are course and unit mastery? (2020). https://khanacademy.zendesk.com/hc/en-us/articles/115002552631-What-are-Course-and-Unit-Mastery-
17. Morrison, H.C.: The Practice of Teaching in the Secondary School. University of Chicago Press, Chicago (1926)
18. Page, E.S.: Continuous inspection schemes. Biometrika **41**(1/2), 100–115 (1954)
19. Pelánek, R., Řihák, J.: Experimental analysis of mastery learning criteria. In: Proceedings of the 25th Conference on User Modeling, Adaptation and Personalization, pp. 156–163 (2017)
20. Piech, C., et al.: Deep knowledge tracing. In: Advances in Neural Information Processing Systems, pp. 505–513 (2015)

21. Reynolds Jr., M.R., Stoumbos, Z.G.: A CUSUM chart for monitoring a proportion when inspecting continuously. J. Qual. Technol. **31**(1), 87–108 (1999)
22. Salden, R.J., Aleven, V., Schwonke, R., Renkl, A.: The expertise reversal effect and worked examples in tutored problem solving. Instr. Sci. **38**(3), 289–307 (2010)
23. Uzun, H.: Personal communication (2020)
24. Washburne, C.W.: The individual system in Winnetka. Elementary Sch. J. **21**(1), 52–68 (1920)
25. Zhang, J., Shi, X., King, I., Yeung, D.Y.: Dynamic key-value memory networks for knowledge tracing. In: Proceedings of the 26th International Conference on World Wide Web, pp. 765–774 (2017)

Towards Practical Detection
of Unproductive Struggle

Stephen E. Fancsali[1]($\boxtimes$), Kenneth Holstein[2], Michael Sandbothe[1],
Steven Ritter[1], Bruce M. McLaren[2], and Vincent Aleven[2]

[1] Carnegie Learning, Inc., Pittsburgh, PA 15219, USA
{sfancsali,msandbothe,sritter}@carnegielearning.com
[2] Carnegie Mellon University, Pittsburgh, PA 15213, USA
{kjholste,bmclaren,aleven}@cs.cmu.edu

Abstract. Extensive literature in artificial intelligence in education focuses on developing automated methods for detecting cases in which students struggle to master content while working with educational software. Such cases have often been called "wheel-spinning," "unproductive persistence," or "unproductive struggle." We argue that most existing efforts rely on operationalizations and prediction targets that are misaligned to the approaches of real-world instructional systems. We illustrate facets of misalignment using Carnegie Learning's *MATHia* as a case study, raising important questions being addressed by ongoing efforts and for future work.

Keywords: Mastery learning · Wheel-spinning · Intelligent tutoring systems · Unproductive struggle

1 Wheel Spinning and Unproductive Persistence

Substantial efforts in the literature on artificial intelligence in education are directed at operationalizing, making inferences about, and responding to what has been called "wheel-spinning," "unproductive persistence," or what we call "unproductive struggle" [1–6]. These efforts focus on situations in which students fail to develop mastery of skills targeted by instruction and practice provided by intelligent tutoring systems (ITSs) and similar systems [1, 3, 6], including Carnegie Learning's *MATHia*, formerly *Cognitive Tutor* [7], *ASSISTments* [8] and *Physics Playground* [9, 10]. However, conclusions drawn in several studies, especially those targeting *Cognitive Tutor*, are difficult to interpret at best, and misleading at worst, due to misalignments between the *operationalizations* and *predictive modeling approaches* commonly used, versus *actual delivery* of instruction and practice in target systems.

Beck and Gong [6] introduced the term "wheel-spinning" to refer to instances in which learners fail to master skills in a "timely" manner. Operationalizing such a notion requires criteria for both mastery and timeliness. Beck and Gong [3, 6], working with data from both *ASSISTments* and *Cognitive Tutor*, use mastery and timeliness criteria associated with elements of *ASSISTments* [8]: a student must respond correctly to three consecutive opportunities to demonstrate mastery of a particular skill; timeliness corresponds to a student reaching mastery within ten opportunities. If a student fails to

© Springer Nature Switzerland AG 2020
I. I. Bittencourt et al. (Eds.): AIED 2020, LNAI 12164, pp. 92–97, 2020.
https://doi.org/10.1007/978-3-030-52240-7_17

demonstrate mastery of a skill within a specified number of opportunities (10 in *ASSISTments*; 15 in *Cognitive Tutor* [3]), they are classified as "wheel-spinning" on that skill. In cases where students did not master a skill and were not presented with at least ten (or 15) opportunities, wheel-spinning status is labeled "indeterminate" (e.g., [3, 6]).

Other options for mastery and timeliness criteria abound, including using Käser et al.'s [5] "predictive stability" and "predictive stability++" instructional policies for "when-to-stop" providing skill practice [12, 13]. These policies improve upon a previous proposal called "predictive similarity" [13], to operationalize unproductive struggle; unproductive struggle occurs when a student reaches the when-to-stop criterion without reaching mastery for that skill.

Zhang et al. [1] observed substantial differences in the relative frequencies with which Beck and Gong's operationalization and Käser et al.'s predictive stability++ label student-skill pairs as "wheel-spinning" across three datasets, finding no clear pattern that a particular operationalization was more or less likely to label instances as wheel-spinning across datasets. In short, unproductive struggle remains ill-defined as a construct – there is no principled operationalization in the literature. Further, as discussed below, no existing approaches are well-aligned to the practical reality of instruction and practice of a widely used real world system, *MATHia*.

2   Carnegie Learning's *MATHia* (Formerly *Cognitive Tutor*)

To begin illustrating the misalignment of existing approaches to Carnegie Learning's *MATHia*, we describe its problem-solving, mastery-based topic progression [14], and "when to stop" instructional policies. *MATHia* [7, 15, 16] is an ITS for middle and high school math that has been a target system in existing analyses (e.g., [1, 3, 6]).

MATHia delivers math content in the form of complex, multi-step problems. Most, but not all, problem-steps are mapped to fine-grained knowledge components (KCs) or skills and provide context-sensitive hints and just-in-time feedback. KC mastery is "traced" according to Bayesian Knowledge Tracing (BKT) [17], which provides a probability estimate that a student has mastered each KC at any given time.

Each academic grade-level of *MATHia*'s standard content is associated with, typically, about 700 KCs, subject to refinement over time (e.g., [18]). Sets of problems and (between two to 15+) KCs are bundled into approximately 70–90 topical workspaces per grade-level, which serve as the unit of student progress in *MATHia*. Problems tend to provide practice on a subset of skills within a workspace, and multiple opportunities to practice a KC are often provided within a single problem. Workspace problem selection tends to "choose" problems that emphasize KCs a student has not yet mastered.

Students master a workspace when BKT's probability estimate of mastery of each KC is greater than the oft-adopted value of 0.95 (e.g., [7, 17]). If a student fails to achieve mastery of all KCs in a workspace before encountering a pre-defined number of problems (typically 25), the student moves to the next workspace without mastery. This represents an instructional "when to stop" policy to move along students who are unproductively struggling, a relatively crude way to ensure that students don't unproductively struggle for too long. Failure to reach mastery is reported to the teacher so that additional instruction can be provided outside of *MATHia*. Early prediction of when such failures are likely and understanding the best information to provide teachers in such cases are active areas of research (e.g., [1, 3, 5, 11]).

3 Misalignments of Existing Approaches to System Design

Existing operationalizations and models that make predictions of unproductive struggle based on these operationalizations (that a student mastered a single KC vs. unproductively struggled on a KC) suffer from one or more of at least three major misalignments, especially (but not exclusively) in contexts where *MATHia* is used.

First, *mastery and timeliness criteria frequently do not match those of the target systems*. Authors have acknowledged this mismatch as a simplifying assumption to avoid implementing a particular system's mastery criteria [6], but its problematic nature has not been scrutinized, with at least one exception beginning to explore this issue [1]. *MATHia* does not use a "three-in-a-row" criterion to determine mastery, and there is no significance to ten (or 15) opportunities in *MATHia*'s instructional "when to stop" policy. In *ASSISTments* data, Almeda [2] finds that learning often appears to occur after ten opportunities, rendering this cutoff questionable. In *MATHia*, three correct opportunities in a row are sufficient to reach a BKT mastery estimate greater than 0.95 under a broad spectrum of KC parameter values, but it is *neither necessary nor sufficient* for three consecutive correct KC opportunities for that KC to be judged as mastered *at workspace completion*. Table 1 illustrates this using a common set of BKT parameters used in *MATHia*, informed by a data-driven clustering analysis [19].

Table 1. Hypothetical sequence of eleven practice opportunities (1 = correct; 0 = incorrect) with BKT P(mastery) estimates after each opportunity using the following KC parameters [19]: P(initial mastery) = 0.201; P(learn) = 0.19; P(guess) = 0.233; P(slip) = 0.226.

Opportunity:	1	2	3	4	5	6	7	8	9	10	11
Correct?:	1	1	0	1	1	0	1	1	0	1	1
P(mastery)	.56	.84	.69	.90	.97	.93	.98	.996	.989	.997	.999

In Table 1, the student first reaches mastery according to *MATHia*'s implementation of BKT at opportunity five, drops below mastery at opportunity six, and subsequently would be judged to have reached mastery. This sequence (and various subsequences) would be judged as wheel-spinning using three-in-a-row correct within ten opportunities [6] and indeterminate within fifteen opportunities [3].

Second, *efforts ignore "when to stop" policies that may already exist in real-world instructional systems*. *MATHia*'s policy focuses on the number of problems a student has completed (regardless of the mix of KCs practiced by those problems). Students may not begin to receive practice on particular KCs until they have already completed a number of problems in that workspace. Because problems address different subsets of

KCs, the number of opportunities for a KC and the number of problems completed are different. If the goal of a stopping criterion is to reduce time students spend unproductively struggling, then *stopping criteria* should focus directly on *problems*, not KCs, at least in systems like *MATHia*. *MATHia* has policies for when to stop providing further practice on a set of KCs, which are grouped together in workspaces. On-going efforts seek to waste less student time by detecting as early as possible that presenting the student with more *problems*, not KC-opportunities, is unproductive.

Third, *predictive models focus on student-skill/KC level outcomes*. Existing operationalizations are applied (and predictions made) at the student-skill/KC level [1, 3, 5, 6]. Gong and Beck [3] report that, for *Cognitive Tutor*, "the wheel-spinning problem is estimated to affect approximately 25% of student-skill pairs." Relying on this estimate, based on the three-in-a-row within 15 KC-opportunities operationalization, they continue, "25%... of student-skill pairs is a large number of lessons from which the learner gains nothing..." [3, p. 73]. Ignoring instructional complexity (e.g., that KCs are not "lessons" and are clustered in workspaces, unlike in systems like *ASSISTments*) and variance across workspaces and students (e.g., that some students and workspaces have much greater rates of non-mastery than others), makes such summary statements exceedingly problematic.

In the 2018–19 academic year, nearly 300,000 learners completed approximately 3.78 million *MATHia* workspaces that use the described mastery learning regime; there are approximately 300 such workspaces across Grades 6–8, Algebra I-II, and Geometry in *MATHia*. Students failed to master the workspace in approximately 424,000 completions (or $\sim 11.2\%$), but even in these cases there is variability in the proportion of KCs that students manage to master before reaching the maximum number of problems. There is also variability in the rate at which students fail to reach mastery across workspaces, with some having near-zero failure rates while others have rates greater than 20%; high rates are indicative to *MATHia* developers that workspaces ought to be a target for learning engineering improvement efforts.

4 Discussion and On-going/Future Work

KCs measure student knowledge but are often clustered within problems, which are clustered in workspaces that serve as the topical unit of student progress in real-world instructional systems. Operationalizing unproductive struggle based on workspace mastery for *MATHia*, we can focus on timely predictions of failures to reach mastery. Actionable models must predict early enough to provide information upon which instructors (and students) can productively act. Models to alert teachers to likely failures to reach workspace mastery are currently deployed in Carnegie Learning's *Live-Lab* teacher orchestration app; empirical evaluation remains future work.

Modeling unproductive struggle serves various goals and end-users. Developers seek to understand *why* certain learning experiences may be ineffective. Teachers make decisions in classrooms for which different information may be actionable at different times. Future research should explore the usefulness of different modeling approaches for different instructional contexts, systems, and use cases.

Acknowledgements. This work was supported by IES Grant R305A180301 and the National Science Foundation under award The Learner Data Institute (award #1934745). Opinions expressed are those of the authors and do not reflect those of the funding agencies.

References

1. Zhang, C., et al.: Early detection of wheel spinning: comparison across tutors, models, features, and operationalizations. In: Lynch, C.F., et al. (eds.) Proceedings of the 12th International Conference on Educational Data Mining, pp. 468–473. IEDMS (2019)
2. Almeda, M.V.Q.: When practice does not make perfect: differentiating between productive and unproductive persistence. Ph.D. Thesis, Columbia University, New York (2018)
3. Gong, Y., Beck, J.E.: Towards detecting wheel-spinning: future failure in mastery learning. In: Kiczales, G., et al. (eds.) Proceedings of the 2nd ACM Conference on Learning @ Scale, pp. 67–74. ACM, New York (2015)
4. Kai, S., Almeda, M.V., Baker, R.S., Heffernan, C., Heffernan, N.: Decision tree modeling of wheel-spinning and productive persistence in skill builders. J. Educ. Data Min. **10**(1), 36–71 (2018)
5. Käser, T., Klingler, S., Gross, M.: When to stop?: towards universal instructional policies. In: Gašević, D., et al. (eds.) Proceedings of the Sixth International Conference on Learning Analytics & Knowledge, pp. 289–298. ACM, New York (2016)
6. Beck, J.E., Gong, Y.: Wheel-spinning: students who fail to master a skill. In: Lane, H.C., Yacef, K., Mostow, J., Pavlik, P. (eds.) AIED 2013. LNCS (LNAI), vol. 7926, pp. 431–440. Springer, Heidelberg (2013). https://doi.org/10.1007/978-3-642-39112-5_44
7. Ritter, S., Anderson, J.R., Koedinger, K.R., Corbett, A.: Cognitive tutor: applied research in mathematics education. Psychon. Bull. Rev. **14**, 249–255 (2007)
8. Razzaq, L., et al.: The assistment project: blending assessment and assisting. In: Looi, C.K., et al. (eds.) Proceedings of the 12th International Conference on Artificial Intelligence in Education, pp. 555–562. ISO, Amsterdam (2005)
9. Shute, V.J., Ventura, M.: Measuring and Supporting Learning in Games: Stealth Assessment. MIT, Cambridge, MA (2013)
10. Palaoag, T.D., Rodrigo, M.M.T., Andres, J.M.L., Andres, J.M.A.L., Beck, J.E.: Wheel-spinning in a game-based learning environment for physics. In: Micarelli, A., Stamper, J., Panourgia, K. (eds.) ITS 2016. LNCS, vol. 9684, pp. 234–239. Springer, Cham (2016). https://doi.org/10.1007/978-3-319-39583-8_23
11. Holstein, K., McLaren, B.M., Aleven, V.: Intelligent tutors as teachers' aides: exploring teacher needs for real-time analytics in blended classrooms. In: Wise, A., et al. (eds.) Proceedings of the 7th International Learning Analytics and Knowledge Conference, pp. 257–266. ACM (2017)
12. Lee, J.I., Brunskill, E.: The impact of individualizing student models on necessary practice opportunities. In: Yacef, K., et al. (eds.) Proceedings of the 5th International Conference on Educational Data Mining, pp. 119–125. IEDMS (2012)
13. Rollinson, J., Brunskill, E.: From predictive models to instructional policies. In: Santos, O.C., et al. (eds.) Proceedings of the 8th International Conference on Educational Data Mining, pp. 179–186. IEDMS (2015)
14. Bloom, B.S.: Learning for mastery. Eval. Comment **1**(2), 1–12 (1968)
15. Anderson, J.R., Corbett, A.T., Koedinger, K.R., Pelletier, R.: Cognitive tutors: lessons learned. J. Learn. Sci. **4**(2), 167–207 (1995)

16. Pane, J.F., Griffin, B.A., McCaffrey, D.F., Karam, R.: Effectiveness of cognitive tutor algebra I at scale. Educ. Eval. Policy Anal. **36**(2), 127–144 (2014)
17. Corbett, A.T., Anderson, J.R.: Knowledge tracing: modeling the acquisition of procedural knowledge. User-Model. User-Adapt. Interact. **4**, 253–278 (1995)
18. Goldin, I., Pavlik Jr., P.I., Ritter, S.: Discovering domain models in learning curve data. In: Sottilare, R.A., et al. (eds.) Design Recommendations for Intelligent Tutoring Systems: Volume 4 - Domain Modeling, pp. 115–126. U.S. Army Research Laboratory, Orlando (2016)
19. Ritter, S., Harris, T.K., Nixon, T., Dickison, D., Murray, R.C., Towle, B.: Reducing the knowledge tracing space. In: Barnes, T., et al. (eds.) Proceedings of the 2nd International Conference on Educational Data Mining, pp. 151–160. IEDMS (2009)

What Happens When Gamification Ends?

Miguel García Iruela[1]([⊠]), Manuel J. Fonseca[2], Raquel Hijón-Neira[1],
and Teresa Chambel[2]

[1] Universidad Rey Juan Carlos, Móstoles, Spain
{miguel.garciai, raquel.hijon}@urjc.es
[2] LASIGE, Facultade de Ciências, Universidade de Lisboa, Lisbon, Portugal
{mjfonseca, mtchambel}@ciencias.ulisboa.pt

Abstract. Nowadays, the application of typical game elements in non-ludic environments has been extended. Gamification has become a very interesting resource to promote engagement and participation in a wide variety of areas including education. For this reason, researchers are increasingly interested in the study of gamification. There are many papers related to the impact that this methodology has on the student's motivation, engagement or satisfaction. The aim of this paper is to analyze four aspects: "Pressure/tension", "Perceived choice", "Perceived competence" and "Effort/importance". The first part of the study analyzes the aspects at two weeks between a test group and a control group. The second part is even more novel, because it analyzes the aspects when the test group is no longer gamified. Most studies focus on what happens when gamifying, but not when a group of students stops gamifying. The results obtained will serve to advance a part of the knowledge about gamification.

Keywords: Gamification · Pressure · Tension · Perceived choice · Perceived competence · Effort · Importance

1 Introduction

Recently, [1] pointed out that gamification research is maturing, transitioning from fundamental "what?" and "why?" questions to more differentiated questions about the implementation of gamification: "how?", "when?", and "how and when not?". In our case, we also encountered a problem without addressing it today in the studies, for example in education, students are analyzed before and during the experience, but not after. In this study, we want to analyze what happens among students when they are no longer gamified, specifically, we analyze 4 aspects: "Pressure/tension", "Perceived choice", "Perceived competence", "Effort/importance".

Motivation has been studied in numerous papers such as [2, 3]. If we focus on education, we find for example [4], that is about the impact of intrinsic and extrinsic motivation on the participation and performance of undergraduate students in an online gamified learning intervention or [5] which investigated the effects of external rewards on fifth graders' motivation, engagement and learning while playing an educational game.

After a review of the articles published in recent years, we hardly find any reference to the moment when gamification stops. For example, in the review [6] that discusses

© Springer Nature Switzerland AG 2020
I. I. Bittencourt et al. (Eds.): AIED 2020, LNAI 12164, pp. 98–102, 2020.
https://doi.org/10.1007/978-3-030-52240-7_18

"how the effectiveness is influenced when the implementation of Gamification in enterprises is stopped", mentions [7], a study that examines patterns of user activity in an enterprise's social network service after the removal of a points-based incentive system. The results of [7] reveal that the removal of the incentive scheme did reduce overall participation. Therefore, we have found a lack of research in motivation at the time that gamification stops in all the areas, including education.

2 Method

The study was conducted in the first semester at the University of Lisbon as part of the database subject. The subject had two weekly sessions, a theoretical-practical session and a practice session. The experience that has been analyzed is about a Moodle course parallel to those face-to-face sessions, over 4 weeks. The course was about the Entity Relationship (ER) and the relational models. In order to encourage student participation, both the test group and the control group were rewarded with part of the final grade if they participated.

Students in this subject are in the second year of computer engineering. Most of the students were men of an approximate age of 20 years. The subject had 200 students, of which 190 were registered. Then, 169 registered students completed the tasks and the survey of the first two weeks. The last two weeks, 113 students completed the experience, so there were 77 dropouts. Due to dropouts, the sample of students in the first survey was larger than in the second. The separation of the students was random, neither sex nor age was considered, since they were mostly men of an approximate age of 20 years.

The students had access to the course out of the hours of the sessions of the subject. The students were divided into two groups. The first group began gamified while the second group was the control group. Both groups had the same tasks to perform. It is intended to analyze what happens when a group of students ceases to be gamified, therefore, after two weeks, the test group ceases to be gamified. In addition to being able to contrast the changes that occur from gamified to non-gamified vs non-gamified to gamified, the control group became gamified at two weeks.

Each week the students had a series of tasks to perform. At the end of the second week and at the end of the fourth week the students conducted a survey. These surveys were the ones that provided us with the data on the aspects to be analyzed. The two tests are based on IMI [8]. Due to the incremental R for each element above 4 for any given factor being quite small [8], we put 4 or more questions for each aspect. "Pressure/tension", "Perceived choice" and "Perceived competence" are measured using 5 questions and "Effort/importance" with 4. Each question had to be answered using a Likert scale from 1 (not at all true) to 7 (completely true).

For the course gamification, different elements have been used that are within the dynamics, mechanics and components of the gamification [9]. For the inclusion of the elements in Moodle, a plug-in called GameMo [10] has been used. The list of elements is as follows: feedback, badges, points, levels, leaderboard, time Limit, locked content and missions

All these elements were used in order to provide a gamified experience within the course of the Moodle platform used. Additionally, each student could see their profile picture, their level, their experience and the experience needed to access the next level on the main page of the course.

3 Results

As mentioned in previous sections, "Pressure/tension", "Perceived choice", "Perceived competence" and "Effort/importance" have been measured using IMI [8] with a scale from 1 (not at all true) to 7 (completely true). In Table 1 we can see the results obtained both in the test and in the control group in the first and second questionnaires.

Table 1. Four aspects evaluated.

	Pressure/tension		Perceived choice		Perceived competence		Effort/importance	
	Avg	σ	Avg	σ	Avg	σ	Avg	σ
Test group 1st	3.40	1.66	4.15	1.63	4.28	1.35	4.44	1.77
Control group 1st	3.56	1.74	4.10	1.73	3.95	1.24	4.38	1.72
Test group 2nd	3.60	1.56	4.03	1.64	3.95	1.24	4.27	1.58
Control group 2nd	3.61	1.63	3.82	1.74	3.94	1.20	4.16	1.61

There is a small difference between both groups in all the factors in the first test. Except for pressure, which is a negative aspect, the test group has a little bit higher rating in all aspects. In the second test, the assessment of the aspects was reduced in both groups except the pressure. The differences between both groups in Pressure and perceived competence in the second test were reduced, while the effort/importance and perceived choice were extended.

At the first test it is possible to see very close values in all the sections between the two groups, except for a wider difference in "Perceived competence". If we analyze using the t-test, we obtain a significant difference in this aspect when comparing the first test of both groups.

In the second test, if we apply the t-test, we observe that only the differences in "Perceived choice" are relevant to have a p-value below 0.05 and "Effort/importance" is close to being significant with a 0.06. Both values are those in which the control group has less valuation.

In the previous data we can see a decrease in both groups in all aspects except in "Pressure/tension" which is considered negative, it undergoes an increase between the first test and the second. The decrease in "Pressure/tension" and "perceived competence" is greater in the test group, while in the rest of the aspects it is higher for the control group. If we apply t-test we did not find significant differences.

4 Conclusions

The objective of this study is to analyze 4 aspects: "Pressure/tension", "Perceived choice", "Perceived competence" and "Effort/importance" of the students when the students cease to be gamified. This study has been carried out at the University of Lisbon with students in the second year of computer science engineering. A test group and a control group have been used to contrast the results obtained.

The first test carried out at two weeks, revealed that there were no significant differences between the gamified group and the control group, except in the aspect of perceived competence. The similarity may be due to the novelty produced by the Moodle course to students regardless of the methodology. In the second test, it reflects a reduction in the positive aspects and an increase in "Pressure Tension" both in the test group and in the control group, but without having significant differences in all aspects in both groups. This small reduction may be due to the loss of the novelty effect among the students mentioned above.

If we focus on the change that occurs between the first test and the second one where the experimental group is no longer gamified, a decrease in all aspects is detected. However, this also occurs in the control group, so it is not possible to identify, in this experience, that the cessation of gamification has affected students.

Therefore, we can conclude that in our experiment no significant differences were found in the 4 aspects analyzed when students stop gamifying. As future work, there is a possibility of studying the effects after stopping gamification in experiences of longer duration or focusing on specific elements of gamification.

Acknowledgment. This work was supported by Ministerio de Economa y Competitividad (TIN2015-66731-C2-1-R), Rey Juan Carlos University (30VCPIGI15), the LASIGE Research-Unit (UIDB/00408/2020 & UIDP/00408/2020), and Madrid Regional Government, through the project e-MadridCM (P2018/TCS-4307). The e-Madrid-CM project is also co-financed by the Structural Funds(FSE and FEDER).

References

1. Nacke, L.E., Deterding, S.: The maturing of gamification research. Comput. Hum. Behav. **71**, 450–454 (2017)
2. Feng, Y., Jonathan Ye, H., Yu, Y., Yang, C., Cui, T.: Gamification artifacts and crowdsourcing participation: examining the mediating role of intrinsic motivations. Comput. Hum. Behav. **81**, 124–136 (2018)
3. van Roy, R., Zaman, B.: Unravelling the ambivalent motivational power of gamification: a basic psychological needs perspective. Int. J. Hum.-Comput. Stud. **127**, 38–50 (2019)
4. Buckley, P., Doyle, E.: Gamification and student motivation. Interact. Learn. Environ. **24**(6), 1161–1175 (2014)
5. Filsecker, M., Hickey, D.T.: A multilevel analysis of the effects of external rewards on elementary students' motivation, engagement and learning in an educational game. Comput. Educ. **75**, 136–148 (2014)

6. Khaleel, F.L., Ashaari, N.S., Tengku Wook, T.S.M., Ismail, A.: User-enjoyable learning environment based on gamification elements. In: 2015 International Conference on Computer, Communications, and Control Technology (I4CT), pp. 221–226, Kuching, Malaysia (2015)
7. Thom, J., Millen, D., DiMicco, J.: Removing gamification from an enterprise SNS. In: Proceedings of the ACM 2012 Conference on Computer Supported Cooperative Work, pp. 1067–1070, Seattle, Washington, USA (2012)
8. Ryan, R.M.: Intrinsic motivation inventory (IMI) (2006). http://selfdeterminationtheory.org/intrinsic-motivation-inventory/. Accessed 25 Feb 2020
9. Werbach, K., Hunter, D.: For the Win: How Game Thinking Can Revolutionize Your Business. Wharton Digital Press, Harrisburg (2012)
10. García-Iruela, M., Hijón-Neira, R.: Proposal of a management interface for gamified environments in Moodle. In: Proceedings of 2018 International Symposium on Computers in Education (SIIE), Jerez, Spain (2018)

Using Eye-Tracking and Click-Stream Data to Design Adaptive Training of Children's Inhibitory Control in a Maths and Science Game

Andrea Gauthier[1]([✉])[iD], Kaśka Porayska-Pomsta[1][iD], Denis Mareschal[2][iD], and The UnLocke Project Team

[1] Knowledge Lab, Institute of Education, University College London, London WC1N 3QS, UK
{andrea.gauthier,k.porayska-pomsta}@ucl.ac.uk
[2] Department of Psychological Sciences, Birkbeck College University of London, London WC1E 7HX, UK
d.mareschal@bbk.ac.uk

Abstract. Computerised educational neuroscience interventions that train within-domain inhibitory control (IC) can improve children's counterintuitive reasoning. However, the HCI or adaptive design of such environments often receive less attention. Eye-tracking and click data were used to compare four versions of an IC-training game in terms of their HCI design and potential for supporting adaptive feedback. Our results provide insights for developing an adaptive system to scaffold pupils' transition towards using IC in un-cued, self-regulated scenarios.

Keywords: Inhibitory control · Counterintuitive reasoning · Educational neuroscience · Game-based learning · Adaptive support

1 Introduction

Inhibitory control (IC) belongs to a set of cognitive skills, known as "executive functions", that are foundational to self-regulated learning (SRL) [1,9,18]. IC is key to maths and science learning where inhibition of pre-existing beliefs or superficial perceptions is necessary for learning and applying counterintuitive knowledge [7,13,14]. There is a keen interest in understanding IC as a component of SRL and in applying Educational Neuroscience (EdN) insights to educational practice. While it is standard to computerise EdN interventions, many of these ignore key principles and methods at the intersection of HCI and AIED. We argue that such principles may be critical to a successful delivery of EdN interventions.

We present work conducted as part of an EdN-focused project (funded by the Wellcome Trust and Education Endowment Foundation), in which we developed a trivia game-based environment for children to train IC skills through exercising "stop and think" behaviours on counterintuitive concepts in science

I. I. Bittencourt et al. (Eds.): AIED 2020, LNAI 12164, pp. 103–108, 2020.
https://doi.org/10.1007/978-3-030-52240-7_19

and maths [16]. Our work examines the relationship between the delivery of diverse visual prompts, their interference with in-game cognitive tasks, and how such interference can be remedied adaptively to promote IC. As such, this work explicitly bridges EdN, HCI and AIED research.

2   Stop & Think IC-Training Environment

"Stop & Think" (*S&T*) is a trivia game-based learning environment that gives children, aged 7–10, structured opportunities to exercise IC on counterintuitive maths and science concepts [16]. The game has two modes: **(1)** TV-trivia show mode where a host character presents quiz questions, while three virtual contestants articulate the reasoning behind their answers through speech bubbles; **(2)** active engagement mode that trains IC by having pupils pause for a few seconds (henceforth–the *S&T mechanic*) before allowing them to answer each question, to encourage them to suppress intuitive thinking and adopt counterintuitive (but correct) concepts. A teacher-led version of this non-adaptive software was evaluated with 6672 children from 89 schools in England. Children played S&T as a whole class for 12 min., 3×/week, for 10 weeks, with a teacher acting as facilitator. The study revealed that training IC in this way improved counter-intuitive reasoning and standardised exam scores [16]. We now investigate how the following HCI features might enhance S&T's IC training in a SRL scenario:

1. **Mandatory interaction: indication of readiness.** In line with the theory of planned behaviour [3], an interaction mechanic where pupils must indicate their readiness to answer, may promote IC through metacognitive awareness.
2. **Pre-attentive cues: motion and colour.** Pre-attentive cues are processed by our visual systems prior to conscious attention to guide gaze [15]. Persistent motion may consistently grab attention [4,15]. Colour has culturally relevant meanings [15,17] that might guide attention, e.g. through the traffic light metaphor for "stop and go" types of activities [10].
3. **Game mechanics: reward systems.** Tangible rewards relay performance information, which may promote IC and metacognitive competencies [8,12]. Penalties create a sense of risk and contextualise the value of rewards [8,11], potentially assisting IC training by motivating pupils to stop and think longer to improve performance and earn greater rewards.

Four versions of S&T implement the above features (Fig. 1): **Condition A** (baseline) uses pulsating motion of a "Stop & Think" icon for four seconds during the S&T mechanic. The screen is 'locked' during this time, then the icon disappears and the screen becomes interactive. **Condition B** builds on A, adding mandatory interaction before the pupil can submit their answer. After the four-second thinking time, the pulsating icon is replaced by a button that reads "I'm ready to answer!". Once pressed, the screen becomes interactive. **Condition C** also includes the mandatory interaction, but uses colour instead of motion to prompt IC behaviour. The common analogy of traffic lights is used on the S&T icon to represent (1) "Stop" (red) during question narration; (2) "Think"

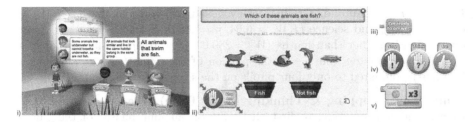

Fig. 1. (i) Game-show mode: contestants express their reasoning; (ii) Task mode: pulsating S&T icon (Condition A–B); (iii) "I'm ready to answer" button (Conditions B–D); (iv) Traffic-light S&T icons (Conditions C–D); (v) Scoreboard (Condition D). (color figure online)

(amber) during the S&T mechanic (the "I'm ready" button pops beside the icon after four seconds); and (3) "Go" (green) when interaction is allowed (after the button is pressed). **Condition D** builds on C by integrating simple rewards (tokens for correct answers) and penalties (loss of bonus multiplier).

3   Study Design and Results

The efficacy of these four conditions at guiding IC was evaluated with children from two English primary schools. We used eye-tracking and click data to investigate which HCI design features encouraged the most consistent IC behaviour, then used these findings to suggest how the game might adapt to support IC.

Participants. 45 participants (19 girls and 26 boys), aged 7–8, were randomised across conditions (11 in Conditions A, B, D; 12 in Condition C).

Procedure. Each pupil's participation lasted about 30 min, including an introduction, randomisation, eye-tracker calibration, 2-min video tutorial on how to play, and 12-min playtime. The eye-tracking station was set up on a laptop running Tobii Pro Studio with compact eye-tracker, in a quiet room.

Measures. Interaction (in-game performance, time spent stopping and thinking) and eye-tracking (fixation duration on areas of interest $-AoI$) data were analysed using Kruskal-Wallis (KW), Wilcoxon signed rank (W), Bonferroni-adjested Mann-Whitney U (U, for pair-wise comparisons), and Spearman correlations (rho). In Tobii Studio, recordings were parsed into four scenes for each task attempt, based on phases of interaction relevant to IC training: (1) Question narration, (2) Mandatory S&T time (first four seconds after narration), (3) Voluntary S&T time (after first four seconds, before "I'm ready" button is pressed), and (4) Activity (while they complete the task). AoI were set for (i) answer-objects (image/number options), (ii) question text box, and (iii) S&T icon. Fixation data were tallied for narration, mandatory, and voluntary S&T phases; as Condition A did not have a voluntary S&T phase, fixations were inevitably lower in this group, so they were excluded from fixation analyses.

In-game Performance. Groups achieved similar scores in maths ($KW = 0.35$, $p = .951$) and science ($KW = 6.64$, $p = .084$). Science scores were generally slightly higher than maths ($W = 280.00$, $p = .081$). 17/45 participants earned a score of zero on the maths portion of the game (simple addition of fractions), compared to only four pupils on the science (fish vs. mammals).

Time Spent Stopping & Thinking (S&T Time). The average total S&T time is the sum of "time to first click" during all four phases of the game, and averaged out over all science/maths tasks. There was no difference across conditions ($KW = 5.29$, $p = .151$) and no relationship between S&T time and performance ($rho = -0.10$, $p = .531$) in maths tasks. Pupils struggled with maths, averaging 28.04 s ($SD = 21.01$) of S&T time. This is much longer than in science ($W = 130.00$, $p < .001$), where pupils averaged 15.72 s ($SD = 4.38$), with a positive relationship between S&T time and in-game performance ($rho = 0.48$, $p = .001$). There was an effect of condition for science ($KW = 11.71$, $p = .008$): Conditions B ($U = -15.27$, $p = .038$), C ($U = -14.81$, $p = .041$), and D ($U = -16.55$, $p = .019$) had longer S&T times than A.

Question Box AoI Fixations. Fixations were similar across groups in both maths ($KW = 0.69$, $p = .709$) and science tasks ($KW = 1.38$, $p = .502$).

Answer Objects AoI Fixations. There was an effect of condition in science ($KW = 9.097$, $p = .011$). Condition C averaged greater fixation duration ($U = 12.470$, $p = .008$) than D. Overall, fixations in maths (5.89 s, $SD = 7.92$) and science (5.63 s, $SD = 2.99$) were similar ($W = 635.00$, $p = .185$).

S&T Icon AoI Fixations. There were no differences between conditions in maths ($KW = 3.50$, $p = .174$) or science ($KW = 3.50$, $p = .174$).

4   Discussion and Conclusions

To inform the design of adaptive support in the context of domain-specific IC training, this study explored how HCI design decisions impacted children's in-game IC behaviours along with their performance. We found that **(1)** long S&T times could either be indicative of IC behaviour (as seen in science tasks, in line with the literature [5,16]) or of confusion (as seen in maths); **(2)** mandatory interaction (i.e. "I'm ready" button) resulted in increased S&T time, supporting the hypothesis that integrating a mechanic that allows pupils to indicate their readiness to answer may encourage planning of interactions [3]; **(3)** Symbolic colour and motion were both effective at promoting IC (B and C generated similar S&T times and fixations on answer objects); and **(4)** Rewards/penalties did not impact behaviours, perhaps because the scoring mechanic did not provide feedback on the IC behaviour itself. Feedback is crucial for meta-learning [2], so future research should consider using more informative displays (like open learner models) to promote reflective thinking [6]. Our results also indicate three aspects of the game that might be adapted to support IC behaviours and aid children in transitioning to un-cued SRL scenarios: **(i)** mandatory S&T time, based on the player's average S&T time together with answer correctness as a measure to calibrate the optimal thinking time; **(ii)** difficulty of the content or level of support given to the pupil, but the system should differentiate between meaningful IC behaviour (as observed in science) and being 'lost' (maths); and **(iii)** visual cues (e.g. S&T icon), which might be scaffolded away once pupils display consistent IC behaviour. This work examined the links between delivery of the diverse visual prompts, their interference with in-game cognitive tasks, and how such interference can be remedied adaptively within a SRL game to promote IC, to explicitly bridge EdN, HCI, and AIED research.

References

1. Allan, N.P., Hume, L.E., Allan, D.M., Farrington, A.L., Lonigan, C.J.: Relations between inhibitory control and the development of academic skills in preschool and kindergarten: a meta-analysis. Dev. Psychol. **50**(10), 2368 (2019)
2. Askew, S., Lodge, C.: Gifts, ping-pong and loops? Linking feedback and learning. In: Askew, S. (ed.) Feedback For Learning, pp. 1–17 (2004)
3. Ajzen, I.: From intentions to actions: a theory of planned behavior. In: Kuhl, J., Beckmann, J. (eds.) Action Control. SSSSP, pp. 11–39. Springer, Heidelberg (1985). https://doi.org/10.1007/978-3-642-69746-3_2
4. Bartram, L., Ware, C., Calvert, T.: Moticons: detection, distraction and task. Int. J. Hum.? Comput. Stud. **58**(5), 515–545 (2003)
5. Brookman-Byrne, A., Mareschal, D., Tolmie, A.K., Dumontheil, I.: Inhibitory control and counterintuitive science and maths reasoning in adolescence. PLoS ONE **13**(6), 1–19 (2018)
6. Bull, S., Mangat, M., Mabbott, A., Abu Issa, A., Marsh, J.: Reactions to inspectable learner models: seven year olds to university students. In: Workshop on Learner Modelling for Reflection, International Conference on Artificial Intelligence in Education, AIED 2005, pp. 1–10 (2005)
7. Diamond, A., Lee, K.: Interventions shown to aid executive function development in children 4 to 12 years old. Science **333**, 959–964 (2011)
8. Gee, J.P.: What Video Games Have to Teach Us About Learning and Literacy. Palgrave MacMillan, London (2007)
9. Jacob, R., Parkinson, J.: The potential for school-based interventions that target executive function to improve academic achievement: a review. Rev. Educ. Res. **85**(4), 512–552 (2015)
10. Jung, T., Huang, J., Eagan, L., Oldenburg, D.: Influence of school-based nutrition education program on healthy eating literacy and healthy food choice among primary school children. Dev. Psychol. **57**(2), 67–81 (2019)
11. Juul, J.: Fear of failing? The many meanings of difficulty in video games. In: Wolf, M.J.P., Perron, B. (eds.) The Video Game Theory Reader, vol. 2, pp. 237–252 (2009). https://doi.org/10.1017/CBO9781107415324.004
12. Proulx, J.N., Romero, M., Arnab, S.: Learning mechanics and game mechanics under the perspective of self-determination theory to foster motivation in digital game based learning. Simul. Gaming **48**(1), 81–97 (2017)
13. Rousselle, L., Palmers, E., Noel, M.P.: Magnitude comparison in preschoolers: what counts? Influence of perceptual variables. J. Exp. Child Psychol. **87**(1), 57–84 (2004)

14. Stavy, R., Babai, R.: Overcoming intuitive interference in mathematics: insights from behavioral, brain imaging and intervention studies. ZDM **42**(6), 621–633 (2010)
15. Ware, C.: Information Visualization: Perception for Design. Elsevier Inc., Amsterdam (2013)
16. Wilkinson, H.R., et al.: Learning mechanics and game mechanics under the perspective of self-determination theory to foster motivation in digital game based learning. J. Cogn. Enhanc. **48**(1), 81–97 (2019). https://doi.org/10.1007/s41465-019-00161-4
17. Wong, B.: Points of view: color coding. Nat. Methods **7**(8), 538 (2010)
18. Zelazo, P.D., Blair, C.B., Willoughby, M.T.: Executive function: implications for education. In: NCER (2016)

Prediction of Group Learning Results from an Aggregation of Individual Understanding with Kit-Build Concept Map

Yusuke Hayashi[✉], Toshihiro Nomura, and Tsukasa Hirashima

Graduate School of Advanced Science and Engineering, Hiroshima University,
Higashihiroshima, Japan
hayashi@lel.hiroshima-u.ac.jp

Abstract. With the development of information and communication technology, we can collect and analyze a variety of data for optimization. It is expected that the prediction of learning with the data enables a deep reflection for enhancing the learning experience. This paper describes a method to predict the group learning results from aggregation of an individual's understanding with the Kit-build concept map (KBmap). KBmap is a reconstruction-type concept map with automated diagnosis of the content. To test this method, we examined the prediction results from the data collected from a classroom lesson. The results show that most of the actual results are in good agreement with the prediction, and the comparison between the actual results and the predictions could be useful for the teacher.

Keywords: Concept map · Kit-build · Collaborative learning · Prediction

1 Introduction

In recent years, the forms of learning in schools have diversified, for example in the form of lectures, collaborative learning, and problem-based learning. In addition, with the evolving learning forms, the role of teachers in the classroom has changed from instructors who impart knowledge to the students to a facilitator for management of learning [1–3].

This study provides an environment for students to work collaboratively with concept maps [10] and for teachers to monitor their interactions. Network analysis analyzes the network structures, including actor-actor (social) network as well as actor-artifact networks. Matsuzawa et al. [8] propose a tool for exploring the network structure of collaborative learning discourses.

Here, we propose a method to predict group learning results from the initial understanding of the members of the group based on a Kit-build concept map [6, 7, 11]. In this method, each student creates a concept map as their initial understanding of the subject. While learning as a group, students compare their concept maps and construct a kit-build concept map representing a consented understanding of what they have learned. The prediction shows the possibilities of the resulting concept maps from the understanding of students at the beginning of the group learning based on the patterns

© Springer Nature Switzerland AG 2020
I. I. Bittencourt et al. (Eds.): AIED 2020, LNAI 12164, pp. 109–113, 2020.
https://doi.org/10.1007/978-3-030-52240-7_20

of individual understanding [4, 5, 9]. This paper also demonstrates an example of the prediction result of data from an actual lesson.

2 Kit-Build Concept Map

The kit-build concept map can provide a guideline for internalizing given information and a method to evaluate it. The kit-build concept map enables students to organize their understanding by reconstruction of the reference concept map called "goal map", and the teacher can assess students' concept maps by their automatic comparison with the reference concept map.

Figure 1 shows the goal map, and a kit made from the goal map in this study. Links and nodes connected to the central topic of the kit were not separated as the basic structure showed the viewpoints to create this map. The viewpoints represented by the connected nodes were "nature," "industry," and "culture." The task of the students for creating a map was to organize the instances of the viewpoints and to find intersections of the viewpoints.

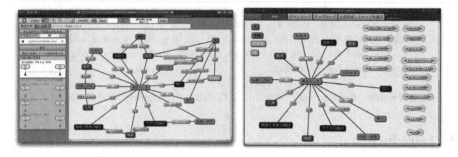

Fig. 1. The goal map and the kit made from the goal map

The KB map system [11] can automatically compare between the maps since the components of the goal map and students map are unified. The comparison may be performed for each proposition, and between students for each link, by comparing the goal map, to realize the group result prediction function. Proposition, which is determined from the above-described problems of group activities, becomes a goal map. Individual maps represent the understanding of each member of the group in the beginning of the learning process. The classification between the propositions, such as "the same proposition as the goal map (GM)," "different proposition from the GM," and "no opinion" is obtained by comparing the individual maps and the goal map. Then, it is possible to aggregate a combination thereof or matching rate for each group.

3   Prediction of the Group Learning Results

Table 1 shows the classification of the proposition made by individuals in the group and pattern them. The propositions are categorized into three types based on the link between concepts: the same propositions as the reference map (the link connects the same concepts as the reference map), different propositions from the reference map (the link connects the different concepts from the reference map), and incomplete propositions (the link does not connect any concepts). For example, in pattern A, all the members have the same proposition as the reference concept map. By contrast, in patterns D–G, there is a conflict of propositions in the group.

Table 1. Proposition patterns in a group

Pattern	Same as the GM	Different from the GM	No opinion
A	Exist	Non-existent	Non-existent
B	Non-existent	Exist	Non-existent
C	Non-existent	Non-existent	Exist
D	Exist	Exist	Non-existent
E	Exist	Non-existent	Exist
F	Non-existent	Exist	Exist
G	Exist	Exist	Exist

We can anticipate the shared understanding of each proposition from the patterns of propositions in the group. The basic rules of prediction in this study are straightforward. If anyone in a group makes a proposition with a link, they select the proposition as their decision. However, if no one has any proposition with a link, they create a correct or wrong proposition or do not create any proposition. For example, in pattern A, their result is uniquely decided into the correct proposition. However, in pattern D, they can create a correct or incorrect proposition.

The proposed prediction calculates the maximum and the minimum result from the proposition patterns in the group. The maximum result occurs when the students in a group choose only correct propositions. The minimum result occurs when they choose some wrong propositions even if a single member in the group has opted for some correct propositions. In the patterns D or G, the maximum result is derived when they choose the correct proposition, and the minimum score is derived when they choose the wrong proposition.

4   Experimental Application to the Lesson Data

This study used the data from a lesson where a total of 70 people from two classes in the second grade of junior high school participated. These lessons were taught as one lesson for each class. The topic was the Tohoku region of Japan in geography. The purpose of this lesson was to frame together the knowledge of nature, industry, traditions, and the culture of the Tohoku region as one structure and to make a common background for the discussion on their proposals for the reconstruction of the region in later lessons. Figure 2 shows the basic flow of the lesson.

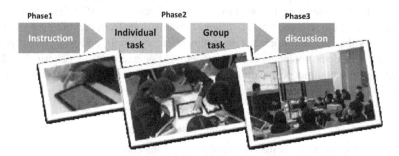

Fig. 2. The basic flow of the lesson.

In this study, we verified the accuracy of the prediction of the group task outcomes. The accuracy is measured by the range of the expected score and its validity. The range is the difference between the possible maximum and the minimum scores calculated from individual maps. The validity is whether the scores of the group maps fall into the predicted ranges.

Figure 3 shows the actual scores of the group results. The triangle indicates the actual group map score. In group A score prediction, the average prediction width was 23%, and the predicted scores were approximately 20 points.

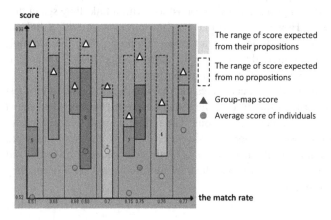

Fig. 3. Prediction of class A (sorted by the match rate)

5   Conclusion and Future Challenges

In this case study, the score of the group activities had 20% width with more than 80% of the group scoring in the range of the predicted score as a result. About 80% of the proposition, even in the detailed analysis, has put the group results with the prediction rules. This shows the validity of the prediction method proposed in this study. In the questionnaire, the teacher pointed out the availability of the prediction graph. The group outcome prediction graph is expected to perform as the representation of the grasping ability of each group and the facilitation of group activities.

Future challenges are the verification of the use of the group outcome prediction function in the classroom by teachers and the learning effect of facilitation of group learning based on the prediction.

References

1. Carey, D.M.: Teacher roles and technology integration: moving from teacher as director to teacher as facilitator. Comput. Sch. **9**(2), 105–118 (1994)
2. Dillenbourg, P., Patrick, J.: Technology for Classroom Orchestration. New Science of Learning, pp. 525–552. Springer, New York (2010). https://doi.org/10.1007/978-1-4419-5716-0_26
3. Grabinger, R.S., Dunlap, J.C.: Rich environments for active learning: a definition. Res. Learn. Technol. **3**(2), 5–34 (1995)
4. Hayashi, Y., Nomura, T., Hirashima, T.: Orchestrating Individual- and group-learning in classroom with kit-build concept mapping. In: Proceedings of AIED2019, pp. 100–104 (2019)
5. Hayashi, Y., Nomura, T., Hirashima, T.: Propositional level analysis of collaborative learning with kit-build concept map. In: Proceedings of the 27th International Conference on Computers in Education (ICCE 2019), vol. 1, pp. 273–281 (2019)
6. Hirashima, T., Yamasaki, K., Fukuda, H., Funaoi, H.: Framework of kit-build concept map for automatic diagnosis and its preliminary use. Res. Pract. Technol. Enhanc. Learn. **10**(1), 1–21 (2015)
7. Yamasaki, K., Fukuda, H., Hirashima, T., Funaoi, H.: Kit-build concept map and its preliminary evaluation. In: Proceedings of ICCE 2010, pp. 290–294 (2010)
8. Matsuzawa, Y., Oshima, J., Oshima, R., Niihara, Y., Sakai, S.: KBDeX: a platform for exploring discourse in collaborative learning. Procedia-Soc. Behav. Sci. **26**, 198–207 (2011)
9. Nomura, T., Hayashi, Y., Suzuki, T., Hirashima, T.: Knowledge propagation in practical use of kit-build concept map system in classroom group work for knowledge sharing. In: Proceedings of ICCE 2014 Workshop, pp. 463–472 (2014)
10. Novak, J.D., Canas, A.J.: The theory underlying concept maps and how to construct them. Technical report IHMC CmapTools (2006)
11. Sugihara, K., et al.: Implementation of kit-build concept map with media tablet. In: Proceedings of WMUTE 2012, pp. 325–327 (2012)

Automatic Classification for Cognitive Engagement in Online Discussion Forums: Text Mining and Machine Learning Approach

Hind Hayati[✉], Mohammed Khalidi Idrissi, and Samir Bennani

Ecole Mohammadia d'Ingénieurs, Université Mohammed V, Rabat, Morocco
hayati.hind@gmail.com

Abstract. For effective learning, students must set learning objectives and adopt the ad hoc cognitive behavior to achieve them. Our research work aims to ensure good scaffolding by offering tutors the opportunity to observe learners' cognitive behaviors, especially their cognitive engagement. In this respect, we propose in the present work an automatic system for classifying learners according to their levels of cognitive engagement. To this end, we focus on the analysis of social interactions within online discussion forums. Hence, the proposed system has two main steps: 1/Learners' vector construction and 2/SVM-based classifier. The results show the efficiency of the proposed system with an accuracy = 0.9 and a cohen's K = 0.89.

Keywords: Text Mining · Machine Learning · Online discussion forum · SVM · Cognitive engagement · Doc2vec · NLP

1 Introduction

The main objective of e-learning platforms is to change the traditional framework of education and make necessary improvements to teaching methods for better learning. However, e-learning remains a complex learning environment in which the learner feels autonomous, isolated, and responsible for his/her educational experience. Therefore, the learner must exhibit enough engagement to counterbalance any other factors resistant to his/her learning. There are three types of engagement: emotional, behavioral, and cognitive. In our work, we toggle the cognitive dimension of engagement since it reveals learners' reflexing and critical thinking. However, the latent nature of engagement and the lack of direct interaction between students and tutors make the prediction of engagement level difficult and challenging (Aleven 2010). Therefore, we focus on the online discussion forum as a tool of asynchronous communication which fosters social interaction.

An online discussion forum is a tool that allows free communication between different participants at any time by keeping track of the various exchanges. Given the degree of learner autonomy during online learning, Larkin-Hein (Larkin-Hein 2001) finds that discussions forum represent a promising way to both achieve emotional attachment and acquire an effective role in the program. Althaus (Althaus 1997) adds that learners learn better through their participation in online discussions because they

© Springer Nature Switzerland AG 2020
I. I. Bittencourt et al. (Eds.): AIED 2020, LNAI 12164, pp. 114–118, 2020.
https://doi.org/10.1007/978-3-030-52240-7_21

are placed in a socio-intellectual environment that encourages active participation, reflection, and equality among different learners.

In our work, we attempt to explore learners' transcripts in order to extract features revealing their cognitive behavior and more especially their level of cognitive engagement. To do that, we propose to automatically classify learners according to cognitive engagement levels based on their social interaction by combining both Text Mining and Machine Learning techniques. We can distinguish four levels of cognitive engagement: **Passive, active, constructive**, and **interactive**.

2 Detecting Learners' Level of Cognitive Engagement

We can't talk about effective and efficient learning without addressing learners' cognitive behavior, particularly their cognitive engagement. This latter reflects the quality and degree of mental effort that a learner can spend during the learning process. Therefore, our main objective is to determine the level of learners' cognitive engagement from their social interactions within discussion forums.

According to ICAP Framework (Chi and Wylie 2014), we can distinguish four levels related to cognitive engagement, namely: **Passive**: for a learner who simply receives the information without analyzing it, interpreting it, or even reacting to it. **Active**: for those who can understand the text, summarize it and focus on what they are learning. **Constructive**: the learner becomes productive and can generate and produce new ideas and construct knowledge. Finally, the **Interactive**, for whom can debate with peers and defend his/her ideas. To automatically classify learners to the four levels above we have two essential phases:

2.1 Learners' Vector Construction

This step is based on feature extraction to model learners and construct vectors. In our system, a learner can be detected by his/her messages categorized according to the cognitive presence phases (Hayati et al. 2019) as well as traces of his/her social interaction within the platform specifically the discussion forum. Therefore, we have two types of attributes:

The Cognitive Presence categorized messages:
For each learner we calculate

- **TE**: number of messages belonging to the Triggering Event phase.
- **EX**: number of messages belonging to the Exploration phase.
- **Int**: number of messages belonging to the Integration phase.
- **Res**: number of messages belonging to the Resolution phase.

The social interaction features:

- **Add_post:** number of added posts.
- **Discussion_view:** number of learner's consultation of the discussions.
- **Thread_count:** number of discussions initiated by the learner.
- **Nbr_peer_interaction:** number of peers interacting with the learner.

- **Nbr_vote:** number of votes collected by the learner.
- **Time_spent:** time spent by the learner in the online forum.

Thus for a learner i we have the vector

$$\overrightarrow{A_i}\left(TE, Ex, Int, Res, Add_{post}, Discussion_{view}, Thread_{count}, Nbr_{peer_{interaction}}, Nbr_{vote}, Time_{spent}\right)$$

2.2 SVM-Based Classifier

This phase relies on the use of SVM as a Machine Learning algorithm for classifying learners as per the four levels of cognitive engagement.

SVM was originally designed for binary classification. Yet, several studies have studied the case of multi-class classification, either by combining binary classifications or by considering all classes at once (Mayoraz and Alpaydm 1999) (Hsu and Lin, n.d.). Indeed, there are two essential approaches, namely "one-vs-one" (OVO) and "one-vs-all" (OVA). OVO consists of definitions for each pair of classes a specific classifier, so, if we have k classes OVO method constructs k(k − 1)/2 classifiers. OVA hinges on constructing for each class a classifier that separates its points from all the others. In fact, if we have k classes OVA approach constructs k classifier.

3 Test and Results

3.1 Data Set Description

To test our system we used data from discussion forum samples of different courses in software engineering. Therefore, to classify learners', we construct a database with all the calculated features whereupon two experts coded according to the four levels of cognitive engagement. The inter-rater agreement was good: percent agreement = 87%. Our data is balanced.

3.2 Training and Testing Phases

After constructing learners-vectors and codding them to the four levels we start the training phase of our SVM classifier after what we will test it and compare in Table 1 accuracy results (classification accuracy, cohen's K, recall precision and f1 score) for the two approaches OVO and OVA.

From the obtained results we can see that the best choice in our context is the OVA approach. To better observe the obtained results, we have detailed the normalized confusion matrix (Fig. 1).

Table 1. Accuracy results for OVA and OVO approaches

	OVA	OVO
F1 Score	**0.90**	0.84
Cohen's K	**0.86**	0.79
Classification Accuracy	**0.90**	0.85
Precision Recall	**0.95**	0.93

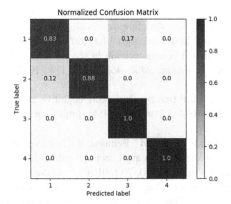

Fig. 1. Normalized Confusion Matrix; 1: passive, 2: active, 3: constructive, 4: interactive

4   General Conclusion

This work sought to explore learners' cognitive engagement within online discussion forums. This later represents a socio-constructivist environment that encourages higher-order thinking behaviors. In fact, this type of asynchronous communication foster conducts like being socially interactive and adding new knowledge constructively. Regarding the literature review, there are four levels of cognitive engagement: Passive, active, constructive, and interactive.

Our research presents a new automated system to predict learners' cognitive engagement while examining their social interactions in online discussion forums and using Text Mining & Machine Learning techniques. These two approaches propose interesting methods for prepossessing text, analyzing data, and discovering knowledge.

Based on a corpus of posts extracted from learners' participation within courses in software engineering offered through an online learning platform, we explore whether the learner is a passive, active, constructive, or interactive participant. The achieved results have demonstrated interesting precision as classification accuracy = 0.9 and Cohen Kappa = 0.89, which shows that the proposed system is very effective with an almost perfect agreement.

Nevertheless, like any other research, there are limitations to this work too. Our approach, focus only on learners' posts in online discussion forums to predict their level of cognitive engagement. Yet, it can be learners who are highly engaged with the course materials even if they never display a good level of cognitive engagement in the discussion forum.

As perspective, we can use our system as an input for the recommended systems. In fact, the reported results can be used to recommend new resources for learners according to their level of engagement.

References

Aleven, V.: Rule-Based Cognitive Modeling for Intelligent Tutoring Systems, pp. 33–62. Springer, Heidelberg (2010). https://doi.org/10.1007/978-3-642-14363-2_3

Althaus, S.L.: Computer-mediated communication in the university classroom: an experiment with on-line discussions. Commun. Educ. **46**(3), 158–174 (1997). https://doi.org/10.1080/03634529709379088

Chi, M.T.H., Wylie, R.: The ICAP framework: linking cognitive engagement to active learning outcomes. Educ. Psychol. **49**(4), 219–243 (2014). https://doi.org/10.1080/00461520.2014.965823

Hayati, H., Chanaa, A., Khalidi Idrissi, M., Bennani, S.: Doc2Vec & Naïve Bayes: learners' cognitive presence assessment through asynchronous online discussion TQ transcripts. Int. J. Emerg. Technol. Learn. (IJET) **14**(08), 70 (2019). https://doi.org/10.3991/ijet.v14i08.9964

Larkin-Hein, T.: On-line discussions: a key to enhancing student motivation and understanding? In: 31st Annual Frontiers in Education Conference. Impact on Engineering and Science Education. Conference Proceedings, F2G-6-F2G-12, 2 May 2001. https://doi.org/10.1109/FIE.2001.963720

Mayoraz, E., Alpaydm, E.: Support Vector Machines for Multi-class Classification (1999). https://www.cmpe.boun.edu.tr/~ethem/files/papers/iwann99.pdf

Explaining Errors in Predictions of At-Risk Students in Distance Learning Education

Martin Hlosta$^{(\boxtimes)}$ iD, Tina Papathoma, and Christothea Herodotou

The Open University, Milton Keynes, UK
{martin.hlosta, tina.papathoma,
christothea.herodotou}@open.ac.uk

Abstract. Despite recognising the importance of transparency and understanding of predictive models, little effort has been made to investigate the errors made by these models. In this paper, we address this gap by interviewing 12 students whose results and predictions of submitting their assignment differed. Following our previous quantitative analysis of 25,000+ students, we conducted online interviews with two groups of students: those predicted to submit their assignment, yet they did not (False Negative) and those predicted not to submit, yet they did (False Positive). Interviews revealed that, in False Negatives, the non-submission of assignments was explained by personal, financial and practical reasons. Overall, the factors explaining the different outcomes were not related to any of the student data currently captured by the predictive model.

Keywords: Learning analytics · At-risk students · Error analysis · Interviews

1 Introduction

Identifying correctly at-risk students has emerged into one of the most prevalent topics in Learning Analytics (LA) and education in general [1]. The identification of at-risk students using Predictive Learning Analytics (PLAs) and followed by a subsequent intervention targeting flagged students (e.g., phone call) could tackle this problem. Many published papers focused on achieving the highest prediction performance, often comparing several learning algorithms. Machine learning models are more likely to exhibit some sort of error hence, the need to understand and explain these errors. In a cross-disciplinary field such as LA, not having the best model could still help understand or even improve student learning. Kitto et al. [2] argued that having imperfect models does not necessarily mean that these should not be deployed. As the LA field is maturing, it becomes essential to understand how models are behaving and how errors occur [3, 4].

Only few studies have examined errors up to now. This paper aims to explain errors in predictions through 12 in-depth interviews with undergraduate online students wrongly predicted as being/not being at risk of failing their next assignment. We treated False Positive (FP) and False Negative (FN) errors separately. Following [5], we refer to FP as students predicted as being at-risk but succeeded, and FN as students that failed despite predicted to succeed. We build on the work of Calvert et al. [6] that

© Springer Nature Switzerland AG 2020
I. I. Bittencourt et al. (Eds.): AIED 2020, LNAI 12164, pp. 119–123, 2020.
https://doi.org/10.1007/978-3-030-52240-7_22

investigated within a single online course why some FP students passed despite predictions showing the opposite and our early quantitative results from [7].

2 Methodology

To analyse the predictive model errors, we used a mixed-methods approach (See Fig. 1). We focused on first year STEM courses and predictions for the first assignment only (A1), when dropout is more likely to happen [8, 9]. The predictions were enhanced by additional data: course context (e.g. the length of the course) and future data from the weeks following the predictions, unknown during the prediction's generation. Predictions for each course were put together in one matrix and only predictions with confidence ≥ 0.85 were selected. A Decision Tree was constructed to distinguish between (1) FP and True Positive (TP) and (2) FN and True Negative (TN).

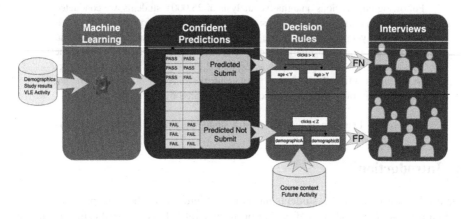

Fig. 1. The schema of the methodology - quantitative analysis followed by interviews.

After getting a favourable opinion from the university's Ethical Committee, we conducted 12 semi-structured interviews with students lasting 20 to 40 min. The interview schedule was developed by two of the authors, piloted with one student, and the analysis followed inter-rater reliability principles. Students were not new to the university, assuming that they would have devised strategies on how to successfully complete their assignment without accessing the Virtual Learning Environment (VLE). Gift vouchers were offered. We grouped participants to (a) students predicted to submit yet they did not submit (FN; N = 7) and (b) students predicted not to submit yet they submitted (FP; N = 5). Following other published work [10], we analysed students as individual case studies creating a distinct profile picture for each student. The following themes emerged from the thematic analysis [11]: motivations for taking the module, studying patterns, reasons for not submitting the assignment, factors that helped or hindered submission, tutor contact, student contact, recommendations for other students so that they submit and proposed module changes. We then plotted this information on a table and identified similarities and differences within and between the two cohorts of students[1].

3   Results

3.1   Quantitative Analysis

Considering the predictions two weeks before the deadline of A1, we analysed 38,073 predictions in 17 courses in 62 presentations between 2017–2019, having 29,247 students (383 FP, 1,507 FN, 2,671 TP and 33,512 TN). The ROC AUC over all predictions was 0.8897. For confident Not Submit predictions, the decision tree classified correctly 50.91% of the FP errors with 75.29% precision (195 students). The strongest attribute was the number of clicks one week before the deadline of the first assignment (confidence 0.82). For the confident Submit predictions, the model distinguished 18.73% of the FN errors with precision 68.73% (1,036 students). The strongest attribute related to a dramatic decrease in students' activity in the last week before assignment 1 (A1) in courses with high activity (confidence 0.83). Both types of errors were associated with a change of student activity after the predictions were generated, and it is worth further examination.

3.2   Qualitative Analysis

Participants (see Table 1) were older than those invited to take part in the study, more successful in their previous courses, female repeating the same course.

Table 1. Invited and interviewed participants – demographic information.

	Age (avg)	Disabled (%)	Female (%)	Previous Pass (%)	Repeat Course (%)	Totals
Invited	38	22	42	64	26	131
Interviewed	45	25	57	70	33	12

FN - Predicted to Submit but did Not Submit: Participants were motivated to study either because they were driven by completing a qualification/degree or out of interest. Their studying patterns were rather random, with no strict schedule. The reasons explaining non-submission were related to family matters/issues (i.e. caring responsibilities), practical issues (i.e. no internet connection at the time of submission) or they were restricted to submit because of student financial issues. FN_2 who took the course out of interest, found it pointless to submit her assignment as it only weighted 7% of the final grade and it was too easy for her. On the contrary, FN_5 found it difficult to

---

[1] The table can be found here: https://docs.google.com/spreadsheets/d/1MwT-luUSl96XYIGhjz24p Xdwbmkn-nLHae9n8gLXiDk .

submit because of her lack of digital skills and absence of detailed guidance. Further, student contact with tutors was minimal and related to requesting an extension to submitting the assignment. FN_11 mentioned that although she contacted her tutor via email, the tutor never replied. Two interviewees reported that their tutor support was helpful with the tutor proactively getting in touch and communicating with them. Interacting with other students was not common for four interviewees. FP_3 reported though that she helped other students and FN_4 used Facebook Groups and forums to communicate socially.

FN students made suggestions for future students to follow the online study guidance and plan ahead for submitting assignments on time. FN_2 who had prior knowledge suggested that assignments should have optional questions for the needs of more advanced students. Two participants would like to have online tutorials with a tutor to guide the assignment submission. FN_5 suggested that the course should be more accessible by adding detailed guidelines on technical aspects for submission. Most participants took the course for the first time apart from one interviewee.

FP - predicted Not to Submit but Submitted: All participants were motivated to take their course in order to get a qualification/degree. Their studying patterns varied mostly studying in the evenings. The reasons they managed to submit related to the fact that this was not the first time they were taking the course. Two of them took the course for the second time. FP_3 was determined to submit as it was their third time taking the course. Two interviewees took the course for the first time. FP_7 on the other hand, did not prepare for the assignment, yet answered the assignment questions as they had some prior knowledge. The other two interviewees submitted after watching videos, consulting books, or with help from external networks.

Contact with tutors was minimal. FP_7 only contacted their tutor for an extension. No interactions with other students were reported. In terms of recommendations, FP_3 suggested that asking for support from their tutor is important although they did not initiate that. FP_8 and FP_9 suggested looking at the VLE material in a timely manner and prepare early on. They proposed more contact with teachers and suggested that audio recordings would be a good addition. Interestingly, the interviewee who was taking the course for the third time, mentioned that assignments should be given more weight towards the final grade. FP_7 suggested that students with prior knowledge or expertise on a topic should be allowed to skip an assignment.

4 Conclusions

None of the predictive errors could be fully explained by only looking at the course data. Errors were explained by factors not currently captured by the university data sets, including personal, technical and financial issues students faced before submission. The factors reported are rather hard to capture automatically and in a timely manner to support students with difficulties. Hence, the role of teachers becomes critical; pastoral and proactive care could identify and resolve such issues on time and enable students to succeed. Existing studies already showcased the significance of teachers' monitoring and intervening with students at risk for better learning outcomes [12]. A university-wide policy accompanied by relevant teachers' training as to when and how teachers should get in touch with their students would ensure that academic connection and social presence are established [13, 14]. Given that we do not gather data from external systems, errors might be hard to prevent in the future. Yet, we could add error explanations especially for students submitting their assignment (e.g. taking the course for a second time).

References

1. Ochoa, X., Merceron, A.: Quantitative and qualitative analysis of the learning analytics and knowledge conference 2018. J. Learn. Anal. 5(3), 154–166 (2018)
2. Kitto, K., Shum, S.B., Gibson, A.: Embracing imperfection in learning analytics. In: Proceedings of the 8th International Conference on Learning Analytics and Knowledge, ACM (2018)
3. Gardner, J., et al.: Modeling and experimental design for MOOC dropout prediction: a replication perspective. In: International Educational Data Mining Society (2019)
4. Taylor, C., Veeramachaneni, K., O'Reilly, U.-M.: Likely to stop? predicting stopout in massive open online courses. arXiv preprint arXiv:1408.3382 (2014)
5. Archer, E., Prinsloo, P.: Speaking the unspoken in learning analytics: troubling the defaults. Assess. Eval. Higher Educ. 1, 1–13 (2019)
6. Calvert, C., Hilliam, R.: Student feedback to improved retention: using a mixed-methods approach to extend specific feedback to a generalisable concept. Open Learn. J. Open Dist. e-Learning 34(1), 103–117 (2019)
7. Hlosta, M., et al.: Why predictions of at-risk students are not 100% accurate? showing patterns in false positive and false negative predictions. In: Companion Proceedings of the 10th International Learning Analytics & Knowledge Conference. Frankfurt, Germany 2020 (Accepted)
8. Walker-Gibbs, B., Ajjawim, R., Rowe, E.: Success and failure in higher education on uneven playing fields (2019)
9. Hlosta, M., Zdrahal, Z., Zendulka, J.: Ouroboros: early identification of at-risk students without models based on legacy data. In: Proceedings of the Seventh International Learning Analytics & Knowledge Conference, ACM (2017)
10. Herodotou, C., et al.: Implementing predictive learning analytics on a large scale: the teacher's perspective. In: Proceedings of the Seventh International Learning Analytics & Knowledge Conference (2017)
11. Braun, V., Clarke, V.: Using thematic analysis in psychology. Qualit. Res. Psychol. 3(2), 77–101 (2006)
12. Herodotou, C., et al.: Empowering online teachers through predictive learning analytics. British J. Educ. Technology (2019)
13. Milem, J.F., Berger, J.B.: A modified model of college student persistence: Exploring the relationship between Astin's theory of involvement and Tinto's theory of student departure. J. College Student Dev. 38(4), 387 (1997)
14. Lukosius, V., Pennington, J.B., Olorunniwo, F.O.: How students' perceptions of support systems affect their intentions to drop out or transfer out of college. Rev. High. Educ. Self-Learn. 6(18), 209–221 (2013)

A General Multi-method Approach to Design-Loop Adaptivity in Intelligent Tutoring Systems

Yun Huang[(⊠)], Vincent Aleven, Elizabeth McLaughlin,
and Kenneth Koedinger

Carnegie Mellon University, Pittsburgh, PA 15213, USA
{yunhuanghci, koedinger}@cmu.edu,
{aleven, mimim}@cs.cmu.edu

Abstract. Design-loop adaptivity, which involves data-driven redesign of an instructional system based on student learning data, has shown promise in improving student learning. We present a general, systematic approach that combines new and existing data mining and instructional design methods to redesign intelligent tutors. Our approach is driven by the main goal of identifying knowledge components that are demonstrably difficult for students to learn and to optimize effective and efficient practice of them. We applied this approach to redesigning an algebraic symbolization tutor. Our classroom study with 76 high school freshmen shows that, compared to the original tutor, the redesigned tutor led to higher learning efficiency on more difficult skills, higher learning gain on unscaffolded whole tasks, and more robust transfer to less practiced tasks. Our work provides general guidance for performing design-loop adaptations for continuous improvement of intelligent tutors.

Keywords: Instructional design · Adaptivity · Data mining · Intelligent tutor

1 The Need for a General Data-Driven Redesign Approach

Design-loop adaptivity [1] uses student learning data to drive instructional decision making for design and iterative improvement of a course or system. It is part of a broader set of endeavors of data-driven instruction and learning designs for continuous improvement in classrooms and schools [2–5]. This paper focuses on the context of *intelligent tutoring systems* (ITSs), a widely adopted and proven technology, where empirical research on data-driven redesign and optimization is still lacking. Numerous data mining methods have been demonstrated to improve prediction accuracy using data from fielded ITSs [6–8], but most stop at better predictions without demonstrating whether and how these methods can improve student learning. One reason for a shortage of such "close the loop" experiments may be that there is no good general guidance for how to convert data-mining outcomes into better tutor design. Prior close-the-loop studies [9–11] were often driven by a limited set of methods or narrow redesign features. This paper demonstrates a general, systematic approach that combines new and existing data mining and instructional design methods to redesign ITSs.

© Springer Nature Switzerland AG 2020
I. I. Bittencourt et al. (Eds.): AIED 2020, LNAI 12164, pp. 124–129, 2020.
https://doi.org/10.1007/978-3-030-52240-7_23

We applied this approach to redesign an algebraic symbolization tutor, and provide empirical evidence of its effectiveness through a classroom study comparing the redesigned tutor to the original tutor.

2   Method: How to Use Data to Improve Intelligent Tutors

Our approach focuses on the continuous improvement of ITSs by mining tutor log data collected from previous iterations. It starts with knowledge component (KC) refinement, followed by content and task selection revisions aiming at more effective and efficient practice of KCs. Our process (Table 1) is generalizable to other domains and other ITSs grounded in a KC approach [12] to instructional design.

Table 1. A general multi-method approach to data-driven redesign of ITSs.

Goals	Methods
1 Refine the knowledge component (KC) model	
Identify difficulty factors to split KCs	Difficulty Factor Effect Analysis
Compare hypothesized KC models	AFM prediction and inspection [13]
2 Redesign content	
Estimate opportunities to mastery, under- and over-practice for each KC in the refined model	Probability-Propagation Practice Estimation
Create focused tasks for difficult KCs with better scaffolding and reduce over-practicing easier KCs	Focused Practice Task Design (with dynamic, composition scaffolding)
Add feedback messages to frequent errors	Error analysis [14, 15]
3 Optimize individualized learning	
Optimize student model parameters	Data-tuning BKT parameters [16]
Optimize task selection based on a student model	Task selection simulation [17]

We applied this process to redesigning the *Algebraic Expressions* unit in Mathtutor [18], a free online tutor based on prior instructional design research [19] (Fig. 1). We utilized prior log data from 356 students with 50,279 student steps. We describe our new methods below, and refer readers to prior work for existing methods.

Difficulty Factor Effect Analysis. A difficulty factor (DF) refers to a property that makes some tasks more difficult than other comparable tasks. We first identified a broad set of potential DFs by coding task features hypothesized to impact difficulty (e.g., requiring parentheses or not). Then we ran a regression for each targeted KC to examine the main and interaction effects of potential DFs on performance, controlling for student proficiencies and learning from prior opportunities. These regressions might be viewed as an efficient simplification of LFA [20]. A KC was split by a set of DFs when there was an interaction or by a DF when there was a main effect.

Probability-Propagation Practice Estimation. We estimated the number of opportunities needed for mastery by fitting parameters of a student model (e.g., BKT [21]) to the data and used the parameters to estimate knowledge for each step. We then compared the estimates to actual opportunities to get the over- or under-practice. Instead of simulating many sequences by propagating simulated outcomes [22], we simulate one sequence by propagating the *probability* of succeeding, and use it as weights to update knowledge (i.e., $P(L)_{new} = P(C)P(L|C)_{new} + P(W)P(L|W)_{new}$). The extrapolation of a KC-student sequence stops when $P(L)_{new} \geq .95$, or the extrapolated opportunities reach a threshold (e.g., 20). Our offline experiments showed that our method reached similar estimations as the method in [22] with higher efficiency.

Focused Practice Task Design. We created new focused problems for hard KCs which eliminate interface steps of easier KCs (Fig. 2). These problems aim to reduce under-practicing hard KCs and over-practicing easier KCs, which were prevalent in the original tutor according to our practice estimation. We introduced *composition scaffolding* (inspired by prior work [14, 23, 24]) to break down problems (Fig. 2a), because our method estimated that many opportunities (≥ 58) would be needed to master each difficult KC (two-operator KCs) in the original tutor.

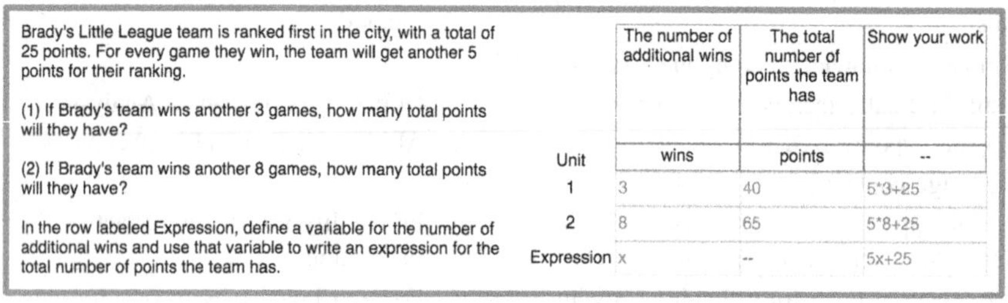

	The number of additional wins	The total number of points the team has	Show your work
Unit	wins	points	--
1	3	40	5*3+25
2	8	65	5*8+25
Expression	x	--	5x+25

Brady's Little League team is ranked first in the city, with a total of 25 points. For every game they win, the team will get another 5 points for their ranking.

(1) If Brady's team wins another 3 games, how many total points will they have?

(2) If Brady's team wins another 8 games, how many total points will they have?

In the row labeled Expression, define a variable for the number of additional wins and use that variable to write an expression for the total number of points the team has.

Fig. 1. A table task in the original tutor (with cells filled in correctly and the toolbar excluded).

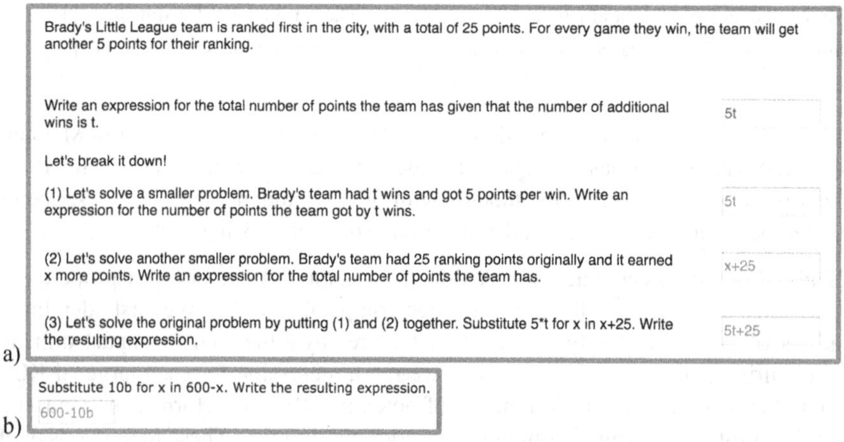

a)

Brady's Little League team is ranked first in the city, with a total of 25 points. For every game they win, the team will get another 5 points for their ranking.

Write an expression for the total number of points the team has given that the number of additional wins is t.   5t

Let's break it down!

(1) Let's solve a smaller problem. Brady's team had t wins and got 5 points per win. Write an expression for the number of points the team got by t wins.   5t

(2) Let's solve another smaller problem. Brady's team had 25 ranking points originally and it earned x more points. Write an expression for the total number of points the team has.   x+25

(3) Let's solve the original problem by putting (1) and (2) together. Substitute 5*t for x in x+25. Write the resulting expression.   5t+25

b)

Substitute 10b for x in 600-x. Write the resulting expression.

600-10b

Fig. 2. Focused tasks target a KC that data reveals is particularly hard. a) A *focused whole task* practices this KC in more realistic problems that require mental steps of easier KCs along with the hard KC. If students fail on the whole task, dynamic composition scaffolding isolates the individual KCs (step 1–3) including the hard one (step 3). b) A *focused part task* practices the hard KC in isolation without the busy work (mental and interface steps) of the easier KCs.

3   Experiment

We conducted a classroom study to investigate whether the data-driven redesigned tutor (treatment condition) yields better learning than the original tutor (control condition). We ran the study in two high school freshman Algebra I classes during three 40-min periods for one week in 2019. Students were randomly assigned to conditions within each class, with 38 students per condition. We used linear mixed models to examine learning gains and two-sample t-tests to examine practice time (Fig. 3).

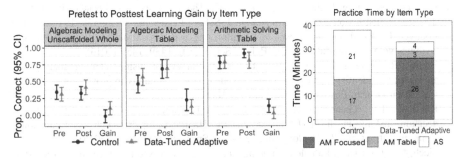

Fig. 3. Redesigned tutor showed advantages in targeted algebraic modeling (AM) skills in terms of learning gains on unscaffolded whole tasks and learning efficiency on table tasks.

Overall, both conditions produced significant learning gains (ps < .01). Students in the treatment condition spent 13% less practice time than students in the control condition (p < .1), with no difference in gains (p = .94). In particular, on more difficult skills, two-operator skills, they spent 19% less time (p < .05) with no difference in gains (p = .78). Treatment students had significant gains on algebraic modeling (AM) in both unscaffolded whole tasks (Fig. 2a without scaffolding steps) and table tasks (Fig. 1) (ps < .05) even with little practice on table tasks. Control students had a significant gain on AM table tasks (p < .001) with no difference from treatment students (p = .14), and no improvement on unscaffolded whole tasks (p = .58) with the gain different from that of treatment students (p < .05). These results suggest that treatment students acquired more robust, transferable learning. Control students had marginally higher gains on arithmetic solving (AS) (p = .096); the treatment condition was designed to shift practice away from these (easier) skills to the harder AM skills.

4   Discussion and Conclusion

We demonstrate a general multi-method approach to design-loop adaptivity and provide empirical evidence of its effectiveness. The results are encouraging, although they are not as pronounced as anticipated. Students spent much less time on the tutor than planned, but our theoretical predictions were based on longer time. Thus, a more stringent test of our approach requires a future longer span study. After all, design-loop adaptivity is intended as an iterative process. Our work provides general guidance for how to convert data-mining outcomes into better tutor design, an important need in AIED/EDM research and practice. Our work may also help define and enhance data-driven learning engineering processes.[1]

References

1. Aleven, V., McLaughlin, E.A., Glenn, R.A., Koedinger, K.R.: Instruction based on adaptive learning technologies. In: Handbook of Research on Learning and Instruction, 2nd edn., pp. 522–560. Routledge, New York (2017)
2. Halverson, R., Grigg, J., Prichett, R., Thomas, C.: The new instructional leadership: creating data-driven instructional systems in school. J. School Leadership **17**(2), 159–194 (2007)
3. Lockyer, L., Heathcote, E., Dawson, S.: Informing pedagogical action: aligning learning analytics with learning design. Am. Behav. Sci. **57**(10), 1439–1459 (2013)
4. Bodily, R., Nyland, R., Wiley, D.: The RISE framework: using learning analytics to automatically identify open educational resources for continuous improvement. Int. Rev. Res. Open Distrib. Learn. **18**(2), 103–122 (2017)
5. Kaufman, T.E., Graham, C.R., Picciano, A.G., Popham, J.A., Wiley, D.: Data-driven decision making in the K-12 classroom. In: Handbook of Research on Educational Communications and Technology, pp. 337–346. Springer, New York (2014)
6. Piech, C., et al.: Deep knowledge tracing. In: Advances in Neural Information Processing Systems, pp. 505–513 (2015)
7. Lindsey, R.V., Khajah, M., Mozer, M.C.: Automatic discovery of cognitive skills to improve the prediction of student learning. In: Advances in Neural Information Processing Systems, pp. 1386–1394 (2014)
8. González-Brenes, J., Huang, Y., Brusilovsky, P.: General features in knowledge tracing to model multiple subskills, temporal item response theory, and expert knowledge. In: The 7th International Conference on Educational Data Mining, pp. 84–91 (2014)
9. Lovett, M., Meyer, O., Thille, C.: The Open Learning Initiative: Measuring the effectiveness of the OLI statistics course in accelerating student learning. J. Interactive Media Educ. **2008** (1) (2008). https://doi.org/10.5334/2008-14. Article no. 13
10. Koedinger, K.R., Stamper, J.C., McLaughlin, E.A., Nixon, T.: Using data-driven discovery of better student models to improve student learning. In: Lane, H.C., Yacef, K., Mostow, J., Pavlik, P. (eds.) AIED 2013. LNCS (LNAI), vol. 7926, pp. 421–430. Springer, Heidelberg (2013). https://doi.org/10.1007/978-3-642-39112-5_43
11. Mostafavi, B., Barnes, T.: Evolution of an intelligent deductive logic tutor using data-driven elements. Int. J. Artif. Intell. Educ. **27**(1), 5–36 (2017)
12. Aleven, V., Koedinger, K.R.: Knowledge component approaches to learner modeling. In: Sottilare, R., Graesser, A., Hu, X., Holden, H. (eds.) Design Recommendations for Adaptive Intelligent Tutoring Systems, vol. 1, Learner Modeling, pp. 165–182. US Army Research Laboratory, Orlando (2013)
13. Stamper, J.C., Koedinger, K.R.: Human-machine student model discovery and improvement using datashop. In: Biswas, G., Bull, S., Kay, J., Mitrovic, A. (eds.) AIED 2011. LNCS (LNAI), vol. 6738, pp. 353–360. Springer, Heidelberg (2011). https://doi.org/10.1007/978-3-642-21869-9_46

---

[1] This work was supported by Bill and Melinda Gates Foundation Prime Award #OPP1196889.

14. Koedinger, K., McLaughlin, E.: Seeing language learning inside the math: cognitive analysis yields transfer. In: Proceedings of the Annual Meeting of the Cognitive Science Society, vol. 32, no. 32 (2010)
15. Koedinger, K.R., Baker, R.S., Cunningham, K., Skogsholm, A., Leber, B., Stamper, J.: A data repository for the EDM community: the PSLC DataShop. Handbook Educ. Data Mining **43**, 43–56 (2010)
16. Cen, H., Koedinger, K.R., Junker, B.: Is over practice necessary? improving learning efficiency with the cognitive tutor through educational data mining. Front. Artif. Intell. Appl. **158**, 511 (2007)
17. Doroudi, S., Aleven, V., Brunskill, E.: Robust evaluation matrix: towards a more principled offline exploration of instructional policies. In: Proceedings of the Fourth (2017) ACM Conference on Learning@ Scale, pp. 3–12 (2017)
18. Aleven, V., Sewall, J.: The frequency of tutor behaviors: a case study. In: Micarelli, A., Stamper, J., Panourgia, K. (eds.) ITS 2016. LNCS, vol. 9684, pp. 396–401. Springer, Cham (2016). https://doi.org/10.1007/978-3-319-39583-8_47
19. Koedinger, K.R., Anderson, J.R.: Illustrating principled design: the early evolution of a cognitive tutor for algebra symbolization. Interact. Learn. Environ. **5**, 161–180 (1998)
20. Cen, H., Koedinger, K., Junker, B.: Learning Factors Analysis – A General Method for Cognitive Model Evaluation and Improvement. In: Ikeda, M., Ashley, K.D., Chan, T.-W. (eds.) ITS 2006. LNCS, vol. 4053, pp. 164–175. Springer, Heidelberg (2006). https://doi.org/10.1007/11774303_17
21. Corbett, A.T., Anderson, J.R.: Knowledge tracing: modeling the acquisition of procedural knowledge. User Model. User-adapted Interact. **4**(4), 253–278 (1994)
22. Lee, J.I., Brunskill, E.: The impact on individualizing student models on necessary practice opportunities. In: International Educational Data Mining Society (2012)
23. Heffernan, N.T., Koedinger, K.R.: The composition effect in symbolizing: the role of symbol production vs. text comprehension. In: Proceedings 19th Annual Conference Cognitive Science Society, pp. 307–312 (1997)
24. Heffernan, N.T., Heffernan, C.L.: The ASSISTments ecosystem: building a platform that brings scientists and teachers together for minimally invasive research on human learning and teaching. Int. J. Artif. Intell. Educ. **24**(4), 470–497 (2014)

Towards Improving Sample Representativeness of Teachers on Online Social Media: A Case Study on Pinterest

Hamid Karimi[(✉)], Tyler Derr, Kaitlin T. Torphy, Kenneth A. Frank, and Jiliang Tang

Michigan State University, East Lansing, USA
{karimiha,derrtyle,torphyka,kenfrank,tangjili}@msu.edu
https://www.teachersinsocialmedia.com

Abstract. Many teachers utilize online social media to supplement their students' needs and enhance their professional activities, curating millions of educational resources. In fact, during the Coronovirus pandemic, online curation of resources provides teachers a repository of materials to provide students in online space. Teachers' engagement online then provides the ability to learn more about how teachers are addressing students' learning needs and potentially improve the quality of the resources they share. Historically, to perform such a study, we often survey some teachers and then leverage their shared resources to investigate education-related research questions. However, this can lead to problems including *sample representativeness* where surveyed teachers may not be representative of the population of teachers in social media. In this paper, we attempt to improve the sample representativeness of teachers on Pinterest. We first survey 541 teachers in the United States as *seed* samples and then collect their online data and social connections on Pinterest. Then, we devise a heuristic that automatically identifies other Pinterest accounts that are likely to be teachers thus improving the sample representativeness. Finally, we evaluate our heuristic with advanced machine learning techniques.

Keywords: Teachers in social media · Sample representativeness · Pinterest

1 Introduction

Unlike traditional resource curation (e.g., asking a colleague or turning to a one's district or state department of education), the diffusion of information from social media to the classroom is significantly more efficient and scaleable. Hence, increasingly, teachers use social media to supplement their instructional resources [7,8,11,16,17]. According to a survey from RAND Corporation [11], more than 87% of elementary school teachers and 62% of secondary school teachers use Pinterest for professional purposes. Furthermore, since the coronavirus

© Springer Nature Switzerland AG 2020
I. I. Bittencourt et al. (Eds.): AIED 2020, LNAI 12164, pp. 130–134, 2020.
https://doi.org/10.1007/978-3-030-52240-7_24

pandemic in 2020, instructional resources and homeschooling are in the top three of the most frequent searches within Pinterest (personal communication, April 1, 2020). Given the breadth of online activities by teachers, particularly within social media, and its direct diffusion into classrooms, it warrants understanding how teachers harness social media to diffuse their classroom ideas, lessons, and practices to a community of colleagues.

To study teachers in social media, researchers usually follow a bottom-up data collection approach where they first survey teachers *offline* and then retrieve their *online* data [2, 3, 12–14]. However, this common bottom-up data collection method is restrictive since there are potentially many other teachers online that are not included in our sampled and surveyed teachers. In other words, the surveyed teachers may not be representative of the population of teachers in online social media. Moreover, the survey process is usually costly and time-consuming. In this paper, we complement bottom-up data collection approaches by offering a scalable top-down approach. More specifically, we first survey 541 teachers across 5 U.S. states and 48 different districts and then using the surveyed teachers as the *seed* samples, we acquire their Pinterest data (a bottom-up approach). We then propose a top-down approach, building a heuristic that automatically identifies new likely teachers on Pinterest beyond our surveyed teachers. Finally, we use advances in machine learning and social network analysis to evaluate the performance of our heuristic.

2   Related Work

Research shows teachers use various online platforms for educational engagement including Facebook, Twitter, and Pinterest. Steinbrecher and Hart [14] showed that in addition to personal usage, teachers use Facebook for some professional activities such as "classroom support and strategy idea generation". Authors in [3] explored Twitter usage by K-16 educators and discovered that many educators use Twitter for professional development. In similar studies [1, 4], it was shown that pre-service teachers use Twitter for some professional career development purposes such as resource sharing and connecting to other teachers. Carpenter et al. [2] indicated that teachers use Pinterest to promote educational materials. In particular, they discovered that many individuals were sharing resources curated in TeachersPayTeachers.com, a crucial virtual resource pool where teachers can sell/buy various educational resources. We have discovered similar results for TeachersPayTeachers.com and Pinterest. Some research has endeavored to identify who is curating educational resources. The authors in [13] explored the characteristics of teachers contributing to TeachersPayTeachers.com and attempted to identify the profile of resource curators. Similarly, Schroeder et al. [12] showed that teachers mostly utilize Pinterest to look for educational resources according to their classroom needs. Frank et al. [6] thoroughly analyzed the role of social networks and in particular Pinterest in providing emerging beneficial opportunities for education. Torphy et al. [16] examined the diffusion of educational resources on Pinterest. Their results indicated that direct connection between teachers spurs resource curation. Other work has examined teachers' social media. The interested reader can refer to [8] for a survey on how to incorporate online social media in educational research.

3   Automated Teacher Identification

Dataset. We surveyed 541 PK-12 teachers across 5 states, 48 districts, and 99 schools. 432 teachers are females, 13 males, and 69 unspecified. For all teachers in our dataset, we acquired their followers and followees (their connections) which resulted in a network with 89,190 nodes (Pinterest users) and 4,379,592 links. Also, for all 89,190 users, we collected their Pinterest data i.e., their shared pins.

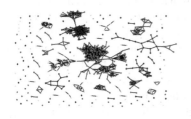

Fig. 1. Network of surveyed teachers on Pinterest where colors represent districts

Top-Down Teacher Identification. As mentioned before, the bottom-up data collection where we first survey teachers offline and then project them into online social media may not properly capture the representativeness of teachers in that online space. To grasp the idea, we visualize the network of our surveyed teachers in Fig. 1. First, we can see there is a considerable number of teachers without any connection to others (96 teachers or around 17% of our surveyed teachers). This is an undesirable property as we expect teachers to connect to their peers and engage in professional career development activities e.g., sharing resources. Second, in general, the network consists of several disjointed sub-networks (components). This disrupts the diffusion of information amongst teachers on Pinterest which plays an essential role in improving the quality of teaching [16]. Third, around 95% of teachers are connected to their peers in the same district, which defies the main strength of social media i.e., breaking physical constraints. Hence, we conclude that we should adamantly attempt to obtain a better picture of the network of teachers on Pinterest as explained in the following.

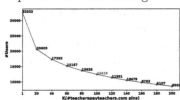

Fig. 2. Number of TPT pins vs the number of users

In line with previous studies [2,13], we discovered that the predominant source of educational resources among teachers is TeachersPayTeachers.com (hereafter referred to as TPT). There are several reasons behind this. First, TPT is the largest marketplace of educational resources offering millions of high-quality PK-12 educational resources. Second, image-oriented characteristics of TPT resources and image-based nature of Pinterest perfectly match these two platforms. Finally, quite often content producers in TPT are teachers/educators who join Pinterest and advertise/share their resources [2]. We also discovered that TPT is the dominant source of resources shared by our surveyed teachers comprising around 50% of the top 5 pin domains. Hence, we hypothesize that the existence of TPT pins in an account is a strong indication that the account belongs to a teacher/educator.

With the above discussion in mind, for all 88,649 other users in our dataset, we process their pins and if for a user the number of his/her TPT pins is more than a threshold K, we mark that user as a teacher. Figure 2 shows the number of users whose K pins' domain is TPT where K changes from 1 to 200. We set K to 100 through which we can mark more than 12,000 users as likely teachers which is almost 23 times larger than the number of surveyed teachers. Note that not necessarily all those marked users are school teachers since they can be other types of educators such as educational organizations, home teachers, parents, and so on. However, as long as their footprint on Pinterest is concerned, they are similar to our surveyed teachers and we keep referring them as *teachers.*

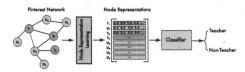

Fig. 3. Evaluating the automated teacher identification

Evaluation. The evaluation process of our automated teacher identification is demonstrated in Fig. 3. First, we use the entire constructed network of Pinterest users (89,190 nodes and 4,379,592 links), and extract some features for nodes in an *unsupervised* manner. Feature extraction from a network is an effective approach and used in different applications [5,9,10,18]. In this paper, we adopt the method proposed by Tang et al. [15] known as LINE (Large-scale information network embedding). The size of the representation for each node is 64. Second, on top of learned node representations, we carry out two classifications using Random Forest as the classifier. Both classifiers are tested against 100 surveyed teachers and 100 non-teachers. The first classifier is trained on the rest of 441 surveyed teachers and 441 identified non-teachers. The second classifier is trained on 5500 teachers and 5500 non-teachers (identified using our heuristic). For *non-teacher* samples, we include those having no TPT pin and no educational pin where being *educational* is marked by the Pinterest internal pin labeling system. The accuracy of the first classifier is just 58% while the second one achieves 76%. Hence, we can conclude that our heuristic for automated teacher identification is reliable as it significantly improves the performance of the teacher classification problem.

In the future, we plan to compare the two datasets, i.e., surveyed teachers and the augmented version, from the perspective of structural properties of the two networks as well as behavioral attributes of teachers. Further, we intend to make sense of the diffusion of information among teachers and characterize resources through their diffusion.

Acknowledgment. Research reported in this paper was supported by the Defense Advanced Research Projects Agency under project ID number (10332.02 RaCHem PHI) and the Center for Business and Social Analytics at MSU 2017 and 2020, the National Science Foundation, and the William T. Grant Foundation under award numbers (NSF REAL– 1420532, WT Grant - 182764).

References

1. Carpenter, J.: Preservice teachers' microblogging: professional development via twitter. Contemporary Issues Technol. Teacher Educ. **15**(2), 209–234 (2015)
2. Carpenter, J., Abrams, A., Dunphy, M.: Educators' professional uses of pinterest. In: Society for Information Technology & Teacher Education International Conference, pp. 1925–1930. Association for the Advancement of Computing in Education (AACE) (2016)

3. Carpenter, J.P., Krutka, D.G.: How and why educators use Twitter: a survey of the field. J. Res. Technol. Educ. **46**(4), 414–434 (2014)
4. Carpenter, J.P., Krutka, D.G.: Engagement through microblogging: educator professional development via twitter. Professional Dev. Educ. **41**(4), 707–728 (2015). https://doi.org/10.1080/19415257.2014.939294
5. Derr, T., Karimi, H., Liu, X., Xu, J., Tang, J.: Deep adversarial network alignment. arXiv preprint arXiv:1902.10307 (2019)
6. Frank, K., Lo, Y.J., Torphy, K., Kim, J.: Social networks and educational opportunity. In: Schneider, B. (ed.) Handbook of the Sociology of Education in the 21st Century, pp. 297–316. Springer, Cham (2018). https://doi.org/10.1007/978-3-319-76694-2_13
7. Greenhow, C., Cho, V., Dennen, P.V., Fishman, B.J.: Education and Social Media: Research Directions to Guide a Growing Field, vol. 121. Teachers College Record (2019)
8. Karimi, H., Derr, T., Torphy, K., Frank, K., Tang, J.: A roadmap for incorporating online social media in educational research. Teachers College Record Year Book (2019)
9. Karimi, H., Derr, T., Brookhouse, A., Tang, J.: Multi-factor congressional vote prediction. In: Proceedings of the 2019 IEEE/ACM International Conference on Advances in Social Networks Analysis and Mining, pp. 266–273 (2019)
10. Karimi, H., VanDam, C., Ye, L., Tang, J.: End-to-end compromised account detection. In: 2018 IEEE/ACM International Conference on Advances in Social Networks Analysis and Mining (ASONAM), pp. 314–321. IEEE (2018)
11. Opfer, V.D., Kaufman, J.H., Thompson, L.E.: Implementation of k-12 state standards for mathematics and english language arts and literacy (2016)
12. Schroeder, S., Curcio, R., Lundgren, L.: Expanding the learning network: how teachers use pInterest. J. Res. Technol. Educ. **51**(2), 166–186 (2019). https://doi.org/10.1080/15391523.2019.1573354
13. Shelton, C.C., Archambault, L.M.: Who are online teacherpreneurs and what do they do? a survey of content creators on teacherspayteachers.com. J. Res. Technol. Educ. 51(4), 398–414 (2019)
14. Steinbrecher, T., Hart, J.: Examining teachers' personal and professional use of facebook: recommendations for teacher education programming. J. Technol. Teacher Educ. **20**(1), 71–88 (2012)
15. Tang, J., Qu, M., Wang, M., Zhang, M., Yan, J., Mei, Q.: Line: large-scale information network embedding. In: Proceedings of the 24th International Conference on World Wide Web, pp. 1067–1077 (2015)
16. Torphy, K., Sihua, H., Liu, Y., Chen, Z.: Examining the Virtual Diffusion of Educational Resources Across Teachers Social Networks Over Time, vol. Special issue, Teachers College Record (2018)
17. Torphy, K.T., Drake, C.: Educators meet the fifth estate: the role of social media in teacher training. Teachers College Record **121** (2019). https://www.tcrecord.org/Content.asp?ContentId=23066
18. Wang, Z., Derr, T., Yin, D., Tang, J.: Understanding and predicting weight loss with mobile social networking data. In: Proceedings of the 2017 ACM on Conference on Information and Knowledge Management, pp. 1269–1278 (2017)

A Framework for Exploring the Impact of Tutor Practices on Learner Self-regulation in Online Environments

Madiha Khan-Galaria$^{(\boxtimes)}$, Mutlu Cukurova, and Rose Luckin

University College London, London, UK
{m.khan.16,m.cukurova,r.luckin}@ucl.ac.uk

Abstract. There is increasing interest in the conceptualization of Self-Regulated learning (SRL) as a dynamic process which unfolds over the course of a learning activity. This is partly because this conceptualization could potentially be operationalized and used as the basis for AI and analytics tools which monitor and scaffold SRL in real-time. However, while there is an abundance of research on theories of SRL, little research explicitly reviews and operationalizes such theoretical considerations. Work is needed to develop frameworks for the practical applications of fundamental SRL theories, helping researchers move from conceptual considerations to operationalization in real world settings. In this paper, we propose a theoretically grounded framework for investigating SRL in the context of online tutoring for upper primary school learners. SRL is interpreted as a social learning construct, and the framework proposed is designed to investigate the influence of tutor practices on the development of learners' SRL. We present the results of a pilot study that explored the applicability of the framework.

Keywords: Self-Regulated learning · Online tutoring · Winne and Hadwin model · Tutor practices · Metacognition · Virtual classroom environment · Process mining

1 Introduction

There is increasing interest in the conceptualization of Self-Regulated learning (SRL) as a dynamic process which unfolds over the course of a learning activity. Mapping out SRL as a dynamic process is of interest, as it may provide opportunities for real time monitoring, evaluation and support of SRL in online learning environments. For example, there may be opportunities for intelligent tools which support tutors in real time as they scaffold learner self-regulation. However, there is limited research on frameworks, which are both theoretically grounded (Matcha et al. 2019), and sufficiently granular to investigate self-regulation in online learning environments.

To address this need, this paper proposes a framework to investigate the impact of tutor practices on learner self-regulation in online environments. Specifically, we focus on an online tutoring environment in which human tutors teach primary school learners (aged 10 years) on a one to one basis, using an interactive whiteboard and tools. We identify signifiers from natural language dialogue between tutor and learner, and

© Springer Nature Switzerland AG 2020
I. I. Bittencourt et al. (Eds.): AIED 2020, LNAI 12164, pp. 135–139, 2020.
https://doi.org/10.1007/978-3-030-52240-7_25

explore the applicability of the framework in a pilot study. Our initial findings are not intended to be generalized to a population, but aim to build on research exploring how to operationalize SRL theoretical models in online environments (Hadwin et al. 2007).

2 Framework Development

The framework has been developed through a two stage, mixed methods approach. Firstly, an established theoretical model is adapted to apply to the online tutoring environment. In the second stage, we use a data driven approach to refine the framework.

The framework developed in this research required a granular, fluid model of SRL which could be applied to real world settings, and use online data. After the review of available theoretical models (Winne and Hadwin 1998; Pintrich 2000; Zimmerman 2000), the Winne and Hadwin (1998) model was identified as a suitable model (Fig. 1).

The Winne and Hadwin model was selected as it is highly granular and suited to the analysis of fine-grained data that is generated from online environments. Further, the model synthesizes all the various components of SRL from the literature into a heuristic framework (Azevedo et al. 2010; Bannert et al. 2014).

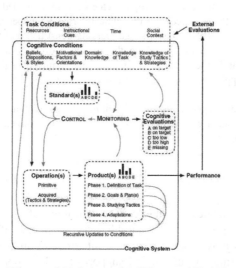

Fig. 1. Winne and Hadwin model (Winne and Hadwin 1998)

The Winne and Hadwin model was adapted to fit our research purposes, namely to investigate the impact of tutor practices on SRL. The model recognizes tutor practices as an external condition impacting learner SRL. Our framework builds on this, and interprets each sub-component to identify tutor practices which may scaffold learner SRL. Following the adaptation of the model, online tutoring sessions were observed to identify fine grained actions. For our empirical work, we partnered with an industrial supplier named Third Space Learning (TSL), which delivers maths tutoring for primary school children aged 10 years old. Learners and tutors log into a shared online environment, and the learner works through a pre-designed online set of questions, with the guidance of a human tutor on an interactive whiteboard. The data available for analysis includes the online resources, natural language dialogue audio between tutor and student, logfile and whiteboard data. TSL sessions were filtered by topic, and the recordings of 50 randomly selected sessions were observed. Fine grained actions that could be observed from the data were mapped to the theoretical framework. This exercise illustrated that there were a number of tutor actions aimed at promoting certain types of engagement by learners which were not yet captured. For example, the theoretical framework did not distinguish between tutors who lectured versus prompting learners to construct meaning. The 'Operations' component was thus broadly defined to refer to the nature of tutor-learner engagement, characterized using the Chi & Wyle ICAP framework (Chi and Wylie 2014). The final framework is presented in Table 1.

Table 1. Framework for exploring tutor practices that influence SRL in online environments

Model	Operational definition of sub-components	Examples of signifiers
Conditions	Tutor actions and utterances scaffolding learner mindset e.g. specific praise)	Tutor utterances': *'Well done for persevering'*. Tutor awarding effort points, pictures and emojis
Operations	Directive engagement - Tutor instructs or explains	Tutor utterances *"To solve this problem, you need to...*
	Active engagement -Tutor prompts learner to physically manipulate the content	Tutor utterances: *"Please underline the key words"*
	Constructive engagement -Tutor prompts learner to construct meaning. The question style can be closed ended/narrow or open ended	Tutor utterances ('narrow'): *'What is x plus y'?" "Is it a or b"* ("open ended"): *"How did you work this out?"*
	Interactive engagement	A dialogue where the learner and the tutor have at least two turns with constructive utterances
Products	Tutor prompts learner to try to understand the question, set goals and plan.	Tutor utterances: *"What does this question mean?" "How will you do this"?*
	Tutor prompts learner to use of study tactic, or to make adaptations to SRL products.	Tutor utterances: *"What method can we use to do this?" "Is there a different way of doing this?"*
Evaluation, Standards	Tutor prompts learner to monitor cognition, metacognition and affect	Tutor utterances: *"How do you feel about this topic?" "Do you need help?"*

3 Pilot Study

We tested the applicability of the framework by applying it to data gathered from tutors manually classified as 'high ranking' and 'mid ranking'. 180 tutors were ranked using student learning outcomes (30%), tutor evaluation test scores (30%), human evaluator scores (30%), and student qualitative ratings for tutors (10%). Tutors in the top ten percentile i.e. with a rank between 1–18, and tutors in the 45th to 55th percentile i.e. with a rank between 81 and 99 were randomly selected. 121 min of audio and whiteboard data from 21 sessions for the selected tutors was extracted and manually tagged using the framework. The data collected was allocated into time bins, as per Table 2:

Table 2. Allocation of session data into time bins

Time bins (mm. ss)	0.00–2.00	2.01–4.00	4.01–6.00	6.01–8.00	8.01–10.33	Total
High ranking tutors (11 sessions)	20.00	20.58	13.04	04.40	02.25	60.31
Mid ranking tutors (10 sessions)	20.00	18.02	10.07	07.09	06.25	61.43

We plotted the tutor practices against the time bins, with the size of the bubble being the average relative frequency of each behavior. Figure 2 shows the results for high ranking and mid ranking tutors. We found that high ranking tutors were more likely to demonstrate practices scaffolding open-ended constructive engagement, such as prompting self-explanation. High ranking tutors embedded monitoring throughout the session, while mid ranking tutors used this practice less regularly. We also found that tutor practices boosting learner mindset (e.g. specific praise) were more prominent amongst high ranking tutors, with a relative frequency of 0.42 for all high-ranking tutors, versus 0.28 for all mid ranking tutors.

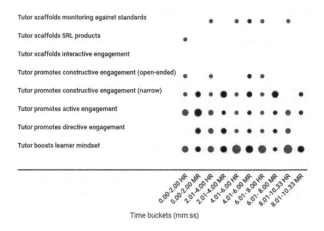

Fig. 2. Average relative frequency of high-ranking tutor practices (purple) vs mid-ranking tutor practices (red). (Color figure online)

The next stage of work will refine the framework to include non-audio traces of SRL behaviour (e.g. use of pointer). We will build the data sample to include low ranking tutors, prior to applying modelling and analytics such as process mining and decision trees. We will examine whether we can effectively use audio and non-audio traces to identify tutor practices scaffolding SRL, and the impact of contextual and macro factors on these practices. We will also analyse the implications of our work for operationalizing SRL in online tutoring environments, and the potential for building intelligent tools, which support human tutors in fostering learner SRL.

References

Azevedo, R., Moos, D., Johnson, A., Chauncey, A.: Measuring cognitive and metacognitive regulatory processes during hypermedia learning: issues and challenges. Educ. Psychol. **45**(4), 210–223 (2010). https://doi.org/10.1080/00461520.2010.515934

Bannert, M., Reimann, P., Sonnenberg, C.: Process mining techniques for analysing patterns and strategies in students' self-regulated learning. Metacognition Learn. **9**, 161–185 (2014)

Chi, M.T.H., Wylie, R.: The ICAP framework: Linking cognitive engagement to active learning outcomes. Educ. Psychol. **49**(4), 219–243 (2014)

Hadwin, A., Nesbit, J., Jamieson Noel, D., Code, J., Winne, P.: Examining trace data to explore self-regulated learning. Metacognition Learn. **2**, 107–124 (2007)

Pintrich, P.R.: Multiple goals, multiple pathways: The role of goal orientation in learning and achievement. J. Educ. Psychol. **92**, 544–555 (2000)

Matcha, W., Uzir, N., Gasevic, D., Pardo, A.: A systematic review of empirical studies on learning analytics dashboards: a self-regulated learning perspective. In: IEEE Transactions on Learning Technologies (2019)

Winne, P.H., Hadwin, A.F.: Studying as self-regulated learning. In: Hacker, D.J., Dunlosky, J., Graesser, A. (eds.) Metacognition in Educational Theory and Practice, pp. 277–304. Lawrence Erl, Hillsdale (1998)

Zimmerman, B.J.: Attaining self-regulation, a socio-cognitive perspective. Handbook of Self Regulation (2000)

Automated Personalized Feedback Improves Learning Gains in An Intelligent Tutoring System

Ekaterina Kochmar[1,2(✉)], Dung Do Vu[1,3], Robert Belfer[1], Varun Gupta[1], Iulian Vlad Serban[1], and Joelle Pineau[1,4]

[1] Korbit Technologies Inc., Montreal, Canada
ekaterina@korbit.ai
[2] University of Cambridge, Cambridge, UK
[3] École de Technologie Supérieure, Montreal, Canada
[4] McGill University & MILA (Quebec Artificial Intelligence Institute), Montreal, Canada

Abstract. We investigate how automated, data-driven, personalized feedback in a large-scale intelligent tutoring system (ITS) improves student learning outcomes. We propose a machine learning approach to generate personalized feedback, which takes individual needs of students into account. We utilize state-of-the-art machine learning and natural language processing techniques to provide the students with *personalized hints*, *Wikipedia-based explanations*, and *mathematical hints*. Our model is used in `Korbit` (https://www.korbit.ai), a large-scale dialogue-based ITS with thousands of students launched in 2019, and we demonstrate that the personalized feedback leads to considerable improvement in student learning outcomes and in the subjective evaluation of the feedback.

Keywords: Intelligent tutoring system · Dialogue-based tutoring system · Natural language processing · Deep learning · Personalized learning and feedback

1 Introduction

Intelligent Tutoring Systems (ITS) [8,21] attempt to mimic personalized tutoring in a computer-based environment and are a low-cost alternative to human tutors. Over the past two decades, many ITS have been successfully deployed to enhance teaching and improve students' learning experience in a number of domains [1,2,5,6,9,12,17,19,22,23], not only providing feedback and assistance but also addressing individual student characteristics [13] and cognitive processes [27]. Many ITS consider the development of a personalized curriculum and personalized feedback [4,5,7,11,18,20,24,25], with dialogue-based ITS being some of the most effective tools for learning [3,14,15,21,26], as they simulate a familiar learning environment of student–tutor interaction, thus helping to improve student motivation. The main bottleneck is the ability of ITS to address

© Springer Nature Switzerland AG 2020
I. I. Bittencourt et al. (Eds.): AIED 2020, LNAI 12164, pp. 140–146, 2020.
https://doi.org/10.1007/978-3-030-52240-7_26

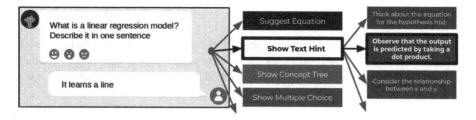

Fig. 1. An example illustrating how the `Korbit` ITS `inner-loop` system selects the pedagogical intervention. The student gives an incorrect solution and receives a text hint.

the multitude of possible scenarios in such interactions, and this is where methods of automated, data-driven feedback generation are of critical importance.

Our paper has two major contributions. Firstly, we describe how state-of-the-art machine learning (ML) and natural language processing (NLP) techniques can be used to generate automated, data-driven *personalized hints and explanations, Wikipedia-based explanations*, and *mathematical hints*. Feedback generated this way takes the individual needs of students into account, does not require expert intervention or hand-crafted rules, and is easily scalable and transferable across domains. Secondly, we demonstrate that the personalized feedback leads to substantially improved student learning gains and improved subjective feedback evaluation in practice. To support our claims, we utilize our feedback models in `Korbit`, a large-scale dialogue-based ITS.

2   `Korbit` Learning Platform

`Korbit` is a large-scale, open-domain, mixed-interface, dialogue-based ITS, which uses ML, NLP and reinforcement learning to provide interactive, personalized learning online. Currently, the platform has thousands of students enrolled and is capable of teaching topics related to data science, machine learning, and artificial intelligence.

Students enroll based on courses or skills they would like to study. Once a student has enrolled, `Korbit` tutors them by alternating between short lecture videos and interactive problem-solving. During the problem-solving sessions, the student may attempt to solve an exercise, ask for help, or even skip it. If the student attempts to solve the exercise, their solution attempt is compared against the expectation (i.e. reference solution) using an NLP model. If their solution is classified as incorrect, the `inner-loop` system (see Fig. 1) will activate and respond with one of a dozen different pedagogical interventions, which include hints, mathematical hints, elaborations, explanations, concept tree diagrams, and multiple choice quiz answers. The pedagogical intervention is chosen by an ensemble of machine learning models from the student's zone of proximal development (ZPD) [10] based on their student profile and last solution attempt.

3 Automatically Generated Personalized Feedback

In this paper, we present experiments on the `Korbit` learning platform with actual students. These experiments involve varying the text hints and explanations based on how they were generated and how they were adapted to each unique student.

Personalized Hints and Explanations are generated using NLP techniques applied by a 3-step algorithm to all expectations (i.e. reference solutions) in our database: (1) keywords, including nouns and noun phrases, are identified within the question (e.g. *overfitting* and *underfitting* in Table 1); (2) appropriate sentence span that does not include keywords is identified in a reference solution using state-of-the-art dependency parsing with `spaCy`[1] (e.g., *A model is underfitting* is filtered out, while *it has a high bias* is considered as a candidate for a hint); and (3) a grammatically correct hint is generated using discourse-based modifications (e.g., *Think about the case*) and the partial hint from step (2) (e.g., *when it has a high bias*).

Table 1. Hint generation. Keywords are marked with boxes

Question	Expectation	Generated hint
What is the difference between overfitting and underfitting ?	A model is underfitting when it has a high bias	Think about the case when it has a high bias

Next, hints are ranked according to their linguistic quality as well as the past student–system interactions. We employ a Random Forest classifier using two broad sets of features: (1) *Linguistic quality features* assess the quality of the hint from the linguistic perspective only (e.g., considering length of the hint/explanation, keyword and topic overlap between the hint/explanation and the question, etc.), and are used by the **baseline model** only. (2) *Performance-based features* additionally take into account past student interaction with the system. Among them, the **shallow personalization model** includes features related to the number of attempted questions, proportion of correct and incorrect answers, etc., and the **deep personalization model** additionally includes linguistic features pertaining to up to 4 previous student–system interaction turns. The three types of feedback models are trained and evaluated on a collection of 450 previously recorded student–system interactions.

Wikipedia-Based Explanations provide alternative ways of helping students to understand and remember concepts. We generate such explanations using another multi-stage pipeline: first, we use a 2 GB dataset on "Machine learning" crawled from Wikipedia and extract all relevant domain keywords from

---

[1] https://spacy.io.

the reference questions and solutions using `spaCy`. Next, we use the first sentence in each article as an *extracted Wikipedia-based explanation* and the rest of the article to *generate candidate explanations*. A Decision Tree classifier is trained on a dataset of positive and negative examples to evaluate the quality of a Wikipedia-based explanation using a number of linguistically-motivated features. This model is then applied to identify the most appropriate Wikipedia-based explanations among the generated ones.

Mathematical Hints are either provided by `Korbit` in the form of suggested equations with gapped mathematical terms for the student to fill in, or in the form of a hint on what the student needs to change if they input an incorrect equation. Math equations are particularly challenging because equivalent expressions can have different representations: for example, y in $y(x + 5)$ could be a function or a term multiplied by $x + 5$. To evaluate student equations, we first convert their LaTeX string into multiple parse trees, where each tree represents a possible interpretation, and then use a classifier to select the most likely parse tree and compare it to the expectation. Our generated feedback is fully automated, which differentiates `Korbit` from other math-oriented ITS, where feedback is generated by hand-crafted test cases [9,16].

4   Experimental Results and Analysis

Our preliminary experiments with the *baseline, shallow* and *deep personalization* models run on the historical data using 50-fold cross-validation strongly suggested that *deep personalization* model selects the most appropriate personalized feedback. To support our claims, we ran experiments involving 796 annotated student–system interactions, collected from 183 students enrolled for free and studying the machine learning course on the `Korbit` platform between January and February, 2020. First, a hint or explanation was selected at uniform random from one of the personalized feedback models when a student gives an incorrect solution. Afterwards, the student learning gain was measured as the proportion of instances where a student provided a correct solution after receiving a personalized hint or explanation. Since it's possible for the ITS to provide several pedagogical interventions for a given exercise, we separate the learning gains observed for all students from those for students who received a personalized hint or explanation before their second attempt at the exercise. Table 2 presents the results, showing that the *deep personalization model* leads to the highest student learning gains at 48.53% followed by the *shallow personalization model* at 46.51% and the *baseline model* at 39.47% for all attempts. The difference between the learning gains of the *deep personalization model* and *baseline model* for the students before their second attempt is statistically significant at 95% confidence level based on a z-test (p = 0.03005). These results support the hypothesis that automatically generated personalized hints and explanations lead to substantial improvements in student learning gains.

Table 2. Student learning gains for personalized hints and explanations with 95% confidence intervals (C.I.).

Model	All attempts		Before second attempt	
	Mean	95% C.I	Mean	95% C.I
Baseline (No personalization)	39.47%	[24.04%, 56.61%]	37.93%	[20.69%, 57.74%]
Shallow personalization	46.51%	[31.18%, 62.34%]	51.43%	[33.99%, 68.62%]
Deep personalization	**48.53%**	**[36.22%, 60.97%]**	**60.47%**	**[44.41%, 75.02%]**

Experiments on the `Korbit` platform confirm that extracted and generated *Wikipedia-based explanations* lead to comparable student learning gains. Students rated either or both types of explanations as helpful 83.33% of the time. This shows that automatically-generated Wikipedia-based explanations can be included in the set of interventions used to personalize the feedback. Moreover, two domain experts independently analyzed a set of 86 student–system interactions with `Korbit`, where the student's solution attempt contained an incorrect mathematical equation. The results showed that over 90% of the *mathematical hints* would be considered either "very useful" or "somewhat useful".

In conclusion, our experiments strongly support the hypothesis that the personalized hints and explanations, as well as Wikipedia-based explanations, help to improve student learning outcomes significantly. Preliminary results also indicate that the mathematical hints are useful. Future work should investigate how and what types of Wikipedia-based explanations and mathematical hints may improve student learning outcomes, as well as their interplay with student learning profiles and knowledge gaps.

References

1. AbuEl-Reesh, J.Y., Abu-Naser, S.S.: An intelligent tutoring system for learning classical cryptography algorithms (CCAITS). Int. J. Acad. Appl. Res. (IJAAR) **2**(2), 1–11 (2018)
2. Agha, M., Jarghon, A., Abu-Naser, S.: An intelligent tutoring system for teaching SQL. Int. J. Acad. Inf. Syst. Res. (IJAISR) **2**(2), 1–7 (2018)
3. Ahn, J.W., et al.: Adaptive Visual Dialog for Intelligent Tutoring Systems. In: Rose, C.P., et al. (eds.) International Conference on Artificial Intelligence in Education, pp. 413–418. Springer, Cham (2018). https://doi.org/10.1007/978-3-319-93846-2_77
4. Al-Dahdooh, R., Abu-Naser, S.: Development and evaluation of the oracle intelligent tutoring system (OITS). Euro. Acad. Res. **4**, 8711–8721 (2017)
5. Al-Nakhal, M., Abu-Naser, S.: Adaptive intelligent tutoring system for learning computer theory. Euro. Acad. Res. **4**, 8770–8782 (2017)
6. Al Rekhawi, H., Abu-Naser, S.: Android applications UI development intelligent tutoring system. Int. J. Eng. Inf. Syst. (IJEAIS) **2**(1), 1–14 (2018)

7. Albacete, P., Jordan, P., Katz, S., Chounta, I.A., McLaren, B.M.: The impact of student model updates on contingent scaffolding in a natural-language tutoring system. In: Isotani, S., Millan, E., Ogan, A., Hastings, P., McLaren, B., Luckin, R. (eds.) International Conference on Artificial Intelligence in Education, pp. 37–47. Springer, Cham (2019). https://doi.org/10.1007/978-3-030-23204-7_4

8. Anderson, J.R., Boyle, C.F., Reiser, B.J.: Intelligent tutoring systems. Science **228**(4698), 456–462 (1985)

9. Büdenbender, J., Frischauf, A., Goguadze, G., Melis, E., Libbrecht, P., Ullrich, C.: Using computer algebra systems as cognitive tools. In: Cerri, S.A., Gouardères, G., Paraguaçu, F. (eds.) ITS 2002. LNCS, vol. 2363, pp. 802–810. Springer, Heidelberg (2002). https://doi.org/10.1007/3-540-47987-2_80

10. Cazden, C.: Peekaboo as an Instructional Model: Discourse Development at Home and at School. Papers and Reports on Child Language Development, No. 17 (1979)

11. Chi, M., Koedinger, K., Gordon, G., Jordan, P., Vanlehn, K.: Instructional factors analysis: a cognitive model for multiple instructional interventions. In: EDM 2011 - Proceedings of the 4th International Conference on Educational Data Mining, pp. 61–70 (2011)

12. Goguadze, G., Palomo, A.G., Melis, E.: Interactivity of exercises in ActiveMath. In: ICCE, pp. 109–115 (2005)

13. Graesser, A.C., Cai, Z., Morgan, B., Wang, L.: Assessment with computer agentsthat engage in conversational dialogues and trialogues with learners. Comput. Human Behav. **76**, 607 – 616 (2017). https://doi.org/10.1016/j.chb.2017.03.041, http://www.sciencedirect.com/science/article/pii/S074756321730198X

14. Graesser, A.C., Chipman, P., Haynes, B.C., Olney, A.: AutoTutor: an intelligent tutoring system with mixed-initiative dialogue. IEEE Trans. Educ. **48**(4), 612–618 (2005)

15. Graesser, A.C., VanLehn, K., Rosé, C.P., Jordan, P.W., Harter, D.: Intelligent tutoring systems with conversational dialogue. AI Magazine **22**(4), 39–39 (2001)

16. Hennecke, M.: Online Diagnose in intelligenten mathematischenLehr-Lern-Systemen. VDI-Verlag (1999)

17. Leelawong, K., Biswas, G.: Designing learning by teaching agents: the Betty's Brain system. Int. J. Artif. Intell. Educ. **18**(3), 181–208 (2008)

18. Lin, C.F., Chu Yeh, Y., Hung, Y.H., Chang, R.I.: Data mining for providing a personalized learning path in creativity: an application of decision trees. Comput. Educ. **68**, 199–210 (2013). https://doi.org/10.1016/j.compedu.2013.05.009, http://www.sciencedirect.com/science/article/pii/S0360131513001309

19. Melis, E., Siekmann, J.: ACTIVEMATH: an intelligent tutoring system for mathematics. In: Rutkowski, L., Siekmann, J.H., Tadeusiewicz, R., Zadeh, L.A. (eds.) ICAISC 2004. LNCS (LNAI), vol. 3070, pp. 91–101. Springer, Heidelberg (2004). https://doi.org/10.1007/978-3-540-24844-6_12

20. Munshi, A., Biswas, G.: Personalization in OELEs: developing a data-driven framework to model and scaffold SRL processes. In: Isotani, S., Millan, E., Ogan, A., Hastings, P., McLaren, B., Luckin, R. (eds.) International Conference on Artificial Intelligence in Education. pp. 354–358. Springer, Cham (2019). https://doi.org/10.1007/978-3-030-23207-8_65

21. Nye, B.D., Graesser, A.C., Hu, X.: AutoTutor and family: a review of 17 years of natural language tutoring. Int. J. Artif. Intell. Educ. **24**(4), 427–469 (2014)

22. Passier, H., Jeuring, J.: Feedback in an interactive equation solver (2006)

23. Qwaider, S.R., Abu-Naser, S.S.: Excel intelligent tutoring system. Int. J. Acad. Inf. Syst. Res. (IJAISR) **2**(2), 8–18 (2018)

24. Rus, V., Stefanescu, D., Baggett, W., Niraula, N., Franceschetti, D., Graesser, A.C.: Macro-adaptation in conversational intelligent tutoring matters. In: Trausan-Matu, S., Boyer, K.E., Crosby, M., Panourgia, K. (eds.) International Conference on Intelligent Tutoring Systems, pp. 242–247. Springer, Cham (2014) https://doi.org/10.1007/978-3-319-07221-0_29

25. Rus, V., Stefanescu, D., Niraula, N., Graesser, A.C.: DeepTutor: towards macro- and micro-adaptive conversational intelligent tutoring at scale. In: Proceedings of the First ACM Conference on Learning@ Scale Conference, pp. 209–210 (2014)

26. Ventura, M., et al.: Preliminary evaluations of a dialogue-based digital tutor. In: Rose, C. et al. (eds.) International Conference on Artificial Intelligence in Education, pp. 480–483. Springer, Cham (2018) https://doi.org/10.1007/978-3-319-93846-2_90

27. Wu, L., Looi, C.-K.: Agent prompts: scaffolding students for productive reflection in an intelligent learning environment. In: Aleven, V., Kay, J., Mostow, J. (eds.) ITS 2010. LNCS, vol. 6095, pp. 426–428. Springer, Heidelberg (2010). https://doi.org/10.1007/978-3-642-13437-1_92

Allowing Revisions While Providing Error-Flagging Support: Is More Better?

Amruth N. Kumar[(⊠)]

Ramapo College of New Jersey, Mahwah, NJ 07430, USA
amruth@ramapo.edu

Abstract. In this study, we studied whether the number of revisions allowed per problem when error-flagging feedback is provided has a significant effect on learning. We used a partial cross-over study and analyzed the data collected by two adaptive tutors on while loops and for loops over six semesters. We found that when students were unfamiliar with the concepts, they solved fewer problems and therefore, learned significantly less when they were provided more opportunities for revision with error-flagging feedback. But, once they became more familiar with the concepts, allowing for more revisions had no deleterious effect on learning.

Keywords: Error-flagging feedback · Revisions · Adaptive tutor

We had conducted several studies of the effect of providing error-flagging feedback, i.e., error-detection but not error-correction support, in the context of code-tracing tutors. In the first study [1], we found that students scored better on tests with rather than without error-flagging support even though the tests did not use multiple-choice format. In a follow-up study [2], we found that when error-flagging feedback was provided, students saved time on the problems that they already knew how to solve, and spent additional time on the problems for which they did not know the correct solution. But, we also found that students may abuse error-flagging support to find the correct solution by trial and error. In a subsequent study [3], we compared not providing error-flagging feedback against providing it with a limit placed on the number of revisions during testing. We found that even with a limit placed on the number of revisions per problem, students revised more often and scored higher with rather than without error-flagging feedback. We found that placing a limit on the number of revisions may discourage students from using error-flagging feedback as a substitute for their own judgment during tests.

In the current study, we wanted to study whether the number of revisions allowed per problem when error-flagging feedback is provided has a significant effect on *learning*. So, we compared error-flagging feedback with 3 revisions allowed per problem versus 5 revisions. We conducted the study using two tutors that did not use multiple-choice format. So, students could not guess the correct answer merely through brute-force trial-and-error in the presence of error-flagging feedback.

The two adaptive problem-solving tutors were on `while` loop and `for` loop. `while` loop tutor covered 9 concepts and `for` loop tutor covered 10 concepts in C++/Java/C#. The tutors presented code-tracing problems on these concepts: in each

I. I. Bittencourt et al. (Eds.): AIED 2020, LNAI 12164, pp. 147–151, 2020.
https://doi.org/10.1007/978-3-030-52240-7_27

problem, they presented a complete program and asked the student to identify the output of the program, one output at a time.

The tutors provided error-flagging feedback while the student was entering the solution to the problem (See bottom right panel in Fig. 1). Once the student submitted the solution, if it was incorrect, the tutors provided step-by-step explanation of the correct solution in the style of a worked example [4, 7].

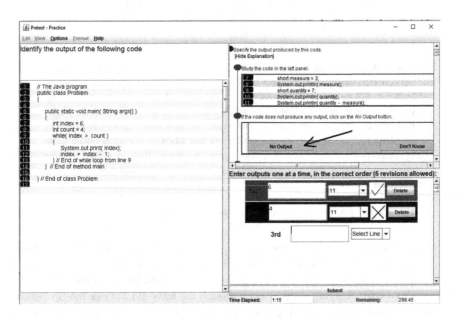

Fig. 1. Error-Flagged answers in bottom right panel

The two tutors were configured to administer pre-test-practice-post-test protocol during each session [5]. During pretest, they administered one problem per concept. During adaptive practice that followed [6], they administered problems on only the concepts on which the student had solved the pretest problem incorrectly. They did so until the student demonstrated mastery of the concept by solving at least 60% of the problems correctly. During posttest, they administered problems on only the concepts mastered during practice. The tutors administered all three stages back-to-back online without interruption.

In this controlled study, the tutors allowed control group to revise the solution of each problem no more than 3 times and experimental group to revise the solution up to 5 times per problem. The interface always displayed the remaining number of revisions allowed for each problem (Title bar of bottom right panel in Fig. 1). The duration of the tutoring session was set to 30 min for control group and 32 min for experimental group in order to accommodate additional revisions. It was also a partial cross-over study: students who were assigned to control group on while loop were assigned to experimental group on for loop and vice versa.

We used the data collected by the two tutors over six semesters: Fall 2014-Spring 2017. The tutors were used by students in introductory programming courses in C++, Java and C#. Typically, students used the tutors as after-class assignments. Students could use the tutors as often as they pleased. Table 1 lists the number of students and the number of times they used the two tutors with each of the two treatments.

Table 1. Number of tutor users and uses in each treatment

	while loop	for loop
Max 3 revisions	1185/2162	1550/2957
Max 5 revisions	1647/2991	1141/2034

If a student solved the pretest problem incorrectly on a concept, solved sufficient number of problems during practice to demonstrate mastery, and went on to solve the post-test problem on the concept with a normalized score of at least 0.8, the student was categorized as having **learned** the concept. For our study, we used the number of concepts learned as a dependent variable.

In while loop tutor, students who were allowed 5 revisions learned significantly fewer concepts per session (1.30) than those who were allowed 3 revisions (1.40, $p = 0.02$). They solved significantly fewer problems than those who were allowed 3 revisions during practice (4.44 ± 0.32 with 3 revisions versus 3.87 ± 0.20 with 5 revisions, $p = 0.003$). One explanation for the differences is that students who were allowed more revisions engaged in more revisions and therefore, took longer to solve problems.

No such differences were found between treatments for for loop tutor. One explanation is that since students used for loop tutor after while loop tutor and the concepts covered by the two tutors were similar, students had less need for revisions in for loop tutor. *Students may revise their answers more when allowed more revisions when the concepts are unfamiliar to them. This may lead them to initially learn fewer concepts per session. But, with increased familiarity of concepts, students do not find the need to revise their answers as much, and any deleterious effect of allowing more revisions on the amount of learning fades.*

Mixed factor ANOVA analysis of while loop data of learned concepts with pretest and post-test score and pretest and post-test time as repeated measures and treatment (3 versus 5 revisions allowed) as between-subjects factor yielded:

- Significant within-subjects effect for score [$F(1,2349) = 3803$, $p < 0.001$]: mean score increased from 0.57 ± 0.01 on pretest to 0.99 ± 0.002 on post-test;
- Significant within-subjects effect for time [$F(1,2349) = 13.66$, $p < 0.001$]: time decreased from 94.95 ± 15.23 s on pretest to 66.64 ± 2.19 s on posttest;
- No significant between-subjects effect of treatment on score [$F(1,2349) = 1.67$, $p = 0.20$] or time [$F(1,2349) = 0.48$, $p = 0.49$] and no significant interaction between pre-post change in score and treatment [$F(1,2349) = 0.82$, $p = 0.37$] or pre-post change in time and treatment [$F(1,2349) = 1.3$, $p = 0.25$].

So, *students solved the post-test problem significantly more correctly and faster than pre-test problem, but there was no difference between treatments.* We found no significant main effect of treatment on the number of practice problems solved on the learned concepts, or the mean score per practice problem. But, we found a significant main effect of treatment on the mean time per practice problem solved [F (1,2683] = 8.29, p = 0.004]: students spent 68.73 ± 2.46 s per problem with 5 revisions compared to 63.80 ± 2.15 s per problem with 3 revisions. *So, students who were allowed 5 revisions spent significantly more time per practice problem than those who were allowed 3 revisions.*

Mixed factor ANOVA analysis of `for` loop data of learned concepts with pretest and post-test score and pretest and post-test time as repeated measures and treatment (3 versus 5 revisions) as between-subjects factor yielded:

- Significant within-subjects effect for score [F(1,2165) = 5140.84, p < 0.001]: mean score increased from 0.52 ± 0.01 on pretest to 1.00 on post-test;
- Significant within-subjects effect for time [F(1,2165) = 269.30, p < 0.001]: time decreased from 106.95 ± 5.80 s on pretest to 55.80 ± 1.95 s on posttest;
- Significant between-subjects effect of treatment on score [F(1,2165) = 5.33, p = 0.02]: Students who were allowed 3 revisions scored a mean of 0.75 ± 0.009 whereas, those who were allowed 5 revisions scored 0.77 ± 0.01. The interaction between pre-post and treatment was also significant [F(1,2165) = 5.09, p = 0.02]: students who were allowed 3 revisions improved from 0.51 on pretest to 0.997 on post-test whereas those who were allowed 5 revisions improved from 0.54 on pretest to 0.997 on post-test. We discounted this result because of ceiling effect, 1.0 being the maximum normalized score per problem.
- No significant between-subjects effect of treatment on time [F(1,2165) = 1.83, p = 0.18] or interaction between pre-post time and treatment [F(1,2165) = 0.53, p = 0.47].

Again, *students solved the post-test problem significantly more correctly and faster than pre-test problem, but the difference between treatments was minimal.* We found no significant main effect of treatment on the number of practice problems solved on the learned concepts, the mean score per practice problem or the mean time per practice problem solved. In contrast, treatment had a significant effect on mean time per practice problem solved on `while` loop tutor, the first tutor to be used by students. This once again reinforces that any negative effect of allowing for more revisions wears out with increased familiarity with the concepts.

Students did not score more per problem when allowed more revisions – so, allowing for revisions with error-flagging feedback was not a substitute for knowing the concepts underlying problems. They did not score less per problem either, although they spent more time per problem on `while` loop tutor. This might suggest that allowing for more revisions with error-flagging by itself may not invite gaming of the system by students, especially when solutions to problems are not of multiple-choice nature.

In this study, we evaluated the effect of allowing a limited number of revisions (as saliently displayed in the user interface of the tutor), not the effect of the number of revisions actually undertaken by students. In the future, we plan to analyze the data to check whether allowing for more revisions invites students to revise more, and if not, the effect of the number of revisions actually undertaken by students on the learning of students.

Acknowledgments. Partial support for this work was provided by the National Science Foundation under grant DUE-1432190.

References

1. Kumar, A.N.: Error-flagging support for testing and its effect on adaptation. In: Proceedings Intelligent Tutoring Systems (ITS 2010), LNCS 6094, pp 359–368 (2010)
2. Kumar, A.N.: Error-flagging support and higher test scores. In: Proceedings Artificial Intelligence in Education (AI-ED 2011), LNAI 6738, pp 147–154 (2011)
3. Kumar, A.N.: Limiting the number of revisions while providing error-flagging support during tests. In: Proceedings Intelligent Tutoring Systems (ITS 2012). LNCS 7315, pp 524–530 (2012)
4. Kumar, A.N.: Explanation of step-by-step execution as feedback for problems on program analysis, and its generation in model-based problem-solving tutors. In: Technology, Instruction, Cognition and Learning. (TICL) J. Special Issue on Problem Solving Support in Intelligent Tutoring Systems, vol. 4, no. 1 (2006)
5. Kumar, A.N.: A model for deploying software tutors. In: IEEE 6th International Conference on Technology for Education (T4E), Amritapuri, India, 12/18-21/2014, pp. 3–9 (2004)
6. Kumar, A.: A scalable solution for adaptive problem sequencing and its evaluation. In: Wade, V.P., Ashman, H., Smyth, B. (eds.) AH 2006. LNCS, vol. 4018, pp. 161–171. Springer, Heidelberg (2006). https://doi.org/10.1007/11768012_18
7. Schwonke, R., Renkl, A., Krieg, C., Wittwer, J., Aleven, V., Salden, R.: The worked-example effect: not an artefact of lousy control conditions. Comput. Human Behav. **25**(2), 258–266 (2009)

Learner-Context Modelling: A Bayesian Approach

Charles Lang[(✉)] [iD]

Teachers College, Columbia University, New York, NY 10027, USA
charles.lang@tc.columbia.edu

Abstract. The following paper is a proof-of-concept demonstration of a novel Bayesian model for making inferences about individual learners and the context in which they are learning. This model has implications for both efforts to create rich open leaner models, develop automated personalization and increase the breadth of adaptive responses that machines are capable of. The purpose of the following work is to demonstrate, using both simulated data and a benchmark dataset, that the model can perform comparably to commonly used models. Since the model has fewer parameters and a flexible interpretation, comparable performance opens the possibility of utilizing it to extend automation greater variety of learning environments and use cases.

Keywords: Context modelling · Personalization · Individualization · Open learner model · Bayes

1 Introduction

1.1 Learner-Context Models

The growth of artificial intelligence in education will be determined to some extent by our ability to expand into new formats and data collection contexts and of machines to model the learner across these disparate environments [9,11]. Here we take a tentative step towards an extensible learner model that would allow individual learner modelling across many different contexts and task types, as well as content domains. We build on work to create a Bayesian Learner-Context model that can support a wide range of task formats [6,7] and provide an alternative to other context modelling attempts [1,3,8]. The purpose of this paper is to introduce the model and benchmark it against other models with respect to prediction accuracy. Based on the results presented here we believe the model can find utility in expanding automated responses due to its simpler parameterization and more flexible interpretation. The research questions we intend to answer are:

1. How does the model perform on simulated data with respect to the recover of exact values? (i.e. if we knew the exact thoughts of learners)
2. How does the model compare to other models based on performance on benchmark data sets?

© Springer Nature Switzerland AG 2020
I. I. Bittencourt et al. (Eds.): AIED 2020, LNAI 12164, pp. 152–156, 2020.
https://doi.org/10.1007/978-3-030-52240-7_28

2 Methods

To capture the relationship between internal and external random variables, we appeal to Bayes rule, construing the internal factors as the learner's *prior knowledge* and the external factors as the *likelihood of the context given the learner's belief*. A Bayesian learner would take input from her environment to calculate a posterior probability of the truth of a hypothesis, given the current that environment $(P(H|D))$, from the likelihood of the data in light of the hypothesis $(P(D|H))$ and their prior belief in the hypothesis from their accumulated experience $(P(H))$ [4]. The likelihood is the degree to which the data confirms or dis-confirms the learner's belief in the hypothesis. The modeller's job then becomes to generate estimates of each individuals' likelihood and prior, to best predict their individual behavior at a task represented by the posterior probability. Within this framework, if we can characterize probabalistically a learner's prior knowledge and how that learner interprets their conditions we should be able to accurately predict their behavior. In other words, modelling learner behavior becomes a matter of resolving *what each individual learner brings to the table vs. what the table brings to each learner*:

$$Behavior \propto Context \times Prior Knowledge \tag{1}$$

The likelihood is what gives this model its ability to cover many different contexts, as long as the contexts can be coded, a probability distribution can be fit to them for each individual learner, represented as the Inverse Bayes Rule [10]:

$$\theta = \frac{\beta - \alpha\beta}{\alpha - 2\alpha\beta + \beta} \tag{2}$$

where θ is the posterior probability, α is the number of times the learner was correct and had experienced the specific context and θ is the prior probability. Code, data and further explanation is available in the following GitHub Repository.

2.1 Data

The data set used for analysis consists of 8,09, 12–14 year olds in the eighth grade of a school district in the North East of the United States during the 2009–10 school year. Student data were collected through ASSISTments, a web-based math tutoring system designed to prepare students for state standardized tests. Data consist of 603,128 log records. Each record is comprised of a timestamp recording when the learner answered the item, an item ID, student ID, the student's answer, the skill (of 153 possible skills) the item was testing and the type of item: multiple choice question, algebraic equation or text answer. All data was retrieved from ASSISTments [5]. No students can be identified.

3 Results

Figure 1A demonstrates certainty as we increase the number of conditions that the model is attempting to resolve while holding the number of hypotheses constant. Figure 1B demonstrates the reduction in error (represented by RMSE) of the estimate of the prior value over the number of items. For a single skill or hypothesis the estimate reaches within 0.1 of the true value within ten items.

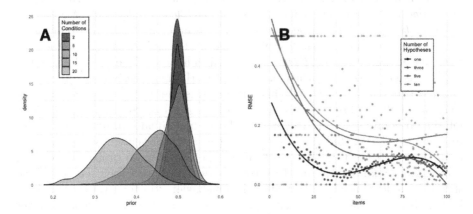

Fig. 1. Simulation results showing the relationship between number of items and the accuracy of belief estimation (A), decreasing error rates estimating prior probabilities over sequences of answers (B).

A comparison to other prediction algorithms on a benchmark prediction task can provide an idea of the relative efficacy of this model. Pardos and Heffernan 2011 have published performance of Bayesian Knowledge Tracing (both individualized and standard) on this same ASSISTments data set with an average cross validated AUC of 0.67 and 0.69 respectively [8]. The context-learner model achieves a cross-validated average AUC of 0.64.

4   Discussion

This paper presents a novel algorithm for predicting learner actions within automated systems, building on previous work that characterized learners as Bayesians [6,7]. The method involves making predictions about individual learners using the sequence of actions and the environment that they are operating in. We further quantified how successful the model is at forecasting learner scores using simulated learner data and a benchmark data set drawn from the ASSISTments online tutoring system.

Since the data is manufactured we have the control to measure how well the model can infer the true belief of the learner. This is not possible in reality but is informative to understand some characteristics of the model and infer what may happen when it is applied. Of particular concern is whether or not the model has useful statistical power, in other words, whether its ability to estimate the learner's state across a given number of skills and conditions given the number of items they have attempted. Whether these estimates have the requisite statistical power to be of use is an interesting and open question that will take more study. What is certain is that it is context driven, whether 100 items is too onerous for the learner depends a lot on what the item is. If it is moves within a game this may not be onerous at all, if each item is a essay question, collecting 100 over a short period of time may well be unrealistic. In the simulation run here it appeared that on average a single skill could be estimated within 0.1 of the true prior value within 15 items.

The validation model demonstrates some interesting characteristics of the method. In opposition to the findings in the simulated data, here there does not seem to be a strong relationship between accuracy and the number of times a skill is tested. Skills with greater number of items devoted to them do not see greater prediction accuracy than those with fewer. One possible reason for this are that all skills had sufficient attempts so there was no observable effect. But there were observable differences across contexts. Different item contexts appear to have different false negative rates. The model does better at predicting the answers to multiple choice questions than text based answers, with text based answers having a higher false negative rate. That we can differentiate contexts according to their accuracy rates suggests that contexts can be parsed by this model to categorize learners. This may provide characterizations that could be used to inform computer decision making. A model like BKT is limited to the insights it can gain to its four parameters - knowing, demonstrating, slipping, and guessing [2]. This model, although having fewer parameters, can provide information across an infinite number of contextual factors because the parameters refer directly to both the learner and the learner's context.

There are three chief benefits of this model. 1. It expands the vocabulary of outcomes that can be quantified beyond things that can be classified as correct/incorrect to anywhere any situation in any behavioral change can be quantified. 2. It allows a distinction to be made between learner proficiency and the impact of the environment that the learner finds herself within and 3. It is an individualised measure that is defined absent reference to other learners so can support flexible, bottom-up analysis of groups. There is currently no method with these characteristics available and it may prove a useful addition to the analytic methodology as it allows us to make more efficacious statements about individual learners, rather than relying on subgroup allocation. The benefits for automated personalization are substantial, but also for context modelling as this is an essential part of the methodology. Since the model requires context to be numerically estimated, context cannot be ignored nor treated as noise.

References

1. Baker, R.S.J., Corbett, A.T., Aleven, V.: More accurate student modeling through contextual estimation of slip and guess probabilities in bayesian knowledge tracing. In: Woolf, B.P., Aïmeur, E., Nkambou, R., Lajoie, S. (eds.) Intelligent Tutoring Systems. pp. 406–415. Lecture Notes in Computer Science, Springer, Heidelberg (2008). https://doi.org/10.1007/978-3-540-69132-7_44

2. Corbett, A.T., Anderson, J.R.: Knowledge tracing: modeling the acquisition of procedural knowledge. User Model. User-Adapted Interact. **4**(4), 253–278 (1994)
3. Fancsali, S.E., Ritter, S.: Context personalization, preferences, and performance in an intelligent tutoring system for middle school mathematics. In: Proceedings of the Fourth International Conference on Learning Analytics and Knowledge, pp. 73–77 (2014)
4. Gopnik, A., Tenenbaum, J.: Bayesian networks, Bayesian learning and cognitive development. Dev. Sci. **10**(3), 281–287 (2007). https://doi.org/10.1111/j.1467-7687.2007.00584.x
5. Heffernan, N.T., Heffernan, C.L.: The ASSISTments ecosystem: building a platform that brings scientists and teachers together for minimally invasive research on human learning and teaching. Int. J. Artif. Intell. Educ. **24**(4), 470–497 (2014). https://doi.org/10.1007/s40593-014-0024-x
6. Lang, C.: An adaptive model of student performance using inverse bayes. J. Learn. Anal. **1**(3), 154–156 (2014)
7. Lang, C.: Opportunities for personalization in modeling students as bayesian learners. In: Proceedings of the Seventh International Learning Analytics & Knowledge Conference, pp. 41–45 (2017)
8. Pardos, Z.A., Heffernan, N.T.: KT-IDEM: introducing item difficulty to the knowledge tracing model. In: Konstan, J.A., Conejo, R., Marzo, J.L., Oliver, N. (eds.) User Modeling, Adaption and Personalization, pp. 243–254. Lecture Notes in Computer Science, Springer, Heidelberg (2011). https://doi.org/10.1007/978-3-642-22362-4_21
9. Roll, I., Wylie, R.: Evolution and revolution in artificial intelligence in education. Int. J. Artif. Intell. Educ. **26**(2), 582–599 (2016). https://doi.org/10.1007/s40593-016-0110-3
10. Tian, G.L., Tan, M.: Exact statistical solutions using the Inverse Bayes Formulae. Stat. Probab. Lett. **62**(3), 305–315 (2003). https://doi.org/10.1016/S0167-7152(03)00044-0
11. Timms, M.J.: Letting artificial intelligence in education out of the box: educational cobots and smart classrooms. Int. J. Artif. Intell. Educ. **26**(2), 701–712 (2016). https://doi.org/10.1007/s40593-016-0095-y

Distinguishing Anxiety Subtypes of English Language Learners Towards Augmented Emotional Clarity

Heera Lee[⊠], Varun Mandalapu, Andrea Kleinsmith, and Jiaqi Gong[⊠]

University of Maryland, Baltimore County, Baltimore, MD 21250, USA
{heera1,jgong}@umbc.edu

Abstract. Public Speaking Anxiety (PSA) and Foreign Language Anxiety (FLA) afflict most English Language Learners (ELLs) during a presentation. However, few tools are available to help multicultural learners clearly identify which type of anxiety they are feeling. In this paper, we present a field study conducted in real language classrooms. We developed machine learning models based on features of electrodermal activity (EDA) to predict non-verbal behaviors manifested as PSA and FLA. The students were labeled with the anxiety categories both PSA and FLA, PSA more, FLA more, or no anxiety. To classify the ELLs into their respective anxiety categories, prominent EDA features were employed that supported the predictions of anxiety sources. These results may encourage both ELLs and instructors to be aware of the origins of anxiety subtypes and develop a customized practice for public speaking in a foreign language.

Keywords: EDA Features · Speaking anxiety · Emotional clarity

1 Introduction

English Language Learners (ELLs) reported more anxiety over speaking than other language skills including reading, writing, or listening [9,14] because Public Speaking Anxiety (PSA) known as social anxiety (e.g., being afraid of audience' attention) [17] and Foreign Language Anxiety (FLA) (e.g., fear of making mistakes in using a foreign language) [1,8,11] are accompanied particularly during presentation performance. Even though ELLs struggle with these subtypes of speaking anxieties, many studies and educators focus on external properties in training [4,6,12,15] rather than careful examination of discrete anxieties [2,7] influencing performance. To improve performance, the ELLs need emotional clarity, which refers to abilities to identify the origins of emotions [3]. By clearly identifying and distinguishing speaking anxieties as the first step, they can determine emotional regulation strategies such as adapting to changing conditions to cope with it [16]. In this context, this study noted the potential to use physiological arousal of electrodermal activity (EDA), which is often considered

© Springer Nature Switzerland AG 2020
I. I. Bittencourt et al. (Eds.): AIED 2020, LNAI 12164, pp. 157–161, 2020.
https://doi.org/10.1007/978-3-030-52240-7_29

as a biomarker to measure individual anxiety levels, [5,13] in a way to support augmented emotional clarity of ELLs. The main research question of this study is "Can EDA features extracted from wearable sensors classify the main source of speaking anxiety (PSA and FLA) among English language learners during an oral presentation in English?"

2 Method

33 students (16 males, 17 female) with intermediate English proficiency were recruited from Speaking classes in the English Language Institute (ELI) at the University of Maryland, Baltimore County (UMBC). The participants were ranged in age from 19 to 43 (mean age ±5.67 years). The experimental protocol was approved by the university's Institutional Review Board. The investigators took the presentation task from the ELI instructors to have an authentic experimental setting. To elicit a natural performance from participants, the location of an audio-video recording device was offset slightly to make the presenters less conscious of the camera and being recorded.

3 Analysis

As shown in Fig. 1 (a), we developed a framework of four sources of anxiety based on manual behavioral annotations of 33 audio-video recordings: eye contact linked to PSA more (P) as a social anxiety, the number of pauses and filler words (i.e. "um" and "ah") linked to FLA more (F), Both anxieties (B), and No anxiety (N).

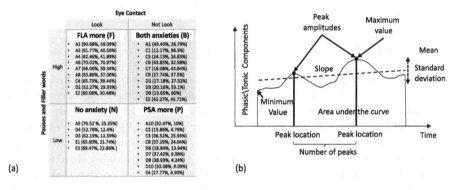

Fig. 1. (a) Four anxiety framework referring to behavioral annotation data as: participant ID (ratio of eye contact (%), the number of pauses and filler words (%)). (b) Ten features of each phasic and tonic from EDA signal

The students were divided into two groups named Look (low PSA) and Not Look (high PSA) based on a 50% ratio of eye contact with the audience in the annotation. These two groups were divided into two subgroups again based on accumulated behavioral annotation on the number of pauses and filler words. These groups were labeled High pauses and filler words (high FLA) and Low pauses and filler words (low FLA). The reference percentage of dividing these coordinates was the 25%, which corresponded with the interviewees' statements.

The EDA data collected from 33 participants underwent multiple cleaning and feature extraction steps. To reduce the severity of artifacts in EDA data, we used a smoothing method based on Hann function with a window size of 1 s. Once we removed artifacts in the EDA signal data, we used a range normalization function to normalize EDA data of all participants to mitigate the individual EDA signal differences between subjects and reduce bias. Once the data was cleaned, we extracted two sets of features from the EDA data. One set consisted of phasic and tonic components of one-dimensional EDA data, and the other set consisted of time-frequency (TF) and energy distribution extracted based on Hilbert Huang Transformation (HHT) method. The phasic and tonic features were further processed to extract mean, standard deviation, minimum and maximum values in a component, locations of minimum and maximum values, mean peak amplitudes, number of peaks, slope, and area under the curve as shown in Figure 1 (b). These EDA features were extracted based on a sliding window of 10 s with an overlap of five seconds that translates to 5326 windows. Similar to the phasic and tonic features, the TF features were extracted based on the same sliding window method.

3.1 Model Development

To understand the importance of different EDA features on ELL anxiety classification, we divide the datasets into multiple subsets based on features and labels. One subset of data consists of all features from Tonic and Phasic components of EDA signal, and time-frequency features from HHT. The other subsets include either tonic-phasic or HHT features. To classify ELL into one of the four anxieties framework,we adopted five machine learning algorithms: Decision Tree, Auto Multilayer Perceptron, Gradient Boosted Tree, Random Forest and Support Vector Machine. All the models are validated using a 10-fold cross-validation method that uses nine subsets of data for training and one for testing, and then it iterates until the algorithm predicts for all samples in a dataset. All the classification algorithms in this study are developed in the RapidMiner data science platform [10]. This study also focuses on identifying features that play a significant role in model prediction using LIME based feature importance method.

4 Result

The performance of each classifier is evaluated based on four metrics: Accuracy, Cohens Kappa, Recall, and Precision. Based on the comparison of these performance metrics between different classifiers on multiple datasets, gradient boosting algorithm outperformed other classifiers as shown in Table 1. Further-more, we also developed binary classifiers to classify 18 ELLs with 2622 samples that belong to either PSA or FLA anxiety types. GBT classifier performed well in predicting ELL anxiety type based on different input feature sets. Table 1 shows that the performance of GBT classifier with all features (HHT + Phasic-Tonic) is the highest. Finally, we also extract the feature importance of both multiclass and binary class GBT model predictions with varying inputs based on a LIME method mentioned in the earlier section. The Table 2 shows the top three supporting features of each classifier.

Table 1. The performance of multi-class and binary class gradient boosting classifier on different feature inputs.

Input Features	Accuracy		Kappa		Recall		Precision	
Class	Multi	Binary	Multi	Binary	Multi	Binary	Multi	Binary
PhasicTonic HHT	60.01	100.00	0.45	1.00	61.67	100.00	85.87	100.00
PhasicTonic	75.76	94.44	0.67	0.89	75.56	94.44	75.56	95.00
HHT	57.78	88.89	0.41	0.78	54.55	88.89	60.42	90.91

Table 2. Top three supporting features of a GBT algorithm on different data subsets based on a LIME method

Class_ Support Attribute	Multi_ Phasic Tonic HHT	Binary_ Phasic Tonic HHT	Multi_ Phasic Tonic	Binary_ Phasic Tonic	Multi_ HHT	Binary_ HHT
1	HHT Feature (0–0.1 Hz)	HHT Feature (0–0.1 Hz)	Min.Tonic component value	Sd. of Tonic data	HHT Feature (0–0.1 Hz)	HHT Feature (0–0.1 Hz)
2	Min. Tonic component value	Slope of Tonic data	Min. Phasic component value	Sd. of Phasic data	HHT Feature (1.8–1.9 Hz)	HHT Feature (1.8–1.9 Hz)
3	Max. Phasic component value	Sd. of Phasic data	Max. Phasic component value	Max. Phasic component value	HHT Feature (1.5–1.6 Hz)	HHT Feature (1.5–1.6 Hz)

5   Conclusion and Future Work

Our findings demonstrate the potential in using EDA to develop a classification model to identify subtypes of speaking anxiety (PSA and FLA). Our future work will focus on developing and evaluating an interactive education system where ELLs can identify their predominant speaking anxiety and apply it to emotional regulation strategies to cope with their anxiety.

References

1. Al-Nouh, N.A., Abdul-Kareem, M.M., Taqi, H.A.: EFL college students' perceptions of the difficulties in oral presentation as a form of assessment. Int. J. Higher Educ. **4**(1), 136–150 (2015)
2. Bosch, N., et al.: Automatic detection of learning-centered affective states in the wild. In: Proceedings of the 20th International Conference on Intelligent User Interfaces, pp. 379–388 (2015)
3. Butler, R.M., et al.: Emotional clarity and attention to emotions in cognitive behavioral group therapy and mindfulness-based stress reduction for social anxiety disorder. J. Anxiety Disorders **55**, 31–38 (2018)
4. Chen, L., Feng, G., Joe, J., Leong, C.W., Kitchen, C., Lee, C.M.: Towards automated assessment of public speaking skills using multimodal cues. In: Proceedings of the 16th International Conference on Multimodal Interaction, pp. 200–203. ACM (2014)
5. Croft, R.J., Gonsalvez, C.J., Gander, J., Lechem, L., Barry, R.J.: Differential relations between heart rate and skin conductance, and public speaking anxiety. J. Behav. Therapy Experimental Psychiatry **35**(3), 259–271 (2004)
6. Damian, I., Tan, C.S.S., Baur, T., Schöning, J., Luyten, K., André, E.: Augmenting social interactions: realtime behavioural feedback using social signal processing techniques. In: Proceedings of the 33rd Annual ACM Conference on Human Factors in Computing Systems, pp. 565–574. ACM (2015)
7. Dixon, L.Q., et al.: What we know about second language acquisition: a synthesis from four perspectives. Rev. Educ. Res. **82**(1), 5–60 (2012)
8. Epp, C.D.: English language learner experiences of formal and informal learning environments. In: Proceedings of the Sixth International Conference on Learning Analytics & Knowledge, pp. 231–235 (2016)
9. Horwitz, E.K., Horwitz, M.B., Cope, J.: Foreign language classroom anxiety. Modern Language J. **70**(2), 125–132 (1986)
10. Mierswa, I., Klinkenberg, R.: Rapidminer studio (2019)
11. Radzuan, N.R.M., Kaur, S.: Technical oral presentations in english: qualitative analysis of malaysian engineering undergraduates' sources of anxiety. Procedia-Soc. Behav. Sci. **29**, 1436–1445 (2011)
12. Schneider, J., Börner, D., Van Rosmalen, P., Specht, M.: Presentation trainer, your public speaking multimodal coach. In: Proceedings of the 2015 ACM on International Conference on Multimodal Interaction, pp. 539–546. ACM (2015)
13. Sevinç, Y.: Language anxiety in the immigrant context: sweaty palms? Int. J. Bilingualism **22**(6), 717–739 (2018)
14. Swain, M.: The inseparability of cognition and emotion in second language learning. Language Teach. **46**(2), 195–207 (2013)
15. Tanveer, M.I., Zhao, R., Chen, K., Tiet, Z., Hoque, M.E.: Automanner: an automated interface for making public speakers aware of their mannerisms. In: Proceedings of the 21st International Conference on Intelligent User Interfaces, pp. 385–396. ACM (2016)
16. Thompson, R.A.: Emotion regulation: a theme in search of definition. Monographs Soc. Res. Child Dev. **59**(2–3), 25–52 (1994)
17. Young, D.J.: An investigation of students' perspectives on anxiety and speaking. Foreign Language Ann. **23**(6), 539–553 (1990)

Siamese Neural Networks for Class Activity Detection

Hang Li[1], Zhiwei Wang[2], Jiliang Tang[2], Wenbiao Ding[1], and Zitao Liu[1(✉)]

[1] TAL Education Group, Beijing, China
{lihang4,dingwenbiao,liuzitao}@100tal.com
[2] Data Science and Engineering Lab, Michigan State University, East Lansing, USA
{wangzh65,tangjili}@msu.edu

Abstract. Classroom activity detection (CAD) aims at accurately recognizing speaker roles (either teacher or student) in classrooms. A CAD solution helps teachers get instant feedback on their pedagogical instructions. However, CAD is very challenging because (1) classroom conversations contain many conversational turn-taking overlaps between teachers and students; (2) the CAD model needs to be generalized well enough for different teachers and students; and (3) classroom recordings may be very noisy and low-quality. In this work, we address the above challenges by building a Siamese neural framework to automatically identify teacher and student utterances from classroom recordings. The proposed model is evaluated on real-world educational datasets. The results demonstrate that (1) our approach is superior on the prediction tasks for both online and offline classroom environments; and (2) our framework exhibits robustness and generalization ability on new teachers (i.e., teachers never appear in training data).

Keywords: Multimodal learning · Neural networks · Class activity detection

1 Introduction

It is essential to equip instructor training with informative dialogic feedback on their classroom activities, which allows teachers to adjust and refine their teaching instructions [1,4,10,17,24]. Prior researches have been demonstrated that pedagogical teaching styles and instructions may significantly influence students' engagements and academic achievements [18,22,26]. Traditionally, providing such feedback is very logistically complex and expensive, as it heavily relies on human annotations [3,14,20,21]. This makes it inapplicable in real-world education scenarios. Thus, in this work, we focus on building an automatic AI driven solution to solve this fundamental class activity detection (CAD) problem. More specifically, we aim at automatically annotating classroom audio recordings by

---

Z. Wang—Work was done when the authors did internship in TAL Education Group.

© Springer Nature Switzerland AG 2020
I. I. Bittencourt et al. (Eds.): AIED 2020, LNAI 12164, pp. 162–167, 2020.
https://doi.org/10.1007/978-3-030-52240-7_30

recognizing different speakers' roles, i.e., student or teacher. CAD solutions produce basic information about the quantities and distributions of classroom conversations, which are one of the essential steps for deep classroom analysis [16].

A large spectrum of models have been developed to solving the CAD problem [2,6,8,22]. Owens et al. proposed a machine learning algorithm that captures distinctive patterns in different instructional techniques and classifies the classroom sound into different class activities [22]. Cosbey et al. targeted on the same classroom sound classification problem as in [22] and adopted deep recurrent neural networks to extract meaningful features from audio frames [6]. Wang et al. conducted CAD by using LENA system [11] and identified three discourse activities of teacher lecturing, class discussion and student group work [30].

However, CAD in real-world scenarios is still extremely difficult because of three challenges: (1) *conversational turn-taking overlap*: Classroom conversations usually contain many frequent talk exchanges between teachers and students, which leads to a number of inextricable speech overlaps; (2) *vocal variability and uniqueness*: Every person's voice is different and unique, which poses a difficult question on the generalization ability of the CAD solution; and (3) *classroom noise*: Both online and offline classrooms in reality are dynamic, complex and noisy. In the attempt to solve the aforementioned challenges, we develop the Siamese neural framework to precisely detect teacher and student activities from classroom audio recordings. The contributions of this work are summarized as follows: (1) It presents a pioneer research on the CAD problem and proposes a novel Siamese neural framework to tackle this problem; and (2) we comprehensively evaluate our framework with different realizations and their benefits on both online and offline real-world, large-scale classroom datasets.

2   The Siamese Neural Framework

In this section, we describe our end-to-end Siamese neural framework for the CAD problem in details. Our framework consists of three key components: (1) feature extraction module that extracts window-level raw embeddings from a pre-train large-scale audio encoding neural network; (2) the representation learning module, which extracts semantic representations from each classroom audio segment; and (3) an attentional prediction module that predicts the activity type for each window. The overall framework architecture is shown in Fig. 1.

Feature Extraction. We first utilize a well-studied voice activity detection (VAD) system to segment audio streams into pieces of utterances and filter out the noisy and silent ones [23,25,27]. Then we transform each segment into frames of pre-defined width and step, and log-mel-filterbank energies of dimension 40 are extracted from each frame. After that, we obtain windows by using non-overlapping sliding windows of a fixed length on these frames. Once we create these audio windows from both teachers' vocal sample segments and classroom recording segments, we extract windows' corresponding low-dimensional dense vocal representations from a pre-trained acoustic neural network.

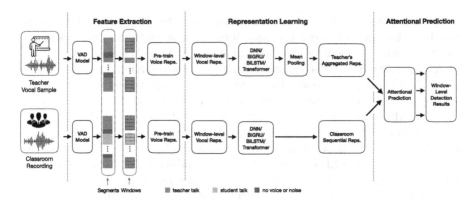

Fig. 1. The overview of our Siamese neural framework. VAD is short for voice activity detection.

Representation Learning. We learn a refined vocal representation for each window by utilizing the contextual dependencies within each segment (either from teachers' vocal samples or classroom recordings). In our framework, any existing sequential modeling function such as long short-term memory (LSTM), gated recurrent unit (GRU), etc. can be used [7,13,29]. By considering the contextual windows across entire segment, we are able to model the changes of tones and pitches in the audio stream smoothly and reduce the noises and outliers in the raw feature extraction component.

Attentional Prediction. We design an attentional prediction module focusing on the window-level class activity detection tasks. Our attentional prediction module is inspired by the intuition that all the audio windows spoken by the teacher share common attributes that are very different from those shared from student's audio windows. Thus, we use teachers' vocal samples as an aggregated query and compute an attention score with each individual window from classroom recordings. The higher the attentional score is, the more likely the audio window is spoken by the teacher. Based on this idea, we first add a mean pooling layer to aggregate all the teacher's vocal sample representations. This yields a robust and representative query embedding of the teacher's voice signals. The obtained vector is used as a voice biometrics query to compute attention scores with each individual window representation. In order to effectively train our framework, we design a cross-entropy loss function as the optimization objective. We use mini-batch stochastic gradient decent algorithm to minimize the objective and update the our model parameters.

3 Experiments

We evaluate our framework with two real-world K-12 education datasets: (1) the *online* dataset, which includes 400 classroom recordings and 300 distinct teachers from a third-party online education platform[1]; and (2) the *offline* dataset that includes 100 recordings and 36 distinct teachers from physical offline classrooms. We randomly select 100 and 10 recordings from *online* and *offline* dataset respectively as our test sets. The prediction results are denoted as "Main". Moreover, in order to evaluate the model generalization ability to new teachers, we further filter out teachers from above test set if the teachers appear in the training set and the prediction results are denoted as "Generalization". We choose to use area under curve (AUC) score to evaluate the model performance [9].

We choose the following approaches as our baselines: (1) *Average*: Vocal representations from feature extraction component are directly used for attentional prediction; (2) *DNN/GRU/LSTM*: A single layer fully connected neural network/a bidirectional GRU/a bidirectional LSTM is used in the representation learning component [5,12,19]. We use 128 neurons and ReLU as the activation function; and (3) *Transformer*: A transformer is used in the representation learning component [28]. We choose to use 2 layers in the transformer and set 4 heads for each layer. We set the dimension of each head to 16.

Experimental Results: The results are shown in Table 1. For the main task, we find that (1) the *Average* performs much worse than any other method. This suggests that the fine-tuned representation learning plays an important role in the final prediction; (2) compared to *GRU*, *LSTM*, and *Transformer*, *DNN* has achieve a lower detection accuracy. This is expected as it is not able to capture the contextual information of windows within each segment; (3) the performance of all methods on *online* dataset is generally better than results on *offline* dataset. We argue that this is because the signal to noise ratio of offline recordings is much higher than the ratio in online recordings [16]; and (4) both *GRU* and *Transformer* have comparable performance, which is consistent with the previous findings [15]. For the generalization task, we have similar observations. The high accuracy achieved by Transformer and LSTM demonstrates the generalization ability of the proposed framework.

Table 1. Experimental results on the *online* and *offline* datasets.

Task	Dataset	Average	DNN	GRU	LSTM	Transformer
Main	Online	0.895	0.926	0.936	0.933	0.942
	Offline	0.713	0.810	0.881	0.858	0.858
Generalization	Online	0.895	0.922	0.932	0.931	0.937
	Offline	0.749	0.840	0.880	0.805	0.882

---

[1] https://www.xes1v1.com/.

4   Conclusion

We present a Siamese framework to tackle the CAD problem. Experiments demonstrate both detection performance and generalization ability of our framework. In the future, we would like to design models that can combine both audio and video data to generate more comprehensive classroom activity feedback.

Acknowledgements. Zhiwei Wang and Jiliang Tang are supported by the National Science Foundation of United States under IIS1714741, IIS1715940, IIS1715940, IIS1845081 and IIS1907704.

References

1. Akalin, S., Sucuoglu, B.: Effects of classroom management intervention based on teacher training and performance feedback on outcomes of teacher-student dyads in inclusive classrooms. Educ. Sci. Theory Pract. **15**(3), 739–758 (2015)
2. Bergman, D.: Comparing the effects of classroom audio-recording and video-recording on preservice teachers' reflection of practice. Teacher Educator **50**(2), 127–144 (2015)
3. Brinko, K.T.: The practice of giving feedback to improve teaching: what is effective? J. Higher Educ. **64**(5), 574–593 (1993)
4. Chen, J., Li, H., Wang, W., Ding, W., Huang, G.Y., Liu, Z.: A multimodal alerting system for online class quality assurance. In: Isotani, S., Millan, E., Ogan, A., Hastings, P., McLaren, B., Luckin, R. (eds) International Conference on Artificial Intelligence in Education, pp. 381–385. Springer, Cham (2019). https://doi.org/10.1007/978-3-030-23207-8_70
5. Chung, J., Gulcehre, C., Cho, K., Bengio, Y.: Empirical evaluation of gated recurrent neural networks on sequence modeling. arXiv preprint arXiv:1412.3555 (2014)
6. Cosbey, R., Wusterbarth, A., Hutchinson, B.: Deep learning for classroom activity detection from audio. In: ICASSP 2019–2019 IEEE International Conference on Acoustics, Speech and Signal Processing (ICASSP), pp. 3727–3731. IEEE (2019)
7. Devlin, J., Chang, M.W., Lee, K., Toutanova, K.: Bert: pre-training of deep bidirectional transformers for language understanding. arXiv preprint arXiv:1810.04805 (2018)
8. Donnelly, P.J., et al.: Automatic teacher modeling from live classroom audio. In: Proceedings of the 2016 Conference on User Modeling Adaptation and Personalization, pp. 45–53 (2016)
9. Fawcett, T.: An introduction to ROC analysis. Pattern Recogn. Lett. **27**(8), 861–874 (2006)
10. Freiberg, H.J., Waxman, H.C.: Alternative feedback approaches for improving student teachers' classroom instruction. J. Teacher Educ. **39**(4), 8–14 (1988)
11. Ganek, H., Eriks-Brophy, A.: The language environment analysis (LENA) system: a literature review. In: Proceedings of the Joint Workshop on NLP for Computer Assisted Language Learning and NLP for Language Acquisition at SLTC, Umeå, 16th November 2016, pp. 24–32. No. 130, Linköping University Electronic Press (2016)
12. Hochreiter, S., Schmidhuber, J.: Long short-term memory. Neural Comput. **9**(8), 1735–1780 (1997)

13. Hu, J., Shen, L., Sun, G.: Squeeze-and-excitation networks. In: Proceedings of the IEEE Conference on Computer Vision and Pattern Recognition, pp. 7132–7141 (2018)
14. Kane, T.J., Staiger, D.O.: Gathering feedback for teaching: combining high-quality observations with student surveys and achievement gains. research paper. met project. Bill & Melinda Gates Foundation (2012)
15. Karita, S., et al.: A comparative study on transformer vs RNN in speech applications, pp. 449–456 (2019). https://doi.org/10.1109/ASRU46091.2019.9003750
16. Li, H., et al.: Multimodal learning for classroom activity detection. In: 2020 IEEE International Conference on Acoustics, Speech and Signal Processing (ICASSP), pp. 9234–9238. IEEE (2020)
17. Liu, Z., et al.: Dolphin: a spoken language proficiency assessment system for elementary education. In: Proceedings of The Web Conference 2020. p. 2641–2647. ACM (2020)
18. Lockheed, M.E.: School and classroom effects on student learning gain: the case of Thailand. World Bank (1987)
19. Murtagh, F.: Multilayer perceptrons for classification and regression. Neurocomputing 2(5–6), 183–197 (1991)
20. Nystrand, M.: CLASS: A Windows Laptop Computer System for the In-Class Analysis of Classroom Discourse. https://dept.english.wisc.edu/nystrand/class.html. Accessed 10 Oct 2019
21. Nystrand, M.: Research on the role of classroom discourse as it affects reading comprehension. Res. Teach. English 40, 392–412 (2006)
22. Owens, M.T., et al.: Classroom sound can be used to classify teaching practices in college science courses. Proc. Nat. Acad. Sci. 114(12), 3085–3090 (2017)
23. Ramırez, J., Segura, J.C., Benıtez, C., De La Torre, A., Rubio, A.: Efficient voice activity detection algorithms using long-term speech information. Speech Commun. 42(3–4), 271–287 (2004)
24. Scheeler, M.C., Ruhl, K.L., McAfee, J.K.: Providing performance feedback to teachers: a review. Teacher Educ. Special Educ. 27(4), 396–407 (2004)
25. Sohn, J., Kim, N.S., Sung, W.: A statistical model-based voice activity detection. IEEE Signal Process. Lett. 6(1), 1–3 (1999)
26. Tanner, K.D.: Structure matters: twenty-one teaching strategies to promote student engagement and cultivate classroom equity. CBE'Life Sci. Educ. 12(3), 322–331 (2013)
27. Tanyer, S.G., Ozer, H.: Voice activity detection in nonstationary noise. IEEE Trans. Speech Audio Process. 8(4), 478–482 (2000)
28. Vaswani, A., et al.: Attention is all you need. In: Advances in Neural Information Processing Systems, pp. 5998–6008 (2017)
29. Veličković, P., Cucurull, G., Casanova, A., Romero, A., Lio, P., Bengio, Y.: Graph attention networks. arXiv preprint arXiv:1710.10903 (2017)
30. Wang, Z., Pan, X., Miller, K.F., Cortina, K.S.: Automatic classification of activities in classroom discourse. Comput. Educ. 78, 115–123 (2014)

Deep-Cross-Attention Recommendation Model for Knowledge Sharing Micro Learning Service

Jiayin Lin[1(✉)], Geng Sun[1(✉)], Jun Shen[1,2(✉)], David Pritchard[2(✉)],
Tingru Cui[3(✉)], Dongming Xu[4(✉)], Li Li[5(✉)], Ghassan Beydoun[6(✉)],
and Shiping Chen[7(✉)]

[1] School of Computing and Information Techonology,
University of Wollongong, Wollongong, Australia
jl461@uowmail.edu.au, {gsun,jshen}@uow.edu.au
[2] Research Lab of Electronics, Massachusetts Institute of Technology,
Cambridge, MA, USA
dpritch@mit.ed
[3] University of Melbourne, Melbourne, Australia
tingru.cui@unimelb.edu.au
[4] UQ Business School, The University of Queensland, Brisbane, Australia
d.xu@business.uq.edu.au
[5] Faculty of Computer and Information Science, Southwest University,
Chongqing, China
lily@swu.edu.cn
[6] School of Information, System and Modelling,
University of Technology Sydney, Sydney, Australia
ghassan.beydoun@uts.edu.au
[7] Data 61, CSIRO, Sydney, NSW, Australia
shiping.chen@csiro.au

Abstract. Aims to provide flexible, effective and personalized online learning service, micro learning has gained wide attention in recent years as more people turn to use fragment time to grasp fragmented knowledge. Widely available online knowledge sharing is one of the most representative approaches to micro learning, and it is well accepted by online learners. However, information overload challenges such personalized online learning services. In this paper, we propose a deep cross attention recommendation model to provide online users with personalized resources based on users' profile and historical online behaviours. This model benefits from the deep neural network, feature crossing, and attention mechanism mutually. The experiment result showed that the proposed model outperformed the state-of-the-art baselines.

Keywords: Recommender system · Neural network · Micro learning · Machine learning · Information retrieval

© Springer Nature Switzerland AG 2020
I. I. Bittencourt et al. (Eds.): AIED 2020, LNAI 12164, pp. 168–173, 2020.
https://doi.org/10.1007/978-3-030-52240-7_31

1 Introduction

As a novel online learning style, micro learning aims to utilize users' fragmented spare time by helping them to carry out effective personalized learning activities [1–3]. Such online learning activities could be formal, informal, and non-formal [4], and online knowledge sharing is one way of non-formal learning. Quora,[1] Zhihu, [2] and Stack-overflow[3] are the most representative and successful online knowledge platforms, where users share knowledge by asking and answering questions. In the meantime, the online platforms continuously recommend questions and topics to the users based on their interests, background, and learning requirements.

As the key to the personalized online learning service, the recommendation strategy determines what information will be finally delivered to the target user [5]. As for a new online learning service in the big data era, conventional recommendation strategies, such as collaborative filtering and content-based filtering [6], are no longer suitable for catering the personalized learning requirements. A recommender system always needs to handle and merge different types and format of information ranging from the user's profile to the resource's profiles. Moreover, higher-order feature interaction is crucial for good performance [7]. How to precisely weight different features is also vital for a recommender system, as different features have various importance levels for a personalized recommendation task [8].

In this paper, we propose a novel model, which combines several advantages from different state-of-the-art recommender systems and offers them in a smooth one-stop manner. The rest of this paper will be organized as follows. Section 2 discusses some prior related work about recommender system used in micro learning. The proposed model is introduced and explained in Sect. 3. The relevant experiment of this study is discussed and analysed in Sect. 4. The conclusions are discussed in Sect. 5.

2 Related Work

The recommendation problem has been investigated for many years in different domains. However, the recommendation task in online education always involves some unique requirements or characteristics [9, 10]. In one prior study [11], the ant colony optimization (ACO) algorithm was proposed to recommend personalized learning paths to users based on the demographic information. The ontology-based method was used to add extra user's profile information and relieve the cold-start problem for micro learning service [12, 13]. Another study [14] investigated the learning path recommendation from micro learning service from an exploitation perspective. So far, there are little efforts on deep learning solutions to this problem.

Feature interaction means features involved in a recommendation task tend to influence each other with various combinations. Factorization machine (FM) [15] uses

---

[1] https://www.quora.com/.

[2] https://www.zhihu.com/.

[3] https://stackoverflow.com/.

embedding techniques to model the latent features in low dimensional space and represents the pair-wise feature interactions by using the inner product. It also shows a satisfactory performance when the dataset is in high sparsity, whereas SVMs fails [15]. However, due to the high computational complexity, in many cases, only 2-order feature interactions are involved in the FM.

Deep learning has demonstrated its powerful strength in modelling non-linear transformation in various AI tasks. Besides using deep neural for a recommendation task in isolation (for example [16]), many researchers argue that combining the advantages of deep neural networks (DNN) with classical methods such as linear model or FM could better learn sophisticated feature interactions [17–19].

3 The Proposed Model

In this study, we aim to effectively combine these functionalities: mining and generating high-order feature interaction, distinguishing the importance difference of both implicit and explicit features, and maintaining the original input information in a single network. To this end, we proposed a new deep cross attention network (DCAN) model for the recommendation task of the online knowledge sharing service. The input of the model contains both user-side and question-side information, and the embedding layer maps such information onto a low dimensional space. The embedding vectors are then passed into the DNN network and crossing network separately for mining latent information and high-order feature interactions. The processed results are combined together, and an attention network is used to distinguish the importance differences of different features. Finally, the output layer is used to make predictions with weighted features.

4 Experiments and Analysis

4.1 Evaluation Metrics and Baselines

Evaluation Metrics. As a binary classification task, the first evaluation metric used is Area Under Curve (AUC), which indicates how much a model is capable of distinguishing the two labels. Another metric used in our experiments is mean squared error (MSE), which directly reflects the prediction error of the involved models. Moreover, we also compared the binary cross entropy of the involved models.

Baselines. We compared our model with several state-of-the-art recommendation models, ranging from DeepFM [17], AutoInt [7], DCN [20], AFM [21], and FM [15]. The characteristics of used baselines are introduced in the previous sections.

Table 1. Experiment results of different models

Model	AUC	MSE	Binary cross entropy
FM	0.6934	0.1243	0.4060
DCN	0.7603	0.1134	0.3690
AFM	0.6881	0.1255	0.4094
AutoInt	0.7613	0.1130	0.3679
DeepFM	0.7404	0.1128	0.3671
Proposed model	**0.7848**	**0.1071**	**0.3442**

4.2 Dataset

The dataset is collected from an online knowledge-sharing platform, which contains around 1.8 million questions and users, and more than 4 million answers for the questions. Nearly 10 million <question, user> pairs are involved in this dataset.

4.3 Experiment Results

Based on the experiment results from Table 1, we can clearly see FM and AFM have lowest AUC values and highest MSE scores. These two models only involve low-order feature interactions. While others involve high-order feature interactions. Hence, high-order (complex) feature interactions are vital in the online learning resource recommendation tasks.

According to Table 1, the AUC scores of our proposed model and AutoInt model are the highest two. These two models refine the results of high-order feature interaction via the attention mechanism [22]. Such performance improvement demonstrates that different features/feature combinations are not equally important for personalized learning service, and attention mechanism can automatically distinguish the importance differences of the latent features or the feature combinations generated by the prior layers of the network.

5 Conclusions

In this study, we proposed a deep cross attention network (DCAN) for recommending personalized online learning resources to online learners. The experiment results clearly demonstrated that our model had potential in handling complex online learning recommendation problem. More specifically, according to the experiment results with authentic online knowledge sharing data, the strengths of DCAN can be concluded into two points: 1.this model can automatically mine and generate high-order feature interactions in both explicit and implicit ways; 2. the proposed model can further distinguish the importance differences of different features.

Acknowledgments. This research has been carried out with the support of the Australian Research Council Discovery Project, DP180101051, and Natural Science Foundation of China, no. 61877051, and UGPN RCF 2018–2019 project between University of Wollongong and University of Surrey. The work was also partially conducted during authors' collaborative visit to MIT and CSIRO.

References

1. Lin, J., et al.: From ideal to reality: segmentation, annotation, and recommendation, the vital trajectory of intelligent micro learning. World Wide Web, 1–21 (2019). http://dx.doi.org/10.1007/s11280-019-00730-9
2. Lin, J., et al.: A survey of segmentation, annotation, and recommendation techniques in micro learning for next generation of OER. In: 2019 IEEE 23rd International Conference on Computer Supported Cooperative Work in Design (CSCWD), pp. 152–157. IEEE (2019)
3. Sun, G., Cui, T., Yong, J., Shen, J., Chen, S.: MLaaS: a cloud-based system for delivering adaptive micro learning in mobile MOOC learning. IEEE Trans. Serv. Comput. **11**(2), 292–305 (2015)
4. Eshach, H.: Bridging in-school and out-of-school learning: formal, non-formal, and informal education. J. Sci. Educ. Technol. **16**(2), 171–190 (2007). https://doi.org/10.1007/s10956-006-9027-1
5. Lin, J., et al.: Towards the readiness of learning analytics data for micro learning. In: Ferreira, J.E., Musaev, A., Zhang, L.-J. (eds.) SCC 2019. LNCS, vol. 11515, pp. 66–76. Springer, Cham (2019). https://doi.org/10.1007/978-3-030-23554-3_5
6. Pazzani, M.J.: A framework for collaborative, content-based and demographic filtering. Artif. Intell. Rev. **13**(5-6), 393–408 (1999)
7. Song, W., et al.: Autoint: automatic feature interaction learning via self-attentive neural networks. In: Proceedings of the 28th ACM International Conference on Information and Knowledge Management, pp. 1161–1170. ACM (2019)
8. Huang, T., Zhang, Z., Zhang, J.: FiBiNET: combining feature importance and bilinear feature interaction for click-through rate prediction. In: Proceedings of the 13th ACM Conference on Recommender Systems, pp. 169–177 (2019)
9. Sikka, R., Dhankhar, A., Rana, C.: A survey paper on e-learning recommender system. Int. J. Comput. Appl. **47**(9), 27–30 (2012). https://doi.org/10.5120/7218-0024
10. Wu, D., Lu, J., Zhang, G.: A fuzzy tree matching-based personalized e-learning recommender system. IEEE Trans. Fuzzy Syst. **23**(6), 2412–2426 (2015). https://doi.org/10.1109/TFUZZ.2015.2426201
11. Zhao, Q., Zhang, Y., Chen, J.: An improved ant colony optimization algorithm for recommendation of micro-learning path. In: 2016 IEEE International Conference on Computer and Information Technology (CIT), pp. 190–196. IEEE (2016)
12. Sun, G., Cui, T., Shen, J., Xu, D., Beydoun, G., Chen, S.: Ontological learner profile identification for cold start problem in micro learning resources delivery. In: 2017 IEEE 17th International Conference on Advanced Learning Technologies (ICALT), pp. 16–20. IEEE (2017)
13. Sun, G., Cui, T., Xu, D., Shen, J., Chen, S.: A heuristic approach for new-item cold start problem in recommendation of micro open education resources. In: Nkambou, R., Azevedo, R., Vassileva, J. (eds.) ITS 2018. LNCS, vol. 10858, pp. 212–222. Springer, Cham (2018). https://doi.org/10.1007/978-3-319-91464-0_21

14. Rusak, Z.: Exploitation of micro-learning for generating personalized learning paths. In: DS 87-9 Proceedings of the 21st International Conference on Engineering Design (ICED 17), 21–25 August 2017, vol 9, pp. 129–138. Design Education, Vancouver (2017)
15. Rendle, S.: Factorization machines. In: 2010 IEEE International Conference on Data Mining, pp. 995–1000. IEEE (2010)
16. Zhang, W., Du, T., Wang, J.: Deep learning over multi-field categorical data. In: Ferro, N., et al. (eds.) ECIR 2016. LNCS, vol. 9626, pp. 45–57. Springer, Cham (2016). https://doi.org/10.1007/978-3-319-30671-1_4
17. Guo, H., Tang, R., Ye, Y., Li, Z., He, X.: DeepFM: a factorization-machine based neural network for CTR prediction. In: Proceedings of the Twenty-Sixth International Joint Conference on Artificial Intelligence, pp. 1725–1731 (2017)
18. Lian, J., Zhou, X., Zhang, F., Chen, Z., Xie, X., Sun, G.: xDeepFM: combining explicit and implicit feature interactions for recommender systems. In: Proceedings of the 24th ACM SIGKDD International Conference on Knowledge Discovery & Data Mining, pp. 1754–1763. ACM (2018)
19. Cheng, H.-T., et al.: Wide & deep learning for recommender systems. In: Proceedings of the 1st Workshop on Deep Learning for Recommender Systems, pp. 7–10. ACM (2016)
20. Wang, R., Fu, B., Fu, G., Wang, M.: Deep & cross network for ad click predictions. In: Proceedings of the ADKDD 2017. pp. 1–7 (2017)
21. Xiao, J., Ye, H., He, X., Zhang, H., Wu, F., Chua, T.-S.: Attentional factorization machines: learning the weight of feature interactions via attention networks. In: International Joint Conference on Artificial Intelligence, pp. 3119–3125 (2017)
22. Vaswani, A., et al.: Attention is all you need. In: Advances in Neural Information Processing Systems, pp. 5998–6008 (2017)

Investigating the Role of Politeness in Human-Human Online Tutoring

Jionghao Lin[1], David Lang[2], Haoran Xie[3], Dragan Gašević[1],
and Guanliang Chen[1(✉)]

[1] Monash University, Clayton, Australia
{jionghao.lin,dragan.gasevic,guanliang.chen}@monash.edu
[2] Stanford University, Stanford, CA, USA
dnlang86@stanford.edu
[3] Lingnan University, New Territories, Hong Kong SAR, China
hrxie2@gmail.com

Abstract. This study aims to investigate the role of politeness in online-tutoring practices by analyzing a large-scale human-human tutorial dialogue dataset. To this end, we employed linguistic theories of politeness to identify the politeness strategies contained in utterances made by tutors and students, and these strategies were further combined to quantify the politeness levels of tutors and students in a tutorial session. The results revealed that tutors had a similar level of politeness at the beginning of all dialogues, while students were more polite at the end if they successfully solved problems.

Keywords: Educational dialogue analysis · Politeness strategies

1 Introduction

Dialogue-based Intelligent Tutoring Systems (ITS), which are expected to act as professional human tutors to teach and interact with students, have been long desired and investigated [7,9,20,21]. Though being popular, most of the existing dialogue-based ITS are still plagued by their ineffectiveness in providing students with personalized learning experiences [1]. The reasons behind such ineffectiveness are multifaceted, among which the lack of sufficient pedagogical expertise was often blamed by researchers [2,5,8,11–14]. In addition to the existing research, we posit that the inability of acting as polite as human tutors might play as another influential role here, which is widely recognized as an integral part of civil behavior in social communications and has been demonstrated essential in several educational settings [10,15–19,22–25]. Instead of directly equipping existing dialogue-based ITS with the ability to deliver polite conversations with students, we first suggest investigating the importance of politeness in human-human online tutoring. Specifically, this paper proposes an approach to measure the politeness level of tutors and students in human-human online tutoring.

I. I. Bittencourt et al. (Eds.): AIED 2020, LNAI 12164, pp. 174–179, 2020.
https://doi.org/10.1007/978-3-030-52240-7_32

Formally, our work was guided by the following research question: *to what extent are tutors and students acting politely in human-human online tutoring?* To answer this question, we relied on a dataset consisting of over 15K dialogues collected in the setting of one-on-one online tutoring. Specifically, we identified the politeness strategies used by tutors and students by applying the linguistic theories of politeness developed in [3], i.e., the application of a politeness strategy can be indicated by the use of certain words and phrases (e.g., *"thank"* and *"appreciate"* are often used to express gratitude). Then, we defined a metric called *UP-Score*, which measures the overall politeness level of tutors and students by taking all of the observed politeness strategies into account. Our work contributes to the literature on dialogue-based ITS with the following main findings: (i) overall, both tutors and students acted politely across the whole tutorial process, among which dialogues with successful problem solving displayed a lower level of politeness than those without; (ii) tutors displayed a similar level of politeness at the beginning of all categories of dialogues, while students were more polite at the end if they successfully solved problems.

2   Approach

In human-human online tutoring, each tutorial session can be regarded as a series of requests, e.g., students request help from tutors to solve problems and tutors also request students to perform certain actions to solve the problems. As indicated in [6], a request from one person to another is likely to and mainly to give rise to negative politeness strategies, which recognize the friendliness with the other person but assume the expressed content would likely pose imposition on the other person [3]. For instance, the negative strategy *Gratitude* is an effective one for a requester (i.e., student) to help balance out the burden placed on a tutor (e.g., *"I would really appreciate if you could help me."*). Therefore, we mainly considered negative politeness strategies here. The embodiment of a politeness strategy can be revealed by the use of certain politeness markers and the positions of these markers. We identified the politeness strategies contained in utterances by employing the politeness strategy classifier constructed by Danescu et al. [6] with Support Vector Machines. In total, we considered a total of 21 politeness strategies in this study, which are explained in detail in [6].

It should be noted that the application of a politeness strategy can incur a sense of both politeness and impoliteness, For instance, when the word *"please"* is placed at the beginning of an utterance (e.g., *"Please do ..."*), it often incurs a sense of impoliteness. To measure the politeness level of an utterance, we further distinguished the 21 strategies into *polite* and *impolite* according to the empirical evidences shown in [6] and defined the **Politeness score** of an **Utterance** (*UP-Score* for short): UP-Score = # Polite strategies - # Impolite strategies. A positive UP-Score implies that the utterance is polite, while a negative value suggests an impolite one. Then, the UP-Scores of utterances generated by tutors or students were aggregated to answer the research question.

3   Dataset and Results

This study used the same tutorial dialogue dataset in [4] for analyses and experiments, which consists of over 15K dialogues crafted by tutors and students working together to solve problems covering subjects like mathematics and chemistry. To gain a better understanding of the role played by politeness in human-human online tutoring, we manually labelled the dialogues to one of the following categories based on the progress made by a student towards solving a problem: (i) *Gap-clarified*, which shows no clue whether the student made any learning progress or not; (ii) *Gap-explained*, the student identified what the underlying problem or error was but did not identified a correct or full solution; and (iii) *Gap-bridged*, the student successfully solved the problem or a similar problem. Most of the dialogues were of the category gap-bridged (57.1%), followed by gap-clarified (22.4%) and then gap-explained (20.5%).

The average *UP-Score* of students and tutors across different dialogues are given in Table 1. When considering all of the utterances made by tutors and students across all dialogues (Row 1), the *UP-Score* is 0.80, which implies that the tutorial sessions took place in a relatively polite atmosphere. Also, tutors were far more polite than students (1.01 vs. 0.49). When delving into the *UP-Score* values of different dialogues, we observe that, surprisingly, Gap-clarified dialogues, where students achieved the least amount of learning, were the most polite one (0.99), followed by Gap-explained (0.76) and then Gap-bridged (0.74). These results motivated us to further check the *UP-Score* of the utterances made by tutors and students at the beginning and the end of the dialogues (Fig. 1).

Table 1. The avg. *UP-Score* of students and tutors across dialogues of different categories. Differences were tested with Mann-Whitney test between any two of the three dialogue categories and are all significant ($p < 0.001$).

	All	G-clarified	G-explained	G-bridged
1. Avg. UP-Score (tutor & student)	0.80 ± 0.30	0.99 ± 0.38	0.76 ± 0.26	0.74 ± 0.24
2. Avg. UP-Score (tutor)	1.01 ± 0.41	1.27 ± 0.54	1.00 ± 0.35	0.91 ± 0.31
3. Avg. UP-Score (student)	0.49 ± 0.39	0.63 ± 0.53	0.39 ± 0.32	0.47 ± 0.33

Figure 1(a) shows that tutors of all types of dialogues displayed a similar level of politeness at the beginning, but the tutors in the Gap-clarified sessions became more polite than the others starting from the 7th utterance. By analyzing the frequent strategies adopted by tutors between 7th and 15th utterances, we found that the tutors in the Gap-clarified sessions used much less impolite strategies of *Direct_Start* and *Direct_Question* than the tutors in the Gap-explained and Gap-bridged sessions. This is probably because, in Gap-explained and Gap-bridged sessions, the tutors had successfully identified the difficulties encountered by students after the first few utterances and started to help students solve problems by giving direct opinions or concrete suggestions, and thus a higher usage of

Direct_Start and *Direct_Question*. When it comes to the end of the dialogues (Fig. 1 (b)), we notice that the politeness of the tutors in the Gap-clarified and Gap-explained sessions had a sudden increase from about 1.0 to 1.8 at the last utterance, while the politeness level of the tutors in the Gap-bridged sessions stayed relatively stable. This is because the polite strategy *Apologizing* was often employed by the tutors at the last utterance of Gap-clarified and Gap-explained dialogues to convey their apologies to the students for not being able to help. Lastly, we can observe that the students in Gap-bridged sessions were much more polite than the others at the end of dialogues, which is in line with our commonsense that students were likely to use strategies like *Gratitude* to express the acknowledgment and appreciation for the help provided by the tutors.

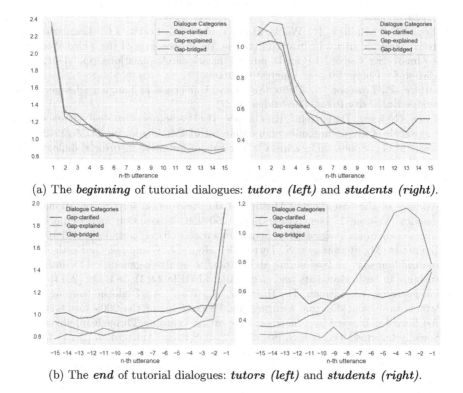

(a) The ***beginning*** of tutorial dialogues: ***tutors (left)*** and ***students (right)***.

(b) The ***end*** of tutorial dialogues: ***tutors (left)*** and ***students (right)***.

Fig. 1. The avg. *UP-Score* of tutors/students at the beginning/end of tutorial sessions.

4   Discussion and Conclusion

Our study brought several implications for online-tutoring practices. Firstly, though Gap-bridged tutors were likely to be less polite by employing more impolite strategies like *Direct_Start*, and *Direct_Question* to guide students after the first few utterances, these tutors had helped the students successfully solve problems. This implies that it may be worthy for online tutors to achieve a balance between polite strategies and impolite strategies so as to deliver effective tutoring to students. Secondly, it would be helpful to encourage students to maintain their politeness since the start of a tutorial session, as we observed that students with successful problem solving (i.e., the Gap-bridged ones) were slightly more polite than those without, though the causal relationship between the politeness levels of students and their performance needs to be further verified.

References

1. Almasri, A., et al.: Intelligent tutoring systems survey for the period 2000–2018 (2019)
2. Boyer, K.E., Phillips, R., Wallis, M.D., Vouk, M.A., Lester, J.C.: Learner characteristics and feedback in tutorial dialogue. In: Proceedings of the Third Workshop on Innovative Use of NLP for Building Educational Applications, pp. 53–61. Association for Computational Linguistics (2008)
3. Brown, P., Levinson, S.: Politeness: Some Universals in Language Usage. Cambridge University Press, Cambridge (1987)
4. Chen, G., Lang, D., Ferreira, R., Gasevic, D.: Predictors of student satisfaction: a large-scale study of human-human online tutorial dialogues. In: EDM (2019)
5. Core, M.G., Moore, J.D., Zinn, C.: The role of initiative in tutorial dialogue. In: EACL (2003)
6. Danescu-Niculescu-Mizil, C., Sudhof, M., Jurafsky, D., Leskovec, J., Potts, C.: A computational approach to politeness with application to social factors. In: Proceedings of the 51st Annual Meeting of the Association for Computational Linguistics (Volume 1: Long Papers), pp. 250–259. Association for Computational Linguistics, Sofia, August 2013. https://www.aclweb.org/anthology/P13-1025
7. Dzikovska, M., Steinhauser, N., Farrow, E., Moore, J., Campbell, G.: Beetle ii: deep natural language understanding and automatic feedback generation for intelligent tutoring in basic electricity and electronics. IJAIED **24**(3), 284–332 (2014)
8. Forbes-Riley, K., Litman, D., Huettner, A., Ward, A.: Dialogue-learning correlations in spoken dialogue tutoring. In: Proceedings of the 2005 Conference on Artificial Intelligence in Education: Supporting Learning Through Intelligent and Socially Informed Technology, pp. 225–232. IOS Press, Amsterdam (2005). http://dl.acm.org/citation.cfm?id=1562524.1562559
9. Graesser, A.C., Chipman, P., Haynes, B.C., Olney, A.: Autotutor: an intelligent tutoring system with mixed-initiative dialogue. IEEE Trans. Educ. **48**, 612–618 (2005)
10. Gupta, S., Walker, M.A., Romano, D.M.: How rude are you?: Evaluating politeness and affect in interaction. In: Paiva, A.C.R., Prada, R., Picard, R.W. (eds.) ACII 2007. LNCS, vol. 4738, pp. 203–217. Springer, Heidelberg (2007). https://doi.org/10.1007/978-3-540-74889-2_19
11. Hennessy, S., et al.: Developing a coding scheme for analysing classroom dialogue across educational contexts. Learn. Cult. Soc. Interact. **9**, 16–44 (2016). https://doi.org/10.1016/j.lcsi.2015.12.001. http://www.sciencedirect.com/science/article/pii/S2210656115300507

12. Katz, S., O'Donnell, G., Kay, H.: An approach to analyzing the role and structure of reflective dialogue. IJAIED **11**, 320–343 (2000). https://telearn.archives-ouvertes.fr/hal-00197333. Pilkington, R. (ed.) Part I of the Special Issue on Analysing Educational Dialogue Interaction
13. Maharjan, N., Rus, V.: A tutorial Markov analysis of effective human tutorial sessions. In: Proceedings of the 5th Workshop on Natural Language Processing Techniques for Educational Applications, pp. 30–34. Association for Computational Linguistics, Melbourne, Australia, July 2018. https://doi.org/10.18653/v1/W18-3704. https://www.aclweb.org/anthology/W18-3704
14. Maharjan, N., Rus, V., Gautam, D.: Discovering effective tutorial strategies in human tutorial sessions. In: The Thirty-First International Flairs Conference (2018)
15. Markus, M.: Politeness in interaction: an analysis of politeness strategies in online learning and teaching (2011)
16. McLaren, B.M., DeLeeuw, K.E., Mayer, R.E.: A politeness effect in learning with web-based intelligent tutors. Int. J. Hum Comput Stud. **69**(1–2), 70–79 (2011)
17. McLaren, B.M., Lim, S.J., Yaron, D., Koedinger, K.R.: Can a polite intelligent tutoring system lead to improved learning outside of the lab? Front. Artif. Intell. Appl. **158**, 433 (2007)
18. Nashruddin, N.: Politeness principles used by EFL teacher in classroom interaction and its implication toward teaching-Learning Process. Ph.D. thesis, Universitas Negeri Makassar (2017)
19. Pearson, N.K., Kreuz, R.J., Zwaan, R.A., Graesser, A.C.: Pragmatics and pedagogy: conversational rules and politeness strategies may inhibit effective tutoring. Cogn. Instr. **13**(2), 161–188 (1995)
20. Rus, V., D'Mello, S., Hu, X., Graesser, A.: Recent advances in conversational intelligent tutoring systems. AI Mag. **34**(3), 42–54 (2013)
21. VanLehn, K., Graesser, A.C., Jackson, G.T., Jordan, P.W., Olney, A., Rosé, C.P.: When are tutorial dialogues more effective than reading? Cogn. Sci. **31**(1), 3–62 (2007)
22. Wang, N., Johnson, W.L., Mayer, R.E., Rizzo, P., Shaw, E., Collins, H.: The politeness effect: pedagogical agents and learning outcomes. Int. J. Hum.-Comput. Stud. **66**(2), 98–112 (2008). https://doi.org/10.1016/j.ijhcs.2007.09.003. http://www.sciencedirect.com/science/article/pii/S1071581907001267
23. Wang, N., Johnson, W.L., Rizzo, P., Shaw, E., Mayer, R.E.: Experimental evaluation of polite interaction tactics for pedagogical agents. In: Proceedings of the 10th International Conference on Intelligent User Interfaces, pp. 12–19 (2005)
24. Yao, L.: How polite you are: A study of learners' politeness strategies used in avatars in the second life virtual world (2018)
25. Yoga, W.I., Ketut, S.I., Hery, S.M.: The implications of politeness strategies among teachers and students in the classroom (2018)

Raising Academic Performance in Socio-cognitive Conflict Learning Through Gamification

Zhou Long[1,2], Dehong Luo[1], Kai Kiu[2,3], Hongli Gao[2,4], Jing Qu[5], and Xiangen Hu[2,6(✉)]

[1] Huaihua University, Huaihua 418000, China
[2] Central China Normal University, Wuhan 430079, China
xiangenhu@gmail.com
[3] Bohai University, Jingzhou 121013, China
[4] Xinxiang Medical University, Xinxiang 453003, China
[5] Peking University, Beijing 100871, China
[6] University of Memphis, Memphis 38152, USA

Abstract. Drawing on the social interdependence theory, we experimentally compared the between-group effects of social learning gamification, competition gamification, and non-gamification on the academic performance in the within-group socio-cognitive conflict learning. Findings show that the positive learning effects of socio-cognitive conflict in within-group are strengthened when the between-group gamification is designed by social learning or competitive strategy.

Keywords: Gamification · Socio-cognitive conflict · Academic performance

1 Introduction

Socio-cognitive conflict occurs within a group when a learner is confronted with different ideas and conceptions that other group members embrace [1]. We have acknowledged the positive power of socio-cognitive conflict in the setting of within-group learning for a long time, but less understood the outsider between-group effects on within-group socio-cognitive conflict learning. Our aim is the generation of testable prediction about how the between-group effects might shape the learning results of within-group socio-cognitive conflict.

We framed the research in the context of between-group gamification because it is a more selective, funny, and constructive between-group avenue. *Gamification*, generally defined as "the use of game design features in non-game contexts" [2], has been used across a variety of scenarios to motivate people to engage in particularly targeted behaviors. Gamification in group learning situations could be driven by social influence-oriented strategies, such as social learning and competition, which are effective at motivating the learner to accomplish target behavior [2, 3]. *Social learning strategy*, based on Bandura's Social Learning Theory, states that people learn from

© Springer Nature Switzerland AG 2020
I. I. Bittencourt et al. (Eds.): AIED 2020, LNAI 12164, pp. 180–184, 2020.
https://doi.org/10.1007/978-3-030-52240-7_33

others through observing what they are performing towards the target behaviors. While *competition strategy*, derived from the human natural motivation to outperform one another, drives them to perform some desired behavior and provides opportunities for users to compete with one another. In the present study, we adopt a mixed-design experiment to testify experiences of socio-cognitive conflicts in the gamification of social learning or competition that are likely to trigger stronger positive academic performance.

2 Method and Results

Undergraduate Participants. 106 undergraduates at a general university in China were recruited to participate in exchange for extra course credits. They all had no related learning experience in the research method (experimental material). Four volunteers were dropped from the dataset because their finishing time of the experiment was over 3 standard deviations above average time. This resulted in a final sample of 102 participants (68 female and 34 males, mean age = 21.08 yrs).

Mixed Design. The study involved a 4 (Socio-cognitive Conflict Induction: true-false, false-true, false-false, true-true) × 3 (Gamification Strategy: social learning strategy, competition strategy, no gamification) mixed design. Participants received all four types of socio-cognitive conflict induction in a Graeco-Latin Square order and were randomly assigned to one of the gamification strategy conditions. Proportional academic performance was computed as (posttest - midtest)/(1 − midtest).

Socio-cognitive Conflict Induction Manipulation. Similar to D'Mello et al. [4], *socio-cognitive conflict induction* was operationalized by varying contradictory information in agent agreement and information correctness during the trialogues (three-party conversation: a participant and two pedagogical peer agents) phase. In the control condition, both animated agents agreed on the correct information (true-true), while in the other three experimental conditions, two agents either disagreed with each other or agreed with the incorrect information. After both agents presented their respective opinions, then one of them would ask the participant to express himself. The contradiction between the agents' opinions was expected to trigger the participant's socio-cognitive conflict (see Fig. 1).

Gamification Strategy Manipulation. Like the within-group factor of socio-cognitive conflict induction, the between-group factor of gamification strategy was also manipulated during the trialogues phase in the experiment. Following Oinas-Kukkonen's guideline, we operationally defined the *social learning strategy* as providing a game board listing effective cognitive strategies adopted by participants in other groups with higher scores, such as critically writing opinions and reasons contrary to group members [3]. The *competition strategy* was operationalized by presenting a leaderboard after each trialogue round. We drew attention to the group who fell behind on the leaderboard by flashing their teams' names and scores. Their name and score were intentionally showed in the last 16–20 positions. This failure feedback was also reinforced by hue - the late five positions were red and the former fifteen white, and by toggling the display of the scores. We chose feedback about failure position in competition here as research suggests that individuals contribute more to the group when the group performance is worse [5] (see Fig. 2).

Fig. 1. Screenshot of the learning interface.   **Fig. 2.** Leaderboard with both color feedback and displayed score. (Color figure online)

Procedure. All research content and procedure were presented via an intelligent tutoring system environment developed for the purposes of this study (see Fig. 1 for a screenshot). The experiment occurred over five phases (total 2.5 h): the participants (1) took a pretest for prior knowledge, (2) acquired research method knowledge through multimedia learning to identify the contradictory of information in later trialogues, (3) took a mid-test to assess and control over academic performance in multimedia learning, (4) attended eight trialogues (each about one concept) that offer contradictory and gamification information to induce the participant's socio-cognitive conflict in between-group different atmospheres (see Fig. 1 and 2), and last (5) took a post-test to check each one's overall academic performance. Each trialogue in the fourth phase began with a description of a research method practice case. The research methods contents mainly consist of fundamental design principles (e.g., random assignment and control groups).

Academic Performance Measurement. We tested the learning content about eight concepts of research method covered in eight trialogues for three times, including pretest, mid-test, and post-test. The academic performance served as the dependent variable was used to assess the benefit of socio-cognitive conflict induction, indicated by the score gap between the post-test and mid-test. Each test had 24 multiple-choice questions with three questions per concept. The three types of items were based on the

Table 1. Means (M) and Standard Deviations (SD) of academic performances.

	SLS ($N = 34$) M (SD)	CS ($N = 34$) M (SD)	NS ($N = 34$) M (SD)	Total ($N = 102$) M (SD)
True-false	.37 (.16)	.39 (.19)	.26 (.2)	.34 (.19)
False-true	.39 (.13)	.33 (.16)	.28 (.22)	.33 (.18)
False-false	.33 (.12)	.2 (.14)	.19 (.11)	.24 (.14)
True-true	.18 (.09)	.21 (.16)	.2 (.09)	.2 (.11)

Notes. SLS = Social Learning Strategy, CS = Competition Strategy, NS = No Gamification.

first three levels of Bloom's Taxonomy (knowledge, comprehension, and application). Three alternate test versions and assignments were counterbalanced across participants.

Results of Academic Performance. To test which strategy of gamification benefited the participant's academic performances and whether these effects were dependent on the socio-cognitive conflict occurrence, we ran a 4 (Socio-cognitive Conflict Induction) × 3 (Gamification Strategy) mixed-model analysis of variance (ANOVA), with repeated measures on the factor of Socio-cognitive Conflict Induction. This analysis yielded a significant interaction between socio-cognitive conflict induction and gamification strategy, $F(6, 297) = 4.46$, $p < .001$, $\eta_p^2 = .09$. Simple-effects analyses suggested that participants experiencing socio-cognitive conflict under the true-false condition reported more learning gains in social learning (Table 1, $M_{SLS-NS} = .12$, $SD = .04$, $p < .05$) and competition strategy gamification groups (Table 1, $M_{CS-NS} = .13$, $SD = .04$, $p < .05$) than the control group. However, socio-cognitive conflict experience under false-false condition only showed better performances in the social learning strategy group (Table 1, $M_{SLS-NS} = .15$, $SD = .03$, $p < .001$) than the control group and a nonsignificant pattern in the competition strategy group. As anticipated, there was no significant difference in the none socio-cognitive conflict experience condition (Table 1, $M_{SLS-NS} = -.02$, $SD = .02$, $p = .79$; $M_{CS-NS} = .01$, $SD = .01$, $p = .98$).

3   Discussion

Drawing on social-functional perspectives on group learning [5] and Social Interdependence Theory [6] in particular, we developed and tested the idea that learners facing within-group socio-cognitive conflicts acquire more knowledge when they are in between-group gamification. Due to using the between-group gamification design, this study extended the preceding studies by addressing the issue of environmental boundary conditions of socio-cognitive conflict in learning. We also obtained additional evidence about the different impacts of the outside between-group gamification environment on the complex learning effects of within-group socio-cognitive conflict. More specifically, under simple and clear socio-cognitive conflict condition (true-false), participants acquired more knowledge about scientific research content in the social learning and competition gamification strategy group rather than the control condition. However, among the participants in the false-false condition of socio-cognitive conflict which were complex and obscure the effect for them was only observed in the social learning gamification strategy group. An explanation could be that when the participants with low knowledge background face complex learning tasks, they need cognitive support more than motivational support.

This conclusion suggests that between-group environments should not be treated as little relevant cues. Instead, they should be incorporated in team learning, theorizing as informative social signals that help learners make sense of both within-group and between-group social situations. The next step is to investigate whether between-group gamification strategies have the power to change other forms of within-group learning activities.

Acknowledgments. We would like to thank the supports from the Project of Research on the Confusion Emotion in the Problem Solving of Normal School Students Adjusted by Intelligent Tutoring System (Grant NO. 18B491), and the Project of Research on the Intervention of Confusion Emotion of Normal School Students under the Context of Intelligent Education (Grant NO. XSP20YBZ175).

References

1. Limón, M.: On the cognitive conflict as an instructional strategy for conceptual change: a critical appraisal. Learn. Instr. **11**(4–5), 357–380 (2001)
2. Deterding, S., Dixon, D., Khaled, R., Nacke, L.: From game design elements to gamefulness: defining "gamification". In: Proceedings of the 15th International Academic MindTrek Conference: Envisioning Future Media Environments, pp. 9–15. ACM, September 2011
3. Oduor, M., Alahäivälä, T., Oinas-Kukkonen, H.: Persuasive software design patterns for social influence. Personal Ubiquitous Comput. **18**(7), 1689–1704 (2014)
4. D'Mello, S., Lehman, B., Pekrun, R., Graesser, A.: Confusion can be beneficial for learning. Learn. Instr. **29**, 153–170 (2014)
5. Cárdenas, J.C., Mantilla, C.: Between-group competition, intra-group cooperation and relative performance. Front. Behav. Neurosci. **9**, 33 (2015)
6. Lewin, K.: Action research and minority problems. J. Soc. Issues **2**(4), 34–46 (1946)

Towards Interpretable Deep Learning Models for Knowledge Tracing

Yu Lu[1,2], Deliang Wang[2], Qinggang Meng[1], and Penghe Chen[1(✉)]

[1] Advanced Innovation Center for Future Education,
Beijing Normal University, Beijing, China
{luyu,chenpenghe}@bnu.edu.cn
[2] School of Educational Technology,
Beijing Normal University, Beijing, China

Abstract. Driven by the fast advancements of deep learning techniques, deep neural network has been recently adopted to design knowledge tracing (KT) models for achieving better prediction performance. However, the lack of interpretability of these models has painfully impeded their practical applications, as their outputs and working mechanisms suffer from the intransparent decision process and complex inner structures. We thus propose to adopt the post-hoc method to tackle the interpretability issue for deep learning based knowledge tracing (DLKT) models. Specifically, we focus on applying the layer-wise relevance propagation (LRP) method to interpret RNN-based DLKT model by backpropagating the relevance from the model's output layer to its input layer. The experiment results show the feasibility using the LRP method for interpreting the DLKT model's predictions, and partially validate the computed relevance scores. We believe it can be a solid step towards fully interpreting the DLKT models and promote their practical applications.

Keywords: Knowledge tracing · Interpretability · Deep learning

1 Introduction

The rapid development of ITS and MOOC platforms greatly facilitates building KT models by collecting a large size of learner's learning and exercise data in a rapid and inexpensive way. Yet, the collected massive and consecutive exercise questions are usually associated with multiple concepts, and the traditional KT models cannot well handle the questions without explicit labels and capture the relationships among a large size of concepts (e.g., 100 or more concepts). Accordingly, deep learning models are recently introduced into the KT domain because of their powerful representation capability [12]. Given the sequential and temporal characteristics of learner's exercise data, the recurrent neural network (RNN) [14] is frequently adopted for building the deep learning based knowledge tracing (DLKT) models. Since it is difficult to directly measure the actual knowledge state of a learner, the existing DLKT models often adopt an alternative solution that minimizes the difference between the predicted and the real

I. I. Bittencourt et al. (Eds.): AIED 2020, LNAI 12164, pp. 185–190, 2020.
https://doi.org/10.1007/978-3-030-52240-7_34

responses on exercise questions. Hence, the major output of DLKT models are the predicted performance on next questions. As a popular implementation variants of RNN, the long short-term memory (LSTM) unit [11] and GRU [7] are widely used in the DLKT models, and have achieved comparable or even better prediction performance in comparison to the traditional KT models [6,12].

Similar as the deep learning models operating as a "black-box" in many other domains [10], the existing DLKT models also suffer from the interpretability issue, which has painfully impeded the practical applications of DLKT models in the education domain. The main reason is that it is principally hard to map a deep learning model's abstract decision (e.g. predicting correct on next question) into the target domain that end-users could easily make sense of (e.g., enabling the ITS designers or users to understand why predicting correct on next question). In this work, we attempt to tackle the above issue by introducing the proper interpreting method for the DLKT models. In particular, we adopt a post-hoc interpreting method as the tool to understand and explain the RNN-based DLKT models, and the experiment results validate its feasibility.

2   Related Work

As indicated earlier, deep learning models are recently introduced into the KT domain, as they have enough capacity to automatically learn the inherent relationships and do not require explicit labels on the concept level. Deep knowledge tracing (DKT) [12] that utilizes LSTM can be regarded as the pioneer work, while some limitations have been reported [15]. Subsequently, other DLKT models [5,6,17,18] are proposed to improve KT performance.

The interpretability can be categorized into *ante-hoc* and *post-hoc* interpretabilities. Among different methods for *post-hoc* interpretability, the LRP method [3] can be regarded as a typical one, where the share of model output received by each neuron is properly redistributed by its predecessors to achieve the relevance conservation, and the injection of negative relevance is controlled by its hyperparameters. LRP method is applicable and empirically scales to general deep learning models. It has been adopted for image classification [1], machine translation [8] and text analysis [2]. In the education domain, researchers have started interpreting KT models [16], but most studies target on the traditional simple-structured Bayesian network-based ones [4,13]. In this work, we mainly focus on explaining the DLKT models by using the LRP interpretability method.

3   Interpreting RNN-Based KT Model

3.1   RNN-Based DLKT Model

A number of DLKT models, such as DKT [12], adopt LSTM or similar architectures (e.g., GRU) to accomplish the KT task. As a typical RNN architecture, the model maps an input sequence vectors $\{x_0, ..., x_{t-1}, x_t, ...\}$ to an output sequence vectors $\{y_0, ..., y_{t-1}, y_t, ...\}$, where x_t represents the interaction between learners and exercises, and $\mathbf{y_t}$ refers to the predicted probability vectors on mastering the concepts. The standard LSTM unit is usually implemented in the DLKT models as follows:

$$f_t = \sigma\left(\mathbf{W_{fh}}h_{t-1} + \mathbf{W_{fx}}\mathbf{x_t} + b_f\right) \tag{1}$$

$$i_t = \sigma\left(\mathbf{W_{ih}}h_{t-1} + \mathbf{W_{ix}}\mathbf{x_t} + b_i\right) \tag{2}$$

$$\widetilde{C_t} = \tanh\left(\mathbf{W_{ch}}h_{t-1} + \mathbf{W_{cx}}\mathbf{x_t} + b_c\right) \tag{3}$$

$$C_t = f_t \odot C_{t-1} + i_t \odot \widetilde{C_t} \tag{4}$$

$$o_t = \sigma\left(\mathbf{W_{oh}}h_{t-1} + \mathbf{W_{ox}}\mathbf{x_t} + b_o\right) \tag{5}$$

$$h_t = o_t \odot \tanh\left(C_t\right). \tag{6}$$

After getting the LSTM output h_t, the DLKT models usually further adopt an additional layer to output the final predicted results y_t as below:

$$\mathbf{y_t} = \sigma\left(\mathbf{W_{yh}}h_t + b_y\right) \tag{7}$$

From the above implementations, we see that the RNN-based DLKT models usually consist of two types of connections: **weighted linear connection**, i.e., Eq. (1), (2), (3), (5), (7), and **multiplicative connection**, i.e., Eq. (4) and (6). The two types would be interpreted by LRP in different ways.

3.2   Interpreting DLKT Models Using LRP Method

Considering the RNN-based DLKT model given in Eq. (1) to (7) and the LRP method, interpreting can be accomplished by computing the relevance as below:

$$R_{h_t} = \frac{\mathbf{W_{yh}}h_t}{\mathbf{W_{yh}}h_t + b_y + \varepsilon * \text{sign}(\mathbf{W_{yh}}h_t + b_y)} * R_{y_t}^d \tag{8}$$

$$R_{C_t} = R_{h_t} \tag{9}$$

$$R_{f_t C_{t-1}} = \frac{f_t C_{t-1}}{C_t + \varepsilon * sign(C_t)} * R_{C_t} \tag{10}$$

$$R_{C_{t-1}} = R_{f_t C_{t-1}} \tag{11}$$

$$R_{i_t \tilde{C}_t} = \frac{i_t \tilde{C}_t}{C_t + \varepsilon * sign(C_t)} * R_{C_t} \tag{12}$$

$$R_{\tilde{C}_t} = R_{i_t \tilde{C}_t} \tag{13}$$

where $R_{y_t}^d$ is the value of the dth dimension of the prediction output y_t, and the item $\varepsilon * sign()$ is a stabilizer. Finally, the calculated relevance value R_{x_t} for the input x_t can be derived as

$$R_{x_t} = \frac{\mathbf{W_{cx}}\mathbf{x_t}}{\mathbf{W_{ch}}h_{t-1} + \mathbf{W_{cx}}\mathbf{x_t} + b_c + \varepsilon * \text{sign}(\mathbf{W_{ch}}h_{t-1} + \mathbf{W_{cx}}\mathbf{x_t} + b_c)} * R_{\tilde{C}_t}$$

Note that the above process is applicable to computing the relevance of the model inputs (e.g., x_{t-1}), while computing $R_{C_{t-1}}$ might be slightly different.

4   Evaluation

We choose the public educational dataset ASSISTment 2009–2010 [9], and the dataset used for training the DLKT model consists of 325,637 answering records on 26,688 questions associated with 110 concepts from 4,151 students. The built DLKT model adopts the LSTM unit with the hidden dimensionality of 256. During the training process, the mini-batch size and the dropout are set to 20 and 0.5 respectively. Considering KT as a classification problem and the exercise results as binary variables, namely 1 representing correct and 0 representing incorrect answers, the overall prediction accuracy achieves 0.75.

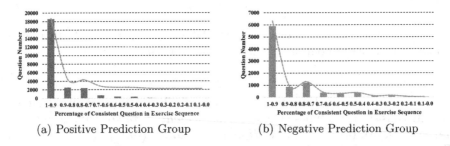

(a) Positive Prediction Group   (b) Negative Prediction Group

Fig. 1. Histogram of the consistent rate on both positive and negative prediction groups

We conduct the experiment to understand the relationship between the LRP interpreting results and the model prediction results. Specifically, we choose 48,673 exercise sequences with a length of 15, i.e., each sequence consisting of 15 individual questions, as the test dataset for the interpreting tasks. For each sequence, we take its first 14 questions as the input to the built DLKT model, and the last one to validate the model's prediction on the 15th question. As the result, the DKLT model correctly predicts the last question for 34,311 sequences, where the positive and negative results are 25,005 and 9,306 respectively. Based on the correctly predicted sequences, we adopt the LRP method to calculate the relevance values of the first 14 questions, and then investigate whether the sign of relevance values is consistent with the correctness of learner's answer. Specifically, we define *consistent question* among the previous exercise questions as "either the correctly-answered questions with a positive relevance value" or "the falsely-answered questions with a negative relevance value". Accordingly, we compute the percentage of such consistent questions in each sequence, and name it as *consistent rate*. Intuitively, a high *consistent rate* reflects that most correctly-answered questions have a positive contribution and most falsely-answered questions have a negative contribution to the predicted mastery probability on the given concept. Figure 1 shows the histogram of the consistent rate on both groups of positive prediction (i.e., the mastery probability above 50%) and negative prediction (i.e., the mastery probability below 50%). Clearly, we see that the majority of the exercise sequences achieve 90%

(or above) consistent rate, which partially validates the question-level feasibility of using LRP method to interpret DLKT model's prediction results.

5   Conclusion

We have introduced a post-hoc interpretability method into KT domain, which is applicable to general RNN-based DLKT models. We demonstrated the promise of this approach via using its LRP method to explain DLKT models. We conducted the preliminary experiments to validate the proposed method.

Acknowledgment. This research is partially supported by the National Natural Science Foundation of China (No. 61702039 and No. 61807003), the Fundamental Research Funds for the Central Universities, and CCF-Tencent Open Fund.

References

1. Arbabzadah, F., Montavon, G., Müller, K.-R., Samek, W.: Identifying individual facial expressions by deconstructing a neural network. In: Rosenhahn, B., Andres, B. (eds.) GCPR 2016. LNCS, vol. 9796, pp. 344–354. Springer, Cham (2016). https://doi.org/10.1007/978-3-319-45886-1_28
2. Arras, L., Horn, F., Montavon, G., Muller, K., Samek, W.: What is relevant in a text document? An interpretable machine learning approach. PLoS ONE **12**(8), 0181142 (2017)
3. Bach, S., Binder, A., Montavon, G., Klauschen, F., Muller, K., Samek, W.: On pixel-wise explanations for non-linear classifier decisions by layer-wise relevance propagation. PLoS ONE **10**(7), 0130140 (2015)
4. Baker, R.S.J., Corbett, A.T., Aleven, V.: More accurate student modeling through contextual estimation of slip and guess probabilities in bayesian knowledge tracing. In: Woolf, B.P., Aïmeur, E., Nkambou, R., Lajoie, S. (eds.) ITS 2008. LNCS, vol. 5091, pp. 406–415. Springer, Heidelberg (2008). https://doi.org/10.1007/978-3-540-69132-7_44
5. Chaudhry, R., Singh, H., Dogga, P., Saini, S.K.: Modeling hint-taking behavior and knowledge state of students with multi-task learning. In: Proceedings of Educational Data Mining (2018)
6. Chen, P., Lu, Y., Zheng, V.W., Pian, Y.: Prerequisite-driven deep knowledge tracing. In: 2018 IEEE International Conference on Data Mining (ICDM), pp. 39–48. IEEE (2018)
7. Cho, K., Van Merriënboer, B., Bahdanau, D., Bengio, Y.: On the properties of neural machine translation: encoder-decoder approaches. arXiv preprint arXiv:1409.1259 (2014)
8. Ding, Y., Liu, Y., Luan, H., Sun, M.: Visualizing and understanding neural machine translation. In: Proceedings of the 55th Annual Meeting of the Association for Computational Linguistics, vol. 1, pp. 1150–1159 (2017)
9. Feng, M., Heffernan, N., Koedinger, K.: Addressing the assessment challenge with an online system that tutors as it assesses. User Model. User-Adap. Inter. **19**(3), 243–266 (2009). https://doi.org/10.1007/s11257-009-9063-7
10. Grégoire, M., Wojciech, S., Klaus-Robert, M.: Methods for interpreting and understanding deep neural networks. Digit. Signal Process. **73**, 1–15 (2018)

11. Hochreiter, S., Schmidhuber, J.: Long short-term memory. Neural Comput. **9**(8), 1735–1780 (1997)
12. Piech, C., et al.: Deep knowledge tracing. In: Advances in Neural Information Processing Systems, pp. 505–513 (2015)
13. Qiu, Y., Qi, Y., Lu, H., Pardos, Z.A., Heffernan, N.T.: Does time matter? Modeling the effect of time with bayesian knowledge tracing. In: Proceedings of Educational Data Mining Workshop at the 11th International Conference on User Modeling, pp. 139–148 (2011)
14. Schuster, M., Paliwal, K.K.: Bidirectional recurrent neural networks. IEEE Trans. Signal Process. **45**(11), 2673–2681 (1997)
15. Xiong, X., Zhao, S., Van Inwegen, E., Beck, J.: Going deeper with deep knowledge tracing. In: EDM, pp. 545–550 (2016)
16. Yang, H., Cheung, L.P.: Implicit heterogeneous features embedding in deep knowledge tracing. Cogn. Comput. **10**(1), 3–14 (2018)
17. Yeung, C.: Deep-IRT: make deep learning based knowledge tracing explainable using item response theory. In: Proceedings of Educational Data Mining (2019)
18. Zhang, J., Shi, X., King, I., Yeung, D.Y.: Dynamic key-value memory networks for knowledge tracing. In: Proceedings of the 26th International Conference on World Wide Web, pp. 765–774 (2017)

Early Prediction of Success in MOOC from Video Interaction Features

Boniface Mbouzao[1](✉), Michel C. Desmarais[1](✉), and Ian Shrier[2](✉)

[1] Polytechnique Montreal, Montreal, Canada
{boniface.mbouzao,michel.desmarais}@polymtl.ca
[2] McGill University, Montreal, Canada
ian.shrier@mcgill.ca

Abstract. The popularity of online learning, such as MOOCs (Massive Open Online Courses), continues to increase among students. However, MOOCs dropout remains high. Prediction of student performance that could feed instructors' dashboards and help them adapt their course structure and material, or trigger help and tailor interventions to specific groups of students, is a valuable research objective. Towards that end, this paper focuses on three predictive metrics (student attendance rate: AR, utilization rate: UR, and watching index: WI) of how students interact with MOOC videos in order to predict which group of students will pass or fail the course. Results show that these metrics, taken after the first week and the midpoint, can be highly effective for predicting the students that will pass or fail the course.

Keywords: MOOC · Video watching traces · Attendance rate · Utilization rate · VBL · Watch index

1 Introduction

Can the analytics of student interaction with videos provide effective predictors of their academic performance? With thousands of students registering for online courses every year, it is of great interest to both MOOC developers and instructors to predict, early on in the course, those students that may drop out or who are instead likely to complete the course successfully. Yet, by using data directly from student behaviours with video-based-learning (VBL), we believe we can predict student performance with minimal research bias while helping the student to avoid failing the course. The interactions during the first week of the course are a key reference point in predicting student performance throughout the course [8], should the student remain enrolled in the MOOC. This can inform the MOOC developers, and instructors, of those students who are likely to persist and perform better in the MOOC if the course was tailored to their learning needs rather than focus on large-volume enrollment to the detriment of successful student performance. The aim of this paper is to investigate characteristics of video utilization that can determine if a student will likely fail or pass at an early stage of the MOOC; even as early as after one week of interaction with VBL modules.

© Springer Nature Switzerland AG 2020
I. I. Bittencourt et al. (Eds.): AIED 2020, LNAI 12164, pp. 191–196, 2020.
https://doi.org/10.1007/978-3-030-52240-7_35

2   Related Work

A fair amount of research is devoted to study student video interactions, including specific characteristics of video watching behaviors.

For instance, Giannakos et al. [4] found a relationship between video interactions, repeated viewing, and the level of cognition required for a specific video segments. Li et al. [13], also studied the link between student behavior patterns and learning performance. Their study included features as: videos lectures, lecture slides, shared assignments and open-forum messages. They concluded that video lectures and lecture slide were the most used by students. He et al. [7] measured the student's utilization of video in a MOOC and its relation to academic performance. They proposed indicators based on student interaction data to measure the utilization of video resources such as: attendance and utilization rates plus watch ratio. Our study measures the utilization and attendance rates for performance prediction. Hughes et al. [9], show how the use of data analysis techniques in MOOCs can help to predict at risk of dropout students before it happens. Some studies used learners' behaviour by defining engagement [12], online social networking [3] to predict performance [10] or predict dropouts [6]. Then it is possible to identify student that might dropouts early enough [11] to give them proper help before it happens [14]. The student performance can be influenced by some features of the videos themselves [5] bringing students to play a video more than others [2,17], or spend more time on video than on other online resources [16].

Beyond video interactions, prediction of success and failure was done by Baker et al. [1] based on student online activity using Soomo Learning Environment. Using many prediction models they show that using the logistic regression model of their propose combined model they can identify up to 59.5% of students who will perform poorly in the course way better than chance performance. Recently, Adithya et al. [18] analyzed students logs of three blended courses to predict student performance, (see also Owen et al. [15] with student profile for performance prediction). The results of their research show that it is possible to predict student performance through student level of use of online system.

3   Methodology

The general objective of this study is to use video interaction metrics to assess the likelihood that a student will succeed in a MOOC. We also aim to evaluate the accuracy of these estimates as a function of the MOOC timeline; earlier estimates are deemed to be less accurate but more useful for remedial purposes. We first describe the three metrics involved and then describe how they are used to define groups. The metrics such as AR and UR are inspired from [7].

The attendance rate $AR_{s,c}$ of a student s on a given week c since the beginning of the course, is the number of videos that the student played over to the total number of videos up to that period in time of the course schedule.

The utilization rate $UR_{s,c}$ of a student s on a given week c since the beginning of the course is the proportion of video play time activity of the student over the sum of video lengths for all videos up to week c.

$$AR_{s,c} = \frac{|W_{s,c}|}{|V_c|} \tag{1}$$

$$UR_{s,c} = \frac{\sum_{i=1}^{n} Wt_{s,i}}{\sum_{j=1}^{N} Vt_j} \tag{2}$$

The watch index (WI) is defined as:

$$WI_{s,c} = UR_{s,c} \times AR_{s,c} \tag{3}$$

Where: $UR_{s,c}$ is utilization rate of student s at week c, Vt_j is the duration of video j, N the total number of videos released up to week c, $Wt_{s,i}$ is the total time student s played video i, n is the number of unique videos that student s played up to week c. $AR_{s,c}$ is the attendance rate of student s after week c, V_c is the course's total number of videos released after week c, $W_{s,c}$ is the collection of different videos watched by student s after week c.

The rule for grouping and testing is taking from the classification of a single student compared to the average value of the group of student. The student that has metrics over the average value of the group of student enrolled in the course is likely to pass the course. The algorithm for groupings student is:

IF $(WI_{i,c} < \overline{WI}$ OR (student i did not submit assignment))
THEN {Student i in GROUP I}
ELSE {Student i in GROUP II}
Where $\overline{WI}$ is the average WI over all students.

4   Data Set

Our study uses the traces of an online course at McGill University on the edX platform that had 30,640 students interacting with learning videos. The course has 138 videos (plus one live session). It has 13 weeks duration. Among students who interacted with the videos, 10,424 students are honors and 970 passed the course. Here, the first week of the course had nine (9) videos with a total length of 41 min. We extracted 2,733,169 different student watching events (play, pause, seek forward/backward, stop). Event data is structured such that we can compute the play time of each student for each video.

5   Results

Table 1 shows the results of classifying students into two groups according to the rule defined above. We find that after a week of data, students who passed the course overwhelmingly fall into group II (78%). The trend is even stronger after week 6 (93%). However, for the students who failed (or dropped) the course, the split is almost even between the two groups. Then, 60% of the students who fail are in Group I, and that ratio grows to 2/3 after the sixth week. We can see that around 4/5 of the students that will succeed the course will be in Group II, whereas around 60% of students who will fail will be in Group I. These results show an improvement compared to previous study using the same kind of metrics to red flag at risk of failing students. Comparing these results to the one that we obtained using the methodology of He et al. [7] (results shown within parenthesis), we see that after the first week there is no majority class separating student who will pass or fail between the two groups. The majority of students who will pass and the majority of student who will fail are all in group II according to He et al. [7] methodology. After six week the results based on their methodology identify majority classes (majority of students who passed are in group II and majority of students who fail are in group I) but there are still 35% of students who passed in group I.

Table 1. Breakdown of success rates and groupings for first and sixth week

	After first week		After six weeks	
	Pass	Fail	Pass	Fail
Group I	22% (15%)	60% (9%)	7% (35%)	67% (93%)
Group II	78% (85%)	40% (91%)	93% (65%)	33% (7%)
	100% (100%)	100% (100%)	100% (100%)	100% (100%)

Values within parenthesis are the results of He et al. [7], reported for comparison purpose.

6   Conclusion

Through quantitative analysis that includes metrics such as Attendance Rate (AR), Utilization Rate (UR), and Watch Index (WI), as defined in this paper, it is possible to identify failure patterns of up to 60% of students who will dropout or fail the course based on the first week student interaction with MOOC videos, based on a total course length of thirteen (13) weeks, and can identify 78% of successful students.

Using the metrics defined, educational institutions can flag students at risk of failing, or dropout, of the MOOC based on the student's interactions with the learning videos in the early stages of the course. Our study shows a better classification compared previous study results of He et al. [7]. Results such as these should help MOOC developers better identify those students that might dropout or fail the course and thus take actions to prevent it.

References

1. Baker, R.S., Lindrum, D., Lindrum, M.J., Perkowski, D.: Analyzing early at-risk factors in higher education e-learning courses. International Educational Data Mining Society (2015)
2. Breslow, L., Pritchard, D.E., DeBoer, J., Stump, G.S., Ho, A.D., Seaton, D.T.: Studying learning in the worldwide classroom: research into edx's first MOOC. Res. Pract. Assess. **8**, 13–25 (2013)
3. Brinton, C.G., Chiang, M., Jain, S., Lam, H., Liu, Z., Wong, F.M.F.: Learning about social learning in MOOCS: from statistical analysis to generative model. IEEE Trans. Learn. Technol. **7**(4), 346–359 (2014)
4. Giannakos, M.N., Chorianopoulos, K., Chrisochoides, N.: Making sense of video analytics: lessons learned from clickstream interactions, attitudes, and learning outcome in a video-assisted course. Int. Rev. Res. Open Distrib. Learn. **16**(1), 260–283 (2015)
5. Guo, P.J., Kim, J., Rubin, R.: How video production affects student engagement: an empirical study of mooc videos. In: Proceedings of the First ACM Conference on Learning@ Scale Conference, pp. 41–50. ACM (2014)
6. Halawa, S., Greene, D., Mitchell, J.: Dropout prediction in MOOCS using learner activity features. Exp. Best Pract. Around MOOCs **7**, 3–12 (2014)
7. He, H., Zheng, Q., Dong, B., Yu, H.: Measuring student's utilization of video resources and its effect on academic performance. In: 2018 IEEE 18th International Conference on Advanced Learning Technologies (ICALT), pp. 196–198. IEEE (2018)
8. Hill, P.: Emerging student patterns in MOOCs: a (revised) graphical view (2013). https://mfeldstein.com/emerging-student-patterns-in-moocs-a-revised-graphical-view/
9. Hughes, G., Dobbins, C.: The utilization of data analysis techniques in predicting student performance in massive open online courses (moocs). Res. Pract. Technol. Enhanced Learn. **10**(1), 10 (2015)
10. Jiang, S., Williams, A., Schenke, K., Warschauer, M., O'dowd, D.: Predicting MOOC performance with week 1 behavior. In: Educational Data Mining 2014 (2014)
11. Kamahara, J., Nagamatsu, T., Kaieda, Y., Ishii, Y.: Behavioral analysis using cumulative playback time for identifying task hardship of instruction video. In: 2010 5th International Conference on Future Information Technology, pp. 1–6. IEEE (2010)
12. Kizilcec, R.F., Piech, C., Schneider, E.: Deconstructing disengagement: analyzing learner subpopulations in massive open online courses. In: Proceedings of the Third International Conference on Learning Analytics and Knowledge, pp. 170–179. ACM (2013)
13. Li, L.Y., Tsai, C.C.: Accessing online learning material: quantitative behavior patterns and their effects on motivation and learning performance. Comput. Educ. **114**, 286–297 (2017)
14. Li, N., Kidzinski, L., Jermann, P., Dillenbourg, P.: How do in-video interactions reflect perceived video difficulty? In: Proceedings of the European MOOCs Stakeholder Summit 2015, pp. 112–121. No. EPFL-CONF-207968, PAU Education (2015)
15. Lu, O.H., Huang, A.Y., Huang, J.C., Lin, A.J., Ogata, H., Yang, S.J.: Applying learning analytics for the early prediction of students' academic performance in blended learning. J. Educ. Technol. Soc. **21**(2), 220–232 (2018)

16. Ozan, O., Ozarslan, Y.: Video lecture watching behaviors of learners in online courses. Educ. Media Int. **53**, 27–41 (2016)
17. Seaton, D.T., Bergner, Y., Chuang, I., Mitros, P., Pritchard, D.E.: Who does what in a massive open online course? Commun. ACM **57**(4), 58–65 (2014)
18. Sheshadri, A., Gitinabard, N., Lynch, C.F., Barnes, T., Heckman, S.: Predicting student performance based on online study habits: a study of blended courses. arXiv preprint arXiv:1904.07331 (2019)

Predicting Reading Comprehension from Constructed Responses: Explanatory Retrievals as Stealth Assessment

Kathryn S. McCarthy[1]([✉]) [iD], Laura K. Allen[2] [iD],
and Scott R. Hinze[3] [iD]

[1] Georgia State University, Atlanta, USA
kmccarthy12@gsu.edu
[2] University of New Hampshire, Durham, USA
laura.allen@unh.edu
[3] Middle Georgia State University, Macon, USA
scott.hinze@mga.edu

Abstract. Open-ended *constructed responses* promote deeper processing of course materials. Further, evaluation of these explanations can yield important information about students' cognition. This study examined how students' constructed responses, generated at different points during learning, relate to their later comprehension outcomes. College students (N = 75) produced self-explanations *during* reading and explanatory retrievals *after* reading. The Constructed Response Assessment Tool (CRAT) was used to analyze these responses across multiple dimensions of language and relate these textual features to comprehension performance. Results indicate that the linguistic features of post-reading explanatory retrievals were more predictive of comprehension outcomes than self-explanations. Further, these models relied on different indices to predict performance.

Keywords: Natural language processing · Science learning · Stealth assessment

1 Introduction

Learning from text is a critical skill, but many students struggle with content-based reading [1]. Prompting students to generate *constructed responses* (e.g., verbal protocols, summaries) is beneficial because it encourages active processing [2, 3] and these responses can also serve as "stealth assessments" [4, 5] of in situ learning that continually update a learner model and drive feedback without needing to wait for more formal checkpoint quizzes or module exams.

In the current study, we explore the use of *explanatory retrieval* prompts as stealth assessments. Explanatory retrievals are a type of constructed response in which students explain what they have just read from memory. As an elaborative or constructive version of retrieval practice, explanatory retrieval may yield superior comprehension as compared to free recall prompts or completing multiple-choice or fill-in-the-blank tests

© Springer Nature Switzerland AG 2020
I. I. Bittencourt et al. (Eds.): AIED 2020, LNAI 12164, pp. 197–202, 2020.
https://doi.org/10.1007/978-3-030-52240-7_36

[6, 7]. Not only is this approach effective, but it is also practical in the sense that asking students to "explain what you have just read about [*topic*]" rather than answer a series of quiz questions reduces the need for instructors or instructional designers to generate numerous items. Finally, these activities may have value as stealth assessments that can track students' learning processes and progress.

Although explanatory retrievals are beneficial for learning, they are often underutilized in the classroom due to the arduous nature of scoring open-ended responses [8]. Fortunately, natural language processing (NLP) tools have afforded an increased use of constructed responses within educational technologies [9, 10]. NLP analyses can be used to automate scoring and provide targeted feedback for a variety of constructed responses including think-alouds [11], self-explanations [12], summaries [13, 14], and essays [15]. Notably, the indices implicated in these analyses vary across constructed response type, presumably because they reflect different strategies and cognitive processes. Taken together, this research demonstrates the potential for analyzing explanatory retrievals as a mode of stealth assessment, but also highlights the need to consider how explanatory retrievals might differ from other forms of constructed response.

Thus, in the current study, we examine how linguistic features of explanatory retrievals (ERs) relate to comprehension test performance. We also examine how ERs compare with another type of constructed response, self-explanation (SE), for which linguistic features have been studied. The prior research guides two primary hypotheses: 1) The linguistic features of the responses will provide information predictive of subsequent comprehension test performance and 2) The features of ERs that predict comprehension performance will differ from the predictive features in SEs. In other words, as a retrieval (i.e., memory-based) process, post-reading ER may bring to bear different strategies and processes than what is found in concurrent SEs.

2   Method

2.1   Design and Procedure

College students (N = 75; M_{age} = 25.04; 72% female; 13% ESL) read two science texts. At nine points in each text, students were directed to generate an SE. After reading, participants were prompted to produce an ER. The instructions specified the goal was not to simply recall as much as possible, but to provide a coherent explanation of the information in the text. After reading and explaining both texts, participants completed multiple-choice comprehension tests for each text. Each test included four memory items and four inference items.

2.2   Data Processing

SEs were combined to create an "aggregated SE" for each text [16–18]. These aggregated SEs and the ERs were submitted to the Constructed Response Analysis Tool (CRAT) [19]. CRAT calculates more than 700 indices related to 1) similarities (key words overlap, latent semantic analysis) between a source text and a constructed response and 2) lexical sophistication and text properties. After the SEs and ERs had been analyzed by CRAT, the dataset was reduced based on multicollinearity and relation to the dependent variable. Thus, when two variables were highly multicollinear ($r > .70$), only the index most strongly related to the dependent variable was retained. Additionally, indices that exhibited a weak or absent relationship with the dependent variable ($r < .10$) were removed from the dataset. After this process, there were 50 CRAT indices remaining for the machine learning analyses.

2.3 Supervised Classification and Validation

Supervised machine learning techniques were used to predict students' comprehension scores. *Caret* for R [20] was used to train Linear Regression, Support Vector Machine (SVM), and Random Forest models. All models were evaluated using leave-one-out cross-validation (LOOCV) in which $k - 1$ instances were used in the training set and the model was tested on the instance not used in the training data. This process was repeated k times until each instance was used as the test set. LOOCV develops models that are more generalizable when applied to new data.

3 Results

On average, students' aggregated SEs contained 172.69 ($SD = 99.75$) words, whereas their ERs contained 90.97 ($SD = 45.52$) words. Word count was included as a control variable in our models; however, it was not an important feature of any of the models.

The response types (SE, ER) were tested independently using the same regression algorithms (Linear Regression, SVM, Random Forest). A summary of model accuracies is presented in Table 1. Overall, the SVM performed the best for both SE and ER data. The CRAT indices accounted for 15% (SE) and 25% (ER) of variance in comprehension scores, suggesting that the properties of the retrievals were more informative of students' comprehension of text content.

Table 1. Description of model accuracy.

Algorithm	Self-Explanation (SE)		Explanatory Retrieval (ER)	
	RMSE	R^2	RMSE	R^2
Linear Regression	1.97	0.04	1.76	0.12
SVM (Polynomial)	**1.67**	**0.15**	**1.52**	**0.25**
Random Forest	1.67	0.13	1.50	0.24

To more closely examine the CRAT indices driving the model predictions, we examined the scaled variable importance of indices in the SVM models. Four of the top five variables in the SE model were adjective keywords from the COCA corpus. They related to *academic adjective keywords, magazine adjective keywords, fiction adjective keywords, news adjective keywords,* and *academic bigram keywords.* In comparison, the top five variables in the ER model were *academic bigram keywords, word imageability, academic keywords, age of acquisition for content words, and fiction keywords.* These results indicate that the descriptive content (i.e., adjectives) of the SEs were most predictive of comprehension scores, whereas the ERs were related to a wider variety of textual information, particularly lexical sophistication.

4   Discussion

This study examined the potential of explanatory retrievals (ERs) to serve as a form of stealth assessment of reading comprehension performance. Given that open-ended retrieval attempts can vary widely in quality [7], automating the evaluation of ER practice can make it more feasible to include ER tasks in the classroom. This study demonstrated modest, but promising results. In particular, our best model (SVM Polynomial) accounted for 15% and 25% of the variance using the properties of SEs and ERs, respectively. These results support the extant work demonstrating that natural language processing techniques can be used to model important comprehension processes [11–15].

A more novel finding in this present study is that, as predicted, different types of constructed responses were not uniformly related to reading comprehension performance. That is, SE responses and ER responses relied on some different features to predict comprehension and did so to different degrees of success. This supports the idea that different constructed responses influence and predict comprehension in different ways. Further work will more closely examine these different linguistic features in context to understand *why* different types of linguistic features are more or less predictive in a particular type of response and how these different processes impact different aspects of learning (i.e., memory vs. inference and application). The goal of this study was to compare and contrast across types of constructed responses and how each might provide different insights into learning processes. However, in future work, we plan to leverage the unique contributions of both in a combined model in which features of SEs and ERs are used to predict performance.

One limitation of note is that LOOCV was conducted at the item level, with the same participants generating multiple items. Further research with larger data sets will examine how these models generalize to entirely independent datasets. In addition, this study relied only on the CRAT tool to analyze linguistic features of the constructed responses. Existing work on analysis of constructed responses [15–18] suggests that our models will have higher accuracy if they include indices that characterize text across multiple dimensions (e.g., lexical, syntax, cohesion). Thus, future work will examine the value of employing additional linguistic analysis tools to account for variance in other dimensions of language.

Overall, the results of this study suggest that ERs can serve as both powerful learning activities and as assessments of developing comprehension. However, more work is needed to improve and refine automated procedures for scoring and providing feedback based on these responses. The ultimate goal of this research is to use these linguistic indices to facilitate nuanced assessments of constructed responses that can drive improved formative feedback and personalization in educational technologies.

Acknowledgements. This research was made possible in part by grants from the Spencer Foundation (201900217) and the Institute for Education Sciences (R305A190063 and R305A180261). The views expressed are those of the authors and do not necessarily reflect the views of the funding agencies.

References

1. Goldman, S.R., Snow, C.E.: Adolescent literacy: development and instruction. In: Polatsek, A., Treiman, R. (eds.) Handbook on Reading, pp. 463–478. Oxford University Press, New York (2015)
2. Bertsch, S., Pesta, B.J., Wiscott, R., McDaniel, M.A.: The generation effect: a meta-analytic review. Mem. Cogn. **35**(2), 201–210 (2007)
3. McNamara, D.S.: Reading Comprehension Strategies: Theories, Interventions, and Technologies. Psychology Press, Hove (2007)
4. Shute, V.J.: Stealth assessment in computer-based games to support learning. Comput. Games Instr. **55**(2), 503–524 (2011)
5. Shute, V.J., Kim, Y.J.: Formative and stealth assessment. In: Spector, J.M., Merrill, M.D., Elen, J., Bishop, M.J. (eds.) Handbook of Research on Educational Communications and Technology, pp. 311–321. Springer, New York (2014). https://doi.org/10.1007/978-1-4614-3185-5_25
6. Endres, T., Carpenter, S., Martin, A., Renkl, A.: Enhancing learning by retrieval: enriching free recall with elaborative prompting. Learn. Instr. **49**, 13–20 (2017)
7. Hinze, S.R., Wiley, J., Pellegrino, J.W.: The importance of constructive comprehension processes in learning from tests. J. Mem. Lang. **69**(2), 151–164 (2013)
8. Hinze, S.R., Wiley, J.: Testing the limits of testing effects using completion tests. Memory **19**(3), 290–304 (2011)
9. Crossley, S.A., McNamara, D.S.: Adaptive Educational Technologies for Literacy Instruction. Routledge, New York (2016)
10. Passonneau, R.J., McNamara, D.S., Muresan, S., Perin, D.: Preface: special issue on multidisciplinary approaches to AI and education for reading and writing. Int. J. Artif. Intell. Educ. **27**(4), 665–670 (2017)
11. Magliano, J.P., Millis, K.K., Levinstein, I., Boonthum, C.: Assessing comprehension during reading with the Reading Strategy Assessment Tool (RSAT). Metacogn. Learn. **6**(2), 131–154 (2011)
12. Jackson, G.T., McNamara, D.S.: Applying NLP metrics to students' self-explanations. In: Applied Natural Language Processing: Identification, Investigation and Resolution, pp. 261–275. IGI Global (2012)
13. Kim, M.K., Gaul, C.J., Kim, S.M., Madathany, R.J.: Advance in detecting key concepts as an expert model: using student mental model analyzer for research and teaching (SMART). Technol. Knowl. Learn. 1–24 (2019). https://doi.org/10.1007/s10758-019-09418-5
14. Li, H., Cai, Z., Graesser, A.C.: Computerized summary scoring: crowdsourcing-based latent semantic analysis. Behav. Res. Methods **50**(5), 2144–2161 (2018)
15. Crossley, S.A., Roscoe, R., McNamara, D.S.: Predicting human scores of essay quality using computational indices of linguistic and textual features. In: Biswas, G., Bull, S., Kay, J., Mitrovic, A. (eds.) AIED 2011. LNCS (LNAI), vol. 6738, pp. 438–440. Springer, Heidelberg (2011). https://doi.org/10.1007/978-3-642-21869-9_62

16. Varner, L.K., Jackson, G.T., Snow, E.L., McNamara, D.S.: Does size matter? Investigating user input at a larger bandwidth. In: Proceedings of the 26th International Florida Artificial Intelligence Research Society (FLAIRS) Conference, pp. 546–549. AAI Press (2013)

17. Allen, L.K., McNamara, D.S.: You are your words: modeling students' vocabulary knowledge with natural language processing. In: Proceedings of the 8th International Conference on Educational Data Mining (EDM), pp. 258–265. Madrid, EDM (2015)

18. Allen, L.K., Snow, E.L., McNamara, D.S.: Are you reading my mind? Modeling students' reading comprehension skills with natural language processing techniques. In: Baron, J., Lynch, G., Maziarz, N., Blikstein, P., Merceron, A., Siemens, G. (eds.) Proceedings of the 5th International Learning Analytics & Knowledge Conference (LAK 2015), pp. 246–254. ACM, Poughkeepsie (2015)

19. Crossley, S.A, Kyle, K., Davenport, J., McNamara, D.S.: Automatic assessment of constructed response data in a chemistry tutor. In: Proceedings of the 9th International Educational Data Mining (EDM) Society Conference, pp. 336–340. EDM (2016)

20. Kuhn, M., et al.: Package 'caret'. R J. (2020)

An Approach to Model Children's Inhibition During Early Literacy and Numeracy Acquisition

Guilherme Medeiros Machado[1][($\boxtimes$)] (iD), Geoffray Bonnin[1], Sylvain Castagnos[1][($\boxtimes$)],
Lara Hoareau[2], Aude Thomas[2], and Youssef Tazouti[2]

[1] LORIA - University of Lorraine, Campus Scientifique, BP239, 54506 Nancy, France
{guilherme.medeiros-machado,bonnin,sylvain.castagnos}@loria.fr
[2] 2LPN (EA 7489), 91 avenue de la Libération, BP32142, 54021 Nancy, France
{lara.hoareau,aude.thomas,youssef.tazouti}@univ-lorraine.fr

Abstract. Early literacy and numeracy skills are developed during childhood at kindergarten level. Among the many factors that influence the development of such skills, the literature shows that the executive function of inhibition – *i.e.* the blocking out or tuning out of information or action that is irrelevant to the learning task – is one of the most important. There are many tests to assess children's inhibition skills; however, such tests are generally time-consuming and have a short lifespan. In this context, we propose a computational approach to model children's inhibition skills by using only student traces from a learning app as input. We propose a mathematical formalization of three related inhibition features, which could be used as input to classification algorithms.

Keywords: Learning · Student model · Inhibition · Executive function

1 Introduction

The development of early literacy and early numeracy skills begins at a very young age. Children's acquisition of competences, such as reading and math, is critical to their long-term academic and career success [10]. A child with problems acquiring literacy and numeracy skills will continue to face academic issues in the future [7]. It is thus essential to identify and help such students.

Among the many factors that influence the acquisition of early literacy and numeracy, the cognitive executive functions play a major role [6]. Executive functions are *"high-level cognitive processes that facilitate new ways of behaving and optimize one's approach to unfamiliar circumstances"* [3].

Miyake and Friedman [8] define three different skills of executive functioning: *updating* (constant monitoring and rapid addition/deletion of working memory contents), *shifting* (flexible switching between tasks or mental sets), and *inhibition* (deliberate overriding of dominant or prepotent responses).

© Springer Nature Switzerland AG 2020
I. I. Bittencourt et al. (Eds.): AIED 2020, LNAI 12164, pp. 203–207, 2020.
https://doi.org/10.1007/978-3-030-52240-7_37

According to the related literature, inhibition is particularly important to child development. Compared to other self-regulatory skills, the inhibition function is found to be the most important variable related to early literacy and early numeracy ability at kindergarten level [1]. Inhibition is generally assessed through specific tests that measure verbal and visuospatial abilities.

There are many specific tests to assess children's inhibition; however, for those under the age of 8, the options are more limited [4]. Moreover, such tests are also time-consuming and deliver results that are valid only for a short-term period of time. So, a computational assessment of inhibition from learning data could be a very interesting tool. The possibility to easily identify children's inhibition skills both in a short-term or in a longitudinal study could allow responses tailored to the needs of children with inhibition dysfunction during their first learning.

Searching the literature, we did not find any papers addressing the automated identification of inhibition. Therefore, we propose a new approach to automatically collect inhibitory features from students traces at kindergarten level. We collected the learning traces from an app used to aid children from 4 to 5 years old in the development of such skills. We identify and derive three distinct features by combining different definitions of inhibition from the literature of psychology and neuroscience. Then, we propose three strategies to model these features based on the students' traces (Sect. 3). To the best of our knowledge, this is the first attempt to isolate inhibitory features.

2   Conceptual Foundation

Early literacy could be defined as the acquisition of the skills, knowledge, and attitudes that are the developmental precursors of conventional forms of reading and writing [11]. On the other hand, early numeracy refers to a lot of concepts and skills that develop together following the same learning trajectory [10].

According to Diamond, inhibition *"involves being able to control one's attention, behavior, thoughts, and/or emotions to override a strong internal predisposition or external lure, and instead do what is more appropriate or needed"* [2]. Another well-known definition of inhibition is given by Miyake et al.: *"one's ability to deliberately inhibit dominant, automatic, or prepotent responses when necessary"* [9]. In both definitions, it is clear that the notion of inhibition is related to a **deliberate** suppression/override of a (wrong) predisposition/response. There is an important difference between this effort-aware suppression of prepotent answers and automatic suppression of a wrong answer. In the first case, the executive function of inhibition is required (interest of this paper). The second case is when a correct behavior/answer is already internalized.

Despite having clear definitions and tests, designing an approach to predict inhibition is still very challenging. How can we identify and isolate the effort-aware behavior to suppress a wrong answer? In this sense, Henry and Bettenay [4] define Executive Dysfunction as the opposite of inhibition functioning, i.e., *deficits in the ability to inhibit well-learned patterns of behavior and derive new ways of solving problems*. The authors affirm that children with such deficits become trapped in "repetitive cycles" of a previously learned pattern, and also have some troubles to accommodate their behavior to novel situations. Such "repetitive cycles", on the other hand, are easier to be identified, from the students' traces, than an effort-aware behavior of inhibition.

3   Proposed Inhibition Features

We describe the three proposed variables used to model the dysfunctional behavior of inhibition. Our input data is made up of student traces resulting from their interaction with a learning application we have developed. In the remainder of this paper, we will use the following notation. Let $S = \{s_1, s_2, ..., s_{|S|}\}$ be the set of all students and $A = \{a_1, a_2, ..., a_{|A|}\}$ the set of all proposed activities. $R_{sa} = \langle r_1, r_2, ..., r_{|R_{sa}|} \rangle$ is the sequence of responses the student s has given to the activity a. Each response $(r_i \in R_{sa})$ also belongs either to the set of possible wrong answers $W_a = \{w_1, w_2, ...w_{|W|}\}$, or to the set of possible correct answers $C_a = \{c_1, c_2, ..., c_{|C|}\}$ of a specific activity. The responses r also carry information about the time demanded to the student answer. We also have $R_{sa} \cap W_a$ the set of wrong answers given by student s in activity a and $R_{sa} \cap C_a$ the set of correct answers given by student s in activity a. Note that this last set is either the empty set, if the student gave no correct answers, or the singleton that corresponds to the correct answer if the student gave the correct answer.

Students that Insisted on the Same Error: In their definition of Dysfunctional Behavior of the Executive Functioning, Henry and Bettenay [4] say that the person "becomes trapped in 'repetitive cycles' of a previous learned pattern". For this reason, we propose to look at the repetitive behaviors and, more specifically, to look at the sum of each sequence of recorded errors in each question.

Considering the dataset is ordered by timestamp, we can formally define: $SE_{sa} = \{r_i \in R_{sa} \cap W_a | \forall j \in \{1, 2, ..., k\}, r_i = r_j\}$. Where SE_{sa} is the same error a student s committed in an activity a. The reason why j starts with 1, is because we are interested in the errors the students committed from their first answer to each activity. The reason for that is once the students make an effort to change their first wrong answer, the executive function of inhibition is already put in place; since the inhibition serves to suppress a "prepotent response". The value k represents the minimum value for the answer to be characterized as a repetitive error. In our case $k = 2$. We get SISE (students that insisted on the same error) our first variable as a function of s: $SISE(s) = \frac{\sum_a |SE_{sa}|}{\sum_a |R_{sa}|}$. We divide $\sum_a |SE_{sa}|$ by the total number of traces/responses of the student s to get the proportion of this variable compared to all other traces.

Students that Failed Very Fast: The second of our three variables is based on Miyake's definition of inhibition (*"one's ability to deliberately inhibit **dominant, automatic, or prepotent** responses when necessary"*). The goal is to identify failures in suppressing the automatic, dominant, or prepotent responses by looking at the time information present in the student traces.

Our hypothesis is the following: the students that answered wrongly, and in a very fast way, present a dysfunctional behavior of inhibition. One prerequisite with this hypothesis is to define what is a "very fast" answer. To accomplish this, we need to look at the dataset and define what a fast answer to each activity is.

Since different activities demand different times to be answered, we need to isolate the set of wrong answers of each activity. Let AW_a be the set of all wrong answers given by the students for exercise a ordered by increasing timestamp. We then use the cut point ϕ_a of the first (lower) quartile as a reference to represent a fast answer to such activity. Quartiles are commonly used to split data because of their insensitivity to outliers and preserve information about the center and spread [5]. Once we get ϕ_a, the student's subset of answers representing a very fast failure attempt is easily defined as: $VF_{sa} = \{r_i \in R_{sa} \cap W \,|time(r_i) \leq \phi_a\}$.

Finally, $\sum_a |VF_{sa}|$ is divided by $\sum_a |R_{sa}|$ to get the proportion of these traces when compared to the whole set of the student traces, then: $SFVF(s) = \frac{\sum_a |VF_{sa}|}{\sum_a |R_{sa}|}$.

Students that Committed the Most Common Error in such Activity: This third variable was also inspired by the definition of inhibition as an effort-aware suppression of a prepotent response, but looking at the *Recorded Answer* information instead of the *Time Demanded to Answer*. The reason to do so is that the prepotent response can be seen as a previous knowledge/belief of the student, which demands effort to be suppressed. This belief can be identified as the most frequent error of each activity. For instance, if one of the activities requires that the student selects a regular pen, but instead, the student selects a pencil, and if most of the students make this same mistake in this activity, then we assume a high effort is required to suppress the response.

To isolate this variable, we need to list each most common error of each activity. Let mc_a be the most common error of each activity a defined as $mc_a = \arg\max_r \sum_{r'} \delta_{rr'}$, where $\{r, r' \in AW_a\}$ and δ is a Kronecker delta function. For each activity a and each student s, we then define the set of responses that correspond to the most common error as $MC_{sa} = \{r_i \in R_{sa} | r_i = mc_a\}$. The third variable is then: $SMCE(s) = \frac{\sum_a |MC_{sa}|}{\sum_a |R_{sa}|}$.

4   Conclusions and Future Work

The design and implementation of a computational approach to model children's inhibition skills is a challenging task. One of the reasons is that there is little literature on the computing field treating this subject. At the same time, this is a critical topic when treating children's skills at early numeracy and literacy. Since this is a subject already broadly explored in neuroscience and psychology fields, we took the seminal definitions of inhibition in these fields and proposed a mathematical formalization of three variables to model a dysfunctional inhibition behavior. To the best of our knowledge, this is the first attempt to model the inhibition behavior. As future work, we are interested in modeling not only the dysfunctional inhibition but also the functional inhibition behavior.

Acknowledgement. This work has received funding from the French Programme of Investments for the Future within the frame of the eFran LINUMEN project.

References

1. Blair, C., Razza, R.P.: Relating effortful control, executive function, and false belief understanding to emerging math and literacy ability in kindergarten. Child Dev. **78**(2), 647–663 (2007). https://doi.org/10.1111/j.1467-8624.2007.01019.x
2. Diamond, A.: Executive functions. Ann. Rev. Psychol. **64**(1), 135–168 (2013). https://doi.org/10.1146/annurev-psych-113011-143750
3. Gilbert, S.J., Burgess, P.W.: Executive function. Curr. Biol. **18**(3), R110–R114 (2008). https://doi.org/10.1016/j.cub.2007.12.014
4. Henry, L.A., Bettenay, C.: The assessment of executive functioning in children. Child Adolesc. Mental Health **15**(2), 110–119 (2010). https://doi.org/10.1111/j.1475-3588.2010.00557.x
5. Krzywinski, M., Altman, N.: Visualizing samples with box plots. Nat. Methods **11**(2), 119–120 (2014). https://doi.org/10.1038/nmeth.2813
6. McClelland, M.M., Acock, A.C., Morrison, F.J.: The impact of kindergarten learning-related skills on academic trajectories at the end of elementary school. Early Child. Res. Q. **21**(4), 471–490 (2006). https://doi.org/10.1016/j.ecresq.2006.09.003. http://www.sciencedirect.com/science/article/pii/S0885200606000627
7. McClelland, M.M., et al.: Predictors of early growth in academic achievement: the head-toes-knees-shoulders task (2014). https://www.frontiersin.org/article/10.3389/fpsyg.2014.00599
8. Miyake, A., Friedman, N.P.: The nature and organization of individual differences in executive functions: four general conclusions. Curr. Dir. Psychol. Sci. **21**(1), 8–14 (2012). https://doi.org/10.1177/0963721411429458
9. Miyake, A., Friedman, N.P., Emerson, M.J., Witzki, A.H., Howerter, A., Wager, T.D.: The unity and diversity of executive functions and their contributions to complex "Frontal Lobe" tasks: a latent variable analysis. Cogn. Psychol. **41**(1), 49–100 (2000). https://doi.org/10.1006/cogp.1999.0734. http://www.sciencedirect.com/science/article/pii/S001002859990734X
10. Purpura, D.J., Napoli, A.R.: Early numeracy and literacy: untangling the relation between specific components. Math. Think. Learn. **17**(2–3), 197–218 (2015). https://doi.org/10.1080/10986065.2015.1016817. http://www.tandfonline.com/doi/full/10.1080/10986065.2015.1016817
11. Whitehurst, G.J., Lonigan, C.J.: Child development and emergent literacy. Child Dev. **69**(3), 848–872 (1998). https://www.ncbi.nlm.nih.gov/pubmed/9680688

Confrustion and Gaming While Learning with Erroneous Examples in a Decimals Game

Michael Mogessie[1](✉), J. Elizabeth Richey[1] (iD), Bruce M. McLaren[1],
Juan Miguel L. Andres-Bray[2], and Ryan S. Baker[2]

[1] Carnegie Mellon University, Pittsburgh, PA 15213, USA
michaelmogessie@cmu.edu
[2] University of Pennsylvania, Philadelphia, PA 19104, USA

Abstract. Prior studies have explored the potential of erroneous examples in helping students learn more effectively by correcting errors in solutions to decimal problems. One recent study found that while students experience more confusion and frustration (confrustion) when working with erroneous examples, they demonstrate better retention of decimal concepts. In this study, we investigated whether this finding could be replicated in a digital learning game. In the erroneous examples (ErrEx) version of the game, students saw a character play the games and make mistakes, and then they corrected the characters' errors. In the problem solving (PS) version, students played the games by themselves. We found that confrustion was significantly, negatively correlated with performance in both pretest ($r = -.62$, $p < .001$) and posttest ($r = -.68$, $p < .001$) and so was gaming the system (pretest $r = -.58$, $p < .001$, posttest $r = -.66$, $p < .001$). Posthoc (Tukey) tests indicated that students who did not see any erroneous examples (PS-only) experienced significantly lower levels of confrustion ($p < .001$) and gaming ($p < .001$). While we did not find significant differences in post-test performance across conditions, our findings show that students working with erroneous examples experience consistently higher levels of confrustion in both game and non-game contexts.

Keywords: Digital learning game · Erroneous Examples · Affect · Affect detection · Confusion · Frustration · Gaming the system · Learning outcomes

1 Introduction

Researchers have investigated the value of solving problems using non-traditional approaches to problem solving. Worked examples [1–3] and erroneous examples [4–6] have been of particular interest. Worked examples demonstrate a procedure to arrive at a correct solution and may prompt students to provide explanations to correct steps of a solution while erroneous examples require them to identify and fix errors in incorrect solutions. The reason these approaches improve learning has been attributed to their role in freeing up cognitive resources that can then be used to learn new knowledge [7]. Factors not specific to a particular approach may also interact with learning. Of these, affect and behavior have garnered the most attention [8–11]. In particular, states of

© Springer Nature Switzerland AG 2020
I. I. Bittencourt et al. (Eds.): AIED 2020, LNAI 12164, pp. 208–213, 2020.
https://doi.org/10.1007/978-3-030-52240-7_38

confusion, concentration and boredom have been shown to persist across computer-based learning environments (dialog tutors, problem-solving games, problem-solving intelligent tutors) [12].

In a recent study, we found that students who were assigned erroneous examples implemented in an intelligent tutor [13] experienced higher levels of confrustion [14], a mix of confusion and frustration, than those who were asked to answer typical problem-solving questions. However, we found that confrustion was negatively correlated with both immediate and delayed learning, albeit less so for students who worked with erroneous examples.

This study, which is a replication of our recent findings but in a game versus ITS context, was motivated by two observations. First, in order to determine whether this relationship is robust, it is important to explore whether our recent findings persist in other digital learning environments. This is because levels of affective states such as frustration and behaviors such as gaming the system have been shown to vary across learning environments and user interfaces [12, 15].

Second, research has shown that students who engage in gaming the system also experience frustration [10], though frustration does not always precede gaming [12]. Therefore, it is interesting to explore if this association persists when erroneous examples are implemented in a digital learning game context.

Participants were divided into four groups where two groups worked with either Erroneous Examples (ErrEx) or Problem Solving (PS) questions only and the other two worked with a mix of either ErrEx then PS or PS then ErrEx questions. We expected that students in all four groups would perform better from pretest to posttest. We then tested the following hypotheses:

H1: Confrustion and gaming will be negatively related to performance, even when controlling for prior knowledge.

H2: Students in any of the conditions that include erroneous examples will experience higher levels of confrustion and gaming the system.

H3: Students in any of the conditions that include erroneous examples will perform better than their PS-only counterparts in the posttest.

2 Methods

The data used in this study was collected in the spring of 2015. Participants were recruited from four teachers' classes at two middle schools, and participated over four to five class sessions. Both schools are located in the metropolitan area of a city in the United States. The analysis for this study included the data of 191 students, divided into four conditions within the game context.

Materials consisted of the digital learning game, Decimal Point [16], and three isomorphic versions of a test administered as a pretest and posttest. The Decimal Point game is laid out on an amusement park map, with 24 mini-games in which students play two rounds of each. All tests and the game used the Cognitive Tutor Authoring Tool (CTAT) [17] as a tutoring backend. The game was designed with focus on common misconceptions middle school students have about decimals [18].

We used gameplay data to generate machine learning models to detect confrustion and gaming the system. In this study, we applied text replay coding [19, 20] to student logs to label 1,560 clips (irr κ = .74). To predict confrustion and gaming, the detectors used 23 features of the students' interaction with the decimal tutor, involving the number of attempts, amount of time spent and restart behavior.

After evaluating the performance of several classification algorithms in terms of Area Under the Receiver Operating Characteristic Curve (AUC ROC) and Cohen's Kappa (κ), we built the confrustion detector using the Extreme Gradient Boosting (XGBoost) ensemble tree-based classifier [21] (AUC ROC = .97, κ = .81) and the gaming detector using the J-Rip classifier [22] (AUC ROC = .85, κ = .62).

3   Results

Confrustion was significantly, negatively correlated with performance on the pretest ($r = -.62$, $p < .001$) and posttest ($r = -.68$, $p < .001$). A multiple regression model tested using confrustion to predict posttest performance while controlling for pretest was also significant, $F(2, 188) = 181.14$, $p < .001$. Within the model, both pretest, ($\beta = .57$, $p < .001$) and confrustion ($\beta = -.32$, $p < .001$) were significant; confrustion was a significant, negative predictor of posttest performance even after controlling for pretest.

Gaming was significantly, negatively correlated with performance on the pretest ($r = -.58$, $p < .001$) and posttest ($r = -.66$, $p < .001$). A multiple regression model tested using gaming to predict posttest performance while controlling for pretest was also significant, $F(2, 188) = 181.14$, $p < .001$. Within the model, both pretest, ($\beta = .59$, $p < .001$) and gaming ($\beta = -.31$, $p < .001$) were significant, indicating that gaming was also a significant, negative predictor of posttest performance even after controlling for pretest.

Mean levels of confrustion and gaming for each condition are reported in Table 1. A one-way analysis of variance (ANOVA) comparing gaming and confrustion levels across conditions indicated a significant effect of condition on confrustion, $F(3, 187) = 14.01$, $p < .001$, and gaming, $F(3, 187) = 10.07$, $p < .001$. Posthoc (Tukey) tests indicated that students in the PS-only condition experienced significantly lower levels of confrustion ($ps < .001$), while there were no differences among the other conditions ($ps > .97$). Similarly, posthoc (Tukey) tests indicated that students in the PS-only condition experienced significantly lower levels of gaming ($ps < .001$), while there were no differences among the other conditions ($ps > .91$).

Table 1. Gaming, confrustion, and test performance by condition.

Measure	PS	ErrEx	ErrEx/PS	PS/ErrEx
Pretest (SD)	23.37 (8.20)	23.39 (9.05)	20.92 (8.00)	20.48 (8.41)
Posttest M (SD)	28.72 (6.18)	27.63 (7.61)	25.75 (7.15)	26.40 (7.43)
Gaming M (SD)	.16 (.11)	.27 (.17)	.28 (.13)	.29 (.13)
Confrustion M (SD)	.24 (.16)	.46 (.26)	.45 (.20)	.47 (.18)

Finally, a repeated-measure analysis of variance (ANOVA) indicated that students across all conditions improved significantly from pretest to posttest, $F(3, 187) = 167.04$, $p < .001$. See Table 1 for means and standard deviations across conditions. A series of ANOVAs indicated no significant differences across conditions on pretest, $F(3, 187) = 1.63$, $p = .18$, or posttest, $F(3. 187) = 1.65$, $p = .18$.

4 Discussion

In this study, we implemented erroneous examples in a digital learning game context and found that students who played the erroneous examples versions of the game experienced higher levels of confrustion. There was also a significant correlation between gaming the system and confrustion. Future research might further explore the relationship between frustration and gaming, as previous research using affect detectors has found that frustration did not tend to precede gaming the system [12].

A previous study using a web-based intelligent tutor showed that students working with erroneous examples performed better than their problem-solving counterparts [6]. This study, however, did not replicate that finding.

While it is not possible to make a direct comparison between confrustion levels in the game and intelligent tutor versions of the ErrEx condition, it is worth noting that students who played the game experienced higher levels of confrustion (M = 0.46, SD = 0.26) than those who used the intelligent tutor (M = 0.34, SD = 0.16) [13]. Since confrustion has been shown to be significantly, negatively correlated with learning, these higher levels of confrustion may explain why we did not see better learning effects of erroneous examples in the game context.

Alternatively, integrating the game interface with a feature where students watch a game character play the game for them may have negatively impacted both the game experience and the intended benefit of erroneous examples.

In an upcoming study, we will explore mechanisms intended to reduce the negative impact of confrustion and gaming on learning with erroneous examples in a digital learning game.

References

1. Sweller, J., Cooper, G.A.: The use of worked examples as a substitute for problem solving in learning algebra. Cogn. Instr. **2**, 59–89 (1985)
2. McLaren, B.M., Lim, S., Koedinger, K.R.: When and how often should worked examples be given to students? New results and a summary of the current state of research. In: Proceedings of the 30th Annual Conference of the Cognitive Science Society, pp. 2176–2181. Cog. Sci. Society, Austin (2008)
3. Renkl, A.: Atkinson. R.K.: Learning from worked-out examples and problem solving. In: Plass, J.L., Moreno, R., Brünken, R. (eds.) Cognitive Load Theory. Cambridge University Press, Cambridge (2010)

4. Isotani, S., Adams, D., Mayer, R.E., Durkin, K., Rittle-Johnson, B., McLaren, Bruce M.: Can erroneous examples help middle-school students learn decimals? In: Kloos, C.D., Gillet, D., Crespo García, R.M., Wild, F., Wolpers, M. (eds.) EC-TEL 2011. LNCS, vol. 6964, pp. 181–195. Springer, Heidelberg (2011). https://doi.org/10.1007/978-3-642-23985-4_15
5. Adams, D., et al.: Using erroneous examples to improve mathematics learning with a web-based tutoring system. Comput. Hum. Behav. **36C**, 401–411 (2014)
6. McLaren, B.M., Adams, D.M., Mayer, R.E.: Delayed learning effects with erroneous examples: a study of learning decimals with a web-based tutor. Int. J. Artif. Intell. Educ. **25** (4), 520–542 (2015)
7. McLaren, B.M., et al.: To err is human, to explain and correct is divine: a study of interactive erroneous examples with middle school math students. In: Ravenscroft, A., Lindstaedt, S., Kloos, C.D., Hernández-Leo, D. (eds.) EC-TEL 2012. LNCS, vol. 7563, pp. 222–235. Springer, Heidelberg (2012). https://doi.org/10.1007/978-3-642-33263-0_18
8. Prensky, M.: Digital game-based learning. Comput. Entertain. (CIE) **1**(1), 21 (2003)
9. Baker, R.S., Corbett, A.T., Koedinger, K.R., Wagner, A.Z.: Off-task behavior in the cognitive tutor classroom: when students "game the system". In: Proceedings of the SIGCHI Conference on Human Factors in Computing Systems, pp. 383–390 (2004)
10. Walonoski, J.A., Heffernan, N.T.: Detection and analysis of off-task gaming behavior in intelligent tutoring systems. In: Ikeda, M., Ashley, K.D., Chan, T.-W. (eds.) ITS 2006. LNCS, vol. 4053, pp. 382–391. Springer, Heidelberg (2006). https://doi.org/10.1007/11774303_38
11. Gee, J.P.: Situated Language and Learning: A Critique of Traditional Schooling. Routledge, Abingdon (2012)
12. Baker, R.S., D'Mello, S.K., Rodrigo, M.M.T., Graesser, A.C.: Better to be frustrated than bored: The incidence, persistence, and impact of learners' cognitive–affective states during interactions with three different computer-based learning environments. Int. J. Hum.-Comput. Stud. **68**(4), 223–241 (2010)
13. Richey, J.E., et al.: More confusion and frustration, better learning: the impact of erroneous examples. Comput. Educ. **139**, 173–190 (2019)
14. Liu, Z., Pataranutaporn, V., Ocumpaugh, J., Baker, R.: Sequences of frustration and confusion, and learning. In: Educational Data Mining (2013)
15. Baker, R.S., et al.: Educational software features that encourage and discourage "gaming the system". In: Proceedings of the 14th International Conference on Artificial Intelligence in Education, pp. 475–482 (2009)
16. McLaren, B.M., Adams, D.M., Mayer, R.E., Forlizzi, J.: A computer-based game that promotes mathematics learning more than a conventional approach. Int. J. Game-Based Learn. (IJGBL) **7**(1), 36–56 (2017). https://doi.org/10.4018/IJGBL.2017010103
17. Aleven, V., McLaren, B.M., Sewall, J.: Scaling up programming by demonstration for intelligent tutoring systems development: an open-access website for middle school mathematics learning. IEEE Trans. Learn. Technol. **2**(2), 64–78 (2009)
18. Isotani, S., McLaren, B.M., Altman, M.: Towards intelligent tutoring with erroneous examples: a taxonomy of decimal misconceptions. In: Aleven, V., Kay, J., Mostow, J. (eds.) ITS 2010. LNCS, vol. 6095, pp. 346–348. Springer, Heidelberg (2010). https://doi.org/10.1007/978-3-642-13437-1_66
19. Lee, D.M.C., Rodrigo, M.M.T., d Baker, R.S.J., Sugay, J.O., Coronel, A.: Exploring the relationship between novice programmer confusion and achievement. In: D'Mello, S., Graesser, A., Schuller, B., Martin, J.-C. (eds.) ACII 2011. LNCS, vol. 6974, pp. 175–184. Springer, Heidelberg (2011). https://doi.org/10.1007/978-3-642-24600-5_21

20. Baker, R.S., Corbett, A.T., Wagner, A.Z.: Human classification of low-fidelity replays of student actions. In: Proceedings of the Educational Data Mining Workshop at the 8th International Conference on Intelligent Tutoring Systems, vol. 2002, pp. 29–36 (2006)
21. Chen, T., Guestrin, C.: XGBoost: a scalable tree boosting system. In: Proceedings of the 22nd ACM SIGKDD International Conference on Knowledge Discovery and Data Mining, pp. 785–794. ACM (2016)
22. Cohen, W.W.: Fast effective rule induction. In: Twelfth International Conference on Machine Learning, pp. 115–123 (1995)

Learning Outcomes and Their Relatedness Under Curriculum Drift

Sneha Mondal[1(✉)], Tejas I. Dhamecha[1(✉)], Smriti Pathak[2], Red Mendoza[3],
Gayathri K. Wijayarathna[3], Paul Gagnon[3], and Jan Carlstedt-Duke[3]

[1] IBM Research, Bangalore, India
{snemonda,tidhamecha}@in.ibm.com
[2] Imperial College, London, UK
[3] Lee Kong Chian School of Medicine,
Nanyang Technological University, Singapore, Singapore

Abstract. A typical medical curriculum is organized as a hierarchy of learning outcomes (LOs), each LO is a short text that describes a medical concept. Machine learning models have been applied to predict relatedness between LOs. These models are trained on examples of LO-relationships annotated by experts. However, medical curricula are periodically reviewed and revised, resulting in changes to the structure and content of LOs. This work addresses the problem of model adaptation under curriculum drift. First, we propose heuristics to generate reliable annotations for the revised curriculum, thus eliminating dependence on expert annotations. Second, starting with a model pre-trained on the old curriculum, we inject a task-specific transformation layer to capture nuances of the revised curriculum. Our approach makes significant progress towards reaching human-level performance.

Keywords: Learning outcome(s) · Data drift · Model adaptation

1 Introduction

The LO-relationship extraction task, recently introduced in [8], seeks to predict the degree of relatedness between learning outcomes (LOs) in a curriculum. The authors examine the curriculum of the Lee Kong Chian School of Medicine, which spans five years of education and covers about 4000 LOs; each LO is a short statement describing a concept that students are expected to master. A hierarchy, designed by curriculum experts, groups these LOs at different levels of granularity. A successful clinical encounter requires students to conceptually relate and marshal knowledge gained from several LOs, spread across years and across distant parts of the curriculum hierarchy. This underscores the need for an automatic LO-relationship extraction tool (hereafter called LReT).

In our earlier work [8], this is abstracted as a classification task, where a pair of LOs is categorized as being strongly related (high degree of conceptual

---

S. Mondal and T. I. Dhamecha—Contributed equally.

© Springer Nature Switzerland AG 2020
I. I. Bittencourt et al. (Eds.): AIED 2020, LNAI 12164, pp. 214–219, 2020.
https://doi.org/10.1007/978-3-030-52240-7_39

similarity), weakly related (intermediate conceptual similarity), or unrelated (no conceptual similarity). An LReT is trained on annotated data obtained from subject matter experts (SMEs), who are both faculty and doctors.

However, this curriculum is periodically reviewed and revised. Modifications are made to both content (emphasising some LOs, dropping others, merging a few), as well as organization (grouping LOs differently, re-evaluating classroom hours dedicated to each). Table 1 compares an old LO with its revised counterpart. Note that the textual formulation (hence underlying concept) of the LO has been modified. Additionally, the LO has been re-grouped under a separate set of verticals - **Longitudinal Course**, **Module**, and **Assessment Type**, while doing away with **Clinical Block**, the only vertical in the previous version.

Table 1. Semantic and curricular change in LOs after curriculum revision

	Old curriculum	Revised curriculum
Learning Outcome (LO)	Identify the main mineralocorticoid in humans and describe its principal actions	Describe the synthesis, principal actions and control mechanisms of glucocorticoids, mineralocorticoids and adrenal steroids
Theme	Scientific Basis of Medicine	Scientific Basis of Medicine
Fundamental	Structure & function of the human body in health (HSF)	Structure & function of the human body in health (HSF)
Fundamental Unit	Anatomy, Physiology, Biochemistry	Biochemistry
Clinical Block	Renal and Endocrine	–
Longitudinal Course	–	Foundations of Clinical Practice (FCP)
Module	–	Endocrine System
Assessment Type	–	Written Exercise, Oral Presentation

As the curriculum drifts, so do relationships between its constituent LOs. An LReT trained on one version of the curriculum may not perform well on the revised version. Re-obtaining SME annotations carries appreciable cognitive and cost overheads, making it impractical to train an LReT from scratch.

We present a systematic approach towards LO-relationship extraction under curriculum drift. Beginning with the SME-labelled dataset on the old curriculum, we employ heuristics to create a pseudo-labelled dataset for the revised curriculum. With some supervision now available, we tune the existing pre-trained model to the nuances of the revised curriculum, and compare its efficacy against human performance.

This aligns with existing work on domain adaptation and transfer learning [6,10]; both study scenarios where training and test data do not derive from the same distribution. In contrast, not only do we adapt the model to a modified domain, but also generate data pertinent to this domain, thus eliminating the need for human intervention. This bridges the gap between building a reliable LReT, and deploying it against a changing curriculum landscape.

2   Silver Standard Dataset Generation

Starting with SME-annotated old LO pairs, which serves as the gold-standard dataset, we proceed in two steps. First, we define a *mapping* that links an LO from the old curriculum (OC) to its closest matching counterpart in the revised curriculum (RC):

$$M(p) = \{r|sim(p,r) \geq sim(p,r'), \ \forall r' \in RC\}, p \in OC. \tag{1}$$

where *sim* is an appropriate semantic textual similarity metric. Intuitively, the mapping score, $sim(p, M(p))$ captures the extent of semantic drift in the content of an LO.

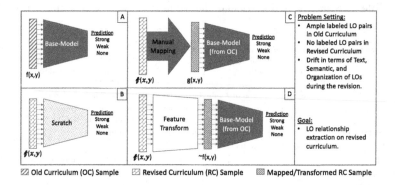

Fig. 1. (A) `base-model` trained on gold-standard data from OC. (B) Model trained from **Scratch** on silver-standard data from RC. (C) Manually map features (**MF**) from RC to OC, and then use `base-model`. (D) Learn a feature transform (**FT**) from RC that approximates OC-like features by leveraging weak correspondence between RC and OC. The base-model can be further smoothed (**FT-S**).

Thereafter, we rely on *pruning*. Recall that the gold-standard dataset ($\mathcal{D}_{old}$) consists of old LO pairs (p, q), along with an SME-annotated class label. A silver-standard dataset for the revised curriculum ($\mathcal{D}_{rev}$) is derived by pruning the mapping scores of an old LO pair at a pre-defined threshold (τ), while retaining its class label. Formally,

$$\mathcal{D}_{rev}(\tau) = \{(M(p), M(q), label) \mid sim(p, M(p)) \geq \tau \text{ and } sim(q, M(q)) \geq \tau\}$$
$$\forall (p, q, label) \in \mathcal{D}_{old}. \tag{2}$$

Effectively, we propagate the SME-label from a LO pair in old curriculum to their corresponding maps in the revised curriculum, only if the both mapping scores exceed the threshold. These pseudo-labeled instances constitute the silver-standard dataset.

3 Proposed Model Adaptation Approaches

The `base-model` (Fig. 1(A)), trained on gold-standard LO pairs of the old curriculum, predicts posterior probabilities for `Strong`, `Weak`, and `None` classes. As a comparative baseline, we train a model from scratch on the silver-standard dataset, without leveraging the `base-model`. We then explore three approaches to adapt `base-model`:

1. **Manual Feature Mapping (MF)**, where we manually map features from the revised curriculum to the old curriculum, and drop features that cannot be mapped (Fig. 1(C)). The resultant feature set can be fed to the `base-model` for predicting LO relatedness in new curriculum.

2. **Feature Transformation (FT):** In this novel approach (Fig. 1(D)), we inject a fully connected layer that transforms the revised feature set to an *approximate* old feature set, which can then be fed to the `base-model`. The silver standard dataset is leveraged to train only this transformation layer, i.e. `base-model` layers are frozen.

3. **Feature Transformation with Smoothing (FT-S):** Once the transformation weights converge to an extent, we unfreeze the `base-model` parameters and train for a few epochs to allow fine-grained updates to the entire network.

4 Experiments and Analysis

Table 2a compares model adaptation techniques outlined in Sect. 3. All approaches that leverage the `base-model` outperform training from **Scratch**, to various degrees. Feature transformation with smoothing (**FT-S**) yields the highest macro-F1, thus establishing that a) the `base-model` encodes some task-specific information independent of the specific curriculum, b) the revised feature-set can be adequately modeled as a linear transformation of the old feature-set, and c) additional smoothing over parameters of the `base-model` allows it to learn curriculum-specific nuances.

Furthermore, as shown in Table 2b, the high variance in model performance stems from the small size of training and test sets for each cross-validation split, and the macro-F1 score is sensitive to samples in the specific test split. We perform paired t-test to ascertain that except for two pairs, FT vs MF ($p = 6.8 \times 10^{-2}$) and FT vs FT-S ($p = 6.6 \times 10^{-2}$), differences between all other technique-pairs are statistically significant at 95% confidence interval.

Finally, for a small held-out set ($n = 229$), we obtain annotations separately from two SMEs and compute the inter-annotator agreement (71.7% macro-F1), which serves as a skyline. As shown in Table 2d, considering one SME as ground-truth and comparing against FT-S's predictions, the human-machine agreement turns out to be 64.4%. Compared to human performance, our reported results are moderately high, with, of course, some further scope of improvement.

Table 2. (a) Macro-average F1 (mean ± standard deviation in %) for `base-model` and several model adaptation approaches (b) per fold Macro-F1 (in %) of Scratch vs FT-S on SS-5. Note the high variance across splits, but consistent improvement of FT-S over Scratch. (c) Human vs human and (d) human vs algorithm agreement.

(a)

Dataset (τ)	Size	Scratch	MF	FT	FT-S
SS-1(0.85)	195	35.5±10.8	45.3±10.8	54.0±16.5	54.4±12.5
SS-2(0.80)	315	35.0±10.3	46.2±10.7	50.7±12.8	54.0±12.3
SS-3(0.75)	466	35.1± 7.6	46.7± 9.1	50.1± 8.2	51.4± 6.8
SS-4(0.70)	692	35.7± 7.7	46.0± 7.0	49.4± 9.6	49.4± 8.8
SS-5(0.65)	963	**35.6± 8.6**	48.1± 4.9	50.4± 5.1	**52.0± 4.2**

Macro-average F1 of `base-model` on gold standard : 59.2±1.2

Gold-standard : 2,276 LO pairs (Strong: 314, Weak: 471, None: 1,491)

(b)

Fold	Scratch	FT-S
1	25.7	49.4
2	23.9	48.3
3	29.2	53.9
4	48.9	54.7
5	42.1	53.7
6	44.3	55.3
7	32.7	48.8
8	43.4	57.1
9	35.6	55.4
10	29.7	43.7
-	35.6±8.6	52.0±4.2

(c)

Confusion Matrix		Annotator 2			
		Strong	Weak	None	Total
Annotator 1	Strong	30	10	0	40
	Weak	7	24	32	63
	None	0	1	125	126
	Total	37	35	157	229

Macro-Average F1= 71.74, Accuracy= 78.16

(d)

Confusion Matrix		FT-S			
		Strong	Weak	None	Total
Annotator 1	Strong	29	3	8	40
	Weak	15	17	31	63
	None	2	1	123	126
	Total	46	21	162	229

Macro-Average F1= 64.4, Accuracy= 73.7

References

1. Bjerva, J., Kouw, W., Augenstein, I.: Back to the future-sequential alignment of text representations. arXiv preprint arXiv:1909.03464 (2019)
2. Chan, J., Bailey, J., Leckie, C.: Discovering correlated spatio-temporal changes in evolving graphs. Knowl. Inf. Syst. **16**(1), 53–96 (2008)
3. Chen, Y., Wuillemin, P.H., Labat, J.M.: Discovering prerequisite structure of skills through probabilistic association rules mining. International Educational Data Mining Society (2015)
4. Gravemeijer, K., Rampal, A.: Mathematics curriculum development. In: Cho, S.J. (ed.) The Proceedings of the 12th International Congress on Mathematical Education, pp. 549–555. Springer, Cham (2015). https://doi.org/10.1007/978-3-319-12688-3_57
5. Käser, T., Klingler, S., Schwing, A.G., Gross, M.: Beyond knowledge tracing: modeling skill topologies with bayesian networks. In: Trausan-Matu, S., Boyer, K.E., Crosby, M., Panourgia, K. (eds.) ITS 2014. LNCS, vol. 8474, pp. 188–198. Springer, Cham (2014). https://doi.org/10.1007/978-3-319-07221-0_23
6. Kouw, W.M., Loog, M.: A review of domain adaptation without target labels. IEEE Trans. Pattern Anal. Mach. Intell. (2019)
7. Kumar, I., Balakrishnan, S.: Beyond basic: a temporal study of curriculum changes in a first-year communication course. Int. J. Res. Bus. Stud. **4**, 14 (2019). ISSN 2455-2992
8. Mondal, S., et al.: Learning outcomes and their relatedness in a medical curriculum. In: Proceedings of the Fourteenth Workshop on Innovative Use of NLP for Building Educational Applications, pp. 402–411 (2019)

9. Pyysalo, S., Ginter, F., Moen, H., Salakoski, T., Ananiadou, S.: Distributional semantics resources for biomedical text processing (2013)
10. Raina, R., Battle, A., Lee, H., Packer, B., Ng, A.Y.: Self-taught learning: transfer learning from unlabeled data. In: Proceedings of the 24th International Conference on Machine Learning, pp. 759–766 (2007)
11. Reis, S.: Curriculum reform: why? what? how? and how will we know it works? Isr. J. Health Policy Res. **7**, 30 (2018). https://doi.org/10.1186/s13584-018-0221-4
12. Stankov, S., Rosić, M., Žitko, B., Grubišić, A.: Tex-sys model for building intelligent tutoring systems. Comput. Educ. **51**(3), 1017–1036 (2008)
13. Zouaq, A., Nkambou, R.: Building domain ontologies from text for educational purposes. IEEE Trans. Learn. Technol. **1**(1), 49–62 (2008)

Promoting Learning and Satisfaction of Children When Interacting with an Emotional Companion to Program

Elizabeth K. Morales-Urrutia[1], José Miguel Ocaña Ch.[2],
Diana Pérez-Marín[3(✉)], and Celeste Pizarro-Romero[3]

[1] Universidad Técnica de Ambato, 182020 Ambato, Ecuador
[2] Ejército Ecuatoriano, 182020 Ambato, Ecuador
[3] Universidad Rey Juan Carlos, 28933 Madrid, Spain
diana.perez@urjc.es

Abstract. Teaching how to program in Primary Education has attracted a great deal of attention in the last years. However, it is still unclear the approach to achieve higher learning and satisfaction levels. In this paper, the proposal is focused on the use of an emotional learning companion called Alcody. To compare whether to insert emotional elements have an equal or more significant effect on students' satisfaction and learning than personalization and execution, 137 children between 10–12 years were randomly split into four groups for three months. The higher learning and satisfaction levels are registered for the students in the group with execution, personalization and emotion management.

Keywords: Learning companion · Teaching programming · Primary Education · Emotions

1 Introduction

Teaching programming to children has attracted a great deal of research interest in the last years [1, 2]. Many approaches are being tried to develop educational environments to teach programming concepts or to allow children to create their own programs. Another area that has received a great deal of research in the last decades is the use of learning companions [3]. A learning companion can be defined as a computer agent in the educational environment that supports the student. It can try to empathize with the student so that the student feels understood (e.g. Jake and Jane [4]).

In the review of the literature, no emotional learning companion has been found to be used to teach children how to program. Our previous work was focused on the design of the educational environment to teach Primary Education children how to program called Alcody [5]. The hypothesis is that by empowering Alcody with an emotional learning companion, the satisfaction and learning levels of the students will be increased. To test the hypothesis, an experiment with 137 children between 10–12 years was carried out in a private school in Ecuador. The higher improvement and satisfaction levels were registered for the students who used Alcody with personalization, execution and emotion management.

© Springer Nature Switzerland AG 2020
I. I. Bittencourt et al. (Eds.): AIED 2020, LNAI 12164, pp. 220–223, 2020.
https://doi.org/10.1007/978-3-030-52240-7_40

2 Alcody

Alcody is an educational environment to teach programming to Primary Education children. The name AlCODy comes from "Algorithms and CODe". Alcody is available on-line, in Spanish, at alcody.site (a demo can be accessed with the user "diana" and the password "123"). A co-design with 66 children between 10–12 years old took place to develop the first prototypes of Alcody [5].

In this study, three new factors are under investigation because of their interest in increasing the learning gains and satisfaction of the students: execution with a new button to run the program (see Fig. 1), personalization with options to change the interface (see Fig. 2 left) and emotion identification from the dialogue with the student (see Fig. 2 right with a sample recommendation message shown by Alcody as the student has told Alcody he is sad and Alcody tries to motivate him).

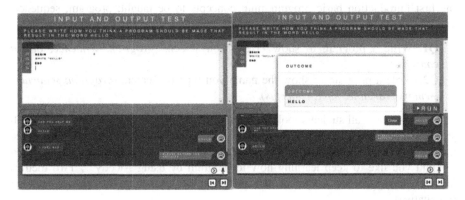

Fig. 1. Questionnaires screen without the run button (left), with the run button (right)

Fig. 2. Personalization (left), Emotion management (right)

3 Experiment

137 children between 10–12 years enrolled in Primary Education participated in the experiment. The reason to carry out the experiment in that school was the willingness of the Head of the School to let them go to the school to teach programming to the students. Half of the sample were boys, and the other half were girls. Children were randomly split into four groups who used different options of Alcody for three months: group TEST-EPNE with execution, personalization, and without emotions; group TEST-EPE with execution, personalization and emotions; group CONTROL without personalization, execution, emotion; and, group TEST-ENPNE with execution and without personalization, emotions.

Each group was at this class with their computers (one computer per child) and they could use it (each group with their configuration of factors) for one hour per week.

The first week, all students took the same pre-test with two questions focused on the first introduction basic programming concepts to be taught: program, sequence, variable, memory, input and output. The test questions were the following:

Q1. Write a program to show "Hello" on screen. *(program, sequence, output concepts)*

Q2. Write a program to show the name you type on screen. *(program, sequence, memory, variable, input concepts).*

The last week all students took the same test with the same questions. Finally, all students were asked to fill in a satisfaction questionnaire with the following three questions: "Do you like using Alcody?", "Do you like to learn programming?" and "Would you like to keep learning how to program by using Alcody?". Two metrics have been registered: scores of the pre-post test (quantitative) and satisfaction (qualitative).

Paired samples t-test for the data are used. A comparative between pre-test and post-test is shown in Table 1. There are very significant differences for all groups ($p < 0.001$). Main conclusion is that all participants improved significantly from the pre-test to the post-test. The size of this significant improvement is measured using d-statistics of Cohen. All values indicate a huge effect. To find out, whether a group

Table 1. t-test: comparative pre-post tests by groups

Group	TEST	N	$\overline{X}$	sd	t test	df	p-value
TEST-EPNE	PRE	32	0.53	0.40	T = 25.142	31	<0.001
	POST	32	7.78	1.59			
TEST-EPE	PRE	36	0.83	0.89	T = 29.250	35	<0.001
	POST	36	9.02	1.40			
CONTROL	PRE	34	1.62	0.90	T = 11.507	33	<0.001
	POST	34	6.07	1.99			
TEST-ENPNE	PRE	35	0.52	0.59	T = 19.432	34	<0.001
	POST	35	7.31	2.03			

improved more than others, a one-way ANOVA is performed. The variation of Alcody used (this is, group variable) is statistically significant ($p < 0.001$). A post-hoc analysis is used to yield more information about these differences. Tukey's HSD tests is used to compare each intervention method with every other intervention twice, exposing significant differences ($p < 0.001$) between all pairs of groups except between TEST-EPNE and TEST-ENPNE.

Finally, from the answers of the children to the satisfaction questionnaires, some qualitative analysis of the satisfaction levels of the groups can be performed. The groups that worked with the new factors were more satisfied using Alcody. All of them answered that they enjoyed using Alcody to learn how to program. Moreover, they showed higher desires to continue learning to program with Alcody unlike the other children who showed less interest in the platform although they could be interested in improving their programming.

4 Conclusion

The satisfaction and learning gains of children learning how to program can be improved by incorporating a learning companion in the educational environment. In an experiment with 137 children between 10–12 years, students using a system with execution, personalization and emotion management had the highest improvement in their scores to a pre-post programming test. Moreover, they also registered the higher satisfaction levels with respect to other group of students.

Acknowledgments. Research funded by the projects TIN 2015-66731-C2-1-R and by the Madrid Regional Government, through the project e-Madrid-CM (P2018/TCS-4307). The e-Madrid-CM project is also co-financed by the Structural Funds (FSE and FEDER).

References

1. Computer Science Teachers Association. Computer science K–8: building a strong foundation (2012). http://csta.acm.org/Curriculum/sub/CurrFiles/CS_K8_Building_a_Foundation.pdf
2. Jacobsen, H.: Five-years-olds learn coding in schools to prepare for future labour market. EurActiv.com - EU News & policy debates, across languages (2014)
3. Chou, C., Chan, T., Lin, C.: Redefining the learning companion: the past, present, and future of educational agents. Comput. Educ. **40**, 255–269 (2003)
4. Arroyo, I., Woolf, B., Royer, J.M., Tai, M.: Affective gendered learning companions. In: Artificial Intelligence in Education (2009)
5. Morales Urrutia, E.K., Ocaña Ch., J.M., Pérez-Marín, D., Tamayo, S.: A first proposal of pedagogic conversational agents to develop computational thinking in children. In: 5th International Conference on Technological Ecosystems for Enhancing Multiculturality (TEEM). ACM (2017)

Automatic Grading System Using Sentence-BERT Network

Ifeanyi G. Ndukwe[1](✉), Chukwudi E. Amadi[2](✉), Larian M. Nkomo[1](✉), and Ben K. Daniel[1](✉)

[1] University of Otago, Dunedin, New Zealand
{glory.ndukwe,larian.nkomo,ben.daniel}@otago.ac.nz
[2] Federal University of Technology, Owerri, Nigeria
emmanuel.amadi@futo.edu.ng

Abstract. The integration of digital learning technologies into higher education enhances students' learning by providing opportunities such as online examinations. However, many online examinations tend to have multiple-choice questions, as the marking of text-based questions can be a tedious task for academic staff, especially in large classes. In this study, we utilised SBERT, a pre-trained neural network language model to perform automatic grading of three variations of short answer questions on an Introduction to Networking Computer Science subject. A sample of 228 near-graduation Information Science students from one research-intensive tertiary institution in West African participated in this study. The course instructor manually rated short answers provided by the participants, using a scoring rubric and awarded scores ranging from 0 to 5. Some of the manually graded students' answers were randomly selected and used as a training set to fine-tune the neural network language model. Then quadratic-weighted kappa (QWKappa) was used to test the agreement level between the ratings generated by the human rater compared with that of the language model, on three variations of questions, including description, comparison and listing. Further, the accuracy of this model was tested on the same questions. Overall results showed that the level of the inter-rater agreement was good on the three variety of questions. Also, the accuracy measures showed that the model performed very well on the comparison and description questions compared to the listing question.

Keywords: Neural network · Natural language processing · Similarity · Short answer grading · BERT

1 Introduction

Language model pre-training and transfer learning have led to significant performance increase in NLP tasks [2,3]. The deployment of self-training methods such as Embeddings from Language Model (ELMo) [6], Generative Pre-trained Transformer (GPT) [8], Bidirectional Encoder Representations from Transformers

© Springer Nature Switzerland AG 2020
I. I. Bittencourt et al. (Eds.): AIED 2020, LNAI 12164, pp. 224–227, 2020.
https://doi.org/10.1007/978-3-030-52240-7_41

(BERT) language model [3], cross-lingual language model (XLM) [4] and XLNet [10] resulted in significant gains in performance. Thus, enabling researchers to smash several benchmarks with minimal task-specific fine-tuning and providing the rest of the NLP community with pre-trained models that could be easily fine-tuned and applied to generate the state-of-the-art results (with fewer data and less computation time). Consequently, generating sentence encoder models that are already trained on a large corpus and subsequently transferred to other tasks. For instance, Conneau et al. [1] showed how universal sentence representations trained using data from the Stanford Natural Language Inference datasets can consistently outperform unsupervised bag-of-words models such as word2vec-SkipGram and unigram term frequency-inverse document frequency (TFIDF) model.

Reimers et al. [9], argued that even though the BERT [3] and RoBERTa [5] language model have laid down new state-of-the-art sentence-pair regression tasks, such as semantic textual similarity, which allow all sentences to be fed into the network, the resulting computing costs overhead is massive. In their work, they proposed Sentence-Bidirectional Encoder Representations (SBERT), as a solution to reduce this bottleneck. SBERT modifies the BERT network using a combination of siamese and triplet networks to derive semantically meaningful embedding of sentences. This adjustment allows BERT to be used for some new tasks which previously did not apply to BERT, such as large-scale semantic similarity comparison, clustering, and information retrieval via semantic search. In this study, we utilised the SBERT language model to perform automatic grading of students short answer questions.

2   Method and Procedures

In this research, three variations of short answer questions, including description, comparison and listing, on an Introduction to Networking Computer Science subject (see Table 1), were administered to a sample of 228 near-graduation Information Science students from one research-intensive tertiary institution in West African. These questions were designed and administered by the course tutor, using the online Google form. Then the course instructor manually rated short answers provided by the students using a scoring rubric. The result of each answer scored one of the six possible ratings, 0, 1, 2, 3, 4, 5.

In order to generate the reference answers that was used as a training dataset to fine-tune our language model, we wrote a python code that randomly selected a maximum of ten distinct student answers for each rating scores. In order words, the code randomly selected 50% of distinct answers that got a particular rating score, and if the total count was greater than ten, it used the top ten selected answers. Otherwise, if the total count was less than ten, it used all the selected answers. The code also appended the standard answer provided by the course tutor to the list of randomly selected answers with ratings of 5. Then the SBERT language model was adapted and used to predict the rating scores. This model mainly functions by performing a search through all the reference answers used to

Table 1. Three variations of questions requiring short answers.

Type	Question
Description	What is server virtualization?
Comparison	Differentiate with examples between IPV4 and IPV6
Listing	Outline at least 5 networking devices that will be used for the integration process

fine-tune the model, in order to determine the one that has the closest similarity, for each provided answer to predict a rating score.

We used the quadratic-weighted kappa (QWKappa) [7,11] for assessing the agreement among the grades assigned by the different raters. Instead of the traditional Cohen's Kappa, we adopt QWKappa, because the former can capture the order information of the scores. For illustration purpose, suppose a response can have scores of up to 3 ratings (0, 1, 2), the first-rater scores a response as 0, the second-rater scores the same response as 1, and the third-rater scores the response as 2. While both the second and third raters disagree with the first-rater, it is clear that the second-rater is more similar than the third-rater. That difference cannot be captured by the traditional Cohen's Kappa, while QWKappa can. Finally, we applied Precision, Recall, and F1 measures to test the accuracy performance of this language model in predicting each variety of the question.

3   Result

Our language model achieved an average score of 0.70 on the QWKappa metric for all the question types, which is considered an outstanding score. The language model predicted comparison questions with the highest accuracy, followed by the description questions. In contrast, the listing question has the lowest accuracy, this result is not surprising, given the nature of the question; "Outline at least five networking devices that will be used for the integration process." The standard answer provided by the instructor had about ten items, and for any five correct answers, the students get a rating of five. Hence, there were several permutations in the answers students provided, and this may have contributed to the low prediction performance of this model on the listing question.

4   Summary

This study found that a pre-trained neural network model can be fine-tuned using minimal reference answers to predict the rating scores of a variety of questions type with reasonable accuracy. Results suggest that students can obtain timely feedback, and lecturers can reduce their workload by utilising automatic grading systems for their students' short type answers. Furthermore, from the observed result on comparing the performance based on the precision, recall, F1-score and accuracy, we conclude that the prediction for the comparison and description answer type outperformed the listing answer type. Although the listing answer type obtained a reasonable score, there is an indication that answers that have several permutations do not necessarily perform well in this model. Hence, cases of complex questions of this nature may not work with an optimal level of accuracy. Despite the success demonstrated, a significant limitation is that this model does not provide reasoning and explanation capabilities, such as feedback to each learner with his particular mistakes. Also, in an online course with low instructor workload, the consistency of grading is very critical for learner's progress. This model generated some false-negative scores, which can be particularly severe due to confusion and time-wasting trying to find out the wrong mistakes in the answers, whereas they were correct. In future research, we hope to validate our proposed model by testing the model performance with standard datasets. We also aspire to see how this model performs in other subject areas. Other interesting aspects may also be explored further, including comparing the performance of this model with other existing models and providing a hint to correct answers.

References

1. Conneau, A., Kiela, D., Schwenk, H., Barrault, L., Bordes, A.: Supervised learning of universal sentence representations from natural language inference data. arXiv preprint arXiv:1705.02364 (2017)
2. Devlin, J., Chang, M.W.: Open sourcing BERT: state-of-the-art pre-training for natural language processing. Google AI Blog, 2 November 2018
3. Devlin, J., Chang, M.W., Lee, K., Toutanova, K.: Bert: pre-training of deep bidirectional transformers for language understanding. arXiv preprint arXiv:1810.04805 (2018)
4. Lample, G., Conneau, A.: Cross-lingual language model pretraining. arXiv preprint arXiv:1901.07291 (2019)
5. Liu, Y., et al.: Roberta: a robustly optimized BERT pretraining approach. arXiv preprint arXiv:1907.11692 (2019)
6. Peters, M.E., Neumann, M., Iyyer, M., Gardner, M., Clark, C., Lee, K., Zettlemoyer, L.: Deep contextualized word representations. arXiv preprint arXiv:1802.05365 (2018)
7. Automated Student Assessment Prize: The Hewlett Foundation: Short Answer Scoring. https://www.kaggle.com/c/asap-sas. Accessed 01 Mar 2020
8. Radford, A., Narasimhan, K., Salimans, T., Sutskever, I.: Improving language understanding with unsupervised learning. Technical report, OpenAI (2018)
9. Reimers, N., Gurevych, I.: Sentence-bert: Sentence embeddings using siamese bert-networks. arXiv preprint arXiv:1908.10084 (2019)
10. Yang, Z., Dai, Z., Yang, Y., Carbonell, J., Salakhutdinov, R.R., Le, Q.V.: Xlnet: Generalized autoregressive pretraining for language understanding. In: Advances in neural information processing systems. pp. 5754–5764 (2019)
11. Zhang, L., Huang, Y., Yang, X., Yu, S., Zhuang, F.: An automatic short-answer grading model for semi-open-ended questions. Interact. Learn. Environ. 1–14 (2019). Taylor & Francis

Extended Multi-document Cohesion Network Analysis Centered on Comprehension Prediction

Bogdan Nicula[1], Cecile A. Perret[2], Mihai Dascalu[1,3(✉)],
and Danielle S. McNamara[2]

[1] University Politehnica of Bucharest, 313 Splaiul Independentei,
060042 Bucharest, Romania
bogdan.nicula@cti.pub.ro, mihai.dascalu@cs.pub.ro
[2] Department of Psychology, Arizona State University, PO Box 871104, Tempe,
AZ 85287, USA
{cperret,dsmcnama}@asu.edu
[3] Academy of Romanian Scientists, Str. Ilfov, Nr. 3,
050044 Bucharest, Romania

Abstract. Theories of discourse argue that comprehension depends on the coherence of the learner's mental representation. Our aim is to create a reliable automated representation to estimate readers' level of comprehension based on different productions, namely self-explanations and answers to open-ended questions. Previous work relied on Cohesion Network Analysis to model a cohesion graph composed of semantic links between multiple reference texts and student productions. From this graph, a set of features was derived and used to build machine learning models to predict student comprehension scores. In this paper, we build on top of the previous study by: a) extending the CNA graph by adding new semantic links targeting specific sentences that should have been captured within the learner's productions, and b) cleaning the self-explanations by eliminating frozen expression, as well as entries which seemed nearly identical to the source text. The results are in line with the conclusions of the previous study regarding the importance of both self-explanations and question answers in predicting the students' reading comprehension level. They also outline the limitations of our feature generation approach, in which no substantial improvements were detected, despite adding more fine-grained features.

Keywords: Multi-document comprehension modeling · Cohesion Network Analysis · Natural Language Processing

1 Introduction

Reading comprehension is a complex task composed of numerous steps, phases, and parallel processes. It involves extracting ideas from a text at multiple levels, including individual sentences, paragraphs as macro-constituents, and even entire documents when multiple texts are considered. Concurrently, a coherent mental representation of

© Springer Nature Switzerland AG 2020
I. I. Bittencourt et al. (Eds.): AIED 2020, LNAI 12164, pp. 228–233, 2020.
https://doi.org/10.1007/978-3-030-52240-7_42

the text is established through connections between various text-based information, as well as with prior knowledge. One key aspect of a reader's mental representation is its coherence, or interconnectedness [1]. Our objective in this project is to develop automated measures of the coherence of readers' mental representation both during and after reading to provide dynamic indicators of readers' level of comprehension.

In our work, we analyze semantic distances (considered a good estimator for coherence) between a set of documents and productions generated by learners under two conditions: a) self-explanations (SEs), generated at specific target sentences while reading the reference documents, and b) open-ended comprehension questions (QAs) that relate to one or more documents. Our aim is to predict multi-document comprehension based on semantic features denoting the links between the reference documents and the student productions. Similar approaches were previously attempted for single text comprehension [2, 3], as well as multiple document scenarios [4].

Cohesion Network Analysis (CNA) [3] was applied in a study by Nicula, Perret, Dascalu and McNamara [5] in a multiple document setting to model the coherence of learner productions, and predict their comprehension level. CNA relies on Natural Language Processing [6] techniques to model discourse in terms of semantic links. CNA is inspired by and transcends Social Network Analysis [7] by considering semantic relatedness between text segments. Its core purpose is to represent cohesion as a graph composed of multiple types of links reflecting semantic distances between elements of different granularity levels (i.e., n-gram sequence, sentence, paragraph, or texts). Several semantic models (such as: LSA [8], Wu-Palmer semantic distance in WordNet [9], word2vec [10] or GloVe [11]) can be used to compute these distances, all of them being available within the ReaderBench framework [12]. For the current study, the CNA graph modeled how information from the reference texts was extracted and structured by readers, while analyzing the links between their productions and the source texts.

Three enhancements were considered while relating to the initial study performed by Nicula, Perret, Dascalu and McNamara [5]. First, we examined the effects of adding features targeting the relation between SEs and specific reference sentences from the target text sequence. This was done in order to better assess whether students' SEs related to relevant information from the prior text. Second, we performed a thorough SE cleaning to check for copy and paste, as well as specific frozen expressions, to provide feedback. Third, a more rigorous and in-depth analysis was performed by calculating the regressions for multiple iterations in an attempt to obtain more informative results less prone to possible outliers.

2 Method

2.1 Corpus

The same corpus in [5] was used, consisting of self-explanations and answers to open-ended questions from 146 students on 4 texts, discussing the same topic. Readers are prompted to write an SE to a sentence at several intervals throughout each text to help them generate inferences within a text. In contrast, the QAs have a target text, but, depending on the question type, they may require linking information from the other texts as well. The students' answers to the 12 questions (3 per text) were graded, resulting in a comprehension score with values ranging from 0 to 12. The students also produced 30 self-explanations on specific target sentences distributed throughout the texts, but these self-explanations were not individually scored.

2.2 Feature Extraction and Selection

A set of features was generated based on the students' responses (i.e., SEs and QAs) reflecting the overlap between the information covered by each response and the information available in the target text. The SE features contain information regarding the semantic similarity between each SE and the four reference texts, the sequences of text targeted by the SEs, and the paragraphs targeted by the SEs. In the case of links between SEs and paragraphs, the extracted features represent aggregate statistics such as the mean, maximum, or standard deviation of the semantic similarity scores corresponding to the links from one SE to all the paragraphs in the targeted text. The information extracted per SE is then aggregated per student by computing the mean, maximum, or standard deviation of these values for all the SEs generated by that student. This results in 272 SE-related features per student.

Compared to previous work, efforts were made to clean up the SEs by eliminating information that is not relevant to our task and by removing SEs that copy-pasted information from the original texts. An approach based on pattern matching with regular expressions was employed to eliminate redundant, uninformative content. In terms of eliminating self-explanations that seemed to be copied, an approach using both n-grams and bag-of-words was applied, eliminating entries that had a high overlap with the source texts. The QA features in the original paper contained information regarding the semantic similarity between the QAs and the 4 texts, and the paragraphs targeted by the QAs. As part of this work, extra information has been added to the model described by [5] in the form of specifying the exact sentences and self-explanations to which a question refers. The semantic distance between the questions and the specified sentences/self-explanations was computed using the same approach. This increased the number of QA-related features from 90 to 330. The extended set of features was passed through the same 2-stage filtering pipeline, which eliminates features with high intra-correlation and features with low correlation to the reading comprehension score. A grid search approach was used to find the most predictive combination of thresholds for the 2 filtering stages. A set of reasonable values were selected for each of the 2 thresholds, and all combinations were tested to determine the best combinations.

3 Results

The 5-fold cross-validation experiments were run 10 times with different random seeds to have more robust results, while the mean and best results were recorded. In this setup, results were slightly different from the ones reported in the original paper, but the conclusions mentioned there still hold using only the original features. When adding the two enhancements (i.e., cleaning of SEs and the extra information regarding links between QAs, SEs, and specific targeted sentences), the best results were slightly below those obtained in the original work; however, the results for all the models except the linear regression improved, implying that threshold selection should be improved. After the extended set of 602 features was generated on the cleaned SEs, the two thresholds for the 2-stage feature filtering were sought using grid search. Depending on the threshold parameters, the filtered set of features varied between 12 and 55 features, but the best performance in all of these experiments was still 2% worse than the results obtained with the original set of features, on the original task (Table 1).

Table 1. Results obtained with features from the 602-feature extended set.

Experimental setup	# SE features	# QA features	Best average performance (MAE)	Best performing model
Original set + intra-corr. < .90 + comp. r > .40	7	13	**1.305**	Linear regression
Extended set + intra-corr. < .90 + comp. r > .40	10	46	1.329	Support Vector Regression
Extended set + intra-corr. < .90 + comp. r > .50	1	19	1.424	Extra trees
Extended set + intra-corr. < .85 + comp. r > .40	8	33	1.319	Support Vector Regression
Extended set + intra-corr. < .95 + comp. r > .40	12	72	1.338	Support Vector Regression
Extended set + intra-corr. < .95 + comp. r > .50	1	32	1.389	Linear regression

* *intra-corr* =intra-correlation above threshold; *comp. r* = reading comprehension score

4   Conclusions

This study confirms some of the conclusions from the original paper [5], namely that the usage of both QA and SE features yields better predictions, while the step of filtering features by intra-correlation helps improve performance. Nevertheless, it seems that that the additional information (i.e., specifically targeting the sentences that should have been referred to by both SEs and questions) is not extremely helpful in the final prediction. A possible explanation resides in the manner in which we extract the semantic data at sentence-level (i.e., average word2vec representations of all words [13]) – which may be too rudimentary.

Nevertheless, we must consider the limitations of this study. Extensions to additional datasets are required to validate and generalize our findings by building machine learning models that take into account more features, without overfitting. This need for larger datasets will also enable a better discrimination as a function of performance. In addition, we will also consider linguistic features (i.e., textual complexity indices), which, in general, are less predictive, but more generalizable.

Despite these limitations, the ultimate value of this extended analysis resides in its potential to provide stealth assessments and scaffolding to students who have not understood the targeted documents. Feedback can be provided either after self-explaining or after the questions and can include additional interventions – such as functionalities to go back and redo a task, or hints, with the aim to provide better answers (reflecting more coherent understanding of the text). The proposed models also deliver more rapid student assessments that provide valuable insights on understanding performance by estimating how well students are capable of conceptualizing and linking ideas from the initial documents.

Acknowledgments. This research was partially supported by a grant of the Romanian National Authority for Scientific Research and Innovation, CNCS – UEFISCDI, project number PN-III-P1-1.2-PCCDI-2017-0689/"Lib2Life - Revitalizing Libraries and Cultural Heritage through Advanced Technologies" within PNCDI III, the Institute of Education Sciences (R305A180144, R305A180261 and R305A190063), and the Office of Naval Research (N00014-17-1-2300). The opinions expressed are those of the authors and do not represent views of the IES or ONR.

References

1. Graesser, A.C., McNamara, D.S., Louwerse, M.M., Cai, Z.: Coh-metrix: analysis of text on cohesion and language. Behav. Res. Meth. Instrum. Comput. **36**(2), 193–202 (2004)
2. Allen, L.K., Jacovina, M., McNamara, D.S.: Cohesive features of deep text comprehension processes. In: 38th Annual Meeting of the Cognitive Science Society, pp. 2681–2686. Cognitive Science Society, Philadelphia, PA (2016)
3. Dascalu, M., McNamara, D.S., Trausan-Matu, S., Allen, L.K.: Cohesion network analysis of CSCL participation. Behav. Res. Methods **50**(2), 604–619 (2018)
4. Hastings, P., Hughes, S., Magliano, J.P., Goldman, S.R., Lawless, K.: Assessing the use of multiple sources in student essays. Behav. Res. Methods **44**(3), 622–633 (2012)
5. Nicula, B., Perret, C.A., Dascalu, M., McNamara, D.S.: *Predicting Multi-document Comprehension:* cohesion network analysis. In: Isotani, S., Millán, E., Ogan, A., Hastings, P., McLaren, B., Luckin, R. (eds.) AIED 2019. LNCS (LNAI), vol. 11625, pp. 358–369. Springer, Cham (2019). https://doi.org/10.1007/978-3-030-23204-7_30
6. Jurafsky, D., Martin, J.H.: An introduction to Natural Language Processing. Computational LINGUISTICS, and Speech Recognition. Pearson Prentice Hall, London (2009)
7. Wasserman, S., Faust, K.: Social Network Analysis: Methods and Applications. Cambridge University Press, Cambridge (1994)
8. Landauer, T.K., Foltz, P.W., Laham, D.: An introduction to latent semantic analysis. Disc. Processes **25**(2/3), 259–284 (1998)
9. Wu, Z., Palmer, M.: Verb semantics and lexical selection. In: 32nd Annual Meeting of the Association for Computational Linguistics, ACL 1994, pp. 133–138. ACL, New Mexico (1994)
10. Le, Q., Mikolov, T.: Distributed representations of sentences and documents. In: International Conference on Machine Learning, pp. 1188–1196. JMLR, Beijing (2014)
11. Pennington, J., Socher, R., Manning, C.D.: Glove: global vectors for word representation. In: The 2014 Conference on Empirical Methods on Natural Language Processing (EMNLP 2014), vol. 14. ACL, Doha, Qatar (2014)

12. Dascalu, M., Crossley, S., McNamara, D.S., Dessus, P., Trausan-Matu, S.: Please readerbench this text: a multi-dimensional textual complexity assessment framework. In: Craig, S. (ed.) Tutoring and Intelligent Tutoring Systems, pp. 251–271. Nova Science Publishers Inc., Hauppauge (2018)
13. Mikolov, T., Chen, K., Corrado, G., Dean, J.: Efficient estimation of word representation in vector space. In: Workshop at ICLR, Scottsdale, AZ (2013)

Supporting Empathy Training Through Virtual Patients

Jennifer K. Olsen[1(✉)] and Catharine Oertel[2]

[1] Ecole Polytechnique Federale de Lausanne, Lausanne, Switzerland
jennifer.olsen@epfl.ch
[2] Interactive Intelligence, Delft University of Technology, Delft, The Netherlands
C.R.M.M.Oertel@tudelft.nl

Abstract. For the training of interpersonal skills, such as those required in the medical field, virtual agents can provide a safe environment for practice. However, many agent systems are not developed with the ability to understand non-verbal input. Being able to automatically parse such input is essential for the practice of interpersonal skills such as empathy. Currently, it is still an open question which prosodic or visual features would aid automatic classification of empathy and how this knowledge can be used to support the practice of these skills. As a first step towards this goal, we report on 42 second-year nursing students practicing their empathy skills with a virtual patient or through collaborative role playing. We found that across both the role playing and simulation, students assessed their empathy as increasing over time but as higher during the role playing. This work contributes to the continued development of virtual agents for the training of interpersonal skills.

Keywords: Virtual agents · Interpersonal skills · Role playing

1 Introduction

As with many areas of vocational education, the medical field has challenges in teaching skills to students in safe environments where the risk from mistakes is minimal and in a way that is scalable. One proposed solution that has been effective across a range of skills has been to use virtual agents [4,14,20,25]. Outside of the medical domain, virtual agents can take on many different roles to support the learning process including those of instructor [1], students for teacher training [9,10], or role-player [24]. Across studies, environments that include virtual agents have been found to enhance learning compared to those that do not [15,29]. Within medical trains, researchers have used virtual patients, a subset of virtual agents, to support both the acquisition of theoretical knowledge [5,27] as well as communication skills [22,31]. Virtual patients provide many advantages to medical training including standardization, accessibility and efficiency, and practice in a safe environment with feedback [5,27].

More recently, research within virtual agents has expanded from focusing primarily on guidance and coaching to using agents' social and affective capabilities

© Springer Nature Switzerland AG 2020
I. I. Bittencourt et al. (Eds.): AIED 2020, LNAI 12164, pp. 234–239, 2020.
https://doi.org/10.1007/978-3-030-52240-7_43

to support learning [18], specifically interpersonal behaviors [2]. For the training of interpersonal skills, students can respond realistically to virtual humans [13] and can improve their target interpersonal skills [17,24]. Furthermore, these skills practiced with the virtual agent may transfer to use with real humans [14].

Moreover, virtual patients can provide increased exposure to cases that take extra care such as those with special needs [28] or dementia. With virtual patients, students are able to practice in a safe environment [31] that prepares them for emotionally-charged real-life encounters and to transfer their skills to a more realistic situation [20]. When training students to deal with sensitive situations specifically, such as those when working with a dementia patient, there is far less work. One specific challenge is to support the training of empathy, which is critical to patient outcomes [16,30]. We define empathy as "a two-phase process: (a) understand and appreciate another person's feelings and emotions and (b) communicate understanding back to the patient in a supportive way" [21] with a focus on the communication through voice. In these situations, the empathy exhibited by the student through both verbal and non-vernal actions is key to fruitful interactions with the patient. Virtual agents have shown mixed results in their ability to support empathy training with higher empathy with real people in some studies [8] and lower in others [19]. One strength of using virtual agents to support empathy training is their ability to provide feedback to students [11,12] and support reflection on their responses [19]. However, virtual patients are still limited in their ability to support complex communication skills [5,7,27].

In this work, we investigate how a virtual agent can be designed and support the training of empathy skills. Specifically, we evaluate the use of a virtual patient for empathy training compared to that of standard practice – collaborative role playing. Our research question is: how does the students' empathy compare over time between the virtual patient condition and the role playing condition? We hypothesize that students will increase their empathy over time but that they will have higher empathy when interacting with real humans [8]. This research contributes to our understanding of using virtual patients to support empathy training.

2   Methods

2.1   Virtual Patient and Collaborative Role Playing Conditions

We developed the patient simulation using Unity with a narrative design, in which decisions the user makes results in different outcomes over time. We represented facial expressions and body posture through a 2-D sketch and speech as both text and audio. The students worked individually with the patient through simple text selections. At each decision point, the student could choose from three answers. We designed the student choices together with experts to represent a range of choices. After making their choice, the students were asked to read out loud the choice that they selected in the way that they would say it to a patient. If they had not liked any of the choices, at this point they were also given the opportunity to rephrase their response. The students could then replay their recording to reflect on the level of empathy. Based on their choice, the next interaction scenario (i.e., dialogue of the patient) would appear on the screen and the facial features of the patient would change subtly to indicate the emotions of the patient (Fig. 1).

Fig. 1. Example screen of the virtual patient.

In the collaborative role-playing, the students were assigned to act out different scenarios in either groups of two or three. In each group there was a patient with dementia and a nurse. When there was a third student, they observed the interaction and took notes. This role-playing set up followed the current school practices. For instructions, we asked the students to speak in High German to standardize the interactions across the different groups as there are multiple dialects of Swiss German. Furthermore, the students were told that they could take advantage of any of the furniture or items in the rooms as props.

2.2   Study Design and Procedure

We collected data from 42 second-year nursing students (16–25 years old) enrolled in a Swiss vocational education program. Of the participants, 37 were female and five male, which is similar to the proportion in the profession. For the experiment, we conducted a within-subject design in which all participants experienced both the virtual patient simulation and the collaborative role playing. We randomly assigned students to experience the virtual patient or the role playing first to counter-balance the order.

For each condition, the students were given three scenarios that were designed to be different across the conditions, but equal. In between each of the scenarios, the students were asked to reflect on the empathy level displayed by the nurse in that scenario on a 1–5 Likert scale [26]. Additionally, they were asked to explain which actions were taken that concretely displayed empathy and which did not display empathy allowing them to reflect on their current actions to elicited self-explanation [6].

3   Results

Our research question related to the impact of the virtual patients on the learning of empathy skills. Specifically, we were interested in the difference between the students' empathy levels between the two conditions, how students' empathy levels changed over time, and if the condition had any impact on this slope. To investigate this question, we used a mixed model to account for the nested nature of the data with each student having multiple scores within each condition. We found a significant impact of time on students' empathy ratings, $t(157) = 5.15$, $p < .001$, with an increase over time. Moreover, we found a significant impact of condition, $t(38) = 3.13$, $p < .01$, with students rating their empathy higher in the role-playing condition. Finally, we found a marginally significant interaction between the time and condition, $t(157) = -1.84$, $p = .07$, with the change over time being positively steeper in the virtual patient condition.

4   Discussion and Conclusion

For virtual agents to support the training of interpersonal skills, it is not enough to only capture the verbal content but to also provide training support for the non-verbal content. In this paper, we conducted a study with 42 nursing students to compare the impact of role playing and virtual patients on their empathy training. Unsurprisingly, we found that the students rated their empathy as being higher in the role-playing condition compared with the virtual patient. One reason for this difference is that the virtual patient did not include many of the channels through which people express empathy. These results support previous work in which students were able to respond empathetically to virtual patients, but not as well as a human [8]. In this case, much of the difference in empathy was also related to the non-verbal aspects of the communication and would be a place for future development of virtual agents. One limitation of our ratings was that they were all self-assessed so may have contained bias, although previous work has shown a correlation between self-assessed communication performance and expert ratings [3,26]. Nevertheless, in this paper, we contribute to the understanding of how virtual agents, specifically the use of virtual patients, can be used to support the learning of interpersonal skills such as empathy. To move in this direction, future work is needed to further develop the non-verbal feedback support within virtual agents.

In this future work, we aim to provide objective ratings of the recorded speech in each condition to further support these results. However, the software is still very limited in being able to provide any feedback around non-verbal features. Extracting prosodic features from the speech samples collected will enable the development of an automatic empathy classifier, similar in approach to the ones developed for engagement [23]. Although gestures and touching cannot be reflected with the virtual patient, the speech support could be greatly strengthened with the automatic detection of prosodic features. Furthermore, we aim to model these student futures to be able to integrate empathy attributes into virtual patients.

Acknowledgements. This project was supported by the leading house DUAL-T research project funded by the Swiss State Secretariat for Education, Research and Innovation (SERI). We would like to thank KOGS (www.kogs.ch) for their excellent collaboration and support in running this study. It would not have been possible without their expert knowledge in health and effort in bringing together input and study opportunities from different inter-company course centres all across the German speaking part of Switzerland.

References

1. Atkinson, R.K.: Optimizing learning from examples using animated pedagogical agents. J. Educ. Psychol. **94**(2), 416 (2002)
2. Aylett, R., Vannini, N., Andre, E., Paiva, A., Enz, S., Hall, L.: But that was in another country: agents and intercultural empathy. In: Proceedings of The 8th International Conference on Autonomous Agents and Multiagent Systems-Volume 1. pp. 329–336. International Foundation for Autonomous Agents and Multiagent Systems (2009)
3. Beaird, G., Nye, C., Thacker II, L.R.: The use of video recording and standardized patient feedback to improve communication performance in undergraduate nursing students. Clin. Simul. Nurs. **13**(4), 176–185 (2017)
4. Berman, A.H., et al.: Virtual patients in a behavioral medicine massive open online course (MOOC): a qualitative and quantitative analysis of participants' perceptions. Acad. Psychiatry **41**(5), 631–641 (2017)
5. Cendan, J., Lok, B.: The use of virtual patients in medical school curricula. Adv. Physiol. Educ. **36**(1), 48–53 (2012)
6. Chi, M.T., Siler, S.A., Jeong, H., Yamauchi, T., Hausmann, R.G.: Learning from human tutoring. Cognit. Sci. **25**(4), 471–533 (2001)
7. Consorti, F., Mancuso, R., Nocioni, M., Piccolo, A.: Efficacy of virtual patients in medical education: a meta-analysis of randomized studies. Comput. Educ. **59**(3), 1001–1008 (2012)
8. Deladisma, A.M., et al.: Do medical students respond empathetically to a virtual patient? Am. J. Sur. **193**(6), 756–760 (2007)
9. Delamarre, A.P., et al.: An interactive virtual training (IVT) simulation for early career teachers to practice in 3D classrooms with student avatars. In: The Thirtieth International Flairs Conference (2017)
10. Dieker, L., Hynes, M., Stapleton, C., Hughes, C.: Virtual classrooms: star simulator. New Learn. Technol.SALT **4**, 1–22 (2007)
11. Foster, A., et al.: Using virtual patients to teach empathy: a randomized controlled study to enhance medical students' empathic communication. Simul. Healthcare **11**(3), 181–189 (2016)
12. Foster, A., Trieu, M., Azutillo, E., Halan, S., Lok, B.: Teaching empathy in healthcare: from mirror neurons to education technology. J. Technol. Behav. Sci. **2**(2), 94–105 (2017)
13. Gillies, M., Pan, X.: Virtual reality for social skills training. In: Proceedings of the Virtual and Augmented Reality to Enhance Learning and Teaching in Higher Education Conference 2018, No. 8, pp. 83–92. IM Publications Open (2018)
14. Johnsen, K., Raij, A., Stevens, A., Lind, D.S., Lok, B.: The validity of a virtual human experience for interpersonal skills education. In: Proceedings of the SIGCHI Conference on Human Factors in Computing Systems, pp. 1049–1058 (2007)

15. Johnson, W.L., Lester, J.C.: Face-to-face interaction with pedagogical agents, twenty years later. Int. J. Artif. Intell. Educ. **26**(1), 25–36 (2016)
16. Kelm, Z., Womer, J., Walter, J.K., Feudtner, C.: Interventions to cultivate physician empathy: a systematic review. BMC Med. Educ. **14**(1), 219 (2014)
17. Kim, J.M., et al.: Bilat: a game-based environment for practicing negotiation in a cultural context. Int. J. Artif. Intell. Educ. **19**(3), 289–308 (2009)
18. Kim, Y., Baylor, A.L.: based design of pedagogical agent roles: a review, progress, and recommendations. Int. J. Artif. Intell. Educ. **26**(1), 160–169 (2016)
19. Kleinsmith, A., Rivera-Gutierrez, D., Finney, G., Cendan, J., Lok, B.: Understanding empathy training with virtual patients. Comput. Hum. Behav. **52**, 151–158 (2015)
20. Kron, F.W., et al.: Using a computer simulation for teaching communication skills: a blinded multisite mixed methods randomized controlled trial. Patient Educ. Couns. **100**(4), 748–759 (2017)
21. Kurtz, S., Draper, J., Silverman, J.: Teaching and Learning Communication Skills in Medicine. CRC Press, London (2017)
22. Menendez, E., et al.: Using a virtual patient system for the teaching of pharmaceutical care. Int. J. Med. Inform. **84**(9), 640–646 (2015)
23. Oertel, C., Scherer, S., Campbell, N.: On the use of multimodal cues for the prediction of degrees of involvement in spontaneous conversation. In: Twelfth Annual Conference of the International Speech Communication Association (2011)
24. Ogan, A., Aleven, V., Kim, J., Jones, C.: Intercultural negotiation with virtual humans: the effect of social goals on gameplay and learning. In: Aleven, V., Kay, J., Mostow, J. (eds.) ITS 2010. LNCS, vol. 6094, pp. 174–183. Springer, Heidelberg (2010). https://doi.org/10.1007/978-3-642-13388-6_22
25. Raij, A.B., et al.: Comparing interpersonal interactions with a virtual human to those with a real human. IEEE Trans. Visual Comput. Graphics **13**(3), 443–457 (2007)
26. Rivera-Gutierrez, D., Kleinsmith, A., Childs, G., Pileggi, R., Lok, B.: Self-assessment through interactive in-action reflections to improve interpersonal skills training. In: 2016 IEEE 16th International Conference on Advanced Learning Technologies (ICALT), pp. 143–147. IEEE (2016)
27. Saleh, N.: The value of virtual patients in medical education. Ann. Behav. Sci. Med. Educ. **16**(2), 29–31 (2010)
28. Sanders, C., Kleinert, H.L., Boyd, S.E., Herren, C., Theiss, L., Mink, J.: Virtual patient instruction for dental students: can it improve dental care access for persons with special needs? Spec. Care Dentist. **28**(5), 205–213 (2008)
29. Schroeder, N.L., Adesope, O.O., Gilbert, R.B.: How effective are pedagogical agents for learning? a meta-analytic review. J. Educ. Comput. Res. **49**(1), 1–39 (2013)
30. Shao, Y.N., Sun, H.M., Huang, J.W., Li, M.L., Huang, R.R., Li, N.: Simulation-based empathy training improves the communication skills of neonatal nurses. Clin. Simul. Nurs. **22**, 32–42 (2018)
31. Stevens, A., et al.: The use of virtual patients to teach medical students history taking and communication skills. Am. J. Sur. **191**(6), 806–811 (2006)

Generating Game Levels to Develop Computer Science Competencies in Game-Based Learning Environments

Kyungjin Park[1]([✉]), Bradford Mott[1], Wookhee Min[1], Eric Wiebe[1],
Kristy Elizabeth Boyer[2], and James Lester[1]

[1] North Carolina State University, Raleigh, NC 27606, USA
{kpark8, bwmott, wmin, wiebe, lester}@ncsu.edu
[2] University of Florida, Gainesville, FL 32601, USA
keboyer@ufl.edu

Abstract. Game-based learning environments hold significant potential for supporting K-12 computer science (CS) education by providing CS learning experiences embedded within engaging virtual worlds. However, many game-based learning environments do not adaptively support individual students based on their specific knowledge and skills. Often, this is because creating game levels is highly labor-intensive, which limits the number of levels created to support student learning. Procedural content generation (PCG) is a promising direction for addressing this challenge by dynamically creating game levels that address specific student needs without requiring extensive development effort. In this paper, we investigate a PCG framework driven by answer set programming (ASP), a variant of logic programming that utilizes well-formed logical rules to express constraints for valid game levels. We demonstrate how variations in CS learning objectives and game-playing skills can be incorporated into ASP-based rules to generate learner-adaptive levels in a middle-grades CS game-based learning environment. Evaluations of the generated levels suggest that the ASP-based level generator not only reliably generates desired CS educational game levels but also synthesizes a large set of diverse game levels. The findings suggest that the ASP-based PCG approach has considerable promise for creating highly engaging and adaptive game-based learning experiences for K-12 CS education.

Keywords: K-12 computer science education · Game-based learning · Procedural content generation · Answer set programming

1 Introduction

Recent years have seen growing interest in game-based learning environments [1–4], which engage students in situated problem-solving challenges within rich virtual worlds [5]. In parallel, there is a growing recognition that computer science (CS) is a fundamental skill required by many career paths, which has intensified the need to develop K-12 students' CS competencies [6–9] and highlighted the potential of game-based learning environments to support CS education [10–12]. However, the

© Springer Nature Switzerland AG 2020
I. I. Bittencourt et al. (Eds.): AIED 2020, LNAI 12164, pp. 240–245, 2020.
https://doi.org/10.1007/978-3-030-52240-7_44

conventional approach of utilizing a linear sequence of game levels is fundamentally non-adaptive and may not effectively address the needs of different students based on their level of concept and skill mastery. This lack of adaptivity may result in undesirable learning experiences (e.g., students adopting a trial-and-error approach without mastering concepts because a game-based learning environment is too difficult). Likewise, students have different levels of game-playing skills, which can affect their learning experiences [13]. Thus, adaptively generating challenges tailored to individual students' knowledge and game-playing skill is crucial for supporting mastery learning and engagement in game-based learning by addressing limitations with "one-size-fits-all" approaches.

Procedural content generation (PCG) automatically generates game content using a range of algorithms that require limited human intervention [14]. In contrast to problem generation in intelligent tutoring systems, in which problems are generated using templates [15, 16], PCG explores the generation of game objects and their layout that collectively constitute a game level. However, level generation in game-based learning environments is challenging for PCG because game levels must exercise the desired learning objectives for individual students as well as target an appropriate level of difficulty for students based on their game-playing skill.

This paper presents a novel approach to generating game levels for game-based learning environments. Our work is the first to introduce a PCG framework that dynamically generates game levels to develop individual students' CS competencies using answer set programming (ASP) [17]. We evaluate our framework with respect to the diversity of generated game levels and the presence of the CS learning objectives as well as the game-playing skill specified as input for each generated level in the context of a game-based learning environment for middle school CS education.

2 ASP-Based Level Generation in Engage

Engage is a game-based learning environment for middle school CS education, the curriculum of which is guided by the K-12 CS Framework [18]. In Engage, students play the role of a protagonist who is sent to an undersea research station, where a rogue villain has severed communication with the facility. In this work, we focus on generating levels for a specific type of challenge shown in Fig. 1a which requires students in the game to connect their wrist computer with a quadcopter device using a pairing

(a)   **(b)**   **(c)**

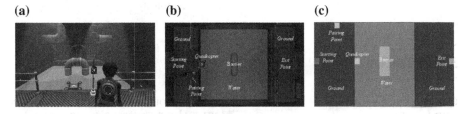

Fig. 1. (a) In-game 3D view of the level, (b) top-down view, and (c) 2D tile-based representation.

point, and program the quadcopter to navigate across a water-filled area while avoiding obstacles. Figure 1b shows a top-down view of the room, which serves as the basis of all the generated levels in this work.

Generated levels incorporate four key learning concepts, *Loop*, *Conditional*, *Sequence* (i.e., requiring minimum of two controls in an unnested structure), and *Nested Control* (i.e., requiring at least one nested control structure), based on the core computer science concepts delineated in the K-12 CS Framework [18], and three game-playing skills (*Low*, *Medium*, *High*) based on the required number of jumps and the width of the path the student's in-game avatar must navigate. To visualize the generated levels, we use a 2D tile-based level representation, as depicted in Fig. 1c.

Answer set programming (ASP) is a declarative programming paradigm, which has its roots in logic programming. In ASP-based PCG, a set of basic requirements and constraints needed for content generation is represented in logical terms (i.e., rules and ground facts) [19]. Then a solver (e.g., Clingo [20]) produces all configurations of content (e.g., game levels) that satisfy the specified constraints. ASP utilizes two constructs: 1) *Choice Rules* to enable non-determinism in choosing ground facts, and 2) *Integrity Constraints* which explicitly define what must not be true in the logical world. Table 1 shows the specific constraints for the four CS learning objectives as well as the three different rulesets for the game-playing skill variations we are considering in ENGAGE.

Table 1. Level category-specific *Choice Rules* and *Integrity Constraints*.

Category	Choice Rules	Integrity Constraints
Loop	The number of repetitive parts	There exists only one path that goes through the repetitive pattern
Conditional	Position of the conditional tile	There exists only one path that passes through the conditional tile
Sequence	Conditional tile exists either at the start of the loop or at the end of loop	There exists only one path that requires a sequence programming
Nested control	Conditional tile exists anywhere within a repetitive pattern	There exists only one path that requires nested control programming
Game skills	Positions where a jump is required Lower the number of connected ground tiles towards *High* level	The character can jump up to one tile The character can move diagonally The character cannot jump diagonally

3   Evaluation

Quantitative Evaluation. We measure the diversity among 100 levels created by the ASP-based level generator using the Clingo [20] solver for each of the 12 categories (four learning concepts combined with three game-playing skills) using a coordinate-based distance metric presented in previous works [21, 22]. The average diversity values of the ASP-generated levels within each category are shown in Table 2. A diversity of 0 indicates that every matched pair of tile types between two levels is identical, while 1 indicates there are no tile types in common across the levels. The average diversity score across all 12 categories is 0.290, which indicates that 29% of tiles (i.e., 113 tiles out of 392 tiles) different between any pair of randomly chosen levels on average. This demonstrates that our model generates levels different to a certain degree consistently. While most categories achieved high diversity scores, *Low* game-playing skill levels across all CS concepts show comparatively lower scores because fewer variations are available within the walkable ground area in these levels.

Table 2. Diversity of 100 levels generated for each of the 12 categories

Loop			Conditional			Sequence			Nested Control			Avg.
Low	Med.	High	Low	Med.	High	Low	Med.	High	Low	Med.	High	
0.132	0.327	0.299	0.234	0.244	0.369	0.135	0.248	0.307	0.135	0.248	0.307	0.290

Qualitative Evaluation. Two domain experts evaluated each level with respect to the presence of the CS learning objectives as well as the game-playing skill required for the level. The evaluators rated each level with game-playing skill (*Low*: 1, *Medium*: 2, *High*: 3) and one binary value for each of the four CS concepts, where 1 indicates the desired concept is present in the level, while 0 is not. The values reported in Table 3 are the averages of the two evaluators' ratings for 100 generated levels. Results for presence of CS concepts suggest that *Sequence, Loop,* and *Conditional* exhibit complete agreements between the human raters, while comparably less agreement occurs for the *Nested Control.* This phenomenon can be explained because some levels have a conditional barrier at the front or end of a path with a repetitive pattern that does not necessarily require use of nested blocks (e.g., it can be solved with a loop followed by a conditional block). Also, we found that there is a small degree of disagreement between *Medium* and *High* game-playing skill levels, while *Low* skill levels were consistently viewed as *Low.*

Table 3. Average human-evaluated presence of CS concepts and game-playing skills (GS).

ASP	Loop			Conditional			Sequence			Nested Control		
	Low (1)	Med. (2)	High (3)	Low (1)	Med. (2)	High (3)	Low (1)	Med. (2)	Hig h (3)	Low (1)	Med. (2)	High (3)
CS	1	1	1	1	1	1	1	1	1	0.55	0.8	0.65
GS	1.05	2.55	2.85	1.2	2.1	2.65	1	2.4	2.95	1	1.95	2.75

4 Conclusion

Game-based learning environments show significant promise for creating engaging learning experiences for students. However, manually crafting a large number of game levels, which is typically required to adaptively support students' mastery learning, is labor-intensive. In this work, we presented an ASP-based PCG framework that automatically synthesizes game levels, and we investigated its generation capabilities for a middle-grade CS game-based learning environment. Evaluation results suggest that the ASP-based level generation framework creates diverse levels, while dynamically synthesizing levels that capture both the learning and game-playing skill-focused specifications. Together, our framework shows significant potential for offering adaptive CS learning experiences with enhanced replayability. In the future, it will be important to investigate robust student modeling techniques to inform the decision-making of the PCG framework to provide student competency-adaptive levels and effectiveness of personalized levels in terms of developing students' CS competencies.

Acknowledgements. This research was supported by the National Science Foundation under Grant DRL-1640141. Any opinions, findings, and conclusions expressed in this material are those of the authors and do not necessarily reflect the views of the National Science Foundation.

References

1. Clark, D.B., Tanner-Smith, E.E., Killingsworth, S.S.: Digital games, design, and learning: a systematic review and meta-analysis. Rev. Educ. Res. **86**(1), 79–122 (2016)
2. Easterday, M.W., Aleven, V., Scheines, R., Carver, S.M.: Using tutors to improve educational games. In: Biswas, G., Bull, S., Kay, J., Mitrovic, A. (eds.) AIED 2011. LNCS (LNAI), vol. 6738, pp. 63–71. Springer, Heidelberg (2011). https://doi.org/10.1007/978-3-642-21869-9_11
3. Nguyen, H., Harpstead, E., Wang, Y., McLaren, Bruce M.: Student agency and game-based learning: a study comparing low and high agency. In: Penstein Rosé, C., Martínez-Maldonado, R., Hoppe, H.U., Luckin, R., Mavrikis, M., Porayska-Pomsta, K., McLaren, B., du Boulay, B. (eds.) AIED 2018. LNCS (LNAI), vol. 10947, pp. 338–351. Springer, Cham (2018). https://doi.org/10.1007/978-3-319-93843-1_25
4. Jackson, G.T., Dempsey, K.B., McNamara, D.S.: Short and long term benefits of enjoyment and learning within a serious game. In: Biswas, G., Bull, S., Kay, J., Mitrovic, A. (eds.) AIED 2011. LNCS (LNAI), vol. 6738, pp. 139–146. Springer, Heidelberg (2011). https://doi.org/10.1007/978-3-642-21869-9_20
5. Spires, H.A., Rowe, J.P., Mott, B.W., Lester, J.C.: Problem solving and game-based learning: effects of middle grade students' hypothesis testing strategies on learning outcomes. J. Educ. Comput. Res. **44**(4), 453–472 (2011)
6. Grover, S., Basu, S., Schank, P.: What we can learn about student learning from open-ended programming projects in middle school computer science. In: Proceedings of the 49th ACM Technical Symposium on Computer Science Education, pp. 999–1004. ACM (2018)
7. Nouri, J., Zhang, L., Mannila, L., Norén, E.: Development of computational thinking, digital competence and 21st century skills when learning programming in K-9. Educ. Inq. **11**(1), 1–17 (2020)

8. Rich, K.M., Strickland, C., Binkowski, T.A., Moran, C., Franklin, D.: K-8 learning trajectories derived from research literature: Sequence, repetition, conditionals. In: Proceedings of the 2017 ACM Conference on International Computing Education Research, pp. 182–190. ACM (2017)

9. Weintrop, D., Hansen, A., Harlow, D., Franklin, D.: Bringing computer science into elementary school classrooms. Am. Educ. Res. Assoc. (2018). https://www.terpconnect. umd.edu/~weintrop/papers/Weintrop_et_al_AERA_2018.pdf

10. Hicks, A., Dong, Y., Zhi, R., Cateté, V., Barnes, T.: BOTS: selecting next-steps from player traces in a puzzle game. In: Proceedings of the Second International Workshop on Graph-Based Educational Data Mining (2015)

11. Bauer, A., Butler, E., Popović, Z.: Dragon architect: Open design problems for guided learning in a creative computational thinking sandbox game. In: Proceedings of the 12th International Conference on the Foundations of Digital Games, pp. 1–6. ACM (2017)

12. Min, W., Frankosky, M.H., Mott, B.W., Wiebe, E.N., Boyer, K.E., Lester, J.C.: Inducing stealth assessors from game interaction data. In: André, E., Baker, R., Hu, X., Rodrigo, M. M.T., du Boulay, B. (eds.) AIED 2017. LNCS (LNAI), vol. 10331, pp. 212–223. Springer, Cham (2017). https://doi.org/10.1007/978-3-319-61425-0_18

13. Rowe, J.P., Shores, L.R., Mott, B.W., Lester, J.C.: Integrating learning, problem solving, and engagement in narrative-centered learning environments. Int. J. Artif. Intell. Educ. 21(1–2), 115–133 (2011)

14. Togelius, J., Kastbjerg, E., Schedl, D., Yannakakis, G.N.: What is procedural content generation? Mario on the borderline. In: Proceedings of the 2nd International Workshop on Procedural Content Generation in Games. ACM (2011)

15. Singh, R., Gulwani, S., Rajamani, S.: Automatically generating algebra problems. In: Proceedings of the Twenty-Sixth AAAI Conference on Artificial Intelligence (2012)

16. Gierl, M.J., Lai, H., Turner, S.R.: Using automatic item generation to create multiple-choice test items. Med. Educ. 46(8), 757–765 (2012)

17. Smith, A.M., Mateas, M.: Answer set programming for procedural content generation: a design space approach. IEEE Trans. Comput. Intell. AI Games 3(3), 187–200 (2011)

18. K-12 Computer Science Framework (2016). https://k12cs.org/

19. Sterling, L., Shapiro, E.Y.: The Art of Prolog: Advanced Programming Techniques. MIT press, Cambridge (1994)

20. Gebser, M., Kaminski, R., Kaufmann, B., Schaub, T.: Clingo = ASP + control: Preliminary report. arXiv preprint arXiv:1405.3694 (2014)

21. Park, K., Mott, B.W., Min, W., Boyer, K.E., Wiebe, E.N., Lester, J.C.: Generating educational game levels with multistep deep convolutional generative adversarial networks. In: Proceedings of the 2019 IEEE Conference on Games (CoG), pp. 345–352. IEEE (2019)

22. Liapis, A., Yannakakis, G.N., Togelius, J.: Enhancements to constrained novelty search: two-population novelty search for generating game content. In: Proceedings of the 15th Annual Conference on Genetic and Evolutionary Computation, pp. 343–350. ACM (2013)

An Evaluation of Data-Driven Programming Hints in a Classroom Setting

Thomas W. Price[1]([✉])[iD], Samiha Marwan[1], Michael Winters[1],
and Joseph Jay Williams[2]

[1] North Carolina State University, Raleigh, USA
{twprice,samarwan,mawinter}@ncsu.edu
[2] University of Toronto, Toronto, Canada
williams@cs.toronto.edu

Abstract. Data-driven programming hints are a scalable way to support students when they are stuck by automatically offering suggestions and identifying errors. However, few classroom studies have investigated data-driven hints' impact on students' performance and learning. In this work, we ran a controlled experiment with 241 students in an authentic classroom setting, comparing students who learned with and without hints. We found no evidence that hints improved student performance or learning overall, and we discuss possible reasons why.

Keywords: Data-driven hints · Computing education

1 Introduction and Background

A fundamental challenge in computer science (CS) education is supporting novice students' learning as they work on independent programming practice. This practice is a common feature of CS courses, but it is challenging for novices working without instructor assistance [3,6,8]. To address this, researchers have designed adaptive, data-driven hints that help students right at the moment they are stuck by offering a personalized suggestion for how to progress or fix an error [14,19]. These are called *data-driven* hints because they are generated from prior students' data [5,11,12,19], allowing them to support diverse solutions [13,19] and scale to support any number of students with little additional instructor effort.

However, because they are generated from data, these hints only suggest how to progress, without the expert-authored explanations and domain principles found in many tutoring systems [22]. This suggests a need for careful evaluation of *data-driven* hints' impact on student performance and learning, especially in authentic classroom settings. However, most prior evaluations have used experts to evaluate the quality of these hints [7,11,12,15,17,23], rather than measuring their effect on learners. Studies that do so provide interesting yet inconclusive

© Springer Nature Switzerland AG 2020
I. I. Bittencourt et al. (Eds.): AIED 2020, LNAI 12164, pp. 246–251, 2020.
https://doi.org/10.1007/978-3-030-52240-7_45

results. One evaluation by Rivers suggests that data-driven programming hints in the ITAP tutoring system had little impact on student learning [18]. However, other work by Marwan et al. suggests that hints can promote learning, but only when carefully designed to scaffold self-explanation [10]. These mixed results not only suggest the need for further evaluation, but also that the effectiveness of hints may depend on their design and the learning context.

In this work, we investigated the efficacy of data-driven programming hints through a controlled study in an introductory CS course. We found that hints had no impact on overall learning or performance, which may have been due to specific choices in the design of hints and low hint quality for students with more complex mistakes.

2   Data-Driven Python Hints

In this study, we used the SourceCheck data-driven hint generation algorithm [12]. SourceCheck takes as input a database of correct student (or expert) solutions to a given problem. When a student asks for a hint, the algorithm identifies a solution that closely matches the structure of the student's current code and suggests small edits to the student's code to bring it closer to that solution. SourceCheck was originally developed for the block-based iSnap tutoring system [14], but in this work we have adapted it to generate hints for the Python programming language and integrated it into a new learning environment. We used students' solutions from a prior semester to generate hints for this study. In a prior technical evaluation, SourceCheck hints were found to be of high-quality compared to other data-driven hint generation approaches, on both iSnap and Python datasets [15], but they have not been evaluated in a large-scale classroom setting.

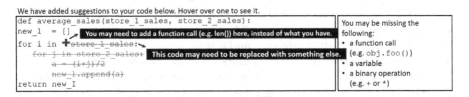

Fig. 1. An example of data-driven Python hints, annotating a student's code. (Color figure online)

In this study, hints were displayed by showing a copy of the student's code, annotated with three types of feedback, as shown in Fig. 1. The hints highlight code that should potentially be: 1) deleted (red strikethrough), 2) replaced (purple strikethrough), or 3) inserted (gray plus). Students can hover over these annotations for further explanation. Students are also shown a list of missing code elements. These suggestions do not directly give away solution code (e.g. add "a boolean value" rather than "False"), reducing the possibility for bottom-out help-abuse [1,4,20]. We chose to provide multiple hints simultaneously, as prior work suggests that students often search through many hints to find one that addresses their current goals [16]. We also chose to show hints each time a student submitted their code to run and test it, given prior work suggesting that many students avoid asking for hints even when they need them [2,9,20].

3   Method

We investigated the following research question: What is the impact of data-driven programming hints on students' overall performance and learning?

Population: Our study took place in an in-person introductory Computer Science course at a large public university in North America, consisting of CS-majors and non-majors with little to no prior programming experience. Our study focused on an optional, online review assignment, which students were given in preparation for their final exam. The class included 1055 students, of whom 401 consented to their data being collected for research and 241 (60.1% of these) participated in the review assignment. Students were randomly assigned to either the Hint condition ($n = 119$), which received hints on some problems, or the Control condition ($n = 122$), which did not.

Procedure: During the review assignment, students completed 4 code writing tasks in an online practice environment. In each problem, students completed a function stub based on a brief description and examples of correct input/output. Each time students submitted their code, it was checked with 4–7 test cases, and the results were reported to the student. Students could submit as many attempts to a given problem as they wanted, revising their solution until it passed all test cases. The review assignment included 2 pairs of related problems (4–5 lines of code), respectively covering: 1) parallel list operations and 2) searching parallel lists. Each pair consisted of an "A" problem, where students could receive hints (depending on their condition), and a subsequent "B" problem, which was used for assessment and provided no hints for either condition. The B problem was a slightly more challenging version of the A problem and therefore allowed us to measure what students learned during the A problem. Students completed two A problems (1A, 2A), with hints in the Hint condition, and then the two corresponding B problems without hints (1B, 2B). The problems were of typical difficulty for the course, and they ranged from 32–46% of students getting them correct on the first attempt (compared to 35% for the average problem in the course).

Measures: We measured students' performance (1A, 2A) and learning (1B, 2B) on a given problem as the number of attempts that they made on that problem until they got it correct (i.e. passed all test cases). Since students almost always got the problem correct *eventually* (98.5% of the time), the number of attempts captures how much the student struggled in that process. It also captures how much feedback they needed, since each attempt received feedback from the data-driven hints (when provided) and test cases (both conditions).

3.1   Results and Discussion

To address our RQ, we compared students' performance on practice problems (1A and 2A), where the Hint condition had hints, and on assessment problems (1B and 2B), which measured hints' impact on learning. As shown in Table 1, the averages are very similar for both conditions, and a Mann-Whitney U-tests show that the difference is not significant on any of the problems, with a small effect size. We also looked at the rate at which students correctly completed problems in each group, since prior work suggests data-driven hints can increase homework completion rates [21]. However, we found little difference between the overall completion rate of the Hint (90.8%) and Control (87.7%) conditions. This suggests that our data-driven hints did not have an overall effect on students' performance or learning.

Table 1. For each problem, and each condition, the mean number of attempts per student (lower is better), p-value from Mann-Whitney U test, effect size, and the number of students who completed the problem correctly.

Problem	Mean attempts (SD)				Completed correctly	
	Hint	Control	p	Cohen's d	Hint (n = 119)	Control (n = 122)
1A	2.26 (1.83)	2.35 (2.72)	0.51	−0.04	117 (98.32%)	122 (100%)
2A	2.79 (2.65)	2.70 (3.79)	0.25	0.03	117 (98.32%)	117 (95.90%)
1B	2.32 (1.95)	2.25 (1.72)	0.77	0.04	109 (91.60%)	111 (90.98%)
2B	3.00 (3.78)	2.64 (2.14)	0.39	0.12	108 (90.8%)	107 (87.70%)

This result contrasts somewhat with prior work, as Marwan et al. found that hints improved students' *immediate performance* (on problems with hints) [10], and Rivers also found suggestive evidence hints increased students' speed on practice problems [18]. We note that the *way* we designed our data-driven hints may have been responsible for some of these differences. For example, our implementation of data-driven hints did not include hand-authored textual explanations (as in [10]). Our results that data-driven programming hints alone did not improve students' *learning* agree with those of both Rivers and Marwan et al. [10,18]. These results may stem from limitations in *data-driven* programming hints in particular, which can be inaccurate or difficult to interpret [16,17]. A manual investigation of the hints offered during our study suggests that the adaptive hints varied across students and were not of equal quality. As in prior work [15], they appeared most useful for students with small mistakes, and may have been confusing for students far from a correct solution.

4   Conclusion and Future Work

This work provides insight into the effectiveness of data-driven programming hints, with additional evidence that these hints alone may not always promote learning, or even performance. The latter result is surprising, given that hints give away part of the correct solution, and it contrasts with prior work [10, 18]. This may be explained by our preliminary finding that hint quality varied across situations, which suggests the need for future work investigating whether contextual factors, such as student prior knowledge and problem difficulty, may mediate hints' usefulness.

References

1. Aleven, V., Koedinger, K.R.: Investigations into Help seeking and Learning with a Cognitive Tutor. In: Papers of the AIED 2001 Workhop 'Help Provision And Help Seeking In Interactive Learning Environments', pp. 47–58 (2001)
2. Aleven, V., Stahl, E., Schworm, S., Fischer, F., Wallace, R.: Help seeking and help design in interactive learning environments. Rev. Educ. Res. **73**(3), 277–320 (2003)
3. Altadmri, A., Kölling, M., Brown, N.C.C.: The cost of syntax and how to avoid it: text versus frame-based editing. In: CELT: COMPSAC Symposium on Computing Education & Learning Technologies; Part of COMPSAC 2016: The 40th IEEE Computer Society International Conference on Computers, Software & Applications (2016)
4. Baker, R.S., Corbett, A.T., Koedinger, K.R.: Detecting student misuse of intelligent tutoring systems. In: Proceedings of the International Conference on Intelligent Tutoring Systems, pp. 531–540 (2004)
5. Choudhury, R.R., Yin, H., Fox, A.: Scale-driven automatic hint generation for coding style. In: Proceedings of the International Conference on Intelligent Tutoring Systems, pp. 122–132 (2016)
6. Collier, S., Downing, M.: A qualitative analysis of students' understanding of conditional control structures. In: Proceedings of the 50th ACM Technical Symposium on Computer Science Education, pp. 1293–1293 (2019)
7. Hartmann, B., Macdougall, D., Brandt, J., Klemmer, S.R.: What would other programmers do? suggesting solutions to error messages. In: Proceedings of the ACM Conference on Human Factors in Computing Systems, pp. 1019–1028 (2010). https://doi.org/10.1145/1753326.1753478
8. Ko, A., Myers, B., Aung, H.: Six learning barriers in end-user programming systems. In: Proceedings of the IEEE Symposium on Visual Languages and Human-Centric Computing, pp. 199–206 (2004)
9. Marwan, S., Dombe, A., Price, T.: Unproductive Help-seeking in Programming: what it is and how to address it? In: To be published in the Proceedings of the 25th Annual Conference on Innovation and Technology in Computer Science Education (2020)
10. Marwan, S., Jay Williams, J., Price, T.: An evaluation of the impact of automated programming hints on performance and learning. In: Proceedings of the International Computing Education Research Conference (2019)
11. Piech, C., Sahami, M., Huang, J., Guibas, L.: Autonomously generating hints by inferring problem solving policies. In: Proceedings of the second (2015) ACM Conference on Learning@ Scale, pp. 195–204 (2015)

12. Price, T., Zhi, R., Barnes, T.: Evaluation of a data-driven feedback algorithm for open-ended programming. In: International Educational Data Mining Society (2017)
13. Price, T.W., Dong, Y., Barnes, T.: Generating data-driven hints for open-ended programming. In: Proceedings of the International Conference on Educational Data Mining (2016)
14. Price, T.W., Dong, Y., Lipovac, D.: iSnap: towards intelligent tutoring in novice programming environments. In: Proceedings of the ACM Technical Symposium on Computer Science Education, pp. 483–488 (2017)
15. Price, T.W., Dong, Y., Zhi, R., Paaßen, B., Lytle, N., Cateté, V., Barnes, T.: A comparison of the quality of data-driven programming hint generation algorithms. Int. J. Artif. Intell. Educ. **29**(3), 368–395 (2019). https://doi.org/10.1007/s40593-019-00177-z
16. Price, T.W., Liu, Z., Catete, V., Barnes, T.: Factors Influencing Students' Help-Seeking Behavior while Programming with Human and Computer Tutors. In: Proceedings of the International Computing Education Research Conference (2017)
17. Price, T.W., Zhi, R., Barnes, T.: Hint generation under uncertainty: the effect of hint quality on help-seeking behavior. In: André, E., Baker, R., Hu, X., Rodrigo, M.M.T., du Boulay, B. (eds.) AIED 2017. LNCS (LNAI), vol. 10331, pp. 311–322. Springer, Cham (2017). https://doi.org/10.1007/978-3-319-61425-0_26
18. Rivers, K.: Automated Data-Driven Hint Generation for Learning Programming. Ph.D. thesis, Carnegie Mellon University (2017). http://krivers.net/files/thesis.pdf
19. Rivers, K., Koedinger, K.R.: Data-driven hint generation in vast solution spaces: a self-improving python programming tutor. Int. J. Artif. Intell. Educ. **27**(1), 37–64 (2015). https://doi.org/10.1007/s40593-015-0070-z
20. Roll, I., Baker, R.S.D., Aleven, V., Koedinger, K.R.: On the benefits of seeking (and avoiding) help in online problem-solving environments. J. Learn. Sci. **23**(4), 537–560 (2014)
21. Stamper, J.C., Eagle, M., Barnes, T., Croy, M.: Experimental evaluation of a automatic hint generation for a logic tutor. Int. J. Artif. Intell. Educ. **22**, 3–17 (2013)
22. VanLehn, K.: The behavior of tutoring systems. Int. J. Artif. Intell. Educ. **16**(3), 227–265 (2006)
23. Watson, C., Li, F.W.B., Godwin, J.L.: BlueFix: using crowd-sourced feedback to support programming students in error diagnosis and repair. In: Proceedings of the International Conference on Web-based Learning, pp. 228–239 (2012)

Deep Knowledge Tracing
with Transformers

Shi Pu[1(✉)], Michael Yudelson[2(✉)], Lu Ou[3], and Yuchi Huang[4]

[1] San Diego, CA, USA
scott.pu.pennstate@gmail.com
[2] Pittsburgh, PA, USA
myudelson@gmail.com
[3] Campbell, CA, USA
lu.ou.psu@gmail.com
[4] ACT, Inc., 500 ACT Drive., Iowa City, IA 52245, USA
yuchi.huang@act.org

Abstract. In this work, we propose a Transformer-based model to trace students' knowledge acquisition. We modified the Transformer structure to utilize 1) the association between questions and skills and 2) the elapsed time between question steps. The use of question-skill associations allows the model to learn specific representation for frequently encountered questions while representing rare questions with their underline skill representations. The inclusion of elapsed time opens the opportunity to address forgetting. Our approach outperforms the state-of-the-art methods in the literature by roughly 10% in AUC with frequently used public datasets.

Keywords: Bayesian Knowledge Tracing · Deep Knowledge Tracing · Transformer

1 Introduction

Bayesian Knowledge Tracing (BKT) is an established approach to modeling skill acquisition of students working with intelligent tutoring systems. However, BKT is far from an ideal solution, and multiple improvements and extensions were suggested to it over the years. One of such extensions is Deep Knowledge Tracing (DKT). The first DKT [6] adopted the Recurrent Neural Network (RNN) architecture from the deep learning community. Recent publications on DKT discuss various RNN architecture modifications to adapt to student learning theories as well as explore new deep learning models. Our work is inspired by both and proposes to use the Transformer architecture to model students' knowledge state.

The Transformer model was first proposed by the Google Brain team [9] to generate better neural translations. It soon became the dominant model in many Natural Language Processing (NLP) problems [2,7]. The main advantage of the Transformer over RNN is its ability to learn long-range dependencies [2].

© Springer Nature Switzerland AG 2020
I. I. Bittencourt et al. (Eds.): AIED 2020, LNAI 12164, pp. 252–256, 2020.
https://doi.org/10.1007/978-3-030-52240-7_46

We modified the Transformer architecture so that it does not directly learn the representation of each question. Instead, it learns the representation of the underlying W-matrix that relates knowledge components to question items, including the cases when multiple knowledge components are associated with an item. This modification allows the model to learn specific representation for frequently encountered questions while represent rare questions with their underline skill representations. Further, we allow the attention weight between question items to decay as students work on questions or problems, which effectively represents forgetting.

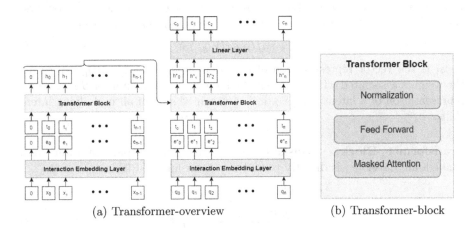

(a) Transformer-overview   (b) Transformer-block

Fig. 1. Transformer architecture

2   Related Work

The original Deep Knowledge Tracing (DKT) Model [6] used an RNN based architecture and claimed to outperform BKT by a large margin. However, latter works [3,10] showed that RNN based DKT is not superior than BKT models over a pool of datasets when data preprocessing errors are taken into account.

Recent work on DKT follows two general patterns. First, a group of studies [4,11] tried to adjust the RNN structure so that it is consistent with the students' learning process. For example, the Dynamic Key-Value Memory Networks [11] explicitly maintained knowledge components and knowledge states. Further, Nagatan and colleagues [4] intentionally modeled students' forgetting behavior in RNN but achieved only limited success.

Another group of DKT papers seeks to leverage recently developed Transformer models [1,5,8]. Pandey and Karypis [5] used a self-attention model which is a simplified version of the Transformer. Ralla and colleagues [8] used Transformer Encoder to pre-train students' interactions. Choi et al. [1] experimented with different alternatives to rewiring the components in the original Transformer. All these works showed inspiring results and motivated this study.

3   Methods

Figure 1 represents a simplified version of our adapted Transformer model. The main inputs to our adapted Transformer model is a sequence tuples $x_i = (q_i, c_i)$, and timestamp t_i. Here, q_i represents the question item a student is trying to answer, and $c_i \in 0, 1$ represents whether the response is correct. The goal of the model is a sequence of correctness estimates, c_{i+1}, representing whether a student correctly solved the next question q_{i+1}. Formally, the Transformer model is trying to predict $P(c_{i+1} = 1 | x_0, .., x_i, t_0, ..., t_i, q_{i+1})$.

Interaction Embedding Layer. A student interaction, x_i, will be first encoded as an index, d_i, and passed to the interaction mapping layer:

$$e_i = softmax(W_{d_i \cdot}) S \qquad (1)$$

e_i is the vector representation of a student interaction x_i. $W_{d_i \cdot}$ represents the weights associated with all latent skills for d_i. Each column of S is a vector representation of a latent skill. So, e_i is a weighted sum of all underlying latent skills.

Transformer Block – Masked Attention. The outputs of Interaction Embedding Layer, e_i, is directly passed to a Transformer Block:

$$q_i = Q e_i, k_i = K e_i, v_i = V e_i \qquad (2)$$

$$A_{ij} = \frac{q_i k_j + b(\Delta t_{i-j})}{\sqrt{d_k}}, \forall j \le i \qquad (3)$$

$$h_i = \sum_{j \le i} softmax(A_{ij}) v_j \qquad (4)$$

the masked attention layer first extracts query q_i, key k_i, and value v_i from the inputs e_i. It then assign an *attention*, A_{ij}, to a past interaction e_j based on two components: 1) $q_i k_j$, the query-key agreement between e_i and e_j, which could be interpreted as the degree of latent skills overlapping between interaction e_i and e_j; 2) A time gap bias, $b(\Delta t_{i-j})$, which adjusts the attention weight by the time gap between interactions e_i and e_j. The hidden representation h_i is a weighted sum of the past value representations of e_j. A Transformer block also have feedforward layer, normalization layer, and residual connections. We recommend readers to read the original paper [9] for more detail.

Linear Layer + Loss. The outputs of a stack of Transformer blocks is feed to the linear layer before calculating the final loss. e_{i+1} and e_{i+1}^* are the results of applying Interaction Mapping Layer to $(q_{i+1}, 1)$ and $(q_{i+1}, 0)$.

$$p_{i+1} = \frac{exp(h_i e_{i+1})}{exp(h_i e_{i+1}) + exp(h_i e_{i+1}^*)} \qquad (5)$$

$$Loss = -\sum_i c_{i+1} log(p_{i+1}) + (1 - c_{i+1}) log(1 - p_{i+1}) \qquad (6)$$

4   Experiments

We ran 5-fold student-stratified cross-validation on three datasets that are frequently used in the literature. Table 1 lists descriptive statistics for the datasets.

ASSISTments2017[1]. Data from the ASSISTment online tutoring system.

STAT F2011[2]. This data is from a college-level engineering statics course.

KDD, A[3]. This data is the challenge set A – Algebra I 2008–2009 data set from the KDD 2010 Educational Data Mining Challenge.

Table 1. Dataset overview and student-stratified 5-fold cross validation

Datasets	Overview				AUC		
	Interactions	Students	Items	Skills	BKT	Literature	Our Model
ASSISTments2017	943K	1,709	4,117	102	0.628	0.734[5]	**0.806**
STAT F2011	190K	333	1,224	81	0.821	0.853[5]	**0.947**
KDD 2010, A	4,420K	3,287	1,379	899	0.744		**0.784**

Table 2. AUC under different architecture

Architecture	ASSISTment 2017	STAT F2011	KDD 2010, A
Transformer: 1-layer original	0.709	0.917	0.772
Transformer: 1-layer + mapping	0.737	0.939	0.772
Transformer: 1-layer + time-bias	0.704	0.931	0.777
Transformer: 1-layer + all	0.773	0.946	**0.784**
Transformer: 6-layer + all	**0.806**	**0.947**	0.775

5   Results and Discussion

Table 1 summarizes our findings and compares them to the start-of-the-art Deep Knowledge Tracing model results in the literature, as well as the Bayesian Knowledge Tracing (BKT) model. Our adapted Transformer model is superior to BKT on all datasets and outperforms the state-of-the-art DKT models from the literature by 9.81% and 11.02% on ASSISTments 2017 and STAT F2011 datasets. The remarkable gain is not due to the structure of the original transformer model. Pandey and Karypis [5]'s self-attention model is roughly equivalent to a 1-layer Transformer. Their reported AUC score on ASSISTments 2017 and STAT F2011 is about 10% worse than our adapted Transformer.

---

[1] https://sites.google.com/view/assistmentsdatamining.
[2] https://pslcdatashop.web.cmu.edu/DatasetInfo?datasetId=507.
[3] https://pslcdatashop.web.cmu.edu/KDDCup/.

To further illustrate this point, we repeat the experiment on the original Transformer with/without the modified components, as illustrated in Table 2. The original Transformer gains an obvious performance boost by adding the *interaction skill mapping* and *time-bias* to its structure.

To conclude, our adapted Transformer architecture generated promising results on frequently used public datasets. For future work, we intend to explore how to efficiently incorporate more feature information into the Transformer architecture, as well as how to represent hierarchical relations between skills in the interaction embedding layer.

References

1. Choi, Y., et al.: Towards an appropriate query, key, and value computation for knowledge tracing. arXiv preprint arXiv:2002.07033 (2020)
2. Devlin, J., Chang, M.W., Lee, K., Toutanova, K.: Bert: Pre-training of deep bidirectional transformers for language understanding. arXiv preprint arXiv:1810.04805 (2018)
3. Khajah, M., Lindsey, R.V., Mozer, M.C.: How deep is knowledge tracing? In: Proceedings of the 9th International Conference on Educational Data Mining, EDM 2016, pp. 94–101 (2016)
4. Nagatani, K., Chen, Y.Y., Zhang, Q., Chen, F., Sato, M., Ohkuma, T.: Augmenting knowledge tracing by considering forgetting behavior. In: The Web Conference 2019 - Proceedings of the World Wide Web Conference, WWW 2019, pp. 3101–3107 (2019). https://doi.org/10.1145/3308558.3313565
5. Pandey, S., Karypis, G.: A self-attentive model for knowledge tracing. arXiv preprint arXiv:1907.06837 (2019)
6. Piech, C., et al.: Deep knowledge tracing. In: Advances in Neural Information Processing Systems, pp. 505–513 (2015)
7. Radford, A., Wu, J., Child, R., Luan, D., Amodei, D., Sutskever, I.: Language models are unsupervised multitask learners. OpenAI Blog $1(8)$, 9 (2019)
8. Ralla, A., Siddiqie, S., Krishna Reddy, P., Mondal, A.: Assessment modeling: fundamental pre-training tasks for interactive educational systems youngduck. In: ACM International Conference Proceeding Series, pp. 209–213 (2020). https://doi.org/10.1145/1122445.1122456
9. Vaswani, A., et al.: Attention is all you need. In: Advances in Neural Information Processing Systems, pp. 5998–6008 (2017)
10. Xiong, X., Zhao, S., Van Inwegen, E.G., Beck, J.E.: Going deeper with deep knowledge tracing. In: International Educational Data Mining Society (2016)
11. Zhang, J., Shi, X., King, I., Yeung, D.Y.: Dynamic key-value memory networks for knowledge tracing. In: 26th International World Wide Web Conference, WWW 2017, pp. 765–774 (2017). https://doi.org/10.1145/3038912.3052580

Relationships Between Body Postures and Collaborative Learning States in an Augmented Reality Study

Iulian Radu[1]([⊠]), Ethan Tu[2], and Bertrand Schneider[1]

[1] Harvard University, Cambridge, MA, USA
iulian_radu@gse.harvard.edu
[2] Tufts University, Medford, MA, USA

Abstract. In this paper we explore how Kinect body posture sensors can be used to detect group collaboration and learning, in the context of dyad pairs using augmented reality system. We leverage data collected during a study (N = 60 dyads) where participant pairs learned about electromagnetism. Using unsupervised machine learning methods on Kinect body posture sensor data, we contribute a set of dyad states associated with collaboration quality, attitudes toward physics and learning gains.

Keywords: Posture · Synchrony · Collaborative learning · Augmented reality

1 Introduction and Research Design

Body postures and gestures are nonverbal communication channels, which have been shown to reveal valuable information about learners' internal states, such as their attitudes towards a learning activity [1], misconceptions [2], comfort with collaborators [3, 4]. Additionally, when students collaborate with other students or teachers, the amount of synchronization between their gestures and postures has been linked to collaborative learning dimensions, such as affect [5], learning gains [1] and quality of collaboration [6, 7]. In studies involving teachers and students, body synchrony has been linked to increased learning gains [5, 10]. However, for some situations body synchrony is negatively correlated with learning. Abney et al. [11] observed dyad movement using computer vision algorithms, and found that synchrony was negatively correlated with learning. Another study [12], which studied Kinect dyad movements, found that body synchronization had no overall effect on any collaborative or learning measures, but found that learning gains were correlated with cycles of "cognition and action", where dyads alternated between reflecting in the activity and interacting with the system. These conflicting results indicate that further research is needed to understand the links between posture and collaborative learning. To perform such research, the traditional method is qualitative coding of video data, which requires large time investment from manual coding. Over the last decade, researchers have been investigating how automated methods can be used to detect body postures and their links to student attitudes and learning [8]. In this paper we expand this research by

I. I. Bittencourt et al. (Eds.): AIED 2020, LNAI 12164, pp. 257–262, 2020.
https://doi.org/10.1007/978-3-030-52240-7_47

contributing new methods for analyzing body posture data from Kinect sensors, and new understanding of the relationships between posture synchronization and collaborative learning.

The goal of this paper is to determine if static postures of paired participants can be used as indicators of group learning, attitudes and collaboration. We perform this investigation in the context of an augmented reality (AR) experience. Decreasing costs and advanced body tracking technology make AR popular for educational use [15], and it is valuable to understand user behaviors under this context. We use data from a previous study (<Anonymized>) where 60 dyads interacted with a homemade speaker system, a common activity in learning physics. Dynamic visual representations of the electromagnetic concepts of the speaker are visualized through the AR headset (Fig. 1).

Fig. 1. Participants wearing the augmented reality headset (left) and interacting with a tangible system which is augmented with virtual information visible through the headset (right)

We measured several dependent measures of collaboration, attitudes and learning gains. For this analysis, all variables were measured at the group level. Collaboration was measured using a validated rating scheme described by Meier, Spada and Rummel [20], measuring collaborative processes on subdimensions such as coordination (i.e. whether participants divided tasks and managed time), information processing (i.e. whether participants shared sharing information and reached consensus), etc. Attitudes towards the user experience were measured using the survey instrument in [21] measuring perception of aesthetics, endurability, focus, novelty, involvement and usability. Learning was calculated as relative learning gains (RLG), which measure the amount of knowledge gained between pre and post tests of electromagnetism knowledge. Relative learning gains were calculated on the overall test score, as well as on specific subdimensions such as the ability to answer transfer questions.

These dependent measures were correlated with dyad participant postures, calculated based on data collected from a Microsoft Kinect sensor, and from the Microsoft Hololens headsets worn by participants. Through these sensors we collected joint coordinates and gaze data from both participants, and calculated dyad posture metrics such as closeness between participants (which may signal how comfortable participants feel with each other), similarity between spine angles (which may indicate that participants mirror each other's posture), orientation towards peers (which may indicate focus on discussion), forward lean (possibly indicating engagement with the task).

2   Method and Results

Participants were recruited from the study pool of a laboratory at a university in the northeastern United States. Participation required subjects to not know each other, have no significant prior physics knowledge, be born on/after 1976, speak English fluently, have at least a bachelor's degree, and wear no bifocal glasses. All participants first individually completed a pre-test, then a 30-min paired activity of answering worksheet questions while interacting with the apparatus, followed by individual post-test. Only data from the paired activity was used for analysis. After data cleaning, the resulting dataset contains 50 dyad sessions: 25 sessions with the AR visualizations and 25 sessions without. Prior to calculating Kinect metrics, the Kinect data was preprocessed to remove noise and disambiguate between the seated participants and researcher.

We explored K-means posture clustering using the "elbow method", exploring combinations of clustering variables and number of clusters k = 2, 3, 4, 5. The optimal configuration involved k = 4 clusters and variables of spine synchrony, mean distance between participants, and discussion orientation (Fig. 2 left). Figure 2 (right lists the significant correlations found between the time in each cluster and the measures, and Fig. 3 shows the video frames at the datapoints that most closely represents each cluster.

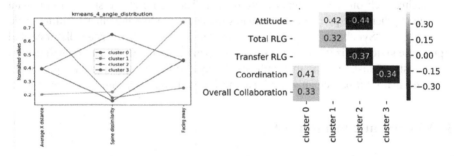

Fig. 2. Left: Showing averages of body feature variables by clusters. Right: Significant correlations ($p < 0.05$) between percentage of time in each cluster vs. dependent measures.

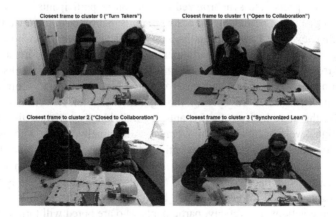

Fig. 3. The video frame closest to each cluster center.

Cluster 0, what we labeled as "Turn Takers", are characterized by **low spine similarity** and **positively correlated with coordination and overall collaboration**. Figure 3 (top left) shows one participant is leaning forward interacting with the setup while the other is watching. This configuration indicates that low spine synchrony could be indicative of a collaboration style where participants take turns interacting with the setup. This is supported by research in [12] where cycles of leaning forward and backward indicated cycles of reflection and action were found across successful dyads.

Cluster 1 "Open to Collaboration", is characterized by **low distance between participants** and participants **facing parallel to each other**, and is correlated with **overall positive attitudes and learning**. Figure 3 (top right) shows both participants are sitting close to each other and are engaged in the task in front of them, and left participant in a thinking pose. This configuration appears to show participants highly focused on the task and which would explain a positive correlation with overall attitude and learning.

Cluster 2 "Closed to Collaboration", is characterized by **high distance between participants** and with participants **facing each other**, and is **negatively correlated with overall positive attitudes** toward the experience. This clustering configuration seems to be indicative of a more negative experience where participants spend some time facing each other yet remain more distant. The figure above shows a dominant interaction where one participant dominates the activity while the other is sitting back.

Cluster 3 "Synchronized Lean", is characterized by **high average distance** and **high spine synchronization**, and is **negatively correlated with overall coordination**. In contrast to Cluster 0, this may indicate the dyad does not spend much time taking turns and that both participants were leaning forward and backward at the same time.

3 Discussion and Future Work

In this paper we used unsupervised machine learning methods on body posture sensor data. We detected different posture clusters associated with collaboration and learning, finding these metrics were correlated to dyad posture variables such as spine similarity, distance between peers, and synchronized orientation of participants.

We found that when participant spines were not synchronized, the dyad pair tended to show higher levels of coordination. This may indicate that dyads who are good at coordinating tend to take turns, as participants move individually before sharing what they gained from their individual explorations. This result aligns with results from [12], where iterating between active and passive states was significantly correlated with learning gains (interpreted as cycling through moments of reflection and action). Alternatively, this may indicate participants are individually active at the same time, leading to high levels of individual movement. Additionally, dyads who were physically closer to each other throughout the activity had better overall attitudes toward the collaborative task. Also, participants who spent more time focused on the activity rather than each other had more positive attitudes. One interpretation is that when people are engaged in the activity, they will be highly focused on the task and enjoying each others' interactions; conversely, participants who are bored will turn to each other to talk more. Dyads also communicated better when leaning forward. People who were leaning forward are likely to be more engaged in the activity, and people who are leaning backward are likely to be more disengaged; this is likely to be reflected in their communication.

The methodology and findings presented in this paper have larger implications for the learning sciences community, as they can serve to indicate markers of successful and unsuccessful collaborations, possibly applicable to other contexts where dyad pairs are learning through interaction with physical objects, and useful to designing systems that monitor student learning through body posture observations. We acknowledge the potential statistical errors introduced by performing large numbers of correlations due to the exploratory nature of our research.

References

1. Won, A.S., Bailenson, J.N., Janssen, J.H.: Automatic detection of nonverbal behavior predicts learning in dyadic interactions. IEEE Trans. Affect. Comput. **5**, 112–125 (2014)
2. Abrahamson, D., Trninic, D., Gutiérrez, J.F., Huth, J., Lee, R.G.: Hooks and shifts: a dialectical study of mediated discovery. Technol. Knowl. Learn. **16**, 55–85 (2011)
3. D'Mello, S., Dale, R., Graesser, A.: Disequilibrium in the mind, disharmony in the body. Cogn. Emot. **26**, 362–374 (2012)
4. Echeverría, V., Avendaño, A., Chiluiza, K., Vásquez, A., Ochoa, X.: Presentation skills estimation based on video and kinect data analysis. In: Proceedings of the 2014 ACM Workshop on Multimodal Learning Analytics Workshop and Grand Challenge, pp. 53–60 (2014)
5. LaFrance, M., Broadbent, M.: Group rapport: Posture sharing as a nonverbal indicator. Group Organ. Stud. **1**, 328–333 (1976)
6. Won, A.S., Bailenson, J.N., Stathatos, S.C., Dai, W.: Automatically detected nonverbal behavior predicts creativity in collaborating dyads. J. Nonverbal Behav. **38**, 389–408 (2014)
7. Delaherche, E., Chetouani, M., Mahdhaoui, A., Saint-Georges, C., Viaux, S., Cohen, D.: Interpersonal synchrony: a survey of evaluation methods across disciplines. IEEE Trans. Affect. Comput. **3**, 349–365 (2012)
8. Wiltermuth, S.S., Heath, C.: Synchrony and cooperation. Psychol. Sci. **20**, 1–5 (2009)
9. Ramseyer, F., Tschacher, W.: Nonverbal synchrony in psychotherapy: coordinated body movement reflects relationship quality and outcome. J. Consult. Clin. Psychol. **79**, 284 (2011)
10. Miles, L.K., Nind, L.K., Henderson, Z., Macrae, C.N.: Moving memories: behavioral synchrony and memory for self and others. J. Exper. Soc. Psychol. **46**, 457–460 (2010)
11. Abney, D.H., Paxton, A., Dale, R., Kello, C.T.: Movement dynamics reflect a functional role for weak coupling and role structure in dyadic problem solving. Cogn. Process. **16**, 325–332 (2015)
12. Schneider, B., Blikstein, P.: Unraveling students' interaction around a tangible interface using multimodal learning analytics. J. Educ. Data Min. **7**, 89–116 (2015)
13. Tomasello, M.: Joint attention as social cognition. In: Moore, C., Dunham, P.J. (eds.) Joint Attention: Its Origins and Role in Development, pp. 103–130. Lawrence Erlbaum Associates Inc., Hillsdale (1995)

14. Schneider, B., Sharma, K., Cuendet, S., Zufferey, G., Dillenbourg, P., Pea, R.: Leveraging mobile eye-trackers to capture joint visual attention in co-located collaborative learning groups. Intern. J. Comput.-Support. Collab. Learn. **13**, 241–261 (2018). https://doi.org/10. 1007/s11412-018-9281-2
15. Radu, I.: Augmented reality in education: a meta-review and cross-media analysis. Pers. Ubiquit. Comput. **18**, 1533–1543 (2014)
16. Ibáñez, M.B., Di Serio, Á., Villarán, D., Kloos, C.D.: Experimenting with electromagnetism using augmented reality: impact on flow student experience and educational effectiveness. Comput. Educ. **71**, 1–13 (2014)
17. Dünser, A., Walker, L., Horner, H., Bentall, D.: Creating interactive physics education books with augmented reality. In: Proceedings of the 24th Australian Computer-Human Interaction Conference, pp. 107–114. ACM (2012)
18. Bellucci, A., Ruiz, A., Díaz, P., Aedo, I.: Investigating augmented reality support for novice users in circuit prototyping. In: Proceedings of the 2018 International Conference on Advanced Visual Interfaces, p. 35. ACM (2018)
19. Beheshti, E., Kim, D., Ecanow, G., Horn, M.S.: Looking inside the wires: understanding museum visitor learning with an augmented circuit exhibit. In: Proceedings of the 2017 CHI Conference on Human Factors in Computing Systems, pp. 1583–1594. ACM (2017)
20. Meier, A., Spada, H., Rummel, N.: A rating scheme for assessing the quality of computer-supported collaboration processes. Int. J. Comput.-Supp. Collaborat. Learn. **2**, 63–86 (2007)
21. O'Brien, H.L., Toms, E.G., Kelloway, E.K., Kelley, E.: Developing and evaluating a reliable measure of user engagement. Proc. Am. Soc. Inf. Sci. Technol. **45**, 1–10 (2008). https://doi. org/10.1002/meet.2008.1450450258

Effect of Immediate Feedback on Math Achievement at the High School Level

Renah Razzaq$^{(\boxtimes)}$ (ID), Korinn S. Ostrow (ID), and Neil T. Heffernan (ID)

Worcester Polytechnic Institute, Worcester, MA 01609, USA
{rrazzaq,ksostrow,nth}@wpi.edu

Abstract. We examine the use of computer-based learning in the classroom and the effect of immediate feedback on student performance. Since it is well known in educational research that it is possible to observe a "Matthew Effect" in which the rich get richer, we wanted to see if feedback was useful for low prior knowledge students, as defined by students whose pretest score was at or below the median. In this counterbalanced randomized controlled trial, 243 tenth and eleventh grade mathematics students were exposed to one of two conditions, as we measured their learning from: 1) immediate feedback (where the computer told them correctness and they could also ask for hints) or 2) practice only (where they received feedback only after taking a posttest). Results suggest that immediate feedback from computer-based learning tasks benefit both high and low prior knowledge students, with low prior knowledge students exhibiting greater gains. The implications of these findings support further investigation into the use of computer-based learning tasks that provide immediate feedback.

Keywords: Computer-based learning · Mathematics education · Technology · Prior knowledge · Urban high school

1 Introduction

Despite widespread acceptance of feedback in computer-based instruction, empirical support for varying types of feedback has been inconsistent and contradictory [1]. Recent meta-analyses claim that the type and timing of feedback can have an effect on student learning [2].

Studies in the field of learning science have posited several questions about feedback. What does productive or effective feedback look like when students are solving a problem or working on a learning task? How does feedback affect student performance? Do the effects of feedback vary from student to student? Ideally, feedback on learning tasks should be constructed for each individual student. Researchers have defined feedback—specifically formative feedback – as information communicated to the student with the intent of modifying their thought process on a learning task and improving their performance. Formative feedback, should be non-evaluative, supportive, timely and targeted [3]. This feedback is commonly offered to students after they started working on a task and is presented in a variety of ways. Examples include informing the student of correctness or errors, providing hints, or providing completed examples of the problem at hand or of a similar problem. Feedback can be presented to

© Springer Nature Switzerland AG 2020
I. I. Bittencourt et al. (Eds.): AIED 2020, LNAI 12164, pp. 263–267, 2020.
https://doi.org/10.1007/978-3-030-52240-7_48

the student during the learning task, immediately after its completion or after some interval of time.

A prior experiment with eighth grade students revealed that computer-supported homework can lead to better results over traditional paper-and-pencil homework [4]. The study compared the use of immediate feedback and tutoring (treatment) to a control condition in which students received feedback the next day in math class. The study was conducted using, ASSISTments, the online learning platform also used in the present work. The original experiment was counterbalanced, with each student receiving each condition. The data collected suggested that students learned significantly more (effect size 0.40) with computer-supported homework. This result had practical significance, suggesting an improvement over widely used paper-and-pencil homework [4].

In other related work, high school students participated in a controlled evaluation of an interactive online tutoring system for math achievement test problem solving [5]. A sample of 202 students completed a pretest, were randomly assigned by their teacher to receive either online tutoring (treatment) or regular classroom instruction without online tutoring support (control). The posttest revealed that students using the online platform performed better than students who received only classroom instruction. The control group showed no improvement on the posttest. The use of multimedia hints predicted pre- to posttest gains and the benefits of tutoring were greatest for students exhibiting the weakest initial math skills [5].

With this past work as context, the present work examines the effects of immediate feedback in comparison to no feedback. Specifically, a randomized controlled trial is used to answer:

Research Question 1: Are there differences in student learning when comparing a computer feedback condition (or "Tutor Mode") to a business-as-usual condition (or "Test Mode") that simply provides practice?
Research Question 2: Is computer feedback effective for both high prior knowledge and low prior knowledge students?

2 Methods and Experimental Design

2.1 Participants

Student inclusion was based on teachers who volunteered to participate in this study. Content used for the assignment in ASSISTments was identical to the content that students would have received if not participating in the study. Participants included 243 students across 10 classrooms. The demographic breakdown was 15.9% African American, 7.1% Asian, 42.6% Hispanic, .2% Native American, 30.2% White, and 4.2% Multi-Race, Non-Hispanic. Fifty-five percent of students in the district from which the sample was drawn identify their first language as a language other than English, 33.4% are English Learners (EL), 18.8% are students with disabilities, 77.5% are considered high needs, and 59.5% are economically disadvantaged.

2.2   Design and Procedure

This study used ASSISTments, an online learning platform that provides correctness feedback and supplemental tutoring. A counterbalanced randomized controlled experiment was used to assign each student to condition. Specifically, this study leveraged a within-subjects design in which each student experienced both the control and the treatment conditions, allowing for measurement of the effect of each condition on each student. Students were successfully randomized into two groups by ASSISTments, as evidenced by a near equal distribution of students in each condition. In the treatment condition, students received math problems in "Tutor Mode," receiving both immediate feedback on the correctness of their answers and optional hints on demand. In Tutor Mode, students were also given: 1) an unlimited number of attempts, and after each attempt students were given an indicator of correctness (yes/no feedback) 2) a button that depicted the existence of multiple hints. If a student was confused, the last hint would provide the answer before to enter before progressing to the next problem. In the control condition, or "Test Mode," students practiced solving the same math problems as those in the treatment, but received feedback only after completing a posttest. In Test Mode, students also only had one attempt to answer each question. Conditions were counterbalanced after five questions, thereby allowing all students to experience each condition. Randomization and counterbalancing were also meant to address any potential order effects of domain content, with students answering questions on either trigonometry or factoring in each condition. Each student had a class period lasting 42 min to complete the experiment but teachers varied in specific pretest and posttest assignment protocol.

3   Results

3.1   Descriptive Statistics and Overall Performance

On average, students scored lower on the pretest (M = .50, SD = .35) than on the posttest (M = .63, SD = .31). Students assigned to Test Mode performed approximately the same as students assigned to Tutor Mode at pretest (M = .51, SD = .40 and M = .50, SD = .38, respectively), but slightly underperformed at posttest (M = .61, SD = .36 and M = .65, SD = .34, respectively).

3.2   Research Question 1

An independent samples t-test revealed that there was no reliable difference in pretest scores among students, p = .46. Subsequently, a repeated measures ANOVA was conducted to assess the difference in posttest scores between the two conditions. The within-subjects factor was test (pretest and posttest) and the between-subjects factor was condition (Tutor Mode (feedback) or Test Mode (no feedback)). Results showed a significant effect of feedback on posttest scores $F(1,241) = 78.32$, $p < .001$.

3.3 Research Question 2

A median split on students' pretest scores was used to differentiate students with high prior knowledge and low prior knowledge. Students above the median (50%) were considered high prior knowledge, while those at or the below the median were considered low prior knowledge. Students with low prior knowledge exhibited lower scores on the posttest (M = .37, SD = .27) than their peers with high prior knowledge (M = .85, SD = .13). A paired-samples t-test revealed a marginally significant effect in learning gains when low prior knowledge students were assigned to Tutor Mode (p = .10).

4 Results

Looking at overall performance, students performed significantly better at posttest than at pretest. While gains in overall performance were expected, results also suggested that Tutor Mode was more effective than Test Mode, answering Research Question 1. Learning gains were observed in both low and high prior knowledge students assigned to Tutor Mode. However, overall, low prior knowledge students exhibited greater gains on average.

This study had limitations that may have affected experimental findings. Pretests and posttests were administered by several different teachers. The amount of time that students were given to take each test was not controlled across teachers. In addition, the timing of test administration was not controlled across teachers; students may have taken the pretest in the beginning, middle, or near the end of class. Further, the experimental design could have been improved with stronger feedback distribution protocols. Each teacher distributed a handout with all correctness feedback to their students after the posttest, instead of providing feedback before the posttest, thereby making the assignment a stronger learning opportunity.

Overall, the implications of the findings presented herein support further investigation into the use of computer-based learning tasks that provide immediate feedback to students in classroom environments.

Acknowledgements. The authors were funded by the NSF (1931523, 1940236, 1917713, 1903304, 1822830, 1759229, 1724889, 1636782, 1535428, 1440753, 1316736, 1252297, 1109483, & 1031398), the US DoE IES (R305A170137, R305A170243, R305A180401, R305A120125, R305A180401, & R305C100024), GAANN (P200A180088 & P200A150306), EIR, ONR (N00014-18-1-2768), and Schmidt Futures.

References

1. Azevedo, R., Bernard, R.M.: A meta-analysis of the effects of feedback in computer-based instruction. J. Educ. Comput. Res. (1995). https://doi.org/10.2190/9lmd-3u28-3a0g-ftqt
2. Van der Kleij, F.M., Feskens, R.C.W., Eggen, T.J.H.M.: Effects of feedback in a computer-based learning environment on students' learning outcomes: a meta-analysis. Rev. Educ. Res. (2015). https://doi.org/10.3102/0034654314564881

3. Shute, V.J.: Focus on formative feedback. Rev. Educ. Res. (2008). https://doi.org/10.3102/0034654307313795

4. Singh, R., et al.: Feedback during web-based homework: the role of hints. In: Biswas, G., Bull, S., Kay, J., Mitrovic, A. (eds.) AIED 2011. LNCS (LNAI), vol. 6738, pp. 328–336. Springer, Heidelberg (2011). https://doi.org/10.1007/978-3-642-21869-9_43

5. Beal, C.R., Walles, R., Arroyo, I., et al.: On-line tutoring for math achievement testing: a controlled evaluation. J. Interact. Online Learn

Automated Prediction of Novice Programmer Performance Using Programming Trajectories

Miguel A. Rubio[✉]

Department of Computer Science, University of Granada, Granada, Spain
marubio@ugr.es

Abstract. Online programming courses have become widely available and host thousands of learners every year. In these courses, participants must solve programming exercises by submitting partial solutions and checking the outcome. The sequence of partial solutions submitted by a student constitutes the programming trajectory followed by the student.

In our work, we define a supervised machine learning algorithm that takes as input these programming trajectories and predicts whether a student will successfully complete the next exercise. We have validated our model with two different datasets: the first one is a set of problems from the online learning platform Robomission with over one hundred thousand exercises submitted. The second one comprises one hundred thousand exercises submitted to the Hour of Code challenge.

The results obtained indicate that our model can accurately predict the future performance of the students. This work provides not only a new method to represent students' programming trajectories but also an efficient approach to predict the students' future performance. Furthermore, the information provided by the model can be used to select the students that would benefit from an intervention.

Keywords: Machine learning · Introductory programming · Novice programmer · Educational data mining · Block-based programming

1 Introduction

Online programming courses have emerged as a popular way to introduce students to programming [1]. These courses present several advantages: they are easily accessible, and students face interesting challenges. Unfortunately, it is not feasible to provide individual support to each student due to the large number of students enrolled in these courses. Automatic systems capable of providing adaptive support could enhance the students' experience and improve their success rate [2].

In order to develop these automatic systems, there is a need to develop models capable of detecting students that will likely fail [3–5]. These models could use the large datasets that students generate when completing programming tasks [6, 7]. Students usually submit several partial solutions before solving a task, creating a programming trajectory for each exercise [8, 9]. These programming trajectories can be analyzed by machine learning systems to find general patterns [10].

© Springer Nature Switzerland AG 2020
I. I. Bittencourt et al. (Eds.): AIED 2020, LNAI 12164, pp. 268–272, 2020.
https://doi.org/10.1007/978-3-030-52240-7_49

In this study we present a supervised machine learning model that predicts the student future programming performance. The model takes the programming trajectory followed by the student and estimates the probability of the student successfully completing the next exercise. The model has been validated using two different datasets obtained from two different online programming environments, Robomission [11], and the Hour of Code challenge from Code.org [12].

Our results indicate that this model can predict accurately whether a student will be able to successfully complete a programming exercise. The information provided by the model can be used to rank students in terms of their performance. Using this ranking one can automatically select a group student that would benefit most from an intervention.

2 Methods

2.1 Data

In this study we worked with two different datasets. The first dataset is a set of programming trajectories submitted by students while completing one exercise in the Hour of Code challenge [13]. Additionally, for each student the dataset contains information about whether the student successfully completed the next task. The exercises and their solutions are shown in Fig. 1. Piech et al. [8] describe this dataset in more detail. The second dataset comprises 85 programming tasks from the Robomission programming platform. Effenberfer [14] gives a thorough description of the dataset.

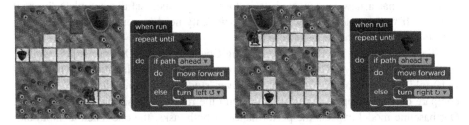

Fig. 1. Hour of code exercise 18 (left) and exercise 19 (right) and example solutions. To solve the exercise the student must program the squirrel to reach the acorn.

2.2 Proposed Model

Our goal is to generate a supervised machine learning algorithm capable of predicting whether the student will successfully complete the next exercise. To this end we will use the programming trajectories followed by the students $T = \{\psi_0, \psi_1 \ldots \psi_n\}$. Where ψ_0 is the state before the student starts to work, ψ_i are the code snapshots submitted by the student and ψ_n is the last snapshot.

The training phase is straightforward: all the programming trajectories present in the training dataset are assembled into a tree. Different branches of the tree contain information about different programming trajectories. Figure 2 describes the process to integrate a new trajectory $\{\psi_0, \psi_1, \psi_5\}$ into a tree. For each code snapshot present in the trajectory we check if there is a branch in the tree with matching snapshots. If there is such a branch, we follow it while the partial solutions match. As soon as we find a partial solution (ψ_5 in this case) that is not present in the branch, a new branch is created.

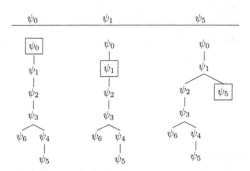

Fig. 2. Steps followed to integrate a new trajectory $\{\psi_0, \psi_1, \psi_5\}$ into the tree. Two different leaves of the final tree present the same partial solution.

Once we have processed all the student trajectories to generate the tree, we store in each node the relevant parameters of the students that ended their programming trajectories in that node. In this study we stored the proportion of students that successfully completed the next exercise. After assembling the tree, we can estimate the probability that a new student with trajectory T_i will successfully complete the next exercise. If we want to classify the student, we only need to compare this probability with the threshold that we have selected.

We have selected the Receiver Operating Characteristic (ROC) curve [15] and the area under the curve (AUC) to measure the performance of the classifier. We have used a 10-fold crossvalidation [16] stratified over students to compute them. We will compare our model optimal performance with the results of a simple baseline model. Our baseline model expects the performance of both tasks, the one taken as input and the predicted one, to be the same.

3   Results

We start examining whether our model is successfully detecting students who fail the next exercise in the Hour of Code challenge. The left side of Fig. 3 shows that the ROC curve is systematically above the identity line ($y = x$). The area under the curve (AUC) of our model in this case is 0.77, with a 95% confidence interval (0.77–0.79). Both the AUC and the confidence interval are greater than 0.5, indicating that our model is performing better than a random classifier. Figure 3 also contain the main results for the baseline model and the optimal threshold. We can see that the baseline model is much closer to the bottom left corner of the figure than the optimal threshold.

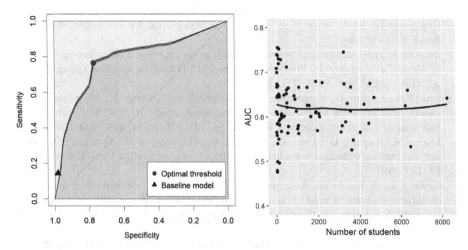

Fig. 3. Left: ROC curve obtained when classifying failing students in the Hour of Code exercise. The cyan region represents the 95% confidence interval. Right: AUC values for all the Robomission tasks vs. the number of students that completed each task. The line represents the loess regression of the data points.

The right side of Fig. 3 shows the AUC obtained for each task in the Robomission dataset versus the number of students that attempted each task. We performed a loess regression [16] looking for a correlation between AUC and the number of students. From the graph we can conclude that there is no such correlation. However, the variability of AUC values depends on the number of students. When the number of students is below 500 the AUC values show high variability. For values over 500 the variability decreases markedly.

4   Conclusions

In this study we present a machine learning algorithm able to predict the future performance of novice programmers using their programming trajectories in just one exercise. The output of the model can be used to rank students according to their predicted performance. The data used by the model can be easily obtained in online programming environments.

We have validated our model using two different datasets from two online learning platforms. Our results indicate that the model can classify students with reasonable accuracy. We have also found that the average performance of our model seems to be independent from the number of students attempting the task.

References

1. Nguyen, A., Piech, C., Huang, J., Guibas, L.: Codewebs: scalable homework search for massive open online programming courses. In: Proceedings of the 23rd International Conference on World Wide Web, pp. 491–502. Association for Computing Machinery, Seoul, Korea (2014)
2. Ihantola, P., et al.: Educational data mining and learning analytics in programming: literature review and case studies. In: Proceedings of the 2015 ITiCSE on Working Group Reports. pp. 41–63. ACM New York, NY, USA (2015)
3. Liao, S.N., Zingaro, D., Laurenzano, M.A., Griswold, W.G., Porter, L.: Lightweight, early identification of at-risk CS1 students. In: Proceedings of the 2016 ACM Conference on International Computing Education Research, pp. 123–131. ACM, New York (2016)
4. Liao, S.N., Zingaro, D., Thai, K., Alvarado, C., Griswold, W.G., Porter, L.: A robust machine learning technique to predict low-performing students. ACM Trans. Comput. Educ. **19**, 18 (2019)
5. Castro-Wunsch, K., Ahadi, A., Petersen, A.: Evaluating neural networks as a method for identifying students in need of assistance. In: Proceedings of the 2017 ACM SIGCSE Technical Symposium on Computer Science Education, pp. 111–116. ACM, New York (2017)
6. Glassman, E.L.: Clustering and visualizing solution variation in massive programming classes (2016)
7. Rivers, K., Koedinger, K.R.: Data-driven hint generation in vast solution spaces: a self-improving python programming tutor. Int. J. Artif. Intell. Educ. **27**, 37–64 (2017)
8. Piech, C., Sahami, M., Huang, J., Guibas, L.: Autonomously generating hints by inferring problem solving policies. In: Proceedings of the Second (2015) ACM Conference on Learning @ Scale, pp. 195–204. Association for Computing Machinery, Vancouver, BC, Canada (2015)
9. Jiang, B., Li, Z., Stamper, J.: Programming pathway clustering using Tree Edit Distance. In: CSEDM 2018: Educational Data Mining in Computer Science Education Workshop, pp. 76–84. ACM, The University at Buffalo, New York (2018)
10. Hosseini, R., Brusilovsky, P., Yudelson, M., Hellas, A.: Stereotype modeling for problem-solving performance predictions in MOOCs and traditional courses. In: Proceedings of the 25th Conference on User Modeling, Adaptation and Personalization. pp. 76–84. ACM, New York (2017)
11. Effenberger, T., Pelánek, R.: Towards making block-based programming activities adaptive. In: Proceedings of the Fifth Annual ACM Conference on Learning at Scale. Association for Computing Machinery, London, United Kingdom (2018)
12. Wilson, C.: Hour of code: we can solve the diversity problem in computer science. ACM Inroads. **5**, 22 (2014)
13. Bau, D., Gray, J., Kelleher, C., Sheldon, J., Turbak, F.: Learnable programming: blocks and beyond. Commun. ACM **60**, 72–80 (2017)
14. Effenberger, T.: Blockly programming dataset. In: 3rd Educational Data Mining in Computer Science Education (CSEDM) Workshop (2019)
15. Robin, X., et al.: pROC: an open-source package for R and S + to analyze and compare ROC curves. BMC Bioinformatics **12**, 77 (2011)
16. Hastie, T., Tibshirani, R., Friedman, J.: The Elements of Statistical Learning. SSS. Springer, New York (2009). https://doi.org/10.1007/978-0-387-84858-7

Agent-in-the-Loop: Conversational Agent Support in Service of Reflection for Learning During Collaborative Programming

Sreecharan Sankaranarayanan[✉], Siddharth Reddy Kandimalla, Sahil Hasan, Haokang An, Christopher Bogart, R. Charles Murray, Michael Hilton, Majd Sakr, and Carolyn Rosé

Carnegie Mellon University, Pittsburgh, PA, USA
{sreechas,skandima,sahilh,haokanga,cbogart,rcmurray,mhilton,
msakr,cprose}@andrew.cmu.edu

Abstract. Dynamic conversational agent-based support for collaborative learning has shown significant positive effects on learning over no-support or static-support control conditions in prior studies. In order to understand the boundary between human-led and AI-led support for collaboration, we compare in this study an approach where the agent's primary role is to help students regulate their own collaboration with two more typical prompting strategies that are used only during a reflection phase: one designed to provide a specific informational focus for the reflection, and the other designed to draw out evaluation, elaboration, and exploration of alternative perspectives. Significant positive effects on learning over and above just the human-led form of support are observed when either of the prompting strategies are used.

Keywords: Conversational agents · Human-AI collaboration · Reflection prompts · Group conversational agents · Adaptive Collaborative Learning Support (ACLS) · Collaborative programming

1 Introduction

In an article in the 25th anniversary issue of IJAIED, Rummel and colleagues contrast two possible futures for adaptive collaborative learning support (ACLS) [11]: In one more dystopian future, an intelligent agent has tremendous AI-enabled capabilities and the resulting blind trust in these abilities leads to practices experienced by students as inscrutable and lacking in nuance. In the second, more utopian vision, the system not only takes into account multiple dimensions of support [4,16] but also balances this adaptivity with user freedom and shared user/system control [11]. While a great many studies have demonstrated a significant positive impact on learning for fully AI-enabled support for collaborative

© Springer Nature Switzerland AG 2020
I. I. Bittencourt et al. (Eds.): AIED 2020, LNAI 12164, pp. 273–278, 2020.
https://doi.org/10.1007/978-3-030-52240-7_50

learning compared to no-support control conditions [1, 7–10], contrasting AI-enabled support to human-led support will allow us to understand the boundary between the two and work towards the more utopian vision.

We situate our study in a synchronous programming activity in an online graduate-level course on Cloud Computing offered at Carnegie Mellon University and its international branch campuses. The activity is divided into several tasks. Within each task, students work in groups of 4 in complementary roles designed with the purpose of assisting each other and furthering the progress of the group as a whole. Thus, the locus of support resides with the students themselves, in an effort to embody the more utopian vision of AI. In this human-led design, the conversational agent only serves as the agent-in-the-loop to provide automated feedback regarding how well students perform their roles – in effect, helping students help each other.

Added to this human-led support, we investigate two more traditional fully AI-enabled conversational agent supports in the form of agent-led reflective discussions at the end of each programming task: one designed to provide a specific informational focus for the reflection, and the other designed to draw out evaluation, elaboration, and exploration of alternative perspectives. The experimental manipulation enables us to test whether the addition of fully automated support produces learning gains over-and-above the human-led support (The Automated Support Benefit Hypothesis).

Results of the 2 × 2 experimental study show that specific portions of the programming activity lend themselves to pre- to post-test learning and within those portions, a significant improvement in learning is observed over-and-above that of the human-led support when either of the two agent-led supports are offered.

2   Method

A summary of the course structure and the location of the study within it is shown in Fig. 1. Within the first sub-unit of the fourth project unit of the course, students work with our synchronous collaborative software development activity, called the Online Programming Exercise (OPE) in an 80-min long session. A total of 101 students from across three campuses completed the activity to build an inverted index using the Scala programming language, and 100 of these students completed the subsequent project.

Based on instructional design best practices [2], we divide the overall programming activity into five different tasks which target five learning objectives (LOs). Each task is divided into a problem-solving phase where students work on the programming task, and a discussion phase where they participate in a reflective discussion based on the task. This task structuring can be considered a macroscript [3] that sequences the activity into learning phases as described in the Script Theory of Guidance [5]. Each LO is assigned two multiple-choice questions on the pre- and post-tests to measure student learning from the activity. Student performance on the subsequent individual project associated with the task then serves as a delayed post-test as show in Fig. 1.

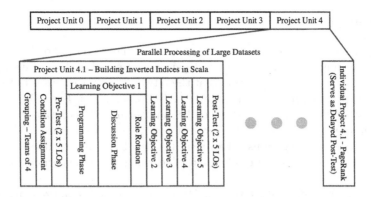

Fig. 1. Course Structure, Pre-Test, Post-Test and Delayed Post-Test Alignment

Within each task, based on the industry paradigm referred to as Mob Programming [6,12–14,17,18], we specified four interdependent roles with well-defined responsibilities that students are assigned to. The *Driver* is the only participant who writes the code, based on high level instructions received from the *Navigator*, who makes decisions on the next course of action based on discussion with the rest of the team members which include the *Researcher* who assists the group with ideation and implementation by consulting external support material, and the *Project Manager* who is responsible for making sure the rest of the team members are complying with and adequately performing their roles. The roles rotate after each task. This role-scaffolding paradigm can be considered a microscript that provides support for the collaboration within a learning phase. The control condition consists of the task structuring macroscript used in combination with the role-scaffolding microscript.

In the experimental conditions, we additionally investigate two more traditional conversational agent supports in the form of discourse level prompts during the discussion phase which can also be considered microscripts. *Information Prompts* support learners in warranting their claims (Ex: *"@Researcher, what is the advantage of writing OS-aware code like you did here?"*) and *Elaboration Prompts* explicitly prompt another learner to build on an existing argument towards knowledge construction (Ex: *@Driver, How would you improve the implemented approach?*) [15].

We tested the Automated Support Benefit Hypothesis with a 2 × 2 factorial design in which the first factor was the presence or absence of information prompts, and the second factor was the presence or absence of elaboration prompts. The teams were randomly placed into the four conditions: 7 groups in the control condition where no prompts were presented, 6 groups presented with elaboration prompts, 5 with information prompts only and 9 groups where both prompts were presented.

3   Results

We first test pre- to post-test learning gains from the exercise. For LOs 3 and 4 there was a significant pre- to post-test gain as measured with a 2-tailed paired t-test, $t = 2.43$, $p < .05$ indicating that these two tasks lent themselves to learning during programming much more than the other tasks. For LO 2, average pre-test score was 1.7, post-test score 1.8, and standard deviation .6. For LO 3, average pre-test score was 1.5, post-test score 1.6, and standard deviation .6. Because of the learning gains achieved in the two LOs, we are able to test our hypothesis regarding the intensification of learning in the experimental conditions.

We used a repeated measures ANCOVA model, with LO and role as random variables, pre-test score (per LO) as a covariate, elaboration prompts and information prompts and the interaction between the two as independent variables, and post-test score (per LO) as the dependent variable. As an aside, there was no statistically significant difference in learning between roles.

In terms of pre- to post-test gains, there was no significant main effect of the elaboration prompt factor; $F(1, 440) = .21$, $p = n.s.$ However, there was a significant interaction effect between the two experimental factors $F(1, 440) = 11.6$, $p < .0001$. In a post-hoc analysis, we determined that both of the conditions with only one type of prompt were associated with significantly more learning than the control condition, and the condition with both types of prompts was not significantly different from control. The effect size of the addition of elaboration prompts over no prompts was .32 s.d., which is a medium effect size. The effect size of the addition of information prompts over no prompts was .42 s.d., which is a medium effect size.

To test the impact on a subsequent individual programming task, we built an ANOVA model, with elaboration prompts and information prompts and the interaction between the two as independent variables, to measure the impact of the experimental manipulation separately on three outcome measures related to task performance: time on subsequent programming task, number of submitted attempts on that task, and score. Here, there was a trend for the elaboration condition to improve performance in terms of time-on-task, number of submission attempts, and score, though none of these were statistically significant. For the information prompts also, the trend was consistently that they were associated with lower time on task, lower number of submissions, and higher scores.

Thus, the use of elaboration prompts or information prompts alone significantly improve on pre- to post-test learning from the task and exhibit positive trends for the subsequent delayed test.

4   Conclusion

Based on the results, we can conclude that agent-led support shows promise for augmenting and significantly improving over primarily human-led support.

Acknowledgements. This work was funded in part by NSF grants IIS 1822831, IIS 1917955 and funding from Microsoft.

References

1. Adamson, D., Dyke, G., Jang, H., Rosé, C.P.: Towards an agile approach to adapting dynamic collaboration support to student needs. Int. J. Artif. Intell. Educ. **24**(1), 92–124 (2014)
2. Carver, S.M.: Cognition and instruction: enriching the laboratory school experience of children, teachers, parents, and undergraduates. In: Cognition and instruction: Twenty-Five Years of Progress. pp. 385–426. Lawrence Erlbaum Associates (2001)
3. Dillenbourg, P., Hong, F.: The mechanics of cscl macro scripts. Int. J. Comput.-Support. Collaborative Learn. **3**(1), 5–23 (2008)
4. Diziol, D., Rummel, N.: How to design support for collaborative e-learning: a framework of relevant dimensions. In: E-collaborative Knowledge Construction: Learning from Computer-Supported and Virtual Environments, pp. 162–179. IGI Global (2010)
5. Fischer, F., Kollar, I., Stegmann, K., Wecker, C.: Toward a script theory of guidance in computer-supported collaborative learning. Educ. Psychol. **48**(1), 56–66 (2013)
6. Hilton, M., Sankaranarayanan, S.: Online mob programming: effective collaborative project-based learning. In: Proceedings of the 50th ACM Technical Symposium on Computer Science Education, p. 1283. SIGCSE 2019, Association for Computing Machinery, New York (2019). https://doi.org/10.1145/3287324.3293774, https://doi.org/10.1145/3287324.3293774
7. Kumar, R., Rose, C.: Architecture for building conversational agents that support collaborative learning. IEEE Trans. Learn Technol. **4**(1), 21–34 (2011)
8. Kumar, R., Rosé, C.P.: Triggering effective social support for online groups. ACM Trans. Interact. Intell. Syst. (TiiS) **3**(4), 24 (2014)
9. Kumar, R., Rosé, C.P., Wang, Y.C., Joshi, M., Robinson, A.: Tutorial dialogue as adaptive collaborative learning support. Front. Artif. Intell. Appl. **158**, 383 (2007)
10. Rosé, C.P., Ferschke, O.: Technology support for discussion based learning: from computer supported collaborative learning to the future of massive open online courses. Int. J. Artif. Intell. Educ. **26**(2), 660–678 (2016)
11. Rummel, N., Walker, E., Aleven, V.: Different futures of adaptive collaborative learning support. Int. J. Artif. Intell. Educ. **26**(2), 784–795 (2016)
12. Sankaranarayanan, S.: Online mob programming: effective collaborative project-based learning. In: Proceedings of the 50th ACM Technical Symposium on Computer Science Education, p. 1296. SIGCSE 2019, Association for Computing Machinery, New York (2019). https://doi.org/10.1145/3287324.3293709, https://doi.org/10.1145/3287324.3293709
13. Sankaranarayanan, S., et al.: Online mob programming: bridging the 21st century workplace and the classroom (2019)
14. Sankaranarayanan, S., et al.: An intelligent-agent facilitated scaffold for fostering reflection in a team-based project course. In: Isotani, S., Millán, E., Ogan, A., Hastings, P., McLaren, B., Luckin, R. (eds.) Artificial Intelligence in Education, pp. 252–256. Springer, Cham (2019). https://doi.org/10.1007/978-3-030-23207-8_47
15. Stegmann, K., Weinberger, A., Fischer, F.: Facilitating argumentative knowledge construction with computer-supported collaboration scripts. Int. J. Comput. Support. Collaborative Learn. **2**(4), 421–447 (2007)

16. Walker, E., Rummel, N., Koedinger, K.: Beyond explicit feedback: new directions in adaptive collaborative learning support (2009)
17. Wilson, A.: Mob programming-what works, what doesn't. In: International Conference on Agile Software Development. pp. 319–325. Springer, Cham (2015). https://doi.org/10.1007/978-3-319-18612-2_33
18. Zuill, W., Meadows, K.: Mob programming: a whole team approach. In: Agile 2014 Conference, Orlando, Florida, vol. 3 (2016)

Toward an Automatic Speech Classifier for the Teacher

Bahar Shahrokhian Ghahfarokhi[(✉)], Avinash Sivaraman,
and Kurt VanLehn

Arizona State University, Tempe, AZ, USA
{bshahrok, asivara6, kvanlehn}@asu.edu

Abstract. Our system classifies audio from microphones worn by the teacher in order to determine (1) whether the teacher is addressing the whole class or talking to individuals or groups of students. In the latter case, it determines (2) whether the teacher is giving formative feedback, giving corrective feedback, chatting socially, or addressing administrative or workflow concerns. This paper reports the initial accuracy of this system against human coding of middle school math classroom behavior. We also compared audio collected through professional hardware versus more accessible alternatives.

Keywords: Intelligent tutoring system · Educational data mining · Multimodal learning analytics

1 Introduction

"Classroom orchestration" refers to the teacher's management of the activities, students and information in classes that integrate small group work, individual work, and whole-class work [1]. Orchestration systems are intended to help teachers and students achieve productive interactions and learning in such classrooms. A key problem addressed by orchestration systems is increasing the teacher's awareness of the state of all the students and their interactions [2]. Awareness is particularly difficult to maintain when students are working in small groups, because much of their interaction is spoken and inaccessible to the teacher. Thus, we are focusing on analysing classroom speech when the main class activity is working in small groups.

In order to focus the research while maintaining its generality, we are exploring just two categorization schemes. Each has been investigated in prior research and seem generally useful for helping teachers maintain awareness.

The first classification scheme divides the teachers' activity into (1) addressing the whole class, (2) talking with students, (3) talking with experimenters and (4) not talking. This classification is useful for several purposes. First, an orchestration system should supress all alerts when the teacher talking to the whole class because teachers would not be able to attend to them. It might send only high priority alerts when the teacher is talking to students, since those conversations are punctuated by times when the teacher is waiting for the students to answer and thus has a limited capacity to attend to alerts. Prior work [3, 4] has focused on similar categories, but included a

I. I. Bittencourt et al. (Eds.): AIED 2020, LNAI 12164, pp. 279–284, 2020.
https://doi.org/10.1007/978-3-030-52240-7_51

category for lecturing and omitted the category for talking to experimenters. Lecturing did not occur in our math classrooms.

The second classification scheme divides teacher's conversation with students into formative interaction, corrective interaction, and several non-instruction categories. The distinction between formative and corrective instruction is traditional and goes by many names. If the teacher points to incorrect work, gives strong hints about correctness or explains how to do correct work, then their instruction is called corrective, didactic or teaching by telling. If teachers elicit explanations from students, encourage them to think more or pose challenging questions without answering them, then their instruction is called formative, teaching by eliciting or formative assessment [5–10]. In the classes we observed, the teachers were all attempting to given formative instruction exclusively. However, we often observed that their conversations with students were corrective. An orchestration system could collect such episodes and present them to the teacher as part of a post-class debriefing sessions. The system might even give teachers feedback on their conversations in the middle of class whenever teacher had some spare time and wanted to get such feedback.

Like many of our predecessors [3, 11, 12, 15], we analysed the speech with acoustic features only. We did not attempt to convert the speech to text and use lexical features, semantic features, or other natural language processing. On the one hand, this probably reduces the accuracy of the classification, particularly for the distinction between formative vs. corrective teacher feedback. On the other hand, this study take place in a live classroom while preserving the privacy of students. It also increases the chance that system is domain general. That is, after it has been trained on classes engaged in one set of lessons and tasks, it can be used without change on a wider set of lessons and tasks. However, testing the generality of our system remains as future work. Here we report its accuracy against human coders.

2   Data Collection and Analysis

2.1   Raw Data Collection

The raw data for this paper was gathered during a class trial of FACT in spring of 2019. This trial consisted of 6, 50-min periods of 8th grade students working on specific sets of mathematics lessons, called Classroom Challenges [10] using our FACT web-based platform [13, 14]. Each period consisted of 9 to 16 groups of mostly two students, but we only had permission to collect multimodal data from 31 groups, out of which we annotated 20 groups (64% of the data), due to reasons like low audio quality or class being too short. 40.4% of all annotated students are male.

During this study, the teachers wore a lavalier microphone and carried a tablet to access FACT and manage classroom lessons and students. While working in a group, students each used their own tablet to access a shared group workspace, typically with their heads down over the tablets while they talked with each other. Most students wore an Audio-Technica PRO 8HEx headset microphone connected to a Tascam DR-40 digital audio interface. Students in 2 groups per classroom wore throat microphones.

In each session 4 groups' interactions were captured using a video camera with its own shotgun mic and a second channel for a boundary mic laid on the group's table. A shoulder-mounted video camera followed the teacher and recorded the lavalier mic's output. Most tablets' screens were also captured by screen recorders. All these recordings were used by the human coders but not by the system. Thus, the human coders had much more information than the system, as befits a gold standard.

2.2 Human Segmentation and Coding

We used ELAN [16] to synchronize all the media files and code them. Although several Elan tiers were used, only two are relevant here.

The Teacher View tier was for classifying the teacher's behaviour into 'Whole Class', 'Admin' and 'Group Interaction'. The 'Whole class' label indicated that the teacher is giving a whole class announcement. This was usually done to explain the activity or the user interface to the students before starting the activity. The Admin category indicated that the teacher was talking to the one the FACT system admins. The Group Interaction label indicated that the teacher was talking to a group or student. Most of the class activity was group work, but this label was used even when students were working individually. In this experiment, teachers never lectured and were rarely silent. This coding created segments of arbitrary length.

We then divided up the 'Group Interaction' segments, which tended to be many minutes long. Using a Teacher Group Interaction tier, we created 30 s segments, because prior work showed that varying the length of segments did not greatly impact accuracy [3, 16]. Human annotators labelled the segments as 'Formative', 'Corrective', 'Overhead', 'Workflow' or 'Chat' coding. A segment was labelled 'Formative' or teaching by eliciting, if for example the teachers instead of giving explanations and feedback, keep students engaged in solving problems, which requires the teachers to analyze the students' work, detect the line of reasoning being followed and then ask questions that push the students further along that line [15]. A segment was labelled 'Corrective' or teaching by telling, if the teacher's instruction is more direct. The 'Overhead' label indicates that the teacher is talking to the individual group about any issues with FACT. The 'Workflow' label indicates that the teacher was discussing the class or tasks (e.g., moving from one task to another) but not giving instruction.

Two human coders labeled 15% of the all the 30-s segments. Inter- rater agreement was considered acceptable with Cohen's kappa $K = 0.75$. For the segments that two coders disagreed with each other, that segment was discussed until both coders agreed on one label, if the agreement was not achieved that segment was not considered for the next step.

2.3 Audio Processing

To process the audio, we initially removed noise using audacity [17]. We extracted acoustic features using openSmile [18]. We created time series features using the tfresh [19] Python package. Since the number of extracted features was quite large, we also used different feature selection algorithms like PCA and Pairwise correlations to reduce the redundancy of the feature set.

3 Result

This section reports the accuracy of our system against the human annotations. Classifiers were machine-learned using random forest, deep learning (forward only, not RNN), KNN, decision tree, additive logistic regression and SVM. Accuracy was measured with 10-fold classification. Random forest yielded the best result for all analyses.

- *Teacher's View* tier: Categorization into 'Whole Class', 'Group Interaction' and 'Admin'.
  - Teacher's audio captured via tablet: Accuracy 0.88, Kappa 0.84
  - Teacher's audio captured via lavalier microphone: Accuracy 0.91, Kappa 0.88.
- *Teacher Group Interaction* tier: Categorization into 'Formative', 'Corrective', 'Overhead', 'Workflow' or 'Chat'
  - Teacher's audio captured via tablet: Accuracy 0.77, Kappa 0.65
  - Teacher's audio captured via lavalier microphone: Accuracy 0.74, Kappa 0.61.

For recording devices, it appears that the tablet's audio was nearly as good as wearing a lavalier mic.

4 Discussion and Comparison to Prior Work

To the best of our knowledge this is one the first studies working on automatic speech classifier for math teachers in middle school classrooms. To evaluate the absolution (as opposed to relative) accuracy, it helps to compare our results to prior work, here we focused on studies analyzing teachers' speech in live classrooms. We must mention that, due to difference in experiment settings, features type, approach, purpose and data annotation, direct comparison of the result is not possible.

Wang et al. [4] trained a classifier to automatically label 30 s segments of teacher's speech, recorded via LENA system, into 'teacher lecturing', 'whole-class' discussion and 'student group work'. Their overall classification accuracy of 84.37% is comparable with our overall classification accuracy of 83.34%.

D'Mello et al. [3, 20–23] also found comparable accuracies to ours. They used linguistic as well as acoustic features of the teacher's speech, and they studied language arts classrooms instead of math.

A challenge for this and similar projects is protecting the privacy of students' speech. Although we only extracted non-lexical features from audio, the database has the full speech audio. Perhaps we can extract the features and discard the audio recording before the end of class to better preserve the students' privacy.

To increase the performance of our classes, other than adding lexical features, we are also planning to extract more features from other multi modal inputs such as our ITS logs, teacher's position, etc.

Acknowledgements. Supported by NSF FW-HTF 1840051.

References

1. Dillenbourg, P., Nussbaum, M., Dimitriadis, Y., Roschelle, J.: Design for classroom orchestration. Comput. Educ. **69**, 485–492 (2013)
2. Prieto, L.P., Holenko Dlab, M., Gutiérrez, I., Abdulwahed, M., Balid, W.: Orchestrating technology enhanced learning: a literature review and a conceptual framework. Int. J. Technol. Enhanc. Learn. **3**(6), 583 (2011)
3. Blanchard, N., D'Mello, S., Olney, A.M., Nystrand, M.: Automatic classification of question & answer discourse segments from teacher's speech in classrooms. International Educational Data Mining Society (2015)
4. Wang, Z., Pan, X., Miller, K.F., Cortina, K.S.: Automatic classification of activities in classroom discourse. Comput. Educ. **78**, 115–123 (2014)
5. Wiliam, D., Lee, C., Harrison, C., Black, P.: Teachers developing assessment for learning: impact on student achievement. Assess. Educ.: Princ. Policy Pract. **11**(1), 49–65 (2004)
6. Cauley, K.M., McMillan, J.H.: Formative assessment techniques to support student motivation and achievement. Clear. House: J. Educ. Strateg. Issues Ideas **83**(1), 1–6 (2010)
7. McMillan, J.H.: Formative Classroom Assessment: Theory into Practice. Teachers College Press, New York (2007)
8. McMillan, J.H.: Classroom assessment. principles and practices for effective instruction. Allyn & Bacon, A Viacom Company, 160 Gould St. (1997). www.abacon.com. Needham Heights, MA 02194
9. Black, P., Wiliam, D.: Assessment and classroom learning. Assess. Educ.: Princ. Policy Pract. **5**(1), 7–74 (1998)
10. Burkhardt, H., Schoenfeld, A.: Assessment in the service of learning: challenges and opportunities or Plus ça Change, Plus c'est la même Chose. ZDM **50**(4), 571–585 (2018)
11. Martinez-Maldonado, R., Dimitriadis, Y., Martinez-Monés, A., Kay, J., Yacef, K.: Capturing and analyzing verbal and physical collaborative learning interactions at an enriched interactive tabletop. Int. J. Comput.-Support. Collab. Learn. **8**(4), 455–485 (2013)
12. Gweon, G., Jain, M., McDonough, J., Raj, B., Rosé, C.P.: Measuring prevalence of other-oriented transactive contributions using an automated measure of speech style accommodation. Int. J. Comput.-Support. Collab. Learn. **8**(2), 245–265 (2013)
13. FACT. http://fact.engineering.asu.edu/. Accessed 27 Feb 2020
14. http://fact.asu.edu/. Accessed Feb 2020
15. Herman, J.L., et al.: The implementation and effects of the mathematics design collaborative (MDC): early findings from Kentucky ninth-grade algebra 1 courses. CRESST Report 845. National Center for Research on Evaluation, Standards, and Student Testing (CRESST) (2015)
16. Martinez, R., Wallace, J.R., Kay, J., Yacef, K.: Modelling and identifying collaborative situations in a collocated multi-display groupware setting. In: Biswas, G., Bull, S., Kay, J., Mitrovic, A. (eds.) AIED 2011. LNCS (LNAI), vol. 6738, pp. 196–204. Springer, Heidelberg (2011). https://doi.org/10.1007/978-3-642-21869-9_27
17. Audacity Team: Audacity (R): free audio editor and recorder [computer program]. Version 2.1.0 (2014). https://sourceforge.net/projects/audacity/. Accessed 27 Feb 2020
18. Eyben, F., Wöllmer, M., Schuller, B.: OpenSmile: the Munich versatile and fast open-source audio feature extractor. In: Proceedings of the 18th ACM International Conference on Multimedia, pp. 1459–1462 (2010)
19. Christ, M., Braun, N., Neuffer, J., Kempa-Liehr, A.W.: Time series feature extraction on basis of scalable hypothesis tests (tsfresh–a python package). Neurocomputing **307**, 72–77 (2018)

20. Donnelly, P.J., et al.: Automatic teacher modeling from live classroom audio. In: Proceedings of the 2016 Conference on User Modeling Adaptation and Personalization, pp. 45–53 (2016)
21. D'Mello, S.K., et al.: Multimodal capture of teacher-student interactions for automated dialogic analysis in live classrooms. In: Proceedings of the 2015 ACM on International Conference on Multimodal Interaction, pp. 557–566 (2015)
22. Blanchard, N., et al.: Semi-automatic detection of teacher questions from human-transcripts of audio in live classrooms. International Educational Data Mining Society (2016)
23. Jensen, E., et al.: Toward automated feedback on teacher discourse to enhance teacher learning. In: Proceedings of the 2020 CHI Conference on Human Factors in Computing Systems, pp. 1–13 (2020)

Constructing Automated Revision Graphs: A Novel Visualization Technique to Study Student Writing

Antonette Shibani[(✉)]

University of Technology Sydney, Ultimo, NSW, Australia
Antonette.Shibani@uts.edu.au

Abstract. This paper introduces a novel technique of constructing *Automated Revision Graphs (ARG)* to facilitate the study of revisions in writing. ARG plots sentences of a written text as nodes, and their similarities to sentences from its previous draft as edges to visualize text as graph. Implemented in two forms: simple and multi-stage, the graphs demonstrate how sentence-level differences can be visualized in short texts to study revision products, processes, and student interaction with feedback in student writing.

Keywords: Natural language processing · Text analysis · Writing · Revision · Automated feedback · Automated Revision Graphs · Visualization

1 Introduction

With data and analytics permeating many aspects of teaching and learning, one area that increasingly uses its capabilities is writing. Writing Analytics makes use of natural language processing and machine learning techniques to assess, provide automated feedback and study student writing [1, 2]. One particular interest in writing analytics is in the study of revision to understand the written products and processes of students. Revision is an important process that contributes to the outcome of the writing by playing a recursive role of reworking and improving the writer's thoughts and ideas [3, 4]. Resource intensive manual observation and coding are now enhanced with advanced data collection and analytics techniques to seamlessly study this revision process. This is seen in recent automation efforts including the study of linguistic properties [5, 6] and visualizing revisions in student writing [7, 8].

However, there is a gap in existing methods to study revised texts and stages of revision in writing. Document-level metrics (such as cohesion, and other linguistic measures) [5] do not distinguish slight changes made to a base text, and require finer grained measures for shorter texts. On the other hand, key strokes and character editing in writing which are used to visualize and study patterns of revision [9–11] are too fine-grained to qualitatively study the actual changes made to the text. To meaningfully interpret what changes a student made to a given short text as a result of an intervention/instruction, the need for automated visualizations to represent the process of drafting and revision at the sentence level arises. This need was identified from our research context where students engaged in a revision task using automated feedback

© Springer Nature Switzerland AG 2020
I. I. Bittencourt et al. (Eds.): AIED 2020, LNAI 12164, pp. 285–290, 2020.
https://doi.org/10.1007/978-3-030-52240-7_52

from AcaWriter [12] (and provided consent for the use of their data as part of a writing intervention [13, 14]). The paper introduces a novel technique for visualizing text as graph called 'Automated Revision Graphs' (ARG) to study revisions at a sentence level for short texts, automating a previous manual prototype [8, 15]. It provides preliminary evidence to demonstrate its usage by generating two forms of ARG: 1) Simple revision graph, which compares two texts to visualize the differences, and 2) Multi-stage revision graph, which visualizes the evolution of a given text over its many drafts.

2   Simple Revision Graph

The first ARG form is a Simple Revision Graph comparing any two short texts (text 1 and text 2, both containing less than 15 sentences each) to visualize the differences between them at a sentence level. The *nodes* of the graph represented as circles denote individual sentences, and are displayed in their order of occurrence in the texts (e.g. Sentence 1, 2, 3,.., expanding downwards). The color of the node represents the text feature we are interested in, and can be adapted to suit different requirements. In the current research context, the node color signifies the number of rhetorical moves in the sentence as students receive automated feedback on this feature. A brown node indicates no rhetorical move made in that sentence, a blue node indicates one rhetorical move, and a green node indicates two or more rhetorical moves. The colored *edges* connecting two nodes in text 1 and text 2 show the similarity/dissimilarity between the sentences represented by them. If there is a yellow edge between two nodes (sentences), it means that the two nodes are the same (no difference between the sentences). If the edge is teal colored, it indicates high similarity between the sentences (minor differences). A purple edge denotes medium similarity or major differences between the texts. A very small similarity means that the sentences are not related and very different (few or no common words between the sentences), and have no edges drawn between them. A sample simple revision graph with descriptions is provided in Fig. 1a.

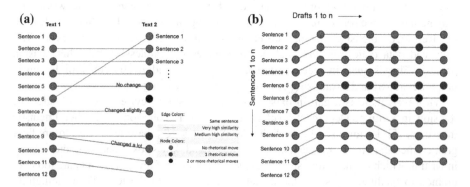

Fig. 1. a) A simple revision graph example and b) sample multi-stage revision graph with iterative changes. (Color figure online)

A simple revision graph helps in studying the different kinds of changes students make at a sentence level on any given base essay. It can visually represent and quantify revision actions such as minor changes, major changes, additions and deletions made in the sentences of the given text, and the presence of rhetorical moves in the revised texts.

3 Multi-stage Revision Graph

The second ARG form of Multi-stage Revision Graph is similar to the simple revision graph described earlier, but extends over multiple text iterations. It is used to study the stages in the revision process over time by comparing one draft to its previous draft. A sample multi-stage revision graph is provided in Fig. 1b, the student has removed the first and the last sentence from the given essay in the first draft requesting feedback (sentence 1 and sentence 12), depicted by missing outgoing edges. In the next draft, the student has introduced a rhetorical move represented by the blue colored node in sentences 2 and 5, with 2 or more rhetorical moves introduced in the subsequent draft in sentence 6 (represented by the green node). No major revisions have been made in the last two drafts as depicted by the unchanged graph structure towards the right end of the multi-stage revision graph.

The multi-stage revision graphs can be used to study the evolution of drafts in the revision process that led to the final product and student interaction with automated feedback based on the frequency of requests. They illuminate the underlying processes involved in the stages of revision after receiving automated feedback. These internal processes show how students apply the feedback on to their writing to revise the given text in different ways, which can be studied in relation to improvements in text quality.

4 Technical Implementation

Construction of ARG involved several steps, making use of Natural Language Processing (NLP) and graphical visualization packages in a Python Jupyter notebook. The code is released open source at https://github.com/AntonetteShibani/AutomatedRevisionGraphs for further development. An overview of steps is provided below:

- **Pre-processing the input text files:** The pre-processing step involved converting the input html files to extract the written text. The cleaned text was parsed to sentences using the TAP API[1], that provides NLP services such as sentence parsing, text metrics, and detection of rhetorical moves in text (More details at [12, 16]).
- **Getting rhetorical moves for all sentences:** The next step invoked Athanor from TAP to identify the rhetorical moves based on a concept-matching framework [17] (http://heta.io/online-training-in-rhetorical-parsing).

---

[1] GraphQL interface of the Text Analytics Pipeline (TAP): https://github.com/heta-io/tap hosted by Connected Intelligence Centre, University of Technology Sydney, Australia.

- **Creating the nodes from sentences:** The next step was to generate nodes for every sentence in the text and set its colour based on the number of rhetorical moves in it. To do this, a nodes csv was created with an index for each node, its actual text (to display while hovering over), and the node category for defining its color.
- **Creating text vectors and calculating similarity scores between sentences:** Next, the edges were generated based on how similar the sentence in the revised text was, to sentences in the previous text, using a cosine similarity score. With no need for semantic similarity measures in the current context (as students were only asked to make structural changes, and not content changes), cosine similarity worked best.
- **Creating the edges based on similarities:** Based on the similarity scores calculated above, edges for the revision graph were created between the nodes of the given text and the revised text using set thresholds. If the similarity score was equal to or greater than the highest similarity threshold (>0.99 for the same sentence, >0.8 for highly similar sentences, >0.6 for medium similarity nodes), an edge was added between the nodes of the two sentences with the corresponding weight. The edges csv consisted of three columns: startnode, endnode and weight, appended for each edge.
- **Rendering the revision graphs:** The next step was to create and render the interactive ARG using the nodes and the edges csv created earlier. This was done using network graphs from a python library called HoloViews[2] with interactive exploration of nodes and edges facilitated by the Bokeh plotting interface[3]. The rendered revision graphs were saved as html files in the specified output folder.
- **Calculating metrics:** An optional step after generating the ARG is to collect quantifiable metrics from the network graph such as the number of nodes with a rhetorical move, number of edges showing absolute similarity with no changes etc.

5   Conclusion

This paper introduced a novel visualization technique of constructing Automated Revision Graphs (ARG) with open-source code to study revisions in student writing in two forms: simple and multi-stage. This visual representation can be used to examine the differences between short texts at a sentence level along with quantifiable metrics, and to study patterns of activities such as addition, deletion and re-organization of sentences in the revision of a given text (for validations with empirical student data, see [18]). In addition, they can be used to study the effects of automated writing feedback on students' revisions at iterative drafting stages by recognizing individual differences in the feedback literacy [19] of students. It can further inform research on the quality of revisions made by students in writing tasks [20] and influence design choices in writing tool development based on user engagement. Future work with improvements made to

---

[2] HoloViews is an open-source Python library (https://github.com/pyviz/holoviews) to visualize graphs.

[3] Bokeh is a Python visualization library to create interactive plots, dashboards, and data applications. More information at https://bokeh.pydata.org/en/latest/.

visual aspects and usability in this preliminary research form of ARG can potentially aid its usage among students and educators for reflecting on revision practices.

Acknowledgements. An extended application of the work presented in this paper has been published in my doctoral thesis [18]. Thanks to Simon Buckingham Shum and Simon Knight for guiding the wider research project on automated writing feedback, which motivated the current work.

References

1. Shibani, A., Liu, M., Rapp, C., Knight, S.: Advances in Writing Analytics: Mapping the state of the field. In: Companion Proceedings of the 9th International Conference on Learning Analytics & Knowledge (LAK19), Tempe, Arizona (2019)
2. Buckingham Shum, S., Knight, S., McNamara, D., Allen, L., Bektik, D., Crossley, S.: Critical perspectives on writing analytics. In: Workshop at the Sixth International Conference on Learning Analytics & Knowledge, pp. 481–483. ACM (2016)
3. Fitzgerald, J.: Research on revision in writing. Rev. Educ. Res. **57**, 481–506 (1987)
4. Flower, L., Hayes, J.R.: A cognitive process theory of writing. Coll. Compos. Commun. **32**, 365–387 (1981)
5. McNamara, D.S., Graesser, A.C., McCarthy, P.M., Cai, Z.: Automated Evaluation of Text and Discourse with Coh-Metrix. Cambridge University Press, Cambridge (2014)
6. McNamara, D.S., Crossley, S.A., McCarthy, P.M.: Linguistic features of writing quality. Writ. Commun. **27**, 57–86 (2010)
7. Zhang, F., Hwa, R., Litman, D.J., Hashemi, H.B.: ArgRewrite: a web-based revision assistant for argumentative writings. In: NAACL-HLT 2016 (Demonstrations), pp. 37–41 (2016)
8. Shibani, A., Knight, S., Buckingham Shum, S.: Understanding students' revisions in writing: from word counts to the revision graph. Technical report, Connected Intelligence Centre, University of Technology Sydney (2018)
9. Caporossi, G., Leblay, C.: Online writing data representation: a graph theory approach. In: Gama, J., Bradley, E., Hollmén, J. (eds.) IDA 2011. LNCS, vol. 7014, pp. 80–89. Springer, Heidelberg (2011). https://doi.org/10.1007/978-3-642-24800-9_10
10. Southavilay, V., Yacef, K., Reimann, P., Calvo, R.A.: Analysis of collaborative writing processes using revision maps and probabilistic topic models. In: Proceedings of the Third International Conference on Learning Analytics and Knowledge, pp. 38–47. ACM (2013)
11. Wininger, M.: Measuring the evolution of a revised document. J. Writ. Res. **6**, 1–28 (2014)
12. Knight, S., et al.: AcaWriter: a learning analytics tool for formative feedback on academic writing. J. Writ. Res. **12**(1), 299–344 (2020)
13. Shibani, A., Knight, S., Buckingham Shum, S., Ryan, P.: Design and implementation of a pedagogic intervention using writing analytics. In: Chen, W., et al. (eds.) 25th International Conference on Computers in Education. Asia-Pacific Society for Computers in Education, New Zealand (2017)
14. Shibani, A., Knight, S., Buckingham Shum, S.: Contextualizable learning analytics design: a generic model, and writing analytics evaluations. In: Proceedings of the 9th International Conference on Learning Analytics and Knowledge (LAK 2019). ACM, Tempe (2019). https://doi.org/10.1145/3303772.3303785

15. Shibani, A., Knight, S., Buckingham Shum, S.: Understanding Revisions in Student Writing Through Revision Graphs. In: Penstein Rosé, C., et al. (eds.) AIED 2018. LNCS (LNAI), vol. 10948, pp. 332–336. Springer, Cham (2018). https://doi.org/10.1007/978-3-319-93846-2_62
16. Shibani, A., Abel, S., Gibson, A., Knight, S.: Turning the TAP on writing analytics. In: Companion Proceedings of the 8th International Conference on Learning Analytics and Knowledge (2018)
17. Sándor, Á.: Modeling metadiscourse conveying the author's rhetorical strategy in biomedical research abstracts. Revue française de linguistique appliquée 12, 97–108 (2007)
18. Shibani, A.: Augmenting pedagogic writing practice with contextualizable learning analytics. Ph.D. thesis. Connected Intelligence Centre. University of Technology Sydney, Sydney, Australia (2019). http://hdl.handle.net/10453/136846
19. Carless, D., Boud, D.: The development of student feedback literacy: enabling uptake of feedback. Assess. Eval. High. Educ. 43, 1315–1325 (2018)
20. Afrin, T., Litman, D.: Annotation and classification of sentence-level revision improvement. arXiv preprint arXiv:1909.05309 (2019)

When Lying, Hiding and Deceiving Promotes Learning - A Case for Augmented Intelligence with Augmented Ethics

Björn Sjödén$^{(\boxtimes)}$

Halmstad University, Halmstad, Sweden
bjorn.sjoden@hh.se

Abstract. If AI systems are to be used for truly human decision-making in education, teachers will need better support for deciding upon educational interventions and strategies on an ethically informed basis. As indicated by a recent call by the AIED Society to focus on the FATE (Fairness, Accountability, Transparency, and Ethics) of AI in education, fundamental issues in this area remain to be explicated, and teachers' perspectives need to be accounted for. The paper offers examples of how AI may serve to promote learning but at the cost of presenting limited or untruthful information to the student. For example, false information about a student's current progress may motivate students to finish a task they would otherwise give up; hiding information from the student that is disclosed to the teacher may decrease students' cognitive load while supporting the teacher's strategic choices, and deceiving the student as to the actual nature of the task or interaction, such as when using virtual agents, can increase students' efforts towards learning. Potential conflicts between such scenarios and basic values of FATE are discussed, and the basis for developing an "augmented ethics" system to support teachers' decision-making is presented.

Keywords: Ethics · Teacher perspectives · FATE · Augmented intelligence · Augmented ethics

1 Introduction

The importance of ethical issues in AIED community motivated a recent call to focus on the FATE (Fairness, Accountability, Transparency, and Ethics) of AI in education. Although FATE makes a nice acronym, it blurs the conceptual relations between these topics (e.g. fairness can be seen as one of several ethical concerns, and accountability as a concept which guides ethical considerations). To guide research and practice, it needs to be situated both in an ethic-theoretical context and in empirical research, and to take into account the perspective of the practitioners – the teachers. Teachers' knowledge of AI and related ethical issues in school needs to increase, and the literature has not clearly addressed the role of the teacher [1, 2]. If AI is to empower

© Springer Nature Switzerland AG 2020
I. I. Bittencourt et al. (Eds.): AIED 2020, LNAI 12164, pp. 291–295, 2020.
https://doi.org/10.1007/978-3-030-52240-7_53

education by augmenting human capabilities, how can ethical standards of human decision-making be ensured? What makes for an ethically informed basis?

This paper aims to address the ethical foundation that can guide empirical research on the teacher's practical knowledge needs, when using presently available AI such as adaptive systems, virtual agents and learning analytics. It argues that the constituents of an augmented ethics system require a broader analysis than that of augmented intelligence in the traditional sense. For instance, there are national curricula, treaties and policy documents, such as the General Data Protection Regulation (GDPR) in Europe and the UN Convention on the Rights of the Child, which must not be neglected to provide useful support for teachers. Hence, ethical theory, teaching practice and policies all need to inform the development of a system that effectively "augments" ethics.

2 Lying, Hiding and Deceiving for the FATE of Learning

There are many opportunities for using AI to enhance student learning at the cost of presenting untruthful, partial or misleading information to the student – in other words, systems that lie, hide or deceive. The message is not to condemn the existence or use of such functions – in fact, teachers have always used deliberate (over-)simplifications and factual misrepresentations in order to help students learn, and so has been done since the early days of AIED [e.g. 3] – but as AIED grows in complexity, and becomes more pervasive in the absence of human reflection and judgment, we need refined conceptual tools to identify and assess potential ethical conflicts with basic human values.

To what extent teachers need support, and of what kind, for taking a position to ethical dilemmas raised by recent AIED, remains an outstanding question. Some cases may appear unethical, such as deliberately inducing confusion in students by staging disagreements between agents [4] or presenting students with erroneous examples [5], but become less problematic for mature learners who are "game", become aware of the manipulations and submit to the pedagogic strategy. Then there are systems which may have personal repercussions far beyond what students and/or their teachers may recognize. A prevalent concern is privacy, relating to learning analytics (LA) [6, 7], for example whether the overall improvement of a learning environment is a valid reason to store and share the exact location of students to facilitate collaboration with peers. Other examples concern the use of Intelligent Tutoring Systems (ITS) that match students with virtual tutors on emotional and cognitive parameters. This raises issues as to when students' interactions with non-human systems are preferred to a human being. As noted in one study, "What is true if the teacher and AI do not agree?" [1].

The message then, in line with other recent work [8], is that ethical use of AI in schools require that teachers' unique human expertise is preserved and promoted. Such expertise is needed for deciding when it is warranted to use misrepresentations or a "deceptive" system for a larger good, in order to secure educational benefits and avoid risks for students' well-being. Next are some examples of such potential conflicts.

Lying refers to deliberately presenting information to the student that is incorrect, with reference to the available data. In principle, this concerns all cases where students are presented with incorrect information and requested to correct it, although the AI "knows" the correct answer. But there are more subtle and specific examples. Studies on learning curves and motivation suggest that students work longer in a problem domain if they make visible progress and are closer to goal (say, 80%) compared to not progressing, further from the goal (say, 40%). Such data can be used for algorithms that – truthfully – match the difficulty of learning tasks to the student's current performance level in a "personally" adaptive system (e.g. Sana Labs, www.sanalabs.com). Would it then be ethically justifiable to present false information about a student's current progress, suggesting that one is closer to the goal than performance indicates, in order to motivate students to finish a task they would otherwise give up?

Hiding refers to presenting selective, but not untrue, information to the student, while processing more data that is relevant to the task but may be presented at a later time and/or to another person (a peer or a teacher). AI systems that serve to identify what data are important to students are implemented in Learning Analytics (LA) and motivate the separation between *student-facing* and *teacher-facing* LA [9]. Hiding information from the student that is disclosed to the teacher may decrease students' cognitive load while supporting the teacher's strategic choices. Should AI therefore be used to determine what data are 'better' communicated to teachers and students, respectively?

Deceiving refers to presenting the student with tasks that are designed to maintain false beliefs or illusions, without making the actual nature of the task or interaction explicit. A form of voluntary deception occurs in all (educational or other) games which involve an "intelligent" opponent that is technically invincible but adapts to the player's performance. The same can be said about collaborative virtual agents, such as Teachable Agents that increase students' efforts [10–12]. An interesting example is BELLA [13] which employs a "super-agent" to adapt to students' knowledge gaps without actual "teaching" by the student. In research, Wizard-of-Oz methodologies exploit student expectations for improving upon existing systems by having human actors simulate AI agents. To what extent are such illusions ethically justifiable to maintain?

3   Towards a System for Augmented Ethics

The wide variety of issues and ethical concerns makes it difficult to define which aspects of FATE to focus on. From consulting ethical-philosophical expertise and standard works [14] four basic values are identified: *privacy, safety, trust* and *fairness*. These values are fundamental in the sense that there is no obvious way of telling which value trumps another one. As to the FATE dimensions, one can argue that, for instance, "Transparency" is not a fundamental ethical value because it could, at the same time, be a risk and a benefit to safety, and a risk to privacy. "Fairness", on the other hand, is a fundamental social value (one cannot be "fair" in isolation), theoretically independent of individual privacy and safety.

Addressing the multiplicity of concerns is helped by distinguishing between pedagogies on the screen-level, "how individual systems work with a single student", and the orchestration-level, "whereby such systems are deployed in the bigger temporal and spatial context of a whole class" [15, p. 6]. The screen/orchestration level distinction thus helps both to direct teachers' attention and to see how accountability is attributed. The results of discussions with teachers can inform ethical guidelines that support decision-making as to what values should be protected, to what costs and benefits.

Figure 1 offers a simplified categorization grid of ethical concerns that emerge from relating teachers' knowledge needs on the screen- and orchestration levels. It is suggested that the teacher take a stand on two questions: *Is the concern a screen-level priority? Is the concern an orchestration-level priority?* It should be emphasized that the yes (✓) or no (✗) to these questions is a deliberate simplification; they are a question of focus rather than exclusion, and they do not definitely tell where concerns belong.

		Screen-level priority	
		✓	✗
Orchestration-level priority	✓	**Privacy** e.g. *Shall teachers be able to see when and for how long a student did her homework? Shall students and their parents be allowed to see how much time the teacher spent correcting the students' homework?*	**Safety** e.g. *How does the system support the student while safeguarding students' independence? How does the system as a substitute for human interactions affect children's formation of self and personal identity?*
	✗	**Trust** e.g. *Is it possible that students will trust an AI-based system so much as to prefer its company to their teacher and their peers? Are AI-based systems more trustworthy than teachers in certain areas of knowledge, e.g. math and computer science?*	**Fairness** e.g. *How should AI resources be distributed to student groups on an equal basis? How do we share teacher and teaching resources fairly among students?*

Fig. 1. A grid for determining types of ethical priorities for AIED, with example questions.

On the screen-level, concerns of *privacy* can be viewed with respect to privacy settings available to the individual but also what data the system stores and what personal data is requested at start. The individual's *trust* in the system is dependent on how well it functions, both for protecting personal data and for producing the expected outcomes. The teacher can assist students with available privacy settings and data storage but cannot directly influence students' trust and expectations, which can only develop from personal experience of working with a system in relation to (human or AI) alternatives.

On the orchestration-level, *safety* can be viewed with respect to how the teacher assesses and manages the risks and threats for all students in a class (arguably, students may have different preferences of privacy and what information they are willing to share, but they should all have an equal level of safety). Safety concerns are about the whole group and the orchestration of all systems used in the classroom. *Fairness* is a value of broader ethical concern than can be addressed by either the student on screen or the teacher beyond her own classroom. Issues of fairness must not be ignored, but teachers need to be aware of the complex social, financial, and cultural context in which they are embedded. For example, teachers and policy makers may need to consider gender equality, and whether the use of AI should be mandatory.

In conclusion, this organization of ethical priorities put the theoretical corner stones on which to base ethical positions with respect to the teacher's responsibilities, the system properties and contextual knowledge needs. Each of the four values deserves attention in its own right. For understanding their meaning in practice and further development, it is suggested that teachers are involved at an early stage and work together with researchers, such as in workshops, in an iterative process of identifying, analyzing, evaluating and re-evaluating ethical concerns. Such a project would have great significance both on a societal level and for covering knowledge gaps on the ethics of AIED.

References

1. Hrastinski, S., et al.: Critical imaginaries and reflections on artificial intelligence and robots in postdigital K-12 education. Postdigital Sci. Educ. **1**(2), 427–445 (2019)
2. Humble, N., Mozelius, P.: Teacher-supported AI or AI-supported teachers?. In: European Conference on the Impact of Artificial Intelligence and Robotics (ECIAIR 2019), pp. 157–164. Academic Conferences and Publishing International Limited, Oxford (2019)
3. Gutwin, C., McCalla, G.: The use of pedagogic misrepresentation in tutorial dialogue. In: Frasson, C., Gauthier, G., McCalla, G.I. (eds.) ITS 1992. LNCS, vol. 608, pp. 507–514. Springer, Heidelberg (1992). https://doi.org/10.1007/3-540-55606-0_60
4. Lehman, B., et al.: Inducing and tracking confusion with contradictions during complex learning. Int. J. Artif. Intell. Educ. **22**(1–2), 85–105 (2013)
5. Adams, D.M., et al.: Using erroneous examples to improve mathematics learning with a web-based tutoring system. Comput. Hum. Behav. **36**, 401–411 (2014)
6. Pardo, A., Siemens, G.: Ethical and privacy principles for learning analytics. Br. J. Educ. Technol. **45**(3), 438–450 (2014)
7. Slade, S., Prinsloo, P.: Learning analytics: ethical issues and dilemmas. Am. Behav. Sci. **57** (10), 1509–1528 (2013)
8. Felix, C.: The role of the teacher and AI in education. In: Blessinger, P., Sengupta, E. (eds.) International Perspectives on the Role of Technology in Humanizing Higher Education. Emerald Group Publishing, Bingley (2020)
9. Bodily, R., Verbert, K.: Trends and issues in student-facing learning analytics reporting systems research. In: Proceedings of the Seventh International Learning Analytics & Knowledge Conference, pp. 309–318. ACM, New York (2017)
10. Chase, C.C., Chin, D.B., Oppezzo, M.A., Schwartz, D.L.: Teachable agents and the protégé effect: increasing the effort towards learning. J. Sci. Educ. Technol. **18**(4), 334–352 (2009)
11. Matsuda, N., et al.: Cognitive anatomy of tutor learning: lessons learned with SimStudent. J. Educ. Psychol. **105**(4), 1152–1163 (2013)
12. Pareto, L.: A teachable agent game engaging primary school children to learn arithmetic concepts and reasoning. Int. J. Artif. Intell. Educ. **24**(3), 251–283 (2014). https://doi.org/10.1007/s40593-014-0018-8
13. Lenat, D.B., Durlach, P.J.: Reinforcing math knowledge by immersing students in a simulated learning-by-teaching experience. Int. J. Artif. Intell. Educ. **24**(3), 216–250 (2014)
14. Rawls, J.: A Theory of Justice. Belknap Press, Cambridge (1972)
15. du Boulay, B.: Escape from the skinner box: the case for contemporary intelligent learning environments. Br. J. Educ. Technol. **50**(6), 2902–2919 (2019)

Understanding Collaborative Question Posing During Computational Modeling in Science

Caitlin Snyder[1]([✉]), Nicole M. Hutchins[1], Gautam Biswas[1],
Mona Emara[2], Bernard Yett[1], and Shitanshu Mishra[1]

[1] Vanderbilt University, Nashville, TN, USA
caitlin.r.snyder@vanderbilt.edu
[2] Damanhour University, Damanhour, Egypt

Abstract. Curricular standards in STEM [9] and computer science have emphasized the role of asking questions to support inquiry learning in K-12 education. In this paper, we examine the role of questioning during collaborative computational modeling of scientific processes through discourse analysis to understand how students grapple with the synergistic application of STEM and CT to build, test, and evaluate their models. To our knowledge, limited research has targeted a systematic understanding of question posing during computational modeling in science. We aim to develop a better understanding of question posing in support of inquiry and problem-solving during model building.

Keywords: Question posing · Synergistic learning · Collaborative learning

1 Introduction

Curricular standards in STEM [9] and computer science (https://k12cs.org/) emphasize the practice of posing questions to aid learning and domain exploration. Developing question posing skills may support critical thinking, which, in turn, impacts student learning and knowledge building [11]. In this paper, we present a systematic analysis of students' question posing as they work together to build computational models of scientific processes [7]. Our focus is on synergistic processes, i.e., the integration of science and CT concepts and practices that students have to develop for successful model building [4, 11, 12]. In this paper, we present a systematic analysis that evaluates learner's collaborative question posing with regards to learning goals i.e. the synergistic processes behind the integration of STEM and CT constructs necessary for successful model building. Our analyses show that transformation questions have an overall greater impact on a group's success in building computational models.

2 Background and Analysis Framework

Successful collaboration requires developing a shared understanding among group members [8] as well as interaction skills that include the encouraging and developing ideas, monitoring progress, and providing constructive feedback [2, 3]. Collaborative

I. I. Bittencourt et al. (Eds.): AIED 2020, LNAI 12164, pp. 296–300, 2020.
https://doi.org/10.1007/978-3-030-52240-7_54

dialogue provides a rich opportunity to understand collaborative processes that are contextualized within learning goals. Leaner-to-learner questions in collaborative dialogue provide insight into group collaboration characteristics in relation to the constructs of the learning domain. In this work we categorize naturally occurring learner-to-learner into two types of questions: confirmation and transformation [10]. Confirmation questions usually require only a shallow understanding of topics. They are used to clarify information, seek reassurance about an idea or ask about the location of a system specific object. Transformation questions require a higher understanding of domain concepts. Such questions challenge actions or statements, pose ideas about domain constructs or guide the modeling processes.

We contextualize students' collaborative question posing in terms of synergistic learning processes. Computational model building of scientific phenomenon has been shown to be an effective framework for integrated knowledge construction of STEM and CT concepts and practices [1, 7]. In previous work studying synergistic learning, we identified three essential applications of synergistic processes during computational modeling: initialization, modeling conditional behavior, and debugging [6, 12]. Each process requires students to integrate their conceptual understanding of physics knowledge with a computational representation to support model building.

3   Study Description and Data Analysis Methods

26 high school sophomore students worked in the C2STEM environment [7] in groups one class day a week for two months to complete a 45-min training unit followed by three kinematics and one mechanics computational modeling units. Students were divided into groups: 8 triads and 1 dyad. Technical issues resulted in removal of 2 triads from our analyses. Model scores were computed using a pre-defined rubric for all modeling tasks that evaluated proficiency in CT and physics separately. We focused our analysis on the 2D motion with constant velocity challenge task where students were instructed to model a boat crossing a river while stopping at two different islands along the way. To be successful in this module students had to calculate the boat's heading angle and resultant velocity while considering the river's current.

Our analysis to understand students' question posing during computational model building is guided by two research questions: (RQ1) *What questioning characteristics linked to CT and physics can we derive from students' discourse, and how does these impact their learning?* (RQ2) *What characteristics of collaboration in the context of synergistic learning can we derive from students' questions?* Learner-to-learner questions were coded by two coders according to three frameworks: (1) question posing (QP): transformation, confirmation, (2) question answering (QA): self-answered, other answered, or not answered, and (3) synergistic learning processes (SLP): initialization, modeling conditional behaviors, and debugging. Inter-rater reliability was checked by calculating Cohen's kappa which resulted in good agreement ($k = 0.73$) for all three forms of coding.

4 Results

Table 1 below shows the final computational model scores and proportions of total questions to total utterances (**Q-to-U**), transformation questions to total questions (**Trans**), and total confirmation questions to total questions (**Conf**) for each group.

Table 1. Model scores and proportions

Performance	Group	Q-to-U	Trans	Conf	Phys score	CT score	Total score
High (over 80%)	5	0.27	0.63	0.37	100%	90%	94%
	2	0.13	0.53	0.47	88%	90%	89%
Middle (80%–60%)	8	0.19	0.43	0.54	75%	70%	72%
	4	0.19	0.43	0.57	63%	60%	61%
Low (under 60%)	1	0.20	0.48	0.52	50%	30%	39%
	6	0.21	0.37	0.63	38%	40%	39%
	7	0.09	0.25	0.75	25%	20%	22%

The two highest performing groups, 2 and 5, had a majority of transformation questions while all other groups had a majority of confirmation questions. This coincides with the findings of [11] that transformation questions require advanced domain knowledge. The majority confirmation questions in the other groups may indicate a shallow understanding of domain or CT constructs for the modeling tasks.

We further investigate how these questions relate to synergistic learning processes by analyzing the proportion of each type of question (confirmation and transformation) during each synergistic process (initialization, debugging and conditional behavior changes) to the total number of questions. In previous work [11], we found that the majority of questions during initialization were classified as confirmation questions. In the context of performance-based analysis, this remains true for all groups except for the highest performers, Group 5 and Group 2, who asked equal or more transformation questions. 50% of Group 5 initialization questions were transformation and Group 2 had 53% while the rest of the groups had less than 44% transformation questions during initialization. During debugging, the groups varied but it is worth noting that the high performing groups (Group 5 and Group 2) and one middle performing group (Group 8) had a majority of transformation questions, 61%, 57% and 60% respectively. We hypothesize that transformation questions during debugging results in higher final model scores because debugging requires advanced domain knowledge to analyze the model behavior based on expected behaviors to locate and correct errors. While working on conditional behavior changes, the groups as whole had a majority of transformation questions (58%). Groups individually varied but it is worth noting that the three worst performing groups had a majority of confirmation questions (Group 1 and 6), or asked no questions while modeling conditional behavior changes (Group 7). 75% of Group 1's questions while working on conditional behavior changes were confirmation questions and 67% of Group 6's questions.

Table 2 shows the correlation between different characteristics of students' question posing pose on their final model. Note that we only include the spearman coefficient, ρ, for transformation questions during each synergistic process since the proportion calculation results in the coefficient for confirmation questions being the negative of the transformation coefficient. Q-to-U does not have a strong correlation, which supports the idea that shallower learning analytic representations miss out on important information. The question posing approach (e.g., transformation and confirmation questions) shows a high correlation with the final model score. Transformation questions during the debugging processes highly correlated with the final score.

Table 2. Correlation between model score (variable 1) and question characteristics

Var 2	Q-to-U	Trans	Conf	Init-trans	Debug-trans	Cond-trans
ρ	0.34	0.87	−0.85	0.71	0.85	0.05
p-value	0.45	0.02	0.02	0.07	0.02	0.76

In regards to RQ2, we calculated the proportion of each question type (transformation vs confirmation) in regards to how it was answered (not, self, other) with respect to all questions of that type. Most transformation questions were answered by other students (62%) with 8% being self-answered and 31% not answered. We hypothesize that transformation questions were more likely to be answered by another group members (e.g., to build consensus or counter-challenge) or not be answered due to the complexity of the question or potential domain misunderstanding(s) by other group members. Most confirmation questions were not answered (50%) with 25% being self-answered and 25% being answered by others. We hypothesize that confirmation questions were more often not answered due to the fact that some confirmation questions are simply think aloud statements and the students may not actually expect a response (e.g., asking about the location of a block found shortly after asking).

5   Discussion and Conclusions

Our results support previous conclusions [11] and extend them by showing the correlation between transformation questions and the success of a group's final model as well analyzing questions in terms of who responded to questions posed. The grounding and alignment of AI-enhanced technologies (e.g., designing and using learning analytics dashboards that include feedback on collaborative processes) with learning theories can support optimization of curriculum design and instruction [5]. This systematic approach demonstrates how an evaluation of key collaborative processes (question posing and group response) can be linked to learning objectives (synergistic learning) to provide comprehensive feedback on possible pedagogical actions. We recognize the limitations in our analysis, including the small sample size, and aim to conduct this systematic analysis with a larger sample size and multiple domains in the future.

Acknowledgements. This research is supported by NSF grant #1640199.

References

1. Basu, S., Biswas, G., Kinnebrew, J.S.: Learner modeling for adaptive scaffolding in a computational thinking-based science learning environment. User Model. User-Adapt. Interact. **27**(1), 5–53 (2017)
2. Garrison, D.R., Akyol, Z.: The Community of Inquiry Theoretical Framework. Handbook of Distance Education, pp. 122–138. Routledge, Abingdon (2013)
3. Grau, V., Whitebread, D.: Self and social regulation of learning during collaborative activities in the classroom: the interplay of individual and group cognition. Learn. Instr. **22** (6), 401–412 (2012)
4. Grover, S., Hutchins, N., Biswas, G., Snyder, C., Emara, M.: Examining Synergistic Learning of Physics and Computational Thinking Through Collaborative Problem Solving in Computational Modeling. American Educational Research Association, Toronto (2019)
5. Hernández-Leo, D., Martinez-Maldonado, R., Pardo, A., Muñoz-Cristóbal, J.A., Rodríguez-Triana, M.J.: Analytics for learning design: a layered framework and tools: analytics layers for learning design. Br. J. Educ. Technol. **50**(1), 139–152 (2019)
6. Hutchins, N., Biswas, G., Maroti, M., Ledezci, A., Bioll, B.: A design-based approach to a classroom-centered OELE. In: International Conference on Artificial Intelligence in Education, pp. 155–159 (2018)
7. Hutchins, N., et al.: C2STEM: a system for synergistic learning of physics and computational thinking. J. Sci. Educ. Technol. **29**(1), 83–100 (2019)
8. Larkin, S.: Collaborative group work and individual development of metacognition in the early years. Res. Sci. Educ. **36**(1–2), 7–27 (2006)
9. NGSS Lead States: Next Generation Science Standards: For States, by States. The National Academies Press, Washington, DC (2013)
10. Pedrosa de Jesus, H., Teixeira-Dias, J., Watts, M.: Questions of chemistry. Int. J. Sci. Educ. **25**, 1015–1034 (2003)
11. Snyder, C., Hutchins, N., Biswas, G., Mishra, S., Emara, M.: Exploring synergistic learning processes through collaborative learner-to-learner questioning. In: Proceedings of the International Conference of the Learning Sciences, Nashville, TN (2020)
12. Snyder, C., Hutchins, N., Biswas, G., Emara, M., Grover, S., Conlin, L.: Analyzing students' synergistic learning processes in physics and CT by collaborative discourse analysis. In: Proceedings of the International Conference on Computer Supported Collaborative Learning, Lyon, France, pp. 360–336 (2019)

Machine Learning and Student Performance in Teams

Rohan Ahuja, Daniyal Khan, Sara Tahir, Magdalene Wang,
Danilo Symonette, Shimei Pan, Simon Stacey$^{(\boxtimes)}$, and Don Engel

University of Maryland Baltimore County, Baltimore, MD, USA
{rahuja2,dkhan1,sarata1,wangmag1,danilo2,shimei,
spstacey,donengel}@umbc.edu

Abstract. This project applies a variety of machine learning algorithms
to the interactions of first year college students using the GroupMe messaging platform to collaborate online on a team project. The project
assesses the efficacy of these techniques in predicting existing measures
of team member performance, generated by self- and peer assessment
through the Comprehensive Assessment of Team Member Effectiveness
(CATME) tool. We employed a wide range of machine learning classifiers (SVM, KNN, Random Forests, Logistic Regression, Bernoulli Naive
Bayes) and a range of features (generated by a socio-linguistic text analysis program, Doc2Vec, and TF-IDF) to predict individual team member
performance. Our results suggest machine learning models hold out the
possibility of providing accurate, real-time information about team and
team member behaviors that instructors can use to support students
engaged in team-based work, though challenges remain.

Keywords: Machine learning · Teamwork · Performance prediction ·
Text mining

1 Introduction

Teamwork skills are vital for college students, both while they are at university
[7] and for their employability and success after graduation [4]. This is true
across the board, for students in a wide variety of disciplines [3,5,6,13]. Despite
great interest in supporting and developing student teamwork skills, there are
relatively few tools available to help instructors do so [2] and the few tools that
do exist are often focused on fairly artificial and controlled experimental settings
rather than robust teaching environments [10] or suffer from other shortcomings
[2,12]. This paper reports on the collection of teamwork data "from the wild" in

This work was supported by the National Science Foundation under Grant No. 1339265.
Any opinions, findings, and conclusions or recommendations expressed in this mate-
rial are those of the authors and do not necessarily reflect the views of the National
Science Foundation. Support was also provided through a Hrabowski Innovation Fund
Innovation and Research Grant from the University of Maryland, Baltimore County.

© Springer Nature Switzerland AG 2020
I. I. Bittencourt et al. (Eds.): AIED 2020, LNAI 12164, pp. 301–305, 2020.
https://doi.org/10.1007/978-3-030-52240-7_55

a deliberately non-intrusive manner, and the subsequent machine learning driven analysis of these data to identify high performing and non-high performing team members. Although just making this discrimination is not on its own enough to support team members and their teams, this is an important initial step towards developing a more broad-ranging program that can do so. We hope with this effort to begin to remedy the dispiriting conclusion of a recent article that "no study has shown that technological support for group regulation can help teams to improve their course-based, collaborative discourse over time [1]."

2   Data Collection

The data for this project come from two semesters of a mandatory, two credit, Pass or Fail class for freshman students in the Honors College at a midsize American university, enrolling about 100 students each year, divided into 12 teams of 8–9 students, each with a non-freshman team leader. The students in the classes came from a very wide variety of majors, and one of the primary requirements of the class was that each team identify a social issue or problem in the city near the campus, research it, and propose a multidisciplinary approach to addressing it. Teams had the entire fifteen-week semester to work on the project. Team member performance was assessed through the Comprehensive Assessment of Team Member Effectiveness (CATME) tool [9]. Twice during the semester, students completed CATME self and peer-assessments, in which they completed a report on their own and their team-members' contributions to the work of their team. CATME calculates a total for each team member for each dimension on the basis of all the assessments a team member receives (including his or her own), averages those scores and then uses an "adjustment factor" to accommodate the fact that some teams may assess more generously than others. CATME scores form a continuum, so to dichotomously categorize team members for analysis we used CATME's "high performer" definition- team members with an average rating of 3.5 out of the available 5 points, and with an overall rating at least half a point above their teammates' average rating. The Fall 2018 class had 36 high performers, and the Fall 2019 class had 22 high performers. (We used the end rather than middle of semester CATME assessments, when team members had the most information on which to base their evaluations.) The class met for two hours every week, but because little of that class time was available for project work, much of the work on team projects took place online, using the GroupMe messaging platform. Data for the project were collected by adding a dummy member to each team's GroupMe group, after obtaining written informed consent from each student. The 94 students who participated in the Fall 2018 GroupMe chats yielded an approximately 5000 message transcript, and the 100 students who participated in the Fall 2019 GroupMe chats generated an approximately 6000 message transcript.

Table 1. 10-fold cross-validation accuracy and macro-f1 scores for machine learning models that were trained to predict high performing team members. The first column shows the features or combination of features that were used as input for machine learning, and the best models were first found individually for several algorithms such as Logistic Regression, K-Nearest Neighbors, SVM, Naive Bayes and Random Forests, using grid searches for hyper-parameter tuning, followed by selection of the best performing model among these different models.

Method	Accuracy	Macro-F1 score
Dummy classifier with "most frequent" strategy	0.698	0.411
Doc2Vec embedding only	0.762	0.699
LIWC only	0.766	0.714
TF-IDF + Doc2Vec embedding	0.928	0.906
TF-IDF only	**0.959**	**0.947**

3   Methods, Analysis and Results

We explored a range of machine learning models to predict high performing students, including Logistic Regression, K-Nearest Neighbors, SVM, Naive Bayes and Random Forests. Based on ten-fold cross-validated Macro-average F1 scores, SVM with Recursive Feature Elimination proved to be the best-performing model overall, with its tendency to reduce overfitting as an added benefit. With the model selected, we trained it to predict high performers using several features, some in combination with others, with the results reflected in Table 1. Among them, TF-IDF scores are frequently used to represent text in text mining and information retrieval. Linguistic Inquiry and Word Count (LIWC) [11] is an off-the-shelf linguistic analysis tool, which categorizes words into roughly eighty different psychologically meaningful categories, signaling attentional focus, attitudes, perceptions, emotionality, social relationships, thinking styles, and authenticity, etc. Doc2vec is a neural network-based text embedding method that automatically learns a dense vector representation of each document/message [8]. Among all the features, TF-IDF scores proved to be the most effective in predicting high performers (0.959 prediction accuracy and 0.947 F1), followed by LIWC features. Although Doc2vec embedding and LIWC both out-perform the Dummy Classifier with "most frequent" strategy baseline significantly, adding them to TF-IDF does not improve performance (see Table 1).

4   Conclusion and Discussion

This project investigates whether machine learning analysis of the text messages of online team member exchanges can discriminate high performing from non-high performing team members. The work demonstrates the potential of such automatic assessments of online student teamwork, and provides some initial pointers about which machine learning approaches are most effective. Near term future work will involve refining these most promising approaches.

One major potential benefit of automatically assessing online teamwork is that it can provide instructors with this information on a real-time or near real-time basis (e.g., in a team performance dashboard), which is important to their making timely decisions about what corrective or supportive actions to take. Furthermore, this benefit is available without the significant outlay of time or energy by instructors it would take for instructors to attempt to assess the quality and trajectory of a team's work themselves. That time and energy can then be devoted to instruction and to the more challenging tasks of determining whether, when and how to intervene.

But several challenges remain. First, we have so far explored only data generated by team members using text-based platforms. This simplified the data collection process, but limited the range of data we had to analyze. In particular, we have so far collected team member interactions neither from online verbal conversations between team members (on Zoom, WebEx, Blackboard Collaborate, etc), nor from in-person conversations between team members. Such conversations are likely to be richer in data, but are technically more challenging to capture and process. In addition, the capture of conversations of this type also raises more serious questions about student expectations of and rights to privacy. Still, as the COVID-19 crisis forces universities to move classes online in the Northern hemisphere's 2020 summer (and perhaps fall), an important if regrettable opportunity to collect data from classes with a teamwork component is presenting itself.

The second challenge is of a different sort- how to represent the findings of these models to instructors in ways which are intelligible and actionable. Using SVM with recursive feature elimination and focusing on TF-IDF features produced the best predictions of high performing team members, but it would be difficult for an instructor to know what to do to support student team members identified as non-high performing, because the features used to make the predictions are so low-level. No matter how predictively potent it is, it is likely that instructors, especially in non-STEM fields, will resist adopting a pedagogical tool if its workings are opaque to them. The challenge, then, is to retain the accuracy of a model like the one that performed best, while making its findings intelligible and usable. For example, somehow grouping the features the model relies on in understandable categories (perhaps, even, categories of the kind employed by LIWC) would allow instructors to identify the kinds of missteps in communicative behavior occurring in student teams. An important focus of future work, then, will be to try to retain the predictive power of low level feature-based models but to add to those models a measure of interpretability and intelligibility that makes them useful instructional tools.

References

1. Borge, M., Ong, Y.S., Rosé, C.P.: Learning to monitor and regulate collective thinking processes. Int. J. Comput.-Support. Collab. Learn. **13**(1), 61–92 (2018). https://doi.org/10.1007/s11412-018-9270-5
2. Britton, E., Simper, N., Leger, A., Stephenson, J.: Assessing teamwork in undergraduate education: a measurement tool to evaluate individual teamwork skills. Assess. Evaluation High. Educ. **42**(3), 378–397 (2017)
3. Earnest, M.A., Williams, J., Aagaard, E.M.: Toward an optimal pedagogy for teamwork. Acad. Med. **92**(10), 1378–1381 (2017)
4. Hart Research Associates: Raising the Bar: Employers' Views on College Learning in the Wake of the Economic Downturn. Hart Research Associates (2009)
5. Hastie, C., Fahy, K., Parratt, J.: The development of a rubric for peer assessment of individual teamwork skills in undergraduate midwifery students. Women Birth **27**(3), 220–226 (2014)
6. Ibrahim, B., DeMiranda, M.A., Lashari, T.A., Siller, Y.J.: Teamwork and engineering design outcomes: examining the relationship among engineering undergraduate students. In: 2017 7th World Engineering Education Forum (WEEF), pp. 628–635. WEEF, Kuala Lumpur (2017)
7. Kuh, G.: High-Impact Educational Practices: What They Are, Who Has Access to Them, and Why They Matter. Association of American Colleges and Universities, Washington, DC (2008)
8. Le, Q., Mikolov, T.: Distributed representations of sentences and documents. In: Proceedings of the 31st International Conference on International Conference on Machine Learning, ICML 2014, vol. 32, p. II-1188–II-1196. JMLR.org (2014)
9. Ohland, M.W., et al.: The comprehensive assessment of team member effectiveness: development of a behaviorally anchored rating scale for self- and peer evaluation. Acad. Manag. Learn. Educ. **11**(4), 609–630 (2013)
10. Stewart, A.E.B., et al.: I say, you say, we say: Using spoken language to model sociocognitive processes during computer-supported collaborative problem solving. In: Proceedings of the ACM on Human-Computer Interaction, pp. 1–19. CSCW (2019)
11. Tausczik, Y., Pennebaker, J.: The psychological meaning of words: LIWC and computerized text analysis methods. J. Lang. Soc. Psychol. **29**(1), 24–54 (2010)
12. Vivian, R., Falkner, K., Falkner, N.: Analysing computer science students' teamwork role adoption in an online self-organized teamwork activity. In: Proceedings of the 13th Koli Calling International Conference on Computing Education Research, Koli Calling 2013, pp. 105–114, Koli, Finland (2013)
13. Weinstein, J., Morton, L., Taras, H., Reznik, V.: Teaching teamwork to law students. J. Leg. Educ. **63**(1), 36–64 (2013)

Scanpath Analysis of Student Attention During Problem Solving with Worked Examples

Samantha Stranc and Kasia Muldner[(⊠)]

Institute of Cognitive Science, Carleton University, Ottawa, Canada
{samantha.stranc,kasia.muldner}@carleton.ca

Abstract. We report on the analysis of scanpath data captured by an eye tracker as students solved problems with access to worked examples. Our work makes two contributions: (1) it reports on scanpath analysis using the MultiMatch tool, (2) it investigates how type of problem-example similarity and assistance influenced attention patterns captured by scanpaths. We show that both problem-example similarity and type of assistance impact scanpaths.

Keywords: Scanpath analysis · Problem solving & worked examples · Assistance

1 Introduction

Eye tracking data can provide valuable data on students' visual attention, which can then be used as input to a user model to detect various student states [1–3]. To date, analysis has focused on *fixation* data [4], namely a moment of attention when the eye stops scanning. Additional insight can be gained by accounting for the *order* of fixations, captured by a *scanpath* [5]. For instance, sequence mining can identify common patterns in scanpaths [3, 6]. A limitation of this method is that it only considers exact sequence matches. However, two scanpaths are rarely identical and this is particularly the case for longer scanpaths, such as ones elicited by complex tasks. Consequently, the results from sequence mining are typically abbreviated to only include sequences consisting of 2 to 4 fixations. This has the potential to miss information on strategies involving longer sequences of fixations. We address this limitation by using fuzzy alignment approaches provided by a scanpath tool called MultiMatch [7]. MultiMatch transforms the original coordinate data into a vector-space representation and then quantifies the similarity between two scanpaths using five features (shape, direction, length, position and duration). Here, we use MultiMatch to analyze the similarity of scanpaths captured as students solved algebra problems in the presence of examples using a basic computer tutor.

Scanpath analysis has been applied in a range of domains like scene analysis [8], decision making [9], reading [10], and analogy making [11]. For instance, Zhou et al. [9] analyzed scanpaths in three different decision-making tasks (e.g., one task involved choosing between risky options under two different conditions). The similarity of scanpaths in a given decision condition were more similar than between the conditions, suggesting that visual attention was affected by type of task. However, more work is

© Springer Nature Switzerland AG 2020
I. I. Bittencourt et al. (Eds.): AIED 2020, LNAI 12164, pp. 306–311, 2020.
https://doi.org/10.1007/978-3-030-52240-7_56

needed to investigate the potential utility of scanpath analysis for educational contexts, something echoed in recent reviews [12].

2 Data and Methods

The instructional context for our work was problem solving with access to worked examples. In this context, learning outcomes depend on student *strategies*, including how much students copy from examples (bad for learning) vs. self-explain from examples or problems (good for learning) [13–15]. To date, these strategies have been investigated using analyses of student utterances [13] and so less is known about students' visual attention in this context. Here, we used data from a between-subjects eye tracking study [16] in which students used a tutoring system to solve 12 algebra problems, with assistance from one example per problem. Half of the problem-example pairs had *high similarity* (example solution could be copied), while the other half had *low similarity* (inferences beyond copying were required to apply the example). Here, we focus on two study conditions: (1) *fade-out assistance* ($n = 20$): students were initially given high-similarity examples, but these transitioned to low similarity after some problems were solved; (2) *fade-in assistance* ($n = 19$): the opposite was the case (low-similarity initially, eventually becoming high similarity). Thus, while the conditions involved the same number of low and high similarity examples, the *timing* of assistance was varied (immediate presentation of high similarity examples, vs. later in the problem sequence).

The original analysis showed that students learned more from *fade-in* assistance than *fade-out* assistance [16] but did not analyze students' strategies. Here, we analyze the scanpaths in each condition (*fade in* vs. *fade out*), using them as a proxy for strategies. Recall that scanpaths are series of fixations on learning materials. If we can show that scanpaths are different, this provides some evidence that strategies are different as well.

We had two key questions: (1) Does problem-example similarity impact scanpaths? (2) Does the type of assistance (fade in vs. fade out) impact scanpaths? Recall that there were 12 problems solved in each condition (*fade in* and *fade out*). We analyzed scanpaths from the 1st and the 9th problem-example pair. The 1st and 9th problem were paired with a high-similarity example in the fade-out condition and a low-similarity example in the fade-in condition. Thus, comparing scanpaths from the 1st problem in each condition allowed us to analyze the effect of problem-example similarity, before any impact of condition took place. Since the two conditions involved a different structuring of assistance (fade in vs. fade out), analyzing scanpaths from the 9th problem-example pair, with the analysis from the 1st pair serving as the baseline, allowed us to investigate the impact of assistance on how problem 9 was solved.

Method. We followed the standard method [9, 17] to analyze the data. We extracted the scanpaths for each problem-example pair per participant in each condition (we capped the scanpath length at 500 fixations to make the analysis feasible; the majority of scanpaths were shorter). We then used MultiMatch to compare all possible pairs of scanpaths (a) *within* a given condition; (b) *between* the two conditions. Each comparison produces one similarity score for each of the 5 MultiMatch features. If students are using a different strategy in the *fade-in* and *fade-out* conditions, then the average scanpath similarity score from *fade-in* condition should be different from *fade-out* condition. However, if the similarity scores are about the same for the *fade-in* and *fade-out* conditions, this shows students are consistent in processing the material *within* each condition, but we don't know if they are using the same strategy in the two conditions. In this case, we also need to compare *between* conditions to obtain a benchmark for the within analyses (for details on this methodology, see [9, 17]). The final step involved analyzing the data using inferential statistics. This analysis is at the *similarity-score* level and so does not violate the independence assumption because each data point corresponds to a participant$_i$-participant$_j$ score that only appears once in the overall analysis (this strategy was used in prior work [17]).

3   Results and Discussion

Recall that MultiMatch produces 5 similarity scores per scanpath-pair comparison, one per feature (shape, direction, length position, duration). The similarity scores range between 0 and 1 (higher = more similar). MultiMatch produces high scores [17] and so the relative difference in scores is more informative than raw scores. We had 3 groups, based on similarity scores from comparing scanpaths *within* the fade-in condition (Sim$_{fade\ in}$), *within* the fade-out condition (Sim$_{fade\ out}$) and *between* the two conditions (Sim$_{between}$). Thus, we used an ANOVA with *comparison group* as the 3-level factor.

Analysis 1. Analysis 1 focused on scanpaths extracted from the first problem-example pair in each condition. The descriptives for the main statistics are in Table 1. The ANOVA on the similarity scores reported significant results for two MultiMatch features: direction, $F(2, 663) = 10.11$, $p < 0.01$, and shape, $F(2, 663) = 50.72$, $p < 0.01$. For direction, pairwise comparisons showed that Sim$_{fade\ out}$ > Sim$_{fade\ in}$ ($p < .01$). Since for problem 1, the *fade-out* group had a high similarity problem-example pair and the *fade-in* group had a low similarity pair, this result shows that scanpaths are more similar when students are given high-similarity examples. While for shape there was also a significant effect of condition, the raw effect size was small. Moreover, scanpaths were significantly different between the conditions, showing that problem-example similarity influenced how students viewed the problem and the example. (The two pairwise comparisons involving Sim$_{between}$ were also significant, but these are not as informative given the significant difference between Sim$_{fade\ in}$ and Sim$_{fade\ out}$).

Analysis 2. The second analysis focused on problem 9. By the time problem 9 was encountered, participants had experienced the effect of assistance type (fade in vs. fade out). Importantly, at problem 9, the corresponding example had the same similarity as for problem 1, and so problem 1 served as a baseline. Descriptives are in Table 1. Because we used problem 1 as the baseline, we ran the analysis on the similarity difference scores (problem 9 – problem 1). The ANOVA reported significant results for 3 MultiMatch features: length, $F(2, 627) = 4.8$, $p < 0.01$, position, $F(2, 627) = 10.8$, $p < 0.01$, and duration, $F(2, 627) = 3.5$, $p = 0.03$. Pairwise comparisons for each

Table 1. Descriptives (mean, stDev) for MultiMatch features. For problems 1 and 9, assistance was low for the fade-in group and high for the fade-out group.

	Shape	Direction	Length	Position	Duration
Problem 1					
fade in	.9873 (.002)	.7506 (.066)	.9851 (.003)	.9163 (.039)	.6627 (.032)
fade out	.9847 (.003)	.7765 (.037)	.9843 (.003)	.9107 (.038)	.6676 (.032)
Problem 9					
fade in	.9866 (.002)	.7374 (.126)	.9842 (.004)	.9181 (.035)	.6738 (.040)
fade out	.9840 (.003)	.7865 (.043)	.9818 (.005)	.8947 (.046)	.6721 (.037)

feature were significant ($p < .01$). For length and position, the difference in similarity scores from problem 1 to problem 9 was significantly greater for the *fade-out* group. This is reflected in the descriptives: for the fade-out group, the average similarity score is bigger for problem 9 than problem 1 for these features, while for the fade-in group, the average similarity score is virtually identical for problem 1 and problem 9. The duration feature, however, demonstrated the opposite pattern with significantly higher change in similarity scores for the *fade-in* group than the *fade-out* group.

To summarize, we found that (1) problem-example similarity affects scanpaths (analysis 1); and type of assistance affects scanpaths (analysis 2). As far as analysis 1, our results confirm prior work showing that difficulty reduces scanpath similarity [17]. The low similarity problem-example pair in the *fade-in* condition was more difficult because it blocked copying of the example (an easy strategy) and so required problem solving (a harder strategy). Analysis 2 examined how assistance influenced change in scanpaths. When the problem-solving session started with low similarity problem-example pairs (*fade-in* group), students were blocked from copying the example solutions. The original analysis [16] found that students subsequently viewed the problem more than the *fade-out* group. Thus, the fade-in group's strategy corresponded to attention to the problem - the present analysis suggests this strategy remained stable over time for the length and position features (there was little difference in scanpaths between problem 1 and 9 for these features). In contrast, for these features, the *fade-out* group's scanpaths changed over time (similarity higher at problem 9 than problem 1), suggesting this group may have started out with one strategy (copying from the high similarity examples they initially received) but revising this strategy when assistance faded out.

Our results show effects for distinct MultiMatch features. Space constraints prevent us from in-depth discussion, but we offer brief interpretations. For analysis 1, direction was one of the informative features. Similarity should be low for this feature when saccades are moving in opposite directions from each other in the target scanpaths. This was occurring more in the *fade-in* group who had the low-similarity example, as the similarity for direction was lower than the *fade-out* group who had the high-similarity example. Thus, type of example influenced the direction of saccades. Additionally, we speculate that length and position, significant for analysis 2, relate to the location of the gaze. Since the *fade-out* group had reduced similarity for these features on problem 9 compared to problem 1, we can speculate they changed their strategy in terms of what they looked at. The implication of our work is that scanpath analysis can identify differences in visual attention for problem-solving tasks. However, more work is needed to identify the benefits and limitations of a scanpath approach.

Acknowledgements. This work was supported with an NSERC Discovery Grant 1507.

References

1. Hutt, S., Mills, C., White, S., Donnelly, P.J., D'Mello, S.: The eyes have it: gaze-based detection of mind wandering during learning with an intelligent tutoring system. In: Proceedings of the 9th International Conference on Educational Data Mining (EDM 2016), pp. 86–93 (2016)
2. Muldner, K., Burleson, B., VanLehn, K.: "Yes!": using tutor and sensor data to predict moments of delight during instructional activities. In: Proceedings of User Modeling, Adaptation and Personalization Conference, pp. 159–170 (2010)
3. Taub, M., Azevedo, R.: How does prior knowledge influence eye fixations and sequences of cognitive and metacognitive SRL processes during learning with an intelligent tutoring system? Int. J. Artif. Intell. Educ. 29(1), 1–28 (2019)
4. Lai, M.L., Tsai, M., et al.: A review of using eye-tracking technology in exploring learning from 2000 to 2012. Educ. Res. Rev. 10, 90–115 (2013)
5. Anderson, N.C., Anderson, F., Kingstone, A., et al.: A comparison of scanpath comparison methods. Behav. Res. 47, 1377–1392 (2015)
6. Steichen, B., Wu, M., Toker, D., Conati C., Carenini, G.: Te, Te, Hi, Hi: eye gaze sequence analysis for informing user-adaptive information visualizations. In: Proceedings of UMAP 2014, pp. 133–144 (2014)
7. Dewhurst, R., Nyström, M., Jarodzka, H., Foulsham, T., Johansson, R., Holmqvist, K.: It depends on how you look at it: scanpath comparison in multiple dimensions with MultiMatch, a vector-based approach. Behav. Res. Methods 44(4), 1079–1100 (2012)
8. Foulsham, T., Underwood, G.: What can saliency models predict about eye movements? Spatial and sequential aspects of fixations during encoding and recognition. J. Vis. 8(2), 6 (2008)
9. Zhou, L., Zhang, Y., et al.: A scanpath analysis of the risky decision-making process. J. Behav. Dec. Making 29(2–3), 169–182 (2016)
10. Von der Malsburg, T., Angele, B.: False positives and other statistical errors in standard analyses of eye movements in reading. J. Mem. Lang. 94, 119–133 (2017)
11. French, R., Glady, Y., Thibaut, J.: An evaluation of scanpath-comparison and machine-learning classification algorithms used to study the dynamics of analogy making. Behav. Res. Methods 49(4), 1291–1302 (2017)
12. Lai, M.L., et al.: A review of using eye-tracking technology in exploring learning from 2000 to 2012. Educ. Res. Rev. 10, 90–115 (2013)
13. Chi, M.T.H., Bassok, M., Lewis, M., Reimann, P., Glaser, R.: Self- explanations: How students study and use examples in learning to solve problems. Cogn. Sci. 13, 145–182 (1989)
14. VanLehn, K.: Analogy events: how examples are used during problem solving. Cogn. Sci. 22(3), 347–388 (1998)
15. VanLehn, K.: Rule-learning events in the acquisition of a complex skill: an evaluation of cascade. J. Learn. Sci. 8(1), 71–125 (1999)

16. Jennings, J., Muldner, K.: From dissimilar to similar: reverse fading assistance improves learning. In: Proceedings of the Cognitive Science Society, pp. 560–566 (2018)

17. Dewhurst, R., Foulsham, T., Jarodzka, H., Johansson, R., Nyström, M.: How task demands influence scanpath similarity in a sequential number-search task. Vision. Res. **149**, 9–23 (2018)

Helping Teachers Assist Their Students in Gamified Adaptive Educational Systems: Towards a Gamification Analytics Tool

Kamilla Tenório[iD], Geiser Chalco Challco, Diego Dermeval[(✉)][iD],
Bruno Lemos, Pedro Nascimento, Rodrigo Santos, and Alan Pedro da Silva

Federal University of Alagoas, Maceió, AL 57072-900, Brazil
{kktas,bll,phbn,rss3,alanpedro}@ic.ufal.br, geiser.gcc@gmail.com,
diego.matos@famed.ufal.br

Abstract. In this paper, we present the results of a case study conducted to validate the effectiveness of our gamification analytics model for teachers proposed in [20]. To conduct this case study, we developed a tool to monitor and adapt gamification designs in gamified adaptive educational systems. Employing this tool, the case study was conducted in a real situation, and the findings suggest that the use of our model and tool improves students' engagement, learning outcomes, and motivation.

Keywords: Adaptive learning systems · Gamification · Gamification analytics

1 Introduction

Gamification is pointed out as a valuable approach to improve students' engagement, motivation, and learning outcomes [1,2,6,13,15]. However, previous studies reported that using gamification in educational technologies does not always assure the expected results' achievement [5,8,14,18]. A promising solution to maximise the gamification benefits is to monitor users' behaviour in the gamified environment and adapt its gamification design when the expected outcomes are not achieved [9,10]. This approach is named gamification analytics and it was defined by Heilbrunn, Herzig, and Schill [10] as "the data-driven processes of monitoring and adapting gamification designs".

Nevertheless, there is a lack of studies that apply the gamification analytics approach in education, and, particularly, in the AIED field [3,9,21]. Therefore, we propose a gamification analytics model for teachers to support them in the process of monitoring the impact of gamification in gamified adaptive learning systems, and adapt the gamification design when considered necessary. Based on this model, a tool was developed, and a case study was conducted to investigate the impact of the use by teachers of the model through the proposed tool regarding students' engagement, learning, and motivation.

I. I. Bittencourt et al. (Eds.): AIED 2020, LNAI 12164, pp. 312–317, 2020.
https://doi.org/10.1007/978-3-030-52240-7_57

2 Gamification Analytics Model for Teachers and GamAnalytics Tool

In the Gamification Analytics Model, teachers may define interaction goals they expect their students achieve, and monitor, during the learning process, if the interaction goals are being achieved through the visualisation of students' interaction with the system's learning resources and game elements. If the outcome is not as expected, teachers may adapt the gamification design through the creation of missions. GamAnalytics is a gamification analytics model-based tool, and the design concepts implemented in the GamAnalytics tool were validated with teachers with respect to their needs and opinions [20]. GamAnalytics tool is integrated to a gamified adaptive educational environment, named Avance (https://avance.eyeduc.com/). This tool includes a class' dashboard and an individual student's dashboard. In the class' dashboard, there are visualisations shown through descriptive data and graphs for each topic of a course, such as number of students registered in the course; the period expected for students to achieve the interaction goals; the class' progress over time in relation to interaction with learning resources; the number and names of students that achieved or not the interaction goals; the number and names of the students that interacted (with success or not) with each learning resource; the number and names of the students that are in each level of gamification. In the individual student's dashboard, there are more visualisations, such as student' basic info; student's gamification info such as points, current level, and position in the ranking; student's progress over time in relation to interaction with learning resources; and student's interaction with each learning resource (see Fig. 1).

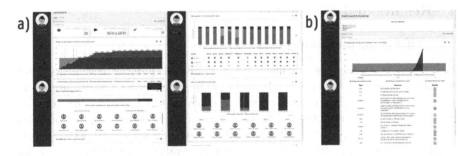

Fig. 1. GamAnalytics Tool: Class (a) and individual (b) students' dashboards showing the topic's interaction goals, students' interaction with resources, and game elements.

3 Method

A case study is conducted to explore the impact of the use by teachers of the gamification analytics model through the GamAnalytics tool regarding students' engagement, learning, and motivation. Ten undergraduate and graduate students of the Federal University of Alagoas enrolled in the *"Gamification in Education"* course are considered in this case study. This study took place for four weeks, which was the expected time for students to master the "Framework, models and processes" and the "Gamiflow" topics.

To conduct the case study, the GamAnalytics tool integrated into the gamified adaptive educational environment (Avance) was used. First, the teacher defined the interaction goals that he expected students to achieve for the domain of each topic (e.g., it was expected that students interact at least with 60% of the resources of the "Gamiflow" topic in 3 weeks). After the teacher's preparation, students completed a demographic questionnaire, and answered the informed consent form. Students also answered a pre-test, reviewed by the teacher, of the two topics. Pre-tests were planned according to the levels of the revised Bloom taxonomy [12] to be balanced with the post-tests.

Afterwards, students started using Avance, and the teacher could visualise students' data through the GamAnalytics tool. When the teacher realised that the outcomes were not as expected, he assigned missions to groups or to a specific student through sending emails. In the email, teacher indicated the expected period of time for the mission, reward, and the set of resources that students should interact to achieve the sent mission. After that, he could visualise the impact of the intervention through the GamAnalytics. For each topic, teachers created 3 different missions depending on students' interaction. At the end, students answered the post-tests, the IMI (*Intrinsic Motivation Inventory*) [7,16,17] and IMMS questionnaires (*Instructional Materials Motivation Survey*) [11,19] to measure participants' motivation – questionnaires validated in the Portuguese language [4].

4   Results and Discussion

4.1   Effects on Engagement

To investigate students' engagement, we measured the number of students' interaction with each topic's resources before and after the teacher's intervention (creation of missions). The results (from Shapiro-Wilk test for normality) indicate that the data concerning the two topics are not from a normal population (First topic: $W = 0.594$, p-value $= 0.000047$; $W = 0.618$, p-value $= 0.000091$/Second Topic: $W = 0.432$, p-value $= 0.020$; $W = 0.432$, p-value $= 0.000058$ – before and after the intervention respectively). A non-parametric Wilcoxon signed-rank test was performed to compare the number of students' interaction before and after the intervention. Concerning the first topic, the Wilcoxon signed-rank test indicates a statistically significant difference ($Z = -2.121$, p-value $= 0.034$) between the number of interactions before and after the teacher's intervention. For the second topic, the test's results also indicated a statistically significant difference ($Z = -2.214$, p-value $= 0.027$) between the number of interactions before and after the intervention. Therefore, students increased significantly their interaction with the resources of the two topics after the teacher's intervention based on the monitoring of students' information, suggesting that students have improved their interaction with the system after teachers intervention.

4.2 Effects on Learning

The results of the pre- and pos-tests taken by students before and after the domain of each topic learned were used to measure the impact on students' learning. Results from a Shapiro-Wilk test show that the data may come from a normal distribution – First topic: $W = 0.965$, p-value $= 0.843$ (pre-test); $W = 0.932$, p-value $= 0.473$ (post-test)/Second topic: $W = 0.909$, p-value $= 0.271$ (pre-test); $W = 0.916$, p-value $= 0.325$ (post-test). A t-test was performed, which indicates that there is a statistically significant difference between the scores of the first topic $(t(9) = -4.116$, p-value $= 0.003)$ and of the second topic $(t(9) = -2.449$, p-value $= 0.037)$. Therefore, our results might suggest that students have improved their understanding on both topics of the "Gamification in Education" course after interacting with resources sent by teachers through missions.

4.3 Effects on Motivation

At the end of each topic, the IMI and IMMS questionnaires were answered by the participants (7-point Likert scale). The internal consistency of all IMI and IMMS questionnaires' subscales was greater than .70. Concerning the IMI questionnaire, the mean overall intrinsic motivation score for the "Frameworks, Models and Process" topic was 4.52. Concerning the second topic, the mean overall intrinsic motivation score for the "Gamiflow" topic was 4.63. These results may suggest that students were more intrinsically than extrinsically motivated during the intervention in the two topics. Concerning the IMMS questionnaire, in the first topic, note that the mean overall motivation level score was 5.19. Whereas, in the second topic, the mean overall motivation level score during the teaching was 4.95. In summary, our results might suggest that the students were motivated (intrinsically and extrinsically) during the intervention in the "Frameworks, Models and Process" and "Gamiflow" topics.

5   Conclusion

In this work, we conducted a case study to validate the impact of a gamification analytics model for teachers to monitor and adapt gamification design for students during the learning process. Our results might suggest that a gamification analytics tools based on this model impacts positively on students' learning, engagement, and motivation – which are of utmost importance since it also shows that teachers may be active users of gamified adaptive learning systems with the aid of gamification learning analytics. As teachers may monitor and adapt gamification design according to how students or groups of students interact with an adaptive system, teachers could be more effective to make opportunistic pedagogical decisions (informed by gamification analytics) that may lead to an increase in learning, engagement, and motivation of the students.

References

1. Bicen, H., Kocakoyun, S.: Perceptions of students for gamification approach: Kahoot as a case study. Int. J. Emerging Technol. Learn. **13**(2), 72–93 (2018). https://doi.org/10.3991/ijet.v13i02.7467
2. Borras-Gene, O., Martinez-Nunez, M., Blanco, A.: New challenges for the motivation and learning in engineering education using gamification in MOOC. Int. J. Eng. Educ. **32**(1), 501–512 (2016). https://www.ijee.ie/contents/c320116B.html
3. Calderón, A., Boubeta-Puig, J., Ruiz, M.: MEdit4CEP-Gam: a model-driven approach for user-friendly gamification design, monitoring and code generation in CEP-based systems. Inf. Softw. Technol. **95**, 238–264 (2018). https://doi.org/10.1016/j.infsof.2017.11.009
4. Chalco, G., Isotani, S.: Gamification of collaborative learning scenarios: an ontological engineering approach to deal with motivational problems in scripted collaborative learning. In: Anais dos Workshops do Congresso Brasileiro de Informática na Educação. vol. 8, p. 981 (2019)
5. Domínguez, A., Saenz-de Navarrete, J., de Marcos, L., Fernández-Sanz, L., Pagés, C., Martínez-Herráiz, J.J.: Gamifying learning experiences: practical implications and outcomes. Comput. Educ. **63**, 380–392 (2013). https://doi.org/10.1016/j.compedu.2012.12.020
6. Fotaris, P., Mastoras, T., Leinfellner, R., Rosunally, Y.: Climbing up the leaderboard: an empirical study of applying gamification techniques to a computer programming class. Technical report (2016)
7. Grolnick, W.S., Ryan, R.M.: Autonomy in children's learning: an experimental and individual difference investigation. J. Pers. Soc. Psychol. **52**(5), 890–898 (1987). https://doi.org/10.1037/0022-3514.52.5.890
8. Hanus, M.D., Fox, J.: Assessing the effects of gamification in the classroom: a longitudinal study on intrinsic motivation, social comparison, satisfaction, effort, and academic performance. Comput. Educ. **80**, 152–161 (2015). https://doi.org/10.1016/j.compedu.2014.08.019
9. Heilbrunn, B., Herzig, P., Schill, A.: Tools for gamification analytics: a survey. In: 2014 IEEE/ACM 7th International Conference on Utility and Cloud Computing, pp. 603–608 (2014). https://doi.org/10.1109/UCC.2014.93
10. Heilbrunn, B., Herzig, P., Schill, A.: Gamification analytics—methods and tools for monitoring and adapting gamification designs. In: Stieglitz, S., Lattemann, C., Robra-Bissantz, S., Zarnekow, R., Brockmann, T. (eds.) Gamification. PI, pp. 31–47. Springer, Cham (2017). https://doi.org/10.1007/978-3-319-45557-0_3
11. Keller, J.M.: Development and use of the ARCS model of instructional design. J. Instruc. Dev. **10**(3), 2–10 (1987). https://doi.org/10.1007/BF02905780
12. Krathwohl, D.R.: A revision of bloom's taxonomy: an overview (2002). https://doi.org/10.1207/s15430421tip4104_2
13. Latulipe, C., Long, N.B., Seminario, C.E.: Structuring flipped classes with lightweight teams and gamification. In: Proceedings of the 46th ACM Technical Symposium on Computer Science Education, SIGCSE 2015, pp. 392–397. ACM, New York (2015). https://doi.org/10.1145/2676723.2677240
14. Orhan Göksün, D., Gürsoy, G.: Comparing success and engagement in gamified learning experiences via Kahoot and Quizizz. Comput. Educ. **135**, 15–29 (2019). https://doi.org/10.1016/j.compedu.2019.02.015

15. Paiva, R., Bittencourt, I.I., Tenrio, T., Jaques, P., Isotani, S.: What do students do on-line? modeling students' interactions to improve their learning experience. Comput. Hum. Behav. **64**(C), 769–781 (2016). https://doi.org/10.1016/j.chb.2016.07.048

16. Ryan, R.M., Connell, J.P.: Perceived locus of causality and internalization: examining reasons for acting in two domains. J. Pers. Soc. Psychol. **57**(5), 749–761 (1989). https://doi.org/10.1037/0022-3514.57.5.749

17. Ryan, R.M., Mims, V., Koestner, R.: Relation of reward contingency and interpersonal context to intrinsic motivation: a review and test using cognitive evaluation theory. J. Pers. Soc. Psychol. **45**(4), 736–750 (1983). https://doi.org/10.1037/0022-3514.45.4.736

18. Snow, E.L., Allen, L.K., Jackson, G.T., McNamara, D.S.: Spendency: students' propensity to use system currency. Int. J. Artif. Intell. Educ. **25**(3), 407–427 (2015). https://doi.org/10.1007/s40593-015-0044-1

19. Song, S.H., Keller, J.M.: Effectiveness of motivationally adaptive computer-assisted instruction on the dynamic aspects of motivation. Educ. Tech. Res. Dev. **49**(2), 5–22 (2001). https://doi.org/10.1007/BF02504925

20. Tenorio, K., Dermeval, D., Monteiro, M., Peixoto, A., Da Silva, A.P.: Raising teachers empowerment in gamification design of adaptive learning systems: a qualitative research. In: Proceedings of the International Conference on Artificial Intelligence in Education (to be published). Morocco (2020)

21. Trinidad, M., Calderón, A., Ruiz, M.: A systematic literature review on the gamification monitoring phase: how SPI standards can contribute to gamification maturity. In: Stamelos, I., O'Connor, R.V., Rout, T., Dorling, A. (eds.) SPICE 2018. CCIS, vol. 918, pp. 31–44. Springer, Cham (2018). https://doi.org/10.1007/978-3-030-00623-5_3

Understanding Rapport over Multiple Sessions with a Social, Teachable Robot

Xiaoyi Tian[1(✉)], Nichola Lubold[2], Leah Friedman[3], and Erin Walker[1]

[1] University of Pittsburgh, Pittsburgh, PA, USA
{xiaoyi-tian,eawalker}@pitt.edu
[2] Arizona State University, Tempe, AZ, USA
nlubold@asu.edu
[3] University of Pennsylvania, Philadelphia, PA, USA
leahf@pitt.edu

Abstract. Social robots have been shown to be effective educational tools. Rapport, or interpersonal closeness, can lead to better human-robot interactions and positive learning outcomes. Prior research has investigated the effects of social robots on student rapport and learning in a single session, but little is known about how individuals build rapport with a robot over multiple sessions. We reported on a case study in which 7 middle school students explained mathematics concepts to an intelligent teachable robot named Emma for five sessions. We modeled learners' rapport-building linguistic strategies to understand whether the ways middle school students build rapport with the robot over time follow the same trends as human conversation, and how individual differences might mediate the rapport between human and robot.

Keywords: Human-robot interaction · Multiple sessions interaction · Rapport · Case study · Long-term hri

1 Introduction

Intelligent social robots have been shown to have positive effects on learning and motivational outcomes [5,12,15] in part because of the socio-emotional support they provide [9,11,12]. One mechanism that may contribute to these positive effects is the rapport, or feeling of connection, that social robots engender with their human collaborators. However, over time, the nature of the relationship between the human and robot might shift (as human-human relationships do), and the importance of rapport may change [19]. Most research on human-robot rapport has been done in single-session studies [9,13,14], and has rarely investigated how learners develop and maintain rapport with a robot. Understanding how children build and maintain relationships during multiple encounters would help maintain engagement and personalize long-term learning experiences.

A widely-accepted human-human rapport framework comes from Tickle-Degnen and Rosenthal's three-factor theory [19], which includes mutual attention, positivity, and coordination. People start building rapport by expressing

© Springer Nature Switzerland AG 2020
I. I. Bittencourt et al. (Eds.): AIED 2020, LNAI 12164, pp. 318–323, 2020.
https://doi.org/10.1007/978-3-030-52240-7_58

mutual attentiveness and interests towards one another. High positivity plays a role in generating a feeling of mutual friendliness and warmth, but in the initial stage of an interaction, there may be less coordination (interlocutors are "in sync" with one another). Over the long term, positivity decreases, coordination increases, and mutual attentiveness remains stable. It's not clear that the same phenomena can be observed in human-robot settings. Thus, our study aims to understand how students verbally build and maintain rapport with a robot in multiple sessions. We conducted an exploratory analysis of 7 middle school students interacting with a social teachable robot over 5 sessions. Our research question was: How do students differ from each other and differ from early to late interaction stages in the way that they build rapport with a teachable robot?

2   Multi-session Study

For this study, a Nao robot named Emma was taught by middle school students how to solve mathematics problems utilizing spoken language [10]. Students sat at a desk with a Surface Pro tablet in front of them. Emma stood on the desk to the right of the participant. Table 1 is an example of exchange between Emma and a learner on a ratio and proportions problem. More details on the system design can be found in [10]. Over multiple sessions, Emma mimicked the [19]'s model of rapport as follows. To implement coordination, we utilized an acoustic-prosodic entrainment module [9], which transforms Emma's utterances to converge to the user's pitch. Entrainment increased over the five sessions. Emma exhibited higher positivity in the initial sessions by exhibiting greater politeness and enthusiastic language (e.g., "Great! Thank you for teaching me") than in later sessions. We operationalized attention as gaze behavior, and did not change Emma's default gaze behavior throughout the sessions.

Table 1. Example dialogue between Emma and a learner, coded with conversational strategies.

Emma:	Interesting. Why do you think *we*[inclusive] do that?
Learner:	Because it's going to be equivalent[responsive]...so that means two times two equals[ask question]?
Emma:	Sweet. I think I get it. *we*[inclusive] multiply two times two, so then is four the answer?
Learner:	Yes, *Emma*[name]. That's correct.

Participants were 7 middle-school students (4 females, 3 males). The mean age was 12.7. Each participant interacted with Emma for five 30-min sessions over several weeks. We grouped session 1, 2 and 3 as early interaction stages, and sessions 4 and 5 as late stages. Participants solved 4–6 problems during each study session, resulting in 186 independent problems in the corpus.

Each problem contains 10.06 user utterances on average. Two coders manually coded conversational strategies indicating behavioral rapport in each utterance in the human-robot tutoring dialogue (Cohen's kappa of all codes was higher than 0.8). The strategies consisted of *off-topic chat, inclusive pronouns (e.g., use of "we" vs "I"), use of Emma's name, praise, apology, refer to past experience, ask a question, respond to Emma's prompt, and adherence to social norms*, drawn from both human-human and human-robot rapport studies [1,3,7,8,17,20]. Example of codes can be found in Table 1. To supplement our manual codes, we incorporated automatic linguistic feature detection using the 2015 LIWC [16] summary language variables (analytical thinking, clout, authenticity, and emotional tone).

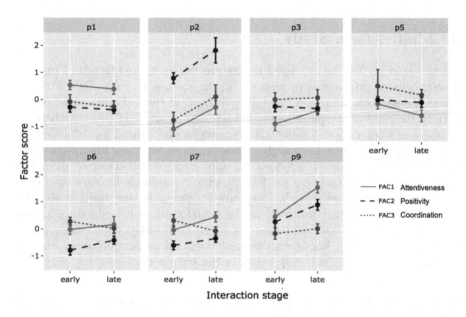

Fig. 1. Rapport factors (with standard errors) across 5 sessions separate by all seven participants. Each factor score across all participant problems has zero mean and unit standard deviation.

We used an Independent Component Analysis (ICA) to map strategies to three rapport factors, revealing how particular behaviors are used as ways of expressing and managing the underlying rapport-building constructs with the robot [2,4]. Linguistic strategies that strongly loaded on factor 1 were *inclusive language, name usage, apology,* and *clout,* and we interpret the factor as **attentiveness**. *Name usage, praise, authenticity* and *emotional tone* were loaded in factor 2, and we interpret this as **positivity**. Markers of off-task coordination load strongly positively on factor 3 (*chat* and *adhere norm*), while markers of on-task coordination load strongly negatively (*responsiveness* and *ask question*). Nevertheless, we do interpret this factor to represent **coordination**, with on-task and off-task coordination interestingly being negatively related. Finally, the *ask question* and *refer to past experience* loaded evenly amongst all factors.

Our next step was to understand how rapport varies from early stage to late stage of interaction. From our ICA model, we computed the source matrix for the 3 extracted rapport components for each 186 participant-problem pair, and aggregated the mean rapport score across all problems in each interaction stage. The results are represented in Fig. 1. We can observe that **attentiveness** went up across the majority of participants. **Positivity** appeared to vary from participant to participant, with some individuals who started from a high score seeing dramatic increases (p2 and p9). **Coordination** decreased in four out of seven learners with large variations (e.g., p5). It is worthy to note that, a decrease in coordination score meant more on-task behaviors, and thus coordination was the only factor to align with human-human rapport theory.

Based on learners' rapport trends and their degree of variation, we clustered them into groups. The *flat* cluster including p1, p3, p6 and p7 tended to adopt one favorable strategy at the beginning of interaction and stick with it over the course of the sessions. These users did not sense their interaction mode changes over time ("At first I already feel how I was with Emma, I just kept that going with the routine." -p6). P2 and p9 were grouped as an *increasing* cluster and p5 as a single *decreasing* case. These users had not interacted with a robot or AI system before but had different expectations and perceptions towards Emma. For example, p2 believed Emma is more friendly than robots he saw in movies. Over the sessions, p2 praised Emma more (frequency from 2% to 8%) and his apologizing behavior disappeared. Similarly, p9 stopped *asking questions* in later sessions. The disappearance of social strategies means the student started to adhere to a "personal norm" (non-apology, no questions) rather than socio-cultural norms [18]. This is a sign that the relationship between "increasing" participants and Emma had moved to more friend-like [20] dyads. On the other hand p5, the decreasing case, had a low expectation of Emma's intelligence and socialness ("She's a robot...I don't think she would have background information or whatever.").

It is important to note that participants' behaviors from session to session are not only due to their rapport states, but also to contextual factors such as energy or mood. For example, in session 3, p6 seldom offered further elaboration except for saying "Yes", seeming bored with the problems or upset on that study day. In session 5, he was very engaged in the task, and was more wordy and responsive ("Yes, but we also can convert it into a decimal, which is 0.125.").

3   Discussion

Our goal was to investigate how middle school learners manage rapport with robots over multiple tutoring sessions. We demonstrated that rapport changes from early to late interaction stages in human-robot tutoring did not follow the same trends as human rapport theory [19]. The variation between individuals on positivity and the increase of attentiveness over time suggested that users may be shifting how they express rapport as their expectations of Emma change. This corresponded to the contrast between users with *flat* rapport trends, who tended to stick with the same linguistic strategies, and users with either *increasing* or *decreasing* rapport trends, who articulated evolving perceptions towards Emma. Given the cross-session variability of individuals and that the majority of rapport studies' focus on an "instant" rapport [6], it is critical to conduct multiple session studies to understand more about human-robot rapport dynamics. This work is a first step towards personalizing rapport-based learning experiences over long-term human robot interactions.

Acknowledgements. This work is supported by the National Robotics Initiative and the National Science Foundation, grant #CISE-IIS-1637809. We would like to thank Mesut Erhan Unal for his guidance in the ICA modeling process.

References

1. Ädel, A.: Rapport building in student group work. J. Pragmat. **43**(12), 2932–2947 (2011)
2. Beckmann, C.F., Smith, S.M.: Probabilistic independent component analysis for functional magnetic resonance imaging. IEEE Trans. Med. Imaging **23**(2), 137–152 (2004)
3. Bracewell, D.B., Tomlinson, M.T., Wang, H.: Identification of social acts in dialogue. Technical report, Language Computer Corporation Richardson United States (2012)
4. Delorme, A., Makeig, S.: Eeglab: an open source toolbox for analysis of single-trial eeg dynamics including independent component analysis. J. Neurosci. Methods **134**(1), 9–21 (2004)
5. Gordon, G., Breazeal, C., Engel, S.: Can children catch curiosity from a social robot? In: 2015 10th ACM/IEEE International Conference on Human-Robot Interaction (HRI), pp. 91–98. IEEE (2015)
6. Gratch, J., et al.: Virtual rapport. In: Gratch, J., Young, M., Aylett, R., Ballin, D., Olivier, P. (eds.) IVA 2006. LNCS (LNAI), vol. 4133, pp. 14–27. Springer, Heidelberg (2006). https://doi.org/10.1007/11821830_2
7. Gremler, D.D., Gwinner, K.P.: Rapport-building behaviors used by retail employees. J. Retail. **84**(3), 308–324 (2008)
8. Lakin, J.L., Chartrand, T.L.: Using nonconscious behavioral mimicry to create affiliation and rapport. Psychol. Sci. **14**(4), 334–339 (2003)
9. Lubold, N., Walker, E., Pon-Barry, H., Ogan, A.: Automated pitch convergence improves learning in a social, teachable robot for middle school mathematics. In: Penstein Rosé, C., et al. (eds.) AIED 2018. LNCS (LNAI), vol. 10947, pp. 282–296. Springer, Cham (2018). https://doi.org/10.1007/978-3-319-93843-1_21
10. Lubold, N., Walker, E., Pon-Barry, H., Ogan, A.: Comfort with robots influences rapport with a social, entraining teachable robot. In: Isotani, S., Millán, E., Ogan, A., Hastings, P., McLaren, B., Luckin, R. (eds.) AIED 2019. LNCS (LNAI), vol. 11625, pp. 231–243. Springer, Cham (2019). https://doi.org/10.1007/978-3-030-23204-7_20
11. McDaniel, B., D'Mello, S., King, B., Chipman, P., Tapp, K., Graesser, A.: Facial features for affective state detection in learning environments. In: Proceedings of the Annual Meeting of the Cognitive Science Society, vol. 29 (2007)

12. Michaelis, J.E., Mutlu, B.: Supporting interest in science learning with a social robot. In: Proceedings of the 18th ACM International Conference on Interaction Design and Children, pp. 71–82. ACM (2019)

13. Ogan, A., Finkelstein, S., Mayfield, E., D'Adamo, C., Matsuda, N., Cassell, J.: "Oh dear stacy!" social interaction, elaboration, and learning with teachable agents. In: Proceedings of the SIGCHI Conference on Human Factors in Computing Systems, pp. 39–48 (2012)

14. Ogan, A., Finkelstein, S., Walker, E., Carlson, R., Cassell, J.: Rudeness and rapport: insults and learning gains in peer tutoring. In: Cerri, S.A., Clancey, W.J., Papadourakis, G., Panourgia, K. (eds.) ITS 2012. LNCS, vol. 7315, pp. 11–21. Springer, Heidelberg (2012). https://doi.org/10.1007/978-3-642-30950-2_2

15. Park, H.W., Rosenberg-Kima, R., Rosenberg, M., Gordon, G., Breazeal, C.: Growing growth mindset with a social robot peer. In: 2017 12th ACM/IEEE International Conference on Human-Robot Interaction (HRI), pp. 137–145. IEEE (2017)

16. Pennebaker, J.W., Boyd, R.L., Jordan, K., Blackburn, K.: The development and psychometric properties of liwc2015. Technical report (2015)

17. Seo, S.H., Griffin, K., Young, J.E., Bunt, A., Prentice, S., Loureiro-Rodríguez, V.: Investigating people's rapport building and hindering behaviors when working with a collaborative robot. Int. J. Social Robot. **10**(1), 147–161 (2018)

18. Spencer-Oatey, H.: (Im) politeness, face and perceptions of rapport: unpackaging their bases and interrelationships (2005)

19. Tickle-Degnen, L., Rosenthal, R.: The nature of rapport and its nonverbal correlates. Psychol. Inq. **1**(4), 285–293 (1990)

20. Zhao, R., Papangelis, A., Cassell, J.: Towards a dyadic computational model of rapport management for human-virtual agent interaction. In: Bickmore, T., Marsella, S., Sidner, C. (eds.) IVA 2014. LNCS (LNAI), vol. 8637, pp. 514–527. Springer, Cham (2014). https://doi.org/10.1007/978-3-319-09767-1_62

Exercise Hierarchical Feature Enhanced Knowledge Tracing

Hanshuang Tong[(✉)], Yun Zhou, and Zhen Wang

AIXUEXI Education Group Ltd., AI Lab, Beijing, China
tonghanshuang2018@163.com, zhouyun.nudt@gmail.com, WangZhen__00@163.com

Abstract. Knowledge tracing is a fundamental task in the computer-aid educational system. In this paper, we propose a hierarchical exercise feature enhanced knowledge tracing framework, which could enhance the ability of knowledge tracing by incorporating knowledge distribution, semantic features, and difficulty features from exercise text. Extensive experiments show the high performance of our framework.

Keywords: Knowledge tracing · Intelligent education · Deep learning

1 Introduction

Knowledge tracing is an essential and classical problem in intelligent education systems. By tracing the knowledge transition process, we could recommend specific educational items to a student based on one's weak knowledge. Existing methods try to solve knowledge tracing problems from both educational psychology and data mining perspectives, such as Item Response Theory (IRT) [7], Bayesian Knowledge Tracing (BKT) [1], Performance Factors Analysis (PFA) framework [9] and Deep knowledge tracing (DKT) [10]. Those models have been proved effective but still have limitations. They do not systematically consider the impact of different attributes of the exercises itself on the knowledge tracing problem. Exercise Enhanced Knowledge Tracing (EKT) [5] is the first method to take exercise text and attention mechanism into consideration. However, EKT extracts features of text by feeding the text of exercise directly into a neural network, which fails to extract hierarchical features from exercise (Fig. 1).

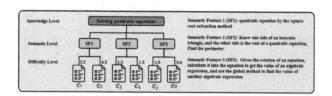

Fig. 1. The illustration of hierarchical features of exercise

I. I. Bittencourt et al. (Eds.): AIED 2020, LNAI 12164, pp. 324–328, 2020.
https://doi.org/10.1007/978-3-030-52240-7_59

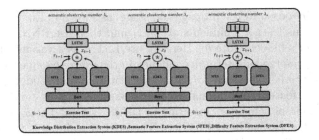

Fig. 2. Exercise hierarchical feature enhanced framework.

2 Exercise Hierarchical Feature Enhanced Framework

Framework Overview. Knowledge tracing task can be summarized as: In an online educational system, suppose we have M students and E exercises in total. Given any learners' exercise record $E = \{(q_1, r_1), (q_2, r_2) \ldots (q_m, r_m)\}$, predict one's performance on q_{t+1}. Here (q_t, r_t) represents that a learner practices question q_t and answers r_t at step t. The entire structure of the framework is shown in Fig. 2. In order to dig deeper into the information in the exercise text, first we utilize Bert [2] to generate embedding vector v_b. Then we feed them into three systems to generate knowledge distribution $v_t \in R^K$, semantic features s_t and question difficulty d_t separately. Let $\varphi(s_t)$ be the one-hot encoding of the semantic cluster where the question belongs at time t. Finally, we concatenate v_t, $\varphi(s_t)$, d_t, and r_t as x_t and feed x_t into a sequence model.

Subsystems Introduction. Two text classification systems, named KDES and DFES, are designed to predict the knowledge distribution and difficulty of the exercise respectively. The semantic feature extractor system (SFES) could be considered as an unsuperviesed clusering problems. The input of those systems is the Bert encoding of the exercise text. The knowledge labeled by teacher and the correct rate of a question [4] serve as ground truth and are predicted using TextCNN [8] in KDES and DFES systems. In KDES system, we use softmax results classified in the trained model to represent the knowledge distribution of an exercise. In DFES systems, we use neural networks to predict difficulty in order to solve the cold start problem. In SFES systems, we cluster the input using a Hierarchical Clustering method by calculating the cos distance between different semantic vectors [6].

$$h_t, c_t = LSTM(x_t, h_{t-1}, c_{t-1}; \theta_t) \tag{1}$$

$$y_t = \sigma(W_{yh} \cdot h_t + b_y) \tag{2}$$

$$loss = -\sum_t (r_{l+1} * log(y_i^T \cdot \varphi(s_{t+1})) + (1 - r_{t+1}) * log(1 - y_i^T \cdot \varphi(s_{t+1}))) \tag{3}$$

Modeling Process. In the propagation stage, as shown in Eq. 1, we process x_t and the previous learner's hidden state h_{t-1} and then use RNN network to get current learner's hidden state h_t. Here we use LSTM as a variant of RNN since it can better preserve long-term dependency in the exercise sequence [3]. Finally, we use h_t to predict y_t which contains information about students' mastery of each semantic feature. Additionally, the dimension of y_t is same as the total number of different semantic clustering in DFES system. The θ_t, W_{yh}, b_y in the equation are the parameters of models. The goal of training is to minimize the negative log likelihood of the observed sequence of student response logs (shown in Eq. 3).

3 Experiment

3.1 Experimental Setting

Since there is no open dataset which could provide exercising records with text information. We derive an experimental dataset containing 132,179 students and 91,449,914 answer records from a large real-world online education system: aix-uexi.com.

The baselines of the experiments are as following: BKT, which is based on Bayesian inference; DKT, which uses recurrent neural networks to model student learning; EKTA, which incoporate exercise text features and attention mechanism into the recurrent neural networks; EHFKT_K/S/D, a simplified version of EHFKT, which only contains KDES/SFES/DFES system. The input of EHFKT series is the concatenation of problem encoding and the ouput of each system; EHFKT_T, which contains all subsystems. It diagnoses the transition of mastery of knowledge, while EHFKT diagnoses transition of the mastery of semantic features.

3.2 Experimental Results

Hierarchical Clustering Result. The SFES system uses Bert and Hierarchical Clustering to obtain semantic features of questions. Figure 3 shows the visualization of the clustering results of 11410 questions. The y-axis corresponds to the classification threshold and x-axis corresponds to each exercise. Table 1 implies the result of clustering when the number of clustering λ_s is 912.

Table 1. The result of clustering

Id	Question content	Knowledge	Cluster
Q35	Calculate factorization of $9a^2 (2x - 3y) + 4b^2 (3y - 2x)$	Factorization	SF3
Q37	Calculate $(2a^3 + a^2) \div a^2$, which of the following is true?	Factorization	SF3
Q38	If $(x^2 + y^2 + 2)(x^2 + y^2 - 2) = 0$, calculate $x^2 + y^2$	Factorization	SF4
Q36	Given two points on $y = -mx^2 + 2x$, calculate m	Factorization	SF5

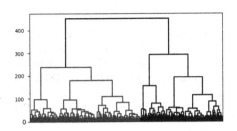

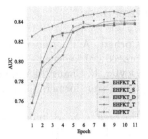

Fig. 3. Hierarchical clustering result   **Fig. 4.** AUC of EHFKT series

EHFKT Result. In this part, our experiment divides the dataset into a training set with 105,744 learners' logs and a test dataset with 26,435 learners' logs. Figure 4 shows the transition of AUC during the training process. Table 2 shows the overall comparing results in this task. The results indicate that EHFKT performs better than other baseline models. Thus, we could draw several conclusions from the result: In the knowledge tracing task, adding hierarchical features can better represent questions; Besides, tracing the mastery of semantic clusterings can predict students' performance more precisely. The reason is that the exercises contained in the same clusters have similar knowledge distribution, difficulty, and semantics; This result also demonstrates the instability of the tracing of knowledge mastery since the difficulty of an exercise is unpredictable.

Table 2. Evaluation metrics of different deep learning methods

Model	AUC	Model	AUC
BKT	0.6325 ± 0.0011	DKT	0.8324 ± 0.0031
EKTA	0.8384 ± 0.0036	EHFKT_S	0.8407 ± 0.0016
EHFKT_K	0.8371 ± 0.0022	EHFKT_D	0.8382 ± 0.0035
EHFKT_T	0.8445 ± 0.0025	EHFKT	$\mathbf{0.8505 \pm 0.0021}$

4   Conclusions

In this article, we propose a novel knowledge tracing framework which could extract the knowledge distribution, semantic features and difficulty from the exercise. Besides, We introduce the diagnosis of semantic features of questions into knowledge tracing, which leads to more accurate performance prediction. Although the meaning of these semantic clusters is beyond people's understanding, in the future we will try extracting the meaning of the exercises in the same cluster by text sumarization technique to make the data-driven clusters result more understandable to human.

References

1. Corbett, A.T., Anderson, J.R.: Knowledge tracing: modeling the acquisition of procedural knowledge. User Model. User-Adap. Inter. **4**(4), 253–278 (1994)
2. Devlin, J., Chang, M.W., Lee, K., Toutanova, K.: Bert: pre-training of deep bidirectional transformers for language understanding. arXiv preprint arXiv:1810.04805 (2018)
3. Hochreiter, S., Schmidhuber, J.: Long short-term memory. Neural Comput. **9**(8), 1735–1780 (1997)
4. Hontangas, P., Ponsoda, V., Olea, J., Wise, S.L.: The choice of item difficulty in self-adapted testing. Eur. J. Psychol. Assess. **16**(1), 3 (2000)
5. Huang, Z., et al.: Ekt:Exercise-aware knowledge tracing for student performance prediction. IEEE Trans. Knowl. Data Eng. (2019)
6. Johnson, S.C.: Hierarchical clustering schemes. Psychometrika **32**(3), 241–254 (1967)
7. Khajah, M.M., Huang, Y., González-Brenes, J.P., Mozer, M.C., Brusilovsky, P.: Integrating knowledge tracing and item response theory: a tale of two frameworks. In: CEUR Workshop Proceedings, vol. 1181, pp. 7–15. University of Pittsburgh (2014)
8. Kim, Y.: Convolutional neural networks for sentence classification. arXiv preprint arXiv:1408.5882 (2014)
9. Pavlik Jr., P.I., Cen, H., Koedinger, K.R.: Performance factors analysis-a new alternative to knowledge tracing. Online Submission (2009)
10. Piech, C., et al.: Deep knowledge tracing. In: Advances in Neural Information Processing Systems, pp. 505–513 (2015)

Relationships Between Math Performance and Human Judgments of Motivational Constructs in an Online Math Tutoring System

Rurik Tywoniw[1]([⊠]) [iD], Scott A. Crossley[1] [iD], Jaclyn Ocumpaugh[2],
Shamya Karumbaiah[2] [iD], and Ryan Baker[2]

[1] Georgia State University, Atlanta, GA 30303, USA
{rtywoniwl,scrossley}@gsu.edu
[2] University of Pennsylvania, Philadelphia, PA 19104, USA
penn.learninganalytics@gmail.com

Abstract. This paper explores how early grade school students' math perfor-mance relates to human ratings of students' affect, identity, and social awareness based on the content of messages to an online tutoring system avatar. There is an expanding body of research which investigates connections between these features and success in mathematics. This study used principle component analysis to identify four components related to motivational constructs. These components were examined using correlations with mathematics performance at three difficulty levels. Data from 572 students were examined, with results indicating little to no links between human judgments of motivational constructs and math performance. These findings have implications for how motivational constructs in math are evaluated and how they can predict mathematics performance.

Keywords: Intelligent tutoring · Principle component analysis · Motivational constructs

1 Introduction

Recent research into math education has put emphasis on the effect of non-cognitive factors on math performance, such as math self-concept and motivation [1–3]. Intel-ligent tutoring systems provide an environment for self-paced learning and growth, and opportunities for interaction which contribute to development [4, 5]. In these online environments, positive sentiment towards the course is associated with positive course outcomes. Wen, Yang, and Rosé [6] examined sentiment analysis of postings in an online course, finding that latent affect features of positive impressions of the course were inversely proportional to course dropout rate. Slater et al. [4] found that students' self-perceptions of the value of math, their math self-concept, and interest in math each correlated with math performance. Crossley et al. [7] similarly found associations with math self-concept and math performance, also incorporating telemetric (click-stream) data from an online tutoring system as predictive of math identity. Missing from previous research is whether math performance is related to human judgments of math

© Springer Nature Switzerland AG 2020
I. I. Bittencourt et al. (Eds.): AIED 2020, LNAI 12164, pp. 329–333, 2020.
https://doi.org/10.1007/978-3-030-52240-7_60

students' affect and identity. As students' use of online and intelligent interactive tutoring tools grows, it is useful to know if these constructs can be seen in student language and if these constructs are related to success. The current study thus asks the following questions: 1) Can human ratings of students' affect, identity, and social awareness be grouped into component macro-features related to motivational constructs? And 2) if such macro-features are discernible, do they relate to math performance?

2   Method

2.1   Data

Data were collected from *Reasoning Mind Foundations* by Imagine Learning, a blended learning platform for students in elementary grades. Students use this platform for self-paced engagement with math. Teachers use system data to monitor student performance and growth. Students can send emails to the Genie, a pedagogical agent who provides math help and encouragement. Messages sent to the Genie are responded to by employees of *Reasoning Mind* who maintain a consistent Genie persona. A more thorough description of the system is given in Khachatryan et al. [8]. The language sample for the analyses in this study come from the messages sent to the Genie tutor. These messages were aggregated into a single file for each student, allowing investigation of the content in individuals' messages, even when the average message by a given individual was short. Overall, the data in this study came from a sample of 572 elementary school students who used the *Reasoning Mind* platform between August 2016 and June 2017. Students attempted A-level (easiest), B-level (mid-level), and C-level (most difficult) math problems and wrote at least 50 words worth of combined messages to the Genie tutor. On average, students wrote 16 words per message. Students math performance scores are students' average performances on the A-, B-, and C-level problems. Data from this study are available upon request from the third and fifth author.

2.2   Human Ratings of Motivational Constructs

All aggregated message files were rated for evidence of students' motivational constructs in mathematics by two human raters. Students' messages were rated for fourteen different constructs, each on a scale from 1 to 5. These included affective features (Delight, Curiosity, Dejection, Engaged Concentration, Confusion, Frustration, Contempt), math identity features (Math Class Interest, Math Domain Interest, Math Self-Concept, And Non-Math Self-Concept), and social awareness features (Responsibility, Success, Cooperation). The two human raters were undergraduate students at a large university in the American South. The raters were trained and normed on similar tutoring messages from a previous data set. There ratings were analyzed for intra-rater reliability using Multi-faceted Rasch Analysis [9]. Intra-rater reliability was satisfactory, with each rater exhibiting an infit of between .5 and 1.5 on each construct, indicating a satisfactory level of model fit and predictability without being invariant in their ratings.

2.3   Analysis

To answer the first research question, we performed dimensionality reduction using Principle Component Analysis (PCA), a statistical procedure which combines variables that are highly correlated into a smaller set of derived components. For inclusion into a component, a cut-off for the eigenvalues of $\lambda > .30$ was set, so only salient indices would be included in components. Each index was only included in the component in which it loaded highest. We calculated weighted component scores by multiplying each index by its respective eigenvalue in the component reported by the PCA. The results of the PCAs are discussed further in the Results section. To answer the second research question, the components resulting from the PCA were compared to math performance scores using Spearman's Rho correlations.

3   Results

3.1   Principal Component Analysis

The PCA was performed on the 13 variables from the raters' judgments of motivational constructs. The Kaiser–Meyer–Olkin test indicated that measuring of sampling adequacy (MSA) was sufficient at MSA = .74. Ten of the variables were retained in the analysis and reduced to four components with eigenvalues at or above 1.0. These four components accounted for 56.58% of the variance in human ratings of motivational constructs. These components were manually named based on indicator variables and are listed in Table 1. The component "Mood" relates to presence of features related to delight in math and the absence of features related to frustration with math. The component "Outcomes" related to the absence of a successful outlook regarding math and the presence of an outlook on math related to engaged concentration, cooperation, and confusion; all concepts related to success-in-the-making. The component "Attitude" relates to absence of contempt for math, and presence of interest in math class. Finally, the component "Declarativity" relates to general interest in the math domain and absence of curiosity.

3.2   Correlations Between Motivational Constructs Ratings and Performance

Correlations between components of motivational constructs with math performance are presented in Table 2. Spearman's Rho was used as a test statistic because the data were not normally distributed. A conservative alpha value was set at .002 using Bonferroni Correction for multiple comparisons. Each of the three math performance scores at different difficulties were pairwise correlated with $\rho > .450$ ($p < .002$). Only two of the motivational components were pairwise correlated. Mood, which involved students' expression of either frustration or delight, correlated strongly with Attitude ($\rho = .478$, p < .002), which similarly involved students' expression of either contempt or interest in the math class. None of the components of motivational constructs were significantly correlated with math performance at any of the three levels.

Table 1. Components from the PCA on human judgments of motivational constructs

Component name and included variables	Percent of variance	Cumulative variance	Eigen loading for indices
1. Mood	25.25	25.25	
a. Frustration (−) (affect)			−.369
b. Delight (+) (affect)			.344
2. Outcomes	13.72	39.17	
a. Success (−) (social)			−.411
b. Engaged concentration (+) (affect)			.319
c. Confusion (+) (affect)			.477
d. Cooperation (+) (social)			.376
3. Attitudes	9.67	48.83	
a. Contempt (−) (affect)			−.457
b. Math Class Interest (+) (identity)			.354
4. Declarativity	7.74	56.58	
a. Math Domain Interest (+) (identity)			.706
b. Curiosity (−) (affect)			−.567

Table 2. Correlations between motivational construct components and math performance.

	A-level[+]	B-level[+]	C-level[+]	Mood	Outcomes	Attitude
B-level[+]	0.599*					
C-level[+]	0.456*	0.487*				
Mood	−0.006	−0.004	−0.001			
Outcomes	0.001	−0.049	−0.004	−0.071		
Attitude	0.010	0.016	0.036	0.478*	0.027	
Declarativity	−0.038	−0.005	−0.111	−0.026	−0.052	0.075

* Significant at $p < .002$, [+] Level of difficulty of performance

4   Discussion

This paper described efforts to relate elementary level students' math performance to human ratings of affect, identity, and social awareness in their messages to a tutor. We successfully derived four components related to motivational constructs. Overall, there were no significant relationships between human judgments of motivational constructs in messages to an online tutoring avatar and math performance at three different level. This finding is in contrast with previous studies which have found more meaningful connections between motivational constructs and math performance [1, 3–5, 7]. However, this only implies that the effect on math performance of externally evaluated motivational constructs found in student writing may be mitigated by other factors which we could not measure, such as prior knowledge and tutoring environment features such as the content of tutor responses. These factors could be the subject of future studies. Considering the informal nature of the writing rated in this study, finer-grained metrics of affective- and identity-related features in language and telemetric data, to predict math achievement may also be effective.

Acknowledgements. This research was supported in part by NSF 1623730. Opinions, conclusions, or recommendations do not necessarily reflect the views of the NSF. We give special thanks to Lucile Petite and Rebecca Wood for their assistance in helping annotate the messages used in this study.

References

1. Spinath, B., Spinath, F., Harlaar, N., Plomin, R.: Predicting school achievement from general cognitive ability, self-perceived ability, and intrinsic value. Intelligence **34**(4), 363–374 (2006)
2. Steinmayr, R., Spinath, B.: The importance of motivation as a predictor of school achievement. Learn. Indiv. Diff. **19**(1), 80–90 (2009)
3. Arens, A.K., Marsh, H.W., Craven, R.G., Yeung, A.S., Randhawa, E., Hasselhorn, M.: Math self-concept in preschool children: Structure, achievement relations, and generalizability across gender. Early Childhood Res. Q. **36**, 391–403 (2016)
4. Slater, S., Ocumpaugh, J., Baker, R., Lib, J., Lab rum, M.: Identifying changes in math identity through adaptive learning systems use. In: Proceedings of the 26th International Conference on Computers in Education (2018)
5. Dowell, N.M.M., Graesser, A.C.: Modeling learners' cognitive, affective, and social processes through language and discourse. J. Learn. Analyt. **1**(3), 183–186 (2014)
6. Wen, M., Yang, D., Rose, C.: Sentiment Analysis in MOOC Discussion Forums: What does it tell us? In: Educational data mining 2014. July 2014
7. Crossley, S.A., Karumbaiah, S., Labrum, M., Ocumpaugh, J., Baker, R.: Predicting math success in an online tutoring system using language data and click-stream variables: a longitudinal analysis. In: Proceedings of Language Data and Knowledge, vol. 70, pp. 1–13. Open Access Series in Informatics (OASIcs) (2019)
8. Khachatryan, G., et al.: Reasoning Mind Genie 2: an intelligent tutoring system as a vehicle for international transfer of instructional methods in mathematics. Int. J. Artif. Intell. Educ. **24**(3), 333–382 (2014)
9. Linacre, J.M.: What do infit and outfit, mean-square and standardized mean? Rasch Measur. Trans. **16**(2), 878 (2002)

Automated Short-Answer Grading Using Deep Neural Networks and Item Response Theory

Masaki Uto$^{(\boxtimes)}$ ⓘ and Yuto Uchida

The University of Electro-Communications, Tokyo, Japan
uto@ai.lab.uec.ac.jp

Abstract. Automated short-answer grading (ASAG) methods using deep neural networks (DNN) have achieved state-of-the-art accuracy. However, further improvement is required for high-stakes and large-scale examinations because even a small scoring error will affect many test-takers. To improve scoring accuracy, we propose a new ASAG method that combines a conventional DNN-ASAG model and an item response theory (IRT) model. Our method uses an IRT model to estimate the test-taker's ability from his/her true-false responses to objective questions that are offered with a target short-answer question in the same test. Then, the target short-answer score is predicted by jointly using the ability value and a distributed short-answer representation, which is obtained from an intermediate layer of a DNN-ASAG model.

Keywords: Deep neural networks · Item response theory · Automated short answer grading

1 Introduction

Short-answer questions are widely used to evaluate the higher abilities of test-takers, such as logical thinking and expressive ability. World-wide large-scale tests, such as the Test of English as a Foreign Language and the Graduate Management Admission Test, incorporate short-answer questions. However, the introduction of this type of question to these large-scale tests has prompted concerns related to scoring accuracy, time complexity, and monetary cost. Automated short-answer grading (ASAG) methods have attracted much attention as a way to alleviate these concerns [1,2].

Conventional ASAG methods have relied on manually tuned features, which are laborious to develop [3,10–12]. However, many deep neural network (DNN) methods, which obviate the need for feature engineering, have been proposed [5,7–9,13]. DNN methods automatically extract effective features for score prediction using a dataset of graded short answers, and have achieved state-of-the-art scoring accuracy [5,7–9,13]. However, further improvement of the accuracy of these methods is required, especially for high-stakes and large-scale examinations because even a slight scoring error will have a large effect on many test-takers.

ⓒ Springer Nature Switzerland AG 2020
I. I. Bittencourt et al. (Eds.): AIED 2020, LNAI 12164, pp. 334–339, 2020.
https://doi.org/10.1007/978-3-030-52240-7_61

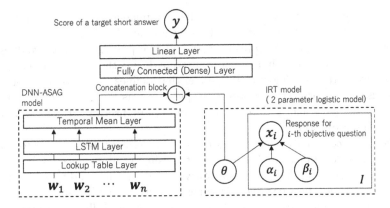

Fig. 1. Architecture of the proposed method.

To improve scoring accuracy, we propose a new ASAG method that combines a conventional DNN model and an item response theory (IRT) model [6]. We focus on short-answer questions given as a part of a test including objective questions. Because a test measures a particular ability, we can assume that short-answer questions and objective questions on the same test measure similar abilities. Thus, estimating the test-takers' ability from the objective questions should be useful for short-answer grading. Based on this assumption, our method incorporates the test-taker's ability, which is estimated using an IRT model from his/her true-false responses for objective questions, into a DNN-ASAG model. Our method is formulated as a DNN framework that predicts a target short-answer score by jointly using the IRT-based ability estimate and a distributed representation of the short-answer text as obtained from an intermediate layer of a DNN-ASAG model. Although the proposed method is suitable for any DNN-ASAG model, we implement it with the most standard long short-term memory (LSTM) ASAG model [9]. The effectiveness of our model is evaluated by using data from an actual experiment. To our knowledge, this is a new approach that focuses on using responses to objective questions to grade short answers.

2   Proposed Method

The architecture of the proposed method is shown in Fig. 1. The method transforms the word sequence in a given short answer to a fixed-length hidden vector M through *a lookup table layer, a LSTM layer,* and *a temporal mean layer*, as in the conventional LSTM ASAG model [9]. Here, *the lookup table layer* transforms each word in a given short answer to a word embedding representation, *the LSTM layer* transforms the embedded word sequence to a sequence of hidden vectors that capture the long-distance dependencies of the words at each time step, and *the temporal mean layer* averages the outputs of the LSTM layer to produce a fixed-length hidden vector M, which can be regarded as a distributed representation of a given short-answer text.

The concatenation block, a newly added component in this method, concatenates the distributed text representation M and an IRT-based test-taker's ability θ which is estimated from his/her true-false responses to objective questions offered together with the short-answer question during the same examination. We use the two-parameter logistic IRT model that defines the probability of a test-taker answering correctly for objective question i as $(1 + \exp[-\alpha_i(\theta - \beta_i)])^{-1}$, where θ is the test-taker's ability, and α_i and β_i are discrimination and difficulty parameters of question i.

The fully connected (dense) layer projects the concatenated vector $M' = [M, \theta]$ to a lower-dimensional hidden vector using a fully connected feedforward neural network. This layer is also newly added in this study to capture the non-linear relation between the test-takers' abilities and short-answer scores.

Finally, *the linear layer* projects the output of the fully connected layer to a scalar value in the range $[0, 1]$ by using the sigmoid function $\sigma(WM' + b)$, where W is the weight matrix and b is the bias.

The model training is conducted by back-propagation with the mean squared error loss function using the training dataset, in which the scores are normalized to the $[0, 1]$ scale. During the prediction phase, the predicted scores are rescaled to the original score range. For the IRT parameter estimation, we use a Markov chain Monte Carlo algorithm [14, 15].

3 Experiments

This section demonstrates the effectiveness of the proposed method by using real data. For this experiment, we used response data from a Japanese reading comprehension test developed by Benesse Educational Research and Development Institute, Japan. This dataset comprises responses given by 511 test-takers (Japanese university students) to three short-answer questions and true-false responses for 44 objective questions. Scores for the short answers were provided by expert raters using three rating categories for two evaluation viewpoints. The total score of the two evaluation viewpoints was also given.

Using the data, we conducted five-fold cross validation to evaluate the Pearson's correlation between the true scores and predicted scores for each evaluation viewpoint and the total score. For model training, the dimensions of the word embedding, the LSTM layer, and the fully connected layer were set to 50, 300, and 50, respectively. The mini-batch size and maximum epochs were 32 and 50, respectively. The dropout probabilities for the lookup table layer and the temporal mean layer were 0.5. The recurrent dropout probability for the LSTM layer was set to 0.1. This experiment was conducted for the proposed method and the conventional method. Furthermore, to evaluate effectiveness of the fully connected (dense) layer, we also conducted the experiment for the proposed method without the dense layer and the conventional method with the dense layer.

Table 1 shows the results. The *Score 1* and *Score 2* columns indicate the results for the two evaluation viewpoints in each question; the *Total* column indicates the results for the sum of the two viewpoints' scores; and the *Avg.*

Table 1. Experimental results

	Question 1			Question 2			Question 3			Avg.
	Score 1	Score 2	Total	Score 1	Score 2	Total	Score 1	Score 2	Total	
Conventional	0.561	0.875	0.604	0.910	0.868	0.815	0.719	0.737	0.694	0.754
with dense	0.568	0.882	0.612	0.909	0.874	0.823	0.715	0.758	0.713	0.762
Proposed	0.576	0.887	0.621	0.912	0.876	0.828	0.710	0.743	0.708	0.762*
w/o dense	0.573	0.873	0.597	0.911	0.865	0.810	0.719	0.733	0.673	0.751

column shows the averaged performance for each method. * indicates that the averaged performance of the method is higher than that of the conventional method at the 1% significance level by the paired t-test.

The table shows that the proposed method has better performance than the conventional method in almost all cases, and the averaged performance of the proposed method is also significantly higher. These results suggest that the proposed method is effective in improving the scoring accuracy. The table also shows that the performance tends to decrease when the dense layer is omitted from the proposed method. Moreover, when the dense layer is added to the conventional method, the performance tends to increase. These results suggest that the incorporation of the fully connected dense layer improves the accuracy. Comparing the proposed method and the conventional method with the dense layer shows that the proposed method provides higher performance in all cases except for *Question 3*, validating the effectiveness of incorporating the IRT-based ability. The drop in performance for *Question 3* might be caused by disagreement between the distribution of IRT ability and that of the observed score. We confirmed that *Question 3* has a strongly skewed score distribution in which the highest score category is overused, whereas the IRT ability follows a normal distribution [4]. Note that test items with strongly skewed score distributions are generally inappropriate because they do not distinguish the ability of test-takers well. Thus, we conclude that incorporating ability values improves the scoring accuracy when target short-answer questions measure ability well.

4   Conclusion

This study proposed a new DNN-ASAG method that integrates the ability of test-takers estimated from true-false responses for objective questions using IRT. An experiment using real data suggested that incorporating ability improves scoring accuracy when a target short-answer question can measure ability well. In future work, we plan to examine the behavior of the proposed method in more detail by applying it to various datasets. We will also examine the potential for scoring bias that might arise from the use of true-false responses.

Acknowledgment. This work was supported by JSPS KAKENHI 17H04726 and 17K20024. We thank Yuki Doka and Yoshihiro Kato at Benesse Educational Research and Development Institute for permission to use the actual data.

References

1. Burrows, S., Gurevych, I., Stein, B.: The eras and trends of automatic short answer grading. Int. J. Artif. Intell. Educ. **25**(1), 60–117 (2015)
2. Dhamecha, T.I., Marvaniya, S., Saha, S., Sindhgatta, R., Sengupta, B.: Balancing human efforts and performance of student response analyzer in dialog-based tutors. In: Penstein Rosé, C., et al. (eds.) AIED 2018. LNCS (LNAI), vol. 10947, pp. 70–85. Springer, Cham (2018). https://doi.org/10.1007/978-3-319-93843-1_6
3. Heilman, M., Madnani, N.: ETS: domain adaptation and stacking for short answer scoring. In: Proceedings of the International Workshop on Semantic Evaluation, pp. 275–279 (2013)
4. van der Linden, W.J.: Handbook of Item Response Theory, Volume One: Models. CRC Press, Boca Raton (2016)
5. Liu, T., Ding, W., Wang, Z., Tang, J., Huang, G.Y., Liu, Z.: Automatic short answer grading via multiway attention networks. In: Isotani, S., Millán, E., Ogan, A., Hastings, P., McLaren, B., Luckin, R. (eds.) AIED 2019. LNCS (LNAI), vol. 11626, pp. 169–173. Springer, Cham (2019). https://doi.org/10.1007/978-3-030-23207-8_32
6. Lord, F.: Applications of Item Response Theory to Practical Testing Problems. Erlbaum Associates, Hillsdale (1980)
7. Lun, J., Zhu, J., Tang, Y., Yang, M.: Multiple data augmentation strategies for improving performance on automatic short answer scoring. In: Proceedings of the Association for the Advancement of Artificial Intelligence (2020)
8. Mizumoto, T., et al.: Analytic score prediction and justification identification in automated short answer scoring. In: Proceedings of the Workshop on Innovative Use of NLP for Building Educational Applications, Association for Computational Linguistics, pp. 316–325 (2019)
9. Riordan, B., Horbach, A., Cahill, A., Zesch, T., Lee, C.M.: Investigating neural architectures for short answer scoring. In: Proceedings of the Workshop on Innovative Use of NLP for Building Educational Applications, Association for Computational Linguistics, pp. 159–168 (2017)
10. Saha, S., Dhamecha, T.I., Marvaniya, S., Sindhgatta, R., Sengupta, B.: Sentence level or token level features for automatic short answer grading?: Use both. In: Penstein Rosé, C., et al. (eds.) AIED 2018. LNCS (LNAI), vol. 10947, pp. 503–517. Springer, Cham (2018). https://doi.org/10.1007/978-3-319-93843-1_37
11. Sakaguchi, K., Heilman, M., Madnani, N.: Effective feature integration for automated short answer scoring. In: Proceedings of the Annual Conference of the North American Chapter of the Association for Computational Linguistics: Human Language Technologies, pp. 1049–1054 (2015)
12. Sultan, M.A., Salazar, C., Sumner, T.: Fast and easy short answer grading with high accuracy. In: Proceedings of the Annual Conference of the North American Chapter of the Association for Computational Linguistics: Human Language Technologies, pp. 1070–1075 (2016)

13. Sung, C., Dhamecha, T.I., Mukhi, N.: Improving short answer grading using transformer-based pre-training. In: Isotani, S., et al. (eds.) AIED 2019. LNCS (LNAI), vol. 11625, pp. 469–481. Springer, Cham (2019). https://doi.org/10.1007/978-3-030-23204-7_39

14. Uto, M.: Rater-effect IRT model integrating supervised LDA for accurate measurement of essay writing ability. In: Isotani, S., Millán, E., Ogan, A., Hastings, P., McLaren, B., Luckin, R. (eds.) AIED 2019. LNCS (LNAI), vol. 11625, pp. 494–506. Springer, Cham (2019). https://doi.org/10.1007/978-3-030-23204-7_41

15. Uto, M., Ueno, M.: Item response theory for peer assessment. IEEE Trans. Learn. Technol. **9**(2), 157–170 (2016)

Automatic Dialogic Instruction Detection for K-12 Online One-on-One Classes

Shiting Xu, Wenbiao Ding, and Zitao Liu[✉]

TAL Education Group, Beijing, China
{xushiting,dingwenbiao,liuzitao}@100tal.com

Abstract. Online one-on-one class is created for highly interactive and immersive learning experience. It demands a large number of qualified online instructors. In this work, we develop six dialogic instructions and help teachers achieve the benefits of one-on-one learning paradigm. Moreover, we utilize neural language models, i.e., long short-term memory (LSTM), to detect above six instructions automatically. Experiments demonstrate that the LSTM approach achieves AUC scores from 0.840 to 0.979 among all six types of instructions on our real-world educational dataset.

Keywords: Dialogic instruction · One-on-one class · K-12 education · Online education

1 Introduction

With the recent development of technology such as digital video processing and live streaming, various forms of online classes emerge [4]. Because of the better accessibility and live learning experience, one-on-one class stands out where students are able to not only study materials at their only own pace, but have opportunities to frequently interact with their teachers facially and vocally [3,13,15]. Online one-on-one class has demonstrated its personalized education experience as supplements to the traditional training from public schools [14].

In spite of the above benefits, online one-on-one classes pose numerous challenges on instructors. On one hand, the instructor qualifications are significantly different from those in public schools. Public school teachers focus on making sure that the majority students are on track and pass their qualification examinations. While one-on-one instructors need to pay detailed attentions to every single student and adjust their teaching paces, styles, or even contents accordingly. Furthermore, students enroll in one-on-one courses for high-frequency interactions. This requires the teachers to encourage and lead students' active participations. On the other hand, a large portion of one-on-one participants are academically low-ranking K-12 students. Most of them are eager to study but don't know how to learn. The one-on-one instructors are responsible to help them build effective study habits. Therefore, in order to scale the qualified supply of one-on-one instructors and provide more effective and personalized education to the general

© Springer Nature Switzerland AG 2020
I. I. Bittencourt et al. (Eds.): AIED 2020, LNAI 12164, pp. 340–345, 2020.
https://doi.org/10.1007/978-3-030-52240-7_62

K-12 students, we develop six in-class dialogic instructions for one-on-one class teachers. Moreover, we build an end-to-end system to automatically detect and analyze the proposed pedagogical instructions.

2 Related Work

Many existing methods have been developed to analyze classroom dialogic instructions. Wang et al. identify teacher lecturing, class discussion and student group work in the traditional classroom by asking teachers to wear the LENA system [8] during the class [22]. Donnelly et al. identify occurrences of some key instructional segments, such as Question & Answer, Supervised Seatwork, etc., by using Naive Bayes models [5]. Owens et al. develop Decibel Analysis for Research in Teaching, i.e., DART, to analyzes the volume and variance of classroom recordings to predict the quantity of time spend on single voice (e.g., lecture), multiple voice (e.g., pair discussion), and no voice (e.g., clicker question thinking) activities [17].

Our work is distinguished from existing research studies because (1) we focus on the K-12 online one-on-one domain and propose six pedagogical instructions explicitly designed for it; (2) our dialogic instruction detection approach is an end-to-end solution that doesn't require any human intervention or any additional recording device.

3 Our Approach

3.1 Dialogic Instructions

By analyzing thousands of online one-on-one class videos and surveying hundreds of instructors, students, parents and educators, we categorize six dialogic instructions for K-12 online one-on-one classes as follows:

- *greeting:* Greeting instructions help teachers manage their teaching procedures before the class, such as greeting students, testing teaching equipments. Examples: "How are you doing?", "Can you hear me?", etc.
- *guidance:* Guidance instructions ask teachers to interact with students when lecturing on a particular knowledge point or a factual answer. Examples: "Do you know the reason?", "Let's see how we can get there?", etc.
- *note-taking:* Note-taking instructions require teachers to help students learn how to take notes and assist them to build effective learning habits. Examples: "Highlight this paragraph.", "Please copy this part", etc.
- *commending:* Commending instructions ask teachers to encourage students and build their confidence. Examples: "Good job.", "Well done.", etc.
- *repeating:* Repeating instructions remind teachers to let students retell the content by themselves, which enhances their understandings. Examples: "Could you please explain that to me?", "Can you rephrase that?", etc.
- *summarization:* Summarization instructions ask teachers to summarize teaching contents and materials at the end of the each class and conclude the main takeaways. Examples: "Let's review the key points", "Let's wrap up.", etc.

3.2   The Dialogic Instruction Detection Approach

The end-to-end dialogic detection pipeline takes class recordings as input and outputs spoken sentences of the above six types of dialogic instructions. The entire workflow is illustrated in Fig. 1, which consists of two key components: *Audio Processing* and *Language Modeling.*

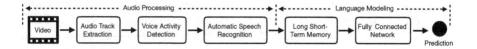

Fig. 1. The workflow of the end-to-end dialogic instruction detection approach.

Audio Processing. Audio processing involves three key steps: (1) extracting audio tracks from video recordings; (2) cutting audio tracks into short-span segments and removing noises and silence segments by a voice activity detection (VAD) algorithm; and (3) transcribing each audio segment by using an automatic speech recognition (ASR) algorithm. Please note that since both students' and teachers' videos are recorded separately, voice overlaps don't exist in the video recordings. This avoids the unsolved challenge of speaker diarization [1,21].

Language Modeling. We conduct language modeling on the transcriptions from the audio processing module. For each word, we first fetch its low dimensional embeddings from a pre-trained word2vec model. After that, we build neural classifiers for each type of dialogic instructions defined in Sect. 3.1. In this work, we use the long short-term memory (LSTM) as our language modeling networks [9,10]. The LSTM models take a sentence as input and sequentially update the hidden state representation of each word by using a well designed memory cell, which is able to capture the long range dependencies within each sentence. The details of LSTM can be found in [9,10]. LSTM model have been successful in language modeling tasks such as text classification [12,24], machine translation [23], etc. Finally, we build a two-layer fully-connected position-wise feed forward network on the last hidden representation of LSTM to conduct the final predictions.

4   Experiments

In this work, we collect 2940 sentences for each type of dialogic instruction by manually annotating class recordings from a third-party online one-on-one learning platform[1]. Each sentence is associated with a binary label, indicating whether the sentence belongs to a dialogic instruction. We use 2352 sentences for

[1] https://www.xes1v1.com/.

training and the rest for validation and testing. Similar to Blanchard et al. [2], we find that publicly available AI engines may yield inferior performance in the noisy and dynamic classroom environments. Therefore, we train our own VAD [20], ASR [25] and word2vec [16] models on the classroom specific datasets.

We compare the LSTM language modeling network with several widely used baselines: logistic regression [11], i.e, *LR*, support vector machine [18], i.e., *SVM*, and gradient boosting decision trees [7], i.e., *GBDT*. Similar to Tang et al. [19], we use area under curve (AUC) score to evaluate the model performance [6].

4.1   Model Performance

Figure 2 shows that our LSTM approach outperforms all other methods on all six types of dialogic instruction detection tasks. Specifically, from Fig. 2, we find that simple instructions are relatively fixed and have little variants, such as "greeting" and "summarization". All the approaches have comparable performance. While for complex instructions with many language variations such as "note-taking", "commending" and "repeating", *LSTM* significantly outperforms other baselines by large margins. We believe this is because the sequential neural networks are able to capture the long contextual language dependence within the sentence, which is very important when dealing with colloquial conversations.

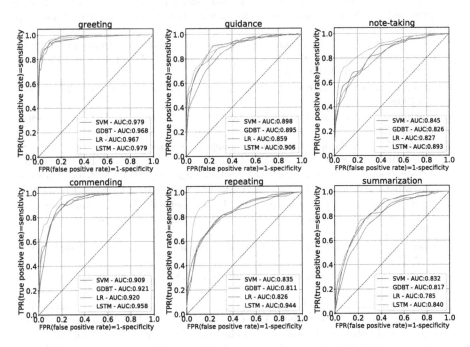

Fig. 2. ROC curves for detection performance of six dialogic instructions.

5   Conclusion

In this work, we propose six dialogic instructions and build an end-to-end solution for online one-on-one instructors. Experiments on a real educational dataset show that our LSTM based approach outperforms other baselines in the proposed six dialogic instructions.

References

1. Anguera, X., Bozonnet, S., Evans, N., Fredouille, C., Friedland, G., Vinyals, O.: Speaker diarization: a review of recent research. IEEE Trans. Audio Speech Lang. Process. **20**(2), 356–370 (2012)
2. Blanchard, N., et al.: A study of automatic speech recognition in noisy classroom environments for automated dialog analysis. In: Conati, C., Heffernan, N., Mitrovic, A., Verdejo, M.F. (eds.) AIED 2015. LNCS (LNAI), vol. 9112, pp. 23–33. Springer, Cham (2015). https://doi.org/10.1007/978-3-319-19773-9_3
3. Chen, J., Li, H., Wang, W., Ding, W., Huang, G.Y., Liu, Z.: A multimodal alerting system for online class quality assurance. In: Isotani, S., Millán, E., Ogan, A., Hastings, P., McLaren, B., Luckin, R. (eds.) AIED 2019. LNCS (LNAI), vol. 11626, pp. 381–385. Springer, Cham (2019). https://doi.org/10.1007/978-3-030-23207-8_70
4. China Education Resources: The largest education system in the world is going online (2012). http://www.chinaeducationresources.com/s/OurMarket.asp. Accessed 5 Feb 2019
5. Donnelly, P.J., et al.: Automatic teacher modeling from live classroom audio. In: Proceedings of the 2016 Conference on User Modeling Adaptation and Personalization, pp. 45–53. ACM (2016)
6. Fawcett, T.: An introduction to ROC analysis. Pattern Recogn. Lett. **27**(8), 861–874 (2006)
7. Friedman, J.H.: Stochastic gradient boosting. Comput. Stat. Data Anal. **38**(4), 367–378 (2002)
8. Ganek, H., Eriks-Brophy, A.: The language environment analysis (lena) system: a literature review. In: Proceedings of the Joint Workshop on NLP for Computer Assisted Language Learning and NLP for Language Acquisition at SLTC, Umeå, 16 November 2016, pp. 24–32. No. 130, Linköping University Electronic Press (2016)
9. Greff, K., Srivastava, R.K., Koutník, J., Steunebrink, B.R., Schmidhuber, J.: LSTM: a search space odyssey. IEEE Trans. Neural Netw. Learn. Syst. **28**(10), 2222–2232 (2016)
10. Hochreiter, S., Schmidhuber, J.: Long short-term memory. Neural Comput. **9**(8), 1735–1780 (1997)
11. Hosmer Jr., D.W., Lemeshow, S., Sturdivant, R.X.: Applied Logistic Regression, vol. 398. Wiley, Hoboken (2013)
12. Lai, S., Xu, L., Liu, K., Zhao, J.: Recurrent convolutional neural networks for text classification. In: Twenty-ninth AAAI Conference on Artificial Intelligence (2015)
13. Li, H., et al.: Multimodal learning for classroom activity detection. In: 2020 IEEE International Conference on Acoustics, Speech and Signal Processing (ICASSP), pp. 9234–9238. IEEE (2020)
14. Liang, J.K., et al.: A few design perspectives on one-on-one digital classroom environment. J. Comput. Assist. Learn. **21**(3), 181–189 (2005)

15. Liu, Z., et al.: Dolphin: a spoken language proficiency assessment system for elementary education. In: Proceedings of the Web Conference 2020, pp. 2641–2647. ACM (2020)
16. Mikolov, T., Sutskever, I., Chen, K., Corrado, G.S., Dean, J.: Distributed representations of words and phrases and their compositionality. In: Advances in Neural Information Processing Systems, pp. 3111–3119 (2013)
17. Owens, M.T., et al.: Classroom sound can be used to classify teaching practices in college science courses. Proc. Natl. Acad. Sci. **114**(12), 3085–3090 (2017)
18. Suykens, J.A., Vandewalle, J.: Least squares support vector machine classifiers. Neural Process. Lett. **9**(3), 293–300 (1999)
19. Tang, C., Ouyang, Y., Rong, W., Zhang, J., Xiong, Z.: Time series model for predicting dropout in massive open online courses. In: Penstein Rosé, C., et al. (eds.) AIED 2018. LNCS (LNAI), vol. 10948, pp. 353–357. Springer, Cham (2018). https://doi.org/10.1007/978-3-319-93846-2_66
20. Tashev, I., Mirsamadi, S.: DNN-based causal voice activity detector. In: Information Theory and Applications Workshop (2016)
21. Tranter, S.E., Reynolds, D.A.: An overview of automatic speaker diarization systems. IEEE Trans. Audio Speech Lang. Process. **14**(5), 1557–1565 (2006)
22. Wang, Z., Pan, X., Miller, K.F., Cortina, K.S.: Automatic classification of activities in classroom discourse. Comput. Educ. **78**, 115–123 (2014)
23. Wu, Y., et al.: Google's neural machine translation system: Bridging the gap between human and machine translation. arXiv preprint arXiv:1609.08144 (2016)
24. Yang, Z., Yang, D., Dyer, C., He, X., Smola, A., Hovy, E.: Hierarchical attention networks for document classification. In: Proceedings of the 2016 conference of the North American Chapter of the Association for Computational Linguistics: Human Language Technologies, pp. 1480–1489 (2016)
25. Zhang, S., Lei, M., Yan, Z., Dai, L.: Deep-FSMN for large vocabulary continuous speech recognition. In: 2018 IEEE International Conference on Acoustics, Speech and Signal Processing, pp. 5869–5873. IEEE (2018)

Exploring the Role of Perspective Taking in Educational Child-Robot Interaction

Elmira Yadollahi[1,2]($\boxtimes$), Marta Couto[1], Wafa Johal[3], Pierre Dillenbourg[2], and Ana Paiva[1]

[1] Group on AI for People and the Society (GAIPS),
INESC-ID & Instituto Superior Técnico, Universidade de Lisboa, Lisbon, Portugal
marta.couto@gaips.inesc-id.pt, ana.paiva@inesc-id.pt
[2] Computer-Human Interaction in Learning
and Instruction Laboratory (CHILI), EPFL, Lausanne, Switzerland
{elmira.yadollahi,pierre.dillenbourg}@epfl.ch
[3] University of New South Wales, Sydney, NSW, Australia
wafa.johal@unsw.edu.au

Abstract. Perspective taking is an important skill to have and learn, which can be applied in many different domains and disciplines. While the ability to recognize other's perspective develops in humans from childhood and solidifies during school years, it needs to be developed in robotic and artificial agents' cognitive framework. In our quest to develop a cognitive model of perspective taking for agents and robots in educational contexts, we designed a task that requires the players (e.g., child and robot) to take the perspective of another, in order to complete and win the task successfully. In a preliminary study to test the system, we were able to evaluate children's performance over four different age groups by focusing on their performance during the interaction with the robot. By analyzing children's performance, we were able to make some assumptions about children's understanding of the game and select the appropriate age group to participate in the main study.

Keywords: Child-robot interaction · Spatial perspective taking · Children · Education · Gamification

1 Introduction and Background

The introduction of robots into education and interaction with children can revolutionize education as we know it. To have robots with capabilities to carry out educational roles, play games, be peers in the activities of a classroom, and at the same time, support learning in different forms is a challenging task. To achieve that we need to equip our robots with cognitive abilities that help them to become true learning companions. To endow the robots with cognitive abilities, we can either focus on the cognitive development, or the interaction capabilities of the robot, or develop both aspects simultaneously. One of the crucial aspects of educational scenarios is maintaining mutual understanding between the child

© Springer Nature Switzerland AG 2020
I. I. Bittencourt et al. (Eds.): AIED 2020, LNAI 12164, pp. 346–351, 2020.
https://doi.org/10.1007/978-3-030-52240-7_63

and the robot. To maintain such an understanding, it is inevitable for the child and the robot to develop a model of each other's mind and perspective.

Developmental psychology defines *Perceptual Perspective Taking* as understanding what other people see and their spatial or visual relationship with the objects in the environment. Taking others visual and spatial perspectives, consists of two levels that correspond to different developmental ages, the extent of perception, and their underlying mechanisms [10,20,21]. "Level 1" develops at around 24 months and corresponds to the ability to judge if an object is visible to another person (visual) or if it is positioned in their front or back (spatial) [14,18,22]. "Level 2" develops from 3–5 to 8–10 years of age and involves the ability to discern how an object, visible to another person, is perceived by them (visual) and to construct a spatial representation of what they perceive (spatial) [4,10,21]. Different tasks, such as three mountain task by Piaget [17] or turtle task [9], have shown that children younger than 4–5 years old were unable to engage in level 2. However, Moll and Meltzoff showed that 36-months-old's were significantly correct in responding to a level 2 test with color filters [12]. As a result, Moll et al. argue that the level of cognitive engagement affects children's performance in level 2 perspective taking tasks [13]. They differentiate between tasks that require confrontation and the ones that only require to take or adopt perspectives. Since children's performance is a function of task complexity, not just the perspective taking itself, we decided to run a pilot to discover the appropriate age for children to participate in our study. Our criteria included the ability to distinguish between left and right and being able to perform the essential task - giving instructions to the robot. However, we wanted children to be at a developmental stage where we can document their choice of perspective and evaluate their learning gain from the interaction.

A great deal of robots in education research has focused on evaluating them as learning companions [8], tutors [2,3,5] and learners [1,6,15] in educational settings. Assigning the robots to any of these roles is subject to the learning objectives and the robot's intelligence. These studies bring an understanding of how robots can be beneficial in educational settings, and the developments still needed. The main goal of this research is to approach the topic of robots in education by generating a decision-making model of perspective-taking for the robot inspired by children's behavior. To elaborate on both topics of perspective taking and robots in education, we have designed the following activity that simulates the collaborative interactions between the child and the robot with spatial perspective taking as a requisite to complete the task. To inform the future design of our perspective taking model and to ensure that we target the right age group, we ran a qualitative pilot study with 7 children from 4 different age groups. In this paper, we briefly describe the design of the task and interaction, our analyses of children's performance, the selection of appropriate age group, and what we learned from the pilot. As a result, we have formulated the following research questions for our pilot study:

RQ1: At which age group are children able to comprehend the task and carry it out without the help of the facilitator?

RQ2: At which age group are children able to correctly differentiate between their left/right and the robot's left/right?

Fig. 1. The experimental set-up with the child side activated (Color figure online)

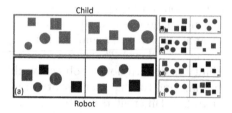

Fig. 2. Medium level: (a) main task with (b) M1, (c) M2 (d) M3 (e) M4 goal cards (Color figure online)

2 Pilot Study

A total of 7 participants (4 female, 3 male) between the ages of 6 and 9 years old took part in this study. They were selected from four different age groups that were going to start 1st, 2nd, 3rd, and 4th grades. The study had received ethical approval from the university's ethics committee and parental consent forms were collected from the parents of the participants prior to the main experiment.

2.1 Study and Task Design

To design an activity involving perspective taking, we consider three concepts observed in the utterances with spatial perspective taking: frame of reference, perspective marking, and perspective taker's role. **Frame of reference** is a set of axes or origin points for addressing position of the objects or their spatial relationships [7,11,23]. Here, we mainly focus on *egocentric* (from the self point of view) and *addressee-centric* (from the other point of view). **Perspective marking** separates the utterances into *implicit* and *explicit* based on the existence of possessive adjectives in the sentence [19]. **Perspective taker's role** corresponds to the differentiation between the *speaker* or *instructor*'s and the *listener* or *manipulator*'s perspectives. Based on these concepts, if the robot tells the child "give me a brick on *your* right", the robot is addressee-centric, explicit, and an instructor/speaker. Children interacted with the robot in a short practice session (child as instructor) and 4 main sessions (child, robot, child, robot as instructor, respectively). We will be looking at children's understanding of the task, recognizing their own and the robot's left/right, and their overall performance.

For the task, we designed a simple game called the *objects game*, which includes moving circles and squares from one side of the screen to the other side, Fig. 1 shows the experimental setup with the child player. The main screen is composed of *squares* and *circles* in two colors: *red* and *yellow*. The game has two difficulty levels, which are a function of the color and shape of the objects presented in that level. Level 1 includes *yellow circles* and *yellow squares* (solved in 2 moves), while level 2 has the additional *red squares* (solved in 3 moves). The goal cards represent the desired final state of the game that players must recreate by moving the objects. Figure 2 shows the main game with 4 out of 6 available goal cards. When the game starts one player guides the other to reach the state represented in the goal card without directly showing it to them. The player with the goal card is called the *instructor*, and the player moving the objects is the *manipulator*. The instructions have three components: the color, the type of the object, and the moving direction. An example of a proper instruction is *"move the yellow circles to the right"*—an implicit utterance that can be either egocentric or addressee-centric.

3   Discussion and Conclusion

To determine the appropriate age group for participating in the main study, we look at two criteria: children's ability to understand the task and to differentiate between their left/right and the robot's left/right. We want children to be able to understand the central concept, be challenged by the difference in perspectives, and make a decision to deal with the difference, either successfully or not. During the interaction, we noticed two participants (6 and 7 years old) had fundamental problems distinguishing between their left/right. Furthermore, the 6 years old child had problems identifying the shapes to produce the instructions. We had a plan to accommodate children with left/right issues by putting stickers on their hand and the robot's hand. Several psychology studies have used this technique in their perspective taking studies [16]. However, it did not solve those children's issues and they were still confused about the robot's difference in perspective. We discussed this issue with the teachers, who advised us that the task was too difficult for children starting 1st and 2nd grades. On the other hand, we observed acceptable performances from children in 3rd and 4th grade. The children in the 3rd grade were able to comprehend the task, they were egocentric at first, but one of them managed to recognize the discrepancy between theirs and the robot's perspective and update their instructions. With 4th grade children, we observed that they effortlessly recognized the robot's different perspective and update theirs. Based on our observation of children's performance and further discussions with the teachers, we decided to select children at 3rd and 4th grade. We excluded younger children due to their issues with left/right and understanding of the task.

Furthermore, we were able to recognize a shortcoming in our interaction that was affecting children's perception of the robot. During the interaction, when the child instructed the robot in implicit egocentric instructions, considering the robot's egocentric perspective, the outcome of the move was opposite of the child's expectation. In such cases, some children were expecting the experimenter to explain why, and most just assumed the robot was faulty. To prevent this, we decided to add some level of transparency to the interaction for the future experiment by making the robot ask for feedback after every move, and in response to a negative feedback convey its egocentric perspective (e.g. "but I moved them to my left/right"). Using the takeaways from the pilot in our next study we plan to explore *how children's choice of perspective is affected by the robotic's choice of perspective.*

Acknowledgements. Special thanks to the staff of *Ideia o nosso sonho* school for their participation and support. This work is supported by Fundação para a Ciência e a Tecnologia (FCT) through funding of the scholarship PD/BD/135150/2017 and project UIDB/50021/2020, and CHILI laboratory in EPFL.

References

1. Yadollahi, E., Johal, W., Paiva, A., Dillenbourg, P.: Anonymous: when deictic gestures in a robot can harm child-robot collaboration. In: Proceedings of the 17th ACM Conference on Interaction Design and Children, pp. 195–206 (2018)
2. Belpaeme, T., et al.: L2tor-second language tutoring using social robots. In: Proceedings of the ICSR 2015 WONDER Workshop (2015)
3. Castellano, G., et al.: Towards empathic virtual and robotic tutors. In: Lane, H.C., Yacef, K., Mostow, J., Pavlik, P. (eds.) AIED 2013. LNCS (LNAI), vol. 7926, pp. 733–736. Springer, Heidelberg (2013). https://doi.org/10.1007/978-3-642-39112-5_100
4. Flavell, J.H., Everett, B.A., Croft, K., Flavell, E.R.: Young children's knowledge about visual perception: further evidence for the level 1-level 2 distinction. Dev. Psychol. **17**(1), 99 (1981)
5. Gordon, G., Breazeal, C.: Bayesian active learning-based robot tutor for children's word-reading skills. In: Twenty-Ninth AAAI Conference on Artificial Intelligence (2015)
6. Hood, D., Lemaignan, S., Dillenbourg, P.: When children teach a robot to write: an autonomous teachable humanoid which uses simulated handwriting. In: Proceedings of the Tenth Annual ACM/IEEE International Conference on Human-Robot Interaction, pp. 83–90 (2015)
7. Levinson, S.C.: Language and space. Ann. Rev. Anthropol. **25**(1), 353–382 (1996)
8. Lu, Y., Chen, C., Chen, P., Chen, X., Zhuang, Z.: Smart learning partner: an interactive robot for education. In: Penstein Rosé, C., et al. (eds.) AIED 2018. LNCS (LNAI), vol. 10948, pp. 447–451. Springer, Cham (2018). https://doi.org/10.1007/978-3-319-93846-2_84
9. Masangkay, Z.S., McCluskey, K.A., McIntyre, C.W., Sims-Knight, J., Vaughn, B.E., Flavell, J.H.: The early development of inferences about the visual percepts of others. Child Dev. **45**, 357–366 (1974)
10. Michelon, P., Zacks, J.M.: Two kinds of visual perspective taking. Percept. Psychophys. **68**(2), 327–337 (2006)
11. Mintz, F.E., Trafton, J.G., Marsh, E., Perzanowski, D.: Choosing frames of referenece: perspective-taking in a 2D and 3D navigational task. In: Proceedings of the Human Factors and Ergonomics Society Annual Meeting, vol. 48, pp. 1933–1937. SAGE Publications Sage, Los Angeles (2004)

12. Moll, H., Meltzoff, A.N.: How does it look? Level 2 perspective-taking at 36 months of age. Child Dev. **82**(2), 661–673 (2011)
13. Moll, H., Meltzoff, A.N., Merzsch, K., Tomasello, M.: Taking versus confronting visual perspectives in preschool children. Dev. Psychol. **49**(4), 646 (2013)
14. Moll, H., Tomasello, M.: Level 1 perspective-taking at 24 months of age. Br. J. Dev. Psychol. **24**(3), 603–613 (2006)
15. Muldner, K., Lozano, C., Girotto, V., Burleson, W., Walker, E.: Designing a tangible learning environment with a teachable agent. In: Lane, H.C., Yacef, K., Mostow, J., Pavlik, P. (eds.) AIED 2013. LNCS (LNAI), vol. 7926, pp. 299–308. Springer, Heidelberg (2013). https://doi.org/10.1007/978-3-642-39112-5_31
16. Newcombe, N., Huttenlocher, J.: Children's early ability to solve perspective-taking problems. Dev. Psychol. **28**(4), 635 (1992)
17. Piaget, J.: Child's Conception of Space: Selected Works, vol. 4. Routledge, Abingdon (2013)
18. Sodian, B., Thoermer, C., Metz, U.: Now I see it but you don't: 14-month-olds can represent another person's visual perspective. Dev. Sci. **10**(2), 199–204 (2007)
19. Steels, L., Loetzsch, M.: Perspective alignment in spatial language. arXiv preprint cs/0605012 (2006)
20. Surtees, A., Apperly, I., Samson, D.: Similarities and differences in visual and spatial perspective-taking processes. Cognition **129**(2), 426–438 (2013)
21. Surtees, A., Samson, D., Apperly, I.: Unintentional perspective-taking calculates whether something is seen, but not how it is seen. Cognition **148**, 97–105 (2016)
22. Tomasello, M.: Origins of Human Communication. MIT Press, Cambridge (2010)
23. Trafton, J.G., Cassimatis, N.L., Bugajska, M.D., Brock, D.P., Mintz, F.E., Schultz, A.C.: Enabling effective human-robot interaction using perspective-taking in robots. IEEE Trans. Syst. Man Cybern.-Part A: Syst. Hum. **35**(4), 460–470 (2005)

Evaluating Student Learning in a Synchronous, Collaborative Programming Environment Through Log-Based Analysis of Projects

Bernard Yett$^{(\boxtimes)}$, Nicole Hutchins, Caitlin Snyder, Ningyu Zhang,
Shitanshu Mishra, and Gautam Biswas

Department of EECS, Institute for Software Integrated Systems, Vanderbilt
University, 1025 16th Avenue South, Nashville, TN 37212, USA
{bernard.h.yett,nicole.m.hutchins,caitlin.r.snyder,ningyu.zhang,
shitanshu.mishra,gautam.biswas}@vanderbilt.edu

Abstract. In this paper we present an initial analysis of synchronous, collaborative programming in a robotics platform. Students worked in dyads and triads to complete a week-long curriculum targeting the learning of cybersecurity and computational thinking concepts, and their application using realistic robotics scenarios. We demonstrate how an analysis of individual student activity data within a group can be extrapolated to understand the group's collaborative problem-solving. We compare our findings to past literature and discuss future implications of collaborative programming research.

Keywords: Collaborative learning · Robotics · Programming action logs · K-12 education · Computational thinking · Cybersecurity

1 Introduction

Collaborative problem-solving is an essential 21st century workforce skill. Collaborative learning and problem solving have proven to be especially useful in the context of programming tasks [6]. Efforts to introduce collaborative programming in K-12 classrooms have led to tools and curricula that support co-located and remote programming tasks. However, limitations exist in the application of these tools in today's classrooms, including the inability to distinguish individual student programming actions in co-located peer-programming environments and the inability of group members to communicate and discuss verbally when they are physically separated [21].

Collaboration represents "a coordinated, synchronous activity that is a result of a continuous attempt to construct and maintain a shared conception of a problem" [14, p. 70]. Research has examined collaborative discourse for improved understanding of problem-solving [16,17] and regulatory [5,13] processes that collaborative teams implement during a programming task. However, to our

© Springer Nature Switzerland AG 2020
I. I. Bittencourt et al. (Eds.): AIED 2020, LNAI 12164, pp. 352–357, 2020.
https://doi.org/10.1007/978-3-030-52240-7_64

knowledge, limited research has examined individual log actions of co-located students participating in a collaborative programming environment to solve problems. In our research, we examine log data of collaborative groups working in a synchronous, block-based programming environment (BBPE), NetsBlox [3], to answer (1) *What can individual student log data tell us about the group's collaborative programming?* and (2) *How do these programming activities impact student learning?* We first provide a brief background on K-12 collaborative programming. This is followed by our log-based analysis of individual students' programming activities, and their implications on collaborative program generation. We conclude with a discussion and future implications of our research.

2   Background

Collaborative programming is an effective pedagogical approach for the learning computer science concepts and practices [6,11,18]. Research has demonstrated significant benefits (i.e., learning gains) during pair programming (two, co-located students sharing one computer) that targets inclusivity [10,18]. However, peer programming studies in K-12 have not considered designing for equality of control of the task [7] and conversational equity [15].

Recent efforts have led to the development of synchronous, collaborative programming environments [2,3,21]. These environments allow students to be co-located but working on separate machines, thus improving equality of control in the programming task while still allowing face-to-face discussions. Initial analysis of these approaches have mainly targeted discourse analysis (e.g., [21]), including comparing this approach to the more well-known pair programming. Understandings of individual student actions, captured through log data, as part of the collaborative programming task are under-researched.

3   Methods

Thirty-eight high school students participated in our intervention aimed at teaching cybersecurity and computational thinking (CT) concepts using a robotic environment as a teaching tool. Students were evaluated in cybersecurity and CT, and the results were computed as average normalized change (ANC) [12] from pre-test to post-test. An overview of the intervention and the BBPE used are presented in [9]. The computed learning gains were statistically significant in both cybersecurity and CT [20].

To analyze student work, we extracted relevant information from their activity logs and modeled the students' actions as solution construction (SC) or solution assessment (SA) actions. SC actions were subdivided into (1) **SC_ computational** actions that include adding, connecting, disconnecting, or removing a block, and (2) **SC_conceptual** actions that refer to creating, modifying, or deleting a custom block definition. SA actions were subdivided into (1) **SA_global** actions for starting a simulation simultaneously for all Sprites, (2) **SA_local** actions for starting a simulation only for the current Sprite, and (3) **SA_stop** actions for stopping all scripts for all Sprites. In addition, **change_view** actions occur when a student changes the working view from one Sprite to another. Since more complex programs tend to have multiple Sprites, this action provides important information about the context of model-building.

We aggregated these results across the four days of group work during the intervention, using the Gini coefficient [4] as a means of comparing the distribution of actions by different students within a particular group. Spearman's ρ [19] was then used to compare results. As a smaller Gini coefficient result indicates more equality in action distribution, a descending approach was used for ranking results. All other categories were treated in the usual ascending manner. The Benjamini-Hochberg (B-H) procedure [1] ($Q = 0.25$) was used for group and individual results separately to control for false positives.

To be considered a group, each member had to contribute at least one action to at least one group project, completed the pre-post-test, and worked together for at least three of the four collaborative days. This process resulted in twelve groups ($n = 12$) with sufficient data to analyze—six dyads and six triads.

For computing the number of actions by each group member, we first excluded any projects that at least one group member did not contribute to. Then, groups were evaluated based on their Gini coefficient, the average number of group actions taken per group member per day (Group Actions), the average ANC of all group members (Average ANC), and the average number of each category of actions taken per group member per day (for example, Group SA_local Actions). In total, eleven tests of significance were conducted.

We also analyzed students at the individual level, to observe if holding particular self-appointed responsibilities within a group improved their own conceptual knowledge as a result. We started with the thirty students making up the groups from the previous analysis. One was disqualified due to perfect scores on the pre-post-tests (resulting in no observable ANC), leaving twenty-nine ($n = 29$) for final analysis. The students were evaluated on pre-post growth in terms of ANC, actions they took as individuals while working on group projects (Individual actions), and the percentage of actions taken by an individual relative to their group (Individual Share of Actions). These measures were further divided into the six categories of actions provided above, resulting in fourteen tests of significance.

4   Results

We begin with a breakdown of the actions performed by students that fell under the previously detailed criteria for inclusion: (1) SA_local = 16,185 actions; (2) SC_computational = 27,377 actions; (3) change_view = 2,490 actions; (4) SA_global = 2,221 actions; (5) SC_conceptual = 782 actions; and (6) SA_stop = 918 actions. The majority of group actions taken were a combination of SA_local and SC_computational (75+% for every group), as well as 75+% for all but one individual student (60+% for that student).

The results for groups as a whole appear in Table 1. The lone significant result ($p < 0.05$) was the relationship between the Gini coefficient and the number of actions taken by a group divided by the number of group members and the number of days that group worked together ($\rho = 0.61, p = 0.04$). However, B-H analysis indicated that this was a false positive. All other results had weak correlations, indicating that no group categories had a significant impact on the ANC of students in those groups.

Table 1. Most significant correlation coefficients of group-based results

Variable 1	Variable 2	Spearman's ρ	p-value
Gini coefficient	Group actions	0.61	0.04
SA_global	Average ANC	−0.34	0.29
Gini coefficient	Average ANC	0.21	0.50
Group actions	Average ANC	0.19	0.56

Finally, we analyze results for individual students (though still within the context of their group work), seen in Table 2. The primary result of significance ($p < 0.01$) compared the average normalized change for each student to the percentage of actions that fall within the SC_computational category ($\rho = 0.47, p = 0.009$). Post hoc B-H procedure confirmed the validity of this result, though it rejected the apparently significant ($p < 0.05$) result corresponding to a student's quantity of SC_computational actions per day ($\rho = 0.38, p = 0.04$). Other results presented here were only weakly positively correlated and were not statistically significant.

Table 2. Most significant correlation coefficients of individual-based results

Variable 1	Variable 2	Spearman's ρ	p-value
ANC	**Share of SC_computational actions**	**0.47**	**0.009**
ANC	Individual SC_computational actions	0.38	0.04
ANC	Overall share of actions	0.31	0.10
ANC	Individual SA_global actions	0.30	0.11
ANC	Overall actions	0.28	0.14

5   Conclusions and Future Work

Our findings indicate that students who heavily participated in model building (SC_computational actions) experienced some pre-post-test gains. This will inform future work as we seek to more systematically evaluate log actions while incorporating both more advanced techniques such as differential sequence mining [8,22] and additional data sources for more accurate action counts. We also seek to combine this log-based approach with discourse analysis [16, 21] to create a comprehensive framework for analyzing students during synchronous, collaborative programming tasks - particularly during solution construction.

Acknowledgements. This material is based in part upon work supported by National Security Agency Science of Security Lablet H98230-18-D-0010 and National Science Foundation grants CNS-1644848, CNS-1521617, and DRL-1640199. Any opinions, findings, and conclusions expressed in this material are those of the author(s) and do not necessarily reflect the views of the US Government.

References

1. Benjamini, Y., Hochberg, Y.: Controlling the false discovery rate: a practical and powerful approach to multiple testing. J. Roy. Stat. Soc.: Ser. B (Methodol.) **57**(1), 289–300 (1995). https://doi.org/10.2307/2346101
2. Boyer, K.E., Dwight, A.A., Fondren, R.T., Vouk, M.A., Lester, J.C.: A development environment for distributed synchronous collaborative programming. In: ITiCSE (2008). https://doi.org/10.1145/1384271.1384315
3. Broll, B., et al.: A visual programming environment for learning distributed programming. In: Proceedings of the 2017 ACM SIGCSE Technical Symposium on Computer Science Education, pp. 81–86 (2017). https://doi.org/10.1145/3017680.3017741
4. Dorfman, R.: A formula for the GINI coefficient. Rev. Econ. Stat., 146–149 (1979). https://doi.org/10.2307/1924845
5. Emara, M., Tscholl, M., Dong, Y., Biswas, G.: Analyzing Students' Collaborative Regulation Behaviors in a Classroom-integrated Open Ended Learning Environment. International Society of the Learning Sciences, Philadelphia (2017)
6. Hanks, B., Fitzgerald, S., McCauley, R.A., Murphy, L., Zander, C.: Pair programming in education: a literature review. Comput. Sci. Educ. **21**, 135–173 (2011). https://doi.org/10.1080/08993408.2011.579808
7. Infante, C., Hidalgo, P., Nussbaum, M., Alarcón, R., Gottlieb, A.: Multiple mice based collaborative one-to-one learning. Comput. Educ. **53**(2), 393–401 (2009). https://doi.org/10.1016/j.compedu.2009.02.015
8. Kinnebrew, J.S., Segedy, J.R., Biswas, G.: Integrating model-driven and data-driven techniques for analyzing learning behaviors in open-ended learning environments. IEEE Trans. Learn. Technol. **10**(2), 140–153 (2015). https://doi.org/10.1109/TLT.2015.2513387
9. Lédeczi, Á., et al.: Teaching cybersecurity with networked robots. In: Proceedings of the 50th ACM Technical Symposium on Computer Science Education, pp. 885–891 (2019). https://doi.org/10.1145/3287324.3287450
10. Liebenberg, J., Mentz, E., Breed, B.: Pair programming and secondary school girls' enjoyment of programming and the subject information technology (IT). Comput. Sci. Educ. **22**(3), 219–236 (2012). https://doi.org/10.1080/08993408.2012.713180
11. Lim, S.: Implementing social learning for more equitable collaboration in introductory computer science education (2019). https://doi.org/10.7298/hjfz-t152
12. Marx, J.D., Cummings, K.: Normalized change. Am. J. Phys. **75**(1), 87–91 (2007). https://doi.org/10.1119/1.2372468

13. Müller, M.M.: A preliminary study on the impact of a pair design phase on pair programming and solo programming. Inf. Softw. Technol. **48**(5), 335–344 (2006). https://doi.org/10.1016/j.infsof.2005.09.008. http://www.sciencedirect.com/science/article/pii/S0950584905001412. eASE 2005

14. Roschelle, J., Teasley, S.D.: The construction of shared knowledge in collaborative problem solving. In: O'Malley, C. (ed.) Computer Supported Collaborative Learning. NATO ASI Series, vol. 128, pp. 69–97. Springer, Berlin (1995). https://doi.org/10.1007/978-3-642-85098-1_5

15. Shah, N., Lewis, C., Caires, R.: Analyzing equity in collaborative learning situations: a comparative case study in elementary computer science. International Society of the Learning Sciences, Boulder (2014). https://doi.org/10.22318/icls2014.495

16. Snyder, C., Hutchins, N., Biswas, G., Emara, M., Grover, S., Conlin, L.: Analyzing students' synergistic learning processes in physics and CT by collaborative discourse analysis (2019). https://doi.org/10.22318/cscl2019.360

17. Tsan, J., Lynch, C.F., Boyer, K.E.: "Alright, what do we need?": A study of young coders' collaborative dialogue. Int. J. Child-Comput. Interact. **17**, 61–71 (2018). https://doi.org/10.1016/j.ijcci.2018.03.001. http://www.sciencedirect.com/science/article/pii/S2212868917300387

18. Werner, L., Denner, J., Campe, S., Torres, D.M.: Computational sophistication of games programmed by children: a model for its measurement. ACM Trans. Comput. Educ. **20**(2) (2020). https://doi.org/10.1145/3379351

19. Wissler, C.: The spearman correlation formula. Science **22**(558), 309–311 (1905)

20. Yett, B., et al.: A hands-on cybersecurity curriculum using a robotics platform. In: Proceedings of the 51st ACM Technical Symposium on Computer Science Education, pp. 1040–1046 (2020). https://doi.org/10.1145/3328778.3366878

21. Zakaria, Z., et al.: Collaborative talk across two pair-programming configurations. In: International Society of the Learning Sciences (ISLS), June 2019. https://doi.org/10.22318/cscl2019.224

22. Zhang, N., Biswas, G.: Understanding students' problem-solving strategies in a synergistic learning-by-modeling environment. In: Penstein Rosé, C., et al. (eds.) AIED 2018. LNCS (LNAI), vol. 10948, pp. 405–410. Springer, Cham (2018). https://doi.org/10.1007/978-3-319-93846-2_76

Adaptive Forgetting Curves for Spaced Repetition Language Learning

Ahmed Zaidi$^{(\boxtimes)}$, Andrew Caines, Russell Moore, Paula Buttery,
and Andrew Rice

ALTA Institute and Department of Computer Science and Technology,
University of Cambridge, 15 JJ Thomson Avenue, Cambridge CB3 0FD, UK
{ahz22,apc38,rjm49,pjb48,acr31}@cam.ac.uk

Abstract. The *forgetting curve* has been extensively explored by psychologists, educationalists and cognitive scientists alike. In the context of Intelligent Tutoring Systems, modelling the forgetting curve for each user and knowledge component (e.g. vocabulary word) should enable us to develop optimal revision strategies that counteract memory decay and ensure long-term retention. In this study we explore a variety of forgetting curve models incorporating psychological and linguistic features, and we use these models to predict the probability of word recall by learners of English as a second language. We evaluate the impact of the models and their features using data from an online vocabulary teaching platform and find that word complexity is a highly informative feature which may be successfully learned by a neural network model.

Keywords: Spaced repetition · Language learning · Forgetting curve · Neural networks · Adaptive learning

1 Introduction

Optimal human learning techniques have been extensively studied by researchers in psychology [4] and computer science [8,16,19,20]. The impact of learning techniques can be measured by how they affect the long-term retention of the learning materials. Measuring retention requires a model of the human forgetting curve, which plots the probability of recall over time. The first version of the forgetting curve was defined by Ebbinghaus [5] but has since been developed further by many researchers who have incorporated additional psychologically grounded variations to the model [3,9,13,14,17]. The ideal forgetting curve should adapt to learning materials as well as user meta-features (including current ability). In this study we examine the task of vocabulary learning. We investigate a range of linguistically motivated features, meta-features, and a variety of models in order to predict the probability a given learner will correctly recall a particular word.

© Springer Nature Switzerland AG 2020
I. I. Bittencourt et al. (Eds.): AIED 2020, LNAI 12164, pp. 358–363, 2020.
https://doi.org/10.1007/978-3-030-52240-7_65

2   Method

We use the Duolingo spaced repetition dataset [15] in order to train and evaluate our features and variety of models. The dataset is filtered for English language learners which results in approximately 4.28 million learner-word datapoints. Our models are a modification of the half-life regression model proposed by Settles and Meeder [16].

2.1   Half-Life Regression (HLR)

The half-life regression model is defined as follows:

$$p = 2^{-\Delta/h} \tag{1}$$

where p is the probability of recall, Δ is the time since last seen (days) and h is the *half-life* or strength of the learner's memory. We denote the estimated half-life by $\hat{h}_\Theta$, and it is defined as:

$$\hat{h}_\Theta = 2^{\Theta \cdot \mathbf{x}} \tag{2}$$

where Θ is a vector of weights for the features $\mathbf{x}$. The features of the model are made up of lexeme tags, one tag for each word in the vocabulary (e.g. the lexeme tag for word *camera* is *camera.N.SG*). The aim of these features is to capture the inherent difficulty of the word.

The HLR model is trained using the following loss function:

$$\ell(\mathbf{x}; \Theta) = (p - \hat{p}_\Theta)^2 + (h - \hat{h}_\Theta)^2 + \lambda||\Theta||_2^2 \tag{3}$$

In practice, it was found that optimising for both p and h in the loss function improved the model. The true value of h is defined as $h = \frac{-\Delta}{log(p)}$. p and $\hat{p}_\Theta$ are the true probability and model estimated probability of recall, respectively.

2.2   HLR with Linguistic/Psychological Features (HLR+)

We now expand on the HLR model by adding additional linguistic, psychological and meta-features to $\mathbf{x}$. We refer to this model as HLR+. The features include *word complexity* scores estimated by a pre-trained model [6], *mean concreteness* scores and *percent known* based on human judgements [2], *SUBTLEX* word frequencies [18] and *user ids*.

The motivation for including complexity as a feature is based on the intuition that the more complex the word, the harder it is to remember. Concreteness is included based on previous work showing that concrete words are easier to remember than abstract words because they activate perceptual memory codes in addition to verbal codes [10]. SUBTLEX is the relative frequency of an English word based on a corpus of 201.3 million words: we hypothesise that more frequent words are more likely to be encountered and reinforced during the time since last seen Δ. Similarly, we expect that 'percent known' (the proportion of respondents familiar with each word based on survey data) will correlate with probability of recall. Lastly, we include user id to capture latent behavioural aspects about the learners.

2.3   Complexity-Based Half-Life Regression (C-HLR+)

In addition to adding new features, we now describe a new model that modifies the p such that it directly incorporates word complexity. Gooding et al. [6] derived *word complexity* to express perceived difficulty. We hypothesise that this will correlate with probability of recall. As the complexity of the word rises, the forgetting curve will become steeper. Therefore, the new model is as follows:

$$p = 2^{-\Delta \cdot C_i / h} \tag{4}$$

where C is the mean complexity for word i. We define estimated half-life $\hat{h}_\Theta$ as $2^{\Theta \cdot \mathbf{x}}$ where $\mathbf{x}$ is a vector composed of all of the features described in Sect. 2.2.

2.4   Neural Half-Life Regression (N-HLR+)

Motivated by the recent success of neural networks, we now describe the N-HLR+ model which replaces $\hat{h}_\Theta = 2^{\Theta \cdot \mathbf{x}}$ with a neural network. The network can be described as follows:

$$\hat{h}_\Theta = ReLU(\mathbf{x} \cdot \mathbf{w_1}) \cdot \mathbf{w_2} \tag{5}$$

where the network contains a single hidden layer. $\mathbf{x}$ is a vector of input features, $\mathbf{w_1}$ is the weight matrix between the inputs and the hidden layer and $\mathbf{w_2}$ is the weight matrix between the hidden layer and the output. We use the same loss function as HLR which optimises for both p and h.

2.5   Evaluation and Implementation

We use mean absolute error (MAE) of probability of recall for a lexical item as our evaluation metric which, despite some known problems [11], is in line with previous work [16]. MAE is defined as: $\frac{1}{D} \sum_D^{i=1} |p - \hat{p_\Theta}|_i$, where D is the total data instances.

We divided the Duolingo English data into 90% training and 10% test. We trained all non-neural models (e.g. HLR, HLR+, C-HLR) using the following parameters which were tuned on the first 500k data points—learning rate: 0.001, alpha α: 0.01, λ: 0.1. For all neural models (e.g. N-HLR), we used—learning rate: 0.001, epochs: 200, hidden dim: 4.

Table 1. Evaluation of forgetting curve models. Pimsleur and Leitner are previous methods of modelling the forgetting curve.

Model	MAE↓
Pimsleur[12]	0.396
Leitner[7]	0.214
Logistic Regression	0.196
HLR[16]	0.195
HLR-lex[16]	0.130

Model	MAE↓
HLR+	0.129
C-HLR+	0.109
N-HLR+	**0.105**
CN-HLR+	**0.105**

3   Results and Discussion

We can see in Table 1 that HLR+ did not perform much better than HLR. By modifying the loss function to include complexity as a parameter in the C-HLR+ model, we considerably improved the performance of our model. This was in line with our hypothesis that more complex words are forgotten faster and thus are an important feature in modelling the forgetting curve.

The N-HLR+ model provided additional improvements to the C-HLR+ model. This is due to the fact that neural models are better at capturing non-linearities between the features and the expected output. Furthermore, when compared to the N-HLR+ model we can see that including complexity into the loss function (CN-HLR+) provides no clear improvements in performance. This is because the model learns to place more importance on the *complexity feature*. We confirm this by analysing the average weights in the hidden layer of the model. The model learns to give greater importance to word complexity, percent known, and concreteness respectively. It does not however, learn much from the user id and SUBTLEX. This is probably due to the fact that a single dimension for capturing user behaviour is not sufficient and that SUBTLEX does not adequately represent learners' experience with English as a second language.

4   Conclusion

We present a new model for adaptively learning a forgetting curve for language learning using a modified HLR loss function and a neural network. We incorporate linguistically and psychologically motivated features and show that word complexity is an important feature in predicting probability of recall for a vocabulary item. Furthermore, we illustrate that neural networks can capture the importance of word complexity while a simple HLR fails to take advantage of that signal. This work lays the foundation for work in neural approaches to understanding language learning over time. Future work in this area includes incorporating high-dimensional user embeddings to capture user specific signals that might influence the forgetting curve, and also different models such as Pareto and power functions which have been proposed in prior work [1].

Acknowledgements. This paper reports on research supported by Cambridge Assessment, University of Cambridge.

References

1. Averell, L., Heathcote, A.: The form of the forgetting curve and the fate of memories. J. Math. Psychol. **55**, 25–35 (2011)
2. Brysbaert, M., Warriner, A.B., Kuperman, V.: Concreteness ratings for 40 thousand generally known English word lemmas. Behav. Res. Methods **46**(3), 904–911 (2013). https://doi.org/10.3758/s13428-013-0403-5
3. Choffin, B., Popineau, F., Bourda, Y., Vie, J.: DAS3H: modeling student learning and forgetting for optimally scheduling distributed practice of skills. In: Proceedings of The 12th International Conference on Educational Data Mining (EDM) (2019)
4. Dunlosky, J., Rawson, K.A., Marsh, E.J., Nathan, M.J., Willingham, D.T.: Improving students' learning with effective learning techniques: promising directions from cognitive and educational psychology. Psychol. Sci. Public Interest **14**(1), 4–58 (2013)
5. Ebbinghaus, H.: Ueber das gedächtnis (1885)
6. Gooding, S., Kochmar, E.: Complex word identification as a sequence labelling task. In: Proceedings of the 57th Annual Meeting of the Association for Computational Linguistics, pp. 1148–1153 (2019)
7. Leitner, S.: So lernt man lernen: angewandte Lernpsychologie-ein Weg zum Erfolg. Herder (1972)
8. Moore, R., Caines, A., Elliott, M., Zaidi, A., Rice, A., Buttery, P.: Skills embeddings: a neural approach to multicomponent representations of students and tasks. In: Proceedings of The 12th International Conference on Educational Data Mining (EDM), vol. 360, p. 365. ERIC (2019)
9. Mozer, M.C., Wiseheart, M., Novikoff, T.P.: Artificial intelligence to support human instruction. Proc. Natl. Acad. Sci. **116**(10), 3953–3955 (2019)
10. Paivio, A.: Imagery and Verbal Processes. Psychology Press, Hove (2013)
11. Pelánek, R.: Metrics for evaluation of student models. J. Educ. Data Min. **7**(2), 1–19 (2015)
12. Pimsleur, P.: A memory schedule. Modern Lang. J. **51**(2), 73–75 (1967)
13. Reddy, S., Levine, S., Dragan, A.: Accelerating human learning with deep reinforcement learning. In: NeurIPS Workshop: Teaching Machines, Robots, and Humans (2017)
14. Rubin, D.C., Wenzel, A.E.: One hundred years of forgetting: a quantitative description of retention. Psychol. Rev. **103**(4), 734 (1996)
15. Settles, B.: Replication data for: a trainable spaced repetition model for language learning (2017). https://doi.org/10.7910/DVN/N8XJME
16. Settles, B., Meeder, B.: A trainable spaced repetition model for language learning. In: Proceedings of the 54th Annual Meeting of the Association for Computational Linguistics (Volume 1: Long Papers), vol. 1, pp. 1848–1858 (2016)
17. Tabibian, B., Upadhyay, U., De, A., Zarezade, A., Schölkopf, B., Gomez-Rodriguez, M.: Enhancing human learning via spaced repetition optimization. Proc. Natl. Acad. Sci. **116**(10), 3988–3993 (2019)
18. Van Heuven, W.J., Mandera, P., Keuleers, E., Brysbaert, M.: SUBTLEX-UK: a new and improved word frequency database for British English. Q. J. Exp. Psychol. **67**(6), 1176–1190 (2014)

19. Zaidi, A.H., Caines, A., Davis, C., Moore, R., Buttery, P., Rice, A.: Accurate modelling of language learning tasks and students using representations of grammatical proficiency. In: Proceedings of The 12th International Conference on Educational Data Mining (EDM) (2019)
20. Zaidi, A.H., Moore, R., Briscoe, T.: Curriculum Q-learning for visual vocabulary acquisition. In: Proceedings of Visually-Grounded Interaction and Language (ViGIL). NeurIPS (2017)

Learning from Interpretable Analysis: Attention-Based Knowledge Tracing

Jia Zhu[1,2] , Weihao Yu[1] , Zetao Zheng[1(✉)] , Changqin Huang[1] ,
Yong Tang[1] , and Gabriel Pui Cheong Fung[3]

[1] Guangzhou Key Laboratory of Big Data and Intelligent Education, School
of Computer Science, South China Normal University, Guangzhou, China
{jzhu,whyu,ztzheng,cqhuang,ytang}@m.scnu.edu.cn
[2] Deceneuron Intelligence Co., Ltd, Hong Kong, China
[3] Department of Systems Engineering and Engineering Management, The Chinese
University of HongKong, Hong Kong, China
pcfung@se.cuhk.edu.hk

Abstract. Knowledge tracing is a well-established problem and non-trivial task in personalized education. In recent years, many existing works have been proposed to handle the knowledge tracing task, particularly recurrent neural networks based methods, e.g., Deep Knowledge Tracing (DKT). However, DKT has the problem of vibration in prediction outputs. In this paper, to better understand the problem of DKT, we utilize a mathematical computation model named Finite State Automaton(FSA), which can change from one state to another in response to the external input, to interpret the hidden state transition of the DKT when receiving inputs. And we discover the root cause of the two problems is that the DKT can not handle the long sequence input with the help of FSA. Accordingly, we propose an effective attention-based model, which can solve the above problem by directly capturing the relationships among each item of the input regardless of the length of the input sequence. The experimental results show that our proposed model can significantly outperform state-of-the-art approaches on several well-known corpora.

Keywords: Knowledge tracing · Interpretable analysis · Self attention

1 Introduction

With the development of modern technologies, online platforms for intelligent tutoring systems(ITS) and massive open online courses are becoming more and

Supported by the National Natural Science Foundation of China (No.61877020, No.U1811263 and No.61772211), the Key-Area Research and Development Program of Guangdong Province, China (No.2018B010109002) and the Science and Technology Project of Guangzhou Municipality, China (No.201904010393), as well as the Guangzhou Key Laboratory of Big Data and Intelligent Education (No.201905010009).

ⓒ Springer Nature Switzerland AG 2020
I. I. Bittencourt et al. (Eds.): AIED 2020, LNAI 12164, pp. 364–368, 2020.
https://doi.org/10.1007/978-3-030-52240-7_66

more prevalent. And knowledge tracing (KT) is considered to be critical for personalized learning in ITS. KT is the task of modeling students' knowledge state based on historical data, which represents the mastery level of knowledge.

One of the well-known methods to solve the KT problem is recurrent neural networks (RNNs) based model called deep knowledge tracing (DKT) [5]. Although DKT achieves impressive performance for the KT task, it still exists the vibration in prediction outputs [9]. This is unreasonable as students' knowledge state is expected to transit gradually over time, but not to alternate between mastering and not-yet-mastered.

To find out the root cause of the problem, we utilize FSA as an interpretable structure which can be learned from DKT because FSA has a more interpretable inner mechanism when processing sequential data [3]. We built an FSA for DKT referring [3] to interpret how elements on each input sequence affect the hidden state of DKT. When an input item was accepted by the FSA, it represents that this item has a positive effect on the final prediction outputs of the model, and vice versa. We display the acceptance rate of every input sequence in Fig. 1. We can draw the conclusion from Fig. 1 that the longer the input sequence, the higher the proportion of rejected items, and the lower prediction accuracy. This phenomenon is consistent with the description in [7], who points out that LSTM [2] has the weakness of capturing feature when the input sequence is too long. Accordingly, we proposed a model to solve the problem of long sequence input in KT and experiments show that our proposed model is effective in solving the problem we discovered above.

Our contributions are three-fold. Firstly, to the best of our knowledge, we are the first group to adopt FSA to provide deep analysis on KT task. By interpreting the learning state change using FSA, we can obtain a better understanding of the problem of existing RNN based methods. Secondly, according to the interpretable analysis, we propose a multi-head attention model to handle the problem of long sequence input in KT. Lastly, we evaluate our model on real-world datasets and the results show that our model improves the state-of-the-art baselines.

2 Proposed Models

In this section, we will describe the KTA in briefly. The overall structure of the model is shown in Fig. 2. (1) **Embedding Layer:** The tuples that contain the questions and the corresponding answers are first projected into real-value vectors, namely one-hot embeddings. (2) **Feature Extraction:** After that, The vectors are fed into a feature extractor, which aims at capturing the latent dependency relationships among the inputs. The main component of the feature extractor consists of N identical blocks. Each block has two sub-layers. The first is a multi-head self-attention mechanism [8], the critical element of the extractor, and the second is a fully connected feed-forward network [8]. Self-attention achieves the extraction of the global relationship by calculating the similarity of each item among the input sequence using the scaled dot-product attention [8]. Here, the attention is calculated h times, which allows the model to

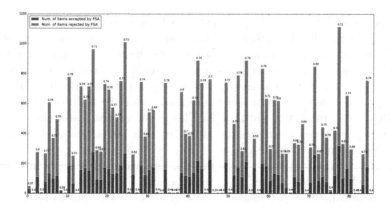

Fig. 1. Accept/Reject States of DKT. The values above each bar represent the proportion of the rejected items in an input sequence.

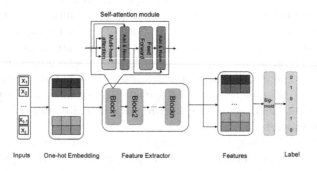

Fig. 2. An illustration of our KTA model.

learn relevant information in different representative sub-spaces, and making it so-called multi-head. **(3) Prediction and Loss:** On the prediction stage, only the topmost outputs of attention sub-layer are taken to a Sigmoid function to make the final decision. The prediction and optimization processes are the same as [9], we would not elaborate here.

3   Experiments

AUC Results. We evaluated our models on four popular datasets which are also used in [9]. We also select four popular methods for comparison, PFA [4], BKT [1], DKT [6], DKT+ [9]. Table 1 displays the AUC results of all the datasets.

According to Table 1, our proposed model achieves excellent results on four datasets on both evaluation metrics except for the Simulated-5. For example, KTA exceeds DKT+ 10% more on ASSIST2015 regards to AUC. Similar situations happened to the F1 score, and our model achieves notable improvement compared with other models. Moreover, we notice that on Simulated-5 dataset, the performance of our model is not very impressive. One reason is that there

Table 1. AUC result and F1 score for all datasets tested.

Model	BKT		PFA		DKT		DKT+		KTA	
	AUC	F1	AUC	F1	AUC	F1	AUC	F1	AUC	F1
ASSIST2009	0.712	0.789	0.658	0.795	0.821	0.834	0.823	0.836	**0.833**	**0.841**
ASSIST2015	0.575	0.828	0.506	0.829	0.736	0.832	0.737	0.830	**0.811**	**0.840**
Statics2011	0.658	0.871	0.521	0.868	0.816	0.886	0.835	0.887	**0.841**	**0.909**
Simulated-5	0.599	0.753	0.522	0.752	0.825	0.794	**0.826**	**0.796**	0.654	0.732

is no long sequence in the dataset. Therefore, our model can not exploit the advantage of capturing the long sequence. Another reason is that all the data have the same length of questions, and every question appears only once. Thus the dependence between data is not as strong as other data.

Prediction Visualization. We also provide prediction visualization, as shown in Fig. 3, in order to give a better sense of the self-attention effect on the prediction results. The figure aims to display the change in the prediction of skill along with the number of questions, e.g., s33. Concretely, our model performs more smoothly compared with DKT.

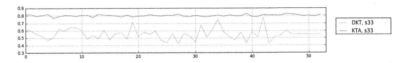

Fig. 3. Line plot for the skill 33 prediction of three models. The student interactions are extracted from ASSISTments 2009. Probability of correctly answering skill 33 is predicted by the trained models.

4 Conclusion

In this paper, we applied the FSA to interpret DKT and through the analysis of FSA, we discover that DKT can not handle the long sequence input. Therefore, we introduce a self-attention model, namely, KTA, which can directly capture the global dependency relationships by computing the similarity among each item of the input regardless of the length of the input sequence. The experimental results show that our proposed model can provide better predictions than existing models.

References

1. Corbett, A.T., Anderson, J.R.: Knowledge tracing: modeling the acquisition of procedural knowledge. User Modeling and User-Adapted Interaction pp. 253–278 (1995)
2. Hochreiter, S., Schmidhuber, J.: Long short-term memory. Neural Comput. **9**(8), 1735–1780 (1997)

3. Hou, B.J., Zhou, Z.H.: Learning with interpretable structure from RNN. arXiv:1810.10708 (2018)
4. Pavlik, P.I., Cen, H., Koedinger, K.R.: Performance factors analysis - a new alternative to knowledge tracing. In: Proceedings of the 14th International Conference on Artificial Intelligence in Education, pp. 531–538 (2009)
5. Piech, C., Bassen, J., Huang, J., Ganguli, S., Sahami, M., Guibas, L.J., Dickstein, J.S.: Deep knowledge tracing. In: Advances in Neural Information Processing Systems, pp. 505–513 (2015)
6. Piech, C., et al.: Deep knowledge tracing. In: Advances in Neural Information Processing Systems, pp. 505–513 (2015)
7. Tang, G., Müller, M., Rios, A., Sennrich, R.: Why self-attention? a targeted evaluation of neural machine translation architectures. arXiv preprint arXiv:1808.08946 (2018)
8. Vaswani, A., et al.: Attention is all you need pp. 5998–6008 (2017)
9. Yeung, C., Yeung, D.Y.: Addressing two problems in deep knowledge tracing via prediction-consistent regularization. arXiv:1806.02180 (2018)

Industry and Innovation Papers

Identifying Beneficial Learning Behaviors from Large-Scale Interaction Data

Miruna Cristus[(⊠)], Oscar Täckström, Lingyi Tan, and Valentino Pacifici

Sana Labs, Stockholm, Sweden
{miruna,oscar,lingyi,valentino}@sanalabs.com

Abstract. Understanding the effect of learning behavior is fundamental to improving learning outcomes. In this paper, we perform a behavioral analysis based on data from a large high-stakes exam preparation platform. By measuring the importance of a set of candidate learning behaviors in predicting final exam outcomes, we identify a suite of beneficial behaviors. In particular, we find that *breadth* (wide coverage of content per week) and *intensity* together with *consistency* (frequent and equal-length practice for a limited period) are most predictive of final exam success rate, among eleven studied behaviors.

Keywords: Learning behavior · Test preparation · Educational data mining

1 Introduction

Sana Labs provides personalized learning through partnership with the world's largest learning content providers. Understanding which learning behaviors lead to successful outcomes is a key focus of our research and development. The combination of online education and machine learning makes it possible to study learners' behaviors and outcomes at an unprecedented scale [17]. This combination holds promise as a way to identify key learning behaviors that can be highly beneficial or detrimental to learning outcomes [11,13]. They can in turn be used to make personalized learning more effective and enjoyable [9]. In this paper, we focus on a behavioral analysis based on data from a large high-stakes exam preparation platform, where Sana provides review sessions that help students bridge their knowledge gaps and retain their acquired knowledge.

2 Online Learning Platform

Sana powers several features on a large-scale online exam preparation platform, where students need to go through a large amount of content, typically over the course of several months. Thus, students need to actively make complex decisions about their learning schedule and what material to cover at a given point in time, to optimize learning outcomes and maximize their exam results.

© Springer Nature Switzerland AG 2020
I. I. Bittencourt et al. (Eds.): AIED 2020, LNAI 12164, pp. 371–375, 2020.
https://doi.org/10.1007/978-3-030-52240-7_67

To guide the students in this decision making process, Sana powers adaptive review sessions tailored to the needs of each student. In these sessions, Sana predicts the current and future knowledge gaps of each student [4,15,16, *inter alia*], and recommends the most appropriate content for remediation; previously seen content is also resurfaced at the optimal time intervals in line with spaced repetition to foster long-term knowledge retention [5,8,10, *inter alia*].

3   Analyzing Learning Behavior

While Sana's recommendation algorithms are based on established research on human learning strategies, it is important to understand student behavior in context to further tailor our recommendations for different use cases. Student interactions constitute a rich source of data from which to derive such insights.

3.1   Data

We collected data from each student interacting with learning material on the platform.[1] This interaction data was enriched with the final exam outcome of each student (pass/fail) to form the core data of our analysis.

To focus on interaction events related only to the observed exam outcome, we disregarded all events registered prior to a break of at least 30 days of studying. We further excluded infrequent users of the platform.[2] After filtering, we obtained a group of 6631 students, totaling over 35 million events over a period of 7 months.

3.2   Method

We defined features to capture different facets of student behavior that were hypothesized to have an impact on learning outcomes. Each behavior was encoded as a numerical feature and the impact of each feature was assessed with the Random Forest permutation importance measure [1].[3]

Specifically, we used Scikit-learn [14] to train a Random Forest classifier to predict the exam outcome (pass/fail) from the full set of features, using a 75–25% train–test split. We tuned the following hyperparameters (optimal value in parenthesis) on the training set: the maximum fraction of features to be considered for a split (0.2), the number of trees (400), and the maximum depth of a tree (50). The optimal setting resulted in 0.93 AUC [6] on the test set.

We repeated the analysis on a smaller group of 1158 students with similar practice frequency, in order to control for the effect of time spent on the platform.

---

[1] Including responses to multiple choice questions, viewing of theory or instructional video, along with outcome, when applicable.

[2] Infrequent users are defined as: students who did not have at least one interaction with each major topic of the exam, students who had used the platform for less than a week, and students who had covered less than 20% of the content on the platform.

[3] This has been shown to be more reliable than impurity-based measures [18].

We obtained 0.91 AUC on the test set, with the optimal hyperparameters being a split fraction of 0.4, 600 trees, and unlimited maximum depth.

Finally, to understand the direction of these effects, we performed t-tests on the averages of each feature between the groups of passing and failing students.

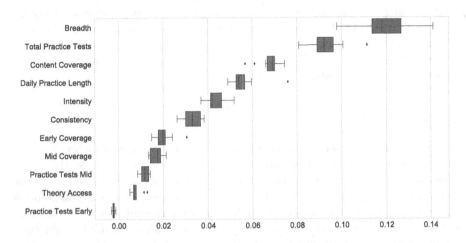

Fig. 1. Permutation importance of evaluated features. See Sect. 3.2–3.3 for details.

3.3 Results

Figure 1 shows the permutation importance of each of the analyzed features. The most effective behaviors identified, all of which are found to have positive effects, are listed below in order of importance (due to space restrictions, we are not able to describe all behaviors in detail):

- **Breadth**: the number of topics (as defined by the curriculum) the student engages with on an average week, without necessarily having completed them.
- **Total Practice Tests**: the number of practice tests taken (a practice test fully mimics the structure and timing of the real exam).
- **Content Coverage**: the percentage of unique content elements (exercises) covered across the entire study path.
- **Daily Practice Length**: the average number of content elements the student interacts with per day.
- **Intensity**: the fraction of days the student has been active on the platform out of the total number of days registered.
- **Consistency**: the reciprocal of one standard deviation of the daily practice length.

Our finding on the importance of breadth and content coverage is consistent with research on interleaved learning [3]. In the case of exam preparation, a breadth-first approach could potentially help by familiarizing the students with the structure of the content or by making associations between different topics.

Additionally, in terms of content type, we found that completing the available practice tests has a positive impact, however with diminishing returns.

Looking at daily practice length, we found that students with the highest total amount of practice do not necessarily have the best exam outcomes: these students often practice less daily, but keep studying for a longer period. It seems that learning intensity matters more than the sheer number of days of studying.

Once the effects of frequency and timing are isolated, consistency becomes important: students who spend roughly the same amount in each practice have better outcomes.[4] These finding may reflect the importance of appropriately spaced repetition on knowledge retention.

4   Limitations

Due to the limitations of data collection, we could not consider factors that are difficult or impossible to measure from the available data, for example, the knowledge state of a student prior to using the platform, their use of external resources, demographics [7], socioeconomic status [2], or motivation [12]. A causal model is also out of scope of the current study for the same reasons. Collecting relevant external information and isolating potential confounding variables would allow us to better identify beneficial learning behaviors that are addressable within the platform. Finally, we hope to verify in future studies whether the present findings are applicable to other learning platform and subjects as well.

5   Conclusion

As online learning platforms are becoming increasingly popular, there is a rising need to tailor both learning paths and content to maximize learning outcomes. In addition to personalization and adaptivity, understanding the effect of overall learning behavior is an important aspect of designing effective strategies, content organization and user experience.

Two key beneficial behaviors have been identified in this study:

1. Cover as much of the content as possible, through a breadth-first approach (interleaved learning).
2. Practice frequently and consistently (i.e. for a similar amount of time in each session).

Our findings validate the algorithms currently employed by Sana for personalized review: these sessions bring out the best content from all topics, facilitating breadth. By predicting knowledge gaps in a topic and surfacing unseen but related material from that topic, the sessions also promote content coverage. We believe that these findings provide a basis for further improvements to recommendation strategies to promote optimal learning behavior.

---

[4] The *consistency* feature has an importance score of 0.1 on the smaller dataset of 1158 students described in Sect. 3.2.

References

1. Breiman, L.: Random forests. Mach. Learn. **45**(1), 5–32 (2001)
2. Broer, M., Bai, Y., Fonseca, F.: A Review of the Literature on Socioeconomic Status and Educational Achievement, pp. 7–17. Springer, Cham (2019). https://doi.org/10.1007/978-3-030-11991-1_2
3. Carvalho, P.F., Goldstone, R.L.: When does interleaving practice improve learning? In: Dunlosky, J., Rawson, K.A. (eds.) The Cambridge Handbook of Cognition and Education. Cambridge Handbooks in Psychology, pp. 411–436. Cambridge University Press, Cambridge (2019)
4. Corbett, A.T., Anderson, J.R.: Knowledge tracing: Modelling the acquisition of procedural knowledge. User Model. User-Adapted Interact. **4**(4), 253–278 (1995)
5. Dempster, F.: Spacing effects and their implications for theory and practice. Educ. Psychol. Rev. **1**, 309–330 (1989)
6. Hanley, J., McNeil, B.: The meaning and use of the area under a receiver operating characteristic (ROC) curve. Radiology **143**(1), 29–36 (1982)
7. Islam, M.A., Rahim, A., Tan, C., Hasina, M.: Effect of demographic factors on e-learning effectiveness in a higher learning institution in malaysia. Int. Educ. Stud. **4**(1), 112–121 (2011)
8. Karpicke, J., Roediger, H.: Repeated retrieval during learning is the key to long-term retention. J. Memory Lang. **57**, 151–162 (2007)
9. Koedinger, K.R., Brunskill, E., Baker, R.S., McLaughlin, E.A., Stamper, J.: New potentials for data-driven intelligent tutoring system development and optimization. AI Magazine **34**(3), 27–41 (2013)
10. Melton, A.W.: The situation with respect to the spacing of repetitions and memory. J. Verbal Learn. Verbal Behav. **9**(5), 1 (1970)
11. Morris, L.V., Finnegan, C., Wu, S.S.: Tracking student behavior persistence and achievement in online courses. Internet Higher Educ. **8**(3), 221–231 (2005)
12. Orhan-Özen, S.: The effect of motivation on student achievement. Factors Effect. Student Achieve.: Meta-Anal. Empirical Stud. **5**, 35–56 (2017)
13. Osmanbegovic, E., Suljic, M.: Data mining approach for predicting student performance. Econ. Rev. J. Econ. Bus. **10**(1), 3–12 (2012)
14. Pedregosa, F., et al.: Scikit-learn: machine learning in Python. J. Mach. Learn. Res. **12**, 2825–2830 (2011)
15. Piech, C., et al.: Deep knowledge tracing. In: Neural Information Processing Systems (2015)
16. Rasch, G.: Studies in mathematical psychology: I. Probabilistic models for some intelligence and attainment tests. Nielsen & Lydiche (1960)
17. Romero, C., Ventura, S.: Educational data mining: A review of the state of the art. IEEE Trans. Syst. Man, Cybern. Part C (Applications and Reviews) 40(6), 601–618 (2010)
18. Strobl, C., Boulesteix, A.L., Zeileis, A., Hothorn, T.: Bias in random forest variable importance measures: illustrations, sources and a solution. BMC Bioinform. **8**(1), 25 (2007)

A Gamified Solution to the Cold-Start Problem of Intelligent Tutoring System

Yang Pian[1], Yu Lu[1,2($\boxtimes$)], Yuqi Huang[1], and Ig Ibert Bittencourt[3]

[1] Advanced Innovation Center for Future Education, Faculty of Education,
Beijing Normal University, Beijing, China
{bianyang,luyu}@bnu.edu.cn

[2] The Joint Laboratory for Mobile Learning, Ministry of Education-China Mobile
Communications Corporation, Beijing, China

[3] Federal University of Alagoas, Maceió, Brazil

Abstract. Today's intelligent tutoring systems provide more intelligent but complex services to learners. These systems encounter two critical issues: 1) the initial lack of new learner's information for running complex services, and 2) new learners failing to actively interact with these complex services due to the initial unfamiliarity. We define such issues as the "cold-start" problem in today's intelligent tutoring systems, and propose a gamified solution to tackle it. By leveraging on the established MDA model, a three-layer framework with narrative elements and task-oriented elements is designed and implemented in an ITS for mathematics. The preliminary evaluations show its effectiveness, and the proposed solution is generally applicable to other ITS systems.

Keywords: Intelligent tutoring system · Cold start · Gamification

1 Introduction

Driven by the fast advancements of artificial intelligence (AI), today's intelligent tutoring system (ITS) [12] delivers more complex and intelligent personalized learning services, such as adaptive learning path guidance, fine-grained learning resource provision, etc. From the perspective of ITS, those intelligent services normally require new learner's personal data as the built model's inputs. Otherwise the models might not be able to output accurate estimates or predictions, and sometimes even cannot operate. From the perspective of new learners, it is relatively hard to get familiar with the novel but complex learning service, which would directly decrease the system usability and painfully hinder the engagement of new learners. We define such phenomenon as the *cold-start problem* of ITS, which refers to (a) system perspective: the system's inability of providing proper learning services for new users due to the initial lack of user information, and (b) user perspective: the user's inability of making highly-engaged and efficient interactions due to the initial strangeness with the system.

© Springer Nature Switzerland AG 2020
I. I. Bittencourt et al. (Eds.): AIED 2020, LNAI 12164, pp. 376–381, 2020.
https://doi.org/10.1007/978-3-030-52240-7_68

The cold-start problem has been considered and studied in some fields, such as e-commerce and digital marketing. From the system perspective, most existing approaches to this problem attempt to optimize the models behind [11,14,15] or directly ask new users to provide the required information, such as personal preference from a mini quiz [3,5]. From the user perspective, it can be regarded as the "user onboarding" issue in product design, that is, helping a new user to become familiar with a complex digital product [6]. One of the most common approaches is to present a novice guidance for users in the initial sign-up or log-in process [10]. However, the previous studies, either from the system perspective or user perspective, have seldom considered the cold-start problem in the context of education, where learner's engagement plays a crucial role during the learning process. On one hand, engagement is closely related to user's concentration [13] in data collecting process, thus it heavily influences the integrity and accuracy of the collected personal information. On the other hand, only the highly-engaged learners could be well motivated to fully utilize the learning functions and services in ITS system [10]. Therefore, to tackle the cold-start problem of ITS, our insight hinges upon enhancing learner's engagement in both data collection process and system novice guidance.

As a method of adopting gaming elements in non-game context [16], gamification is an effective and practical way to enhance learner's engagement. The previous studies have found that the gaming elements could successfully engage users to rate more items for recommender system [2,4] and to complete the onboarding process of digital product [10]. We therefore propose a gamified solution to address the cold-start problem in ITS. The proposed solution is based on a well-established gamification design model called MDA [7], and implemented as an interactive novice guidance for learner's initial log-in process. A three-layer gamification design is utilized to enhance the engagement of system-learner interaction, so as to (a) acquaint the learner with system key functions, and (b) implicitly collect necessary learner information.

2 Solution Design

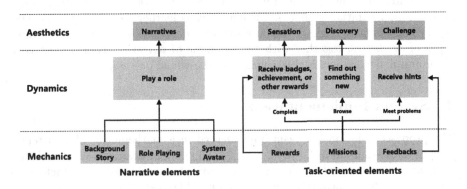

Fig. 1. The gamification design based on MDA framework.

Briefly speaking, our designed solution is based on the MDA model of gamification design, where MDA stands for mechanics, dynamics and aesthetics. From bottom up, mechanics refer to the concrete gaming elements implemented in the user interface. Dynamics are related to the interactions between users and the system. Aesthetics describe the user emotions when experiencing different dynamics. To enhance learner engagement in ITS, we design and implement six gaming elements in Mechanics Layer, which could result in multiple system-learner interactions in Dynamics Layer and deliver four types of experiences in Aesthetics Layer, as indicated in Fig. 1. Specifically, the six gaming elements are basically categorized into two types, namely *narrative elements* and *task-oriented elements*, for tackling the ITS cold-start problem from user perspective and system perspective respectively.

Narrative Elements. To address the cold-start problem from the user perspective, narrative elements are designed to enable learner quickly getting familiar with the ITS environment and understanding its key services. First of all, an appropriate **background story** needs to be composed according to the system characteristics. In the story, the system can be visualized as a **system avatar**, and the user conducts **role playing** to interact with the system avatar. Then the system avatar could accomplish the tasks of introducing the system main services, encouraging system-learner interactions via text chats or voice conversations. Narrative elements create the sense of immersion during the system novice guidance, making those abstract parts of the system vivid to learners. An aesthetic of narrative can be aroused by implementing narrative elements.

Task-oriented Elements. Task-oriented elements are designed to collect learner information for solving the cold-start problem from the system perspective. After identifying what types of learner information should be collected, the required information will be divided into several groups. The collecting of each information group will be respectively gamified as a **mission**, with **rewards** for accomplishing the mission and **feedbacks** for encountering difficulties. Note that it is better to develop the mission design on the basis of narrative elements, which could help learners understand the mission quickly and better engage in the process of data collection. During system-learner interaction, these three task-oriented elements can arouse three types of experiences: Sensation brings about learner's initial freshness. Challenge leads learner to think and try. Discovery continuously triggers the curiosity of a deeper exploration. These three types of aesthetics, together with the aesthetic of narrative, complement each other and make learners highly-engaged in the whole process.

3   System Implementation

The proposed solution has been implemented in a mathematics ITS currently serving for learners from Grade 7 to 9 [9]. The system designers identified that there are 4 system functions (e.g. learning path planning, learning obstacle diagnosis) needed to be introduced, and the required learner information are divided into 3 groups (e.g. personal information, current knowledge status). Based on our proposed gamification design model, Table 1 illustrates the six gaming elements in this implementation.

The **background story** refers to the **system avatar**, called Little R, dreaming to be an astronaut in the mathematics universe. As a partner of Little R (**role playing**), a new registered learner would be invited to visit 4 landmarks (corresponding to the 4 key system functions) with Little R in the mathematics universe, thus have a general understanding about the system and its services.

Then, Little R will invite the learner to complete 3 **missions** (corresponding to 3 groups of learner information) with it. The **reward** of accomplishing each mission is a part of a spacesuit. Therefore, after all of the 3 missions are completed, the learner will win an entire spacesuit for Little R, as shown in Fig. 2. Meanwhile, **feedback** will be provided when the learner encounters problem or intends to quit, which motivates the learner to complete the entire mission and ensures the integrity of the collected information. After the novice guidance, Little R will continue assisting the learner in the subsequent learning process.

Table 1. Gaming elements implementation in an ITS for mathematics.

Narrative elements		Task-oriented elements	
System avatar	Little R	**Missions**	Three missions of space cruise.
Background story	Little R dreams to be an astronaut in the mathematics universe	**Rewards**	An entire spacesuit (get a component for each mission)
User's role playing	Little R's partner during her space cruise	**Feedbacks**	Corresponding hints when encountering difficulties

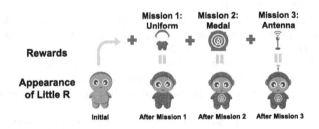

Fig. 2. The process of collecting rewards to make a spacesuit.

By implementing our designed solution, 92.5% of required learner information has been obtained on average. The test results of In-game GEQ [8] (M = 4.1, SD = 0.7 for Sensory and Imaginative Immersion; M = 4.0, SD = 1.0 for Flow) on 13 learners (6 males, 7 females) preliminarily indicate high learner engagement in the gamified guidance. Moreover, the test results of System Usability Scale [1]

(M = 4.2, SD = 0.8 for positive options; M = 1.9, SD = 1.1 for negative options) on the same group of learners also indicate a high usability of the designed solution.

4   Conclusion

In this work, we specifically define a cold-start problem in today's ITS, and then propose a novel gamified solution to tackle it. By leveraging on the MDA model, we design and implement a three-layer gamified solution to enhance new ITS learner's engagement in data providing and service acquaintance, where the preliminary evaluation results indicate its feasibility and effectiveness. The designed solution and its two key types of elements are generally applicable to today's ITS system that still suffers from the cold-start issue, and thus are valuable for the practical system designers.

Acknowledgement. This research is supported by the National Natural Science Foundation of China (No. 61702039), the Fundamental Research Funds for the Central Universities and Tencent.

References

1. Brooke, J., et al.: SUS-a quick and dirty usability scale. Usability Eval. Ind. **189**(194), 4–7 (1996)
2. de C.A. Ziesemer, A., Müller, L., Silveira, M.S.: Just rate it! Gamification as part of recommendation. In: Kurosu, M. (ed.) HCI 2014. LNCS, vol. 8512, pp. 786–796. Springer, Cham (2014). https://doi.org/10.1007/978-3-319-07227-2_75
3. Duolingo: https://www.duolingo.com/. Accessed February 2020
4. Feil, S., Kretzer, M., Werder, K., Maedche, A.: Using gamification to tackle the cold-start problem in recommender systems. In: Proceedings of the 19th ACM Conference on Computer Supported Cooperative Work and Social Computing Companion, pp. 253–256 (2016)
5. Hdioud, F., Frikh, B., Ouhbi, B., Khalil, I.: Multi-criteria recommender systems: A survey and a method to learn new user's profile. Int. J. Mob. Comput. Multimedia Commun. (IJMCMC) **8**(4), 20–48 (2017)
6. Hucko, M., Gazo, L., Simun, P., Valky, M., Moro, R., Simko, J., Bielikova, M.: YesElf: Personalized onboarding for web applications. In: Adjunct Publication of the 27th Conference on User Modeling, Adaptation and Personalization, pp. 39–44 (2019)
7. Hunicke, R., LeBlanc, M., Zubek, R.: MDA: a formal approach to game design and game research. In: Proceedings of the AAAI Workshop on Challenges in Game AI, vol. 4, p. 1722 (2004)
8. IJsselsteijn, W., De Kort, Y., Poels, K.: The game experience questionnaire. Eindhoven: Technische Universiteit Eindhoven, pp. 3–9 (2013)
9. Pian, Y., Lu, Y., Chen, P., Duan, Q.: Coglearn: a cognitive graph-oriented online learning system. In: 35th IEEE International Conference on Data Engineering, ICDE 2019, Macao, China, April 8–11, 2019, pp. 2020–2023. IEEE (2019)
10. Renz, J., Staubitz, T., Pollack, J., Meinel, C.: Improving the onboarding user experience in MOOCs. In: Proceedings EduLearn (2014)

11. Shinde, S.K., Kulkarni, U.: Hybrid personalized recommender system using centering-bunching based clustering algorithm. Expert Syst. Appl. **39**(1), 1381–1387 (2012)
12. VanLehn, K.: The relative effectiveness of human tutoring, intelligent tutoring systems, and other tutoring systems. Educ. Psychol. **46**(4), 197–221 (2011)
13. Wang, A.I., Lieberoth, A.: The effect of points and audio on concentration, engagement, enjoyment, learning, motivation, and classroom dynamics using kahoot. In: European Conference on Games Based Learning, vol. 20. Academic Conferences International Limited (2016)
14. Zhang, Z.K., Liu, C., Zhang, Y.C., Zhou, T.: Solving the cold-start problem in recommender systems with social tags. EPL (Europhys. Lett.) **92**(2), 28002 (2010)
15. Zhao, W.X., Li, S., He, Y., Chang, E.Y., Wen, J.R., Li, X.: Connecting social media to e-commerce: Cold-start product recommendation using microblogging information. IEEE Trans. Knowl. Data Eng. **28**(5), 1147–1159 (2015)
16. Zichermann, G., Cunningham, C.: Gamification by Design: Implementing Game Mechanics in Web and Mobile Apps. O'Reilly Media Inc., Sebastopol (2011)

Bridging Over from Learning Videos to Learning Resources Through Automatic Keyword Extraction

Cleo Schulten[1], Sven Manske[1(✉)] , Angela Langner-Thiele[2], and H. Ulrich Hoppe[1]

[1] University Duisburg-Essen, Duisburg, Germany
{schulten,manske,hoppe}@collide.info
[2] Evonik Digital GmbH, Evonik Industries AG, Essen, Germany
angela.thiele@evonik.com

Abstract. The presented system and approach facilitate intelligent, contextualized information access for learners based on automatic learning video analysis. The underlying workflow starts with automatically extracting keywords from learning videos followed by the generation of recommendations of learning materials. The approach has been implemented and investigated in a user study in a real-world VET setting. The study investigated the acceptance, perceived quality and relevance of automatically extracted keywords and automatically generated learning resource recommendations in the context of a set of learning videos related to chemistry and chemical engineering. The results indicate that such extracted keywords are in line with user-generated keywords and summarize the content of videos quite well. Also, they can be used as search key to find relevant learning resources.

Keywords: Video analysis · Content analysis · Keyword extraction · Learning resource recommendation · Vocational education · Digital transformation

1 Introduction

The ongoing digital transformation of industrial work aims at reaching new levels of process automation [1] and comprises the adoption of digital technologies in business processes, organizational structures, business domains and the society as a whole [2]. The digital transformation demands major changes in habits and ways of working and calls for new digital competences and digital literacy in newly evolving skill profiles. This needs to be reflected in vocational education and training (VET). Major companies such as Evonik[1] have started to equip their apprentices with digital tools such as mobile devices to support mobile learning using digital internet and communication technologies in workplaces and training settings. This comes with specific challenges but also has a potential for triggering innovation in VET. The adoption of new digital technologies, particularly when pioneering digital initiatives inside an organization,

---

[1] Evonik Industries AG (2020). https://corporate.evonik.com/en. Retrieved: 2020-02-26.

© Springer Nature Switzerland AG 2020
I. I. Bittencourt et al. (Eds.): AIED 2020, LNAI 12164, pp. 382–386, 2020.
https://doi.org/10.1007/978-3-030-52240-7_69

may lead to a more heterogeneous and scattered landscape with different digital islands that are not well connected. Beyond technical interoperability, the point is to integrate learning and instructional process in a technical environment that enables "educational interoperability" [3].

Videos are a more and more popular format of media and have a high potential to support and enrich professional training and education [4]. This is not limited to high-end, polished materials, but can also include learner-generated videos [5]. Such learner-generated videos have been analyzed using semi-automatic methods combining human coding and automatic content analysis order, e.g. to detect missing pre-knowledge and misconceptions [6]. To extract semantic concepts and relations, DBPedia Spotlight uses NLP techniques to spot (compound) terms in texts and to relate it to structured data from DBPedia [7]. Similar techniques have been applied to discover learning resource recommendations based on textual learning materials [8]. However, many recommender systems in the context of learning materials usually take user preferences such as the rating of materials into account [9]. Consequently, such approaches have difficulties providing good recommendations if the amount of data, particularly user ratings, is quite low. Content-based recommender systems typically analyze item descriptions and often transform this into a vector space model, whereas the recommendation quality highly depends on the quality of the description [10]. According to Kopeinik, Kowald, and Lex standard recommendation algorithms are not well-suited to provide learning resource recommendations [11]. Particularly for sparse-data learning environments, they propose ontology-based recommender systems to better describe the learners and learning resources. Semantic technologies using AI help to automatically process content given by the learning context or learner-generated artefacts [12].

The research presented in this paper stems from an academia-industry cooperation with Evonik, a large company in the chemical industry. The overarching goal of this cooperation is to design and implement well-adapted technologies to support digitalization in VET. Video-based learning was taken as a starting point in a joint endeavour between in-company instructors, apprentices and researchers. Videos have been created by apprentices as well as instructors and are shared on a collaboration platform. Automatic information extraction from these learning videos is used as a key to recommending relevant learning materials as a value-adding function.

2   Video-Analysis and Contextualized Information Access

Our approach to extract information and to generate recommendations from learning videos is based on the following general workflow: (1) segmentation of the video; (2) transcription (speech-to-text); (3) keyword extraction; (4) representation of the data. In the first step, the video file is segmented and de-multiplexed into separate video and audio streams. Second, each audio segment will be transcribed using a speech-to-text API and stored in the file system. Third, keywords are extracted from the transcripts using DBPedia Spotlight and classical tf-idf measure. Finally, the keywords will be represented in the learning environment, e.g. as lists of learning resource recommendations or interactive tag clouds.

The recommendations for learning materials are generated through keyword-based search in the sense of a content-based recommender system. This helps to easily connect new and already existing search APIs to the learning environment. Open Search is one of the approaches to easily integrate such an already existing API. Using existing knowledge sources in already implemented management services is crucial for companies in order to preserve a predominance in a certain field of business. To discover learning resources, multiple searches with the extracted keywords are performed using the Google Custom Search API, followed by a ranking of the different results. Each search can be parametrized, e.g., to prioritize certain domains in the results.

3 Evaluation

To evaluate the keyword extraction and recommendation mechanisms, an online questionnaire was set up. In it we included the recommenders results for four chemistry related videos which were presented in a randomized order to reduce order effects.

Initially the participants received a brief textual instruction. For each video the participants were asked to watch the video before giving their own keyword suggestions, then rating the quality of the extracted keywords and of the top 10 proposed learning resources. The keywords were to be rated as "important in relation to the topic", "suitable but not important" or "irrelevant to the topic". The learning resources could be rated as "suitable and helpful", "suitable but not helpful" or "unsuitable".

Subsequently, the participants were presented a shortened version of the ResQue questionnaire [13]. The included items were related to the constructs Quality of Recommendation, Perceived Usefulness, Transparency and Attitudes. Finally, demographic questions regarding gender, age and occupation. 32 apprentices completed the questionnaire (n = 32, 19 males, age range 16–31 with $M = 21.03$, $SD = 3.614$).

Table 1. Rating of keywords and learning resources

	Keywords			Resources		
	Important in relation to the topic	Suitable but not important	Irrelevant to the topic	Suitable and helpful	Suitable but not helpful	Unsuitable
Video 1	61,98%	28,13%	9,90%	55,31%	30,00%	14,69%
Video 2	58,81%	30,40%	10,80%	45,00%	32,81%	22,19%
Video 3	48,38%	30,93%	20,69%	62,81%	26,88%	10,31%
Video 4	66,25%	26,10%	7,66%	57,19%	27,5%	15,31%
Overall	58,86%	28,89%	12,26%	55,08%	29,30%	15,63%

Perceived Quality of the Extracted Keywords and Generated Information. In the rating systems for keywords and resources two of the three options can be considered positive, with one of the two being more neutral than the other, while the third is negative. The combined score shows that the participants on average rate 87.74% of the keywords and 84.69% of the resources for one of the four videos positively. The aggregated results are depicted in Table 1.

Among the more poorly rated keywords are mainly those that are not directly related to the main topic. For example, in video 3 which deals with oxidation and has 29 keywords total, the keywords 'oxidation', 'chemic reaction' and 'oxygen' are rated really good while 'vitamin', 'candle wax' and 'English' are rated rather poorly.

Evaluation of the Recommender System (ResQue). The constructs measured by items adapted from ResQue each have a mean score of at least 3, as can be seen in Table 2. The low diversity score relates to an open question where a participant remarked that some of the resources had very similar content. The higher accuracy score fits the positive ratings of keywords and resources.

Table 2. ResQue results

	M	SD
Quality of Recommendation	3.23	0.58
Accuracy	3.81	1.00
Novelty	3.09	1.09
Diversity	3.00	0.75
Perceived Usefulness	3.14	1.11
Transparency	3.50	1.19
Attitudes	3.40	0.72

4   Conclusion and Discussion

The results show that the majority of the proposed keywords and resources are rated positively. The videos being informative yet not very high level do contain excerpts that digress from the main topic. Therefore, it makes sense that the system does find some keywords that do not match the topic and seem misplaced for participant or user.

The results of the ResQue questionnaire showed moderate but slightly positive scores. While this can be perfectly accurate it should also be noted that the participants neither interacted with the tool themselves nor were they informed in detail on the option to use the tool with any media other than videos. Both of which might influence the rating if it were included in further studies. Additionally, the rating might be influenced by the state of knowledge of the trainees.

References

1. Hirsch-Kreinsen, H.: Digitization of industrial work: Development paths and prospects. J. Labour Mark. Res. **49**(1), 1–14 (2016)
2. Parviainen, P., Tihinen, M., Kääriäinen, J., Teppola, S.: Tackling the digitalization challenge: How to benefit from digitalization in practice. Int. J. Inf. Syst. Proj. Manage. **5**(1), 63–77 (2017)

3. Milrad, M., Hoppe, H.U., Gottdenker, J., Jansen, M.: Exploring the use of mobile devices to facilitate educational interoperability around digitally enhanced experiments. In: Proceedings of WMTE 2004, pp. 182–186. IEEE Press (2004)
4. Erkens, M., Manske, S., Bodemer, D., Hoppe, H.U., Langner-Thiele, A.: Video-based competence development in chemistry vocational training. In: Proceedings of ICCE 2019 (2019)
5. Malzahn, N., Hartnett, E., Llinás, P., Hoppe, H.U.: A smart environment supporting the creation of juxtaposed videos for learning. In: Li, Y., et al. (eds.) State-of-the-Art and Future Directions of Smart Learning. Lecture Notes in Educational Technology, pp. 461–470. Springer, Singapore (2016)
6. Erkens, M., Daems, O., Hoppe, H.U.: Artifact analysis around video creation in collaborative STEM learning scenarios. In: Procedings of ICALT 2014, pp. 388–392. IEEE (2014)
7. Mendes, P.N., Jakob, M., García-Silva, A., Bizer, C.: DBpedia spotlight: Shedding light on the web of documents. In: Proceedings of 7th International Conference on Semantic Systems, pp. 1–8 (2011)
8. Ahn, J.-W., et al.: Wizard's apprentice: Cognitive suggestion support for wizard-of-Oz question answering. In: André, E., Baker, R., Hu, X., Rodrigo, M.M.T., du Boulay, B. (eds.) AIED 2017. LNCS (LNAI), vol. 10331, pp. 630–635. Springer, Cham (2017). https://doi.org/10.1007/978-3-319-61425-0_79
9. Ghauth, K.I., Abdullah, N.A.: Learning materials recommendation using good learners' ratings and content-based filtering. Educ. Tech. Res. Dev. 58(6), 711–727 (2010)
10. Pazzani, M.J., Billsus, D.: Content-based recommendation systems. In: Brusilovsky, P., Kobsa, A., Nejdl, W. (eds.) The Adaptive Web: Methods and Strategies of Web Personalization. LNCS, vol. 4321, pp. 325–341. Springer, Heidelberg (2007). https://doi.org/10.1007/978-3-540-72079-9_10
11. Kopeinik, S., Kowald, D., Lex, E.: Which algorithms suit which learning environments? A comparative study of recommender systems in TEL. In: Verbert, K., Sharples, M., Klobučar, T. (eds.) EC-TEL 2016. LNCS, vol. 9891, pp. 124–138. Springer, Cham (2016). https://doi.org/10.1007/978-3-319-45153-4_10
12. Manske, S., Hoppe, H.U.: The "Concept Cloud": supporting collaborative knowledge construction based on semantic extraction from learner-generated artefacts. In: 2016 IEEE 16th International Conference on Advanced Learning Technologies (ICALT), pp. 302–306. IEEE (2016)
13. Pu, P., Chen, L., Hu, R.: A user-centric evaluation framework for recommender systems. In: Proceedings of the 5th ACM Conference on Recommender Systems, pp. 157–164. ACM (2011)

A Large-Scale, Open-Domain, Mixed-Interface Dialogue-Based ITS for STEM

Iulian Vlad Serban[1(✉)], Varun Gupta[1], Ekaterina Kochmar[1,2], Dung D. Vu[1,3], Robert Belfer[1], Joelle Pineau[1,4], Aaron Courville[1,4], Laurent Charlin[1,4], and Yoshua Bengio[1,4]

[1] Korbit Technologies Inc., Montreal, Canada
iulian@korbit.ai
[2] University of Cambridge, Cambridge, UK
[3] École de Technologie Supérieure, Montreal, Canada
[4] MILA (Quebec Artificial Intelligence Institute), Montreal, Canada

Abstract. We present Korbit, a large-scale, open-domain, mixed-interface, dialogue-based intelligent tutoring system (ITS). Korbit uses machine learning, natural language processing and reinforcement learning to provide interactive, personalized learning online. Korbit has been designed to easily scale to thousands of subjects, by automating, standardizing and simplifying the content creation process. Unlike other ITS, a teacher can develop new learning modules for Korbit in a matter of hours. To facilitate learning across a wide range of STEM subjects, Korbit uses a mixed-interface, which includes videos, interactive dialogue-based exercises, question-answering, conceptual diagrams, mathematical exercises and gamification elements. Korbit has been built to scale to millions of students, by utilizing a state-of-the-art cloud-based micro-service architecture. Korbit launched its first course in 2019 and has over 7,000 students have enrolled. Although Korbit was designed to be open-domain and highly scalable, A/B testing experiments with real-world students demonstrate that both student learning outcomes and student motivation are substantially improved compared to typical online courses.

Keywords: Intelligent tutoring system · Dialogue-based tutoring system · Natural language processing · Reinforcement learning · Deep learning · Personalized · Interactive learning · Data science · STEM

1 Introduction

Intelligent tutoring systems (ITS) are computer programs powered by artificial intelligence (AI), which deliver real-time, personalized tutoring to students. Traditional ITS implement or imitate the behavior and pedagogy of human tutors. In particular, one type of ITS are dialogue-based tutors, which use natural language conversations to tutor students [13]. This process is sometimes

I. I. Bittencourt et al. (Eds.): AIED 2020, LNAI 12164, pp. 387–392, 2020.
https://doi.org/10.1007/978-3-030-52240-7_70

called "Socratic tutoring", because of its similarity to Socratic dialogue [17]. Newer ITS have started to interleave their dialogue with interactive media (e.g. interactive videos and web applets) – a so-called "mixed-interface system". It has been shown that ITS can be twice as effective at promoting learning compared to the previous generation of computer-based instruction and may be as effective as human tutors in general [12].

However, despite the fact that ITS have been around for decades and are known to be highly effective, their deployment in education and industry has been extremely limited [14,16]. A major reason for this is the sheer cost of development [5,14]. As observed by Olney [14]: *"Unfortunately, ITS are extremely expensive to produce, with some groups estimating that it takes 100 h of authoring time from AI experts, pedagogical experts, and domain experts to produce 1 h of instruction."* On the other hand, lower-cost educational approaches, such as massive open online courses (MOOCs), have flourished and now boast of having millions of learners. It is estimated that today there are over 110 million learners around the world enrolled in MOOCs [18]. However, the learning outcomes resulting from learning in MOOCs depend critically on their teaching methodology and quality of content, and remains questionable in general [2,3,9–11,15]. In particular, recent research indicates that MOOCs having low levels of active learning, little feedback from instructors and peers, and few peer discussions tend to yield poor learning outcomes [10,15]. Further, it is well-known that student retention in MOOCs is substantially worse than in traditional classroom learning [8]. By combining low cost and scalability with the personalization and effectiveness of ITS, we hope Korbit may help to effectively teach and motivate millions of students around the world.

2   The Korbit ITS

Korbit is a large-scale, open-domain, mixed-interface, dialogue-based ITS, which uses machine learning, natural language processing (NLP) and reinforcement learning (RL) to provide interactive, personalized learning online. The ITS has over 7,000 students enrolled from around the world, including students from educational institutions and professionals from industry partners. Korbit is capable of teaching topics related to data science, machine learning, and artificial intelligence. The modular platform will soon be expanded with many more topics.

Students enroll on the Korbit website by selecting either a course or a set of skills they would like to study. Students may also answer a few questions about their background knowledge. Based on these, Korbit generates a personalized curriculum for each student. Following this, Korbit tutors the student by alternating between short lecture videos and interactive problem-solving exercises. The outer-loop system decides on which lecture video or exercise to show next based on the personalized curriculum. Work is currently underway to adapt the curriculum during the learning process (Fig. 1).

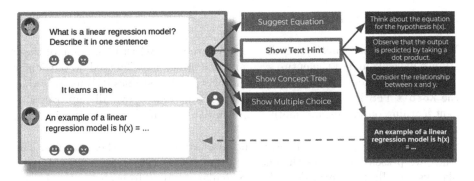

Fig. 1. An example of how the `Korbit` ITS inner-loop system selects the pedagogical intervention. The student gives an incorrect solution and afterwards receives a text hint.

During the exercise sessions, the `inner-loop` system manages the interaction. First, it shows the student a problem statement (e.g., a question). The student may then attempt to solve the exercise, ask for help, or skip the exercise. If the student attempts to solve the exercise, their solution attempt is compared against the expectation (i.e. reference solution) using an NLP model. If their solution is classified as incorrect, then the `inner-loop` system will select one of a dozen different pedagogical interventions. The pedagogical interventions include textual hints, mathematical hints, elaborations, explanations, concept tree diagrams, and multiple choice quiz answers. The pedagogical intervention is chosen by an ensemble of machine learning models based on the student's profile and last solution attempt. Depending on the pedagogical intervention, the `inner-loop` system may either ask the student to retry the initial exercise or follow up on the intervention (e.g., with additional questions, confirmations, or prompts).

The `Korbit` ITS is related to the work on dialogue-based ITS, such as the pioneering AutoTutor and the newer IBM Watson Tutor [1,6,7,13,19]. Although `Korbit` is highly constrained compared to existing dialogue-based ITS, a major innovation of `Korbit` lies in its modular, scalable design. The `inner-loop` system is implemented as a finite-state machine. Each pedagogical intervention is a separate state, with its own logic, data and machine learning models. Each state operates independently of the rest of the system, has access to all database content (including exercises and videos) and can autonomously improve as new data becomes available. This ensures that the system gets better and better, that it can adapt to new content and that it can be extended with new pedagogical interventions. The transitions between the states of the finite-state machine is decided by a reinforcement learning model, which itself is agnostic to the underlying implementation of each state and also continues to improve as more and more data becomes available.

3   System Evaluation

We have conducted multiple studies to evaluate the `Korbit` ITS. Some of these studies have evaluated the entire system while others have focused on particular aspects or modules of the system. Taken together, the studies demonstrate that the `Korbit` ITS is an effective learning tool and that it overall improves student learning outcomes and motivation compared to alternative online learning approaches.

In this paper we limit ourselves and discuss only one of these studies. The study we present compares the entire system (`Full ITS`) against an xMOOC-like system [4]. The purpose of this particular study is to evaluate 1) whether students prefer the `Korbit` ITS or a regular MOOC, 2) whether the `Korbit` ITS increases student motivation, and 3) which aspects of the `Korbit` ITS students find most useful and least useful. In an ideal world, `Korbit` ITS would be compared against a regular xMOOC teaching students through lecture videos and multiple choice quizzes in a randomized controlled trial (a randomized A/B testing experiment). However, it is not possible to compare against such a system in a randomized controlled trial, because it would create confusion and drastically offset student expectations. Therefore, in this study, we compare the `Full ITS` against a reduced ITS, which appears identical to the `Full ITS` and utilizes the same content (video lectures and exercise questions), but defaults to multiple choice quizzes 50% of the time. Thus, students assigned to the reduced ITS spend about half of their interactions in an xMOOC-like setting. We refer to this system as the `xMOOC ITS`.

Table 1. A/B testing results comparing the `Full ITS` against the `xMOOC ITS`: average time spent by students (in minutes), returning students (in %), students who said they will refer others (in %) and learning gain (in %), with corresponding 95% confidence intervals. The * and ** shows statistical significance at 90% and 95% confidence level.

System	Time spent	Returning students	Will refer others	Learning gain
xMOOC ITS	22.98 ± 4.18	26.98% ± 3.44%	44.83% ± 9.00%	**39.14% ± 2.35%**
Full ITS	**39.86 ± 3.70**	**31.69% ± 1.92%***	**54.17% ± 4.05%**	

The experiment was conducted in 2019 with n = 612 participants. Students who enrolled online were randomly assigned to either the `Full ITS` (80%) or `xMOOC ITS` (20%). Students came from different countries and were not subject to any selection or filtering process. Apart from bug fixes and speed improvements, the system was not modified during the experiment to limit confounding factors. After studying for about 45 min, students were shown a questionnaire to evaluate the system.

Table 1 shows the experimental results. The average time spent in the `Full ITS` was 39.86 min compared to 22.98 min in the `xMOOC ITS`. As such, the `Full ITS` yields a staggering 73.46% increase in time spent. In addition, the percentage of returning students and the percentage of students who said they would refer others to use the system is substantially higher for the `Full ITS` compared to the `xMOOC ITS`. These results were also confirmed by the feedback provided by the students in the questionnaire. Thus, we can conclude that students strongly prefer `Korbit ITS` over xMOOCs and that the `Korbit ITS` increases overall student motivation.

Table 1 also shows that the average student learning was observed to be 39.14%. The learning gain is measured as the proportion of instances where a student provides a correct exercise solution after having receiving a pedagogical intervention from the `Korbit ITS`. Thus, the pedagogical interventions appear to be effective.

Finally, in the questionnaire, 85.31% of students reported that they found the chat equally or more fun compared to learning alone and 66.67% of students reported that the chat helped them learn better sometimes, many times or all of the time. For the `Full ITS`, 54.17% of students reported that they would refer others to use `Korbit ITS`. In addition, students reported that the `Korbit ITS` could be improved by more accurately identifying their solutions as being correct or incorrect and, in the case of incorrect solutions, by providing more personalized feedback.

References

1. Ahn, J.-W., et al.: Adaptive visual dialog for intelligent tutoring systems. In: Penstein Rosé, C., et al. (eds.) AIED 2018. LNCS (LNAI), vol. 10948, pp. 413–418. Springer, Cham (2018). https://doi.org/10.1007/978-3-319-93846-2_77
2. Cavanaugh, J.K., Jacquemin, S.J.: A large sample comparison of grade based student learning outcomes in online vs. face-to-face courses. Online Learn. 19(2), n2 (2015)
3. Colvin, K.F., Champaign, J., Liu, A., Zhou, Q., Fredericks, C., Pritchard, D.E.: Learning in an introductory physics MOOC: all cohorts learn equally including an on-campus class. Int. Rev. Res. Open Distrib. Learn. 15(4), 263–283 (2014)
4. Daniel, J.: Making sense of MOOCs: Musings in a maze of myth, paradox and possibility. J. Interact. Media Educ. 2012(3), 18 (2012)
5. Folsom-Kovarik, J.T., Schatz, S., Nicholson, D.: Plan ahead: pricing ITS learner models. In: Proceedings of the 19th Behavior Representation in Modeling & Simulation (BRIMS) Conference, pp. 47–54 (2010)
6. Graesser, A.C., Chipman, P., Haynes, B.C., Olney, A.: AutoTutor: an intelligent tutoring system with mixed-initiative dialogue. IEEE Trans. Educ. 48(4), 612–618 (2005)
7. Graesser, A.C., VanLehn, K., Rosé, C.P., Jordan, P.W., Harter, D.: Intelligent tutoring systems with conversational dialogue. AI Mag. 22(4), 39–39 (2001)
8. Hone, K.S., El Said, G.R.: Exploring the factors affecting mooc retention: A survey study. Comput. Educ. 98, 157–168 (2016)
9. Kirtman, L.: Online versus in-class courses: an examination of differences in learning outcomes. Issues Teach. Educ. 18(2), 103–116 (2009)

10. Koedinger, K.R., Kim, J., Jia, J.Z., McLaughlin, E.A., Bier, N.L.: Learning is not a spectator sport: Doing is better than watching for learning from a MOOC. In: Proceedings of the Second (2015) ACM Conference on Learning@ Scale, pp. 111–120 (2015)
11. Koxvold, I.: MOOCs: opportunities for their use in compulsory-age education. Department for Education (2014)
12. Kulik, J.A., Fletcher, J.: Effectiveness of intelligent tutoring systems: a meta-analytic review. Rev. Educ. Res. **86**(1), 42–78 (2016)
13. Nye, B.D., Graesser, A.C., Hu, X.: AutoTutor and family: a review of 17 years of natural language tutoring. Int. J. Artif. Intell. Educ. **24**(4), 427–469 (2014)
14. Olney, A.M.: Using novices to scale up intelligent tutoring systems. In: Interservice/Industry Training, Simulation, and Education Conference (I/ITSEC) (2018)
15. Otto, D., Bollmann, A., Becker, S., Sander, K.: It's the learning, stupid! discussing the role of learning outcomes in moocs. Open Learn. J. Open Dist. e-Learn. **33**(3), 203–220 (2018)
16. Ritter, S., Anderson, J.R., Koedinger, K.R., Corbett, A.: Cognitive tutor: applied research in mathematics education. Psychon. Bull. Rev. **14**(2), 249–255 (2007)
17. Rosé, C.P., Moore, J.D., VanLehn, K., Allbritton, D.: A comparative evaluation of socratic versus didactic tutoring. In: Proceedings of the Annual Meeting of the Cognitive Science Society, vol. 23 (2001)
18. Shah, D.: By The Numbers: MOOCs in 2019. Class Central MOOC Report (2019)
19. Ventura, M., et al.: Preliminary evaluations of a dialogue-based digital tutor. In: Penstein RoséPenstein Rosé, C., et al. (eds.) AIED 2018. LNCS (LNAI), vol. 10948, pp. 480–483. Springer, Cham (2018). https://doi.org/10.1007/978-3-319-93846-2_90

Doctoral Consortium Papers

Contingent Scaffolding for System Safety Analysis

Paul S. Brown[1]([✉]), Anthony G. Cohn[1], Glen Hart[2], and Vania Dimitrova[1]

[1] University of Leeds, Leeds LS2 9JT, UK
{sc16pb,a.g.cohn,v.g.dimitrova}@leeds.ac.uk
[2] Defence Science and Technology Laboratory (DSTL), Wiltshire SP4 0JQ, UK

Abstract. System safety analysis is a creative process that can often be undertaken by people who are not experts in the system under analysis whilst also learning the analysis methodology. With the increase of system complexity, the high demand for analyses conducted at a scale and the potentially catastrophic consequences of inadequate analysis, there is an urgent need for supporting the development of system analysis skills. Technological solutions can effectively scaffold this ill-defined domain. We propose a generic framework for Contingent Scaffolding capable of providing flexible learning support while conducting system safety analysis. This has been implemented into an intelligent agent, Oswin, which offers **O**ntology-driven **s**caffolding **wi**th interactive **n**udges.

Keywords: Contingent Scaffolding · System safety · STPA · Ontology

1 Problem Statement

System safety analysis is conducted to understand the behaviour of increasingly complex systems to mitigate or prevent undesirable behaviour. The consequences of inadequate analysis can be catastrophic. To support the analyst several methodologies have been created, one of which is System-Theoretic Process Analysis (STPA) [4]. STPA is relatively new, gaining results comparable with other methodologies and revealing insights they missed [3,8].

Analysts require expert-level knowledge and skills regarding their chosen methodology, chosen model, modelling, as well as the system under consideration. Given that STPA is an emerging methodology, there are a growing number of people wishing to learn it and its associated model. Expertise regarding the system also cannot be assumed given that STPA can be conducted from the design phase, on large systems distributed over teams, and on complex systems requiring expertise in multiple fields.

STPA is an ill-defined task [6] with an ambiguous starting state, an unknown goal state, an advisory non-strict procedure, and no known correct solution. It is an ill-defined domain [6]: STPA is generic to all analyses and thus contains incomplete declarative knowledge regarding a particular analysis, including the system under analysis. System safety is an ill-defined problem [5], in STPA safety

© Springer Nature Switzerland AG 2020
I. I. Bittencourt et al. (Eds.): AIED 2020, LNAI 12164, pp. 395–399, 2020.
https://doi.org/10.1007/978-3-030-52240-7_71

is re-characterised as a control problem, alternative characterisations include Swiss-cheese and dominoes [4].

Contingent Scaffolding is presented by Wood *et al.* [11] as a process enabling the learner to accomplish a task beyond their current capabilities, which is one key goal of supporting the non-expert analyst. It has been successfully applied in Intelligent Tutoring Systems, where it provides graded support for multi-step problem solving in formalised domains [2]. Thus it is used by Oswin as a strategy for delivering feedback as interactive nudges regarding the violation of constraints.

Wood and Wood expounded the principals of "contingent scaffolding" [12] as:

- Help is provided expeditiously when the learner is in trouble
- Help is increased as the learner requires, until the solution is reached
- As the learner succeeds, support is withdrawn

The learner's behaviour is observed to determine whether intervention is required, the tutor then moves through the levels of support. The number of levels vary, between 4 and 5 [12] or 6 [1]; the only guidance being that they should increase in depth or interference until physical intervention is undertaken. There has also been concern in implementations regarding a lack of flexibility [2,10]. It arises from the capability of a learner to approach a problem in an unexpected but valid way. This PhD project takes into account these concerns in the proposed contingency scaffolding framework outlined below. It uses constraints based on situational calculus and a domain ontology to provide scaffolding flexibility in the context of system safety analysis.

2 Proposed Solution and Methodology

Within this project an AI agent, Oswin (**O**ntology-driven **S**caffolding **W**ith **I**nteractive **N**udges), has been prototyped to provide learning support to the non-expert STPA analyst. The intention is to enable them to produce a product beyond their current abilities, whilst improving their knowledge of STPA and the system under analysis, as well as improving their safety-analytic and modelling skills. Oswin uses a constraint-based Contingent Scaffolding framework to accomplish this.

Previous work on ill-defined domains and tasks indicates various strategies have been successful, including constraints [5] which can check if certain properties of a solution are present or not. The violation of some constraint indicates a need for intervention [7]. Oswin is provided constraints as logical-queries over a user-extended ontology, including strong constraints such as a situation can't be both safe and hazardous, as well as advisory constraints such as not analysing more than 7–10 hazards.

The range of help the ontology is capable of supporting exceeds enforcing constraints. It is also capable of providing a reference to factual, conceptual and procedural knowledge as understood by Oswin to ensure a common conceptualisation. Furthermore, it both enables explanations for Oswin's reasoning, and guiding the learner through formulating their own arguments regarding causality or the categorisation of systems. Finally it enables some re-use of systems and their behaviour from previous analyses, encouraging analogous reasoning over multiple analyses: especially beneficial to those specialising in particular system domains such as autonomous vehicles.

The dual issues of flexibility and expeditious intervention are accounted for by the on-line evaluation of constraints [7], and following violations immediately with Contingent Scaffolding. Within this framework, the contingency is formally defined using Situation Calculus. Reiter's definition [9] allows complex reasoning over a log of interactions, including queries over prior situations, which is used to determine fading.

Regarding levels of support for the Contingent Scaffolding Framework, in the absence of specific guidance on the levels to use, successful behaviour of human tutors is used to inform the hierarchy. Due to the nature of the ill-defined domain this hierarchy also accounts for the limitation that it is not always possible to provide a solution as physical intervention. Messages for the first three levels are automatically generated from the constraint, the highest level requires a database of adaptable code snippets that can be executed in the UI to provide physical intervention.

A prototype Oswin has been implemented in Logtalk, based upon the Prolog implementation by Reiter of Situation Calculus [9]. The implementation is split into a Situation Calculus Ontology Authoring tool and a Contingent Scaffolding framework, both of which will be defined in Situation Calculus. The ontology has been defined in Description Logics, OWL, and Prolog. Additional ontological reasoning has been defined in set-builder notation and Prolog.

A prototype interface has also been implemented to facilitate evaluating the efficacy of the provided support, see Fig. 1. It is proposed to test the system on non-expert cohorts who will be provided with STPA training and an example system. Following which they will conduct an analysis independently. Half will have access to Oswin and all will have access to a human with system expertise, simulating an analyst within an organisation. Detailed logs will be gathered via the Situation Calculus implementation, which will then be studied for evaluation.

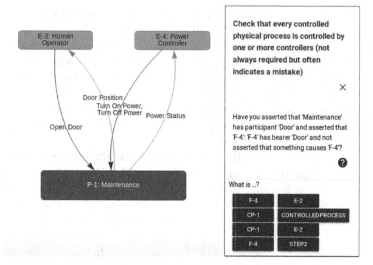

Fig. 1. The UI with Oswin showing level 1 and 2 feedback for a missing "close door" action, which causes "F-4". The user believes they have finished defining all relevant control actions, Oswin believes they have missed one. The ineloquent question asked by Oswin is generated from and reflects the successful unification of the constraint query used to arrive at its belief. The available interactions Oswin provides are to request more help, dismiss the nudge (Oswin may be wrong), or to lookup a relevant term. By defining the missing control action, the feedback nudge will dismiss itself with no direct interaction.

3   Expected Contributions and Future Work

The main contribution of this PhD project to AIED is a framework for ontology-driven scaffolding with interactive nudges for developing system safety analysis skills. It uses situational calculus and a domain ontology to specify situations requiring scaffolding and to automatically generate interactive nudges. While the framework is illustrated in system safety analysis, providing a formal, logical specification enables generalisation to similar ill-defined domains and tasks (e.g. debugging, software security, design).

Currently we have a working prototype of Oswin, using the framework in the system safety domain. Preliminary testing has been conducted with a representative STPA example (interlock system [4]) by a small group of system safety analysis novices. Our immediate work is an evaluation of the efficacy of the application in the challenging domain provided by STPA. It is expected that Oswin users' final ontological models representing the outcome of the system safety analysis will be close to expert ones. Additional analysis will consider non-productive behaviour, timings, and resolution of interventions. We also consider retention of learning and re-use of system safety analysis patterns and components across different scenarios.

Acknowledgements. The authors gratefully acknowledge the financial support provided: an EPSRC CASE studentship partially funded by the Defence Science and Technology Laboratory (Dstl). The advice provided by experts at Dstl is also acknowledged.

References

1. Daniels, H.: Vygotsky and Pedagogy. Routledge, London (2010)
2. Du Boulay, B., Luckin, R.: Modelling human teaching tactics and strategies for tutoring systems. Int. J. Artif. Intell. Educ. **12**, 235–256 (2001)
3. Fleming, C.H., Spencer, M., Thomas, J., Leveson, N., Wilkinson, C.: Safety assurance in NextGen and complex transportation systems. Saf. Sci. **55**, 173–187 (2013)
4. Leveson, N.: Engineering a Safer World. The MIT Press, Cambridge (2017)
5. Lynch, C., Ashley, K.D., Pinkwart, N., Aleven, V.: Concepts, structures, and goals: Redefining ill-definedness. Int. J. AI Educ. **19**(3), 253–266 (2009)
6. Mitrovic, A., Weerasinghe, A.: Revisiting ill-definedness and the consequences for ITSs. In: Artificial Intelligence in Education: Building Learning Systems that Care from Knowledge Representation to Affective Modelling, pp. 375–382 (2009)
7. Ohlsson, S.: Constraint-based modeling: From cognitive theory to computer tutoring - and back again. Int. J. Artif. Intell. Educ. **26**(1), 457–473 (2015)
8. Pawlicki, T., Samost, A., Brown, D.W., Manger, R.P., Kim, G.Y., Leveson, N.G.: Application of systems and control theory-based hazard analysis to radiation oncology. Med. Phys. **43**(3), 1514–1530 (2016)
9. Reiter, R.: Knowledge in Action. The MIT Press, Cambridge (2001)
10. Wood, D.: Commentary: Contribution of scaffolding to learning and teaching: Interdisciplinary perspectives. Int. J. Educ. Res. **90**, 248–251 (2018)
11. Wood, D., Bruner, J.S., Ross, G.: The role of tutoring in problem solving. J. Child Psychol. Psychiatry **17**(2), 89–100 (1976)
12. Wood, H., Wood, D.: Help seeking, learning and contingent tutoring. Comput. Educ. **33**(2–3), 153–169 (1999)

The Exploration of Feeling of Difficulty Using Eye-Tracking and Skin Conductance Response

Chou Ching-En[✉] and Kaska Porayska-Pomsta

UCL Knowledge Lab, UCL Institute of Education, London, UK
Joechou0929@gmail.com

Abstract. Metacognitive experience (ME) plays an important role in self-regulated learning. To date, through mainly self-reporting methodology, metacognition assessment lacks objective evidence and therefore hinder the discussion of its subjective and implicit nature. In exploring ME, eye-tracking and skin conductance response (SCR) offer certain advantages over self-reporting methods. However, to date, most studies tend to focus on utilizing these measures to explore metacognitive skills (MS) rather than ME. Also, while some studies do explore ME with these measures tend to utilize the data from a summative perspective rather than aligning the data with the real-time ME behaviours. Based on previous works in this field, this research will discuss how feeling of difficulty (i.e. a type of ME) functions in real-time based on the hypothesis that eye-tracking and SCR data can provide objective measures. Through such, a better understanding of how FOD functions could be gained and therefore contribute to the support of learners' metacognitive competencies.

Keywords: Metacognition · Metacognitive experience · Feeling of difficulty (FOD) · Eye-tracking · Skin conductance response (SCR)

1 Introduction

Metacognition is a complex and multifaceted construct, which can be defined as "thinking about thinking (Flavell 1979, p. 906)". In addition, metacognition has the characteristic of being both a domain-general and domain-specific skill that functions on both conscious and unconscious levels (Brown 1987; Efklides and Misailidi 2010). However, while metacognitive skills (MS) is widely discussed, metacognitive experience (ME) on the other hand receive lesser attention (Efklides 2006). Furthermore, the assessment of metacognition is dominated by self-reporting methodologies which lack objective evidence. As a result, this doctoral research has the following two aims. The first is to target the lesser attention ME, especially feeling of difficulty (FOD), and untangle its fuzzy construct while discuss it in a versatile yet unified way by including methodologies and insights from different disciplines. Secondly, with the support of biometric data such as *eye-tracking data* (e.g. De Rooij et al. 2018; Nelson et al. 2013; Chua and Esolinger 2015) and *skin conductance response* (SCR) data (e.g. Lakie 1967; Morris et al. 2008), a more exhaustive ME assessment might be achieved through combing these kinds of objective evidence with the traditional self-reporting methodologies.

© Springer Nature Switzerland AG 2020
I. I. Bittencourt et al. (Eds.): AIED 2020, LNAI 12164, pp. 400–404, 2020.
https://doi.org/10.1007/978-3-030-52240-7_72

2   Literature Review

Metacognition is comprised of *metacognitive knowledge* (MK), which refers the offline knowledge of cognition, *metacognitive skill* (MS), which supports the control of cognition, and *metacognitive experience* (ME), which is the product of online cognition monitoring (Efklides 2009; Flavell 1979). Among these components, what apart ME from the rest is it is both affective and cognitive in nature (Efklides 2005). Taking FOD as an example, from the affective perspective, it is represented in the form of negative emotion and, from a cognitive perspective, it indicates how well a cognitive process is performed. It is this affective nature of FOD enables the possibility of utilizing eye-tracking and SRC data, which has strong indication for emotion, for its assessment. However, from a study design point of view, what factors trigger FOD is a major issue here. According to Efklides (2005), cognitive discrepancy/interruption (i.e. the lacking cognitive processing fluency) is a particularly influential factor (Efklides and Misailidi 2010). That is, FOD is likely to occur when a cognitive processing result contradicts with what one has planned. For example, when solving a math problem, a learner may initially plan for taking it casually as s/he used to be good at math but later feel frustrated as this problem is actually beyond s/he math ability. However, assuming a stimulus can correctly trigger FOD, another issue here is how to address the functioning of unconscious FOD. According to Efklides (2005), it is when a feeling is strong enough to be aware can FOD emerge on a conscious level. This implies that FOD might emerge on an unconscious level and cannot be reported by one as the "feeling" is not yet felt. This is another reason for including biometrical evidence which may fill the gap for illustrating the whole FOD occurrence process (i.e. from unconscious to conscious level) before one can report the arise of FOD. A pilot study involving an eye-tracker was conducted based on the theoretical framework discussed above. Nonetheless, as the study tasks (i.e. learning material drawn from an online math learning platform called Mathigon and the topic of graph theory was chosen as it includes different types of learning tasks such as reading comprehension, multiple-choice and learning games) was presented in a rather exploratory environment, it was hard to pinpoint the exact FOD arising period from the eye-tracking data. For instance, the increasing pupil size pattern can be found and related to the time when a FOD stimulus is presented (see Fig. 1). Furthermore, a fluctuated pupil pattern can be spotted which may indicate one is regulating their learning process affected by the arise of FOD and attempting to guide the process back on track. However, this interpretation is only a speculation and is even harder for the participant to report. For example, in Fig. 1, the red box on the left indicating when the participant shifts her focus from reading text to the diagrams below and try to figure out what these diagrams mean. From the self-report by her, the difficulty level was increasing and therefore FOD arise. Yet, there was no explanation given by the participant about the three peaks circled in the left red box of Fig. 1. As a result, the revised study proposal in the later section needs to set the study setup more strictly to minimize other factors that could potentially contribute to the forming of FOD.

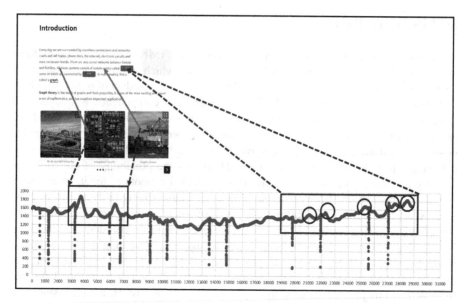

Fig. 1. A sample of the learning material and the pupil size data

3 Methodology

3.1 Research Aims, Hypothesis and Questions

As mentioned previously, to date, there exists an extensive body of metacognition research apply eye-tracking and SCR, which demonstrate the potential of including biometrical evidence to support metacognition assessment. As a result, along with the discussion above, the proposed research aims at investigating how eye-tracking, SCR and self-report can be adopted for exploring FOD on both a conscious and unconscious level. The hypothesis made here is through the design of the activities (see next section for more detail), participants' FOD can be elicited and the data acquired can indicate both the occurrence and intensity of FOD. Two overarching questions provide the focus for this research: (1) Does triangulate eye-tracking, SCR and self-report data can provide indications about how FOD functions?; (2) can the acquired data illustrate the whole FOD arising process both consciously and unconsciously? In sum, the implication from this research may support learners to better understand their FOD functioning and subsequently promote self-regulated learning. Moreover, data from eye-tracking and SCR regarding FOD functioning can shed light on metacognition assessment by providing a more objective perspective.

3.2 Study Design

Participants will be recruited who are in university or graduate level. Metacognition plays an important role in life-long learning (Evans 2018) and it is a lack of ability among the target group (Jaberi and Gheith 2015). As being the last stop of formal education, the potential contribution of this study can support improving metacognitive competence and therefore benefits to the target group. To ensure that FOD behaviours can be observed, both the claims of cognitive discrepancy can trigger FOD (Efklides and Misailidi 2010) and learning-through-teaching can promote metacognitive awareness (Leelawong and Biswas 2008) are adopted. The stimulus will be drawn from Mathigon (Legner 2012) which was used in the pilot study. The context is graph theory and networks which includes four topics. However, to deliver the stimulus in a more restricted way, instead of letting participants explore the given task freely, the learning material from Mathigon will be divided into smaller pieces and each study trails will only last for a certain time (this will be determined by conducting another pilot study). The participants will first get familiar with the given task on a pc connected to an eye-tracker and an SCR equipment. Eye-tracking and SCR data along with screen and video recording of the interaction will be recorded. These data will be used for supporting the later stimulated recall interview (SRI) at the end of each study phases. Participants will then explore the given task as teachers and later report difficult parts spotted with according FOD level rating. Next, participants will take problems that aim at causing cognitive discrepancy and later report the accordingly FOD level rating.

3.3 Data Analysis

Eye-tracking features will be selected based on Eivazi and Bednarik (2011) with the focus on pupillary data along with mean and sum fixation duration, mean between fixation and total eye-movement path distance, number and rate (divided by the duration) of fixations, fixation position within the trails, and pupil dilation. SRC data will be analysed according to Whittlesea and Rayner (1993) work. The reason for applying two types of biometric instruments that both related closely to emotion assessment is to minimize other factors that could influence FOD. That is, to triangulating eye-tracking data, SRC data along with the self-report FOD level, the affective nature of FOD can be focused. Through such, the first research question might be answered through the triangulated data. And the second research question might be tackled via exploring the data's pattern in a set time to see if there are any features can be spotted before FOD is reported.

4   Conclusions

The current proposal aims at exploring the potential of including eye-tracking and SCR together into metacognition research. Besides discussing metacognition from different yet related disciplines, the main goal here is to access metacognition functioning from a more objective perspective. In this way, the implication can be drawn from in assisting learners' metacognitive competence while providing a new approach to metacognition assessment which can be beneficial for their self-regulated learning.

References

Brown, A.L.: Metacognition, executive control, self-regulation and other more mysterious mechanisms. In: Weinert, F.E., Kluwe, R.H. (eds.) Metacognition, Motivation and Understanding, pp. 65–116. Erlbaum, London (1987)

De Rooij, A., Schraffenberger, H., Bontje, M.: Augmented metacognition: exploring pupil dilation sonification to elicit metacognitive awareness. In: Proceedings of the Twelfth International Conference on Tangible, Embedded, and Embodied Interaction, pp. 237–244 (2018)

Efklides, A., Misailidi, P.: Cognitive interruption as an object of metacognitive monitoring: feeling of difficulty and surprise. In: Efklides, A., Misailidi, P. (eds.) Trends and Prospects in Metacognition Research, pp. 171–208. Springer, Boston (2010). https://doi.org/10.1007/978-1-4419-6546-2_9

Efklides, A.: Emotional experiences during learning: multiple, situated and dynamic. Learn. Inst. **15**, 377–380 (2005)

Efklides, A.: Metacognition and affect: what can metacognitive experiences tell us about the learning process? Educ. Res. Rev. **1**, 3–14 (2006)

Efklides, A.: The role of metacognitive experiences in the learning process. Psicothema **21**, 76–82 (2009)

Efklides, A.: Interactions of metacognition with motivation and affect in self-regulated learning: the MASRL model. Educ. Psychol. **46**, 6–25 (2011)

Eivazi, S., Bednarik, R.: Predicting problem-solving behavior and performance levels from visual attention data. In: Proceedings of the 2nd Workshop on Eye Gaze in Intelligent Human Machine Interaction at IUI 2011 (2011)

Chua, E.F., Esolinger, L.: Building metamemorial knowledge over time: Insights from eye tracking about the bases of feeling-of-knowing and confidence judgments. Front. Psychol. **6**, 1206 (2015)

Evans, G.: Windmills of your mind: metacognition and lifelong learning. In: Proceedings of the Canadian Engineering Education Association (CEEA) (2018)

Flavell, J.H.: Metacognition and cognitive monitoring: a new era of cognitive-developmental inquiry. Am. Psychol. **34**, 906–911 (1979)

Jaberi, N., Gheith, E.: University Students' Level of Metacognitive Thinking and their Ability to Solve Problems (2015)

Leelawong, K., Biswas, G.: Designing learning by teaching agents: the betty's brain system. I. J. Artif. Intell. Educ. **18**, 181–208 (2008)

Morris, A., Cleary, A., Still, M.: The role of autonomic arousal in feelings of familiarity. Conscious. Cogn. **17**(4), 1378–1385 (2008)

Nelson, T., Narens, M.E., Eproust, J., Esodian, B.: Examining implicit metacognition in 3.5-year-old children: an eye-tracking and pupillometric study. Front. Psychol. **4**, 145 (2013)

Legner, P.: Mathigon (2012). https://mathigon.org

Whittlesea, B., Rayner, Keith: Illusions of familiarity. J. Exp. Psychol. Learn. Mem. Cogn. **19**(6), 1235–1253 (1993)

Lakie, W.L.: Relationship of galvanic skin response to task difficulty, personality traits, and motivation, research quarterly. Am. Assoc. Health, Phys. Educ. Recreation **38**(1), 58–63 (1967)

Sense of Agency in Times of Automation: A Teachers' Professional Development Proposal on the Ethical Challenges of AI Applied to Education

Ana Mouta[1(✉)], Eva Torrecilla Sánchez[2(✉)],
and Ana María Pinto Llorente[2(✉)]

[1] Doctoral School, University of Salamanca, Salamanca, Spain
id00771513@usal.es
[2] Faculty of Education, University of Salamanca, Salamanca, Spain
{emt,ampintoll}@usal.es

Abstract. The possibilities given by artificial intelligence are becoming enactments of what once were just distant fictional displays. Even if we restrict the context to Artificial Intelligence in Education (AIEd) the horizon is still wide. But which society layers and ethical frameworks are being considered in the process of conceiving AIEd scope? Committed with this debate, this research focuses the ethical challenges of AIEd in terms of sense of agency development across formal education.

Keywords: Artificial intelligence · Education · Ethics · Sense of agency · Training

1 Introduction: Who's Accountable for Automation Applied to Learning Processes?

The latest technological advancements emerging as daily commodities are so far-reaching that our ways of thinking, feeling, acting and relate with others may be transformed at a very silent and rapid pace. But what investments are being made to determine the kind of culture, usage and ethics people want, need and may be able to spread through their technology mediated performances? In fact, works on ethical assessment of new tech, including AI-powered environments, are gaining traction [1, 2]. Education-wise huge worldwide governmental investments were made for the deployment of laptops, broad access to Internet and educational software, some integrating AI [3], intelligent tutoring systems [4], and robots [5]. Although we may consider relevant some achievements over the last 25 years, AIEd is quite a new discipline and a research overview revealed a lack of critical reflection of its challenges and risks [6, 7]. In fact, AIEd is covering an unprecedent range of cognitive functions and easing some routine tasks through automated grading, feedback loops, virtual facilitators, personalised learning, customised materials, and proctoring. But ideologies, fantasies, and projections about what the future should or is expected to be inform the

I. I. Bittencourt et al. (Eds.): AIED 2020, LNAI 12164, pp. 405–408, 2020.
https://doi.org/10.1007/978-3-030-52240-7_73

development of these technological solutions. So, who may be accountable for AIEd development and scope? How is sense of agency being enhanced or constrained in the processes it enables? And how is our Judgement of Agency [8] being respected by its automations? In fact, many studies emphasised the sense of agency role in user experience and interface design [9] and some found a conundrum in the association of automation and sense of agency [10, 11]. This PhD research is being developed under the premise that sense of agency is at the heart of learning, enabling experiences of signification that may foster lifelong orientation for learning. It also considers sense of agency core for legal and ethical structures [12]. So, this research aims at contributing to the public debate on AIEd, so that its researchers/developers become more sensitive and critical towards ethical learning-related issues. Furthermore, it intends to foster teachers' critical thinking on AIEd, by directly recognising their current attitudes and levels of awareness on the matter. Teachers are expected to be empowered to decide whether they want to use AIEd or not, to recognise the ways these technologies enter and may transform classrooms and learners and how they may integrate these resources into their pedagogical practices.

2   Research Goals and Methodology: Designing the Futures We Long for

2.1   Research Goals

This work aims at understanding if and how ethical impact assessment of AIEd influences primary teachers' awareness on the challenges AIEd may pose [13] to sense of agency. The specific goals comprise: (1) the exploration of contexts, applications, drivers, ethical issues, and controls that may be critical to evolve in the discussions of AIEd, particularly in what relates to sense of agency. (2) The enhancement of teachers' capacity to explore AI impact on learning, across students' different developmental tasks. (3) The design of professional development content that promotes teachers' capability to intentionally consider AI ethical challenges in their pedagogical practices, preserving the conditions that enable students' sense of agency.

2.2   Methodology

The research methodology will be mainly qualitative, comprising data triangulation. On the first phase it will be used a grounded theory-based design of a framework for teachers' Continuing Professional Development (CPD). This part will include the following variables: the narrative shared participatory methods and the capability of ethically reason upon AI applied to Education. Given the fact that this research's theoretical corpus is on its first growing years, the option for the Delphi method seemed accurate, enabling the identification of guiding theories, variables, causal relationships, constructs, instruments and generating a common language for discussion [14]. The structure is planned as follows: 1.1. Selection of a group of circa 15 experts from different geographical realities (snowball method), with experience on education, philosophy of technology, tech applied to education or in AI software development.

1.2. Participants will be challenged (email) to express their opinions on AIEd – *i.e.*, AIEd techs and applications, user contexts, usage drivers, ethical issues involved, and existing controls. 1.3. This data will enable the construction of a survey questionnaire. 1.4. Participants will (a) rethink their first responses, (b) choose the 2 main critical items for each criterion, and (3) conclude on the drivers, the potential ethical challenges, and the current existing controls. Data will be analysed through descriptive statistics that will be further shared with the experts. 1.5. These new ideas will be voted by the group to define a final list on each criterion and further create a hypothetical dilemma reflecting an ethical challenge posed by AIEd. 1.6. Participants will vote 3 dilemmas (better exploration of AIEd ethical challenges). 1.7. Results will be shared with the entire group.

Then, providing directions on CPD needs, a focus group of circa 7–10 teachers will be presented 3 ethical dilemmas (resulting from the previous research design). This will constitute a common basis to identify what AI tech might be like and speak about the AIEd construct. Teachers will be invited to choose the most impactful dilemma in terms of learning implications, justifying their choices. They are expected to highlight potential consequences to students' sense of agency resulting from the use of that tech under the described circumstances (or others). Then, teachers will be also invited to explore the needs of a school community in what concerns AIEd. This content will be analysed (CAQDAS) to explore teachers' current attitudes towards AIEd and related CPD needs.

The content resulting from the Delphi and focus group phases will be the basis for designing a socio-constructivist eLearning course. Its methodologies will create opportunities to explore and evaluate teachers' capacity to intentionally integrate the potential and limits of using AI. A group of around 20 teachers or education internship students will be invited to complete this online course (MOOC platform). A qualitative data collection moment on attitudes towards AIEd will be included in the initial and final phases of the course structure. Throughout the course teachers will (1) identify AIEd applications, (2) explore its potential and challenges in terms of learning, and (3) specifically identify the effects of AIEd ethical challenges upon sense of agency. Then, a group of around 5 teachers will be invited to a final semi-structured interview to grasp teachers' attitudes towards AIEd regarding learning experiences' processes. The eLearning characteristics that might have contributed to those results will be explored along with the teachers' perception on their capability and will to continue dealing with the ethical challenges AI may pose to formal educational environments. The questions will also comprise the main criteria teachers consider relevant for CPD on AIEd.

3 Conclusions

This research is expected to mainly reinforce understanding on the critical ethical dimensions of AI applied to Education, in what concerns the role of sense of agency in the signification of a learning experience. It will reflect upon the perspective of different educational stakeholders, namely teachers, and it will try to contribute to the public debate and further research on AIEd. That will be done through the development of conceptual insights and theoretical frameworks to analyse and incorporate its critical dimensions into deliberate pedagogical practices.

References

1. Brey, P.: Ethics of emerging technologies. In: Hansson, S.O. (ed.) Methods for the Ethics of Technology. Rowman and Littlefield International (2017)
2. Reisman, D., Schulz, J., Crawford, K., Whittaker, M.: Algorithmic impact assessment: a practical framework for public agency accountability (2018). https://ainowinstitute.org/aiareport2018.pdf
3. Becker, B.: Artificial intelligence in education: what is it, where is it now, where is it going? In: Ireland's Yearbook of Education 2017–2018, pp. 42–46. Education Matters (2017)
4. Craig, S.: Tutoring and Intelligent Tutoring Systems. Nova Science Publishers, New York (2018)
5. Vitanza, A., Rossetti, P., Mondada, F., Trianni, V.: Robot swarms as an educational tool: the Thymio's way. Int. J. Adv. Robot. Syst. (2019). https://doi.org/10.1177/1729881418825186
6. Humble, N., Mozelius, P.: Artificial Intelligence in Education – a Promise, a Threat or a Hype? (2019). https://doi.org/10.34190/eciair.19.005
7. Zawacki-Richter, O., Marín, V.I., Bond, M., Gouverneur, F.: Systematic review of research on artificial intelligence applications in higher education – where are the educators? Int. J. Educ. Technol. Higher Educ. 16, 39 (2019). https://doi.org/10.1186/s41239-019-0171-0
8. Synofzik, M., Vosgerau, G., Newen, A.: Beyond the comparator model: a multifactorial two-step account of agency. Conscious. Cogn. 17, 219–239 (2008). https://doi.org/10.1016/j.concog.2007.03.010
9. Moore, J.W.: What is the sense of agency and why does it matter? Front. Psychol. 7 (2016). https://doi.org/10.3389/fpsyg.2016.01272
10. Berberian, B., Sarrazin, J.-C., LeBlaye, P., Haggard, P.: Automation technology and sense of control: a window on human agency. PLoS ONE 7, e34075 (2012). https://doi.org/10.1371/journal.pone.0034075
11. Sahaï, A., Desantisb, A., Grynszpand, O., Pacheriea, E., Berberian, B.: Action co-representation and the sense of agency during a joint Simon task: comparing human and machine co-agents. Conscious. Cogn. 67, 44–55 (2019). https://doi.org/10.1016/j.concog.2018.11.008
12. Frith, C.D.: Action, agency and responsibility. Neuropsychologia 55, 137–142 (2014). https://doi.org/10.1016/j.neuropsychologia.2013.09.007
13. Aiken, R., Epstein, R.: Ethical guidelines for AI in education: starting a conversation. Int. J. Artif. Intell. Educ. 11, 163–176 (2000). https://www.researchgate.net/publication/228600407_Ethical_guidelines_for_AI_in_education_Starting_a_conversation
14. Cabero, J., Infante, A.: Empleo del Método Delphi y su empelo en la investigación en comunicación y educación. Revista Electrónica de Tecnología Educativa 48, 1–16 (2014). https://idus.us.es/bitstream/handle/11441/32234/edutec-e_n48_cabero-infante.pdf?sequence=1&isAllowed=y

Improving Students' Problem-Solving Flexibility in Non-routine Mathematics

Huy A. Nguyen[(⊠)] [iD], Yuqing Guo, John Stamper,
and Bruce M. McLaren

Carnegie Mellon University, Pittsburgh, PA 15213, USA
hnl@cs.cmu.edu

Abstract. A key issue in mathematics education is supporting students in developing general problem-solving skills that can be applied to novel, non-routine situations. However, typical mathematics instruction in the U.S. too often is dominated by rote learning, without exposing students to the underlying reasoning or alternate ways to solve problems. As a first step in addressing this problem, we present a cognitive task analysis study that investigates how students without a mathematics-related background solve novel non-routine problems. We found that most students were able to identify the underlying pattern that yields the final solution in each problem. Furthermore, they tended to use various forms of visualization in their draft work, but occasionally made computational mistakes. Based on these results, we propose our plan for developing an instructional platform that leverages learning science principles to train students in problem-solving abilities.

Keywords: Problem-solving flexibility · Strategy · Non-routine mathematics

1 Introduction

The ability to tackle non-routine problems – those that cannot be solved with a known method or formula and require analysis and synthesis as well as creativity [9] – is becoming increasingly important in the 21st century [5]. However, when faced with a non-routine problem, U.S. students tend to apply memorized procedures incorrectly rather than modify them or develop new solutions [8]. One possible source for this difficulty is the typical instructional focus in U.S. schools on memorization and application of routine procedures [2, 6, 7]. Such an approach makes students proficient at executing rote procedures, but it does little to help them understand the conceptual basis for the procedures or to think creatively about novel problems - both of which are essential for developing problem-solving flexibility.

An important first step in addressing this issue is to assess how students currently approach non-routine problem solving, so that we can design the appropriate learning interventions. In this work, we present an empirical cognitive task analysis where participants were asked to think aloud while solving a series of non-routine problems from discrete mathematics. We chose this domain because discrete math problems can often be tackled from multiple perspectives while not requiring any advanced background beyond the high school curriculum [3]. Based on the findings from this study,

© Springer Nature Switzerland AG 2020
I. I. Bittencourt et al. (Eds.): AIED 2020, LNAI 12164, pp. 409–413, 2020.
https://doi.org/10.1007/978-3-030-52240-7_74

we propose our plan for developing a tutoring system for non-routine problem-solving ability. Then, we discuss the system's broader implications and the challenges we need to address in deploying this system at scale.

2 Assessing Students' Problem-Solving Skills

We conducted interview sessions with three students at a private university in a midwest US city. None of the students had a mathematics-related background. The participants were asked to solve three non-routine mathematics problems on paper in one hour. They were also encouraged to think aloud and write down their draft work. The three problems in our study, taken from [3], and a brief summary of their sample solutions, are as follows.

Problem 1: *In an air show there are twenty rows. The first row contains one seat, the second three seats, the third five seats, the fourth seventh seats, and so on. How many seats are there in total?*

Sample solution: In the first row there is **1** seat. In the first two rows there are $1 + 3 = $ **4** seats. In the first three rows there are $1 + 3 + 5 = $ **9** seats. In the first four rows there are $1 + 3 + 5 + 7 = 16$ seats. In the first five rows there are $1 + 3 + 5 + 7 + 9 = $ **25** seats. Based on this pattern, in the first k rows there are k^2 seats. In our case, there are 20 rows and therefore 400 seats in total.

Problem 2: *Find all integers between 1 and 99 (inclusive) with all distinct digits.*

Sample solution: there are 99 integers between 1 and 99 in total, and 9 of them have non-distinct digits, namely 11, 22, 33, ..., 88, 99. Hence, the remaining 90 integers have distinct digits.

Problem 3: *What is the digit in the ones place of 2^{57}?*

Sample solution: Looking at the sequence of powers of 2–2, 4, 8, 16, 32, 64, 128, 256, 512, 1024, ... – we see that the corresponding sequence of digits in the ones places is 2, 4, 8, 6, 2, 4, 8, 6, 2, 4, ... In other words, this sequence is a cycle of length 4. Therefore the last digit of 2^{57} is that of 2^{53}, which is that of 2^{49}, ..., which is that of 2^1, which is 2.

We then analyzed recordings of the participants' think-aloud and their draftwork, from which we derived the following insights:

Pattern Identification. Participants were aware that they had to find a pattern or formula to solve the problems, because it was not feasible to directly compute the final answer. All participants were able to identify the expected pattern for each problem as outlined above, except for one student who failed to do so for Problem 1. While this participant realized that the number of seats on row k is the k-th positive odd number, this pattern alone was insufficient to solve the problem.

Visualization. Participants tended to visualize the problem by drawing examples and making lists or tables (Fig. 1). They expressed that these visualizations were crucial in helping them identify the correct pattern and solve the problem.

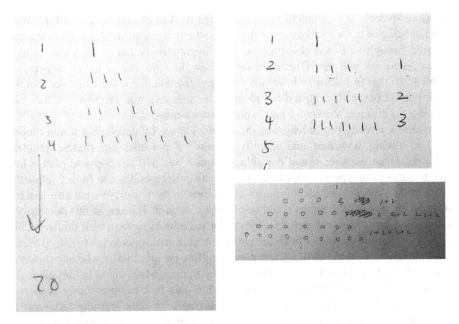

Fig. 1. Participants' attempts at visualizing the problem in their draftworks.

Computation. Participants occasionally made computational mistakes while calculating the initial sequence values, especially in Problem 3. As a consequence, they could not identify any pattern based on the wrong values, and took some time to realize the mistake. All students who corrected their mistakes were able to subsequently solve the problem.

In summary, we found that participants were aware of the idea behind identifying patterns, and they all did so via some kind of visualization. On the other hand, computational mistakes, while not directly related to our learning objectives, can be detrimental to the overall problem-solving process. From these insights, we propose the following next steps.

3 Developing a Tutoring System for Flexible Problem-Solving

Moving forward, our plan is to iteratively conduct more cognitive task analysis interviews and develop a prototype of the system. Our initial conceptualization of how the system will work is as follows. A single round of exercise in the system incorporates four learning stages, all of which are built on established learning principles: 1) Reviewing a worked example of a non-routine mathematics problem, 2) Explaining the worked example to a partner, 3) Solving a new problem which is isomorphic to the worked example problem, and 4) Explaining the isomorphic solution to a partner. Between rounds, the student can review previous solutions, look at materials related to the problem space, or practice basic math skills. This design is intended to (1) formally introduce students to a complete solution through worked examples, (2) reinforce their understanding of the worked example through self-explanation, and (3) assess students' learning through an isomorphic problem. Our hypothesis is that through the learning system, students will get a better sense of how to *approach* a novel non-routine problem, so that in case they have not yet found the solution – for example, like the participant in our study who did not identify the true pattern in Problem 1 – they can still adopt a different viewpoint and explore other strategies.

We have already begun mapping the problem space by developing a non-routine problem-solving flowchart and identifying sets of potential non-routine problem solutions. Once we have tested our solution space, we will develop and pilot a low fidelity paper prototype version of the system with college students to further refine the mathematical content and identify areas for revision to the design. We are also looking at which technological features could be useful for students learning in this domain. As a first step, our system will include a canvas for students to perform their draftwork on, as well as a simple calculator interface with basic arithmetic operations to help students avoid computational mistakes. An important follow-up question is whether students' draftwork can be analyzed to infer their thinking process, which could in turn guide the design of appropriate feedback mechanics. While this task has previously been performed manually by domain experts [1], employing a machine learning technique to automate it to some extent would greatly enhance the system's adaptive support functionality and scalability.

4 Conclusion

This research will provide concrete, generalizable evidence about the utility and implementation of worked examples, multiple solutions, and self-explanation to promote skills in non-routine problem solving. Results will inform future tutoring system design by identifying how and when the instructional features are most beneficial for developing problem-solving skills. We also intend to have a practical impact by distributing a tutoring system that is accessible to a wide range of students, including lower-performing students who would typically not be exposed to these types of problems and strategies [1, 4]. In addition, we will provide a teacher's guide to support educators in using the system adaptively to support their instructional goals.

References

1. Arslan, C., Yazgan, Y.: Common and flexible use of mathematical non routine problem solving strategies. Am. J. Educ. Res. **3**, 1519–1523 (2015)
2. Crooks, N.M., Alibali, M.W.: Defining and measuring conceptual knowledge in mathematics. Dev. Rev. **34**, 344–377 (2014)
3. Johnson, K., Herr, T.: Problem Solving Strategies: Crossing the River with Dogs: and Other Mathematical Adventures. Key Curriculum Press, New York (2001)

4. Kolovou, A., Van Den Heuvel-Panhuizen, M., Bakker, A.: Non-routine problem solving tasks in primary school mathematics textbooks–a needle in a haystack. Math. Prob. Solving Primary School **8**, 45 (2011)
5. Neubert, J.C., Mainert, J., Kretzschmar, A., Greiff, S.: The assessment of 21st century skills in industrial and organizational psychology: complex and collaborative problem solving. Ind. Organ. Psychol. **8**, 238–268 (2015)
6. Richland, L.E., Stigler, J.W., Holyoak, K.J.: Teaching the conceptual structure of mathematics. Educ. Psychol. **47**, 189–203 (2012)
7. Stigler, J., Hiebert, J.: Understanding and improving classroom mathematics instruction: an overview of the TIMSS video study. In: ACER National Conference 1997, pp. 52–65 (1997)
8. Stigler, J.W., Givvin, K.B., Thompson, B.J.: What community college developmental mathematics students understand about mathematics. MathAMATYC Educ. **1**, 4–16 (2010)
9. Woodward, J., et al.: Improving Mathematical Problem Solving in Grades 4 through 8. IES Practice Guide. NCEE 2012-4055. What Works Clearinghouse (2012)

Workshop Papers

Optimizing Human Learning: Third International Workshop Eliciting Adaptive Sequences for Learning (WASL 2020)

Jill-Jênn Vie[1]([✉]), Fabrice Popineau[2], Hisashi Kashima[3], and Benoît Choffin[2]

[1] Inria Lille, Lille, France
jill-jenn.vie@inria.fr
[2] CentraleSupélec/LRI, Orsay, France
{fabrice.popineau,benoit.choffin}@lri.fr
[3] Kyoto University, Kyoto, Japan
kashima@i.kyoto-u.ac.jp

Abstract. Machine learning is promising for empowering education, however it requires a solid specification of the problem at hand. What are good metrics or losses for optimizing knowledge retention? What are the specific issues when dealing with adaptive environments? This workshop attempts at discussing challenges related to optimizing human learning. https://humanlearn.io

Keywords: Adaptive learning · Reinforcement learning · Knowledge tracing

1 Objectives

What should we learn next? In this current era where digital access to knowledge is cheap and user attention is expensive, a number of online applications have been developed for learning. These platforms collect a massive amount of data over various profiles, that can be used to improve learning experience: intelligent tutoring systems can infer what activities worked for different types of students in the past, and apply this knowledge to instruct new students. In order to learn effectively and efficiently, the experience should be adaptive: the sequence of activities should be tailored to the abilities and needs of each learner, in order to keep them stimulated and avoid boredom, confusion and dropout. In the context of reinforcement learning, we want to learn a policy to administer exercises or resources to individual students [1–3].

Educational research communities have proposed models that predict mistakes and dropout, in order to detect students that need further instruction. Such models are usually calibrated on data collected in an offline scenario, and may not generalize well to new students. There is now a need to design online systems that continuously learn as data flows, and self-assess their strategies when interacting with new learners. These models have been already deployed

© Springer Nature Switzerland AG 2020
I. I. Bittencourt et al. (Eds.): AIED 2020, LNAI 12164, pp. 417–419, 2020.
https://doi.org/10.1007/978-3-030-52240-7

in online commercial applications (ex. streaming, advertising, social networks) for optimizing interaction, click-through-rate, or profit. Can we use similar methods to enhance the performance of teaching in order to promote lifetime success? When optimizing human learning, which metrics should be optimized? Learner progress? Learner retention? User addiction? The diversity or coverage of the proposed activities? What the issues inherent to adapting the learning process in online settings, in terms of privacy, fairness (disparate impact, inadvertent discrimination), and robustness to adversaries trying to game the system?

Student modeling for optimizing human learning is a rich and complex task that gathers methods from machine learning, cognitive science, educational data mining and psychometrics. This workshop welcomes researchers and practitioners in the following topics (this list is not exhaustive):

- abstract representations of learning
- additive/conjunctive factor models
- adversarial learning
- causal models
- cognitive diagnostic models
- deep generative models such as deep knowledge tracing
- item response theory
- models of learning and forgetting (spaced repetition)
- multi-armed bandits
- multi-task learning
- bandits & reinforcement learning

2   Questions

- How to put the student in optimal conditions to learn? e.g. incentives, companion agents, etc.
- When optimizing human learning, which metrics should be optimized?
  - The progress of the learner?
  - The diversity or coverage of the proposed activities?
  - Fast recovery of what the student does not know?
  - Can a learning platform be solely based on addiction, maximizing interaction?
- What kinds of activities give enough choice and control to the learner to benefit their learning (adaptability vs. adaptivity)?
- Do the strategies differ when we are teaching to a group of students? Do we want to enhance social interaction between learners?
- What feedback should be shown to the learner in order to allow reflective learning? e.g. visualization, learning map, score, etc. (Should a system provide a fake feedback in order to encourage the student more?)
- What student parameters are relevant? e.g. personality traits, mood, context (is the learner in class or at home?), etc.
- What explicit and implicit feedbacks does the learner provide during the interaction?

- What models of learning are relevant? E.g. cognitive models, modeling forgetting in spaced repetition.
- What specific challenges from the ML point of view are we facing with these data?
- Do we have enough datasets? What kinds of datasets are missing? In particular, aren't the current datasets too focused on STEM disciplines?
- How to guarantee fairness/trustworthiness of AI systems that learn from interaction with students? This is especially critical for systems that learn online.

3   About the Program Committee

To contact us, join our mailing list: optimizing-human-learning.

Jill-Jênn Vie is a researcher in machine learning at Inria Lille, SequeL team. His research focuses on learning fair representations of users that evolve over time, with applications to education and recommender systems. He authored several publications about knowledge tracing.

Fabrice Popineau is a professor at CentraleSupélec and researcher in the LAHDAK team of LRI, Orsay. He is interested in adaptation, personalization and companion agents for online educational platforms.

Hisashi Kashima is a professor at the Department of Intelligence Science of Technology, Kyoto University. His research interests are machine learning and human computation, and their applications to learning analytics.

Benoît Choffin is a PhD student in Computer Science at CentraleSupélec (University of Paris-Saclay) in France, under the supervision of Yolaine Bourda and Fabrice Popineau. Benoét is interested in leveraging machine learning methods for improving the way humans learn. In particular, he is currently developing adaptive spacing algorithms for skill mastery: these algorithms personalize skill reviewing schedules to suit the students' strengths and weaknesses and optimize long-term mastery. His research work has been awarded the Best Full Paper Award at EDM 2019.

References

1. Clement, B., Roy, D., Oudeyer, P.Y., Lopes, M.: Multi-armed bandits for intelligent tutoring systems. J. Educ. Data Min. **7**(2) (2015)
2. Whitehill, J., Movellan, J.: Approximately optimal teaching of approximately optimal learners. IEEE Tran. Learn. Technol. **11**(2), 152–164 (2017)
3. Tabibian, B., Upadhyay, U., De, A., Zarezade, A., Schölkopf, B., & Gomez-Rodriguez, M., : Enhancing human learning via spaced repetition optimization. In: Proceedings of the National Academy of Sciences, vol. 116(10), pp. 3988–3993 (2019)

Empowering Education with AI Technology – IEEE LTSC

Robby Robson[1]([⊠]), Xiangen Hu[2], Jim Goodell[3], Michael Jay[4],
and Brandt Redd[5]

[1] EduWorks, Corvallis, OR 97333, USA
robby.robson@eduworks.com
[2] The University of Memphis, Memphis, TN 38152, USA
xiangenhu@gmail.com
[3] Quality Information Partners, Fairfax, VA 22038, USA
jimgoodell@qi-partners.com
[4] MatchMaker Education Labs, Bellingham, WA 98226, USA
michael@matchmakeredlabs.net
[5] MatchMaker Education Labs, Provo, UT 84604, USA
brandt@redd.org

Abstract. The goal of this proposed workshop is to explore opportunities to empower educational systems with the most advanced AI technologies and to explore how to standardize on these systems, technologies, and practices, including adaptive learning systems, AI-based recommendation engines, and systems that use machine learning to model student interactions and preferences to improve learning outcomes. Relevant topic areas will cover some aspects of the research that directly or indirectly define, inform and advance the current relevant IEEE standards for the application of AI in learning technologies, which may include (but are not limited to) the following: 1) AI architecture, methodology and models that improve the scalability, performance, and explainability, and that enable components to plugin and interact with AI engines used in learning technology systems, especially AI-driven adaptive instructional systems; 2) Federated Machine Learning (FML) and Explainable AI (XAI); 3) Standards, practice, and methodology for accessing, collecting, storing, utilizing, sharing, and securing child and student data. Standards that provide stakeholders with certifiable and responsible child and student data governance methodologies, specific metrics, and conformance criteria; 4) Standards for evaluating and reporting the use of AI in educational systems; 5) Practices and methodologies that capture the nuanced and political nature of educational institutions while addressing the needs of the learner and educator.

Keywords: Adaptive instructional systems · Data governance and privacy · Explainable AI · Open source · Standardization · Interoperability · Machine learning

© Springer Nature Switzerland AG 2020
I. I. Bittencourt et al. (Eds.): AIED 2020, LNAI 12164, pp. 420–423, 2020.
https://doi.org/10.1007/978-3-030-52240-7

1 Introduction

AI-enabled education tools have recently attracted attention for their potential to improve education quality and enhance traditional teaching and learning methods. These offerings are now being rolled out at scale in commercial and non-commercial products. Having achieved this level of maturity, standards for common interfaces, components, and processes serve as a foundation for new research and innovation while reducing the risk of adopting AI-based educational products and helping to avoid wasteful duplication of effort. Interoperability gained through thoughtfully developed standards makes it possible to reuse existing technologies and content so they can be integrated into existing educational ecosystems. This can reduce costs and accelerate advances in the field of AI in Education by enabling researchers and innovators to more easily test and evaluate new strategies and technologies through a wide variety of implementations in real-world environments generating large data sets. The standardization effort is also deeply connected with and informed by the AIED research in the corresponding areas.

2 Workshop Chairs

Dr. Robby Robson is a researcher and innovator in the broad field of learning technology who has contributed to numerous standards and technologies that are widely used today. He holds a doctorate in mathematics from Stanford University, is CEO and co-founder of Eduworks Corporation, former chair of the IEEE Learning Technology Standards Committee, and currently serves on the IEEE Standards Association Board of Governors. **Dr. Xiangen Hu** is a professor in the Department of Psychology, Department of Electrical and Computer Engineering and Computer Science Department at The University of Memphis (UofM) and senior researcher at the Institute for Intelligent Systems (IIS) at the UofM and is professor and Dean of the School of Psychology at Central China Normal University (CCNU). **Mr. Jim Goodell** is the Senior Education Analyst at Quality Information Partners. Mr. Goodell leads standards development for the US Department of Education's Common Education Data Standards (CEDS) and works with stakeholders from early learning, K12, postsecondary, and workforce organizations. He is Vice-Chair of the IEEE Learning Technology Standards Committee, Chair of the Competency Data Standards Workgroup, and Chair of the Adaptive Instructional Systems Interoperability Workgroup. **Mr. Michael Jay** is the CEO of MatchMaker Education Labs. He left the classroom in 1986 to join Apple Computer's Classroom of Tomorrow (ACOT) research and development project, served as Apple's Education Competitive Analyst, and led major curriculum-related marketing initiatives. **Mr. Brandt Redd** is the CTO of MatchMaker Education Labs, a new startup involved in competency definitions and facilitating directories of learning resources. He is the creator and coordinator of the EdMatrix.org directory of Learning Technology Standards. Mr. Redd was formerly CTO of the Smarter Balanced Assessment Consortium and Senior Technology Officer for Education at the Bill & Melinda Gates Foundation.

3 Program Committee Members

- **Richard Tong**, IEEE LTSC Chair, Chief Architect and General Manager of US Operations at Squirrel AI Learning
- **Robert Sottilare**, IEEE AIS Chair, Soar Technology
- **Shelly Blake-Plock**, Technical Advisory Group (TAG) for xAPI
- **Elliot Robson**, Eduworks
- **Lixin Fan**, Explainable AI WG
- **Yang Qiang**, Federated Machine Learning WG
- **Zitao Liu**, TAL
- **Songfan Yang**, TAL
- **Ronghuai Huang**, Beijing Normal University
- **Victor Lu**, Beijing Normal University
- **Avron Barr,** IEEE Learning Technology Standards Committee
- **Art Graesser**, University of Memphis
- **Bruce McLaren**, Carnegie Mellon University
- **Mark Lee**, IEEE TLT
- **Tianyi Ivy Tang**, Squirrel AI Learning
- **Zachary Pardos**, UC Berkeley
- **Alicia Sanchez**, DAU
- **Sae Schatz**, ADL
- **Keith Brawner**, U.S. Army CCDC SC
- **David Dockterman**, Harvard University
- **Erlend Overby** - ISO SC36 Chair
- **Delmar Larson**, University of California, Davis, and Founder of LibreTexts

4 Proposed Format

- Paper Presentations: 3–5 (30 min Each)
- Invited Talks: We intend to have 5–7 speaker to present their expert insights
- Panel Discussions: Panel discussion sessions are intended to explore various heated topics in the implementation of AI in the field of education, ongoing initiatives, and projects.
- Poster sessions: Optional for papers that could not fit into the main session - Allow breakout rooms.

5 About the Hosts

IEEE Learning Technology Standards Committee (LTSC) focuses on supporting the evolution of learning technologies. The LTSC supports the IEEE's mission by developing global technical standards, recommended practices, and guides for learning technology. The IEEE LTSC actively cooperates with academic, industrial research labs and government agencies to promote and transform learning research to scalable and practical learning technologies in use.

Squirrel AI Learning by Yixue Group is the first and market-leading K12 EdTech service company that specializes in intelligent adaptive education in China. For the second year in a row, Squirrel AI Learning is the hosting partner and primary sponsor for this workshop at AIED.

Second Workshop on Intelligent Textbooks

Sergey Sosnovsky[1]([⊠]), Peter Brusilovsky[2], Richard G. Baraniuk[3],
and Andrew S. Lan[4]

[1] Utrecht University, Princetonplein 5, Utrecht 3584 CC, The Netherlands
s.a.sosnovsky@uu.nl
[2] University of Pittsburgh, 135 North Bellefield Ave, Pittsburgh
PA 15260, USA
peterb@pitt.edu
[3] Rice University, 6100 Main Street, Houston, TX 77005, USA
richb@rice.edu
[4] University of Massachutsetts Amherst, 140 Governors Dr,
Amherst, MA 01003, USA
andrewlan@cs.umass.edu

Abstract. Textbooks have evolved over the last several decades in many
aspects. Most textbooks can be accessed online, many of them freely. They
often come with libraries of supplementary educational resources or online
educational services built on top of them. As a result of these enrichments, new
research challenges and opportunities emerge that call for the application of
AIEd methods to enhance digital textbooks and learners' interaction with them.
Therefore, we ask: How to facilitate the access to textbooks and improve the
reading process? What can be extracted from textbook content and data-mined
from the logs of students interacting with it? This workshop will seek research
contributions addressing these and other research questions related to the idea of
intelligent textbooks. It seeks to bring together researchers working on different
aspects of learning technologies to establish intelligent textbooks as a new,
interdisciplinary research field.

Keywords: Digital and online textbooks · Open educational resources (OER) ·
Modelling and representation of textbook content · Assessment generation ·
Adaptive presentation and navigation · Content curation end enrichment

1 The Motivation

Textbooks and instructional texts in general remain one of the main methods of
instruction, but – just like other educational tools – they have been evolving over the
last several decades in many aspects (how they are created, published, formatted,
accessed, and maintained). Most textbooks these days have digital versions and can be
accessed online. Plenty of textbooks (and similar instructional texts, such as tutorials)
are freely available as open educational resources (OERs). Many commercial textbooks
come with libraries of supplementary educational resources or even distributed as parts
of online educational services built on top of them. The transition of textbooks from
printed copies to digital and online formats has facilitated numerous attempts to enrich

© Springer Nature Switzerland AG 2020
I. I. Bittencourt et al. (Eds.): AIED 2020, LNAI 12164, pp. 424–426, 2020.
https://doi.org/10.1007/978-3-030-52240-7

them with various kinds of interactive functionalities including search and annotation, interactive content modules, automated assessments and more.

As a result of these enrichments, new research challenges and opportunities emerge that call for the application of *artificial intelligence* (AI) methods to enhance digital textbooks and learners' interaction with them. There are many research questions associated with this new area of research; examples include:

- How can one facilitate the access to textbooks and improve the reading process?
- How can one process textbook content to infer knowledge underlying the text and use it to improve learning support?
- How can one process increasingly more detailed logs of students interacting with digital textbooks and extract insights on learning?
- How can one find and retrieve relevant content "in the wild", i.e., on the web, that can enrich the textbooks?
- How can one better understand both textbooks and student behaviors as they learn within the textbook and create personalized learner experiences?

Our workshop will seek research contributions addressing these and other research questions related to the idea of intelligent textbooks. While the pioneer work on various kinds of intelligent textbook technologies has already begun, research in this area is still rare and spread over several different fields, including AI, human-computer interaction, information retrieval, intelligent tutoring systems, and user modeling. This workshop will bring together researchers working on different aspects of intelligent textbook technologies in these fields and beyond to establish intelligent textbooks as a new, interdisciplinary research field.

2   Description of the Workshop Content and Themes

We intend to make this workshop the first in a series. Therefore, we aim at gathering researchers from a wide range of communities that are interested in all aspects of intelligent textbooks. The workshop themes include but are not limited to:

a) Modelling and representation of textbooks: examining the prerequisite and semantic structure of textbooks to enhance their readability;
b) Analysis and mining of textbook usage logs: analyzing the patterns of learners' use of textbooks to obtain insights on learning and the pedagogical value of textbook content;
c) Collaborative technologies: building and deploying social components of digital textbooks that enable learners to interact with not only content but other learners;
d) Generation, manipulation, and presentation: exploring and testing different formats and forms of textbook content to find the most effective means of presenting different knowledge;

e) Assessment and personalization: developing methods that can generate assessments and enhance textbooks with adaptive support to meet the needs of every learner using the textbook;

f) Content curation and enrichment: sorting through external resources on the web and finding the relevant resources to augment the textbook and provide additional information for learners.

2nd International Workshop on Education in Artificial Intelligence K-12 (EduAI)

Gerald Steinbauer[1]([✉]), Sven Koenig[2], Fredrik Heintz[3], Julie Henry[4], Tara Chklovski[5], and Martin Kandlhofer[1]

[1] Institute of Software Technology, Graz University of Technology, Graz, Austria
{steinbauer,kandlhofer}@ist.tugraz.at
[2] Computer Science Department, University of Southern California, Los Angeles, USA
skoenig@usc.edu
[3] Computer Science Department, Linköping University, Linköping, Sweden
fredrik.heintz@liu.se
[4] Namur Digital Institute, University of Namur, Namur, Belgium
julie.henry@unamur.be
[5] Technovation, Los Angeles, USA
tara@technovation.org

Abstract. In recent years, Artificial Intelligence (AI) has gained the attention of the public, and become a major topic of discussion. AI already has a significant influence on various areas of life and across different sectors and fields. The rapidity with which AI is impacting our everyday life as well as our working world poses a tremendous challenge for our society and educational system. This second edition of the EduAI workshop aims to address that challenge by bringing together researchers, teachers, and practitioners who are actively involved with and/or interested in K-12 AI education. The aim is to foster a mutual exchange of knowledge, ideas and views between those groups to discuss and find a common ground for how to best implement AI education.

Keywords: AI literacy · AI education · Digital citizenship education

1 Introduction

In recent years, Artificial Intelligence (AI) has gained the attention of the public, and become a major topic of discussion. AI already has a significant influence on various areas of life and across different sectors and fields. The rapidity with which AI is impacting our everyday life as well as our working world poses a tremendous challenge for our society and educational system. Sound knowledge about AI, its principles and concepts, the ability to apply AI techniques and methods, coupled with the ability to analyze their long-term benefits, are becoming 21st century key skills. They are the basis for creating career opportunities and fostering a broad common understanding of AI applications and products.

© Springer Nature Switzerland AG 2020
I. I. Bittencourt et al. (Eds.): AIED 2020, LNAI 12164, pp. 427–429, 2020.
https://doi.org/10.1007/978-3-030-52240-7

As a consequence, this also enables people to better estimate potential opportunities and possible risks of those upcoming technologies. Access to basic AI literacy, education and tools will also reduce the danger of social or economic exclusion of certain groups of people, especially women and minorities. In this context it is essential to introduce fundamental concepts and techniques of AI from an early age. In doing so, a convenient byproduct will be the involvement of the child's caregivers – parents and educators, who will also become AI-literate.

2   Aims and Scope

Teaching fundamental AI concepts and techniques has traditionally been done at the university level. Education in AI at the K-12 level is still quite rare. However, in recent years several initiatives and projects pursuing the mission of K-12 AI education have emerged. The main goal of this workshop is to bring together people who are actively involved with and/or interested in K-12 AI education (researchers, teachers, educators, practitioners) and top AI scientists, fostering a mutual exchange of knowledge, ideas and views between those groups. The workshop aims to present initiatives, projects, ideas and best practice examples, to get input from leading AI education researchers, and to discuss current work, possible cooperation and future directions in the context of AI education in schools. Furthermore, it aims to discuss and find a common ground for how to best implement AI education at the K-12 level.

3   Topic Areas

Topics of interests include (but are not limited to):

- K-12 AI educational initiatives and projects
- AI curricula
- AI teaching concepts and materials
- Social, ethical and economic aspects of AI, human factors
- Software and hardware tools in AI education and how those tools could improve teaching
- AI in education
- Best practices for training educators to teach about AI
- Parental involvement in AI-literacy
- Approaches dealing with the question of what should be taught to prepare youth for a digitized world

4   Topic's Importance to AIED Community

Education organizations, AI experts and even governments develop and deploy AI curricula and programs for a K-12 audience. The workshop proposes to step back and intentionally create curricula and programs that not only provide

K-12 students with basic AI literacy, but also allow them to apply AI tools and techniques to real-world problems. Most real-world problems are ill-defined, with incomplete information, operating at multiple scales, across different disciplines in dynamic ways, and may not have well-defined end states. Humans have trouble solving problems that involve multiple time scales, inferring functional relationships from time series data, or predicting trajectories of dynamic systems. They spend considerable effort in developing mathematical models and technologies to compensate for these weaknesses, but not enough attention in educating students to develop these capacities [2]. They tend to create single-variable interventions or inventions that do not take into account their impact on complex or imbricate systems. This "command and control" approach focuses on controlling a target variable, and may be successful at first, but tends to create spin-off problems over time, and at disastrous scale [1]. Effects of this have been seen in the recent examples of biased datasets and algorithms.

Building on the 1st International Workshop on Education in Artificial Intelligence K-12 (EduAI) [3], the workshop proposes a gathering of experts from AI, education and complex systems thinking so a set of best practices to prepare students for a complex world where they will be living and working alongside AI and significant automation are collectively developed.

Sound knowledge about AI principles and concepts, the ability to apply AI techniques and methods to real-world problems, coupled with the ability to collaborate and deploy AI-based solutions are the basis for creating career opportunities and fostering a broad common understanding of AI applications in society. As a consequence, this also enables people to better estimate potential opportunities and possible risks of those upcoming technologies. But it is not enough to just provide access to basic AI literacy, education and tools to students. Their parents, educators and other adults in their lives need to be engaged. Many of whom will be impacted by automation and will need to "upskill". This co-learning model will broaden and open up the conversation around AI, will reduce the danger of social or economic exclusion of certain groups of people, especially women and minorities, resulting in deeper capacity building, and eventually more innovation.

References

1. Gunderson, L.H., Holling, C.S.: Panarchy: Understanding Transformations in Human and Natural Systems. C, Island Press, Washington D (2002)
2. Ornstein, R., Ehrlich, P.: New World-New Mind: Moving Toward Conscious Evolution (1989)
3. EDUAI-19: 1st internat. Workshop on Education in AI K-12. (2019). http://eduai.ist.tugraz.at/index.php/workshop-program-2019/. Accessed 11 May 2020

Author Index

Abdi, Solmaz II-3
Ahmed, Umair Z. I-106
Ahuja, Rohan II-301
Akcayir, Gokce I-346
Al-Doulat, Ahmad I-3
Aleven, Vincent I-240, II-92, II-124
Al-Hariri, Lara I-610
Alhazmi, Sohail II-10
Al-Hossami, Erfan I-3
Allen, Laura K. II-197
Alshaikh, Zeyad II-15
Amadi, Chukwudi E. II-224
An, Haokang II-273
An, Sungeun II-20
Andres-Bray, Juan Miguel L. II-208
Andrzejewska, Magdalena II-25
Arrington, Catherine M. I-500
Azad, Sushmita I-16
Azevedo, Roger I-67

Bae, Chan II-69
Baek, Jineon II-69
Bailey, James I-296, I-423
Baker, Ryan I-411, II-329
Baker, Ryan Shaun I-228, I-423, I-437,
     I-574, II-208
Banerjee, Ayan I-29
Baraniuk, Richard G. II-424
Barnes, Tiffany I-472
Basu, Satabdi I-598
Bates, Robert II-20
Belfer, Robert II-140, II-387
Benedetto, Luca I-43
Benedict, Aileen I-3
Bengio, Yoshua II-387
Bennani, Samir II-114
Beydoun, Ghassan II-168
Biswas, Gautam I-411, I-598, II-296, II-352
Bittencourt, Ig Ibert I-79, I-448, II-376
Bogart, Christopher II-273
Bonnin, Geoffray II-203
Bosch, Nigel I-204

Botarleanu, Robert-Mihai II-31
Botelho, Anthony F. I-562
Boyer, Kristy Elizabeth II-240
Brown, Paul S. II-395
Brusilovsky, Peter II-424
Buckingham Shum, Simon I-360
Buttery, Paula II-358

Cader, Andrzej II-37
Caines, Andrew II-358
Camus, Leon II-43
Cappelli, Andrea I-43
Carlstedt-Duke, Jan II-214
Carpenter, Dan I-55, I-67
Carvalho, Paulo F. I-460
Castagnos, Sylvain II-203
Chalco Challco, Geiser II-312
Challco, Geiser Chalco I-79
Chambel, Teresa II-98
Chanaa, Abdessamad II-49, II-54
Charlin, Laurent II-387
Chatterjee, Rishabh I-92
Chen, Binglin I-16
Chen, Guanliang II-174
Chen, Jiahao I-269
Chen, Penghe II-59, II-185
Chen, Shiping II-168
Chhatbar, Darshak I-106
Chi, Min I-472
Ching-En, Chou II-400
Chiu, Jennifer L. I-598
Chklovski, Tara II-427
Chng, Edwin I-118, II-64
Cho, Junghyun II-69
Choi, Youngduck II-69
Choffin, Benoît II-417
Cohn, Anthony G. II-395
Conati, Cristina I-282
Condor, Aubrey II-74
Courville, Aaron II-387
Couto, Marta II-346
Cremonesi, Paolo I-43

Cristus, Miruna   II-371
Crossley, Scott A.   I-437, II-31, II-329
Cui, Tingru   II-168
Cukurova, Mutlu   II-135

Daniel, Ben K.   II-224
Dascalu, Maria-Dorinela   II-80
Dascalu, Mihai   II-31, II-80, II-228
Del Bonifro, Francesca   I-129
Demmans Epp, Carrie   I-346
Dermeval, Diego   I-524, II-312
Derr, Tyler   II-130
Desmarais, Michel C.   II-191
Dhamecha, Tejas I.   II-214
Di Mitri, Daniele   I-141
Dillenbourg, Pierre   II-346
Dimitrova, Vania   II-395
Ding, Wenbiao   I-269, II-162, II-340
Dorodchi, Mohsen   I-3
Doroudi, Shayan   II-86
Dou, Wenwen   I-3
Dowell, Nia   I-333
Drachsler, Hendrik   I-141

Echeverria, Vanessa   I-360
Effenberger, Tomáš   I-153
El Faddouli, Nour-Eddine   II-49, II-54
Elizabeth Richey, J.   II-208
Emara, Mona   II-296
Emerson, Andrew   I-55, I-165
Engel, Don   II-301

Fancsali, Stephen E.   II-92
Filighera, Anna   I-177, I-512, II-43
Fonseca, Manuel J.   II-98
Fowler, Maxwell   I-16
Frank, Kenneth A.   II-130
Friedman, Leah   II-318
Fu, Weiping   I-269
Fung, Gabriel Pui Cheong   II-364

Gabbrielli, Maurizio   I-129
Gagnon, Paul   II-214
Gao, Hongli   II-180
García Iruela, Miguel   II-98
Gašević, Dragan   II-174

Gautam, Dipesh   I-191
Gauthier, Andrea   II-103
Geden, Michael   I-67
Glazewski, Krista D.   I-55
Gliser, Ian   I-204
Goel, Ashok   II-20
Gong, Jiaqi   II-157
Goodell, Jim   II-420
Graesser, Art C.   I-321
Gu, Lin   I-309
Guo, Yuqing   II-409
Gupta, Sandeep K. S.   I-29
Gupta, Varun   II-140, II-387

Hallifax, Stuart   I-216
Hamilton, Margaret   II-10
Hammock, Jen   II-20
Hanegbi, Nathan   I-296
Harpstead, Erik   I-586
Hart, Glen   II-395
Hasan, Sahil   II-273
Hayashi, Yusuke   II-109
Hayati, Hind   II-114
Heffernan, Neil T.   I-562, II-263
Heintz, Fredrik   II-427
Henderson, Nathan   I-165, I-228
Henry, Julie   II-427
Heo, Jaewe   II-69
Herodotou, Christothea   II-119
Hijón-Neira, Raquel   II-98
Hilton, Michael   II-273
Hinze, Scott R.   II-197
Hirashima, Tsukasa   II-109
Hlosta, Martin   II-119
Hmelo-Silver, Cindy E.   I-55
Hoareau, Lara   II-203
Holland, Jay   I-386
Holstein, Kenneth   I-240, II-92
Hoppe, H. Ulrich   II-382
Hossain, Sameena   I-29
Hou, Xinying   I-255
Hu, Xiangen   II-180, II-420
Huang, Changqin   II-364
Huang, Gale Yan   I-269
Huang, Yuchi   II-252
Huang, Yun   II-124

Huang, Yuqi   II-376
Hutchins, Nicole   II-352
Hutchins, Nicole M.   II-296

Indulska, Marta   I-486
Isotani, Seiji   I-79

Jay, Michael   II-420
Johal, Wafa   II-346

Kai, Shimin   I-574
Kandimalla, Siddharth Reddy   II-273
Kandlhofer, Martin   II-427
Kar, Purushottam   I-106
Karduni, Alireza   I-3
Karimi, Hamid   II-130
Karumbaiah, Shamya   I-437, II-329
Kashima, Hisashi   II-417
Kennedy, Gregor   I-423
Khalidi Idrissi, Mohammed   II-114
Khan, Daniyal   II-301
Khan-Galaria, Madiha   II-135
Khosravi, Hassan   I-486, II-3
Kim, Byungsoo   II-69
Kiu, Kai   II-180
Kleinsmith, Andrea   II-157
Kochmar, Ekaterina   II-140, II-387
Koedinger, Kenneth   I-460, I-586, II-124
Koenig, Sven   II-427
Koprinska, Irena   I-374
Kumar, Amruth N.   II-147
Kurzum, Christopher   I-309

Labrum, Matthew   I-437
Lallé, Sébastien   I-282
Lamrani, Imane   I-29
Lamtara, Jesslyn   I-296
Lan, Andrew   I-610
Lan, Andrew S.   II-424
Lang, Charles   II-152
Lang, David   II-174
Langner-Thiele, Angela   II-382
Lavoué, Elise   I-216
Lee, Heera   II-157
Lee, Seewoo   II-69
Lee, Seung   I-165
Lee, Youngnam   II-69
Leemans, Sander J. J.   I-486
Lehman, Blair   I-309

Lemos, Bruno   II-312
Lester, James   I-67, I-165, I-228, II-240
Lester, James C.   I-55
Li, Guoliang   I-269
Li, Haiying   I-321
Li, Hang   II-162
Li, Li   II-168
Lin, Jiayin   II-168
Lin, Jionghao   II-174
Lin, Yiwen   I-333
Lisanti, Giuseppe   I-129
Liu, Haochen   I-269
Liu, Jiefei   II-59
Liu, Yulin   I-309
Liu, Zitao   I-269, II-162, II-340
Llorente, Ana María Pinto   II-405
Lobczowski, Nikki G.   I-460
Long, Zhou   II-180
Lothian, Delaney   I-346
Lu, Xiwen   I-562
Lu, Yu   II-59, II-185, II-376
Lubold, Nichola   II-318
Luckin, Rose   II-135
Luo, Dehong   II-180

Ma, Xingjun   I-296
Madaio, Michael   I-92
Maher, Mary Lou   I-3
Mandalapu, Varun   II-157
Mangaroska, Katerina   I-360
Maniktala, Mehak   I-472
Manske, Sven   II-382
Mareschal, Denis   II-103
Martinez-Maldonado, Roberto   I-360
Marwan, Samiha   II-246
Mbouzao, Boniface   II-191
McBride, Elizabeth   I-598
McBroom, Jessica   I-374
McCarthy, Kathryn S.   II-197
McElhaney, Kevin W.   I-598
McLaren, Bruce M.   I-255, II-92, II-208, II-409
McLaughlin, Elizabeth   II-124
Mcleod, Owen   I-346
McNamara, Danielle S.   II-31, II-80, II-228
Medeiros Machado, Guilherme   II-203
Mendoza, Red   II-214
Meng, Qinggang   II-185
Mills, Caitlin   I-204
Min, Wookhee   I-165, II-240

Minogue, James   I-165
Mishra, Shitanshu   I-411, II-296, II-352
Mitrović, Antonija   I-386
Mogessie, Michael   II-208
Mondal, Sneha   II-214
Monteiro, Mateus   I-524
Moore, Russell   II-358
Moore, Steven   I-398
Morales-Urrutia, Elizabeth K.   II-220
Mott, Bradford   II-240
Mott, Bradford W.   I-55
Mouta, Ana   II-405
Muldner, Kasia   II-306
Munshi, Anabil   I-411
Murray, R. Charles   II-273

Nascimento, Pedro   II-312
Nawaz, Sadia   I-423
Ndukwe, Ifeanyi G.   II-224
Nguyen, Huy A.   I-255, I-398, II-409
Nicula, Bogdan   II-228
Niu, Xi   I-3
Nkomo, Larian M.   II-224
Nomura, Toshihiro   II-109
Nur, Nasheen   I-3

O'Leary, Stephen   I-296
Ocaña Ch., José Miguel   II-220
Ocumpaugh, Jaclyn   I-411, I-437, II-329
Oertel, Catharine   II-234
Ogan, Amy   I-92
Okano, Masashi   I-549
Olsen, Jennifer K.   II-234
Ostrow, Korinn S.   II-263
Ou, Lu   II-252

Pacifici, Valentino   II-371
Paiva, Ana   II-346
Paiva, Ranilson   I-448
Pan, Shimei   II-301
Papathoma, Tina   II-119
Paquette, Luc   I-228, I-411
Park, Kyungjin   II-240
Park, Seoyon   II-69
Pathak, Smriti   II-214
Paudyal, Prajwal   I-29
Pedro da Silva, Alan   II-312

Pedro, Alan   I-524
Peixoto, Aristoteles   I-524
Pelánek, Radek   I-153
Peng, Yan   II-59
Pérez-Marín, Diana   II-220
Perret, Cecile A.   II-228
Pian, Yang   II-376
Pineau, Joelle   II-140, II-387
Piromchai, Patorn   I-296
Pizarro-Romero, Celeste   II-220
Popineau, Fabrice   II-417
Porayska-Pomsta, Kaśka   II-103, II-400
Price, Thomas W.   II-246
Pritchard, David   II-168
Pu, Shi   II-252

Qu, Jing   II-180

Rachatasumrit, Napol   I-586
Radu, Iulian   II-257
Razzaq, Renah   II-263
Redd, Brandt   II-420
Rensing, Christoph   I-177, I-512
Rice, Andrew   II-358
Richey, J. Elizabeth   I-255, I-460
Ritter, Steven   II-92
Robson, Robby   II-420
Rosé, Carolyn   II-273
Rowe, Jonathan   I-67, I-165, I-228
Rubio, Miguel A.   II-268
Rugaber, Spencer   II-20
Rummel, Nikol   I-240
Rus, Vasile   I-191, II-15
Ruseti, Stefan   II-80

Sadiq, Shazia   I-486, II-3
Sakr, Majd   II-273
Saleh, Asmalina   I-55
Sánchez, Eva Torrecilla   II-405
Sandbothe, Michael   II-92
Sankaranarayanan, Sreecharan   II-273
Santos, Rodrigo   II-312
Sanz Ausin, Markel   I-472
Schiano, Michael   I-309
Schneider, Bertrand   I-118, II-64, II-257
Schneider, Jan   I-141
Schulte, Jurgen   I-360

Schulten, Cleo   II-382
Serban, Iulian Vlad   II-140, II-387
Serna, Audrey   I-216
Seyam, Mohamed Raouf   I-118
Shabaninejad, Shiva   I-486
Shahrokhian Ghahfarokhi, Bahar   II-279
Shen, Jun   II-168
Shibani, Antonette   I-360, II-285
Shin, Dongmin   II-69
Shrier, Ian   II-191
Sivaraman, Avinash   II-279
Sjödén, Björn   II-291
Skawińska, Agnieszka   II-25
Smilek, Daniel   I-204
Smith, Shelby   I-204
Snyder, Caitlin   II-296, II-352
Solovey, Erin   I-500
Sopka, Sasa   I-141
Sosnovsky, Sergey   II-424
Sparrow, Anaka   I-346
Specht, Marcus   I-141
Srivastava, Namrata   I-423
Stacey, Simon   II-301
Stamper, John   I-398, II-409
Steinbauer, Gerald   II-427
Steuer, Tim   I-177, I-512
Stranc, Samantha   II-306
Sun, Geng   II-168
Symonette, Danilo   II-301

Täckström, Oscar   II-371
Tahir, Sara   II-301
Talks, Benjamin   I-296
Tamang, Lasagn   II-15
Tan, Lingyi   II-371
Tang, Jiliang   I-269, II-130, II-162
Tang, Yong   II-364
Tanner Jackson, G.   I-309
Tärning, Betty   I-537
Tazouti, Youssef   II-203
Tenório, Kamilla   I-524, II-312
Ternblad, Eva-Maria   I-537
Thevathayan, Charles   II-10
Thomas, Aude   II-203
Tian, Xiaoyi   II-318
Toggerson, Brokk   I-610
Tong, Hanshuang   II-324

Torphy, Kaitlin T.   II-130
Trausan-Matu, Stefan   II-80
Trebing, Kevin   I-141
Tsuprun, Eugene   I-309
Tu, Ethan   II-257
Turrin, Roberto   I-43
Tywoniw, Rurik   II-329

Uchida, Yuto   II-334
Unal, Deniz Sonmez   I-500
Uto, Masaki   I-549, II-334

VanLehn, Kurt   II-279
Varatharaj, Ashvini   I-562
Vie, Jill-Jênn   II-417
Viola, Adam   I-610
Vu, Dung Do   II-140, II-387

Walker, Erin   I-500, II-318
Wammes, Jeffrey D.   I-204
Wang, Deliang   II-185
Wang, Magdalene   II-301
Wang, Yeyu   I-574
Wang, Zhen   II-324
Wang, Zhiwei   II-162
Weigel, Emily   II-20
Weitekamp, Daniel   I-586
West, Matthew   I-16
Wiebe, Eric   II-240
Wijayarathna, Gayathri K.   II-214
Wijewickrema, Sudanthi   I-296
Williams, Joseph Jay   II-246
Winters, Michael   II-246

Xie, Haoran   II-174
Xu, Dongming   II-168
Xu, Qi   II-59
Xu, Shiting   II-340

Yacef, Kalina   I-374
Yadollahi, Elmira   II-346
Yang, Songfan   I-269
Yao, William   I-118
Ye, Zihuiwen   I-586
Yett, Bernard   II-296, II-352
Yu, Ji Hyun   I-423

Yu, Renzhe   I-333
Yu, Weihao   II-364
Yudelson, Michael   II-252

Zaidi, Ahmed   II-358
Zeylikman, Sofya   II-64
Zhang, Ningyu   I-411, I-598, II-352

Zhao, Jing   I-309
Zheng, Zetao   II-364
Zhou, Yun   II-324
Zhu, Jia   II-364
Zilles, Craig   I-16
Zingaro, Stefano Pio   I-129
Zylich, Brian   I-610

Printed in the United States
By Bookmasters